TEACH

What'

TEACH offers instructors scholarly content and unmatched currency in a succinct magazine format that engages students. *TEACH* consistently asks students to reflect on their experiences and engage in a dialogue about critical issues in education.

Join the Dialogue

Have you experienced the support of a community or a group of people outside school who cared about you and made sure you succeeded at something? Was that ongoing support, or was it for a special occasion?

"Join the Dialogue" poses essential questions that you should consider as you begin a career in teaching.

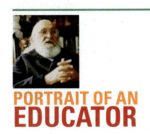

PORTRAIT OF AN EDUCATOR

"Portrait of an Educator" highlights people who have made and continue to make an impact and difference in education.

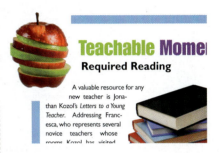

Teachable Mome[nt]
Required Reading

A valuable resource for any new teacher is Jonathan Kozol's *Letters to a Young Teacher*. Addressing Francesca, who represents several novice teachers whose rooms Kozol has visited.

"Teachable Moment" articles highlight key topics and events in teaching and education.

Promising Practices
The Psychology of It

The American Psychological Association (APA) recently established a special task force to attempt to answer the question "What is the core knowledge from psychology that teachers need to know?" The task force, which includes 18 deans of colleges of education, began by identifying the core areas of psychology that are relevant to teacher preparation:

1. Learning theory: How do human beings learn what they learn?
2. Child/adolescent development: How does the age and develop-

"Promising Practices" feature unique strategies and programs focused on improving education.

A QUESTION OF . . .
What are the benefits of teaching?

"I can't think of a more rewarding profession. Working with children can be quite challenging, but watching them learn and interact with others is awesome."

—*Kathy Cushman, fourth-grade teacher*

"A Question of…" vignettes provide unique insights and advice from real, practicing teachers.

Did you know?

Acknowledging how much support first-year teachers need, Texas A&M University–Corpus Christi developed a program called SOS: Strategies of Success, designed to support beginning teachers. The program has been working. The school conducted a study in 2005 to determine how likely program participants were to stay in teaching.* For the three cohort groups studied, SOS program participants had a 98 percent retention rate, compared to 88 percent for graduates of the teacher education program who did not participate in SOS, and 70 percent for new teachers across the state of Texas.

"Did You Know" provides short, engaging real world data relevant to the chapter.

What About Me?
Creating Responsible Citizens

What should be a school's role in creating responsible citizens? Some of the following issues controversial among various parts of society for different reasons, for example, because of limited funding or understaffing. Particular problems arise, however, when certain groups believe that what a school is teaching oversteps the boundaries of what many people assume to be the domain of family or religious community. Put a checkmark next to the items that you believe students should learn or that should be offered during a public school education:

- Sexual and puberty education
- Out-of-school field trips or recreational activities, such as dances
- Social studies courses that address controversial issues
- Advanced courses in math and engineering
- Advanced Placement classes and computer courses
- Physical education and nutrition
- After-school tutoring and summer courses
- Classes on child-rearing skills for pregnant students
- Technical courses such as auto shop or welding

"What About Me?" asks you to recall your personal experiences as a student and your opinions on key issues.

You Decide

Is "teaching democracy" an appropriate expectation for our schools, along with all the core material that has to be covered?

...aration, and ...Or they ask ...ss myriad ...for exam-...cation and ...tackling ...of obesity ...f what food ...and through ...nutrition, or ...buraging a range ...that trouble adults.

Schools appropriately including ensurin developing stu knowledge a helping yo safe and pr inducting yo democratic theless, the ing in a demo to be central i schooling and te

"You Decide" asks your opinion on a controversial topic.

Readings

Will I Join a Union?
From "WHY TEACHERS SHOULD OR[GANIZE]"
BY MARGARET HALEY

Margaret Haley's 1904 speech to the National Educati many teachers a century ago. It also reflects Haley's ho type of schooling could be achieved through a public i

"Readings" from leading educators and researchers, past and present, offer insights into critical issues that have affected and will continue to affect education and a teacher's role in the classroom.

TEACH

VICE PRESIDENT, EDITORIAL **Michael Ryan**

PUBLISHER **David S. Patterson**

SENIOR SPONSORING EDITOR **Allison McNamara**

EXECUTIVE MARKET DEVELOPMENT MANAGER **Sheryl Adams**

EXECUTIVE MARKETING MANAGER **James Headley**

MARKETING MANAGER **Yasuko Okada**

DEVELOPMENT EDITOR **Vicki Malinee, Van Brien & Associates**

EDITORIAL COORDINATOR **Sarah Kiefer**

EDITING, DESIGN, AND PRODUCTION MANAGER/PHOTO EDITOR **Melissa Williams**

PROJECT MANAGER **Melissa Higey, Lachina Publishing Services**

COVER DESIGN **Preston Thomas**

INTERIOR DESIGN **Elise Lansdon**

PHOTO RESEARCH **Lisa Jelly Smith and Nancy Null**

SENIOR PRODUCTION SUPERVISOR **Louis Swaim**

COMPOSITION & ILLUSTRATION **Lachina Publishing Services**

PRINTING **RR Donnelley & Sons**

The credits section begins on page 452 and constitutes an extension of the copyright page. Front Cover Photo: John Cumming/Getty Images; Back Cover Photo: Peter Cade/Getty Images

We are indebted to our REVIEWERS: Phyllis Adcock, University of Nebraska-Omaha • Peggy Akerman, Pensacola Junior College • Antonette Aragon, Colorado State University • Kathryn Birmingham, Florida State College-Jacksonville • Melanie Bishop, Lindenwood University • Robin Boggs, Brevard Community College • Paul Thomas Bole, University of New Orleans • Tony Boyd, KCTCS-Maysville Community and Technical College • Diann Brown, Bowling Green State University • Joan Brownstein, University of St. Thomas • Ellen Burkhouse, Marywood University • Edelia Carthan, Jackson State University • Dominique Charlotteaux, Broward Community College • Patricia Walsh Coates, Kutztown University • Marlene Cousens, Yakima Valley Community College • Charles Craig, Jr., Tennessee Tech University • Dorothy Valcarcel Craig, Middle Tennessee State University • Araceli Cumbo, State College of Florida-Venice • Rob Danin, University of Colorado-Colorado Springs • Kimberly Davis, Lake Land College • Francine DeFrance, Cerritos College • Swen Digranes, Northeastern State University • Judy Divine, University of Southern Indiana • Karen Dunlap, Texas Woman's University • Holly Eckles, Western Oregon University • Jim Elsberry, Indiana Wesleyan University • Louis Evans III, Lone Star College Cy-Fair • B. L. Fish, Jackson State University • Jill Flygare, University of Utah • Robin Ford, New York University • Cindi Fries, Northeastern State University • Marilyn Friga, University of Central Arkansas • Daniel Glisczinski, University of Minnesota-Duluth • Dana Grayson, New York University • Mary Elizabeth Hendrix, Missouri Western State University • Sharon Hirschy, Collin County Community College-Plano • Linda Hoover, Shippensburg University • Carolyn Huber, State College of Florida-Manatee • Denise Hughes-Tafen, West Virginia University-Morgantown • Jeanine Huss, Western Kentucky University • John Huss, Northern Kentucky University • Jeannette Jones, Northwest Vista College • Patricia Jungkeit, East Tennessee State University • Jennifer Kidd, Old Dominion University • Shannon Knight, Collin County Community College-Plano • Merryl Kravitz, New Mexico Highlands University • Kacy Larson, North Iowa Area Community College • Tony Latiker, Jackson State University • Nancy Lauter, Montclair State University • M. Jerome Leavy, University of South Florida • Rebecca Lewis, Boston College • Ann Loving, J. Sargeant Reynolds Community College • Penni Major, Lone Star College Cy-Fair • Karyn Schweiker Marra, Frostburg State University • David Martin, Kennesaw State University • Elizabeth McDonald, New York University • Linda McMillan, Kutztown University • Harrison Means, University of Nebraska-Omaha • Annalisa Mendiola, University of Texas-San Antonio • Heather Merrill, Glendale Community College • Christine Meus, Purdue University-Calumet-Hammond • Barbara Meyer, Illinois State University • Harriet Morrison, J. Sargeant Reynolds Community College • Cindi Nicotera, Harrisburg Area Community College • Pedro Noguera, New York University • Terry Nourie, Illinois State University • Eucabeth Odhiambo, Shippensburg University • Sansanee Ohlson, Bowling Green State University • Kwadwa Okrah, Indiana University-South Bend • Lois Oestreich, Salt Lake Community College • Nancy Oreshack, Glendale Community College • Glenda Orgill, Yakima Valley Community College • Carlos Ovando, Arizona State University • Darlene Pabis, Westmoreland County Community College • Mary Parker, Del Mar College • Lynn Patterson, Murray State University • Jocelyn Lee Payne, Northeastern State University • Susan Perlis, Marywood University • Darlene Peters, University of West Florida • Naomi Jeffery Petersen, Central Washington University • David Powell, Southeast Missouri State University • Geoff Quick, Lansing Community College • Ginny Richerson, Murray State University • Dutchie Riggsby, Columbus State University • Anne Rothstein, Lehman College-CUNY • Wendi Rowlett, Valencia Community College-Winter Park • Melissa Rugh, Westmoreland County Community College • Cynthia Schubert-Irastorza, National University • Ann Schulte, California State University-Chico • Pat Seiber, Murray State University • Ann Selleck, Lansing Community College • Susan Sheffield, State College of Florida-Manatee • Susan Sies, Carroll Community College • Sandra Smith, Tennessee Tech University • Jane Spruill, Pensacola Junior College • Theresa Stahler, Kutztown University • Paula Stickles, Millikin University • Ann Taylor, Southern Illinois University • Robert Townsend, Indiana Wesleyan University • Rosemary Traoré, University of North Carolina-Charlotte • Lantana Usman, University of Northern British Columbia • Dorothy (Jean) Waddell, State College of Florida-Manatee • Mary Ware, SUNY Cortland • Leslie Haley Wasserman, University of Akron • Laura Wendling, California State University-San Marcos • Jeremy Wendt, Tennessee Tech University • Betsy Were, Pensacola Junior College • Andrew Whitehead, East Stroudsburg University • Margaret Wilder, University of Georgia • Elaine Wilkinson, Collin County Community College-Plano • Jane Wilson, Saint Petersburg College Gibbs • Eric Yeager, Collin County Community College-Plano • Marilyn Yokel, Millikin University

TEACH

BRIEF CONTENTS

Meet JIM FRASER

Name: James W. Fraser. But you can call me Jim.

Occupation: When people ask, I say I'm a teacher. The rest comes after that. Currently, I am a Professor of History and Education at New York University.

Hobbies: Snorkeling whenever I can get some place warm. I love hanging out with fish. Reading murder mysteries by a warm fire when I can't.

Childhood Ambition: Be a preacher or president of the United States. I achieved one of my goals. Guess which one...

Family: My wife, Katherine Hanson is a writer and an artist (my office walls are well decorated). I have three daughters and one son and three grandchildren—two girls and a boy. And, of course, my dog, Pebble.

Last book read: More Than Title IX: How Equity in Education has Shaped the Nation by Katherine Hanson. The Appeal, by John Grisham.

Favorite film: Casablanca or The Sting . . . . I'm never sure—I know, it's kind of pathetic but I like old films better than new ones.

Favorite album: I listen to whatever someone else is playing or whoever is playing on Prairie Home Companion.

Favorite teacher: Mrs. Kelley, my 8th grade teacher in California Bob Lynn and Bob Handy, my professors in graduate school

Latest accomplishment: It has been pretty hard to accomplish anything recently except finishing this book! I have managed to visit teacher education programs in ten states this year and that keeps me on my toes.

Favorite quote: From my wife: "I can always tell when you had a good day teaching. You come home in a terrific mood and you're exhausted." I can't imagine not teaching!

CONTENTS

FEATURES >>

Teachable Moment

What About Me?

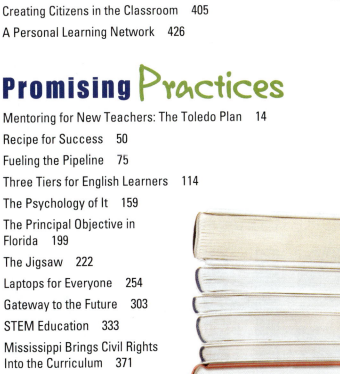

1

TEACHING

W hy do I want to do this?" Almost everyone who begins any professional program—certainly a program leading to a career in teaching—asks that basic question. "Why would I consider teaching?" is a critical first question in the list of questions and issues we explore in this book.

Although anyone who enters teaching does so for his or her own personal reasons, there are key similarities among people in any particular profession. Thus, it is important to understand why other people have selected a career similar to the one you are considering. You want to know why they like teaching—or don't. This chapter is designed to help you hear the voices of current teachers and teachers from generations past as they talk about why they became teachers, what they liked about the work once in it, and why they stayed in the profession (if they did indeed stay). In the process, you will think about how to answer the same question for yourself: *Why do I want to be a teacher?*

For insights into why others have chosen to teach—and have stayed with it—the **Readings** section of this chapter offers a starting point. Ranging from the reflections of successful teachers like William Ayers, Melinda Pellerin-Duck, and Herbert Kohl to the latest research on why people stay in teaching or leave it, the **Readings** will show you real teachers' motivations, joys, satisfactions, and also frustrations and hopefully will prod you to ask yourself new questions as you consider this career that can change so many lives.

IS IT FOR ME?

FOCUS >>

- Why do people become teachers today?
- Why do some people leave teaching?
- What has motivated people to teach at different times in the past?
- Should I be a teacher?

>> Why Do People Become Teachers Today?

By signing up for this class, you've already determined that a career in teaching is something that sparks your interest. Why is that? What is it about teaching—or at least what you think you know about teaching—that sounds appealing? Is it the opportunity to "mold young minds," or rather the chance to open them? Is it the comfort of being part of a professional community more than 5 million active members strong? Is it an avenue for you to share your passion for (you fill in the blank) with the rest of the world?

In 2001, the National Education Association (NEA) asked current public school teachers to identify the main reasons they had originally decided to become teachers (each person could list up to three reasons). Several clear themes emerged, including:

- a desire to work with young people, 73%
- the value or significance of education in society, 44%

Did you know?

There are 3 million public school teachers in the United States. Approximately 1 out of every 60 people in the United States is a teacher.

Reasons Why People Become Teachers

	1971	1981	1991	2001
Desire to work with young people	72%	70%	66%	73%
Value or significance of education in society	37%	40%	37%	44%
Interest in subject-matter field	35%	44%	34%	36%
Influence of teacher in elementary or secondary school	18%	25%	27%	32%
Never really considered anything else	17%	20%	24%	19%
Influence of family	21%	22%	23%	20%
Long summer vacation	14%	22%	21%	21%
Job security	16%	21%	17%	17%
Opportunity for a lifetime of self-growth	21%	13%	8%	11%

Source: "Status of the American Public School Teacher 2000–2001," National Education Association.

Teachable Moment

Start the Dialogue

You've probably noticed there are a lot of questions in this book. There's a good reason for this. The purpose of this text is not simply to spew forth what professors or publishers think you need to know but rather to address the real questions first-year education students—like you—are asking; questions like:

"How will I control my class?"

"Are schools sometimes unfair to students?"

"How can I be sure that I'm reaching all my students?"

"Why do some people leave teaching?"

As we tackle these important questions, we'll engage in a three-way dialogue involving (1) your own educational autobiography (looking at what you have learned—and where and how you may have learned it—during your years as a student), (2) what can be learned by carefully observing schools and the lives of students and teachers in these schools, and (3) the most current research literature about how students learn, how schools succeed and fail, and the changing demographic and political realities that form the background for education in the United States today.

The teaching profession has changed dramatically during the past generation, and it's crystal clear that today's teacher needs to be *more informed* about effective instructional practices and educational

expectations, *more prepared* to manage and motivate a diverse group of students, and *more active* in developing professional opportunities that benefit everyone involved in the education process.

So come join the dialogue!

QUESTIONS

- How long have you been considering a career in teaching?
- At this point in your education, how sure are you about a career in teaching? Fifty percent? More? Less?
- What other professions are you (or have you been) interested in? Do these have similarities with teaching?

- interest in a subject-matter field, 36%
- the positive influence of a former teacher in elementary or secondary school, 32%[1]

These reasons have changed over the last 35 years, but not very much. In every survey since 1971, about 70% of teachers have ranked "a desire to work with young people" as a primary reason for deciding to teach. Similarly, between 34% and 44% of teachers have listed the value or significance of a teacher's work in society as a reason they became a teacher, and similar numbers have listed inter-

est in their subject-matter field. Interestingly, the greatest change has been in the impact of a former teacher, which has grown from only 18% in 1971 to 32% in 2001, almost one-third of teachers.

It is also interesting to note the other reasons listed. Over the years, approximately one-fifth of all teachers have said that they never really considered any career except teaching, and a similar number list the influence of their family. Only a slightly smaller number list a long summer vacation and job security in their responses. Clearly, people decide to become teachers for many reasons.

PORTRAIT OF AN EDUCATOR

Paulo Freire

For more than a century, many educators have stressed the importance of encouraging students to ask questions and engage in discussion within an academic subject rather than merely to read and memorize facts and spit them back on exams. Brazilian educator Paulo Freire (1921–1999) described in detail what he called "banking" in education, in which teachers simply make "deposits" in the blank brains of their students:

> Education is suffering from narration sickness.... Education thus becomes an act of depositing, in which the students are the depositories and the teacher is the depositor. Instead of communicating, the teacher issues communiqués and makes deposits which the students patiently receive, memorize, and repeat. This is the "banking" concept of education, in which the scope of action allowed to students extends only as far as receiving, filing, and storing the deposits.... In the banking concept of education, knowledge is a gift bestowed by those who consider themselves knowledgeable upon those whom they consider to know nothing.

Freire contends that the creation of "dialogue" must replace the banking model. Dialogue, however, does not negate the role of the teacher. The teacher brings his or her unique expertise to the dialogue, including knowledge of the larger world, the academic disciplines, the experiences of other people in other contexts, and the pedagogical techniques essential to engaging people in an effective dialogue. At the same time, the teacher must come to the dialogue always ready to learn from the context and experiences of the students and, as Freire says, "with humility."

Freire sees a powerful connection between the style of **pedagogy** (teaching) used in school and the way the larger society operates. Schools can teach students to be passive, to accept things the way they are, and to defer to distant authority, or schools can teach students to be active, to ask why things are as they are, and to demand change when it is needed. In his most famous book, *Pedagogy of the Oppressed*, Freire describes the extraordinary importance of dialogue not only for schools but also for the role education can play in creating a more democratic society for schools, teachers, and students to live in.

> **pedagogy** The art and science of teaching, including the methods, principles, and styles used for instruction. Often used as *how* to teach vs. *what* to teach (content).

> Through dialogue the teacher-of-students and the students-of-the-teacher cease to exist and a new term emerges: teacher-student with students-teachers. The teacher is no longer merely the-one-who-teaches, but one who is himself taught in dialogue with students, who in turn while being taught also teach. They become jointly responsible for a process in which all grow.

Freire did not come to his educational ideas easily. He was born in Recife, Brazil, in 1921. After a brief career as a lawyer, he taught high school from 1941 to 1947. He then took on responsibility for adult literacy in some of the highly illiterate poor communities in northeast Brazil. Freire quickly found that traditional methods of teaching literacy—starting with the alphabet and simple words—did not work with adults. They quickly became bored and saw little point to the exercises. Freire turned instead to asking people to think about the most pressing issues in their communities. In one famous example, a community needed a well. Freire focused the literacy campaign around writing a letter to the government demanding a new, deeper well. Freire's link of educational success with activism got him in trouble with the political authorities, and after the military coup in Brazil in 1964 he was briefly jailed and then forced into exile. It was in exile that he further developed his educational ideas, writing *Pedagogy of the Oppressed* in 1970.

After 15 years in exile, Freire was allowed to return to Brazil, where he continued to teach and write about the important link between literacy and liberation. In 1988, he was elected Secretary of Education (Superintendent of Schools) for the city of Sao Paulo, Brazil, where he had the opportunity to put many of his educational ideas into practice in a large urban public school system.

THE JOYS OF WORKING WITH YOUNG PEOPLE

When teachers talk about their desire to work with children or adolescents, they usually are talking about much more than simply "feeling good" at the end of the day. Most people who become teachers have a deep commitment to young people and their future and find acting on that commitment rewarding. Ayla Gavins, who has taught for a dozen years in several different small elementary schools in the Boston area, says she teaches in part because "I love to laugh." Teaching allows her to interact with kids who are "naturally humorous in the ways they discover and make sense of the world." But she also teaches because "Every day that I teach, I learn something new about myself. I am slightly changed every time I get to know a student. As a teacher I exude my values and what is important to me."[2]

What About Me?

Why Do *I* Want to Teach?

Matters to Me	Reason for Teaching	Really Doesn't Matter to Me
_____	Teaching and supporting our young people is the best way I can contribute to society.	_____
_____	Working with young people will keep *me* young.	_____
_____	The skills and experience will easily transfer to other professions.	_____
_____	I had a great teacher that I want to emulate.	_____
_____	My family thinks this is a good fit for me.	_____
_____	I love learning, and a teaching environment will give me learning opportunities.	_____
_____	There will always be a need for teachers, so there's job security.	_____
_____	I'd like to move eventually into an administrative position in education, such as a principal or superintendent.	_____
_____	I want to have my summers available for other interests.	_____
_____	I like to be in charge of a group.	_____
_____	I'm really excited about a specific subject area and want to share that with others.	_____
_____	I've just always wanted to be a teacher.	_____
_____	Teaching gives me the flexibility to live anywhere I want to.	_____
_____	I want to make a difference in someone's life.	_____
_____	Other:	
_____	Other:	
_____	Other:	

Now go back and rank the reasons that do matter to you. What are your top three reasons for considering a career in teaching?

A QUESTION OF . . .

What are the benefits of teaching?

"I can't think of a more rewarding profession. Working with children can be quite challenging, but watching them learn and interact with others is awesome."

—*Kathy Cushman, fourth-grade teacher* ◼

William Ayers, who has taught in the Chicago area for many years, reflects a similar understanding of teaching when he writes in the first **Reading** of this chapter from his book *To Teach: The Journey of a Teacher:*

People are called to teaching because they love children and youth, or because they love being with them, watching them open up and grow and become more able, more competent, more powerful in the world. They may love what happens to themselves when they are with children, the ways in which they become better, more human, more generous.[3]

Anyone who has spent time teaching has experienced a few—if not many—of those magic moments.

Parker Palmer, another long-time teacher, describes the satisfaction that leads many to teaching and keeps them there throughout their careers. In his best-selling book *The Courage to Teach*, he helps us understand what many teachers may have had in mind when they reported in their NEA interviews being motivated by the satisfaction that comes from a career focused on young people and their education. He writes: "I am a teacher at heart, and there are moments in the classroom when I can hardly hold the joy.

When my students and I discover uncharted territory to explore, when the pathway out of a thicket opens up before us, when our experience is illuminated by the lighting-life of the mind—then teaching is the finest work I know."[4]

For most of us who teach, this discovery of uncharted territory alongside our students is also one of the great joys that keeps bringing us back again and again over the course of a long career. The moment when student and teacher connect—the moment when, often after considerable struggle, a student "gets it," whether the "it" is how to read a difficult word, understand an abstract concept in mathematics, or make the sometimes dry words of educational theory come alive—is truly one of life's most satisfying. However, Palmer is honest enough to admit that not all moments are like that. There are times when "the classroom is so lifeless or painful or confused—and I am so powerless to do anything about it—that my claim to be a teacher seems a transparent sham." Every honest teacher can describe such moments. But for most of us, on balance, the moments of engagement far outweigh the moments of pain, and the satisfaction is substantial.

THE VALUE OF TEACHING IN SOCIETY

*"I teach in the hope of making
the world a better place."*

—William Ayers[5]

In interview after interview, many teachers indicate that, while they clearly enjoy teaching, they have reasons for being a teacher that go beyond personal satisfaction. Jennifer Welborn, a middle-school science teacher, says: "I teach because it gives me a purpose. Teaching gives me a really good reason to get up and try my best every day. I may be naïve, but I believe that what I do day in and day out does make a difference. Teachers do change lives forever."[6]

Teacher Melinda Pellerin-Duck, whose essay is included in the **Readings**, says: "I teach because I see extraordinary possibilities in my students. . . . As a teacher, I have the most fortunate experience of nurturing our future." Many teachers share that idealism, and it certainly is one important part of the satisfaction of teaching. Talk with fellow students entering teacher education programs in colleges and universities across the country and you will find many young people—and more than a few middle-age career changers—who are entering teaching because they want to "nurture our future" and hope to make the world a better place. They see teaching, much more than some other, more lucrative professions, as a way to do this. At almost any school in the United States, you will find teachers who reflect all the joys that Welborn, Gavins, and Ayers describe, who love watching young lives develop, who like what happens to themselves personally as they interact with the fast-changing people called students, and who see these interactions as a way to make the world a better place in which to live.

Concern about the significance of education to society is reflected in Herbert Kohl's *The Discipline of Hope: Learning from a Lifetime of Teaching*, excerpted in the **Readings**. Kohl writes that: "These are not easy times in which to keep hope alive in poor or even middle-class communities. . .And yet I have hope." His hope is based on the many examples of teachers, parents, and others working together to create educational environments that reflect their aspirations for what children can and should be able to do. "Schools of hope," he says, "are places where children are honored and well served." Schools of this sort are built by the teachers who enter—and stay in—teaching because they believe that their work has significant value in society as well as in the lives of individual children.

Another long-time teacher and educational researcher, Jean Anyon, argues that if one truly cares about building a better society, teaching is an excellent place to start. She asks, "Why should we put education—and concerned educators—at the center of efforts to build a unified movement for **social justice**?" Her answer to this question rests on her compelling sense that schools are places where many of the most pressing issues of society—and the people who care about them—come together. She also notes that putting education at the center of efforts for social change makes good sense because so many teachers already care about building a better society. "I, like many others, entered teaching 'to change the world.'" There are teachers in every city today who teach a critical, thought-provoking **curriculum**, and

social justice education Education programs and models focused on the development of a more fair and equitable society for all citizens, with freedom, more equal income distribution, and equal opportunity.

curriculum A collection of lessons, skills, and evaluations which fulfill the objectives of a particular subject.

who utilize the classroom to discuss issues their students face." And these teachers have access to other teachers, to parents, and to community leaders. Teachers, Anyon seems to say, can indeed succeed in doing work of significance to society.[7]

INTEREST IN SUBJECT-MATTER FIELD

It should not be surprising that while about one-third of all teachers listed their interest in their academic subject as a reason to teach, there is a major difference between high school teachers and elementary teachers. In the NEA survey, 60% of high school teachers said that their interest in subject matter was a prime reason to enter teaching, while only 22% of elementary teachers gave this reason. Middle school teachers were in the middle, with 43% saying they became teachers because of their interest in a specific academic subject. Given the structure of schooling, these differences make perfect sense. High school teachers, and to some extent middle school teachers, usually teach only one or two subjects. A high school teacher may teach chemistry and physics, or social studies, history, and perhaps English Literature. But it would be highly unlikely for any high school teacher to teach all of these subjects. Elementary teachers, on the other hand, nearly always teach all of these and other subjects to the same group of students, even if they occasionally have experts in the arts or mathematics join them for an hour or two a week. For a person who loves a specific field of academic study, high school teaching is one of the best places to indulge that passion—be it for history, mathematics, biology, or the Spanish language—and share it with a large audience.

Teacher Jennifer Welborn says:

> I like teaching science. It's hands-on and interesting for many kids. But I want my students to do more than just have fun in science. I want them to come away with some big ideas they can apply later on in real-life situations. I feel it's important for kids to know that science is one way of knowing—a way of gaining knowledge about the material world.[8]

Other teachers like teaching English, social studies, or elementary-level reading. But all good teachers like teaching their subjects and feel that it is important for their students to know what they have to offer. Without a passion for their subjects, teachers would quickly find their profession a drudgery.

Educational researcher Robert Fried describes many different ways teachers can be passionate about their work. One of these ways is having a passion for their subject matter:

> You can be passionate about your field of knowledge: in love with the poetry of Emily Dickinson or the prose of Marcus Garvey; dazzled by the spiral of DNA or the swirl of van Gogh's cypresses; intrigued by the origins of the Milky Way or the demise of the Soviet empire; delighted by the sound of Mozart or the sonority of French vowels; a manic for health and fitness or wild about algebraic word problems. . . .[9]

A passion for knowledge and for sharing that knowledge with young people has taken many teachers far in their work.

On the other hand, as Herbert Kohl indicates in the **Reading** in this chapter, many teachers—and Kohl is one of them—find the integration of different subjects more intriguing than any one subject:

> I still don't know how children learn to read, even though I can teach them to do it, so I hope to learn more about the actual process. I would like to teach calculus to six-year-olds and nonlinear differential equations to eight-year-olds; introduce particle physics and complexity theory into the elementary school curriculum; create and test science and math programs, beginning in kindergarten, that are based on how contemporary scientists work and think. . . .

A passion for subject matter is definitely not limited to high school teaching.

OTHER INFLUENCES

Some people discover an interest in teaching in the middle of their active careers, others in the middle of college, and others almost from birth. Some people are inspired

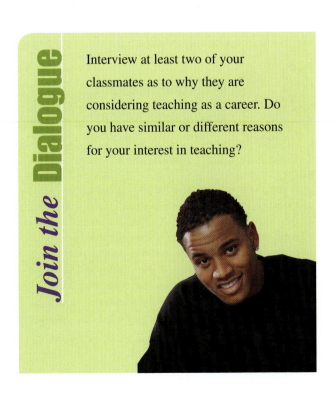

Join the Dialogue

Interview at least two of your classmates as to why they are considering teaching as a career. Do you have similar or different reasons for your interest in teaching?

to teach by a teacher they have had, are encouraged by a family member, or simply feel "I've always wanted to be a teacher." In her **Reading** essay, Melinda Pellerin-Duck says, "I could not see myself doing anything else but teaching; it is my vocation. It is part of my life, my soul, and my heart." She also sees herself as coming from a long line of teachers, even if many of them were not formal, paid teachers:

> *I am descended from a slave who withstood tremendous odds, lived and raised her family, and gave her family heirlooms not of material wealth but of the wealth of words, stories, prayers, and love. This woman, my great-great-grandmother, who had no formal education, was my first teacher, one who helped me understand the power of love, sacrifice, and vocation that teaching truly is.*

Other teachers might not use quite the same language, but Judy Logan, in *Teaching Stories*, describes herself as a born teacher. She writes:

> *Although my mother attended one year of junior college, no one in my parents' families had ever graduated from college. Still, somehow my parents conveyed to me that there was no question but that I would go to college and, in my mind, there was never a question that I would grow up to be a teacher. Since second grade, when I fell in love with the kindness of my instructor, Miss Miles, I had wanted to be a teacher. In the 1950s, this was the best career I could imagine for myself. Teaching was a traditional woman's profession at that time, but in my family it was still traditional for a woman to be a homemaker.*

A QUESTION OF . . .

Why did you want to be a teacher?

"I have never had a moment when I wanted to become a teacher; I have simply always been one. Even as a child I helped friends with school work or shared my notes from class. In fact, it is a family joke that I give more information than anyone wants to hear, correct more children than my own, and encourage strangers as though they were cherished friends. Teaching is a natural bent of my personality and pursuing a career in education was only a selfish indulgence."

—*Laura Morris, middle school math teacher* ■

Many of us can remember a teacher or two who first inspired us to want to do the same work ourselves. Many can also remember a family member who encouraged us to consider teaching, as well as relatives who thought we were crazy to even think about teaching. But for Logan, and for many of us, it was also an early opportunity to actually teach—in a community group, a tutoring program for younger people, or another informal setting—that made us think teaching was what we were meant to do. The experience of student teaching confirmed what Logan had felt since second grade. As a graduate student, she was assigned a student-teaching placement: "While I always knew I wanted to be a teacher, it wasn't until I taught that I realized how right this was for me. I can't explain this. I was a potter who had discovered clay, a swimmer in water, a gardener with her hands in the dirt . . . ." With her initial interest confirmed in this way, Logan began what turned out to be a 24-year tenure as a high school teacher in San Francisco. She is far from alone in telling this sort of story.

Jennifer Welborn, on the other hand, like many other teachers, tried several careers before settling on teaching. Some, like Welborn, tried hard not to be teachers. She writes, "I've taken many a twist and turn in my career path to becoming a middle school science teacher, including two stints in private schools and a job with a college textbook publisher." She even cried when a career counselor told her she should be a teacher. But in the end, having tried other lines of work, Welborn came back to teaching with a clear conviction that it was right for her. She says, "At this point in my life, I cannot think of anything I would rather do. Teaching is a compelling profession. I've come back to classroom teaching three times in my life. I'm here now for the long haul."[10]

>> Why Do Some People Leave Teaching?

Teaching is not for everyone. While thousands of teachers would agree with Ayers, Pellerin-Duck, and the other teachers mentioned, there are others who would not. Sometimes the issue is a matter of individual preference—teaching is simply not as satisfying to some people as it is to others. Certainly not everyone has Judy Logan's experience of immediately feeling at home in the classroom; for some of us it takes a year or two, or even longer, to feel at home as a teacher. Some people plan to teach for a year or two and then move on to something else. However, the current reality is that too many people leave teaching, especially in the early years of their careers, and many of those who leave had planned to stay. Between 40% and 50% of all new teachers leave within the first 5 years. This is a serious problem not only for our society, which needs more qualified teachers, but also for those individuals who may have spent several years in college or graduate school preparing to teach. That is why it is important to ask early in a teacher preparation program, "Is this for me?" and "What kind of school will be most supportive of my work?"

Perhaps the most thorough research on teacher attrition (as the teacher drop-out rate is called) has been done by Richard M. Ingersoll. In the article that is included in the **Readings** at the end of this chapter, Ingersoll and his coauthor, Thomas M. Smith, summarize their surveys of those who leave teaching.[11] They report four primary reasons why new teachers leave the profession:

- personal reasons, such as health or family matters
- school staffing actions, including the elimination of a position or firing
- other job opportunities
- dissatisfaction (a general term that encompasses a multitude of things but that accounted for almost one-third of all those who left teaching)

While it is clear from this research that some people leave teaching for reasons that are hard to change, such as deciding to stay at home with their own young children, other reasons have to do with frustrations about the structure of schools or the way people feel they are being treated as a teacher.

Those who said they left teaching because of dissatisfaction were asked to list up to three reasons for their decision. More than three quarters said they were unhappy with the poor salaries they were receiving. Slightly over one-third listed problems with student discipline, while over one quarter mentioned a lack of support from the school's administration, such as having a principal who was too rigid or critical or a principal who could never be found when help was needed. (People could give multiple answers, so the percentages sum to far more than 100%.) Concerns about student motivation were listed by 17% of the dissatisfied. Other issues, such as class size or the lack of opportunity for advancement or time for preparation, received very low numbers.

"What does all this mean for me?" you might (and should) be asking. Teaching brings extraordinary joy and satisfaction. For some people, it is a vocation in the truest sense, something they believe they are meant to do. However, like any career, teaching has its frustrations, and some of the concerns reported in recent studies bother some people more than others. So as you ask "Do I really want to be a teacher?" consider the issues we discuss next.

Connections

In Chapter 7, we'll discuss why establishing clear expectations for students is critical to maintaining discipline.

Did you know?

In 18 states, the majority of teachers are age 50 and older. Most of these states are in the Northeast and Northwest. West Virginia tops the list, with almost 68% of its teachers in this age group.

Join the Dialogue

Set up an appointment with someone who is currently teaching at the elementary, middle, or high school level. Ask (1) Why did you become a teacher? and (2) Are you still happy with your decision? What advice and words of wisdom does he or she give you that relate to this point in your exploration?

How Can I Make a Difference?

The Tsunami Is Coming

Not only do almost 50% of incoming teachers head back out the door within their first five years, but experts also predict that a "tsunami"-size teacher shortage could hit the United States by the year 2015. More than half of current teachers are Baby Boomers age 50 and older and will be eligible for retirement in the next decade or so. More than 100,000 veteran teachers may be gone after the 2010–11 school year. One report indicates that we may be facing a shortage of 280,000 math and science teachers.

The good news: Schools will need to fill those jobs. The U.S. Department of Labor predicts that elementary teachers, secondary teachers, and post-secondary teachers will be three of the top nine occupations for college graduates in terms of growth.

The bad news: A huge number of highly experienced teachers will be leaving the classroom—and our students—behind. With them will go years of both academic and on-the-job training, as well as wisdom and advice that are priceless.

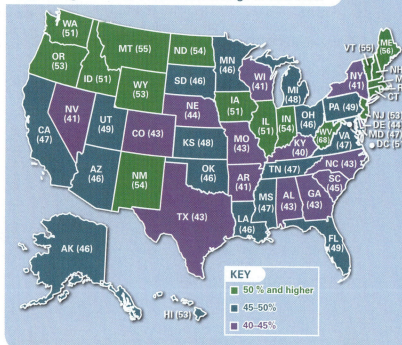

Percentage of Public School Teachers Age 50 and Older

KEY
- 50 % and higher
- 45–50%
- 40–45%

Source: U.S. Department of Education, Schools, and Staffing Survey, 2003–2004; NCTAF analysis.

DISCUSSION QUESTIONS

- As someone who may be entering teaching in the next few years, what would you do to access that experienced talent that might not be available in the classroom right next door?

- What should incoming teachers suggest, ask for, or fight for that will help them be better prepared and more effective in interacting with their students?

Sources: Der Bedrosian, Jeanette. (2009, April 6). "A 'Tsunami' of Boomer Retirements Is on the Horizon." *USA Today,* from USAToday .com. National Commission on Teaching and America's Future. (April 2008). "Learning Teams: Creating What's Next." Washington, D.C. Pytel, Barbara. "Baby Boomer Teachers Retiring." http://suite101.com; accessed July 21, 2007.
Rothberg, Steven. "Top Nine Growth Occupations for College Graduates." http://MyCollegeRecruiter.com; accessed May 6, 2009.

SALARIES

Am I going to be happy with a teacher's salary? While teachers' salaries have risen dramatically over the last decades and the benefits, including health insurance and **pensions**, are better than for most other kinds of work, teachers are not likely to ever make as much money as lawyers, doctors, or people in the business world. There is, of course, extraordinary satisfaction to be found in teaching that many of us believe is "priceless" and cannot be found anywhere else. That satisfaction is a major reason why every year many individuals leave higher-paying but less meaningful jobs to enter teaching. It's important to be realistic as you think about the sources of satisfaction—both financial and nonfinancial—that matter to you.

pension Regular income normally provided to retired employees by a previous employer.

Increases in the Average Teacher's Annual Salary

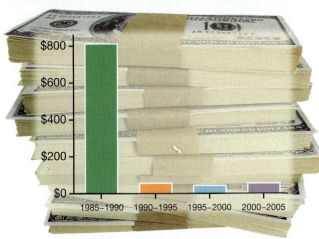

Source: American Federation of Teachers, "Survey and Analysis of Teacher Salary Trends 2007." Copyright 2008.

Did you know?

The average teachers' salary in the United States is $51,000. The highest paid teachers (top of the scale for long-time teachers) are in Santa Ana, California, earning around $95,000. The lowest-paid, entry-level teachers are in Albuquerque, New Mexico, where teachers' salaries start at around $30,000.

SUPPORT

Am I going to be able to find the kind of support that will help me stay in teaching and be successful at it? This question is harder for you to answer at this point, but it is worth thinking about now. Traditionally, teacher induction—that first year on the job after all the courses and supervised student teaching are over—has been "sink or swim." For many, the first year is when you show up at the school that hired you, get the keys to your classroom, and then are on your own. Teaching has not had the equivalent of a doctor's years of hospital residency or a lawyer's work as a highly supervised junior partner.

But that is changing. More and more school districts are creating mentoring programs, in which a new teacher is paired with a senior teacher who can spend time in the classroom, advise how to handle a difficult lesson or a difficult student, and counsel how to succeed in the work. Many schools also offer induction programs in which new teachers can support each other, learn from experts, and discuss their initial difficulties. Ellen Moir, executive director of the New Teacher Center at the University of California at Santa Cruz, describes five essential stages of a comprehensive system of professional development:

Connections

In Chapter 9, we'll see how teachers' salaries compare to those of other major professions.

1. *recruitment*—when someone first considers becoming a teacher
2. *pre-service preparation*—when someone participates in an undergraduate, graduate, or alternative program to receive an initial license to teach
3. *induction*—being hired and getting through the critical first year
4. *professional development*—continued mentoring and support
5. *instructional leadership*—as one grows in skill and confidence to be a leader among peers

Right now, you are most likely at the second stage in this list. At every level, it is important that teachers receive support from thoughtful mentors so that they will neither leave teaching nor stagnate in one position.[12] When looking at a first job, asking some hard questions of the school and district is absolutely critical. You want to find the position that will support you and encourage you to succeed and continue to grow so that you can take charge of your professional life.

The Ingersoll and Smith survey makes it very clear that those who have the responsibility for schools—school administrators, school boards, and state education agencies and legislatures—need to take a number of critical steps. These include raising teachers' salaries, supporting teachers in handling discipline, and developing better ways for

Mentoring for New Teachers: The Toledo Plan

The Toledo (Ohio) Federation of Teachers and the Toledo Public Schools have developed a program of peer evaluation based on the **teachers' union's** belief that experienced teachers are in the best position to screen new entrants into the profession. This program began in 1981, when the Toledo Federation successfully negotiated the first peer-evaluation system of its kind in the United States. Under the Toledo Plan, every first-year teacher in Toledo has a consultant who works with him or her to help develop a sense of personal strengths and weaknesses as well as a plan for professional growth to assure that the district's performance standards can be met. In answer to the question "What is the evaluation component of the program?" the Toledo union responds: "The evaluation process is one of continuous mutual goal-setting based on detailed observations and follow-up conferences where the consulting teacher and intern can establish goals for improvement based on specific evaluation criteria."

Consulting teachers are chosen from teachers who have at least 5 years of experience and outstanding evaluations and references from fellow teachers and their principal. They are then assigned to full-time duties as consultants and work

closely with new teachers on teaching procedures, classroom management, knowledge of subject matter, and continuing academic preparation. The Toledo Plan is governed by an Internal Board of Review that includes five union representatives and four representatives from the superintendent's office. Toledo's leaders—in both the union and the district—are convinced that their program is a key part of the district's growing academic success and brings "positive benefits to students by improving the quality of instruction and promoting the professional growth of the teaching staff." The plan has also dramatically reduced district–union tensions over personnel issues. Toledo's union leaders believe that, in order to succeed, a mentoring plan must have widespread support from teachers, the union, and the administration and that the union must be strong enough to retain the confidence of its members. For more information, go to **www.tft250.org**.

teacher union Professional unions that negotiate for the teachers in a school district as a group in order to provide job security and certain benefits to teachers and act as their voice in government.

administrators to interact with teachers. Teachers who receive good preparation for teaching and who then receive support during their crucial early years as teachers, including thoughtful district-wide induction programs or mentoring from a senior colleague, are much less likely to leave teaching than are those who do not.[13]

There are no easy answers to the questions regarding salary and support. Educator Barbara McEwan reflects on what happens to teachers when they run into serious difficulty for the first time: "Some throw in the towel at this point and leave the profession. . . . Some do the minimum amount of work necessary to get by. . . . Others roll up their sleeves, work hard, continually find new challenges, and love what they do almost every minute of their professional lives."[14] No one wants to prepare for a career and then, early on, simply "throw in the towel." Even worse, no one wants to "do the minimum amount of work" and wait to retire. Yet it takes hard work and careful planning to make teaching a career in which it is possible to "love every minute"—or at least most minutes.

YouDecide

In 1776, few teachers stayed in the profession more than 5 years. Today, 40–50% leave during that time frame. Coincidence?

As many as 40% of the graduates of Harvard College in the 140 years between its founding in 1636 and the American Revolution in 1776 taught at some point in their lives. None of them had any formal preparation for teaching. It was assumed that because they had been students themselves, they could figure out what needed to be done as a schoolteacher. For example, John Adams, who would go on to a career as a lawyer, revolutionary politician, and second president of the United States, spent three years teaching school in Worcester, Massachusetts, following his graduation from Harvard College. In March 1756, Adams wrote in his diary: "Is it not then the highest Pleasure my Friend to preside in this little World. . .and fire the new born soul with a noble ardor and Emulation. The World affords no greater Pleasure."[16] Not all of Adams's comments about teaching were as positive as this one, but his sense of satisfaction with the profession is evident even after two and a half centuries. For all the pleasure he received from teaching, Adams moved on quickly. He had brought to teaching neither the preparation nor the commitment that an expanded school system would need in later generations.

>> Historically Speaking: What Has Motivated People to Teach at Different Times in the Past?

Unfortunately, there was no NEA survey or other similar study of the reasons people entered or left teaching in the 18th, 19th, or early 20th centuries. Many people undoubtedly became teachers for many different reasons at different times in the past. While we will never know all their stories, we are fortunate that the stories of many teachers have been recorded. From these stories, we can learn a great deal about why teachers taught in earlier times.

THE NATION'S FIRST TEACHERS

Two hundred fifty years ago, before the United States became a nation, teaching was often something young women did at home and young men did between the end of college and the beginning of what they saw as their real career, often as a lawyer or minister. Few paid teachers in the colonial era stayed in the profession for more than 5 years before moving on.[15] Teaching allowed young men who had recently graduated from college to earn the money needed to continue their education or to keep themselves gainfully employed while waiting for better opportunities.

John Adams, second president of the United States, was a teacher in his first job after graduation from college. Much later, President Lyndon B. Johnson also taught school before entering politics.

TEACHING BECOMES A WOMEN'S PROFESSION

In the 19th century, teaching was transformed from a primarily male to a primarily female profession. In 1830, the vast majority of teachers in the United States were men. By 1850 approximately 60% of teachers were women, and by 1900 more than 75% of the nation's teachers were women.[17] One woman who played a key role in the gender change of the profession was Catharine Beecher. Beginning in the 1830s, Beecher set out to create opportunities for middle-class, single women like herself, who were expected to marry or stay in the home of relatives as the maiden aunt—a pretty narrow set of options. Though she accepted, or pretended to accept, the cultural expectations of the time, based on the belief that women's nature was dramatically different from that of men, Beecher wanted to create a new professional independence within the social norms. In 1835, she wrote: "Woman, whatever are her relations in life, is necessarily the guardian of the nursery, the companion of childhood, and the constant model of imitation. It is her hand that first stamps impressions on the immortal spirit, that must remain forever."[18] Thus, she argued, school boards should hire women to be teachers. As teachers, women could still operate in their own sphere—as that sphere was defined in the 19th century—but do so with other people's children, not only their own. Beecher also reminded the ever-cash-strapped school boards that women would work for much less money than men would. In her writings and her negotiations with school boards, Beecher struck a bargain that gave women far greater opportunities than they had had in the United States before 1830, but it also relegated teaching to a lower-salaried profession. Unfortunately, the results are still with us today.

The shift in teaching from a male to a female profession began in the Northeast but quickly included the whole nation. According to a Massachusetts state census taken in 1865, at the end of the Civil War, teaching was the third most popular job (and the most popular "white collar" job) for all women who worked outside the home, a considerable proportion in such a highly industrialized state. As historian Michael Katz has observed, the "middle-class girl who wanted to work at something respectable had little choice; teaching it almost had to be."[19] And what was true in Massachusetts became true for the country. In the 19th century, over a fairly short period of time, teach-

Students sit on make-shift chairs in a one-room school room.

An African American teacher instructs her students in 1866.

ing became what another historian, Nancy Hoffman, has called "Woman's 'True' Profession," and women came to make up the vast majority of teachers.[20]

In the early years of the 19th century, women—like the men who had gone before them—underwent relatively little preparation for their jobs. In time, educational reformers such as Catharine Beecher, Emma Willard, Horace Mann, and Mary Lyon began to organize some of the first teacher-preparation programs in the United States, the earliest forerunners of today's teachers' colleges and schools and departments of education. The first women teachers were hired through a very informal system. Usually someone with political connections in the rural district, town, or city would put out the word that a teacher was needed. Especially in cities, political connections were essential to getting the job. The young women were strictly supervised, and most left after only a few years on the job. Until the middle of the 20th century, many school districts expected a woman to leave teaching if she got married.

THE FIRST "PEACE CORPS"— TEACHERS FOR THE MIDWEST AND SOUTH

As the United States expanded and changed in the 1830s and 1840s, young women became teachers at schools in their hometowns, but they also sought meaningful work,

freedom, and adventure as teachers in new places. Communities in the new territories and states—Ohio, Indiana, Illinois, Michigan, Wisconsin, and Minnesota—needed to establish schools to teach children to read, write, and share in the relatively new American democracy. How could these schools find teachers? No one was willing to pay high salaries to attract them, and no one pretended that working conditions would be comfortable.

Once again, Catharine Beecher—along with William Slade, a former governor of Vermont—came to the rescue. In 1848, they created the Board of National Popular Education. It was designed as a kind of early "Peace Corps" to recruit young women as teachers and send them west to "civilize" the frontier. Young women could escape the intense supervision of their families and home communities and at the same time serve the nation. Many young women believed that they were making the world a better place by sharing learning and American cultural assumptions with young people who might not otherwise learn. It was a powerful combination, and many responded to the call.

In 1849, one of the National Board's teachers wrote home from her assignment in the then frontier town of St. Paul, Minnesota: "My labors have been abundantly blessed during the past season. . . . This is a great country to make one grow. All the faculties are brought into action. I feel as if it was one of heaven's best blessings, that I was sent here, where there can be no shirking of labor—no release

Teachable Moment

Charlotte Forten Grimké

Charlotte Forten was born a free African American in Philadelphia in 1837. With her family's support she attended Salem Normal School (now Salem State College) and then taught at the racially integrated Epes Grammar School in Salem, one of the very few racially integrated schools in the United States at the time. When she learned of the opportunity to go south in the midst of the Civil War in order to teach newly freed slaves in South Carolina, she wrote in her journal: "At any cost I will go." And she did, volunteering with the New England Freedmen's Aid Society. While the majority of northern women who went south to teach were White, Forten was not the only African American among them. The selections from her journal that follow give a sense of what her southern teaching experience meant for her. The first entry was written in Salem and relates to her decision to go south. The next three entries were written after she had arrived in war-torn South Carolina.

Sunday, August 17 [1862]. *My twenty-fifth birthday. Tisn't a very pleasant thought that I have lived a quarter of a century, and am so very, very ignorant. Ten years ago, I hoped for a different fate at twenty-five. But why complain? The accomplishments, the society, the delights of travel which I have dreamed of and longed for all my life, I am now convinced can never be mine. If I can go to Port Royal, I will try to forget all these desires. I will pray that God in his goodness will make me noble enough to find my highest happiness in doing my duty. Since Mrs. J. has given me such sad accounts of the sufferings of the poor freed people my desire of helping them has increased. It is but little I c'ld do, I know, but that little I w'ld do with all my heart.*

Friday, October 31 [1862]. *Miss Towne went to Beaufort today, and I taught for her. I enjoyed it much. The children are well-behaved and eager to learn. It will be a happiness to teach here.*

Wednesday, November 5 [1862]. *Had my first regular teaching experience, and to you and you only friend beloved, will acknowledge that it was* not *a very pleasant one. Part of my scholars are very tiny—babies, I call them—and it is hard to keep them quiet and interested while I am hearing the larger ones. They are too young even for the alphabet, it seems to me.*

Thursday, November 27 [1862]. *Thanksgiving Day. . .This morning a large number—Superintendents, teachers, and freed people, assembled in the little Baptist church. It was a sight that I shall not soon forget—that crowd of eager, happy faces from which the shadow of slavery had passed. "Forever free!" "Forever free!" Those magical words were all the time singing themselves in my soul, and never before have I felt so truly grateful to God.*

QUESTIONS

- If you had lived in 1862, would you have gone south like Grimké, or would you have stayed in your school in Salem, Massachusetts?
- Can you think of teaching situations today where a person might leave his or her "comfort zone" of experiences to take on unknown challenges?

from responsibility, and no lack of room to work in."[21] For this woman, the challenge and responsibility of teaching gave her life a meaning and purpose that she never would have found staying safely in New England, even though many also wrote home about the terrible loneliness of being separated from family and friends. The sense that teaching challenges a person to the extent that "all faculties are brought into action" is perhaps an earlier version of Parker Palmer's reasons for saying that "teaching is the finest work I know." It remains to this day one of the key attractions of the profession.

During and after the Civil War, a similar campaign was launched to send teachers to the states of the former Confederacy to teach the newly freed slaves. Early in the war—as soon as the Northern troops freed the first slaves, in 1862—the leaders of the Union army found a thirst for literacy among those who had so recently been held in slavery. Those few slaves who had learned to read and write were teaching other slaves as the Northern troops arrived, and they never stopped teaching. The first teachers in the new South were newly freed Blacks, not northern Whites. African American teachers had a special answer to the question "Why teach?" As the Civil War was coming to a close, Mrs. E. Garrison Jackson, an African American from Rhode Island, applied for a job teaching in the South, saying, "I think it is our duty as a people to spend our lives in trying to elevate our own race." Fanny Jackson Coppin, an African American woman who educated generations of teachers as principal of the Institute for Colored Youth in Philadelphia from 1865 to 1902, reminded her students: "You can do much to alleviate the condition of our people. Do not be discouraged." The civil rights movement of the 1950s and 1960s grew in part out of this earlier dedication to teaching, fostering yet another generation of teachers committed to "elevate our own race." The belief that teaching can be of value in society has long been a reason for doing it.[22]

IMMIGRATION TRANSFORMS TEACHING

After the Civil War, hundreds and later thousands of **immigrants** came to the United States from across the Pacific—from China and Japan—to work in the gold fields, on the railroads, and in the emerging industries of the West Coast. In the 1880s and 1890s, the United States was further transformed by the arrival of even more thousands of immigrants from across the Atlantic, primarily from southern and eastern Europe. Catholics from Italy, Orthodox Christians from Greece, Jews from Poland and Russia, and many others from countries small and large were fleeing **persecution** and the terrible poverty that plagued the majority of people in countries still governed for the benefit of a small ruling elite.

Many different groups of immigrants came to the United States, and their labor was needed in the factories and shops that were transforming the American economy. At the same time, established residents of the United States were worried about the changes. Could the nation incorporate so many new immigrants, with their different cultures, and still remain "American" as the older residents defined it? Others thought they had already found a solution to "Americanizing" the immigrants. Early in the 1800s, at the time of the great Irish immigration, political leaders had devised a solution to **assimilating** immigrants from

> **immigrants** People who move from country of their birth to a new country of permanent residence.
>
> **persecution** Subjugation or mistreatment of a group of people based on factors such as race, religion, or beliefs.
>
> **assimilation** Minority groups forced or voluntarily blending into the dominant society by adopting social practices and beliefs.

In a New York City classroom, students attentively watch their teacher from crowded pews.

non-English parts of Europe into a nation still dominated by English culture. Boston's Mayor Josiah Quincy announced that "all children must be taught to respect and revere law and order," while Edward Everett Hale told the school committee that it was their responsibility to "save society not with the cannon and the rifle, but with the spelling book, the grammar, and the Bible."[23] Immigrant students must be required to attend school if this solution was to work.

In Chapter 9, we'll look at the role unions play in a teacher's life today.

Connections

As the number of schools grew to accommodate the children of these new immigrants, the opportunities for careers in teaching also expanded. In 1870 there were 126,822 teachers in the United States, while by 1900 the number had more than tripled to 450,000.[24] Teaching continued to offer the combination of personal freedom and the excitement of fostering learning that has long drawn people to the profession. One Boston teacher reflected on her first day in the classroom in 1889:

> *The odd thing about the first class is that while other classes may fade more or less from the memory, that first group given to the young green girl in a September of long ago, emerges strong and clear. . . . There was positively not a thing to worry about except to acquit oneself with credit in a happily chosen profession. Of course the pay was small or so it seems today. But at that time it seemed to me ridiculously large: thirty-eight dollars a month was the handsome beginning. . . . When I reached the master's office and told him it was hard to wait for the school term to begin, he shook with ill-suppressed laughter. That puzzled me. What was funny? Did he not feel that way too?[25]*

Across a century and a half, in both rural and urban locations, teaching has been blessed with those who join it each year finding it "hard to wait for the school term to begin."

PROGRESSIVE EDUCATION AND THE EMERGENCE OF THE HIGH SCHOOL

During the first decades of the 20th century, two important developments changed the nature of teaching and thereby impacted the reasons for becoming a teacher. The first was the progressive education movement, a multifaceted campaign to improve the quality of schools and the present and future lives of students. The second was the emergence of the high school as an important part of education in the United States.

Progressive Education Progressive education meant many different things. In essence, it was part of a larger effort to improve the quality of American life—especially urban life, which swept the United States around 1900. There was growing concern among teachers that the immigrant children should not simply be "Americanized" but should be shown respect for the culture they brought to this country. There was also an interest in more innovative styles of teaching to help students be happier and more successful in school. In 1899, John Dewey, perhaps the best-known voice of progressive education, described his goal for a progressive school when he wrote of the need to reorganize schools as "an embryonic community life, active with types of occupations that reflect the life of the larger society and are permeated throughout with the spirit of art, history, science." Suddenly, teaching was an attractive profession for people who wanted to make a difference, to create in small school communities the model for a larger society that, in Dewey's words, is "worthy, lovely, and harmonious."

Progressive educators also wanted to make teaching a more inviting profession for those entering it. Ella Flagg Young, progressive superintendent of the Chicago Public Schools, wrote in 1901 that teachers needed to be given more professional respect and freedom, with "close supervision" (a form of school administration that attempted to regulate every aspect of teachers' lives) replaced by a structure in which the teacher corps was "unfettered in its activity in striving to realize those things which will evolve themselves in a free play of thought. . . ." Margaret Haley, the leader of the Chicago teachers, argued for a teachers' union as the key to teachers gaining power and respect in their work lives. In 1910, New York City teacher Grace Strachan campaigned successfully for "equal pay for equal work" and an end to paying women teachers lower wages than men for the same job. By the end of the progressive era in the 1920s, teaching had become a much more appealing profession for many.[26]

High Schools While the first institutions known as high schools emerged in the United States as early as the 1830s, it was really after 1900 that high schools became widespread across the country. It is hard for us today to comprehend, but only in the 1930s did the majority of Americans begin attending high school at all, and only in the 1950s did the majority graduate from high school. As high schools—and later junior high schools or middle schools—became more common, some teachers were given important new opportunities. High school teachers, especially in cities, usually taught only one or two subjects, so teachers who had a love of a particular subject—be it history or mathematics or the sciences—could specialize in a way that no elementary teacher could. In addition, high school teachers were paid more than elementary teachers, sometimes substantially more.

One reason for the higher pay was the more advanced education expected of high school teachers; another was the higher prestige awarded to high school teaching. One example is Fern Persons, who spent the first years of her teaching career, between 1914 and 1926, as an elementary teacher in four different schools. In 1926, after further study at Western Michigan College and Olivet College, she became a high school math teacher at Olivet (Michigan) High School, where she subsequently became princi-

The Peace Corps has given many Americans the opportunity to teach abroad. For many, it is their first teaching experience and the beginning of a lifetime career in teaching.

pal and later district superintendent.[27] Even if they did not become principals or superintendents, many other teachers, women and men alike, followed the same basic career path, beginning in an often rural elementary school and moving in time to cities and to high schools where they were paid more and treated with more respect.

While the salaries of elementary and high school teachers were equalized later in the 20th century, the work continued to be quite different in the two institutions and remains so today. Happily, as the salary and prestige differences have all but disappeared, a prospective teacher can decide whether to prepare for a career in elementary, middle school, or high school teaching based on personal preference for the type of teaching involved—preferences related to subject matter and to spending time engaging young people of particular age and developmental stages.[28]

MOVEMENTS OF THE 1960s

Many aspects of life in the United States were transformed, some quite dramatically, in the 1960s. Yet few observers focus on the substantial changes in the teaching profession resulting from several intersecting developments in those years. Like many movements in the 1960s, those that impacted teaching had roots that went far back.

The Peace Corps   In the 19th century, many young teachers—mostly women but also some men—had found opportunities for service and adventure by going to teach in schools of the new territories of the Midwest and later the post–Civil War South. In the 20th century, teachers and aspiring teachers found equally adventurous opportunities traveling abroad. While the Peace Corps, founded in the 1960s, was perhaps the most far-reaching effort to send Americans overseas to bring American culture and styles of education to different countries, it was far from the first such

effort. Beginning in the 1890s, Protestant missionaries, with strong federal support, traveled to the Philippine Islands (newly acquired from Spain as a result of war in 1898), bringing a new style of education to the islands. Throughout the 20th century, similar efforts to export U.S.-style education, culture, and democracy were spearheaded by cadres of teachers. For the last half-century, the Peace Corps has offered important opportunities for adventure and service. It has also brought back to the United States teachers with a much more sophisticated sense of the values of other nations and cultures, and often a humbler sense of the potential arrogance of U.S. efforts to transform others who may not be as interested in being transformed.[29]

Increasing Educational Requirements

Ever since the first specialized school to prepare teachers opened in the 1830s with a 1-year curriculum, the standards for entry into teaching had been slowly rising. But it was during the 1950s that state after state finally raised the bar by requiring every new teacher to complete a baccalaureate degree prior to starting teaching. It is hard to imagine people entering teaching without a college degree, but that was the norm until the middle of the 20th century. As late as the 1930s, most new teachers had completed only 2 years of college, and a quarter of the nation's teachers—especially those teaching in rural areas—did not have even that much education. Then suddenly, after World War II, every state changed the rules, and every new teacher needed a college degree. The results became apparent in schools throughout the following decades. In 1961, almost 15% of the nation's teachers still had less than a bachelor's degree; 10 years later, fewer than 3% were without a degree, and by 1981 the number was less than 1%, with more and more teachers seeking a master's degree. The nation's teachers were better prepared than ever before.[30]

Nancy Pelosi, Speaker of the U.S. House of Representatives, and Sonia Sotomayor, the first Hispanic woman to serve on the U.S. Supreme Court.

The Women's Movement

In the 1830s and 1840s, when Catharine Beecher proposed to school boards around the country that they should hire women instead of men as teachers, she was seeking to open a profession to women who previously had been excluded from most forms of work outside the home and farm. In the 1950s and 1960s, the women's movement transformed the professional opportunities for women more than at any earlier time. While more jobs had opened to women in the decades between 1830 and 1960, most newspapers still ran separate "men's jobs" and "women's jobs" sections in the want-ads, and the realm of acceptable women's work was substantially limited. Today, women make up the majority of those studying in medical and law schools and serve in a wide range of professional and governmental positions, from university presidents to hospital administrators to U.S. Supreme Court justices and even Speaker of the U.S. House of Representatives. Women today have options that were unimaginable to their mothers and grandmothers.

As a result of the changes brought about by the women's movement, women who decide to teach do so because they want to, not because, as women, it is their only option. And men have the freedom to become teachers—including elementary and early childhood teachers—that their fathers and grandfathers never enjoyed. However, women still are not as widely represented in the most prestigious and highly-paid professions, and teachers still are underpaid in part because teaching is seen as "women's work" by too many. Men receive quizzical looks when they say they are teachers, especially if they are elementary teachers. Nevertheless, the professional freedom—for teachers and nonteachers,

women and men—is greater than in 1960 or at any previous time in the nation's history. And this new freedom has had a positive impact on both individual teaching careers and the diversity of the staff of many schools.

The Civil Rights Movement

After the 1954 U.S. Supreme Court ruling in *Brown* v. *Board of Education,* deliberate racial segregation in the schools became illegal in the United States. After years of resistance, states across the South, where the majority of legally segregated schools existed, began to integrate the schools. However there were unintended consequences of the movement to end racial segregation in the schools. All too often, the new integration resulted in sending Black students to White schools and closing Black schools. In many cases, closing the Black schools also meant firing the Black teachers. Sometimes the teaching staff was integrated along with the student body; however, the Black teachers often were relegated to second-class status, and the Black principal became the assistant principal to the White school leader. In the decade following the *Brown* decision,

---

Connections

In Chapter 3, we'll discuss the real people behind the *Brown* v. *Board of Education* case. In Chapter 11, we'll see how *Brown* v. *Board of Education* reflects the extraordinary role that politics and government—at all levels—play in shaping schools in the United States.

Join the Dialogue

Research the story of a teacher from the past. Do you think the reasons he or she became a teacher would apply today?

31,584 African American teachers lost their jobs in southern and border states. The problem of teaching being far too often a White profession, in spite of the growing ethnic diversity of the nation's students, persists to the present day.[31]

It is also important to note here that the larger civil rights movement had an impact on the job description of teachers that is not always recognized. As we discuss in Chapters 3 and 4, before the 1960s many students were excluded from school informally or formally. Students who arrived in the United States not speaking English, students with a disability, and students who did not find the culture of the school a comfortable place were allowed to simply drop out, with few questions asked. Teachers were expected to teach those for whom school worked well and not worry about the others. Today, teachers are expected to teach every child, to "leave no child behind." This change in the job description of teachers is yet to be fully recognized.

For the last two centuries, women and men have entered the teaching profession because they enjoy being with young people, because teaching provides an opportunity to share in the excitement of learning, because it offers a level of freedom not otherwise available to them, and because, through teaching, they might "make the world a better place," especially for the growing numbers of young people who are attending school longer. Today, the new and higher standards teachers are expected to meet—standards being enforced within a growing shortage of qualified teachers—stand to transform teaching and the reasons for teaching, yet again.

>> Should I Be a Teacher?

Don't worry. No one expects you to have the magical answer to this question yet. However, as you think about the reasons other people have given for choosing, staying in, or leaving teaching, it is important that you ask yourself these questions: "Why am I considering teaching?" "How will I find out if it is

What About Me?

- What about teaching most appeals to you?

- What excites you when you think about standing in front of your own classroom?

- What is the least appealing thing about teaching? What about it scares you?

right for me?" The reality is that as much as you think about these questions, you may never find the answers until you try teaching. There is no substitute for standing in front of a group of children or youth and seeing what it is like, whether or not your experience is as positive as Judy Logan's or as fulfilling as Parker Palmer's. Today more and more teacher preparation programs are offering the first experience of actually being with young people—of actually teaching—earlier and earlier in the program. It is important to ask when your program will give you this opportunity.

It is of great value to be able to observe real teachers and students in actual school settings, and it is even more valuable to become a participant in the teaching–learning process. Tutoring one student, assisting a teacher with a lesson, working with a small group of students during or after school—any one of these can give you the chance to experience that wonderful moment when a child or adolescent "gets it" for the first time. Whenever you first have the opportunity to stand in front of a class, it is your job to prepare for the experience so that it will be as successful as possible, so that you allow yourself, as Parker Palmer says, to know teaching as the finest work there is even if there are also moments (as Palmer also recognizes) of pure agony. Only when you are informed by a personal sense of the range of experiences and of the feelings teaching creates in you, as well as by stories of what has worked and not worked for other teachers, can you make a wise and informed decision about your own future in this fascinating field.

Herbert Kohl, who has taught school for some 40 years, acknowledges that these are not easy times to be a teacher, yet he sees many reasons to be hopeful. In *The Discipline of Hope: Learning from a Lifetime of Teaching*, he talks about what he calls "schools of hope." He describes such schools

A QUESTION OF . . .

When did you decide you wanted to be a teacher?

"I didn't know for sure that I wanted to teach until I got into the classroom during my student teaching practicum. I had done all the education coursework and still wasn't sure of my career choice until that semester. I found that I loved working with teenagers—I appreciate their idealism, their intelligence, their silliness. It was empowering to have a place in their lives."

—*Dawn Striker, science and math teacher*

as "places where students can work hard without being harassed . . . [and] teachers and staff are delighted to work and are free to innovate while at the same time they are willing to take responsibility for their students' achievement." He also talks about his own hopes to "create a diverse, compassionate, nonracial community of learners where students honor themselves, respect each other, love what they are learning, are passionate about justice, and prepare themselves for compassionate, connected adult lives." Few other professions hold out such promise. All wise educators warn that teaching is difficult work, but they also say, again and again, how wonderfully rewarding and hopeful the work can be.[32]

In the end, however, the main reason for you to consider teaching as a career is the one the best teachers have always given. At the core of this work lie the joy and satisfaction that come from seeing a child's excitement at truly mastering something new. This will remain the ultimate reward of teaching. Perhaps Kohl said it best: "There's no end to the delights and joys of teaching, no limit to the challenges we will continue to face in order to serve children well, and no limit to the creativity and love adults can and should bring to helping children grow through teaching, which is at its heart the discipline of hope." It is a rare privilege to pursue a career that offers so much.

REVIEW >>

- **Why do people become teachers today?**

  Over the years, people have become teachers for many different reasons. Nevertheless, certain basic reasons seem to remain true across time and in different locations. People are drawn to teaching because it seems to be "the work they were always cut out for," because "they enjoy being with young people and watching them learn and grow," or because "they want to change the world." These reasons are not very different from one another. Few people enter teaching in order to become rich or famous. Yet many of us are drawn to the wonderfully engaging work of supporting young people in their learning and, through that support, making the world a better place, one child at a time.

- **Why do some people leave teaching?**

  Sadly, it is also true that too many of those who enter teaching find that they cannot stay and make a career of it. Sometimes the lack of administrative support, low salaries, or poor working conditions wear teachers out. Increasingly, however, school districts are seeking to address these issues by paying teachers better salaries, improving the conditions of teachers' work lives, and offering the kinds of strong continuing induction and mentoring programs that help novice teachers succeed in the early years of their work so that they can stay and prosper in the profession. And teachers have often played a major role in changing the schools and the teaching profession for the better.

- **Historically speaking, what has motivated people to teach at different times in the past?**

  Over the decades many different people have become teachers for different reasons. In the early years of the United States many men became teachers for a year or two until a better job became available. Women became teachers because it was virtually the only job available to them, and over time women made up the majority of teachers. After the Civil War, teachers saw the opportunity to use schools as a means to expand the meaning of freedom, especially for newly freed slaves. Some people became teachers because they felt a call to help new immigrants or because they wanted to make schools more humane places for often bored students. In the 1960s, the civil rights movement expanded the diversity of the student body and the responsibilities of teachers, and a new generation embraced the challenge. Increasingly teaching has come to be a profession with high entrance requirements in which people stay for a lifetime. Throughout history, however, teaching has always been a place where people have derived great satisfaction from helping individual students grow and learn new things and from helping to expand the meaning of freedom and justice for communities.

- **Should I be a teacher?**

  It is important for you, as a prospective teacher, to think realistically about how you will respond to these complaints that have been voiced by other teachers. Are teacher salaries realistic for you? How do you think you will respond to a difficult student or a difficult principal? Is there a way to pick a first teaching job—to find the right school or the right district—where support for new teachers is available? The material offered throughout this book will help you in the important process of answering these difficult questions.

Why Do People Become Teachers Today?

From *TO TEACH: THE JOURNEY OF A TEACHER*

BY WILLIAM AYERS

William Ayers is a teacher in Chicago. He has taught at every level from preschool to university and it is clear that he loves teaching and thoughtfully reflects on his chosen profession. During the 2008 presidential campaign, Ayers's name became a well-known name because of his leadership in the radical antiwar politics of the 1960s. Many years later he served on a rather large educational board with Barack Obama, and the presidential candidate was criticized because of his association with this "radical." A lifelong educator, Ayers has written compellingly about the importance of his profession. The selection that follows, from his book *To Teach: The Journey of a Teacher*, describes his own decision to become a teacher and his commitment to stay with the profession.

Teachers are asked hundreds, perhaps thousands, of times why they chose teaching. The question often means: "Why teach, when you could do something more profitable?" "Why teach, since teaching is beneath your skill and intelligence?" The question can be filled with contempt and cynicism or it can be simply a request for understanding and knowledge: "What is there in teaching to attract and keep you?" Either way, it is a question worth pursuing, for there are good reasons to teach and equally good reasons not to teach. Teaching is, after all, different in character from any other profession or job or occupation, and teaching, like anything else, is not for everyone.

There are many reasons not to teach, and they cannot be easily dismissed, especially by those of us who love teaching. Teachers are badly paid, so badly that it is a national disgrace. We earn on average a quarter of what lawyers are paid, half of what accountants make, less than truck drivers and shipyard workers. Romantic appeals aside, wages and salaries are one reflection of relative social value; a collective, community assessment of worth.

Teachers also suffer low status in many communities, in part as a legacy of sexism: Teaching is largely women's work, and it is constantly being deskilled, made into something to be performed mechanically, without much thought or care, covered over with layers of supervision and accountability and bureaucracy, and held in low esteem.

Teachers often work in difficult situations, under impossible conditions. We sometimes work in schools that are large, impersonal, and factory-like; sometimes in schools that resemble war zones.

The complexity of teaching can be excruciating, and for some that may be sufficient reason not to teach (for others, it is one of teaching's most compelling allures).

These are some of the reasons not to teach, and, for me at least, they add up to a compelling case. So, why teach? My own pathway to teaching began long ago in a large, uniquely nurturing family, a place where I experienced the ecstasy of intimacy and the irritation of being known, the power of will

and the boundary of freedom, both the safety and the constraints of family living. I was the middle child of five children, and I had opportunities to learn as well as opportunities to teach. In my family, I learned to balance self-respect with respect for others, assertiveness with compromise, individual choice with group consciousness.

I began teaching in an alternative school in Ann Arbor, Michigan, called the Children's Community. It was a small school with large purposes; a school that, we hoped, would change the world. One of our goals was to provide an outstanding, experience-based education for the young people we taught. Another was to develop a potent model of freedom and racial integration, a model that would have wide impact on other schools and on all of society. We thought of ourselves as an insurgent, experimental counterinstitution; one part of a larger movement for social change.

The year was 1965, and I was twenty years old. For many young people, teaching was not only respectable, it was one of the meaningful, relevant things a person could do. Many schools then, as now, were inhumane, lifeless places. But we were crusading teachers. We felt that we could save the schools, create life spaces and islands of compassion for children and, through our work, help create a new social order. We were intent on living lives that did not make a mockery of our values, and teaching seemed a way to live that kind of life. We were hopeful and altruistic and we were on a mission of change.

Today, teaching may not seem so attractive, nor so compelling in quite the same way. Not only are the schools in even worse shape than before, and the problems seemingly more intractable, but there is a narrow, selfish spirit loose in the land. Idealists are "suckers" in the currency of the day, and the notion that schools should be decent, accessible, and responsive places for all children is just more pie-in-the-sky. With a combative social Darwinism setting the pace in our society, and a cynical sense that morality has no place in our public lives, teaching today can seem a fool's errand.

Source: From William Ayers, *To Teach: The Journey of a Teacher*, New York: Teachers College Press.

But it is not. Teaching is still a powerful calling for many people, and powerful for the same reasons that it has always been so. There are still young people who need a thoughtful, caring adult in their lives; someone who can nurture and challenge them, who can coach and guide, understand and care about them. There are still injustices and deficiencies in society, in even more desperate need of repair. There are still worlds to change—including specific, individual worlds, one by one—and classrooms can be places of possibility and transformation for youngsters, certainly, but also for teachers. Teaching can still be world-changing work. Crusading teachers are still needed—in fact we are needed now more than ever.

And this, I believe, is finally the reason to teach. People are called to teaching because they love children and youth, or because they love being with them, watching them open up and grow and become more able, more competent, more powerful in the world. They may love what happens to themselves when they are with children, the ways in which they become better, more human, more generous. Or they become teachers because they love the world, or some piece of the world enough that they want to show that love to others. In either case, people teach as an act of construction and reconstruction, and as a gift of oneself to others. I teach in the hope of making the world a better place.

From "THE COLORS AND STRANDS OF TEACHING"

BY MELINDA PELLERIN-DUCK

Melinda Pellerin-Duck has remained far from the national spotlight. A teacher in the High School of Commerce in Springfield, Massachusetts, she was named the Massachusetts Teacher of the Year for 2003–2004. She sees her commitment to teaching as rooted in stories from her family dating back to the time when her great-great-grandmother was a slave in Louisiana and in her experience as a student of the Sisters of St. Joseph at Holy Name Elementary School in Springfield. In this article, her sense of calling and her creative approach to curriculum come through loud and clear.

I was meant to be a teacher. It has not been one experience, but many that have taught me this. Life's lessons have made me the person I am, and continue to transform me into the teacher I am becoming. Lessons from students, family, and friends have taught me that patience is a virtue to be embraced in my classroom every day. I've learned perseverance, even when the struggle seems insurmountable. I've learned love, and I've had this love reinforced by the gifts each child brings to my classroom experiences. I've learned about hope, and I know not to judge a person by outside distractions because it is inner beauty that counts. As a teacher, I continue to search for it in each student. These are the lessons I try to instill in each miracle that walks across the threshold of my classroom.

I have always believed that classrooms must transcend traditional convention. Students should participate actively in their own learning; they cannot just sit passively while knowledge is being poured into them. Instruction must be well planned, relevant, interesting, and exciting. To be an outstanding teacher, you must see your students as fellow travelers and learners. In my classroom, we are all "in this together."

A successful teacher understands there is always room for improvement. I am never satisfied with the notion that the longer I teach, the more expert I become. I am not an expert, but I am striving to learn more and to become experienced. I live in the "learning-mode." I am motivated to learn more because I am a teacher reaching for higher standards for myself and for my students. There is nothing more rewarding than helping transform students who

thought they could never create anything meaningful into confident and excited historians. A lesson in world history on the art of Michelangelo finds me jumping on a desk, lying face up, showing students how Michelangelo created his masterpiece. Students are engaged, excited, answering difficult questions about art, style, and form. The students add their own crucial analysis to the work and I, as their teacher, am in awe of them. This is a gift, a miracle.

The rewards of teaching are many. Watching our school's mock trial team, a team that was never supposed to win or achieve, compete against suburban school systems with many more advantages and economic resources makes my heart skip a beat. I have watched the team transform into a confident, well-prepared legal team. It has become a formidable adversary. As the team members advance to the final round of statewide competition, I am inspired by their dedication, their spirit, and their performance. I am like a proud parent watching them soar. In 1995, the team placed second for the Commonwealth of Massachusetts.

Some may question why I continue teaching. My answer is

Source: Melinda Pellerin-Duck, "The Colors and Strands of Teaching," in Nieto, pp. 127–133.

that I teach because I see extraordinary possibilities in my students. I could not see myself doing anything else but teaching; it is my vocation. It is part of my life, my soul, and my heart. It is challenging, at times difficult, but the rewards are overwhelming. As a teacher, I have the most fortunate experience of nurturing our future. If we do it well, combining unforgettable and meaningful instruction with a sense of community, our students will become not only stewards of their destiny, but productive citizens of our nation and the world.

Too often, I hear that old quotation, "Those who can't, teach." It has been used in popular film and culture to poke fun at and criticize our profession. Yet ours is a vocation, a vocation of love; true teachers know this. Those who instruct, who nurture, who hope patiently and lovingly each and every day understand the quotation is really, "Those who *can*, teach." Those who can, find joy in walking into a room with open minds. They teach. Those who can, take students from "I can't" to "I can." They teach. Those who can, counsel and dispense positive discipline, while staying well after school hours with students. They

teach. Those who can, struggle with self-doubt but endure. Those who can, worry about their lesson plans and whether a particular student will have enough clothing to wear, or whether there will be heat in that student's home. Those who can, teach and they do it everyday. I am lucky enough to be one of those who "can."

QUESTIONS

1. Look at the reason William Ayers gives for not teaching? How do you react to those concerns?

2. What are your thoughts about Ayers's assertion that, in spite of all the reasons not to teach, teaching is worth doing?

3. What do you think when you read Pellerin-Duck's comment "I was meant to be a teacher." Does that ring true for you, or is teaching a more recent interest?

Why Do Some People Leave Teaching?

From "THE WRONG SOLUTION TO THE TEACHER SHORTAGE"

BY RICHARD M. INGERSOLL AND THOMAS M. SMITH

Richard Ingersoll, a professor at the University of Pennsylvania, has written a number of books and articles on the problem of teacher turnover and the way this turnover creates a shortage that would not otherwise exist. In this article and in his book *Who Controls Teachers' Work? Power and Accountability in America's Schools*, he and his coauthor not only analyze why teachers leave but also give very clear advice to school leaders and districts as to what they could do to change the situation.

In recent years, researchers and policymakers have told us again and again that severe teacher shortages confront schools. . . . They point to a dramatic increase in the demand for new teachers resulting from two converging demographic trends: increasing student enrollments and increasing numbers of teachers reaching retirement age. Shortfalls of teachers, they say, are forcing many school systems to lower their standards for teacher quality (National Commission on Teaching and America's Future, 1997).

A closer look at the best data available suggests that the conventional wisdom on teacher shortages, although partly correct, also errs in important ways. The demand for teachers has indeed grown. Since 1984, both student enrollments and teacher retirements have increased (Snyder, Hoffman, & Geddes, 1997). Substantial numbers of schools with teaching openings have experienced difficulties finding qualified candidates to fill their positions (Ingersoll, 1999). But the data also show that increases in student enrollment and teacher retirements are not the primary causes of the high demand for new teachers and subsequent staffing difficulties. A larger part of the problem is teacher attrition (leaving

the profession)—which is particularly high among teachers in their first few years of service.

Understanding Employee Turnover

The teaching occupation suffers from chronic and relatively high annual turnover compared with many other occupations. Total teacher turnover is fairly evenly split between two components: *attrition* (those who leave teaching altogether); and *migration* (those who move to teaching jobs in other schools). Teaching is also a relatively large occupation: It represents 4 percent of the entire civilian work force. There are, for example, more than twice as many K–12 teachers as registered nurses and five times as many teachers as either lawyers or professors (U.S. Bureau of the Census, 1998). The sheer size of the teaching force, combined with the relatively high annual turnover rate within the teaching occupation, means that large numbers of employees flow into, between, and out of schools each year.

Of course, not all employee turnover is a bad thing. Too little turnover in any organization may indicate stagnancy. Effective organizations usually benefit from a limited

Source: Richard M. Ingersoll and Thomas M. Smith, "The Wrong Solution to the Teacher Shortage," *Educational Leadership*, May 2003, Vol. 60, No. 8, pp. 30–33. For a complete listing of the references for this Reading, go to *www.mhhe.com/teach1e2010*.

degree of turnover, which eliminates low-caliber performers and brings in new blood to facilitate innovation. High levels of employee turnover, however, suggest that an organization has underlying problems; in turn, this high turnover can cause turmoil and lead to problems in how the organization functions (Mobley, 1982; Price, 1977).

Industries and organizations take employee turnover seriously because of its high costs, some of which are more apparent than others. Employee turnover has especially serious consequences in workplaces that require extensive interaction among participants and that depend on commitment, continuity, and cohesion among employees. From this perspective, the high turnover of teachers in schools does not simply cause staffing problems but may also harm the school environment and student performance.

Attrition Among Beginning Teachers

The turnover problem, although high for the entire teaching occupation, affects beginning teachers more than others. Teaching has always lost many of its newly trained members early in their careers, long before the retirement years (Johnson & Birkeland, in press; Lortie, 1975; Murnane, Singer, Willett, Kemple, & Olsen, 1991).

We used the SASS/TFS [Schools and Staffing Survey/Teacher Follow-up Survey] data to provide a rough estimate of the cumulative attrition of beginning teachers in their first several years of teaching. The data suggest that after just five years, between 40 and 50 percent of all beginning teachers have left the profession. Why do beginning teachers leave at such high rates?

Perhaps the best way to discover why employees depart from jobs is to ask them. Many organizations do this through exit interviews. Similarly, the Teacher Follow-up Survey administered a questionnaire to a national sample of U.S. teachers who had left their teaching jobs the year before. Among other questions, it asked teachers to list the main reasons (up to three) for their departure. For this analysis, we focused on new teachers who left teaching after their first year.

About 19 percent of these beginners who left teaching said that they did so as a result of a school staffing action, such as a cutback, layoff, termination, school reorganization, or school closing. Another 42 percent cited personal reasons, including pregnancy, child rearing, health problems, and family moves.

Around 39 percent said that they left to pursue a better job or another career, and about 29 percent said that dissatisfaction with teaching as a career or with their specific job was a main reason. These final two reasons—pursuit of another job and dissatisfaction—together play a major role in about two-thirds of all beginning teacher attrition.

The survey asked the 29 percent who listed job dissatisfaction as a major reason for leaving about the source of their dissatisfaction, again giving them the option of listing up to three reasons. More than three-fourths linked their quitting to low salaries. But even more of them indicated that one of four different school working conditions was behind their decision to quit: student discipline problems;

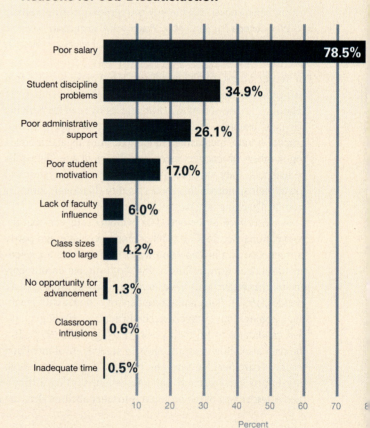

Reasons for Job Dissatisfaction

Poor salary — 78.5%
Student discipline problems — 34.9%
Poor administrative support — 26.1%
Poor student motivation — 17.0%
Lack of faculty influence — 6.0%
Class sizes too large — 4.2%
No opportunity for advancement — 1.3%
Classroom intrusions — 0.6%
Inadequate time — 0.5%

Percent

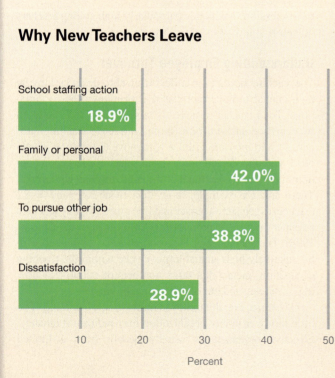

Why New Teachers Leave

School staffing action — 18.9%
Family or personal — 42.0%
To pursue other job — 38.8%
Dissatisfaction — 28.9%

Percent

lack of support from the school administration; poor student motivation; and lack of teacher influence over school wide and classroom decision making.

These findings on dissatisfaction-related attrition are important because they point to "policy-amenable" issues. The conventional wisdom places the roots of the teacher shortage outside schools, within larger demographic trends. By contrast, these data suggest that the roots of the teacher shortage largely reside in the working conditions within schools and districts. These two explanations for the teacher shortage point to different prescriptions for fixing the problem.

What Can Schools Do?

The data on new teacher attrition suggest that efforts to recruit more teachers—which have been the focus of much policy—will not, by themselves, solve the staffing problems plaguing schools. The solution must also include teacher retention. In short, recruiting more teachers will not solve the teacher crisis if 40–50 percent of these teachers leave in a few short years. The image that comes to mind is that of a bucket rapidly losing water because of holes in the bottom. Pouring more water into the bucket will not do any good if we do not patch the holes first.

Although the data confirm that raising teacher salaries offers one effective way to plug these holes, this strategy would be expensive, especially given the sheer size of the teacher population. The working conditions identified by new teachers as factors in their decision to leave teaching—lack of administrative support, poor student discipline and student motivation, and lack of participation in decision making—may offer a more effective focus for improvement efforts (Ingersoll, 2003).

Increasing support from school administrators for new teachers, for example, might range from providing enough classroom supplies to providing mentors. Mentors are especially crucial. Life for beginning teachers has traditionally been described as a sink-or-swim proposition. Indeed, data from SASS/TFS show that mentoring does make a difference.

Plugging holes through these kinds of changes will not be easy. But the good news, from the perspective of this analysis, is that schools are not simply the victims of inexorable demographic trends. The management and organization of schools play a significant role in the genesis of school staffing problems but can also play a significant role in their solution. Improving teachers' working conditions would contribute to lower rates of new teacher turnover, thereby diminishing school staffing problems and improving the performance of schools.

Induction program
11.9%
17.6%

Mentoring program
11.8%
18.6%

5   10   15   20

Percentage of Attrition

■ Teacher Participated   ■ Teacher Did Not Participate

QUESTIONS

1. How do you respond to the problems described by Ingersoll and Smith?

2. Are there ways to find a school district that offers the kind of supportive programs Ingersoll and Smith describe? How important do you think these programs will be to you?

3. Do you know someone who taught for a year or two and then stopped? Are that person's reasons for leaving similar to or different from those described in this article?

4. Ingersoll and Smith say that many of the reasons teachers leave could be fixed by schools and districts. As a future teacher, are there things you can do to improve the situation this article describes?

Should I Be a Teacher?

From THE DISCIPLINE OF HOPE: LEARNING FROM A LIFETIME OF TEACHING

BY HERBERT KOHL

Herbert Kohl began his teaching career in New York City in the 1960s. He wrote a book about his first-year experience, *Thirty Six Children*, which became a best seller because of its graphic description of the frustrations of urban teaching 4 decades ago. In the years since then, Kohl has devoted his life to improving schools, improving teaching, and, most of all, improving the lives of children. As this passage reflects, he still has great hopes, both for himself and for the nation's children, as he begins his 5th decade as a teacher.

These are not easy times in which to keep hope alive in poor or even middle-class communities. The most common question I am asked these days is whether the schools are worse now than they were when I began teaching. My answer is

Source: Herbert Kohl, *The Discipline of Hope: Learning from a Lifetime of Teaching* (New York: Simon & Schuster, 1998), pp. 331–333.

no; they are just about as bad. But now there are more local efforts to provide decent schools based on the notion that all children can learn than I have ever seen before. Unfortunately, the world beyond the school is much harsher toward children, much more cynical about the future, and much more indifferent to those children who do not have privilege, support, or special gifts that will enable them to succeed. The ordinary child, my child, your child, our children have a much harder time of it than I have ever seen before, and their needs are not being met by most schools.

And yet I have hope—hope that we will look intelligently at what *is* working, especially for poor children, and learn from those special places how to shape learning for children in the spirit of hope. I hope that we as adults will then make it our business to transform society into the place of hope that we have prepared them for.

A common characteristic of all these schools and educational programs, which I call schools and classrooms of hope, is that staff, parents, and community are in common accord that every child can learn. They all see their role as making the doable possible, and this is reflected in how their students come to believe in themselves as learners. This is in contrast with the majority of schools for the poor, where the staff is demoralized and projects the belief that only a small number of the children can learn. In such schools the community and parents are often considered the enemies; this turns the school into a sad, isolated place that perpetuates failure.

Schools of hope are places where children are honored and well served. They have a number of common characteristics, no matter where they are to be found across the country. They are safe and welcome places, comfortable environments that have a homey feel. They are places where students can work hard without being harassed, but also places where the joy of learning is expressed in the work of the children and in their sense of being part of a convivial learning community. They are places where the teachers and staff are delighted to work and are free to innovate while at the same time they are willing to take responsibility for their students' achievement. If you talk to children in schools like these, they express a pride of place and sense of ownership that are also manifest in how the rest of the community regards the school. Parents feel welcome and often have a role in school governance. Community volunteers are abundant. Hope, projected primarily through the children's learning, is also manifest in how the physical environment of the school is treated with respect.

We do have many schools of hope across the country, and many teachers who try to build classrooms of hope within more hostile and indifferent schools. It is essential to seek out these places, to support them, and to learn from them. Simply acknowledging that there are places where public education works is not a formula for school change. Besides, particular formulas do not work anyway. You have to know the community you serve, know what you want to teach or need to teach. You have to understand the times in which you work and your responsibilities as a citizen to fight for your children. Most of all, you have to love to be there with them, have to be delighted in their presence and feel the awe at their growth that any gardener does in experiencing the unfolding of a beautiful flower or the emergence of a delicious fruit or vegetable. It takes hard, careful, loving work to nurture hope and bring learning into the school— but what a birthing, what a pleasure, what fun despite all the struggles. And because teaching is so full of love, so hope-centered, and so difficult, it is also one of the most painful vocations. Despite the best teaching and the most passionate learning, this society has a way of wasting young talent. To teach well and care about children has a double edge that keeps one militant as well as romantic, that tempers what you know children can do with worry about what might happen to them after school, on the streets, in the job market, and in their own personal lives.

The hundreds of young people I have taught do dozens of different things, and it is a delight to see many of them embodying the central driving ideas of my life's work as an educator: that everyone can learn; that you can become the person you want to be and do work that you love; that whatever you do with your life, you can also do things for others; and that being thoughtful and possibly controversial and unpopular can be morally more sensible than being passive and conforming.

There are many things I hope to do with children over the next fifteen or twenty years. I still don't know how children learn to read, even though I can teach them to do it, so I hope to learn more about the actual process. I would like to teach calculus to six-year-olds and non-linear differential equations to eight-year-olds; introduce particle physics and complexity theory into the elementary school curriculum; create and test science and math programs, beginning in kindergarten, that are based on how contemporary scientists work and think—that is, I want to incorporate technology, mathematics, genetics, and the interdisciplinary sciences such as biochemistry and physical biology into children's ways of thinking from the beginning of their formal schooling.

I would also like to create a watershed curriculum based on a study of the history, nature, and future of the places students live in and the dreams they can develop about convivial communities; set up hundreds of poetry and writing groups of the sort I've been doing for years and continue to do; direct a production of *The Tempest* with five young theater troupes, each working on one act, each act set in a different time and place but with color-coded costumes, and each group working independently of the others and then coming together to perform the entire play; and create an extracurricular high school arts and math program that takes up as much time and excites as much passion and commitment as athletics and in which students regularly travel to other schools to participate in the arts.

Those are just the beginning. I would like to work with other teachers to develop a pervasively diverse and excellent literature curriculum that integrates reading, writing, thinking, and discussion and connects them not to critical theory, but to everyday life, personal identity, culture, and community; to set up a school and teacher-education program centered on social justice, the arts, literature, and modern science and mathematics.

Finally, and most centrally, I would like to understand more about how to deal with youth rage and violence and try to use this understanding to make life more nurturing for my students. I would like to create a diverse, compassionate, nonracial community of learners where students honor themselves, respect each other, love what they are learning, are passionate about justice, and prepare themselves for compassionate, connected adult lives. To paraphrase Neruda, I wouldn't mind being a butterfly or an apple—or, even better, a gadfly or a mango.

With these, as with all of the challenges of teaching and learning, I'm looking forward to beginning again. There's no end to the delights and joys of teaching, no limit to the challenges we will continue to face in order to serve children well, and no limit to the creativity and love adults can and should bring to helping children grow through teaching, which is at its heart the discipline of hope.

QUESTIONS

1. What do you think of what Herbert Kohl calls "the discipline of hope"? Do you agree with him?

2. Can you imagine staying in teaching, as Kohl has, for an entire career?

3. Can you imagine trying, as Kohl has, to build the kind of classrooms that can change the conditions young people experience in school?

2

GOOD TEACHING

There is a saying among teachers that people enter the profession for one of two reasons: either they remember a teacher who changed their lives and want to be like that person, or they remember a terrible teacher and want to be sure that no child is subjected to the misery they experienced. Whether this is completely true or not, many of us do have fond memories of a special teacher who made a difference in our lives, although others may be remembered less fondly. Indeed, much has been written that romanticizes teachers and their influence.

However, some have argued that teachers and schools cannot make much of a difference. They claim that larger social and economic forces, such as poverty, are too powerful for schools to counteract, that teachers are not able to offer what students need, or that the key to reform is a "teacher proof curriculum." Do teachers really make a difference in the lives of their students? New research reveals more clearly than ever before that teaching—when it is done well—definitely does matter and that teachers can make an extraordinary difference in the lives of their students, in spite of poverty or other social forces.

The **Readings** included in this chapter address each of these questions. The Education Trust, based in Washington, D.C., and led by Kati Haycock, is but one of many centers whose research has led to an almost unanimous conclusion that teachers make much more of a difference than many observers and scholars in previous generations realized. According to Haycock, "Good teaching matters. . .a lot." Of course, concluding that good teachers do make a substantial difference only gives rise to another, far more complex, question: What do good teachers do that makes them so good? We'll begin answering that question in this chapter and pursue it further in subsequent chapters.

Offering students the best education possible is the fundamental ethical responsibility of every teacher. Included in the **Readings** for this chapter is the Code of Ethics for Educators adopted by the state of New York, which outlines six main principles regarding a teacher's ethical responsibility.

As we look at the research regarding the impact of good teaching and discuss what constitutes good teaching, we must remember

WHAT IS ITS IMPACT?

FOCUS >>

- What does the evidence say about the difference a good teacher can make?
- What is a "good teacher"?
- How does a good teacher involve parents and the community?

that no one teaches in a vacuum. It is no longer acceptable for a teacher to say, "I can't make a difference because there are too many external factors in a child's life that get in the way of learning." Thus, teachers who do not look carefully at the context within which they will teach—such as the family and community in which the children in their classroom spend the majority of their time, the support that may or may not be there for learning, and the opportunities to build on the work of other important people in students' lives— are missing the opportunity to offer students the best education possible. Reviewing James Comer's wise advice in the **Readings** section about the appropriate place of parents in the education of their children and his detailed report about how he engaged parents in the schools he worked with allows us to explore further the complex web of relationships surrounding good teachers and good schools.

>> What Does the Evidence Say About the Difference a Good Teacher Can Make?

Educational researcher Sonia Nieto tells the story of Beatriz Campuzano, a high school senior whose father came to the United States from Mexico with less than a third-grade education. Early in her own schooling, Campuzano ran into the low expectations and barriers that too often are part of the educational experience of all students, but especially students who are immigrants, who are poor, or whose first language is not English. But in Campuzano's life, there was that one teacher who made the difference:

> In the sixth grade, my English teacher, Mr. Wilke, helped me to understand that I was capable of achieving anything. I began to believe in myself. My self-esteem grew as Mr. Wilke told me day after day that I was a "gift to the world." I loved education because it made me feel smart. Knowing that I had knowledge made me feel invincible.[1]

Many of us have been fortunate to have a Mr. Wilke in our life. But, in the end, do the Mr. (and Mrs. and Ms.) Wilkes really make a difference? Would the outcome be the same for the student no matter how motivating or qualified the teacher? What does the research say about how important the Mr. Wilkes of this world really are—and have been over time—to the majority of students?

HISTORICALLY SPEAKING: THE "GOOD OLD DAYS"

More than a century and a half ago, Horace Mann told school boards that they needed to view themselves as "sentinels stationed at the door of every schoolhouse in the State, to see that no teacher ever crosses its threshold, who is not clothed, from the crown of his head to the sole of his foot, in garments of virtue." Mann also offered more practical advice. He wisely insisted that teachers should know the subjects they were going to teach, that they "should be able to teach *subjects*, not manuals merely." He also insisted that teachers needed to know how to teach: "Aptness to teach involves the power of perceiving how far a scholar understands the subject-matter to be learned, and what, in the natural order, is the next step he is to take."[2]

Throughout much of the century after Mann wrote about the qualities of a good teacher, school leaders seemed to use his **rhetoric** but ignore his advice. One-room schoolhouses in which a single teacher

rhetoric The art of using effective verbal or occasionally written language in order to persuade or influence others.

My Learning Autobiography

As you begin to think about the type of teacher you will become—and want to become—you first need to reflect on your own educational experiences when you were on the other side of the desk, as a student.

Start by asking yourself questions about the key learning moments in your life:

- What are some of the most important things that I have learned thus far?
- Who helped me learn them?
- Where were these lessons learned? In school? In other organizations? With my family? Alone?
- What are my educational experiences that I would consider "positive"? Why? What was a teacher's involvement?
- What are my educational experiences that I would consider "negative"? Why? What was a teacher's involvement?

Begin to record these various experiences, lessons, and influences. Be creative in how you approach this ongoing exercise—create lists, journal, make a visual time line, or find other ways to make the refection meaningful.

Discuss your experiences with fellow classmates, either in a class discussion, a study group, or casual conversation. Use this opportunity to get to know one another, to build support systems, to share insights regarding the best (and sometimes the worst) learning experiences, and to begin developing a personal philosophy about education and teaching that will change and evolve to guide you throughout your career.

---

taught all the grades were replaced with graded schools (like those most of us attended) in which teachers became specialists in the first or second or third grade. As urban school systems grew, they were organized in ways that would lead to the conclusion that individual teachers—and their proficiency in any one subject—did not make much difference at all. Every teacher in the same grade level was expected to teach exactly the same lesson, at the same time, in the same way. And growing school systems added more and more supervisors—principals, superintendents, assistant superintendents (nearly all of whom were male)—who were expected to closely supervise the female classroom teachers and keep them in line.

Many objected to this deskilling of teachers. In 1904, Margaret Haley, the feisty and tough-minded founder of the Chicago Federation of Teachers, complained about policies that made "the teacher an automaton, a mere factory hand, whose duty it is to carryout mechanically and unquestioningly the ideas and orders of those clothed with the authority of position. . . ." Until the situation changed, Haley and many other progressive educators insisted, the schools would not be democratic and would not be using one of their greatest resources: the ability of teachers to make a difference for their students.[3]

"TEACHER-PROOF CURRICULUM"

Sadly, this limited view of teachers and their potential to impact student learning did not disappear at the turn of the 20th century. From the 1950s to the 1970s, many argued for what they called a "teacher-proof curriculum" so that students could be protected from supposedly poorly prepared or uncreative teachers. Glenn Seaborg, who won a Nobel Prize for his research in chemistry and served as the chair of the U.S. Atomic Energy Commission, complained that "there was and is a feeling that it's not so important that the teacher understand the subject matter, as long as they're good at conveying it." Alan Friedman of the New York Hall of Science,

Teachable Moment

Selling the Subject

A salesperson can sell anything as long as he or she has the skills and flashy marketing. It isn't necessary to understand how the product works or what the customers' needs are.

In essence, that's the philosophy behind a "teacher-proof" curriculum. A teacher who knows how to teach and has "product support"—such as a video, beautifully illustrated textbooks, or detailed lesson plans—doesn't really need to have a firm grasp of the actual "product" (such as science or history) or the "customer" (the students).

But is it really true that all a successful salesperson needs are good communication skills and the right "props"? That may suffice for the short term, but what happens when the customer has questions about how the product works? Or when it breaks down? Or when the user's manual is so poorly designed that the client needs one-on-one help? Or when customers conclude that they don't have any need for the product—and never did? In fact, the most successful salespeople—whether they are selling cars or the wonders of the solar system—use their product knowledge to determine what will fulfull their clients' needs and to educate their clients as to why the solution will work.

And besides, teachers can't forward their "customers" to a "help desk" or "tech support."

QUESTIONS

- Although the thought of a "teacher-proof curriculum" might seem offensive, would a teacher feel a sense of comfort from not being expected to have mastered a subject prior to teaching it?
- What qualities do a successful salesperson and a successful teacher share?

---

remembering the same effort to "teacher-proof" the curriculum, lamented that "the idea was that if you had an activity, a filmstrip, and a book, that was sufficient, and even if the teacher was afraid of science, they could do a good job."[4]

TEACHERS, SCHOOLS, AND THE WAR ON POVERTY

In 1964, President Lyndon B. Johnson declared a national war on poverty, a massive federal program inspired by the **civil rights movement** and designed to dramatically reduce social and economic inequality in the nation. Johnson, who had been a schoolteacher long before he became a politician, believed

that one of the keys to ending poverty was improving education and that, given the right resources, schools and teachers could better the educational attainment and future lives of students. In 1965, with one of his own schoolteachers standing by his side, Johnson signed the Elementary and Secondary Education Act, the first major federal financial support for schools. He said, "As President of the United States, I believe deeply no law I have signed or will ever sign means

> **civil rights movement** A movement in the United States, beginning in the 1930s, growing rapidly in the 1950s and 1960s, and continuing through the 1980s, that meant to secure civil and human rights for all people regardless of race or gender—primarily associated with African American efforts.

more to the future of America."[5] Here was faith in the power of schools and teachers to make a difference.

However, more was involved in the federal war on poverty than faith in education. As part of the funding of Johnson's programs, the U.S. Congress also authorized a massive study of the impact of education on reducing poverty. The result of this congressional mandate for research was one of the best-financed and most thorough studies of American education—James S. Coleman's *Equality of Educational Opportunity*, published in 1966. Surprising and disappointing to Coleman, as well as to many in the Johnson administration and to educators across the country, Coleman's study essentially concluded that there was very little, if any, **causative correlation** between educational inputs such as facilities and numbers of teachers—the benefits of expanded funding that could be measured most easily—and educational outputs as measured by student achievement.

> **causative correlation** A relationship wherein one variable (such as educational achievement) is directly affected and influenced by another variable (such as income).

While many debated the conclusions of the Coleman Report, the Carnegie Corporation of New York funded a group of researchers, led by Harvard's Christopher Jencks, to duplicate, test, and expand on Coleman's research. Jencks's 1972 book, *Inequality: A Reassessment of the Effects of Family and Schooling in America*, was even more depressing to educators than the original Coleman Report. Jencks concluded that while it was certainly true that educational opportunity was unequally distributed across the nation, it was also the case that "inequality in educational opportunity is not responsible for most of the inequality in educational results that we see all around us" and that "equalizing educational opportunity will not do much to equalize the results in economic competition." Essentially, Jencks said, schools can't "fix" an unequal society, especially in regard to economic inequality.

Jencks himself argued that the obvious conclusion of his research was that only fundamental changes in the American economy, including income redistribution, would improve the life chances of poor and marginalized people in the United States. Many others, however, also concluded that Coleman and Jencks had virtually proven that schools and the teachers who taught in them made no meaningful difference in the lives of students.

President Lyndon Johnson, a former school teacher, signs the Elementary and Secondary Education Act in 1965.

Ronald Edmonds, who later conducted his own research on the characteristics of those schools that did make a difference for poor students, complained that whatever the motivation behind Jencks's work, it had the potential to let schools

Connections

In Chapter 4, we'll explore what other groups besides racial minorities benefited from the 1960s legislation.

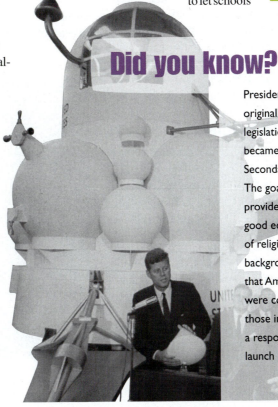

Did you know?

President John F. Kennedy originally developed the legislation that eventually became the Elementary and Secondary Education Act. The goal was twofold: (1) to provide every child with a good education, regardless of religious, racial, or class background; and (2) to ensure that American students were competitive with those in other countries, as a response to the Soviets' launch into space of Sputnik.

The Coleman Report by James Coleman (seen here with a group of students) was widely interpreted to mean that schools could do little to improve the lives of poor children and children of color.

ity students. . . . Nothing schools do makes a very big difference." But it depends on how the question is asked. Haycock continues: "Recently, however, a number of large-scale studies provide convincing proof that what we do in education does matter. Schools—and especially teachers, it turns out—really DO make a difference. Earlier educational researchers just didn't have very good ways of measuring the variables." The end-of-chapter **Reading** describes the many studies that have convinced Haycock of the error of earlier approaches. She voices her frustration that for too long too many researchers have clung to "dog-eared copies of the Coleman Report" and insisted that schools could not make a difference for poor children or for their chances for success in life.[7]

What has changed is the kind of research that Haycock and her colleagues have conducted and the questions they have asked. Other researchers, notably William L. Sanders, Ronald F. Ferguson, and Linda Darling-Hammond, have reached similar conclusions as Haycock by looking at statewide or national data that provide much more information about individual teachers than was previously available. Instead of generalizing as Coleman and Jencks did about

"off the hook" for any responsibility for effective teaching—especially in poor and nonwhite communities—and as such represented a tremendous disservice. Given how vital schooling was to all young people, especially to those born into poverty, Edmonds believed it was essential that educators be held accountable for what their students learned and failed to learn.[6] It would be a long time before the views of Edmonds and others who agreed with him came to be dominant, but slowly some of the conclusions reached by Coleman and Jencks began to be challenged. Coleman and Jencks had looked at some of the easier data to study, such as the total funds expended on education and the impact on all poor children and children of color in the country or in a school district. However, if we look more carefully at the differences from classroom to classroom and teacher to teacher, a very different picture emerges.

NEW RESEARCH, DIFFERENT CONCLUSIONS

The view of what teachers can and cannot accomplish has only recently begun to change. New research indicates that Coleman and Jencks were simply wrong. Teachers *do* make a substantial difference in the learning of their students, no matter what external factors might get in the way. The difference—one that Coleman and Jencks did not examine—involves the very significant question "*Which teachers?*" Coleman and Jencks looked at whole school districts. When more recent researchers looked at individual teachers, they found significant differences, even within the same school.

Kati Haycock of the Education Trust describes the change in our understanding of the role of good teachers in the lives of their students that has emerged from recent research: "For decades, educators, educators-in-training and the public more broadly have been relentlessly fed the same message about achievement among poor and minor-

Kati Haycock of the Education Trust is one of the nation's leading advocates for the important difference *good* teachers can make in the lives of all students.

all poor students who attended a school or a district, these researchers have gotten much more specific. They have looked at differences in student performance in two different classrooms in the same school, as well as at entire schools and school districts where special efforts have been made to ensure that many students have especially well qualified teachers. The differences have proved to be pretty amazing. A teacher just down the hall from another can have a significantly different impact on her or his students, regardless of the economic background or race of the students. Summarizing research that has been conducted by several different researchers working independently in different parts of the country, Haycock concludes:

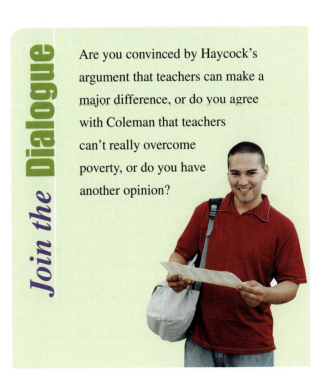

You Decide

Does good teaching make enough of a difference to counter the impact of poverty in the education of poor children?

> *If we but took the simple step of assuring that poor and minority children had teachers of the same quality as other children, about half of the achievement gap would disappear. If we went further and assigned our best teachers to the students who most need them (a step, by the way, that makes sense to most people outside of education), there's persuasive evidence to suggest that we could entirely close the gap.*[8]

The conclusion of this research is fairly unambiguous. On one hand, those who entered teaching a decade ago (people who may have studied Coleman and Jencks as part of their preparation) inevitably faced the nagging question of whether anything they could ever do would make a difference in the lives of the students they would teach. The research at that time seemed to say no. But today, for those who are teachers or who are considering teaching, the research points in a very different direction. Do teachers make a difference? The answer is clear: "Good ones do. . .and they make a very big difference." This conclusion also puts a heavy burden on every teacher. If teaching makes a powerful difference when it is done expertly and well, then the responsibility is on us—quite dramatically on us—to be the best possible teachers, well prepared and ready to do whatever is needed to help our students succeed. The outcome, it turns out, is in our hands. Teachers can make a difference—a very significant difference.

In the end, the debate between those who are most convinced by the research of Coleman and Jencks and those who find the research of Haycock, Sanders, Ferguson, and others more careful and compelling will probably continue as long as there are schools and teachers. One recent study of teachers' attitudes conducted by the Public Agenda Foundation found that teachers were divided in their views. Indeed, they split almost evenly when asked, "Is student achievement mostly determined by such things as parental involvement and socioeconomic factors, or

is teacher quality just as important?" Forty-two percent of practicing teachers said that external factors were most important, while 54% answered that teacher quality is just as important.[9] Part of the difference is in the way the question is asked. It is quite a different matter to ask "Do all teachers make a difference?" than to ask "Do teachers with certain skills and abilities and commitments make a difference?" It is also true that this is probably not an either-or debate. To say that teachers can make a meaningful difference for students is not the same thing as saying that teachers can or should make all of the difference in what students learn. Likewise, to say that poverty or prosperity or other external variables make a huge difference in learning is not to say that teachers cannot make a major difference—for good or for ill—in spite of such variables.

Sonia Nieto, who has spent many years teaching teachers and observing teachers in schools, says that early in her career as a teacher educator she began to doubt that teachers could make much of a difference for young people. However, as she continued to work with teachers, she changed her mind. While her ideas are tempered by a realistic sense of the limitations to what teachers can do—limitations that Haycock may underestimate—teachers still can make an extraordinary difference. Nieto says, "I believe more strongly than ever in the power of teachers.

Join the **Dialogue**

Are you convinced by Haycock's argument that teachers can make a major difference, or do you agree with Coleman that teachers can't really overcome poverty, or do you have another opinion?

This is because I have seen breathtaking teachers in action, and I have witnessed firsthand what they can achieve."[10]

Perhaps the right way to answer the question "Do teachers make a difference?" is with a qualified yes. A tempered optimism and an understanding that the larger society makes a difference *and* that teachers make a difference is probably the most realistic way to proceed. To assume that teachers make all the difference for students is to set ourselves up for constant failure and frustration. But to enter teaching—or stay in teaching—believing that teachers cannot make a difference is to engage in meaningless activities. This leads us to the most important and difficult questions, which have to do with when and how teachers make a difference—indeed, to the very nature of what constitutes good teaching.

>> What Is a "Good Teacher"?

If it is true that good teaching matters—a lot—then the obvious question is, What constitutes good teaching? Or, according to current policy language, what is a "highly qualified teacher"? Though researchers differ on the details, there is surprising consensus about what a good teacher should know and be able to do.

Can you think of teachers—schoolteachers or educators in more informal settings—who made a difference in your life? What were the unique characteristics of these teachers? Would they have made the same difference if you had grown up in a different family or community or in different socioeconomic circumstances?

Join the Dialogue

A QUESTION OF . . .

What are the drawbacks of teaching?

"Having been valedictorian of my high school class of 500 and voted Most Likely to Succeed, I feel as if society feels that successful people may teach for a while, but they do not stay in the classroom. To do so reflects a lack of ambition. This is reinforced by the pay structure. The only way to advance (except for salary step increases or taking college classes) is to go into administration. Those of us who love to teach and excel in the classroom will never realize the financial rewards of excellence in teaching. However, as we teachers know, we did not go into teaching for the money, and if that were our primary goal, we would have chosen another field. We may not make lots of money, but we do make a difference in the lives of each of our students. This is my reward."

—*Phyllis Hoyt, middle school mathematics teacher* ■

TEACHERS NEED TO KNOW THEIR SUBJECT

Looking at teachers in Texas and Alabama whose students were most successful on the state examinations, researcher Ronald Ferguson found that the teachers themselves had scored well on their own tests. This could be interpreted to mean that people who are good test takers have a greater ability to teach their students how to take tests. However, there is probably much more to it than that. Teachers who have strong verbal and mathematics skills and know their subject matter very well seem to be much more effective than teachers who are less prepared and/or less confident.

Other researchers have found a correlation not only between a teacher's test-taking success and that of his or her students but also between other measures of teacher content knowledge and student success. In some fields, such as mathematics and the sciences, the research is clear that teachers who know more have more success with their students. Dan D. Goldhaber and Dominic J. Brewer's detailed examination of the National Educational Longitudinal Study of 1988 (discussed by Kati Haycock in the **Readings**) led them to see a

PORTRAIT OF AN EDUCATOR

Ella Flagg Young

A century before Kati Haycock and other researchers were documenting the significant difference individual teachers could make in the lives of their students, Chicago educator Ella Flagg Young (1845–1918) based her whole career on her belief in the importance of individual teachers in the lives of their students. Young was involved with the Chicago public schools for 53 years as a teacher, a principal, and finally superintendent of schools.[11]

Ella Flagg Young did not seem destined for a career in education. She was often sickly as a child, and her parents educated her at home. When the family moved to Chicago, Young entered the Brown grammar school but dropped out after a few months. She was bored, she said, because she already knew everything the school was attempting to teach her. She first tried to start teaching when she was 15 years old, in 1860. She took the Chicago teachers exam and passed it easily. In many parts of the United States, teachers as young as 15 were common, but Chicago required a teacher to be at least 16 years old. Given her success on the exam, the superintendent invited Young to attend the Chicago Normal School, from which she graduated in 1862. Immediately after graduating, she began teaching elementary school in Chicago. One of her first classes at the Foster School was the "cowboy class," so named not because the young male students acted like cowboys but because they were cowboys.

Herding cattle was something young males still did within the city limits of Chicago in the 1860s. Young continued her career, teaching at a number of schools, and later was promoted to school principal.

From 1899 to 1905, Young was a professor at the University of Chicago. She then served as principal of the Chicago Normal School from 1905 to 1909—the leading teacher preparation program for Chicago teachers, from which she herself had graduated. Finally, in 1909, she was elected superintendent of the Chicago public schools, becoming the first woman to lead a large urban school system in the United States.

Young became famous for her attacks on "close supervision," the assumption among most superintendents that individual teachers should be mere cogs in a well-oiled machine managed by a single educational leader who knew what was best for all students. In her 1901 book *Isolation in the School*, Young argued against close supervision because she believed that individual teachers, given the responsibility and the freedom to act, could make all the difference in the lives of children. She insisted that "the school cannot take up the question of the development of training for citizenship in a democracy" while treating teachers as "citizens in an aristocracy."

Once she became superintendent, Young set up teachers councils to give classroom teachers at the elementary and secondary levels a meaningful voice in the policy decisions of the Chicago schools—an unheard-of innovation in a top-down educational world. While many of the male leaders of Chicago's business and educational establishments attempted to undermine her during her term as superintendent out of anger over her support for teachers, a tax increase to fund increased teacher salaries, and the Chicago's teacher union, teachers, parents, and many of Chicago's progressive reformers worked hard to support her. Young's steadfast belief that good teachers really could make a difference for their students and should be given the freedom and responsibility to do so earned her intense loyalty from most of Chicago's 6,000 teachers, who felt that for the first time in their professional careers they were being treated with respect by the school system.

In 1910, Young became the first woman elected president of the National Education Association. She was a close colleague of many of Chicago's progressive leaders, including John Dewey, who taught at the University of Chicago, and Jane Addams, the leader of Hull House (a social and human services organization) and the first American woman to receive the Nobel Peace Prize.

---

clear link between what teachers had studied and how well their students learned. They concluded, "In mathematics and science, it is the teacher subject-specific knowledge that is the important factor in determining tenth-grade achievement." Another study (also reported by Haycock) traced the achievement of elementary school students in Dallas, Texas. One group of third-graders who averaged around the 55th percentile in mathematics was taught for the next 3 years by teachers who had a high level of mathematical knowledge and were viewed as highly effective teachers. At the end of fifth

grade, these students scored, on average, in the 76th **percentile**. Another group of students who started at about the same point—the 57th percentile in mathematics—were taught for the same amount of time by teachers who were viewed as the least effective mathematics teachers. At the end of fifth grade, this latter group scored at only the 27th percentile. Those who have been arguing for

> **percentile** A ranking system commonly used for testing purposes which expresses an individual's position by the number of people at or below that position.

teachers had known more about effective instructional practices. Even students who have done well in school might have developed much more if their teachers had known the latest research on how people learn and the best ways to teach them.[14]

Knowing how to teach (i.e., having a mastery of pedagogy as well as content) is essential to effective teaching. Another scholar, Lee Shulman, coined the term "pedagogical content knowledge" for the ability to not only know a subject but also

some time that high school teachers should have a college major in the subject they teach and that elementary school teachers also need broad content knowledge in the range of elementary school subjects were shown to be correct.[12]

Another important education scholar, Linda Darling-Hammond, also focuses on the need for teachers who know their subject and know it well. She writes that "as long as over 50,000 people a year who lack training for their positions have entered teaching on emergency or substandard licenses, as is now the case, we will never have the corps of teachers that our young people need." In the United States today, 25% of all high school teachers do not have at least a minor in the field they are teaching, and the percentage is 30% for mathematics, a subject for which research shows subject matter knowledge to be especially important. Fifty-six percent of high school students taking physical science are taught by "out of field" teachers. Darling-Hammond also notes that the teachers who know the least about their subject are concentrated in schools with the highest enrollments of students of color. In these schools, students have a less than 50% chance of having a science or mathematics teacher who holds a license and degree in the field in which he or she teaches. It's not surprising, then, that students in these schools do not seem to do as well in school.[13]

TEACHERS NEED TO UNDERSTAND HOW TO TEACH

Knowledge of subject matter, while essential to good teaching, is not sufficient. Teachers also need to know how to teach, how to connect with young people. In the introduction to *How People Learn*, which is included in the **Readings** for Chapter 5, John D. Bransford and his colleagues write that they believe many young people who have had difficulty in school might have done much better if their

A QUESTION OF . . .

Was there a teacher who had a memorable impact on you?

"One teacher who made an early and lasting impact on my understanding of art, creativity, and indeed pedagogy, was a woman named Helen. My mother enrolled me in her pottery class when I was about 13 that took place at a local college.

"One day, we were told to make animals. I went about sculpting the expected prototype: a four legged thing, kind of a standing dog, frozen awkwardly. Helen approached, issued a rather annoyed look, and pinched its neck, stretching the clay upward and around with her thumb. Then she walked away. Within a second, she'd given the thing life—even at that age, I could recognize the transformation of something soulless into strong, daring expression. Its neck twisted dramatically. The creature was suddenly endowed with a kind of violent confusion. I didn't touch it. It went straight to the kiln, and when I brought it home, my mother, a modern dance choreographer, marveled at it, and praised my expressiveness. I never revealed the effect of Helen's touch.

"In retrospect, I'm grateful to Helen for taking such a role in my 'authorship,' for invading my space, for giving me a dose of her raw artistic integrity. It was a moment of mindful apprenticeship—it's no small thing to feel connected to creativity, even when someone else provides you with this degree of momentum. Indeed, the next time around, my work showed far more of my own courage.

"Occasionally, when I see a student struggling with her writing, I take the pen, craft a new sentence for her, then walk away. I'm aware that this sort of behavior flies in the face of progressive workshop instruction, but it feels right, and I can tell my kids appreciate the intensity of my help. I'm a writer, no? I'm a writer, and it's my job to share the tools of my craft, and, as often as possible, to give students the sensation of writing well. That's the Helen in me."

—Avi Kline, high school writing and English teacher

Connections

In Chapter 5, we'll review a number of theories about how students learn and how teachers can serve many learning styles.

know how to communicate it to others. Knowing something is not the same as knowing how to ensure that others learn it. The latter skill is acquired only through a mix of academic study and guided clinical practice in school settings—watching good teachers teach, trying to teach while being observed and critiqued, and trying again. The combination of knowledge and teaching skill is essential to effective, sustained student learning.[15]

Regarding these issues, the differences among the researchers are small compared to the similarities. While not everyone would agree with Haycock when she says that the right teacher can offset virtually *any* impact of poverty or discrimination that students have experienced in their lives, few of today's researchers would argue against the proposition that having a teacher who knows the subject matter very well, knows how to teach it very well, and is deeply committed to successful teaching is *the most* important guarantee of student success. Does teaching matter? The answer clearly is yes.

TEACHERS NEED TO BE PASSIONATE ABOUT WHAT THEY DO

As important as knowledge of subject matter and pedagogical skill may be, they are simply elements of good teaching. Another stream of research focuses on the less tangible, but just as important, aspect of a teacher's commitment—what Robert Fried calls "a teacher's passion." As he says in *The Passionate Teacher* (in the **Reading** in Chapter 13):

> *Yet as I look into hundreds of classrooms, watch teachers working with all kinds of students, when I ask myself what makes the greatest difference in the quality of student learning—it is a teacher's passion that leaps out. More than knowledge of subject matter. More than variety of teaching techniques. More than being well-organized, or friendly, or funny, or fair.* Passion.[16]

Some researchers may question whether passion counts for *more than* knowledge of subject matter or specific pedagogical skills, but few would challenge the essential mix of passion, skill, and knowledge in the definition of good teaching.

Any discussion of good teaching quickly leads us to ask, "who were my *best* teachers?" and "What made them different?" While there are many answers to these questions, certain themes are repeated over and over when we start thinking about outstanding teachers—our own or ones we have observed teaching others.

In a recent, extensive study of college students by Richard Light, reported in his *Getting the Most Out of College*, students were asked about exceptional professors. Light asked, "Can you think of any particular faculty member who has had a particularly important impact on you, in shaping the way you think about yourself, or life, or the world around you, or your future?" Eighty-nine percent

In a recent survey of college students, 89% could easily name an instructor who had made an impact on them.

of the students questioned quickly identified a particular professor. Among the stories he heard, Light quoted one undergraduate whose summary of his appreciation for a certain professor mimicked the stories of hundreds of other

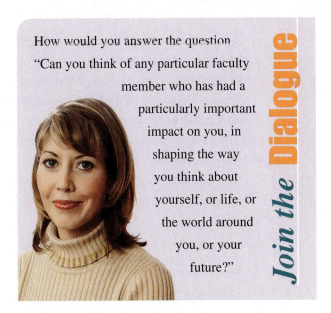

How would you answer the question "Can you think of any particular faculty member who has had a particularly important impact on you, in shaping the way you think about yourself, or life, or the world around you, or your future?"

Join the **Dialogue**

How Can I Make a Difference?

The Lesson You Never Forget

Marta Cruz-Janzen, a professor in the Department of Teacher Education at Florida Atlantic University, tells of her experiences with the negative messages she received in school in Puerto Rico as a young Latina girl whose first language was Spanish and whose family was poor. Everything seemed to reinforce low expectations. Success in school—and certainly aiming for college—was not for her, it seemed.

Then one teacher made a difference. Cruz-Janzen says, "I never forget my fourth grade teacher. She told me, 'I want you to start looking at universities in the United States,' and she brought me catalogs about all the universities on the mainland. She told me that if I was going to do that, I needed to learn English and she started teaching me English at a very young age, but it stayed with me."

Cruz-Janzen transferred to a high school in New York City. After graduation, she attended Cornell University, received her master's degree at Columbia University, and earned her Ph.D. at the University of Denver. She was a teacher and a principal and now teaches other aspiring teachers. Her career was possible, at least in part, because one fourth-grade teacher knew she could make a difference.

Katherine Hanson, coauthor of the book that describes Marta Cruz-Janzen's story, responds to the question "What can a teacher do?" by proposing three actions:

1. Learn more about your own expectations or stereotypes of students or groups.
2. Test your assumptions about who is likely to do well, making sure not to favor one group of students over another.
3. Learn what resources are available to students who may need extra or a different kind of help or support so you can refer students to them.

As this example shows, teachers can make an extraordinary difference—even if it's only one child at a time.

Sources: Hanson, Katherine, Guilfoy, Vivian, & Nair-Pillai, Sarita. (2009). *More than Title IX: How Equity in Education Has Shaped the Nation.* Lanham, MD: Rowman & Littlefield. Interview with Katherine Hanson, June 24, 2009.

students: "I will never forget him, because he never tried to tell us what to think. Rather, he worked hard to come up with ways to help us learn how to think creatively."

Students in the study described the way professors created an atmosphere of joint responsibility for the construction of the course, their ability to connect serious curriculum to the lives and experiences of students, and the way they helped students understand how people in their field think about topics in their field. Students welcomed debate, disagreement, and a lack of predictability in their professors' thinking and the inclusion of interdisciplinary topics that helped broaden class discussions. Light reported, "Details vary, but the most common hope students express is that each class, by its end, will help them to become a slightly different person in some way. This hope transcends the subject matter of the class, or a student's background, or even whether the student is a wise old senior or an incoming freshman"[17]—or a first- or second-grader.

TEACHERS NEED AN ETHICAL COMMITMENT TO THEIR WORK

In addition to a teacher's knowledge of subject matter, understanding of pedagogy, and passion for teaching, a fourth element of good teaching must not be ignored. Teachers need to be deeply ethical professionals who reflect their ethical commitment to their students in the way they do their work.

In 2002, the New York State Board of Regents adopted a new Code of **Ethics** for Educators (see the **Readings** section, page 59). It reveals just how much the view of teachers has changed since the days when Horace Mann called for every teacher to be clothed "in garments of virtue." In the New York code, virtue is not enough. If teaching really does matter and if teachers really do make a difference—or at least have the potential to make a difference—then they must embrace the opportunity to make a difference for all students, not merely as models of distant virtue but as active, engaging participants in the teaching and learning process.

> **ethics** Addresses what constitutes right or wrong behavior in both a professional or personal environment.

To that end, the New York code begins with a call for every educator to nurture the intellectual, physical, emotional, social, and civic potential of each student. It goes on to insist that to do so educators must "commit to their own learning in order to develop their practice." Ethical educators who follow this code are expected to collaborate with colleagues, other professionals, and parents and community members in fostering a vibrant intellectual and ethical foundation for learning.

If teachers are merely models of virtue, as Mann seemed to assume, then this vibrant intellectual and ethical commitment

> **Connections**
>
> In Chapter 10, we will explore a teacher's professional ethics as related to both legal ramifications and issues of fairness.

Did you know?

The most prominent code of ethics for teachers is the National Education Association's Code of Ethics of the Education Profession. It starts with:

"The educator, believing in the worth and dignity of each human being, recognizes the supreme importance of the pursuit of truth, devotion to excellence, and the nurture of the democratic principles. Essential to these goals is the protection of freedom to learn and to teach and the guarantee of equal educational opportunity for all. The educator accepts the responsibility to adhere to the highest ethical standards."

Source: National Education Association.

Join the Dialogue

Applying the New York Code of Ethics for Educators, would you say that your teachers have been ethical?

Teachable Moment
Breaking the Code

Inappropriate language on school grounds. Smoking at school functions. Embarrassing a teacher or a student. These may appear to be the acts of a teenager, but they are actually the negative behaviors teachers in Alabama can be reprimanded for, fired over, or even have their teaching certificate revoked.

Alabama's Code of Ethics has officially been in place since 2005. However, in 2009, the Alabama Board of Education voted to place the ethical standards into the state administrative code for public schools, much to the dismay of the state teacher's union, who argued that the language of the code is too vague. While something like smoking at a school function is pretty clear cut (i.e. either the teacher was smoking or not), what it means to embarrass a student can be wide open to many interpretations. Certainly no good teacher *means* to embarrass any student, but students can be sensitive, teachers can get harried, and words can be taken in different ways.

In this situation, the Alabama code was pretty much a top-down affair which more than likely fueled resistance from teachers. However, teachers are hired and paid from tax funds and, in a democratic society, public policy is set by elected officials. According to Governor Bob Riley, "This makes it part of the law so that every teacher understands what is expected of them."

Source: "Alabama Board of Education Beefs Up Ethics Rules for Teachers," Phillip Rawls, The Associated Press, montgomeryadvertiser .com, July 15, 2009

QUESTIONS

- Should a Teachers' Code of Ethics be considered a legal document with legal ramifications for violating it, or should it be truly considered like a "code" to follow? Should these decisions be made on a local, state, or federal level? Should teachers have a voice in developing such a code and in deciding when it has been violated?
- Does your state have a Teacher's Code of Ethics? If so, how is it enforced? Who was involved in developing the code and who will make future revisions?

---

is far too much to ask of them. If teachers are merely cogs in a well-oiled machine administered by others, as some of those against whom Margaret Haley rebelled seemed to assume, or if teachers are so insignificant that they need "teacher-proof curricula" to protect their students, then a code like this is simply irrelevant. Indeed, if teachers are limited by external factors—by the class and race of their students—as Coleman and Jencks seemed to assume, then this code makes outrageous and unacceptable demands on them. If, on the other hand, researchers and philosophers like Kati Haycock and Robert Fried are right, if teachers can make the most important difference in the learning of their students, then this code of ethical conduct is right on target.

When things go wrong around us and, for whatever reason, our students fail to learn, we would love to be able to say, "It's not my fault." Of course, at times circumstances beyond our control affect things in the classroom, in spite of our best efforts, and learning does not take place. However, the clear conclusion of the current research is that those moments are much rarer than many like to acknowledge. An awesome responsibility goes with teaching. It is a sobering fact, but it is also encouraging. In the end, who wants to be part of a profession that really does not make much of a difference? If "good teaching matters . . . a lot," then teaching can be some of the most meaningful, ethical, and powerful work there is to do.

>> How Does a Good Teacher Involve Parents and the Community?

A WEB OF RELATIONSHIPS

Educator and author Jacqueline Jordan Irvine adds another significant element to the definition of good teaching: The best teachers understand that they are part—an important part, but only one part—of a web of significant relationships in a young person's life. In her book *In Search of Wholeness*, Irvine writes about what she calls "other mothering," a sense of personal attachment and kinship that many African-American teachers feel toward African-American children in their classrooms. As Irvine describes it:

> *These African American teachers were attached both to the individual child as well as the race. Their willingness to "adopt" was not solely because of their desire to help a child but also to advance the entire race. These "other mothers" had strong beliefs about their students' ability to achieve despite widely publicized data, such as the black-white achievement gap, that could have convinced them otherwise.*[18]

As Irvine has also noted, not all effective teachers—African American or otherwise—choose to see themselves as second mothers to their students. But all teachers can learn something from the concept of "other mothering." When a teacher has high expectations and sees a student as connected to a web of social relationships within a family and community, the teacher can draw on resources unavailable to a teacher who focuses his or her instruction on each student as an isolated individual.

Teachers who make connections among the subjects being taught, the individual needs of their students, and the community context in which their students are living are going to be the most successful. On another occasion, Irvine wrote that "effective teachers love and care about the student whom they teach, and they also love and are excited about the subject that they teach." The two attributes cannot be divided if learning is to be achieved.

If Irvine is right—and there is ample evidence that she is—then teachers need to know the subjects they teach very well and need to know their students in the context of their families and communities equally well. Only when all aspects of a student's life are connected—the material the student needs to master and the context in which the student decides that the learning matters—can successful teaching really take place.

PARENTS AND CAREGIVERS

The first and most important network in every child's life is the family. Yet families and schools do not automatically work easily or well together. In communities in which both parents (or caregivers) and teachers share a similar socio-economic background and cultural experience, common purpose can be based on common assumptions. For all their very real problems, the segregated African-American schools of the pre–*Brown* decision South often reflected this strength because of the existence of a unified African-American community. However, in too many other cases, parents and teachers have different backgrounds, seem to speak a different language, and cannot be expected to automatically trust each other.

Have you experienced the support of a community or a group of people outside school who cared about you and made sure you succeeded at something? Was that ongoing support, or was it for a special occasion?

Join the Dialogue

In one of the **Readings** for this chapter, child psychiatrist James P. Comer describes what can happen when people begin to try to build stronger bridges between home and school. As he notes, "In the most severely dysfunctional schools, parents, teachers, and administrators don't like, trust, or respect one another." This distrust leads to a culture in which students do not learn very much and in which everyone blames everyone else for the problem. This sense of powerlessness in turn leads to ever more anger and less progress.[19]

It was in a school with just these problems that Comer and his colleagues succeeded in building bridges between parents and school teachers and administrators in New Haven, Connecticut. Their "Comer model" and the program based on it are now a national framework for how such connections can be built. However, as Comer reminds us, the work is not easy.

A generation ago, many aspiring teachers were taught how to "deal with parents," as if parents were some sort of problem or irritant in the otherwise smooth functioning of the schools. As Comer and others found, this approach was not effective. Parents, especially poor and marginalized parents, were hardly mollified by the efforts of school leaders and teachers to "deal with" them. More fundamentally, there was a profound flaw in the idea that parents were a problem to be managed rather than the most natural and important ally a teacher could have. To assume that every parent will view teachers as allies would certainly be naive. Indeed, in many cases, such as when the school is dominated by professionals with low expectations for their students, parents should not trust school officials. However, researchers and activists like Comer have shown that, with patience, a powerful alliance can be built between school and home, teacher and parent. When that happens, the child is the beneficiary.

Many parents, especially parents who themselves have not had particularly positive experiences in school, can be resentful of schools and the professionals who work in them. If parents were not treated with respect when they were students or if their school was a place that had low expectations for them or related to them as failures, they certainly will approach schools and teachers with wariness as adults. After he got over his initial shock at how deep the divide was between parents and schools, Comer discovered that if a program to include parents were to succeed it needed to be based on respect—real and deep respect, not merely the illusion of respect. Parents and staff needed to be brought together in schools in ways that made the schools a community. Power needed to be shared.

Recently, a group of researchers focused on the different ways African-American and Chinese-American parents view their involvement in schools. For many Asian Americans, the notion of attending meetings at school or participating in school governance is antithetical to powerful cultural traditions, and they much prefer a "backstage/

Join the **Dialogue**

Students whose parents are involved in their schooling—including attending meetings and volunteering—tend to have fewer behavioral problems and better academic success and are more likely to complete high school. Students also tend to perform better if their fathers as well as their mothers are involved, regardless of whether the student lives with one or both parents. What can teachers do to encourage parental participation?

behind-the-scene" approach. And it is not only Asian parents who feel that way. Studies of Mexican and Haitian immigrant families have found that they too are cautious about becoming active at their children's school, wanting instead to respect what they see as the quite separate spheres of home and school. While some parents may come to feel very comfortable participating actively in the life of their children's school, other parents will see their role as supporting the school's message at home by helping with homework and ensuring that it is done, setting high standards for their children, and promoting discipline and respect, for example. It is essential that teachers not confuse a parent's reluctance to take part in what any one school considers parent involvement activities with lack of interest or concern for their children.[20] As Comer says in another article, "While we strongly support the practice of direct parental involvement in the work of schools, there is evidence that children from families. . .that facilitate academic learning at home often do well in school without direct parental involvement."[21]

Based on his decades of work and research, however, Comer is more convinced than ever of the value of the active participation of parents in the lives of schools, especially schools serving poor and often marginalized young people. He concludes:

A significant body of research suggests that parent participation in school improves the academic achievement of students. Additional research shows that life success is more likely when students receive continual, constructive support from meaningful adults who serve as role models and motivators. . . . Parents with experience in program schools also serve as dependable defenders of teachers.[22]

While teachers need to find as many ways as possible to build bridges to parents—to welcome them into the life of schools on the parents' terms, not merely on the school's terms— teachers as professionals also need to respect a wide range of parental involvement. Even as teachers welcome and encourage parental involvement, the lack of such **activism** on the part of parents who for whatever reason simply cannot or will not be involved can never be an excuse for failure. However, parent involvement, when it does happen, can dramatically improve the atmosphere for learning.

activism Using action to achieve a goal or result.

YouDecide

Should parents help run a school—for example, by evaluating teachers?

A COMMUNITY NETWORK

In 2000, a book appeared that quickly became a best seller in large part because it spoke so well to a generalized and lingering uneasiness that many people in the United States had come to feel. The book was *Bowling Alone*, by Harvard professor Robert D. Putnam. Putnam wrote:

Over the last three decades a variety of social, economic, and technological changes have rendered obsolete a significant stock of America's social capital. Television, two-career families, suburban sprawl, generational changes in values—these and other changes in American society have meant that fewer and fewer of us find that the League of Women Voters, or the United Way, or the Shriners, or the monthly bridge club, or even a Sunday picnic with friends fits the way we have come to live. Our growing social-capital deficit threatens educational performance, safe neighborhoods, equitable tax collection, democratic responsiveness, everyday honesty, and even our health and happiness.[23]

While Putnam consistently pleaded that his book shouldn't be read as a nostalgic paean to a romantic past when community bonds were stronger and people spent more time in small communities, from bowling leagues to churches, almost every reviewer took it just that way. Many Americans, it seemed, longed for the days when more time

Promising Practices

Recipe for Success

According to Karen Mapp, coauthor of *Beyond the Bake Sale: The Essential Guide to Family-School Partnerships*, "When families are involved in their children's education, their good attitude about schools transfers to their children." Mapp says it's not that parents necessarily are hard to reach but rather that educators are not always open to parents.

That's not the case with Bonnie McReynolds, a fifth-grade teacher in Phoenix, Arizona. McReynolds created her "PIE Program," which stands for "Partners in Education." "I've always felt that parental involvement was the answer to many problems facing teachers and students," says McReynolds, including both academic and social problems.

Parents or caregivers are offered five pieces of the PIE:

1. **Decision making.** Parents are encouraged to set goals for their children *and* for the teacher that go beyond those goals the teacher has already set. The goals (including everyone's responsibilities) are stated at the start of the school year in a signed "contract" between parents, teachers, and students.

2. **Supporting.** Parents are presented with the research that supports the need for their involvement in their children's education at home and at school. They are then provided with tips and resources to help them create a supportive home environment that reinforces for their children the idea that school and education are important.

3. **Teaching.** A parent is a child's number one teacher. Thus, parents are provided with information on how to make education a priority and part of the daily routine, such as by designating a time and a place for doing homework, reading with a child, making sure homework is understood and finished, and talking about what is being done at school. Parents can also get actively involved in the classroom as volunteer tutors, as lecturers sharing their own expertise, and in many other ways.

4. **Learning.** Parents who are more competent in handling the information will feel more confident sharing it with their children. Parents are encouraged to take classes (offered through adult education programs, community colleges, etc.) to demonstrate to their children how important learning is. Or they can take classes *with* their children—computer classes or hobby classes are two possibilities. Teachers can be creative and offer educational field trips designed for both student and parent participation.

5. **Communicating.** An open-door policy allows parents to come into the classroom at any time. Parent newsletters that include information about the concepts being taught and how those concepts can be reinforced and practiced at home, a schedule of after-school help sessions, and news about a special program in which kids are rewarded for positive behaviors reinforce the concept that two-way communication is essential to success.

McReynolds has seen tremendous success with the PIE Program. One parent says: "We worked together as a team. I've never had such a great relationship with my son."

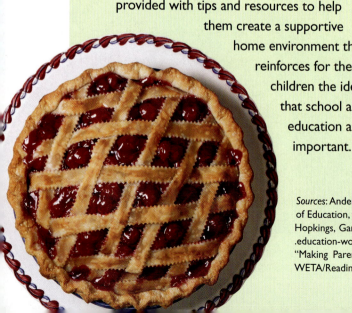

Sources: Anderson, Jill. (2007, April 30). "Beyond the Bake Sale." Harvard Graduate School of Education, www.gse.harvard.edu/news_events/features/2007/04/30_bakesale.html.
Hopkings, Gary. (2004). "Parental Involvement Is as Easy as PIE!" Education World, www.education-world.com/a_curr/curr030.shtml.
"Making Parents Partners." Reading Rockets Professional Development Webcast Series, WETA/Reading Rockets, www.readingrockets.org/webcasts/2003?trans=yes.

Teachable Moment

It Takes a Community

In her study of African American schooling in the segregated South prior to the implementation of the *Brown v. Board of Education* decision, researcher Vanessa Siddle Walker paints a portrait of a powerful kind of community involvement. Few have any nostalgia for the South of the pre–civil rights era, when schools, churches, and communities were segregated by race and when "separate but equal" really meant rigidly separate and very unequal in terms of resources, access to opportunity, and the "pursuit of happiness." Yet, she notes, it was partly as a result of the terrible discrimination of segregation and the need to unite in the face of that assault that the African American community came together in support of its schools.

Walker describes the case of Caswell County, North Carolina, where often desperately poor parents came together to raise the funds needed to ensure that the school their children attended was first-rate, even if this fundraising was a kind of "double taxation" because they paid taxes that mostly supported the white schools. The school's teachers and administrators also made connections to parents and families at multiple levels. One parent remembered the long-time principal of the school, Nicholas Longworth Dillard: "He visited my home a lot of times. He would get around. Then another thing he would do—if his children's [relatives] or somebody passed, he would try to make it to the churches to the funerals. He had a closeness to people."

Looking back at this example of a time when the community, parents, and teachers were united in support of their school's young people, Walker concludes:

Long-time residents of this Caswell County community who participated in the CCTS [Caswell Country Training School] culture remember the interaction between school and community as a collaborative relationship, a kind of mutual owner-

ship in which the community and the school looked out for each other's needs—the parents depended on the school's expertise, guidance, and academic vision, and the school depended on the parents' financial contributions, advocacy, and home-front support. They were united in a common mission to provide a quality education for their children.

Caswell County was far from unique. Across the segregated South, in many African-American communities, the sense of a common mission gave focus to all their efforts.

QUESTIONS

- What would it take to build similar community support—a similar sense of "mutual ownership"—for schools in the more prosperous, sometimes much less closely connected communities in which most North Americans live in the 21st century?
- What is a teacher's role in fostering such communities?

Source: Walker, Emilie V. Siddle. (1993, Summer). "Caswell County Training School, 1933–1969: Relationships Between Community and School." *Harvard Educational Review 63:* 2, 161–182, citations pp. 174, 175.

was spent in small face-to-face communities around shared common interests. Putnam's ideas are terribly important for anyone who wants to see teachers and schools make a difference for young people. Our educational future is indeed at risk if we do not take time to talk to our neighbors.

At the end of *Bowling Alone*, Putnam calls on everyone to play a role in building a more engaged community, which could include a community of support for schools. He wrote:

> "So our challenge is to restore American community for the twenty-first century through both collective and individual initiative. I recognize the impossibility of proclaiming any **panacea** for our nation's problems of civic disengagement. . . . Figuring out in detail how to renew our stock of social capital

panacea Easily espoused remedy or "cure-all" for current problems.

is a task for a nation and a decade, not a single scholar, a single book, or even a single group."[24]

Yet one critical group in any such enterprise will certainly be teachers. As the professionals closest to the schools and the young people who inhabit them, teachers cannot wait passively for such community support to develop. They must be among those who take primary responsibility for fostering community engagement.

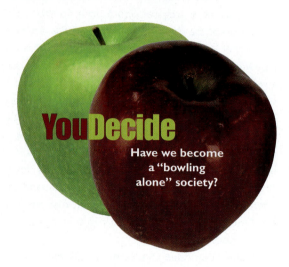

YouDecide
Have we become a "bowling alone" society?

REVIEW >>

- **What does the evidence say about the difference a good teacher can make?**

  Over the years, educators and researchers have had different opinions as to whether teachers—and education—have any impact on a student's success in life, especially for students living in poverty. Although Horace Mann contended that teachers should be able to teach subjects, that was not the trend; rather, teachers were expected to teach uniformly, with some administrators later supporting a "teacher-proof curriculum" focused on teaching itself rather than the subject mastery of the teacher. With legislation from the Johnson administration focused on education and poverty, the Coleman and Jencks reports seemed to say that teachers had little or no impact on a student's lot in life. Years later, research by Kati Haycock and others concluded that not simply teaching but *good* teaching matters—a lot.

- **What is a "good teacher"?**

  A good teacher has a command of the subject matter he or she is teaching, not simply the ability to "stay one chapter ahead of the students" but rather to be able to travel with students on those adventures on which their active imaginations may lead them. A good teacher possesses a strong passion for his or her work so that young people will experience an invigorating interest in the subject and understand that the teacher has an equally determined interest in their success. Teachers also need to be deeply ethical professionals whose commitment to their students is reflected in the way they do their work.

- **How does a good teacher involve parents and the community?**

  An effective teacher has an understanding of and respect for the parents, the community, and the surrounding world that shape each of his or her students and with which the teacher must connect in order to be successful.

What Does the Evidence Say About the Difference a Good Teacher Can Make?

From "GOOD TEACHING MATTERS . . . A LOT"

BY KATI HAYCOCK

As the following article makes clear, Kati Haycock's research points to a powerful answer to the question of what difference good teaching makes. Haycock and her colleagues at the Education Trust, a national center for educational research and advocacy, have concluded that good teaching makes a greater difference than anything else—greater than the impact of poverty, race, or any other factor. While articles like this call for national policies that will ensure a first-rate teacher in every classroom, they also implore all current and future teachers to take their work more seriously than ever before.

For decades, educators, educators-in-training and the public more broadly have been relentlessly fed the same message about achievement among poor and minority students: "Because of poverty and other neighborhood conditions, these students enter school behind other students. As they progress through the grades, the deficits accumulate, leaving them further and further behind other students." Their conclusion? Nothing schools do makes a very big difference.

As an organization, we have questioned the prevailing explanation for some time. "If poverty always overwhelms everything else," we ask, "what explains the 89% pass rate on the Texas state assessment by the Loma Terrace School in El Paso where almost 90% of the children are poor? Or what about the 95% fourth grade pass rate on the same exam by the entire Mission Independent School District with a 94% poverty rate? And why, if schools really don't make a difference, are the low-income students in Community School District #2 in New York City performing so much higher now than were their counterparts a decade ago?"

Always, the response is the same. "It's that superstar principal/superintendent (choose one). We can't expect those kinds of feats from the mere mortals who lead most of our schools."

But what if that answer is wrong? What if these schools are succeeding not on the force of someone's personality, but simply by teaching students what they need to know to perform at high levels? What if, in other words, poor and minority students are performing below other students not because something is wrong with them or their families, but because most schools don't bother to teach them what they need to know?

By now, those of you who are familiar with our work know that we are absolutely convinced—by both research and extensive experience in classrooms all over the country—that poor and minority youngsters will achieve at the same high levels as other students if they are taught at those levels. In our groundbreaking report, Education Watch: The Education Trust National and State Data Book, we document the clear relationship between low standards, low-level curriculum, under-educated teachers and poor results. We argue, further, that if states and school districts work hard on these three issues, they can close the achievement gap.

Most of the time, we have felt as Ron Edmonds undoubtedly felt: surrounded by researchers clinging to dog-eared copies of the *Coleman Report* and arguing that nothing works.

Recently, however, a number of large-scale studies provide convincing proof that what we do in education does matter. Schools—and especially teachers, it turns out—really DO make a difference. Earlier educational researchers just didn't have very good ways of measuring the variables.

We have chosen to focus this issue of *Thinking K–16* on what all of the studies conclude is the most significant factor in student achievement: the teacher. We focus here not because we think improvements in teachers' capabilities or changes in teacher assignment patterns are, by themselves, a silver bullet, but because such changes are clearly more important to increasing student achievement—especially among poor and minority students—than any other.

We focus on teacher qualifications here also because this is an issue within our power to change. If we but took the simple step of assuring that poor and minority children had teachers of the same quality as other children, about half of the achievement gap would disappear. If we went further and assigned our best teachers to the students who most need them (a step, by the way, that makes sense to most people outside of education), there's persuasive evidence to suggest that we could entirely close the gap.

Thought provoking, yes? Read on.

Good Teaching Matters . . . a Lot

Parents have always known that it matters a lot which teachers their children get. That is why those with the time and skills to do so work very hard to assure that, by hook or by crook, their children are assigned to the best teachers. (That is also at least part of the

Source: Katie Haycock, "Good Teaching Matters", *Thinking K–16*, Vol. 3, Issue 2, Summer 1998, pp. 1–13 and "The Real Value of Teachers", Vol. 8, Issue 1, Winter 2004, pp. 1–2.

reason why the children of less skilled parents are often left with the worst teachers, but more on that later.)

Professional educators typically reject these notions. When parents ask for their children to be assigned to a particular teacher, or to be moved out of the classroom of another, most principals counsel them not to worry. "Your child will learn what he or she needs to from any of our teachers."

Recent research from Tennessee, Texas, Massachusetts, and Alabama proves that parents have been right all along. They may not always know which teachers really are the best, but they are absolutely right in believing that their children will learn a lot from some teachers and only a little from others—even though the two teachers may be in adjacent classrooms. "The difference between a good and a bad teacher can be a full level of achievement in a single school year," says Eric Hanushek, the University of Rochester economist notorious for macroanalyses suggesting that virtually nothing seems to make a difference.[1]

Teacher Effects: Tennessee

Tennessee is one of the few states with data systems that make it possible to tie teachers to achievement in their classrooms. Moreover, the state's value-added approach for assessing student achievement allows observers to look at the gains students make during a particular school year. William L. Sanders, director of the Value-Added Research and Assessment Center at the University of Tennessee, Knoxville, has studied these data extensively. By grouping teachers into quintiles based on their effectiveness in producing student learning gains, his work allows us to exam-

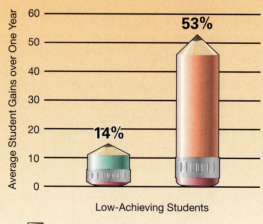

The Effect of Different Teachers on Low-Achieving Students
Tennessee

Source: William L. and Rivers, Joan C. "Cumulative and Residual Effects of Teachers on Future Student Academic Achievement," 1996, Table 1, p. 9.

ine the impact of teacher effectiveness on the learning of different types of students, from low- to high-achievers.

The chart shows the effect teachers from different quintile levels have on low-achieving students. On average, the least effective teachers (Q1) produce gains of about 14 percentile points during the school year. By contrast, the most effective teachers (Q5) posted gains among low-achieving students that averaged 53 percentile points.

The Tennessee data show dramatic differences for middle- and high-achieving groups of students, too. For example, high-achieving students gain an average of only 2 points under the direction of Q1 (least effective) teachers but an average of 25 points under the guidance of Q5 (most effective) teachers. Middle achievers gain a mere 10 points with Q1 teachers but in the mid-30s with Q5 teachers.

There is also considerable evidence that, at least in Tennessee, the effects of teachers are long-lived, whether they advance student achievement or squash it. Indeed, even two years after the fact, the performance of fifth-grade students is still affected by the quality of their third-grade teacher. The chart shows the examples of different patterns of teacher effectiveness for one metropolitan system.

As Sanders points out, students whose initial achievement levels are comparable have "vastly different academic outcomes as a result of the sequence of teachers to which they are assigned."[2] Differences of this magnitude—50 percentile points—are stunning. As all of us know only too well, they can represent the difference between a "remedial" label and placement in the "accelerated" or even "gifted" track. And the difference between entry into a selective college and a lifetime at McDonald's.

Teacher Effects: Dallas

A variety of recent studies in Texas show similar differences in achievement between students taught by teachers of differing quality. Borrowing from some of Sanders's techniques, researchers in the Dallas Independent School District recently completed their first-ever study of teacher effects on the ability of students to perform on assessments. In sharing their findings, Robert Mendro, the district's executive director of institutional research, said, "what surprised us the most was the size of the effect."[3]

For example, the average reading scores of a group of Dallas fourth graders who were assigned to three highly effective teachers in a row rose from the 59th percentile in fourth grade to the 76th percentile by the conclusion of sixth grade. A fairly similar (but slightly higher achieving) group of students was assigned three consecutive ineffective teachers and fell from the 60th percentile in fourth grade to the 42nd percentile by the end of sixth grade. A gap of this magnitude—more than 35 percentile points—for students who started off roughly the same is hugely significant.

Cumulative Effects of Teacher Sequence on Fifth-Grade Math Scores
Tennessee

Student Gains Over Three Years

- Students With 3 Very Ineffective Teachers: **29%**
- Students With 3 Very Effective Teachers: **83%**

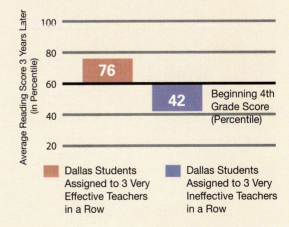

Effects on Students' Reading Scores (Grades 4–6)
Dallas

Average Reading Score 3 Years Later (in Percentile)

- **76** — Dallas Students Assigned to 3 Very Effective Teachers in a Row
- **42** — Dallas Students Assigned to 3 Very Ineffective Teachers in a Row
- Beginning 4th Grade Score (Percentile)

Source: William L. and Rivers, Joan C. "Cumulative and Residual Effects of Teachers on Future Student Academic Achievement," 1996, Figure 1, p. 12.

Source: Heather Jordan, Robert Mendro, & Dash Weerasinghe, "Teacher Effects on Longitudinal Student Achievement" 1997.

The impact of teacher effectiveness is also clear in mathematics. For example, a group of beginning third-graders in Dallas who averaged around the 55th percentile in mathematics scored around the 76th percentile at the end of fifth grade after being assigned to three highly effective teachers in a row. By contrast, a slightly higher achieving group of third-graders—averaging around the 57th percentile—were consecutively taught by three of the least effective teachers. By the conclusion of fifth grade, the second group's percentile ranking had fallen to 27th. This time the youngsters, who had scored nearly the same as beginning third graders, were separated by a full 50 percentile points just three years later.

What Makes for Teacher Effectiveness?

None of these studies has yet advanced to the obvious next step: identifying the qualities that make for an effective teacher. But other researchers have used Texas's extensive database on both teachers and students to examine the impact of specific teacher characteristics on student achievement. Together with work from Alabama and North Carolina, this research helps us to get underneath the matter of teacher effectiveness.

1. Strong Verbal and Math Skills

The first thing that is clear when you look across the various studies is the critical importance of strong verbal and math skills. Harvard's Ronald F. Ferguson, for example, has looked closely at the relationship between student achievement and teacher performance on a basic literacy examination (the Texas Examination of Current Administrators and Teachers, which was administered to all teach-

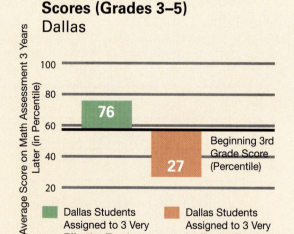

Effects on Students' Math Scores (Grades 3–5)
Dallas

Average Score on Math Assessment 3 Years Later (in Percentile)

100
80
76
60
40
27
20

Beginning 3rd Grade Score (Percentile)

Dallas Students Assigned to 3 Very Effective Teachers in a Row

Dallas Students Assigned to 3 Very Ineffective Teachers in a Row

Source: Heather Jordan, Robert Mendro, & Dash Weerasinghe, "Teacher Effects on Longitudinal Student Achievement" 1997.

ers and administrators in Texas in 1986). Ferguson found a significant positive relationship between teacher test scores on TECAT and student scores on the Iowa Test of Basic Skills (ITBS), with higher scoring teachers more likely to produce significant gains in student achievement than their lower scoring counterparts. Indeed, a change of one standard deviation in a district's teacher scores produced a corresponding change of .17 standard deviation in student scores, when other differences were controlled.[4]

Ferguson got similar results in an analysis of the impact of teacher and classroom qualities on student achievement scores in Alabama. As in the Texas studies, he found a strong positive relationship between teacher test scores (in this case, ACT scores) and student achievement results.[5]

2. Deep Content Knowledge

There is also considerable research showing how important teachers' content knowledge is to their effectiveness with students, especially at the middle and senior high school levels. The data are especially clear in mathematics and science where teachers with majors in the fields they teach routinely get higher student performance than teachers who did not. Goldhaber and Brewer examined this relationship using data from the National Educational Longitudinal Study of 1988 (NELS), an ongoing survey of individuals who were in eighth grade in 1988. Goldhaber and Brewer found a significant positive relationship between teachers' degrees and students' achievement in technical subjects. They concluded that "in mathematics and science, it is the teacher subject-specific knowledge that is the important factor in determining tenth-grade achievement."[6]

The data are less clear in English and social studies; in these subjects students taught by majors don't show consistently better scores than students taught by teachers who majored in something else. However, other evidence suggests that content is no less important in these two disciplines. For example, a recent study in Hawaii asked social studies teachers to rate their own level of understanding about various historical periods and teaching methods, then compared teacher expertise to student achievement. Not surprisingly, there was an almost perfect match: students performed best in the domains where teachers indicated the most expertise.[7]

3. Teaching Skill?

All of this seems to beg the question: what about teaching knowledge and skills? Is content knowledge really sufficient for effective teaching? Clearly not. One only has to spend a few semesters in higher education to see that the deep content knowledge inherent in the Ph.D. doesn't necessarily lead to effective teaching.

That said, the large-scale studies we have reviewed are not particularly helpful in identifying ways to quantify teaching expertise. Neither education courses completed, advanced education degrees, scores on professional knowledge sections of licensure exams nor, interestingly, years of experience seem to have a clear relationship to student achievement. Perhaps the work going on at the National Board for Professional Teaching Standards or Lee Shulman's work on "pedagogical content knowledge" at the Carnegie Foundation for the Advancement of Teaching will advance our understanding of—and options for developing and measuring—teaching knowledge and skill.

In the meantime, we suggest that educational leaders not get sidetracked: there is more than sufficient evidence about the importance of deep content knowledge and strong verbal skills to serve as a foundation for immediate action. At the very least, we know enough to call the question with faculty in the arts and sciences, who, after all, are responsible for developing both content knowledge and verbal skills among intending teachers. It is also enough to justify a second look at hiring and assignment criteria. If good teachers matter, we need to be sure that we are getting the best we can.

Inequities in Distribution

Our emerging understanding of the critical importance of good teachers has especially profound implications for poor and minority youngsters. For no matter how quality is defined, these youngsters come up on the short end. While the teaching force in high-poverty and high-minority communities certainly includes some of the most dedicated and talented teachers in the country, the truth is that these teachers are vastly outnumbered by under- and, indeed, unqualified colleagues.

These patterns are clear in national data tabulations on out-of-field teaching specially prepared for the Education Trust earlier this year by Richard Ingersoll, a professor at the University of Georgia. As is evident in the adjacent table, minority and poor youngsters—the very youngsters who are most dependent on their teachers for content knowledge—

Percentage of Classes Taught by Teachers Lacking a Major in Field, 1993–1994

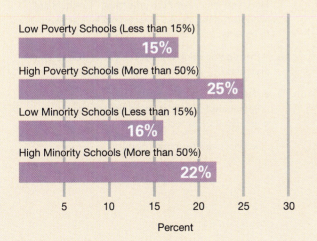

Source: Richard Ingersoll, University of Georgia, Unpublished, 1998.

are systematically taught by teachers with the least content knowledge.

Similar inequities show up at all grade levels in the state-level studies described above, and many more. For example, in Tennessee, black students are almost twice as likely to be taught by ineffective "Q1" teachers as are white children, and are considerably less likely to be taught by the most effective teachers.

The patterns look quite similar in Texas, where, according to researchers John Kain and Kraig Singleton, African American and Latino children are far more likely to be taught by teachers who scored poorly on the TECAT examination. Indeed, as the percentage of non-white children in the school increases, the average teacher score declines.[8] Finding the same patterns in his analysis, Ferguson wrote that "[i]n Texas, and certainly in other places too, attracting and retaining talented people with strong skills to teach in the districts where black students are heavily represented is part of the unfinished business of equalizing educational opportunity."[9]

Race More Than Class?

Contrary to the assumptions that many people may make, inequities in the distribution of teacher expertise are not driven wholly by finances. If they were, we would expect that poor minority children would have teachers of about the same quality as poor white children. But such is not always the case.

In their analysis of Texas data, Kain and Singleton found disturbing differences. Poor white children, it turns out, appear to have a higher likelihood of having well qualified teachers than poor black children.[10]

Similar patterns are evident in teacher quality data from other states. For example, it is clear that students who attend predominantly minority secondary schools in Virginia are more likely to be taught by underqualified teachers than students who attend high-poverty secondary schools. The same is true in Pennsylvania and Oklahoma: students in high-minority secondary schools are more likely to be taught by teachers without a college major in the subject they are teaching.

The problems in central cities are particularly acute, according to a 1995 report from the National Governors Association. "Emergency hiring, assignment of teachers outside their fields of preparation, and high turnover in underfunded schools conspire to produce a situation in which many poor and minority students are taught throughout their entire school careers by a steady stream of the least qualified and experienced teachers."[11]

A More Equitable Distribution of Teacher Expertise

What would happen if minority and poor children had teachers of the same quality as other children? A large part of the gap would simply disappear. The estimates vary somewhat depending upon the statistical model used, but in no case is the effect minor.

- Ferguson's modeling for several metropolitan Alabama districts suggests that an increase of 1 standard deviation in the test scores of teachers who teach black children would produce a decline of about two-thirds in the black/white test score gap in that state.[12]
- Strauss's study of student achievement in North Carolina suggested that a 1% relative increase in teacher scores on the NTE would bring about a 5% relative decline in the percentage of students who fail standardized competency exams.[13]

In other words, much of what we have blamed on children and their families for decades is actually the result of things we have done to them. As a nation, we have deprived our neediest students of the very ingredient most important to learning: a highly qualified teacher.

In his analyses of the Texas data base, Ferguson found a small number of school districts that are exceptions to the general pattern (see chart). A look at how their youngsters benefit from a steady diet of higher performing teachers gives us a glimpse of how the national data for poor and minority students *could* look. . .if we had the will.

For a complete listing of the references for this Reading, go to **www.mhhe.com/teach1e2010**.

Long-Range Effects of Low-Scoring and High-Scoring Teachers on Student Achievement
Texas

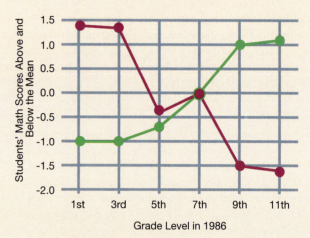

Source: Ronald F. Ferguson, "Evidence That Schools Can Narrow the Black-White Test Score Gap, 1997.

African American Students Are More Likely to Have Underqualified Teachers
Tennessee

Least Effective Teachers (Q1)
- White Students: 15.9
- African American Students: 26.7

Most Effective Teachers (Q5)
- White Students: 22.4
- African American Students: 14.4

■ White Students
■ African American Students

Source: William L. and Rivers, Joan C. "Cumulative and Residual Effects of Teachers on Future Student Academic Achievement," 1996, Table 1, p. 23.

QUESTIONS

1. Have you ever heard the argument "Teachers and schools cannot make a difference if kids grow up in poverty"?

2. What do you think of Haycock's response to that argument?

3. Is the United States—or are most local communities—ready to make the kind of commitment Haycock calls for?

4. Are Hancock's proposals realistic?

What Is a "Good Teacher"?

From **"NEW YORK STATE CODE OF ETHICS FOR EDUCATORS"**

In 1998, the Board of Regents of the State of New York called for a new Code of Ethics for Teachers. During the next several years, the staff and members of the State Professional Standards and Practices Board of Teaching reviewed other state codes, consulted with colleagues across the state, and offered many opportunities for public comment so that as many educators as possible would have a voice in the development of a new code. After a long and inclusive process, the final version of this code was adopted by the Board of Regents in 2002.

Statement of Purpose

The Code of Ethics is a public statement by educators that sets clear expectations and principles to guide practice and inspire professional excellence. Educators believe a commonly held set of principles can assist in the individual exercise of professional judgment. This Code speaks to the core values of the profession. "Educator" as used throughout means all educators serving New York schools in positions requiring a certificate, including classroom teachers, school leaders and pupil personnel service providers.

Principle 1: Educators nurture the intellectual, physical, emotional, social, and civic potential of each student.

Educators promote growth in all students through the integration of intellectual, physical, emotional, social and civic learning. They respect the inherent dignity and worth of each individual. Educators help students to value their own identity, learn more about their cultural heritage, and practice social and civic responsibilities. They help students to reflect on their own learning and connect it to their life experience. They engage students in activities that encourage diverse approaches and solutions to issues, while providing a range of ways for students to demonstrate their abilities and learning. They foster the development of students who can analyze, synthesize, evaluate and communicate information effectively.

Principle 2: Educators create, support, and maintain challenging learning environments for all.

Educators apply their professional knowledge to promote student learning. They know the curriculum and utilize a range of strategies and assessments to address differences. Educators develop and implement programs based upon a strong understanding of human development and learning theory. They support a challenging learning environment. They advocate for necessary resources to teach to higher levels of learning. They establish and maintain clear standards of behavior and civility. Educators are role models, displaying the habits of mind and work necessary to develop and apply knowledge while simultaneously displaying a curiosity and enthusiasm for learning. They invite students to become active, inquisitive, and discerning individuals who reflect upon and monitor their own learning.

Principle 3: Educators commit to their own learning in order to develop their practice.

Educators recognize that professional knowledge and development are the foundations of their practice. They know their subject matter, and they understand how students learn. Educators respect the reciprocal nature of learning between educators and students. They engage in a variety of individual and collaborative learning experiences essential to develop professionally and to promote student learning. They draw on and contribute to various forms of educational research to improve their own practice.

Principle 4: Educators collaborate with colleagues and other professionals in the interest of student learning.

Educators encourage and support their colleagues to build and maintain high standards. They participate in decisions regarding curriculum, instruction and assessment designs, and they share responsibility for the governance of schools. They cooperate with community agencies in using resources and building comprehensive services in support of students. Educators respect fellow professionals and believe that all have the right to teach and learn in a professional and supportive environment. They participate in the preparation and induction of new educators and in professional development for all staff.

Principle 5: Educators collaborate with parents and community, building trust and respecting confidentiality.

Educators partner with parents and other members of the community to enhance school programs and to promote student learning. They also recognize how cultural and linguistic heritage, gender, family and community shape experience and learning. Educators respect the private nature of the special knowledge they have about students

Source: "What Is a Teacher's Ethical Responsibility?" Used by permission of the New York State Education Department and the New York State Professional Standards and Practices Board of Teaching.

and their families and use that knowledge only in the students' best interests. They advocate for fair opportunity for all children.

Principle 6: Educators advance the intellectual and ethical foundation of the learning community.

Educators recognize the obligations of the trust placed in them. They share the responsibility for understanding what is known, pursuing further knowledge, contributing to the generation of knowledge, and translating knowledge into comprehensible forms. They help students understand that knowledge is often complex and sometimes paradoxical. Educators are confidantes, mentors and advocates for their students' growth and development. As models for youth and the public, they embody intellectual honesty, diplomacy, tact and fairness.

QUESTIONS

1. Is it reasonable to ask a teacher to do everything that the New York Code seems to expect?

2. Are clear expectations like this helpful, or do people already know what's expected?

3. Why do you think leaders in New York State saw a need for such a code?

4. Are there any principles you would like to add to (or subtract from) the code?

How Does a Good Teacher Involve Parents and the Community?

From "THE REWARDS OF PARENT PARTICIPATION"

BY JAMES P. COMER

James P. Comer is a medical doctor and Professor of Child Psychiatry at Yale University. Beginning in the late 1960s, Comer turned more of his attention to schools and schooling, asking what it will take for schools to serve poor and marginalized children in the United States effectively. What began as a small effort in his own city of New Haven, Connecticut, has spread to over a thousand schools that now use the "Comer model." Many see the reforms Comer advocates as a key element in building more effective schools for the young people of the 21st century.

In 1968–1969, King Elementary School in New Haven, Connecticut, became one of two low-performing schools to pilot our Yale Child Study Center School Development Program. The families served by the school were almost all poor and African American. In a school that served about 300 students, 15 parents turned out for that year's school winter holiday program.

Three years later, with no change in the demographics, more than 400 parents, kin, and friends attended the same program. By this time, families were involved in almost all aspects of the school's work.

Through previous Child Study Center work in schools, we had learned that we could not enforce parental involvement through administrative mandates or by touting the benefits of participation. Thus, the School Development Program did not immediately impose an intervention designed to improve parent participation. Instead, our five-person team moved into King Elementary and provided mental health and social services.

Working with students, parents, and school staff, we experienced small successes and gradually built mutual respect and trust. All participants were then able to collaborate in creating a positive community. Because parents sensed that they were welcome and could contribute something of value, they became more involved in the work of the school and in the education of their children.

Some people argue that times have changed and that schools today have more difficulty getting parents involved—that parents are busier, younger, and often living in more dysfunctional settings. But in our work, we still observe the same transition from reluctance to enthusiastic participation when we make coordinated, systematic efforts to create inclusive school cultures.

Parents in Dysfunctional Schools

The School Development Program has now worked in more than 1,000 schools. More than two-thirds have been high-minority, low-income elementary schools. In general, these sites were characterized by a dysfunctional culture in which parent participation was either minimal or negative.

Even when dysfunctional schools don't have overwhelming behavior problems, many parents stay away. Some of these parents had poor experiences in schools themselves. Although they would like to see their children have better experiences, they don't expect this to happen. Often, the education and social status of people who work in the school intimidate undereducated and poor parents. Differences in race, religion, income, and ethnicity might cause tension. Some parents are under economic stress and have little time or energy. Because of these and many other factors, low-income urban parents need compelling reasons to get involved in their children's schooling (Epstein & Salinas, 2004).

In the most severely dysfunctional schools, parents, teachers, and administrators don't like, trust, or respect one another. The culture of low academic and social performance reinforces all things negative and generates blame. Understandably, parents avoid such settings except when they become angry or when they believe they need to protect their children from unfair treatment. Parents may even threaten to physically attack teachers. When people feel powerless and do not expect to make progress

Source: "The Rewards of Parent Participation," by James P. Comer. In March, 2005 issue of *Educational Leadership*, 62(6) p. 38–42, copyright 2005 by ASCD. Learn more about ASCD at www.ascd.org.

through participation and negotiation, they may gain satisfaction through overly assertive and aggressive interactions (Hirschhorn & Barnett, 1993).

An incident in one of our pilot schools illustrates this combative disposition. Toward the end of the third year of the School Development Program, I gave a report on the progress of the school. All of the parents seemed pleased, except for one parent who angrily challenged me throughout the presentation, as she had often done in the past. But as the two of us cleaned up the meeting room together, she said, "See you next year. I sure enjoy fighting with you!"

Today, the notion that parents have an important role to play in schools has gained increasing acceptance. But even when schools expect and encourage parent participation, many educators don't quite understand how it is supposed to work. Teachers fear adversarial relationships, or "somebody looking over my shoulder." Some schools want parents to cooperate by keeping their children under control but resist involving the parents in discussions about school organization, management, culture, teaching, and learning. When parents receive these mixed or disingenuous messages, they sense that they are unwanted. Thus, many schools that believe they are encouraging parents to participate nevertheless find that the parents don't respond (Mapp, 1997).

From the beginning of our work in schools, we were struck by this mixture of parents' hesitancy to get involved and educators' subtle and even unintentional resistance to parental involvement. But on the positive side, we were equally struck by the fact that parents, school staff, and students all wanted to succeed. We found that if parents could be involved in ways that threatened neither the parents nor the teachers, parental involvement would reach a critical mass that could transform even the most dysfunctional school.

The Child Development Perspective

In the School Development Program, a growing understanding of the problems leading to parental paralysis and dysfunction helped us develop a nine-element framework for change (see "The SDP Framework for Change"). The framework is based on the theory that student academic performance, behavior, and preparation for school and life can be greatly improved when the adult stakeholders work together in a respectful, collaborative way to create a school climate or culture that supports development, good instruction, and academic learning.

The basis of our theory of change—and the rationale for meaningful parent participation in the work of schools—is our developmental perspective. We put child development at the center of parent and educator thinking about school improvement. In our program schools, teams often discuss the role of parents as a child's first teachers. We explain that children are born into the world thinking and learning in order to survive; that they bond to their caretakers; that they identify with, imitate, and internalize the caretakers' attitudes and values. Interactions with their children enable caretakers to help children grow along crucial developmental pathways—physical, social-interactive, psycho-emotional, ethical, linguistic, and cognitive (Comer, Joyner, & Ben-Avie, 2004).

Academic learning is an acquired interest that students usually gain through social, emotional, and cognitive interactions with meaningful others. Thus, academic learning and healthy development are inextricably linked. Parents and teachers must work together, seamlessly supporting development at home and at school.

Insights from Experience

In School Development Program schools, the existing parent association is rejuvenated as the Parent Team. Through their representatives on the School Planning and Management Team, parents help to create a year-long, schoolwide schedule of activities designed to support instruction and to create positive relationships in the school. But perhaps more important, they support this comprehensive school plan, particularly its social component. They organize a set of activities to inform parents—discussions about child-rearing, work readiness, how to access out-of-school services, and the like.

The Parent Team also works with teachers to plan the usual back-to-school, Thanksgiving, and other holiday events as purposeful parts of the comprehensive school plan that support students' developmental needs. This differs from other schools, where social activities often have no clear purpose beyond entertainment and therefore are vulnerable to being eliminated in response to pressures for more academics.

Parental input has helped us to identify several simple but important conditions that could limit the benefits of social activities. For example, before trust is established, the parents tend to gather on one side of the room and the staff on the other. A parent-teacher matching process can make

Experience has also taught us to have realistic expectations. Early on, we were concerned about the overall level of parent participation. Although some parents attended events regularly and some activities attracted many parents, we were unable to achieve the high level of parental participation that we believed was optimal. Eventually, however, we realized that this behavior was inevitable in organizations. We therefore created participation goals at three levels that took this natural pattern into account:

Level 1: Parents provide general support by attending parent-teacher conferences, monitoring their children's homework, and supporting fund-raising activities. They participate in calendar events, such as school concerts and awards ceremonies. This level attracts the largest number of parents.

Level 2: Parents serve as volunteers in daily school affairs—for example, by providing office support, going along on field trips, or working as library assistants. It is important to give these parent volunteers meaningful tasks that they are capable of accomplishing and to place them with compatible staff members.

Level 3: Parents participate in school decision making by serving on the School Planning and Management Team or on other school committees. Parent representation in the governance and management of the school should be as broadly based as possible (School Development Program, 2001).

A Broad Range of Benefits

A significant body of research suggests that parent participation in school improves the academic achievement of students (Henderson & Mapp, 2002). Additional research shows that life success is more likely when students receive continual, constructive support from meaningful adults who serve as role models and motivators (Adger, 2001).

The School Development Program's long experience has established that parent participation in schools can be helpful to students, school staff, and the parents themselves—often in unexpected ways. Highly involved parents can be some of the most effective advocates for education. District administrators and elected officials tend to respond much more positively to school requests when those requests come from parents and staff members together. At one school, a new parent forcefully proposed to the Parent Team that they march on City Hall because the superintendent had not responded to the school's problem of overcrowding. A veteran parent helped her consider the downside of such action; instead, they sent a letter to the superintendent and copies to the city alderperson and mayor and received a prompt and positive response.

Parents with experience in program schools also serve as dependable defenders of teachers. For example, when angry parents misguidedly attack a teacher's discipline measures, other parents in school leadership positions may help the complaining parents focus on how they can help

the intent clear and encourage better interaction. One school gives teachers and parents numbers and asks those teachers and parents with matching numbers to sit and engage with each other during the event. We have noted that parents turn out more often when food is served, particularly when they are involved in its preparation—for instance, through potluck dinners or ethnic festivals. They are also more likely to attend events when their children are on the program. The need to care for other children in the family can prevent some parents from attending events; providing a babysitter at school during the event can overcome this obstacle.

An important component of the Parent Team is a staff liaison, who helps parents develop such skills as using an agenda, promoting input from all members, considering benefits and negative consequences of various proposals, setting priorities, making decisions, and interacting constructively with staff members. When parents gain the necessary skills to carry out their own programs and to participate in the larger school program, the staff liaison becomes less active. Providing this support to facilitate success is particularly crucial in schools serving many undereducated families. These parents are often capable and proud, but they initially lack the skills and confidence needed to fully participate in school programs. Because they are proud, the support must be subtle, goal-oriented, and temporary.

their children become more responsible instead of blaming the school.

Another bonus of parent participation in School Development Program schools has been the positive, powerful impact of the experience on the lives of the parents themselves. For example, after a Politics and Government curriculum unit that parents helped to design and attended themselves, some of the participants registered and voted in city and state elections for the first time in their lives. Involvement in school activities has also motivated many parents to further their own education and to secure jobs and promotions that they previously believed were out of reach. One low-income parent went from high school dropout status to a master's degree and a professional career. Two of her children are now engineers; another is a lawyer, and the fourth is a physician.

Such parents cite as major factors in their success the respect and sense of belonging they received from school staff members. Parents gained confidence as they engaged in school activities. They discovered that they had competencies they were not using, and they also developed new skills. As parents support the activities that the school provides for their children, they are exposed to larger opportunities and they open their minds to their own possibilities. Parental involvement in School Development Program schools not only improves teaching and learning; it can also transform families' lives.

For a complete listing of the references for this Reading, go to **www.mhhe.com/teach1e2010**.

QUESTIONS

1. Haycock argues that ensuring that a school has high-quality teachers can virtually wipe out the impact of racism and poverty in the achievement of students. Comer seems to argue that restructuring schools to engage parents can do much the same thing. Do you think they agree or disagree with each other? Why?

2. Comer talks about the strange mix of the hesitancy of many parents to get involved and the hesitancy of teachers to have them become involved. What do you think is the greatest barrier to increased parent involvement in schools? Is it a factor that Comer mentions, or could there be other reasons?

3. Is it possible for parents to be too involved in the life of a school?

3

STUDENT DIVERSITY

The simplest answer to the question "Who will I teach?" is "a diverse group of young people." But diversity is a complex issue. Diversity can mean different things, depending on the classroom and the school. Many schools are segregated in ways that reduce or mask diversity. Some cities, states, and regions are extraordinarily diverse; others are more homogeneous. Schools in Maine and Vermont reflect those states' communities, which are predominantly White. In Washington, D.C., the majority of the population is African American, and the school population is only 5% White. Some forms of diversity, such as racial and gender diversity, can be obvious. Other forms of diversity, such as sexual orientation, religion, or diversity of cultural assumptions, are often far less obvious. The best teacher is one who knows how to embrace and honor diversity and how to engage a diverse group of young people and create in a classroom a small model of the larger, diverse democracy that schools are expected to foster.

Scholars, political leaders, parents, and teachers often debate the nature of diversity and the ways in which diversity should be recognized, or ignored, in schools. Among the **Readings**, "Globalization, Immigration, and Education," by Marcelo M. Suárez-Orozco, helps us understand the extraordinary changes happening in the U.S. population, especially among young people who attend school today. The next article pulls us more deeply into one of the many types of diversity that teachers face—the experience of gay and lesbian students in school. In "Dude, You've Got Problems," *New York Times* columnist Judith Warner demands that schools take the needs of these students much more seriously than they have to date. In the final **Reading**, "The Silenced Dialogue," scholar Lisa Delpit discusses some of the ways White and Black teachers look at race and the best ways to teach in a racially diverse classroom.

WHO WILL I TEACH?

FOCUS >>

- Will my classroom be like the ones I attended?
- Who attends school today?
- How can I be sure that I am reaching all my students?

>> Will My Classroom Be Like the Ones I Attended?

Many of us have a vivid memory of our favorite class. It may have been in first or second grade, when we were learning to read; or it may have been in middle school, when we started to feel "grown up" and independent; or perhaps it was in high school, when we came to love a specific subject. Most aspiring teachers have at least one memory of school that gives them positive inspiration for the work they want to do in the future.

You may see yourself standing at the front of that very room, filled with students who look and act a lot like the students you went to school with. You may have attended a school that was relatively diverse in terms of students' race or socioeconomic background. Or you may have spent your days with classmates very much like yourself.

Whatever your experience, remember that schools and their students are constantly changing. As we see in this chapter, classrooms have become extraordinarily diverse in a way that no one could have predicted a generation ago. High levels of immigration to the United States from Central and South America as well as from Asia have fundamentally changed the ethnic make-up of the nation's student body, if not the mix in every school. At the same time, schools in some places are becoming more homogeneous as efforts of past decades to end racial segregation slip away because of new social movements.

Given these changes, you need to understand that the classrooms of today and tomorrow are going to be very different from those of even 10 years ago, especially in terms of the **diversity** of students (and students' needs) that you will encounter. The answer to the question "Will my classroom be the like the ones I attended?" is more than likely a resounding no.

> **diversity** Refers to the wide range of differences between people, most often associated with racial and ethnic identities, but also including variations in gender, beliefs, customs, sexual orientation, income, and other intangible distinctions.

There are many reasons for the changing demographics in today's schools. For one thing, more students are coming to school than ever before. The National Center for Health Statistics reports that more babies were born in 2007 than in any other year in American history, even more than in the peak of the post–World War II baby-boom year of 1957. People are also moving to the United States from other parts of the world in record numbers. The New York City public school system has students who were born in 102 of the 104 countries represented at the most recent Olympics. Schools in some of the most prosperous suburbs, which have long served an all-White student body, now include students who are the children of South Asian or African American doctors, lawyers, and other highly educated professionals. Small farming towns have as many students who were born in Latin America as they do students who were born locally. Long-term residents of the United States are also moving around more and intermarrying more frequently. Traditional notions of **ethnicity** are fading.

> **ethnicity** Real or presumed characteristics and customs that identify members as part of a racial or cultural group.

Beyond population demographics, a number of social movements have led schools to include more students who do not come to school speaking English, or who have a physical handicap or learning disability, in what were previously considered "regular education" classrooms. As a result of these changes, the nation will need a growing number of teachers in the coming years, and those teachers need to be well prepared to embrace a diverse group of learners.[1]

>> Who Attends School Today?

RACE AND ETHNICITY

By 2030, when many readers of this book will be in the middle of their teaching careers, the number of school-aged students in the United States who are not of European American background will exceed the number of European American children by a substantial margin. In each age group of 1 year olds through 5 year olds, the non–European Americans (often called minority youth, though they will be the majority by 2030) will exceed the White population by one-half million or more.

These changing demographics are part of an extraordinary change in the overall U.S. population. In 1995, all "minority groups" made up 26% of the nation's people. By 2050, that percentage is expected to rise to 47%, with the greatest changes among young people. The emergence of what is sometimes called a "majority-minority" student enrollment has been a long time coming, and this growing racial and ethnic diversity is but one of several indicators of the changing nature of today's and tomorrow's students.

The percentage of non–European American students in the public schools has grown from 22% in 1972 to 31% in 1986 to 43% in 2006. At the same time, the percentage of White students has declined from 78% to 57%. (Note that all of these numbers are percentages. The actual number of students—including White students—has grown through all of these years.)

The most dramatic change is the growing number of Hispanic students who today represent one out of five students. In 1972, Hispanic students made up only 6% of the nation's student body; that percentage had grown to 11% in 1986 and 20% in 2006. The percentage of African American students has remained static, at around 17%. In 2006, Asian and Pacific Islander students constituted about 4% of the total, and this percentage is expected to grow, also quite dramatically, in the near future. Another group that is likely to grow comprises those who are of "more than one race" or "other," as the number of children of parents of many different racial and ethnic

categories grows in the next generation. For a student who may have a father of mixed Chinese and English origins and a mother from Latin America, for example, the very idea of race makes little sense. Finally, American Indian/Alaska Natives make up about 1% of today's students.

The rapid growth in the racial and ethnic diversity of American students has come about for many reasons. More European Americans are not having children or are having smaller families, compared with other Americans, whereas many so-called minority families, especially Hispanic families, are much larger. In addition, in recent decades the United States has seen the largest number of immigrants in

Difference Between Minority and Non-Minority Populations by Age

Legend: Minority More Than Non-Minority; Non-Minority More Than Minority

2030

2050

Source: U.S. Department of Commerce, Minority Business Development Agency, Minority Population Growth: 1995 to 2000.

The racial and ethnic make-up of students has changed in different regions of the United States. Many African American families have relocated in the past 30 years, with an increase in the number of such families in the Northeast and Midwest. The percentage of Black students remained constant in the South, at one-quarter of the total, and dropped slightly in the West. (Again, percentages, not actual numbers, are reported here. The total numbers of Black and White students increased significantly across the country and in all regions over the past 30 years.) The percentage of Asian students has grown throughout the country but especially in the West. The percentage of Hispanic students has also grown, and this group now represents well over one-third of all public school students in the West. (Hispanics constitute a majority in New Mexico and are represented in significant numbers in California and Texas.)

history. The two dominant features that characterize this most recent wave of immigration are (1) its intensity—the immigrant population grew by over 30% in the 1990s, and (2) the shift in the sources of new immigration. Prior to 1965, the majority of immigrants were Europeans or Canadians, whereas today more than 50% of immigrants are from Latin America and 25% are from Asia.

Although this combination of immigration and differential birth rates has changed the racial and ethnic make-up of the school-aged population of the United States, no one school reflects exactly that diversity. There are many segregated, predominantly White schools, just as there are segregated, primarily Black and mostly Hispanic schools. Many schools come very close to having homogeneous student bodies. Schools are also, perhaps even more, segregated by the economic backgrounds of their students. Most poor students are concentrated in major cities or rural parts of the country, whereas in other areas of the nation's major cities, as well as in many suburbs, students come from much more prosperous families.

The Changing Face of Public School Children

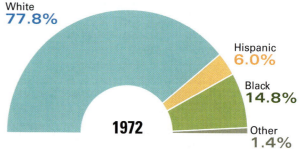

White 77.8%

Hispanic 6.0%

Black 14.8%

1972

Other 1.4%

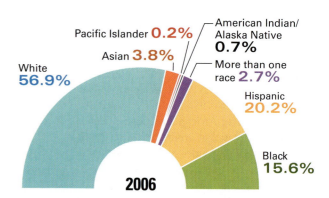

Pacific Islander 0.2%

American Indian/ Alaska Native 0.7%

Asian 3.8%

More than one race 2.7%

White 56.9%

Hispanic 20.2%

Black 15.6%

2006

Source: U.S. Department of Commerce, Census Bureau, Current Population Survey (CPS), October Supplement, 1972–2006.

The Changing Face of Public School Children - by Region

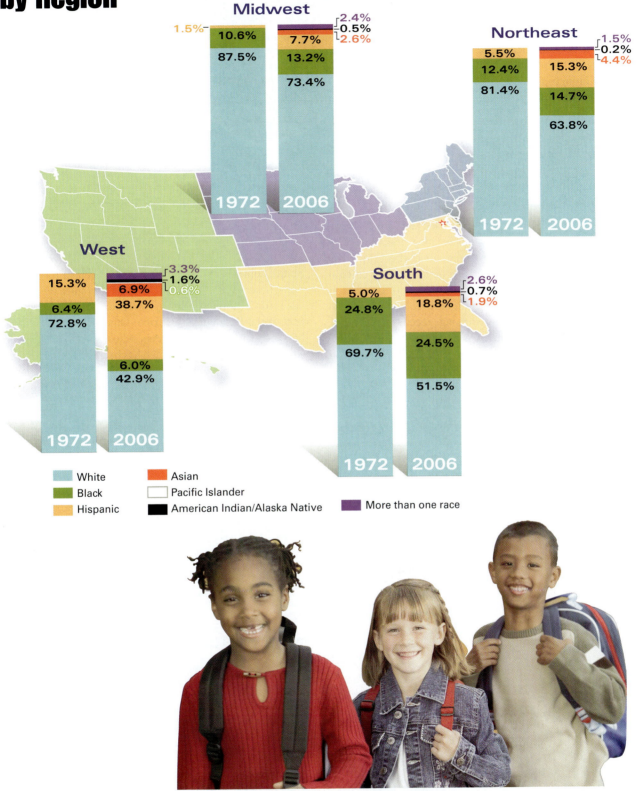

Midwest

1972: 1.5% | 10.6% | 87.5%

2006: 2.4% | 0.5% | 2.6% | 7.7% | 13.2% | 73.4%

1972   2006

Northeast

1972: 5.5% | 12.4% | 81.4%

2006: 1.5% | 0.2% | 4.4% | 15.3% | 14.7% | 63.8%

1972   2006

West

1972: 15.3% | 6.4% | 72.8%

2006: 3.3% | 1.6% | 0.6% | 6.9% | 38.7% | 6.0% | 42.9%

1972   2006

South

1972: 5.0% | 24.8% | 69.7%

2006: 2.6% | 0.7% | 1.9% | 18.8% | 24.5% | 51.5%

1972   2006

Legend:
- White
- Black
- Hispanic
- Asian
- Pacific Islander
- American Indian/Alaska Native
- More than one race

Source: U.S. Department of Commerce, Census Bureau, Current Population Survey (CPS), October Supplement, 1972–2006

Black Americans Demographic charts can mask as many differences as they illustrate. For example, people of many different backgrounds are included in a single category of "Black Americans." Many Black Americans are African Americans who are the descendants of slaves brought to these shores between the 1500s and the 1800s. More Africans than Europeans came to North America prior to the American Revolution, and their descendants have been in this country longer than there has been a country, far longer than the ancestors of many European Americans. However, other Americans who are classified as Black are the descendants of more recent immigrants or are immigrants themselves. For the past century, there has been a steady movement of people back and forth between the United States and the now mostly independent islands of the Caribbean. These citizens, often called Afro-Caribbean, bring to their schooling their own quite different cultural experiences and expectations and, in many cases, their differing languages, such as Haitian Creole or Jamaican-accented English. Finally, among recent immigrants, many come to the United States directly from Africa. Their families have lived for generations in nations and cultures where Africans were the majority and where the experience with racism was with European colonialism—English or French or occasionally Italian or German—rather than American slavery and segregation. An urban teacher, Black or White, who has a number of students who have immigrated from Senegal, and whose families

YouDecide

Are most schools really going to be "majority-minority" in my lifetime?

want to be sure that they maintain their native-born mastery of the French language, needs skills different from those of another teacher who may have many students whose African American grandparents migrated north from Alabama or Mississippi. The fact that both groups of students are classified as "Black" is not the most significant information these teachers need to know.

Hispanics The number of students classified as Hispanic is growing rapidly, both in total numbers and in the percentage of all students. People of many different backgrounds classify themselves, or are classified by others, as Hispanic or, as many prefer, Latino. Some Latino or Hispanic students, especially in the southwestern United States, come from families that have been here for generations, in some cases living in the same area since the current states of California, Arizona, New Mexico, and Texas were part of the Republic of Mexico. Other Hispanic children have parents and grandparents who came to the United States from Puerto Rico, which has been part of the United States since the Spanish-American War of 1898 and whose residents are U.S. citizens. Many others are from Cuban families, most of whom came to the United States after the Communist Revolution in Cuba in 1959. Still others are the children of immigrants from every country of Central and South America, who have come to the United States,

The U.S. population is expected to rise from 296 million in 2005 to 438 million by 2050, with 82% of the increase coming from immigrants.

PORTRAIT OF AN EDUCATOR

Septima Clark

Septima Poinsette Clark began her teaching career in 1918 when she was 20 years old. She first taught in an isolated rural school on Johns Island, off the coast of South Carolina. Clark had been a teacher in the African American schools of the segregated South for many years when she took a job as a seventh grade teacher in Charleston, South Carolina, in 1947. As she described her work there, "But soon my assignment was changed, and I was put in charge of a group of problem pupils in grades four through seven." She was proud of the progress she made with her students, but she would soon confront new problems.

As the National Association for the Advancement of Colored People (NAACP) was winning the court battles that would eventually lead to the 1954 *Brown v. Board of Education* decision, many African American teachers faced a difficult decision regarding their participation in the organization. As Clark described it:

> There weren't too many black people who considered the NAACP worthwhile. They were still afraid, you know, so it was a very small group at first. But after many years of work by its lawyers, the United States Supreme Court ruled, in 1954, that racial segregation in public schools was unconstitutional. After that decision, the school authorities in South Carolina passed out questionnaires to every teacher requiring us to list all the organizations we belonged to. I refused to overlook my membership in the NAACP, as some of the teachers did. I listed it.

Source. Septima Clark and the Civil Rights Movement: Ready from Within, ed. Cynthia Stokes Brown, 1990, African World Press.

> The next year the South Carolina legislature passed a law that said that no city or state employee could belong to the NAACP. You see, our legislature was joining others across the Deep South in a systematic campaign to wipe out the NAACP....
>
> It wasn't too long before I got my letter of dismissal. The Board of Education wrote me that it would not be renewing my contract to teach remedial reading at the Henry Archer School. My goodness, somehow or other it really didn't bother me.

Clark never returned to public school teaching after her dismissal in 1955, but her career as an educator in the civil rights movement was just beginning. While she was attending a workshop at the Highlander Center in Tennessee, one of the centers of civil rights organizing in the South, along with Eleanor Roosevelt and representatives from the Sea Islands where she had first taught, it quickly became clear that there was a desperate need for adult literacy education if African Americans were to claim the voting rights for which the movement was fighting. Many states used literacy tests to keep blacks from voting. Along with a few other African American educators, Clark took the lead in organizing Citizenship Schools on the Sea Islands and eventually across the South. In order to achieve a high level of literacy for these adult students and to keep the focus on the goal of their active political participation, Clark and her colleagues decided not to use traditional textbooks, but rather have the students learn to read by studying the United Nations Universal Declaration of Human Rights and the South Carolina state constitution.

In 1961, Highlander turned the Citizenship School program over to the Southern Christian Leadership Conference and she and Andrew Young, who had recently been hired at Highlander and who went on to serve in the U.S. Congress and as U.S. Ambassador to the United Nations, shifted to the SCLC staff. For Clark, gaining the right to vote—a difficult enough task for southern blacks in the 1950s—was only the first step. She also taught people to ask questions like "Do you have an employment office in your town?" or "How come the pavement stops where the black section begins?" Her focus was always on helping people in "asking questions like that, and then knowing who to go to talk to about that, or where to protest it." Education, Clark believed, was a key element, but only an element, in a long road to freedom that wound through the schools, the voting booth, and the political organization of her people.

---

as most immigrants have, to seek greater political freedom and economic opportunity—to make a better life for themselves and their descendents. Today, the majority of Hispanic students in Florida, especially in the Miami area, are of Cuban descent; the majority in New York and many other parts of the Northeast are from Puerto Rican families; and the majority in the West are of Mexican descent. But like all other residents of the United States, Hispanic families move around, and it is easy to find Mexican children in New England, Cuban children in the Northwest, or

Did you know?

One in five students in the United States is Hispanic. The Census Bureau predicts that, by 2025, one out every four students will be Hispanic.

children from any other Hispanic community in any of the nation's fifty states.

Native Americans   American Indians and Alaska Natives—descendents of people who have been in the United States the longest—comprise 1% of all students (although their actual numbers are growing). For centuries, European diseases, to which they had no immunity, and European-style military operations, to which their arms were no match, reduced the original American Indian population to less than 10% of what it was when Columbus landed. In the late 19th century, federal policy began very slowly to change. Government boarding schools had sought to transform American Indian youth into models of European American culture but failed miserably. Many American Indian adults today can tell stories of being beaten at the boarding school for speaking in their tribal language instead of English, but proudly recall maintaining their language in spite of the harsh rules.

Beginning in the 1960s, more and more Indian tribes were given control of their own schools, including the right to hire teachers and develop curricula that honored their culture and traditions. Schools like the Rough Rock Demonstration School of the Navajo Nation, in which the curriculum and policies of the school were under the direct control of Navajo people, became models of a new form of Indian schooling. Today, tribes are building schools that reflect their culture and beliefs in everything from the

....

National Origin of U.S. Hispanics and Latinos (right)

Areas of the U.S. with the Most Hispanics and Latinos. Green bars indicate areas with the fastest growing Hispanic populations. (below)

Hispanic Categories in the United States

Dominican 2%

Salvadoran 3%

Cuban 3.5%

Puerto Rican 9%

All other Hispanic 18.5%

Mexican 64%

Source: Estimated Hispanic Population as of July 1, 2006. U.S. Census Bureau, 2007.

Hispanic Population by State

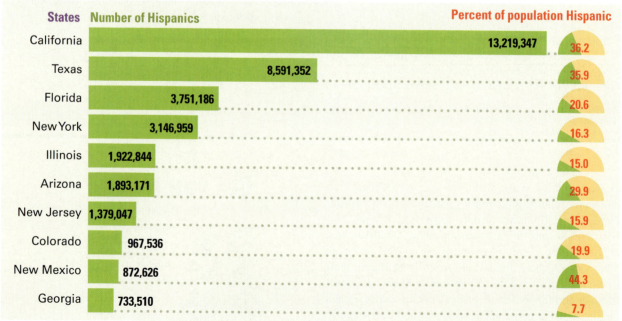

States	Number of Hispanics	Percent of population Hispanic
California	13,219,347	36.2
Texas	8,591,352	35.9
Florida	3,751,186	20.6
New York	3,146,959	16.3
Illinois	1,922,844	15.0
Arizona	1,893,171	29.9
New Jersey	1,379,047	15.9
Colorado	967,536	19.9
New Mexico	872,626	44.3
Georgia	733,510	7.7

Source: Pew Hispanic Center tabulations of 2007 American Community Survey (1% IPUMS).

Promising Practices

Fueling the Pipeline

By 2025, Hispanics (or Latinos) are expected to comprise about 20% of the U.S. workforce. However, currently only about half of Latino adults have high school diplomas. This number can be accounted for in part by the large number of recent immigrants in the Latino community, but the dropout rate among Hispanic students in U.S. schools is far too high. If the trend continues, many Latinos will be marginalized from active participation in civic life and from good jobs.

ENLACE (Engaging Latino Communities for Education) is a program primarily funded by the W. K. Kellogg Foundation that establishes partnerships among Hispanic-serving institutions. The resulting coalitions, which include colleges and universities, K–12 school districts, communities, and businesses, provide Hispanic students and their families with guidance and support from preschool through college graduation.

A critical academic juncture for Hispanic students is ninth grade, when many drop out of high school, primarily due to an unfamiliar environment, a decrease in community and family support, and schools that aren't prepared to meet their needs. Some ENLACE programs provide ninth graders with mentors, such as upperclassmen or college students, who help with the transition and act as role models.

Source: "Program Links Hispanic Families to Education Resources," by Ellen R. Delisio, 2005, *Education World*, retrieved September 1, 2009, from http://www.educationworld.com/a_issues/issues/issues201.shtml.

In Santa Ana, California, where 80% of students are Hispanic, the ENLACE program is designed to link points along the "educational pipeline," from pre-K to graduate school. According to program director Lilia Tanakeyowma, "The concept is to prepare all students as if they are going to college." Their program is a collaboration of ENLACE staff members, teachers, and parents from the Santa Ana school district, along with Santa Ana College faculty. Through their combined efforts, the Santa Ana school system has upgraded its mathematics curriculum, requiring all eighth graders to take algebra and providing tutors when necessary. In addition, high school graduation requirements now mirror the requirements for admission to a California state university.

Programs have been established in thirteen school districts in seven states with the highest populations of Latino students: Arizona, California, Florida, Illinois, New Mexico, New York, and Texas. ENLACE, which also has its roots in the Spanish word *enlazar*, meaning "to link or weave together, to connect in such a way that the new entity is stronger than its parts" is providing one step toward building a more educated workforce and productive society.

The Muckleshoot Indian Tribe's K–12 school in Washington is a complex rich in symbolism. The design of each building supports tribal identity and traditions, and the campus incorporates the surrounding landscape.

architecture to the curriculum to the staff. Federal aid for education and the growing prosperity of many tribes, often due to the success of their gambling industries, are supporting the construction of beautiful buildings that reflect American Indian values in a way that was unimaginable even a few years ago. In Wisconsin, the Indian Community School is built on a 124-acre site that maintains the wetlands, hills, prairies, and woodlands on which the Oneida, Menomonee, and Stockbridge-Munsee Indian tribes have long lived. In western New York, the Seneca Nation is building a school that will focus on its storytelling culture and ensure that stories are passed on in both English and tribal languages. American Indian communities are growing, and many remain closely connected to their tribes and their tribal cultures, religion, and traditions and are creating schools that foster this sense of community.

Ronald Takaki, a leader in multicultural studies, was the third generation of his family to live in the United States.

Asians   Asian Americans are by far the fastest-growing group and, in the near future, will more than likely comprise a much larger percentage of the nation's students, especially in the West. Some Asian students are from Chinese and Japanese families that have been in the United States for many generations. The historian Ronald Takaki tells the story of taking a taxi from an airport to a conference he was attending:

> *"How long have you been in this country?" he [the taxi driver] asked. "All my life," I replied, wincing. "I was born in the United States." With a strong southern drawl, he remarked: "I was wondering because your English is excellent!" Then as I had many times before, I explained, "My grandfather came here from Japan in the 1880s. My family has been here, in America, for over a hundred years." He glanced at me in the mirror. Somehow I did not look "American" to him; my eyes and complexion looked foreign.*[2]

Although teachers will encounter young Ronald Takakis among their Asian students, other Asian children are themselves immigrants or the children or grandchildren of immigrants, such as the Vietnamese and Cambodian families whose lives were uprooted by the war in Vietnam in the 1960s and early 1970s or others, including many from southern Asia—India and Pakistan—who have come to the United States very recently.

How Can I Make a Difference?

Seeing the Forest through the Vines

"One of my favorite teaching experiences was with a third-grade girl whose primary language was Hindi. Although her parents had lived in America for more than 12 years and were fluently bilingual, they preferred to speak Hindi when they were together as a family. They had many ties to India and their daughter spent several weeks of every summer there visiting her grandparents. On one occasion, I was working to help this young student prepare for a social studies test. It involved describing regions of the United States, including the forested Northeast.

I was surprised by the trouble she had remembering the vocabulary associated with the region—words like deer, fox, raccoon, meadow, deciduous tree, and evergreen. This bright young girl needed additional practice, so I decided to have her draw the forest to engage some kinetic and visual modes of learning. I joined her in this venture and we sat across from each other drawing with our colored pencils. My page had the leafy trees and evergreens I knew so well; a deer, a fox, and a raccoon who was peering from behind a branch. Several minutes into the exercise I looked across the desk to see what she had drawn. To my surprise there were vines, colorful birds, and monkeys swinging across her forest page. We were both using the word forest, but her concept came from her summer vacations in India where she visited a tropical forest, what I might call a rainforest. It was suddenly clear to me why she would find deer, fox, raccoon, meadow, and evergreen hard to put into her "picture" or vocabulary of what a forest looks like. It also became clear that although we were using the same words, we were each bringing to our conversation worlds of unspoken concepts that were nothing alike."

—Third-grade teacher

QUESTIONS

- Have you ever had an experience when you suddenly realized that you and another person were using the same simple word, like *forest*, with a completely different meaning? What was the result?

- What would have happened if the teacher had not asked the student to draw a picture and then taken the time to look at what the student drew? Do teachers have the time to do this? If not, should they make the time or find other ways to communicate?

Asian students often complain that they face a number of stereotypes based on the way issues of race are treated in schools and in the larger society. Some are seen as part of the "model minority," the students who are "always good at math" and generally take schools seriously. However, these stereotypes make little sense, given that there are 30 Asian groups and 21 Pacific Islander groups. Generalizing about these many different groups of people, as if all Asians are alike, is terribly misleading.

Some Asian students also report a sense of being pulled in two different directions—by a family that wants them to maintain certain traditions yet also succeed in their new home and by a school that wants to "Americanize" them. The result can be a family that sees its children as conforming too much to the dominant culture and a school that still sees Asian students as "other." As one student reported, "It was very weird—on the weekend I was American to my people and during the week I was a foreigner [in school]."[3]

More Than One Race The charts in this chapter also include a new category of "more than one race," which comprises 2.7% of all students. Today, more and more young people are resisting a single ethnic category, seeing ethnic labels as something that someone else, especially someone in authority, seeks to place on them. Looking at urban communities in the United States and how they have changed over the past 20 years, researchers Shirley Brice Heath and Milbrey W. McLaughlin write, "Marriages across different races, nationalities, and languages dramatically increased in number, and parents often did not want their children boxed under one ethnic label. Children with one African American parent and one Puerto Rican parent and several Portuguese or Dominican Republican friends saw only psychological hazard in proclaiming a single label for themselves." The

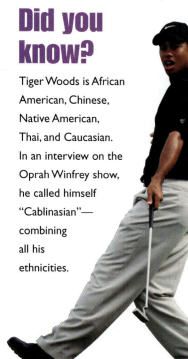

Did you know?

Tiger Woods is African American, Chinese, Native American, Thai, and Caucasian. In an interview on the Oprah Winfrey show, he called himself "Cablinasian"— combining all his ethnicities.

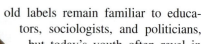

You Decide

Are all racial and ethnic groups discriminated against in one way or another?

old labels remain familiar to educators, sociologists, and politicians, but today's youth often revel in their diversity and, as youth of every generation, enjoy trying on different identities at different points in their own development. Thus Heath and McLaughlin report, "A large urban school district, for example, in the last decade passed a regulation that students could change their designated ethnicity only once every three years."[4]

Even as it is important for teachers to understand, respect, and value the ethnic diversity of today's school students, and the individual students in a classroom, it is also equally, perhaps even more, important for teachers to understand that the meaning of ethnicity for individuals and communities is based on an ever-changing and often illusive set of categories. Based on their own studies of youth culture and their interviews with young people, Heath and McLaughlin have wisely warned all who seek to work with young people:

> *Ethnicity seemed, from the youth perspective, to be more often a label assigned to them by outsiders than an indication for their real sense of self. Many young people told us repeatedly, "Ethnicity ain't what it's really all about." . . . Being the local tough kid's younger brother, the girlfriend of a prominent gang member, or a player on a winning local ball team counted more heavily in daily street life than one's label of ethnic membership. Many young people pointed out that at one time their communities may have been identified with a single ethnic group but that what they see today are different groups continually moving in and out of their housing projects and neighborhoods. They have learned to "hang with all kinds," "to be local," to get along, and to survive.*[5]

All this makes understanding and engaging young people important and difficult business for any teacher. To ignore ethnicity, as to ignore any other attribute, is disrespectful and courts disaster. But to impose an ethnic name or a set of expectations, based on perceived ethnicity, on an individual student or a class is equally disrespectful and disastrous. Many things matter to our students. Having adults who take the time to know them as individuals and what they care about is high on the list.[6]

CONTINUING RACIAL SEGREGATION IN THE SCHOOLS

In 1903, W.E.B. Du Bois, one of the nation's leading African American educators, wrote "the problem of the Twentieth Century is the problem of the color-line." The United States was a nation marred by deep racial segregation and

What Do You Want to Be Called?

White, Black, Hispanic, Asian, Native American, Pacific Islander. At some point in your life, you've probably had to check off your race or ethnicity on a form. But what if none of those labels truly reflects your own personal identity or accommodates the majority of us who have come from multiple backgrounds? For example, some people of Central and South American origin prefer to be called Hispanic; others prefer Latino. Many prefer to use a specific place of origin, such as Guatemalan, Mexican, Puerto Rican, Cuban, and so on. In the same way, some descendents of the first residents of this country prefer American Indian; others prefer First Peoples and others, Native Americans. Many prefer specific tribal names, such as Sioux, Navajo, Apache, or Wampanoag. Today, many people are from families of mixed racial and ethnic origins and do not want to be called by the name of any one group. The term *Blasian* is now used by many of Black and Asian descent.

Most people agree that everyone has a right to be called what they want to be called and not to have a group name imposed on them by someone else. How would you "label" yourself in one (or many) words?

---

discrimination Unfair treatment that is based on differences in gender, race, or class or other differences rather than individual merit.

racial integration The mixing, intentional or accidental, of members of different ethnic or racial groups in a single setting.

discrimination, and Americans spent most of the century wrestling with the issue. Schools in much of the country had been racially segregated, and in many states, Black children (and Latino children and Japanese children in the far west) were assigned to separate and far inferior school buildings, when there even were schools for them.

The U.S. Supreme Court's 1954 decision in *Brown v. Board of Education* ended the legal foundation, though not the reality, of racial segregation in schooling. It took more than a decade before the Court's ruling came to be enforced in many parts of the country. Throughout the late 1950s and beyond, politicians in the South and the North campaigned on a promise that racial integration would never come to their communities. Virginia Senator Harry F. Byrd, Sr., organized a resistance movement that led some

Virginia communities simply to close all schools. Arkansas governor Orval Faubus tried to block Black students from entering Little Rock High School until President Eisenhower sent U.S. Army troops to escort the students to school. In 1963, Governor George Wallace of Alabama gained national prominence by "standing in the school house door" to block students. Nevertheless, the Court's ruling stood.

For some 20 years after *Brown*, slow and steady progress was made toward greater **racial integration** in the schools. Sadly, however, the movement to integrate public schools has not only stalled, but it has shifted backward. In 2009, primarily to catch the attention of the new Obama administration, Gary Orfield, who has spent decades researching school integration, wrote, "Fifty-five years after the Brown decision, blacks and Latinos in American schools are more segregated than they have been in more than four decades. . . . Segregation is fast spreading into large sectors of suburbia and there is little or no assistance for communities wishing to resist the pressures of resegregation and ghetto creation in order to build successfully integrated schools and neighborhoods." Orfield is far from the only

Teachable Moment

Brown v. Board of Education of Topeka, Kansas

On May 17, 1954, Chief Justice Earl Warren delivered the unanimous opinion of the United States Supreme Court:

We come then to the basic question presented: Does segregation of children in public schools solely on the basis of race, even though the physical facilities and other "tangible" factors may be equal, deprive the children of the minority group of equal educational opportunities? We believe that it does.... We conclude that in the field of public education, the doctrine of "separate but equal" has no place. Separate educational facilities are inherently unequal.

This far-reaching ruling in the case of *Oliver Brown et al. v. Board of Education of Topeka, Kansas* effectively declared the laws of almost half the states—not only in the South but in places like Kansas and Washington, D.C.—to be illegal. At the time of the *Brown* decision, seventeen states required their schools to be racially segregated and only sixteen states prohibited racial segregation in the schools.

The *Brown* case was a merger of five different cases challenging school segregation in Delaware, Kansas, South Carolina, Virginia, and the District of Columbia. In Virginia, 16-year-old Barbara Johns had organized a student strike in 1951 to demand a new school building for the very unequal schools serving the Black community in Prince Edward County. In the case that gave the decision its name, Linda Brown, a third-grade student in Topeka, Kansas, had to travel far past the nearest, all-White, school to attend the Black school to which she was assigned.

Brown was also far from the first challenge to racial segregation in the schools. In 1855, African Americans in Boston finally won a long battle to end legal segregation of the schools. Very soon after the Civil War, as Reconstruction-era state legislatures in the South began to create public school systems for Black and White students, they also created racially segregated systems that were challenged from the beginning. In the case of *Plessy v. Ferguson* in 1896, the U.S. Supreme Court ruled that state-mandated racial segregation in public facilities was legal ("separate but equal"). Beginning in the 1930s, the National Association for the Advancement of Colored People Legal Defense Fund, led by Charles H. Houston and Thurgood Marshall, began a meticulous campaign to overturn the school segregation that so many states mandated. They won their first victory in 1948 in a case against the University of Oklahoma; the ruling guaranteed all taxpayers the right to state-funded law schools. In 1946, the Court prohibited the segregation of Mexican American children in California. In 1950, in *Sweatt v. Painter*, the Court said that the segregated law schools of Texas deprived African American law students of a first-rate education. And finally, in the 1954 *Brown* decision, the Court said that all segregated schooling violated the U.S. Constitution's Fourteenth Amendment guarantee that "No State shall abridge the privileges or immunities of citizens of the United States."

QUESTIONS

- Had you heard of the *Brown* decision before reading this book? Had you thought it was based on just one incident or that it was the culmination of many cases?
- If the Supreme Court said that school segregation was unconstitutional in 1954, why do many schools in the United States still seem to be segregated by race today?

researcher pointing out the resegregation of American public education that has been going on for the past two or three decades. But he has compiled a massive amount of evidence to make the case. The statistics are startling: 38.5% of Blacks and 40.0% of Latino students attend schools where more than 90% of the students are non-White. Only a small minority of students—seldom over 20% of the students of any race in any part of the country—attend schools that can truly be called multiracial.

For Orfield and other researchers, the practice of segregating students, especially poor students and those of color, not only into racially segregated schools but also into schools that lack many basic resources, "where everyone is poor, teachers transfer out as soon as they can, parents are powerless. . .is deeply harmful to students." As an aspiring teacher, you need to be well aware of this reality. Whether you pursue a career in a racially segregated school like the ones Orfield describes or in another kind of racially segregated school—one serving predominantly White students—you need to understand the larger legal and cultural structures into which you are entering. In the end, Orfield says, only leadership will change this situation, and teachers will need to be among these leaders.[7]

GENDER AND SEXUALITY

Although the gender make-up of the nation's student body is not changing the way that racial and ethnic groupings are, when future teachers ask "*who* will I teach," it is also important to look at the changing *understanding* of gender and sexuality among today's young people. The fact that boys and girls go to school together, sit in the same classrooms, read the same books, and hear from the same teachers does not mean that boys and girls experience school in the same way. Girls and boys experience schooling differently because of differences in the way they experience life; the way they develop, especially in adolescence; and the way they respond to the world around them.

Contemporary views of sexuality are obviously different from those of the past. Whereas almost any mention of youth sexuality used to be taboo, many of today's young people are sexually active (and quite vocal about it). Not long ago, pregnant teens were excluded from school; today they can sit side by side with their peers. At least three states now allow same-sex couples to marry. Only a generation ago, virtually any mention of homosexuality in schools was unimaginable. Children with two mothers or two fathers now appear in more and more classrooms. In this ever-changing world, boys and girls experience schooling differently because an ever-changing youth culture views issues of gender and sexuality differently.

Heath and McLaughlin write, "While ethnicity had come to be more and more a fluid academic concept after the 1960s, gender in both theory and practice escalated as a public issue and sociopolitical concern. . . . Lived experiences every day told the young that their gender mattered as much as if not more than their ethnicity to their patterns of survival and their identity."

Heath and McLaughlin, like many other scholars, make an important distinction between the biological differences between females and males and the changing social expectations of females and males at different points in history. As they say, "*masculine* and *feminine* are learned behaviors and are continuously variable."[8]

HIDDEN DIVERSITIES

Many young people need special attention from teachers because they may be prone to discrimination that is sometimes hard for teachers to see, even when students are ridiculing other students.

Lesbian, Gay, Bisexual, and Transgendered Students There have always been gay and lesbian students, but for most of the nation's history, students whose sexual orientation was other than heterosexual quickly recognized the social forces stacked against them. Most pretended, with varying degrees of success, to pass for what was considered "normal," as abnormal as it might be for them.

You Decide
What are the benefits of segregating schools?

Connections
In Chapter 4, we'll look at some of the issues related to teaching boys and girls differently.

Did you know?
Of all the developed nations, the United States has the highest rate of teen pregnancy, twice that of England and Canada and eight times that of Japan and the Netherlands. Only one-third of teenage mothers finish high school.

Beginning in the 1970s, a movement of homosexual people "coming out of the closet" developed. Gay and lesbian students began demanding their rights in schools, sometimes with success and sometimes with disastrous results. The survey entitled "From Teasing to Torment" indicates just how hard it is to be a student in today's schools. The survey found that 65% of teens reported that they had been harassed during the past school year because of appearance, gender, sexual orientation, race, disability, religion, or a similar issue; one-third of teens reported that students in their school are frequently harassed because of their perceived or actual sexual orientation.[9] As the survey indicates, **harassment** in general and sexual harassment in particular takes many forms in school. The most common form of harassment reported in the study was for appearance: "the way they look or their body size." The next most common reason was for sexual orientation. The tragic results of this sort of harassment are reported in one

harassment The act of persistently attacking, threatening, or annoying another person or group of people.

You Decide

Should a gay or lesbian teacher come out to his or her students? When is sharing one's personal life too much?

of the **Readings** for this chapter: a *New York Times* column by Judith Warner reporting on the suicides of very young students who felt that they simply could not take the bullying in their school.

Much harassment happens out of the earshot of teachers, as seems to be the case in the examples reported by Warner, so that teachers do not hear students make negative remarks as frequently as the students report hearing them. Teachers, however, rate the problem of bullying and harassment as more serious than students do. Future teachers need to think carefully about how they will respond, not only to harassment but also to the manifold needs and strengths of students who do not fit the sexual "norms" of macho males and passive females and who may be attracted as much or more to people of their own gender as to those of the opposite sex.

Religious Minorities Another hidden group of students are those who do not fit cultural assumptions about what is "normal" religious practice. In the 19th century, many Roman Catholic students found the public schools to be bastions of Protestantism, including a curriculum that reflected a Protestant prejudice against "papist" religion. Most Jewish students who arrived later in the same century found more secular public schools. Nevertheless, well into the 20th century, many Catholic students found themselves saying Protestant-sounding prayers in class and many Jewish students sang carols in the annual Christmas pageant. In more recent times, especially since Supreme Court decisions in the early 1960s outlawed school-sponsored devotional exercises, schools have been more welcoming places for people of a range of religious persuasions (including those espousing no religious affiliation). Sometimes the cost of this openness has been a refusal to engage in discussions that are important or to recognize that, since the beginning of civilization, people have asked questions about gods,

Eleven-year-old Carl Joseph Walker-Hoover tragically committed suicide after continually being harassed by fellow students, who called him "gay" and made fun of his clothes.

Did you know?

There are an estimated 4,200 different religions in the world. Christianity has the most followers (2 billion people) followed by Islam (1.3 billion people).

Try to visit an elementary or a secondary school classroom. Are some of the diverse students discussed in this chapter visible to you? Who might be excluded from the classroom you visited? Why? Who might feel the need to hide their identity in that classroom and school? Why?

Future teachers need to prepare to embrace a classroom that may include:

- students with a wide range of disabilities, including possibly a student in a wheelchair, a blind student, a student with attention-deficit/hyperactivity disorder, or a student who learns more slowly than others in the class

- students who are gay, lesbian, bisexual, or transgendered, or whose parents are a single-sex couple, as well as those who believe that any sexual expressions outside of traditional marriage are sinful

- students from homes where any of the world's religions are practiced, as well as those from homes where all talk of religion is frowned upon

- students who arrived in the United States quite recently from Central America, South Asia, or any of a hundred other places, as well as those whose ancestors have lived in the United States for many generations

- students who do not speak any English, or who are determined to maintain both English and the language of their home, as well as those who are monolingual English speakers

- students who have very strong feelings of ethnic identity as African American, European American, Asian American, or Latino, as well as those for whom ethnic identity is an almost meaningless category

purpose, and the meaning of life (and afterlife). Schools continue to discriminate, however, and many teachers find themselves wishing they knew better how to proceed, such as when as a Sikh student is punished for wearing a ritual knife, or a Muslim girl is chastised for wearing a headscarf, or a conservative religious student, such as a Protestant fundamentalist or a Navajo traditionalist, finds the biology class discussion of evolution unresponsive to his or her concerns. In a nation changing as quickly as the United States, teachers need to know a great deal about the extraordinary variety of religious traditions, practices, beliefs, and nonbeliefs of the students they will teach.[10]

Ethnic, gender, sexual identity, and religious differences are not the only diversities that can lead to some students' being marginalized in today's classrooms. Students who were once excluded from school because they could not speak English are now included. Students with physical disabilities, emotional problems, or severe psychological conditions were often excluded from schools until quite recently. Today, thanks to a continuing civil rights movement among the disabled and their advocates, these children have a place in school and are often mainstreamed in regular classrooms along with their peers.

Connections

In Chapter 4, we'll explore the impact of inclusion and a teacher's responsibility to instruct students with a variety of abilities.

A QUESTION OF . . .

How do you think education has changed since you first started teaching?

"Education in elementary schools has dramatically changed over the last 30 years. Educators are more aware of different learning styles and are more willing to address those differences in all the many areas of education. Also the children that we used to say "fell between the cracks" are now being helped with research-based interventions. Committed leadership is the key to finding time, resources, and the energy that it takes to address these very real concerns of many of the students. Whereas in the past the classroom was mostly one culture, now many cultures are represented and the teacher must be able to relate to those cultures. Being able to educate students keeps evolving and teachers have to be willing to leave the comfort of their teaching style to address the needs of the student. New teachers—be flexible!"

—*Lindy Stacy, first grade teacher* ∎

- students, both boys and girls, who love school and thrive in it, and those who hate school and reject many aspects of the school's culture for what they see as good reasons

>> How Can I Be Sure That I Am Reaching All My Students?

A recent survey of new teachers found that many of them were saying, "I wasn't prepared for the challenges of teaching in a diverse classroom." It is intriguing to note, however, that new teachers from urban areas reported that they were much better prepared to respond well to diversity than those who began teaching in the suburbs. People who planned on urban careers may have sought out more experiences with diversity or may have graduated from programs that emphasized attention to diversity. The fact that less than a third of teachers in affluent schools said that they were prepared for the diversity they found in their schools says a great deal—about their preparation and also about the growing diversity of the nation's schools.[11] No matter where you plan to teach—in an urban, a suburban, or a rural school—a diversity of students will most likely be in the classroom with you.

LOOKING AT OURSELVES

To effectively embrace the diversity of your students, you must first look carefully at your own "place" in the diverse world of today. It is one thing for a new teacher to try to be respectful of, and to engage, all students. It is quite another thing for a teacher to examine where she or he falls personally. Tessie Liu, a professor at Northwestern University in Chicago, talks about the way in which the failure to examine one's own position in the world can be dangerous. She says that there is a special danger for students who are White and middle class to think that "they themselves embody the universal norm," even though they are sympathetic to the needs and concerns of others. Nevertheless, of these White and middle-class students, she says, "In their heart of hearts, they believe that white establishes not merely skin color but the norm from which blacks, browns, yellows, and reds deviate." Liu also sees that "many male students accept the reality of **sexism**, feel bad about it for women, but think that they are not touched by it. Even though they sympathize, for these students poverty, racism, and even sexism are still other people's problems." Distancing from problems—and people—in this way, Liu and many other educators would argue, is almost

sexism A term created in the mid-20th century to describe the belief that one gender is inherently superior to the other and is often acted out by discriminatory, unfair, and, sometimes, abusive actions.

Join the **Dialogue**

Consider one situation in which you have been part of the dominant society and one in which you were subject to discrimination. How did each experience feel? What could a teacher or an adult leader have done to make you more aware in the first instance and more comfortable in the second?

a sure way to guarantee that one will fail to connect with one's students.[12]

For White teachers—and teachers who are part of the majority in other ways, be it heterosexual teachers, teachers without disabling conditions, or teachers who have never struggled with the English language—it may be difficult to see oneself as in some ways quite privileged. In *Other People's Children*, a book that has come to be important to many educators, and a selection from which is included in the **Readings** for this chapter, Lisa Delpit argues that several aspects of such privilege are important to anyone thinking about the dynamics of contemporary education. Included in Delpit's list is her belief that "Those with power are frequently least aware of—or least willing to acknowledge—its existence. Those with less power are often most aware of its existence."

This is an issue that every teacher needs to think about, whether he or she is of the majority or the minority group on any specific form of diversity. As Delpit says, "For many who consider themselves members of liberal or radical camps, acknowledging personal power and admitting participation in the culture of power is distinctly uncomfortable." While Delpit is writing primarily about issues of race, the same things can often be said of straight teachers, able-bodied teachers, teachers for whom English is their first language, male teachers, and so on. None of us wants to see ourselves as privileged, but honesty is essential.

The issue here is not one of guilt. Indeed, guilt is quite unhelpful and the educator who keeps apologizing for his or her position is unhelpful in the extreme. Simply worrying about one's guilt, or lack of it, is a diversion from the real issue, as Delpit notes, which is an ability to listen and "really hear." This means you must be willing to reconsider your power, educational philosophy, and relationship to others, whether they are students, parents, or other teachers. Really hearing means being ready to consider that you might be wrong about (for example) the best strategy to teach reading to a particular student or class, or your assumptions about what kind of classroom structure students need at a given time in their lives, or the background and strengths and weaknesses a student brings to class on a given day. It is not a matter of being a pushover; rather it is a matter of being willing to engage deeply in a sometimes-painful dialogue and to really speak and really listen.[13]

Several years ago, Peggy McIntosh, a White teacher, wrote a short piece, "Unpacking the Invisible Knapsack," that was designed to help teachers look at their often unexamined privileges as an important means of seeing themselves as their students may see them. Reflecting on her own experience as a White feminist trying to get men to see their privileges, McIntosh came to realize that she, as a White woman, had never before examined her own race privilege and that many Whites—like many men—learn how to avoid recognizing their privileges. Thus, she sought to "unpack" the bag of privileges that Whites carry, whether they know it or not, or whether they want it or not. She posed questions such as whether one could go shopping and not be followed around the store or whether one can apply for a job or a credit card and not worry if race will be an issue. The point here again is not to feel guilty about what one has received in life. However, it is essential to be self-aware of privileges easily assumed and self-aware of hidden and not-so-hidden differences that can make interaction with students awkward or ineffective, especially students who may be aware that they do not share the same privileges. In the process of such self-reflection, we gain new insights that can help engage students, both those who are most like us and those who are most different, as well as parents, other teachers, and members of the community where we find ourselves teaching.[14]

SEEING DIVERSITIES

In her book, *Educating Teachers for Diversity: Seeing with a Cultural Eye*, Emory University professor Jacqueline Jordan Irvine addresses the statement she has heard often from aspiring teachers, "Race is not an issue until someone brings it up. What difference does it make anyway?" Irvine responds to this kind of statement, which she has heard so often:

Many teachers erroneously believe that if they recognize the race of their students or discuss issues of ethnicity in their classroom, they might be labeled as insensitive or, worse, racist. However,

YouDecide

Do all White people benefit from what is termed "White privilege"?

when teachers ignore their students' ethnic identities and their unique cultural beliefs, perceptions, values, and worldviews, they fail as culturally responsive pedagogists. Colorblind teachers claim that they treat all students "the same," which usually means that all students are treated as if they are, or should be, both White and middle class.

Clearly for Irvine and for the future of our students, something much more sophisticated is needed. Not all students are White, and not all students want to be treated as if they are White or as if White is the norm. Our goal as educators must be to develop that more sophisticated approach to our students and the education that we offer them.[15]

In the **Readings**, Lisa Delpit says something very similar. If Irvine hears some teachers say, "Race is not an issue until someone brings it up," or claim to be "color-blind," Delpit hears, "I want the same thing for everyone else's children as I want for mine." This may be a noble sentiment, born of the best of intentions. Nevertheless, Delpit warns:

To provide schooling for everyone's children that reflects liberal, middle-class values and aspirations is to ensure the maintenance of the status quo, to ensure that power, the culture of power, remains in the hands of those who already have it. Some children come to school with more accoutrements of the culture of power already in place—"cultural capital," as some critical theorists refer to it—some with less. . . . But parents who don't function within that culture often want . . . to ensure that the school provides their

A QUESTION OF . . .

What are the benefits of a diverse classroom?

"I feel blessed to work in a school that has so much cultural diversity. It gives me the opportunity to learn about the cultures of my students as well as share my culture with them. It brings our community closer together to share food, songs, dances, and traditions with one another. It also allows the students to learn to embrace people who are different from themselves."

—*Valerie Geschwind, fourth-grade teacher* ■

children with discourse patterns, interactional styles, and spoken and written language codes that will allow them success in the larger society.[16]

Different students come to school with different needs. Those who, for whatever reason, come to school without certain "cultural capital" need the keys to that storehouse of information and skills as much as they need anything else out of schooling. To deny them that in the name of ignoring race or giving all students the same thing is to permanently tip the scales in favor of some children and against others.

Irvine calls for teachers to be both caring and competent, and it is probably important to add the word *curious.* A teacher who wants to learn about his or her students—who wants to learn *from* his or her students—will teach them a model of respect for diversity that will go a long way toward building an engaging classroom.

A final note is important to remember. It is all too easy to fall into the trap of viewing groups of people as neat and separate packages; to think of immigrants as one group, people of color as another, boys and girls as another, and students with disabilities or different beliefs as yet another. But human beings do not fall into such neat categories. In one classroom, a teacher may well have a wheelchair-bound African American lesbian; a Russian-speaking, near-sighted, Pentecostal boy; and a recent immigrant from India who is a very literate Hindu with a learning dis-

ability; along with students representing any of a hundred of other interesting and challenging mixes. Human beings come in all sizes and shapes and characteristics, all rolled into one beautiful, unique person.

So, who will my students be? A group of young people more diverse, more interesting, and more engaging than one can ever imagine, waiting for someone to build a classroom for them that respects them, engages them, and teaches them.

Did you know?

There are numerous sources to help a teacher understand the many diversities of his or her students and to be effective in today's diverse classrooms. The National Center for Educational Statistics issues regular reports titled *The Condition of Education.* These reports are a goldmine of data on today's students and the schools they attend.

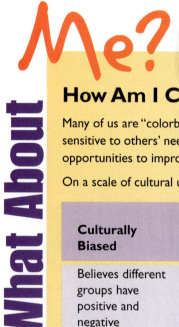

What About Me?

How Am I Culturally Connected?

Many of us are "colorblind," thinking that not bringing up race, ethnicity, or culture as an "issue" means that we are sensitive to others' needs and concerns. However, just the opposite is true. Ignoring our diversity only denies us the opportunities to improve interactions and to create a better society for all.

On a scale of cultural understanding, where do you fall and why?

Culturally Biased	Culturally In Denial	Culturally Aware	Culturally Sensitive and Respectful	Culturally Responsible and Active
Believes different groups have positive and negative characteristics as a whole.	Believes there is no problem; everyone should be the same.	Attempts to understand and increase awareness that experiences differ for people based on their culture.	Respects people from diverse cultural and social backgrounds; seeks out contacts with people from diverse backgrounds; encourages people to value and respect their cultural identity.	Acts on commitment to eliminate oppression; seeks to include full participation of diverse cultural groups in decision making.

Source: Ferrett, Sharon K. Peak Performance: Success in College and Beyond, 7e, McGraw-Hill, 2010, page 432.

REVIEW >>

- Will my classroom be like the ones I attended?

  The classrooms of today and tomorrow are more than likely going to be very different in many ways from those of even 10 years ago, especially regarding the diversity of students (and students' needs). Although many schools will continue to become more diverse, some will become even more homogeneous as social movements that made positive improvements in education during the past 50 years are countered by other social forces today.

- Who attends school today?

  In recent years, birth rates and immigration (including shifts in where immigrants are coming from) have increased significantly, and changing demographics indicate that the percentage of many "minority" groups (especially Hispanics and Asians) are growing rapidly. These changes are being reflected in the classroom. Thus, any future teacher must be prepared to embrace enthusiastically recent immigrant students along with students whose families have been in the United States for generations, girls as well as boys, students of all races, students who reject ethnic identifications, students who do not come to school speaking English, and students with a wide range of disabilities (or conditions perceived by the dominant society as disabling). A teacher must also be able to embrace gay and straight students, students of many different religions (or none), and students with a wide range of other diversities, including students who have chosen a lifestyle with which the teacher may disagree.

- How can I be sure that I am reaching all my students?

  Simply saying, "I am colorblind" or "I am gender blind," is not acceptable. Students need and want to be embraced in their uniqueness, and this means recognizing who they are in many different ways. To fail to respect a student's culture or language or physical characteristics or deepest beliefs is to be disrespectful in ways that may disengage a student completely. However, no teacher can know everything there is to know about every culture, condition, and characteristic that may be represented in a classroom. A teacher must be prepared to see students as individuals who define themselves by many different characteristics and are defined by the larger society by many more. And a teacher must think continually about how to mold a diverse classroom into a small society that models the kind of inclusive and welcoming behavior that we wish the larger society would adopt.

Who Attends School Today?

From "GLOBALIZATION, IMMIGRATION, AND EDUCATION"

BY MARCELO M. SUÁREZ-OROZCO

Marcelo M. Suárez-Orozco is the Courtney Sales Ross Professor of Global Education at New York University. Along with his wife, Carola Suárez-Orozco, he has directed one of the largest research inquiries into the current movement of immigrants into the United States. Their most recent book, *Learning a New Land: Immigrant Students in American Society*, was published in 2008.

The "New" Immigration

At the turn of the millennium, the United States had the largest number of immigrants in history. By the year 2000, the "foreign-stock" (foreign born plus the U.S.-born second generation) population of the United States reached nearly 55 million people (Portes & Rumbaut, 2001).

When it comes to immigration in the global era, race and ethnicity, along with class and gender, continue to matter. They matter, first and foremost, because the vast majority of immigrants are from the non-European, non-English-speaking "developing world." In the new *argot* of American multiculturalism, they are "people of color." Whether new immigrants have a cultural category to conceive of themselves as "people of color" or not is quite irrelevant; that is the category that will be mirrored at them (C. Suárez-Orozco, 2000).

Immigrants today are a highly heterogeneous population that defies easy generalizations. They include highly educated, highly skilled workers drawn by the explosive growth in the knowledge-intensive sectors of the economy. They are slightly more likely to have advanced degrees than the native-born population. These immigrants come intending to thrive. Immigrants now, especially those from Asia, are among the best-educated and most skilled folk in the United States. They are overrepresented in the category of people with doctorates. Thirty-two percent of all scientists and engineers working in California's Silicon Valley are immigrants (Saxenian, 1999).[1] Roughly one-third of all Nobel Prize winners in the United States have been immigrants; in 1999, *all* (100%!) of the U.S. winners of the Nobel Prize were immigrants. Perhaps with the exception of the highly educated immigrants and refugees escaping Nazi Europe, immigrants in the past tended to be more uniformly poorly educated and relatively less skilled than they are today (see Borjas, 1995). Never in the history of U.S. immigration have so many immigrants advanced so fast—both in terms of educational attainment and status mobility.

At the same time, the new immigration contains large numbers of poorly schooled, semiskilled, or unskilled workers, many of whom are in the United States without proper documentation. In 2000, over 22 percent of all new immigrants in the United States had less than a ninth-grade education.

These are workers, many of them from Latin America, drawn by the service sector of the U.S. economy, which seems to have an insatiable appetite for foreign folk. They typically end up in poorly paid jobs that lack insurance and basic safeties. Unlike the low-skilled factory jobs of yesterday, the kinds of jobs typically available to low-skilled immigrants today do not hold much realistic promise for upward mobility.[2] These immigrants tend to settle in areas of deep poverty and racial segregation (Orfield, in press). Concentrated poverty is associated with the "disappearance of meaningful work opportunities" (Wilson, 1997, p. 1). When poverty is combined with racial segregation, the outcomes can be devastating—regardless of immigrant or native-born status—as observed by Massey and Denton:

> *No matter what their personal traits or characteristics, people who grow up and live in environments of concentrated poverty and racial isolation are more likely to become teenage mothers, drop-out of school, achieve only low levels of education, and earn lower adult incomes. (1993, p. 3)*

Globalizing Youth

Immigrant children are the fastest growing sector of the U.S. child population (Landale & Oropesa, 1995). Roughly one in five children in the United States today lives in an immigrant-headed household (Suárez-Orozco & Suárez-Orozco, 2001). By the end of the 1990s there were roughly three million foreign-born children and 11 million U.S.-born children of foreign-born parents (Portes & Rumbaut, 2001). Immigrant children are now present in substantial numbers in school districts throughout the country. In California, for example, the number of English-language learners (ELL) jumped from fewer than 500,000 in 1985 to about 1.5 million a decade later (Rumbaut, 1995). They now make up over 20 percent of the California school population.

From "Globalization, Immigration, and Education: The Research Agenda," by Marcelo Suárez-Orozco, 2001, *Harvard Educational Review, 71*, pp. 345–364.

While California leads the nation in terms of numbers of immigrant students, no area of the country is untouched by immigration. Nationwide, there are now over 3.5 million ELL youth enrolled in U.S. schools.

In the New York City public schools, approximately 48 percent of all children come from immigrant households (Suárez-Orozco & Suárez-Orozco, 2001). Immigrant children are highly diverse in terms of language—over one hundred different languages are represented in New York City schools—country of origin, ethnicity, religion, and socioeconomic background. Although immigration tends to be highly concentrated in a handful of states (California, New York, Florida, Texas, and Illinois), immigrant youth are found in all areas of the nation and in diverse school systems. For example, today nearly 40 percent of all schoolchildren enrolled in Dodge City, Kansas, come from immigrant backgrounds (Suárez-Orozco & Suárez-Orozco, 2001).

In the last few years there have been a number of studies examining the adaptation of immigrant children in schools. The data suggest a complex picture. In broad strokes, we can say that immigrant children today fit a trimodal pattern of school adaptation. Some immigrant children seem to do quite well in school, surpassing native-born children in terms of grades, performance on standardized tests, and attitudes toward education (Kao & Tienda, 1995). Other immigrants tend to overlap with native-born children (see Rumbaut, 1995; Waters, 1999). Yet others tend to achieve below their native-born peers (Kao & Tienda, 1995; Portes & Zhou, 1993; Rumbaut, 1995; Suárez-Orozco & Suárez-Orozco, 1995; Vernez, Abrahamse, & Quigley, 1996). Perhaps not surprisingly, the children of today's highly educated immigrants tend to perform better in schools than the children of less skilled immigrant workers, especially those from Latin America (see Portes & Rumbaut, 2001).

In general, studies examining patterns that lead to school success tend to emphasize "the ideologies of opportunity" and "cultures of optimism" that motivate immigrant parents to migrate (Gibson, 1988; Kao & Tienda, 1995; M. Suárez-Orozco, 1989; Suárez-Orozco & Suárez-Orozco, 1995; Tuan, 1995; Waters, 1999). Some scholars have argued that successful adaptation among immigrants may relate to the patterns of cultural, economic, and social capital they are able to deploy in the new land (Portes & Rumbaut, 2001). Other scholars more specifically single out immigrant "cultural values" said to promote educational success (Sue & Okazaki, 1990). Yet others suggest that some immigrant families succeed by developing culturally specific strategies that inoculate their children against the hostilities and negative attitudes they encounter in the new culture (De Vos, 1992). Other studies note that successful immigrant families and communities are able to maintain social control by orienting their youth away from various negative interpersonal and cultural aspects of the host culture (Zhou & Bankston, 1998). This line of work suggests that immigrant parents who are able to maintain their own cultural patterns of social sanctioning and who actively resist a whole array of dystopic cultural practices and beliefs in the host country—specifically attitudes toward authority, discipline, homework, peer relations, and dating—tend to have children who are more successful in schools.

Scholars working in the area of immigrant school underachievement have explored a variety of relevant factors. Some have examined the structural barriers to advancement facing many poor immigrants of color today (Orfield, in press). Poor, low-skilled immigrants of color have few options other than to send their children to schools located in drug-, prostitution-, and gang-infested neighborhoods.[3] All too many schools attended by poor immigrant children today can only be characterized as sites overwhelmed by a "culture of violence."[4] Many newly arrived immigrant youth find themselves deeply marginalized in toxic schools that offer inferior education. These schools affect the opportunities and experiences of immigrant children in several immediate ways: they tend to have limited resources, classrooms are typically overcrowded, textbooks and curricula are outdated, and computers are few and obsolete. Many of the teachers do not have credentials in the subjects they teach. Clearly defined tracks sentence students to noncollege destinations. For example, lacking English skills, many immigrant students are often enrolled in the least demanding or competitive classes, which eventually excludes them from courses needed for college. These schools generally offer few (if any) Advanced Placement courses, which are critical for entry in many of the more competitive colleges. The guidance counselor-student ratio is impossibly high. Because the settings are so undesirable, teachers and principals routinely transfer out in search of better assignments elsewhere. As a result, in many such schools there is little continuity or sense of community. Children and teachers in these schools are often preoccupied with ever-present violence, and morale is often very low (see Suárez-Orozco & Suárez-Orozco, 2001).

Other researchers have focused on the sociocultural and linguistic practices involved in the schooling of children in poor and highly segregated inner-city schools—the schools in which many newly arrived immigrants, especially those from the Afro-Caribbean and Latin American regions, tend to enroll (Trueba, 1989). Yet others have carefully examined the devastating consequences of racism on the long-term trajectories of immigrants of color. Sociologist Mary Waters (1999), for example, considered transgenerational changes in attitudes toward schooling and opportunities in the new land among Caribbean immigrants as they endured persistent forms of American racism. Carola Suárez-Orozco (2000) examined how newly arrived immigrant children become keenly aware of negative stereotypes about them. These studies suggest that immigrant optimism and faith in the educational system as the route to status mobility may diminish over time and across generations—especially among those subject to persistent forms of symbolic and structural violence.

The issue of variability in school adaptation and outcomes among groups has received some attention in the scholarly literature. In a series of well-known works, John Ogbu and his colleagues have argued that in a number of settings "immigrant minorities" tend to perform better in schools than non-immigrant—or "involuntary"—minorities (see Gibson & Ogbu, 1991; Ogbu & Simons, 1998). However, to date there has been little systematic attention to changes over time as different groups of immigrant youth adapt to U.S. schools.

Yet some recent data suggest an unsettling pattern in need of further robust empirical and theoretical treatment: Among immigrants today, length of residence in the United States seems associated with *declining* health, school achievement, and aspirations (see Kao & Tienda, 1995; Portes & Rumbaut, 2001; Rumbaut, 1995; Steinberg, 1996; Suárez-Orozco & Suárez-Orozco, 1995; Waters, 1999). In other words, acculturation today seems to lead to detrimental health, more ambivalent attitudes toward school, and lower grades.

In the area of immigration and health, for example, we find a number of counterintuitive results. Immigrants, while they tend to share a number of "at-risk" characteristics, such as high rates of poverty and segregation, tend nevertheless to be healthier than their non-immigrant counterparts (Hayes-Bautista, in press). Immigrant youth also tend to be healthier than their non-immigrants peers. A recent national study of health among 20,000 randomly selected U.S. teens reveals an alarming trend:

Foreign-born youth experience fewer physical health problems, have less experience with sex, are less likely to engage in delinquent and violent behavior and are less likely to use controlled substances than native-born youth. Findings of health deterioration rather than improvement were remarkably consistent. Among foreign-born youth, statistical analysis showed the longer the time since arrival in the United States, the poorer was the adolescents' physical health and the greater the likelihood of engaging in risky behaviors. Specific health measures analyzed were general health, missed school due to health or emotional problems, learning difficulties, obesity, asthma and health risk behaviors involving sexual intercourse, unprotected sex, delinquency, violence and substance abuse. ("Health and Well-Being," 1998, p. 3)

Latino youth paid an especially high price for acculturation. Foreign-born Mexican youth, for example, were less likely than native-born Mexican American youth to be obese, suffer from asthma, have had sex, or have engaged in violent or delinquent acts. In the area of schooling, Steinberg (1996) reports the findings of a national survey of over 20,000 teenagers:

Foreign-born students—who, incidentally, report significantly more discrimination than American-born youngsters and significantly more difficulty with the English language—nevertheless earn higher grades in school than their American-born counterparts. . . .

The more Americanized students—those whose families have been living here longer—are less committed to doing well in school than their immigrant counterparts. Immigrants spend more time on homework, are more attentive in class, are more oriented to doing well in school, and are more likely to have friends who think academic achievement is important.

The adverse effects of Americanization are seen among Asian and Latino youngsters alike (that is, within each of the two largest populations of immigrant youth in this country), with achievement decreasing, and problems increasing, with each successive generation. Instead of finding what one might reasonably expect—that the longer a family has been in this country, the better the child will be faring in our schools—we find exactly the reverse. Our findings, as well as those from several other studies suggest that becoming Americanized is detrimental to youngsters' achievement, and terrible for their overall mental health. (pp. 97–98)

In an ambitious study of over five thousand immigrant and second-generation students in San Diego, California, and Dade County, Florida, sociologists Alejandro Portes and Rubén Rumbaut (2001) found that "U.S. nativity and long term residence among the foreign-born increase English skills but significantly lower grades. . . . These findings strongly suggest that second-generation children gradually lose their achievement drive with increasing acculturation" (p. 239). In a different voice, the Reverend Virgil Elizondo, rector of the San Fernando Cathedral in San Antonio, Texas, articulates the same point: "I can tell by looking in their eyes how long they've been here. They come sparkling with hope, and the first generation finds hope rewarded. Their children's eyes no longer sparkle" (quoted in Suro, 1998, p. 13). While the pathbreaking work of Portes and Rumbaut (2001; see also Rumbaut, 1995), as well as findings by Steinberg (1996) and Kao and Tienda (1995), independently report similar findings, more sophisticated longitudinal and, especially, interdisciplinary data are needed to explore this urgent issue.[5] What is perhaps most alarming about the new schooling and health data is 1) they seem to affect all major immigrant groups, and 2) they reveal that the work of acculturation today tends to produce "dystopic" rather than "utopic" results (M. Suárez-Orozco, 2000). While many immigrant children do brilliantly in school, others over time seem to display more negative adaptations (Suárez-Orozco & Suárez-Orozco, 2001).

Concluding Thoughts

Globalization links traditional urban issues such as immigration, race, segregation, and poverty to broader transnational formations. It is indeed the globalization of capital—along with the emergence of new communication and information technologies and transportation networks—that is largely behind the largest migratory wave in U.S. history. Immigrants—and especially their children—are now important actors in the new global stage.

The preponderance of evidence suggests that some immigrant children, especially those originating in families with more education, resources, connections, and skills, will indeed thrive in the era of globalization. These immigrant youth are outperforming native-born children not only in terms of grades, but also as winners of the nation's most prestigious science competitions (two of the three top Intel Science prizes in March 2000 went to immigrant youth) and as freshmen in the nation's most exclusive colleges. These highly educated and skilled youth are likely to move rapidly into the more desirable sectors of the global economy, generally bypassing the traditional transgenerational modes of immigrant status mobility.[6]

There are, however, reasons to worry. Substantial numbers of immigrant youth began enrolling in public schools when large inner-city districts were in deep crisis—some near collapse. Many of these schools are overpopulated and understaffed. Qualified teachers are needed, and the best teachers often leave as soon as they can (Orfield, in press). Bilingual education, eternally controversial in the United States, has faced a head-on challenge in California—the state most heavily affected by immigration.

[See the discussion of bilingual education and specifically the challenge and debates in California in Chapter 4.]

In many schools that immigrant students attend, there is little teaching and learning going on (M. Suárez-Orozco, 1989). The dominant lessons tend to be about discipline ("management") and social control. Many of the routines the students are subjected to can only be characterized as mindless and pointless. The little teaching that goes on is neither culturally relevant to the immigrant students' backgrounds nor pertinent to the realities of the global culture and global economy these youth will eventually have to face. Consequently, unacceptable numbers of immigrant youth, especially those coming from poor backgrounds, are leaving school before acquiring the tools needed to navigate today's bitterly competitive global economy.

For a complete listing of the references for this Reading, go to **www.mhhe.com/teach1e2010.**

QUESTIONS

1. What information in this article most surprised you? What information seemed least surprising to you?

2. Have you been in classrooms that reflect the diversity that Suárez-Orozco describes here?

3. What skills would you want to be sure to have if you were teaching a class made up mostly of recent immigrants such as those described here?

4. When Suárez-Orozco discusses the loss in achievement suffered by second-generation immigrant children, what do you think accounts for that? Can you think of ways that schools might be organized to turn that situation around?

Who Attends School Today?

From "DUDE, YOU'VE GOT PROBLEMS"

BY JUDITH WARNER

In April 2009, many newspapers reported the story of a bright and active 11-year-old boy, Carl Joseph Walker-Hoover, who killed himself after a long period of harassment at the school he attended. Judith Warner, well-known *New York Times* columnist, highlighted Carl's story, along with previous stories of other young students, to focus readers on the problems facing students, schools, and the larger society that tolerates and, she says, inadvertently fosters the kind of intolerance that has led to these tragic deaths and to years of fear and sadness for far more young people.

Early this month, Carl Joseph Walker-Hoover, an 11-year-old boy from Springfield, Massachusetts, hanged himself after months of incessantly being hounded by his classmates for being "gay." (He was not; but did, apparently, like to do well in school.)

In March, 2007, 17-year-old Eric Mohat shot himself in the head, after a long-term tormentor told him in class, "Why don't you go home and shoot yourself; no one will miss you." Eric liked theater, played the piano and wore bright clothing, a lawyer for his family told ABC news, and so had long been subject to taunts of "gay," "fag," "queer" and "homo."

Teachers and school administrators, the Mohats' lawsuit now asserts, did nothing.

We should do something to get this insanity under control.

I'm not just talking about combating bullying, which has been a national obsession ever since Columbine, and

From "Dude, You've Got Problems," by Judith Warner, April 16, 2009, *New York Times*.

91

yet seems to continue unabated. I'm only partly talking about homophobia, which, though virulent, cruel and occasionally fatal among teenagers, is not the whole story behind the fact that words like "fag" and "gay" are now among the most potent and feared weapons in the school bully's arsenal.

Being called a "fag," you see, actually has almost nothing to do with being gay.

It's really about showing any perceived weakness or femininity—by being emotional, seeming incompetent, caring too much about clothing, liking to dance or even having an interest in literature. It's similar to what being viewed as a "nerd" is, Bennington College psychology professor David Anderegg notes in his 2007 book, "Nerds: Who They Are and Why We Need More of Them": "'queer' in the sense of being 'odd' or 'unusual,'" but also, for middle schoolers in particular, doing "anything that was too much like what a goody-goody would do."

It's what being called a "girl" used to be, a generation or two ago.

"To call someone gay or fag is like the lowest thing you can call someone. Because that's like saying that you're nothing," is how one teenage boy put it to C.J. Pascoe, a sociologist at Colorado College, in an interview for her 2007 book, "Dude, You're a Fag: Masculinity and Sexuality in High School."

The message to the most vulnerable, to the victims of today's poisonous boy culture, is being heard loud and clear: to be something other than the narrowest, stupidest sort of guy's guy, is to be unworthy of even being alive.

It's weird, isn't it, that in an age in which the definition of acceptable girlhood has expanded, so that desirable femininity now encompasses school success and athleticism, the bounds of boyhood have remained so tightly constrained? And so staunchly defended: Boys avail themselves most frequently of epithets like "fag" to "police" one another's behavior and bring it back to being sufficiently masculine when someone steps out of line, Barbara J. Risman, a sociologist at the University of Illinois at Chicago, found while conducting extensive interviews in a southeastern urban middle school in 2003 and 2004. "Boys were showing each other they were tough. They were afraid to do anything that might be called girlie," she told me this week. "It was just like what I would have found if I had done this research 50 years ago. They were frozen in time."

Pascoe spent 18 months embedded in a Northern California working-class high school, in a community where factory jobs had gone south after the signing of NAFTA, and where men who'd once enjoyed solid union salaries were now cobbling together lesser-paid employment at big-box stores. "These kids experience a loss of masculine privilege on a day-to-day level," she said. "While they didn't necessarily ever experience the concrete privilege their fathers and grandfathers experienced, they have the sense that to be a man means something and is incredibly important. These boys don't know how to be that some-thing. Their pathway to masculinity is unclear. To not be a man is to not be fully human and that's terrifying."

That makes sense. But the strange thing is, this isn't just about insecure boys. There's a degree to which girls, despite all their advances, appear to be stuck—voluntarily—in a time warp, too, or at least to be walking a very fine line between progress and utter regression. Spending unprecedented amounts of time and money on their hair, their skin and their bodies, at earlier and earlier ages. Essentially accepting the highly sexualized identity imposed on them, long before middle school, by advertisers and pop culture. In high school, they have second-class sexual status, Pascoe found, and by jumping through hoops to be sexually available enough to be cool (and "empowered") yet not so free as to be labeled a slut, they appear to be complicit in maintaining it.

Why—given the full array of choices our culture ostensibly now allows them—are boys and girls clinging to such lowest-common-denominator ways of being?

The strain of being a teenager, and in particular, a pre-teen, no doubt accounts for much of it; people tend to be at their worst when they're feeling most insecure. But there's more to it than that, I think. Malina Saval, who spent two years observing and interviewing teenage boys and their parents for her new book "The Secret Lives of Boys," found that parents played a key role in reinforcing the basest sort of gender stereotypes, at least where boys were concerned. "There were a few parents who were sort of alarmist about whether or not their children were going to be gay because of their music choices, the clothes they wore," she said. Generally, she said, "there was a kind of low-level paranoia if these high-school-age boys weren't yet seriously involved with a girl."

It seems it all comes down, as do so many things for today's parents, to status.

"Parents are so terrified that their kids will miss out on anything," Anderegg told me. "They want their kids to have sex, be sexy."

This generation of parents tends to talk a good game about gender, at least in public.

Practicing what we preach, in anxious times in particular, is another thing.

QUESTIONS

1. If you were Carl Joseph's teacher what might have tipped you off that he needed support? What could you have done to help him?

2. Have you heard students called "fag" or otherwise bullied for their sexual orientation—or perceived sexual orientations?

3. Have you heard or seen students being bullied or picked on for other reasons in school?

4. Have you personally experienced harassment in school? For what reason? (Or was there no reason?)

How Can I Be Sure That I Am Reaching All My Students?

From "THE SILENCED DIALOGUE: POWER AND PEDAGOGY IN EDUCATING OTHER PEOPLE'S CHILDREN"

BY LISA DELPIT

Lisa Delpit is the executive director of the Center for Urban Education and Innovation at Florida International University in Miami, Florida. Former recipient of the MacArthur Award and author of *Other People's Children: Cultural Conflicts in the Classroom* and *The Skin That We Speak: Thoughts on Language and Culture in the Classroom*, she is one of the most thoughtful and provocative educational researchers today. In this article, as in her other works, she asks the hard questions with which every aspiring teacher must wrestle in order to be a responsible teacher.

A black male graduate student who is also a special education teacher in a predominantly black community is talking about his experiences in predominantly white university classes:

> There comes a moment in every class where we have to discuss "The Black Issue" and what's appropriate education for black children. I tell you, I'm tired of arguing with those white people, because they won't listen. Well, I don't know if they really don't listen or if they just don't believe you. It seems like if you can't quote Vygotsky or something, then you don't have any validity to speak about your own kids. Anyway, I'm not bothering with it anymore, now I'm just in it for a grade.

A black woman teacher in a multicultural urban elementary school is talking about her experiences in discussions with her predominantly white fellow teachers about how they should organize reading instruction to best serve students of color:

> When you're talking to white people they still want it to be their way. You can try to talk to them and give them examples, but they're so headstrong, they think they know what's best for everybody, for everybody's children. They won't listen; white folks are going to do what they want to do anyway.
>
> It's really hard. They just don't listen well. No, they listen, but they don't hear—you know how your mama used to say you listen to the radio, but you hear your mother? Well they don't hear me.
>
> So I just try to shut them out so I can hold my temper. You can only beat your head against a brick wall for so long before you draw blood. If I try to stop arguing with them I can't help myself from getting angry. Then I end up walking around praying all day "Please Lord, remove the bile I feel for these people so I can sleep tonight." It's funny, but it can become a cancer, a sore.

> So I shut them out. I go back to my own little cubby, my classroom, and I try to teach the way I know will work, no matter what those folk say. And when I get black kids, I just try to undo the damage they did.
>
> I'm not going to let any man, woman, or child drive me crazy—white folks will try do that to you if you let them. You just have to stop talking to them, that's what I do. I just keep smiling, but I won't talk to them.

A soft-spoken Native Alaskan woman in her forties is a student in the Education Department of the University of Alaska. One day she storms into a black professor's office and very uncharacteristically slams the door. She plops down in a chair and, still fuming, says, "Please tell those people, just don't help us anymore! I give up. I won't talk to them again!"

And finally, a black woman principal who is also a doctoral student at a well-known university on the West Coast is talking about her university experiences, particularly about when a professor lectures on issues concerning educating black children:

From *Other People's Children: Cultural Conflict in the Classroom*, by Lisa Delpit, 1995, New York, The New Press, pp. 21–47.

If you try to suggest that's not quite the way it is, they get defensive, then you get defensive, then they'll start reciting research.

I try to give them my experiences, to explain. They just look and nod. The more I try to explain, they just look and nod, just keep looking and nodding. They don't really hear me.

Then, when it's time for class to be over, the professor tells me to come to his office to talk more. So I go. He asks for more examples of what I'm talking about, and he looks and nods while I give them. Then he says that that's just my experience. It doesn't really apply to most black people.

It becomes futile because they think they know everything about everybody. What you have to say about your life, your children, doesn't mean anything. They don't really want to hear what you have to say. They wear blinders and earplugs. They only want to go on research they've read that other white people have written.

It just doesn't make any sense to keep talking to them.

Thus was the first half of the title of this text born: "The Silenced Dialogue." One of the tragedies of this field of education is that scenarios such as these are enacted daily around the country. The saddest element is that the individuals that the black and Native Alaskan educators speak of in these statements are seldom aware that the dialogue *has* been silenced. Most likely the white educators believe that their colleagues of color did, in the end, agree with their logic. After all, they stopped disagreeing, didn't they? . . .

How can such complete communication blocks exist when both parties truly believe they have the same aims? How can the bitterness and resentment expressed by the educators of color be drained so that the sores can heal? What can be done?

I believe the answer to these questions lies in ethnographic analysis, that is, in identifying and giving voice to alternative worldviews. Thus, I will attempt to address the concerns raised by white and black respondents to my article "Skills and Other Dilemmas." My charge here is not to determine the best instructional methodology; I believe that the actual practice of good teachers of all colors typically incorporates a range of pedagogical orientations. Rather, I suggest that the differing perspectives on the debate over "skills" versus "process" approaches can lead to an understanding of the alienation and miscommunication, and thereby to an understanding of the "silenced dialogue."

In thinking through these issues, I have found what I believe to be a connecting and complex theme: what I have come to call "the culture of power." There are five aspects of power I would like to propose as given for this presentation:

1. Issues of power are enacted in classrooms.
2. There are codes or rules for participating in power; that is, there is a "culture of power."
3. The rules of the culture of power are a reflection of the rules of the culture of those who have power.
4. If you are not already a participant in the culture of power, being told explicitly the rules of that culture makes acquiring power easier.
5. Those with power are frequently least aware of—or willing to acknowledge—its existence. Those with less power are often most aware of its existence.

The first three are by now basic tenets in the literature of the sociology of education, but the last two have seldom been addressed. The following discussion will explicate these aspects of power and their relevance to the schism between liberal educational movements and that of non-white, non-middle-class teachers and communities.[1]

1. Issues of power are enacted in classrooms.

These issues include: the power of the teacher over the students; the power of the publishers of textbooks and the developers of the curriculum to determine the view of the world presented; the power of the state in enforcing compulsory schooling; and the power of an individual or group to determine another's intelligence or "normalcy." Finally, if schooling prepares people for jobs, and the kind of job a person has determines her or his economic status and, therefore, power, then schooling is intimately related to that power.

2. There are codes or rules for participating in power; that is, there is a "culture of power."

The codes or rules I'm speaking of relate to linguistic forms, communicative strategies, and presentation of self; that is, ways of talking, ways of writing, ways of dressing, and ways of interacting.

3. The rules of the culture of power are a reflection of the rules of the culture of those who have the power.

This means that success in institutions—schools, workplaces, and so on—is predicated upon acquisition of the culture of those who are in power. Children from middle-class homes tend to do better in school than those from non-middle-class homes because the culture of the school is based on the culture of the upper and middle classes—of those in power. The upper and middle classes send their children to school with all the accoutrements of the culture of power; children from other kinds of families operate within perfectly wonderful and viable cultures but not cultures that carry the codes or rules of power.

4. If you are not already a participant in the culture of power, being told explicitly the rules of that culture makes acquiring power easier.

In my work within and between diverse cultures, I have come to conclude that members of any culture transmit information implicitly to co-members. However, when implicit codes are attempted across cultures, communication frequently breaks down. Each cultural group is left saying, "Why don't those people say what they mean? As well as, "What's wrong with them, why don't they understand?"

Anyone who has had to enter new cultures, especially to accomplish a specific task, will know of what I speak. When I lived in several Papua, New Guinea villages for extended periods to collect data, and when I go to Alaskan villages for work with Native Alaskan communities, I have found it unquestionably easier, psychologically and pragmatically, when some kind soul has directly informed me about such matters as appropriate dress, interactional styles, embedded meanings, and taboo words or actions. I contend that it is much the same for anyone seeking to learn the rules of the culture of power. Unless one has the leisure of a lifetime of "immersion" to learn them, explicit presentation makes learning immeasurably easier.

And now, to the fifth and last premise:

5. *Those with power are frequently least aware of—or least willing to acknowledge—its existence. Those with less power are often most aware of its existence.*

For many who consider themselves members of liberal or radical camps, acknowledging personal power and admitting participation in the culture of power is distinctly uncomfortable. On the other hand, those who are less powerful in any situation are most likely to recognize the power variable most acutely. My guess is that the white colleagues and instructors of those previously quoted did not perceive themselves to have power over the nonwhite speakers. However, either by virtue of their position, their numbers, or their access to that particular code of power of calling upon research to validate one's position, the white educators had the authority to establish what was to be considered "truth" regardless of the opinions of the people of color, and the latter were well aware of that fact.

To explore those differences, I would like to present several statements typical of those made with the best of intentions by middle-class liberal educators. To the surprise of the speakers, it is not unusual for such content to be met by vocal opposition or stony silence from people of color. My attempt here is to examine the underlying assumptions of both camps.

"I want the same thing for everyone else's children as I want for mine."

To provide schooling for everyone's children that reflects liberal, middle-class values and aspirations is to ensure the maintenance of the status quo, to ensure that power, the culture of power, remains in the hands of those who already have it. Some children come to school with more accoutrements of the culture of power already in place—"cultural capital," as some critical theorists refer to it[2]—some with less. Many liberal educators hold that the primary goal for education is for children to become autonomous, to develop fully who they are in the classroom setting without having arbitrary, outside standards forced upon them. This is a very reasonable goal for peo-

ple whose children are already participants in the culture of power and who have already internalized its codes.

But parents who don't function within that culture often want something else. It's not that they disagree with the former aim, it's just that they want something more. They want to ensure that the school provides their children with discourse patterns, interactional styles, and spoken and written language codes that will allow them success in the larger society.

"Child-centered, whole language, and process approaches are needed in order to allow a democratic state of free, autonomous, empowered adults, and because research has shown that children learn best through these methods."

People of color are, in general, skeptical of research as a determiner of our fates. Academic research has, after all, found us genetically inferior, culturally deprived, and verbally deficient. But beyond that general caveat, and despite my or others' personal preferences, there is little research data supporting the major tenets of process approaches over other forms of literacy instruction, and virtually no evidence that such approaches are more efficacious for children of color.[3]

Although the problem is not necessarily inherent in the method, in some instances adherents of process approaches to writing create situations in which students ultimately find themselves held accountable for knowing a set of rules about which no one has ever directly informed them. Teachers do students no service to suggest, even implicitly, that "produce" is not important. In this country, students will be judged on their product regardless of the process they utilized to achieve it. And that product, based as it is on the specific codes of a particular culture, is more readily produced when the directives of how to produce it are made explicit.

"It's really a shame but she (that black teacher upstairs) seems to be so authoritarian, so focused on skills and so teacher directed. Those poor kids never seem to be allowed to really express their creativity. (And she even yells at them.)"

This statement directly concerns the display of power and authority in the classroom. One way to understand the difference in perspective between black teachers and their progressive colleagues on this issue is to explore culturally influenced oral interactions.

In *Ways with Words*, Shirley Brice Heath quotes the verbal directives given by the middle class "townspeople" teachers:[4]

- "Is this where the scissors belong?"
- "You want to do your best work today."

By contrast, many black teachers are more likely to say:

- "Put those scissors on that shelf."
- "Put your name on the papers and make sure to get the right answers for each question."

Is one oral style more authoritarian than another?

But those veiled commands are commands none-theless, representing true power, and with true consequences for disobedience. If veiled commands are ignored, the child will be labeled a behavior problem and possibly officially classified as behavior disordered. In other words, the attempt by the teacher to reduce an exhibition of power by expressing herself in indirect terms may remove the very explicitness that the child needs to understand the rules of the new classroom culture.

And now to the final comment I present for examination:

"Children have the right to their own language, their own culture. We must fight cultural hegemony and fight the system by insisting that children be allowed to express themselves in their own language style. It is not they, the children, who must change, but the schools. To push children to do anything else is repressive and reactionary."

A statement such as this originally inspired me to write the "Skills and Other Dilemmas" article. It was first written as a letter to a colleague in response to a situation that had developed in our department. I was teaching a senior-level teacher education course. Students were asked to prepare a written autobiographical document for the class that would also be shared with their placement school prior to their student teaching.

One student, a talented young Native American woman, submitted a paper in which the ideas were lost because of technical problems—from spelling to sentence structure to paragraph structure. Removing her name, I duplicated the paper for discussion with some faculty members. I had hoped to initi-ate a discussion about what we could do to ensure that our students did not reach the senior level without getting assistance in technical writing skills when they needed them.

I was amazed at the response. Some faculty implied that the student should never have been allowed into the teacher education program. Others, some of the more progressive minded, suggested that I was attempting to function as gatekeeper by raising the issue, and had internalized repressive and disempowering forces of the power elite to suggest that something was wrong with a Native American student just because she had another style of writing. With few exceptions, I found myself alone in arguing against both camps.

No, this student should not have been denied entry to the program. To deny her entry under the notion of upholding standards is to blame the victim for the crime. We cannot justifiably enlist exclusionary standards when the reason this student lacked the skills demanded was poor teaching at best and institutional racism at worst.

However, to bring this student into the program and pass her through without attending to obvious deficits in the codes needed for her to function effectively as a teacher is equally criminal—for though we may assuage our own consciences for not participating in victim blaming, she will surely be accused and convicted as soon as she leaves the university. As Native Alaskans were quick to tell me, and as I understood through my own experiences in the black community, not only would she not be hired as a teacher, but those who did not hire her would make the (false) assumption that the university was putting out only incompetent Natives and that they should stop looking seriously at any Native applicants. A white applicant who exhibits problems is an individual with problems. A person of color who exhibits problems immediately becomes a representative of her cultural group.

To summarize, I suggest that students must be *taught* the codes needed to participate fully in the mainstream of American life, not by being forced to attend to hollow, inane, decontextualized subskills, but rather within the context of meaningful communicative endeavors; that they must be allowed the resource of the teacher's expert knowledge, while being helped to acknowledge their own "expertness" as well; and that even while students are assisted in learning the culture of power, they must also be helped to learn about the arbitrariness of those codes and about the power relationships they represent.

I am also suggesting that appropriate education for poor children and children of color can only be devised in consultation with adults who share their culture. Black parents, teachers of color, and members of poor communities must be allowed to participate fully in the discussion of what kind of instruction is in their children's best interest. Good liberal intentions are not enough. In an insightful 1975 study entitled "Racism without Racists: Institutional Racism in Urban Schools," Massey, Scott, and Dornbusch found that under the pressures of teaching, and with all intentions of "being nice," teachers had essentially stopped attempting to teach black children.[5] In their words; "We have shown that the oppression can arise out of warmth, friendliness, and concern. Paternalism and a lack of challenging standards are creating a distorted system of evaluation in the schools." Educators must open themselves to, and allow themselves to be affected by, these alternative voices.

In conclusion, I am proposing a resolution for the skills/process debate. In short, the debate is fallacious; the dichotomy is false. . . . The dilemma is not really in the debate over instructional methodology, but rather in communicating across cultures and in addressing the more fundamental issue of power, of whose voice gets to be heard in determining what is best for poor children and children of color. Will black teachers and parents continue to be silenced by the very forces that claim to "give voice" to our children? Such an outcome would be tragic, for both groups truly have something to say to one another. As a result of careful listening to alternative points of view, I have myself come to a viable synthesis of perspectives. But both sides do need to be able to listen, and I contend that it is those with the most power, those in the majority, who must take the greater responsibility for initiating the process.

To do so takes a very special kind of listening, listening that requires not only open eyes and ears, but open hearts and minds. We do not really see through our eyes or hear through our ears, but through our beliefs. To put our beliefs on hold is to cease to exist as ourselves for a moment—and that is not easy. It is painful as well, because it means turning yourself inside out, giving up your own sense of who you are, and being willing to see yourself in the unflattering light of another's angry gaze. It is not easy, but it is the only way to learn what it might feel like to be someone else and the only way to start the dialogue.

Teachers are in an ideal position to play this role, to attempt to get all of the issues on the table in order to initiate true dialogue. This can only be done, however, by seeking out those whose perspectives may differ most, by learning to give their words complete attention, by understanding one's own power, even if that power stems merely from being in the majority, by being unafraid to raise questions about discrimination and voicelessness with people of color, and to listen, no, to *hear* what they say. I suggest that the results of such interactions may be the most powerful and empowering coalescence yet seen in the educational realm—for *all* teachers and for *all* the students they teach.

For a complete listing of the references for this Reading, go to **www.mhhe.com/teach1e2010**.

QUESTIONS

1. If you are a student of color, have you ever experienced the kind of silencing that Delpit describes in this article? What was your reaction?

2. If you are a white student, have you experienced similar silencing for another reason, such as a time when you just knew something was right but somehow others would not listen to or hear you? What was your reaction?

3. Can you think of a time when you may have silenced someone else?

4. Do you agree with Delpit that students who are "not part of the culture of power" may need explicit instruction in the rules of the dominant culture? Can you imagine giving such instruction to a group of children or adolescents? What would that look like?

5. Is it true that those with power may be unaware of it while those without power are quite aware? Can you give examples of when this is, or is not, true? What does that mean for teachers who come from a dominant culture and teach students from a less powerful part of society?

4

INCLUDING EVERYONE

In Chapter 3, we explored issues of diversity primarily in terms of race and ethnicity or status as a recent or not-so-recent immigrant, as well as a range of sometimes hidden diversities, including sexual orientation, religious preference, and the cultural background of a student's family. In this chapter, we continue the discussion of diversity but with a different focus. We look at several groups of students who were often easily excluded from many schools until the 1960s and 1970s, including students who arrive at school not speaking English, students with disabilities, and girls who experienced marginalization because of their gender. We explore the legislation and programs designed to maximize their education, including controversies regarding their effectiveness.

The **Readings** for this chapter introduce you to three key debates surrounding inclusion and exclusion in schools today. First, we examine a significant debate about what it means for schools to be gender fair. In the first essay, Michael Gurian and Kathy Stevens argue that today's focus needs to be on how boys, rather than girls, are left behind. In response, Sara Mead argues that although the needs of some boys, especially African Americans, are severe, the Gurian and Stevens research overlooks significant barriers to academic success that female students continue to face. In the next pair of **Readings**, two contemporary scholars take differing perspectives on the best way to serve students who come to school speaking little or no English. Although virtually no one today argues that such students should simply be "on their own," Orhan Agirdag argues strongly for a true bilingual program that helps students maintain their home languages while also learning English. On the other side, Kevin Clark argues for an intensive immersion in the English language for these students while leaving any attention to their first languages to their home and family. In the final article, Thomas Hehir argues that the biggest barrier to treating students with special needs well in school is the persistent myth that somewhere out there are a large number of "normal students" against which all others should be measured.

WHO SOMETIMES GETS OVERLOOKED IN SCHOOL?

FOCUS >>

- Who was traditionally left out of American schools?
- What legal actions made school available for everyone?
- What does it mean for schools to be gender fair?
- What are the ongoing debates over bilingual education?
- What is the best education for students with disabilities?

>> Historically Speaking: Who Was Left Out of American Schools?

Prior to the 1960s, many people, including teachers, assumed that the purpose of public schooling was to provide the best possible education to those students who were prepared to receive it. Half a century ago, although most Americans attended elementary school, more than half dropped out before finishing high school. If students did not stay in school because they did not understand instruction in English, or because a disability made school painful if not impossible, or because they felt school was "not for them," or because they were simply bored or disengaged, many people thought that was just fine. There were plenty of jobs in an industrial economy for students with only a modest education. Schooling, they said, "was not for everyone."

Many people thought it was okay if girls did not receive an education equal to that of boys, even when they were in the same schools and classrooms. After all, career opportunities for women were limited by the social expectations of the day. Most middle-class European American girls were expected to settle happily into the role of stay-at-home wives and mothers while poor girls and girls of color were expected to work as domestics or in factories or in other menial jobs. And it was certainly okay in many places to tell immigrant students or students who were the children of immigrants whose home language was not English that their only choice was to "sink or swim," to learn English very quickly or leave school for whatever education their home and immigrant communities might offer. It was also okay if students with various disabilities simply left school. Students in wheelchairs who could not climb the stairs, blind students or dyslexic students who could not read the texts, students who had deep-seated emotional problems that made conforming to the routines of school

virtually impossible, and students who were, for whatever reason, slower to learn than their classmates were often simply told to "go home," that the education offered in the public schools was not for them. As we see in the following sections, these were the realities faced by far too many young people not too long ago.

Primarily due to the intensive focus on the **inclusion** of all students (not just racial minorities) that grew out of the civil rights movement, and including the most recent **federal legislation**, a growing consensus has emerged that "no child should be left behind." Indeed, most people now view it as a serious problem when any student drops out without completing high school. As a result, many students who had previously been excluded from school— or at least were allowed to easily exclude themselves—are now expected to stay in school.

> **inclusion** Ensuring that all students, regardless of perceived ability, race, gender, or other differences, are offered the same education, usually in the same setting, and engaged and connected with the larger school community and given the same opportunities and education.
>
> **federal legislation** A law put into place by the federal government.

In 1870, only 2% of students graduated from high school. By 1970, that percentage had grown to more than 75%. However, several important pieces of information are buried in these statistics. At the beginning of the 20th century, only about 6% of students completed high school. However, high schools were still not available in many parts of the country, outside of big cities. Even in the cities, most people saw a high school diploma as a luxury for a privileged few. Completing 8 years of school was plenty for most people, including, ironically, most teachers of the day. Only in the 1920s, as high schools became much more widespread, not just in big cities but in small towns and rural areas, did a quarter of the nation's 17-year-olds finish high school. It took another 50 years to get to the point where three-quarters finished high school, a proportion that has remained relatively stable since then.

100 Years of Graduates

Year	High School Graduation Rates (% of 17-Year-Olds)	Year	High School Graduation Rates (% of 17-Year-Olds)
1870	2.0%	1920	16.3%
1880	2.5%	1930	28.8%
1890	3.5%	1940	49.0%
1900	6.3%	1950	57.4%
1910	8.6%	1960	63.4%
		1970	75.6%

Source: *Historical Statistics of the United States: Colonial Times to 1970,*
U.S. Department of Commerce, 1976, Washington, DC.

Connections

In Chapter 10, we explore the issues surrounding dropout rates today and efforts to keep kids in school.

The fact that we now assume that every student should at the very least complete high school has fundamentally changed the job description of every classroom teacher. Schools, especially classroom teachers, have been expected to make significant adjustments to accommodate the needs and interests of this widely diverse group of students. Whereas teachers were previously expected to teach those who were easily engaged and able to learn what was in the lessons and those who could also accommodate themselves to the physical surroundings and cultural assumptions of the schools, teachers are now expected to teach everyone—the better prepared and the underprepared, the able and the less able, the willing and the unwilling—and to do it to higher and higher standards so that many more students will graduate with the skills and knowledge needed to compete in a highly technical, **postindustrial society**.

postindustrial society The restructuring of the economy and society that is occurring as the United States makes the transition from a manufacturing-based economy to a service-based economy.

>> What Legal Actions Made School Available for Everyone?

In the 1960s and 1970s, a set of far-reaching changes in the economy, the cultural assumptions of society, and eventually the laws governing schools brought about a fundamentally new understanding of the answer to the question "Who should be in school?" By the end of the 1970s, the answer had become "everyone." A number of federal laws and U.S. Supreme Court decisions not only helped to create but also reflected the changes in expectations for schools that are at the heart of this chapter. Although many schools fail dramatically to live up to these expectations and educators and members of the larger public continue to argue about the values behind these changes, no one can deny that the

The Right to an Education

A series of court cases and legislation increased significantly the number of students attending school.

- 1964: Civil Rights Act of 1964 prohibits discrimination against students in school based on their race, color, sex, or national origin.
- 1968: Bilingual Education Act provides federal funds to encourage programs for students who do not speak English when they arrive in school.
- 1972: Title IX of the Education Amendments says that no one can be excluded from any school program on the basis of his or her sex.
- 1974: U.S. Supreme Court in *Lau v. Nichols* rules that schools must attend to the needs of students who do not speak English; programs for English language learners are no longer voluntary.
- 1975: U.S. Congress passes Public Law 94-142, which requires a "free appropriate public education" for every child in the United States no matter what his or her handicap—physical, mental, or emotional.

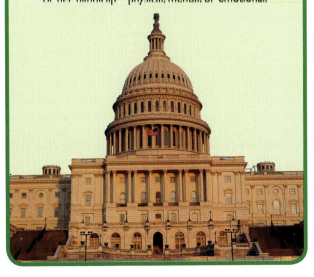

changes that took place between 1964 and 1975 fundamentally transformed schooling in the United States.

The tone for this era was set when the landmark Civil Rights Act of 1964 prohibited discrimination against students based on race, color, sex, or national origin. Subsequently, Title IX of the Education Amendments of 1972 said that no one could be excluded, on the basis of his or her sex, from the benefits of any program in any school that received federal funds (and virtually every school in the United States receives federal money). Then, the U.S. Supreme Court's 1974 decision in *Lau v. Nichols*, combined with the 1968 Bilingual Education Act, said that school districts could not ignore the needs of students who did not speak English. And Section 503 of the Rehabilitation Act of 1973, followed by Public Law 94-142, the Education for All Handicapped Children Act (1975), said that every child, in spite of any handicapping condition, deserved a "free appropriate public education" designed specifically to meet his or her needs.

Looking back at the changes that took place in American education in the decade before 1975, Martha Ziegler, executive director of the Federation for Children with Special Needs in Boston and a longtime educational advocate, commented, "In November 1975, when the Education for All Handicapped Children Act was enacted into law, we had finally reached the ultimate objective for education in a democracy: Zero reject."[1] The nation's understanding of whom schools served and how they served them changed dramatically.

>> Boys and Girls Together: What Does It Mean for Schools to Be Gender Fair?

Most U.S. schools, unlike those in some countries, have long educated boys and girls in the same classrooms. So, if girls and boys sit next to each other in the same classroom with the same teacher, how can there be any problems regarding **educational equity**? The answer to that question is complex.

educational equity Students are regarded as equal in value and status and treated as thus.

Debates about unfair gender differences in education are not new. In 1910, the Chicago reformer Jane Addams told the National Woman's Trade Union League,

There is an agricultural school in one of our Eastern cities, where the girls and boys are taught the possibilities of breadwinning as agricultural laborers, agriculturalists, gardeners, florists, or whatever you will. When it comes to the boy, he learns the chemistry of the soil, and gets down to

the fundamental things in those particulars, but the girl is taught cooking and sewing. I am not saying that cooking and sewing are not necessary, but when we cheat a girl out of the training she ought to have for her breadwinning capacity, and substitute something that has nothing to do with the trade she is trying to learn, then we make a great and grave mistake.[2]

A half-century later, the 1964 Civil Rights Act included sex as well as race, color, and national origin when it outlawed discriminatory practices, especially in employment. However, in the early years, the Equal Employment Opportunities Commission, which was established to enforce the law, failed to give gender complaints serious attention and instead focused primarily on the still prevalent cases of racial discrimination.

With the founding of the National Organization of Women (NOW) in 1966, the women's movement had become a force to be reckoned with, growing dramatically in both the numbers of people involved and the political sophistication of the activists. By the 1970s, women had gained further political clout as more women were elected to Congress and as legislators of both genders began to pay more attention to women's votes. In the 1960s, Edith Green from Oregon, one of the senior women in the U.S. House of Representatives, heard a group of **school superintendents** say they were proud of special programs their schools ran to keep boys from dropping out of school. When Green specifically asked them about the girls, they responded that classes for

school superintendent Individual with executive and administrative responsibilities for a school district or a state, sometimes named commissioner of education or chief state school officer at the state level. Usually chosen by a board of education but in some cases chosen by the mayor of a city or—especially at the state level—sometimes through popular election.

girls were not nearly as important because the boys "are going to have to be the breadwinners." Several years later, Green got her opportunity to respond when she became the chief sponsor of what would be Title IX of the Education Amendments of 1972, passed by both houses of Congress and signed into law by President Richard Nixon.

THE IMPACT OF TITLE IX

When Title IX of the Education Amendments was passed, gender was added to the list of categories protected by federal law. From then on, schools and colleges receiving any federal funds were prohibited from discriminating against either employees or students on the basis of their sex. Despite resistance in many forms, Title IX has slowly transformed education in the United States.

When people hear the words *Title IX*, they usually think of athletics and sports facilities. Indeed, in 1972, only about 294,000 American high school girls took part in interscho-

PORTRAIT OF AN EDUCATOR

Edith Green

Edith Green began her career as a public school teacher in Salem, Oregon, in 1929. Like many women of her generation, Green attended college for only 2 years prior to taking a job as a public school teacher (which was the norm for teachers until well after World War II). Like many teachers of the time, Green later returned to college and graduated from the University of Oregon in 1939. She later became director of public relations for the Oregon Education Association, a position that launched her political career.

Green was elected as a Democrat to the U.S. House of Representatives from Oregon in 1954. Once in Congress, however, Green's interest in education, and especially in the status of women in education, never wavered. She was one of the spon-

Source: Biographical Directory of the United States Congress, 1774–present, U.S. Congress, retrieved June 8, 2009, from http://bioguide.congress.gov/ scripts/biodisplay.pl?index=G000407; and *More Than Title IX: How Equity in Education Has Shaped the Nation,* by Katherine Hanson, Vivian Guilfoy, and Sarita Nair-Pillai, 2009, Rowman & Littlefield.

sors of the Higher Education Facilities Act of 1963 and the Higher Education Act of 1965. Throughout the 1960s, Green grew increasingly angry about the fact, as she said in 1969, that "[i]t was perfectly legal to discriminate in any education program against girls or women!"

In 1970, Representative Green held congressional hearings on the treatment of women and girls in education and employment. Along with Representatives Patsy Mink and Shirley Chisholm and Senators Birch Bayh and George McGovern, Green sponsored Title IX of the Higher Education Act, which was signed into law in 1972, banning discrimination on the basis of gender in any school or college that received federal funds. As she said, "All I want and all I ask is that if two individuals, a man and a woman, come to college or university and they have equal credentials and apply for admissions, that they shall be treated as equals." Although Title IX was attached to a higher education measure, it covered all levels of education. While best known for mandating equal budgets for women's and men's sports, Title IX required equality at every level of education from kindergarten programs to graduate programs in all areas of study.

QUESTIONS

- How important do you think Green's experience as a school teacher in Oregon was to her involvement with the congressional hearings? What is the value of having people in powerful, political positions with a background in school teaching? Do you think it makes a difference?

- Green was frustrated by school superintendents' attitudes that men "had to be the breadwinners." Can you imagine school leaders saying things like that today? Have people's attitudes changed or have they learned to be more careful about the way they say things?

lastic sports; today, about 3 million girls play sports. But Title IX is much more far-reaching than sports.

With the passing of Title IX, traditional gender segregation in health, physical education, and vocational subjects became illegal, as did discriminatory guidance counseling or discrimination against pregnant and parenting teens. Although contact sports continued to be separate, athletic program clubs could not be, and schools needed to provide equal opportunities to girls and boys to participate in sports.

Prior to Title IX, girls who became pregnant were often forced to leave school or, at best, to attend segregated—and well-hidden—classes. Title IX prohibited that practice. Although schools can still offer voluntary classes for pregnant and parenting teens, no girl can be kept out of any program, class, or extracurricular activity because of bearing a child. These were no small victories in schools where girls who became pregnant were routinely expelled.

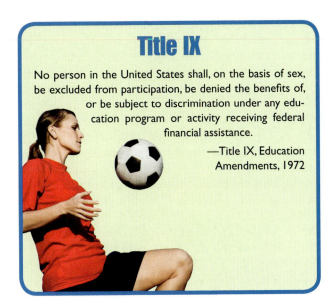

Title IX

No person in the United States shall, on the basis of sex, be excluded from participation, be denied the benefits of, or be subject to discrimination under any education program or activity receiving federal financial assistance.

—Title IX, Education Amendments, 1972

Until passage of Title IX, many high school students were taught "gender-appropriate" behavior in segregated classes for boys and girls. These young women are being given a lesson on babysitting and child-rearing.

Title IX also required schools to change the way **vocational education** was offered. Prior to the implementation of Title IX, vocational classes had usually been highly sex segregated and had reinforced stereotypes of appropriate sex role behavior. Boys took wood shop, girls took home economics, and that was that. In 1974, 80% of all female students in vocational education were in home economics courses (50%) or low-level clerical courses (30%). The idea that there might be more options for all students or that both boys and girls might gain a lot by learning how to saw and how to cook was not considered in most places. Title IX opened up options for both boys and girls.

> **vocational education** Training for a specific job or industry; comprises manual or practical activities.

As Title IX was first being implemented, T. J. Wirtenberg studied the immediate impact of the change to sex-integrated classes mandated by Title IX. The effects were dramatic. Girls who took the newly integrated vocational education courses gained skills, described themselves as being more logical, and took a greater interest in nontraditional fields than girls in segregated home economics classes. Boys also expanded their interests and sense of competence. Amazingly, the differences became evident very early in the classes. Within the first 2 weeks, students in the integrated classes showed change in terms of skill, self-confidence, and interest. Clearly, something important happened for girls and boys when traditional sex role stereotypes were removed from course assignments, even before the content of the courses was changed.

Although the U.S. Office for Civil Rights was charged with implementing Title IX, it was mostly outside pressure, led by groups like NOW's Project on Equal Educa-

tional Rights, that led to real change. At the same time, federal grants to schools, colleges, and universities, but also to individuals and community organizations, funded through the Women's Educational Equity Act (WEEA), enabled schools to comply more fully with the new laws in thoughtful and well-researched ways.[3]

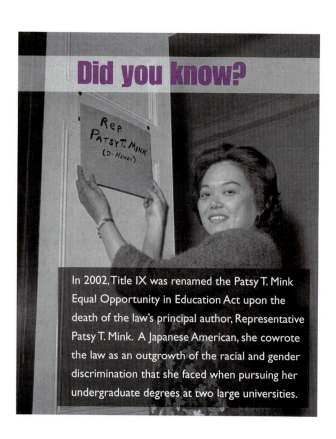

Did you know?

In 2002, Title IX was renamed the Patsy T. Mink Equal Opportunity in Education Act upon the death of the law's principal author, Representative Patsy T. Mink. A Japanese American, she cowrote the law as an outgrowth of the racial and gender discrimination that she faced when pursuing her undergraduate degrees at two large universities.

"Entitled" IX?

Since the passage of Title IX in 1972, girls' participation in sports has soared. In that year, girls accounted for 7% of all participants in high school sports. By 2007, girls' share had grown to 41%, according to the National Federation of State High School Associations.

In the suburbs, roughly the same numbers of girls and boys play sports. A 2007 survey by Harris Interactive of more than 2,000 schoolchildren nationwide showed that 54% of boys and 50% of girls in the suburbs described themselves as "moderately involved" athletes.

However, much greater discrepancies were observed in urban areas. Only 36% of city girls in the survey described themselves as moderately involved athletes, compared to 56% of the boys. Girls in cities from Los Angeles to New York "are the left-behinds of the youth sport movement in the United States," said Don Sabo, a professor of health policy at D'Youville College in Buffalo, who conducted the study, which was commissioned by the Women's Sports Foundation.

In the suburbs, girls' participation in sports is so commonplace in many communities that the concern isn't over equal access but rather that some girls are playing too much. In urban areas, girls' sports are still often seen as a luxury rather than an entitlement. Many urban schools lack free transportation and uniforms for their athletes, as well as full seasons of regularly scheduled games. Navigating these logistics is often the biggest hurdle, especially when frequent last-minute cancellations can occur because team members are stuck in traffic.

Coaches and organizers of youth sports in cities say that although many immigrant and lower-income parents see the benefit of sports for sons, they often lean on daughters to fill needs in their own hectic lives, like tending to siblings or cleaning the house. Also, because parents are often unable to attend games, they are especially concerned for their daughters' safety and thus often restrict their attendance.

According to the Women's Sports Foundation, girls who participate in sports receive a number of benefits. Research has shown that girls who play sports usually do better in school—with improved learning, memory, and concentration—and are more likely to graduate high school. Girls who play sports learn teamwork, goal-setting, and leadership skills that help them not only on the playing field but also in their future careers. In addition to the health benefits of regular physical activity, sports participation helps build a young woman's confidence through commitment, accomplishments, and social experiences.

QUESTIONS

- In what ways can you, as a teacher, link concepts learned through sports and physical activity to other areas of study, such as mathematics, business, and science? Can you link life skills—such as leadership, confidence, and commitment—to other areas of your students' lives?
- How can you help students and their parents advocate for more equitable support for girls' teams and to increase school and community support for girls' athletics?

As with other civil rights victories, changes in the treatment of girls in school have endured a sustained attack. In 1979 and again in 1981, Nevada senator Paul Laxalt proposed legislation to "withhold funds to any program that teaches children values that contradict demonstrated community beliefs, or to buy any textbooks that denigrate, diminish, or deny the historically understood role differences between the sexes." Had it passed, Laxalt's legislation would have allowed states and school districts "the right, with parental consultation, to limit or prohibit intermingling of the sexes in sports or other school related activities, free of Federal interference." President Ronald Reagan's administration tried multiple ways to undermine WEEA, and the program eventually ended under President George W. Bush.

Programs focused on **gender equity** in schools continue to be the subject of great controversy, but schools are without question different places, for girls and for boys, than they were prior to the passage of Title IX. Researcher Patricia Cayo Sexton is likely right when she says, "[D]espite some conspicuous problems, females are probably treated in a more **egalitarian** way in schools than in other institutions, including religious, familial, economic, and political institutions."[4]

gender equity Provision of equal responsibilities, opportunities, and benefits to students regardless of gender.

egalitarian The belief that all people are equal in value and merit.

GENDER EQUITY

In their 1994 book *Failing at Fairness*, Myra and David Sadker do not mince words when they say, "Sitting in the same classroom, reading the same textbook, listening to the same teacher, boys and girls receive very different educations." They report, "Girls are the majority of our nation's schoolchildren, yet they are second-class citizens." Their conclusion is based, among other things, on a careful look at the time teachers spend focused on boys, as opposed to girls, during a given day and the kinds of responses boys and girls elicit from their teachers, even when they are sitting in the same classroom.

More recently, however, other scholars have begun to write about the "boy problem." This shift is partly due to the fact that gender discrimination hurts not just girls. Although many arguments have been made about what is happening to boys in light of changes in our understanding and beliefs about gender in the larger culture, gender and gender differences clearly remain important for both sexes. A new postfeminist image of the macho male may well be leading some boys, perhaps relatively large num-

You Decide

Do boys-only and girls-only classes provide better instruction?

bers, to give up on schooling, to view academic success as a sign of being weak or feminized. Some versions of this new machismo can be found across all races and socioeconomic classes. New statistics may seem to say that boys are failing in school at faster rates than girls.

The articles on gender equity included in the **Readings** for this chapter provide clear evidence of the significance of gender inequity in the schools, even as they provide strikingly different interpretations of the evidence and different understandings of the current state of affairs. The two **Readings** provide quite different perspectives on the meaning of gender equity in the 21st century. While voicing some appreciation for the Sadkers's work, Michael Gurian and Kathy Stevens offer research and statistics, in their article "With Boys and Girls in Mind," that lead them to conclude, "Our boys are now losing frightening ground in school, and we must come to terms with it—not in a way that robs girls, but in a way that sustains our civilization and is as powerful as the lobby we have created to help girls." If fairness in the 1980s and 1990s led educators to define gender equity as focusing especially on the educational achievement of girls, Gurian and Stevens seem to say that achieving equity requires a major focus on the learning needs and on the decline in achievement among boys.

Sara Mead, however, directly challenges Gurian and Stevens' research and data in her article "The Truth about Boys and Girls." Mead concludes that "the truth is far different from what these accounts suggest. The real story is not bad news about boys doing worse; it's good news about girls doing better." According to Mead, both boys and girls are improving in their academic work, indeed for the most part improving fairly dramatically, but compared to boys, "girls have just improved their performance on some measures even faster." What one scholar sees as a crisis for boys another sees as a healthy closing of a once huge gap. Mead, however, is hardly a Pollyanna. She notes real problems, especially in the educational achievement of African American and Latino boys, but she contends that crisis will best be addressed in the context of race rather than gender.

Indeed, many current studies seem to indicate that girls are having greater success in school than boys. They drop out less often, they get in trouble less often, and they seem less dissatisfied. Some people today are calling for boys-only schools, or girls-only schools, as a way to attend to the needs of one gender at a time. Whatever the future brings, it will demand that teachers continue to attend to both the girls and the boys in their classes, and to find ways to be fair in the structure of their schools and in their individual interactions

Teachable Moment

Committing to Gender Fairness

Ed Little is a longtime elementary school principal in Washington state. As he describes it, he came to see gender inequity as a serious roadblock to the education of both girls and boys in a school where he became the principal. With his faculty, he studied the problem, developed an action plan, and saw things change.

The first time I really took a critical look at gender equity and its limits for students was when I was a principal at the Martin Luther King Elementary. It was my first year as principal, and there were some issues going on that bothered me. There seemed to be some separation in the building based on gender issues. I just felt uncomfortable with how some of the staff members were treating girls differently in terms of expectations in particular areas, especially in math and science. I looked at the test scores, I saw that some of our girls were not performing as well as the boys, and that bothered me. So I had the staff do a study from October to May, looking at how our girls were doing. We asked ourselves if we were giving the same opportunities, the same level of intensity to our girls as our boys. We found out that we were not holding the girls accountable for a lot of things that we were [with] the boys....

I then contacted Gene Liddell, who worked out of our Superintendent of Public Instruction's office. She invited a team of my teachers to a weekend workshop on team building around gender equity.

We spent three days with Gene, and with others from the state of Washington, and I have never been impacted more, nor has a group of teachers been impacted more, in terms of that experience with gender equity issues and team building. That was the most powerful weekend in my life in terms of education!

It got our team committed to making some significant changes in the building. We really worked on gender equity issues and started infusing it into the elementary curriculum. Students and teachers quit looking at negatives and built on strengths. Within about six months, the culture and climate of the building really changed, and we saw very few putdowns, either from kid to kid or adult to kid. We saw a lot of positive rewards and positive comments from staff to students and students to students. That's how I got interested in gender equity.

Source: *More Than Title IX: How Equity in Education Has Shaped the Nation*, by Katherine Hanson, Vivian Guilfoy, and Sarita Pillai, 2009, Rowman & Littlefield, pp. 74–79.

QUESTIONS

- Think of the school where you observed most recently—either the school you attended or one where you are now observing. Specifically, think about the ways boys and girls are treated or the way they interact. Do you see anything that should bother you in the way that Ed Little was bothered at Martin Luther King Elementary School?

- Ed Little singles out the different expectations for girls and boys in math and science. Can you think of a time when you were held to higher or lower standards in a subject than were students of the opposite sex? Were boys or girls treated differently or held to different expectations? By whom?

with students. Most of all, it will require constant attention to the difficult question of just what is fairness, after all.[5]

>> Learning the Language: What Are the Ongoing Debates Over Bilingual Education?

AMERICA: A LAND OF MANY LANGUAGES

Bilingual programs have existed in schools in the United States far longer than most people realize. Beginning in the early 1500s, Europeans speaking Spanish, Portuguese, Dutch, French, and English, accompanied by Africans speaking Ashanti, Yoruba, Kru, and other African languages, encountered American Indians speaking innumerable different languages of their own. As schools were founded in these lands, instruction also took place in many different languages. In 1664, when the English conquered New Amsterdam and renamed it New York, at least 18 languages were spoken on Manhattan Island, not counting the Indian languages. German language schools opened in Philadelphia as early as 1694, and by the mid-1800s, most major cities, including Baltimore, Cincinnati, Cleveland, Indianapolis, Milwaukee, and St. Louis, offered schooling in both German and English, while Louisiana supported schools that taught in both French and English.

After 1848, when most of the land in the current states of California, Arizona, New Mexico, Texas, Utah, and Colorado was ceded to the United States by the Republic of Mexico at the end of the U.S.-Mexican War, most of the people who lived in those areas spoke only Spanish. In response, dual systems of Spanish and English schooling were developed, especially in New Mexico, which, in 1906, also set up a dual system of teacher preparation. As researcher Diego Castellanos said, "For much of the 19th century. . .American public education allowed immigrant groups to incorporate linguistic and cultural traditions into the schools. . .wherever immigrant groups possessed sufficient political power—be they Italian, Polish, Czech, French, Dutch, German—foreign languages were introduced into elementary and secondary schools, either as separate subjects or as languages of instruction."[6]

Japanese language schools were introduced in California early in the 20th century despite considerable opposition and hostility from supporters of **nativism**. The strong American tradition of local control of schools, and the strength of different linguistic groups in different localities, meant that what we now call bilingual education had a sufficiently strong constituency in many places (although, in the 18th and 19th centuries, it was often monolingual instruction in a language other than English).

This linguistic diversity was not without its critics. Throughout the 19th century, anti-immigrant groups demanded that people who

> **nativism** Inherent favoring of the practices and culture of native-born inhabitants of a region rather than recent immigrants—in this case, European Americans were the only ones considered to be native-born inhabitants, rather than the Native American population.

You Decide

Have we always lived in a multilingual society?

were in America speak English, whether they had arrived via immigration or, as was the case for Mexicans of the Southwest or residents of Puerto Rico, through the conquest of previously Spanish-speaking lands. American Indians were often educated in schools that forced them to speak and learn only in English and that were consciously designed to wipe out every vestige of the Indians' language, customs, beliefs, and culture. Early in the 20th century, Theodore Roosevelt said, "We have room for but one language in this country and that is the English language, for we intend to see that the crucible turns our people out as Americans, of American nationality." When the United States entered World War I on the side of England and against Germany, anti-German feeling led to attacks on German-language schooling. Through the 1920s and 1930s, bilingual schooling virtually disappeared in the United States; it was illegal in some places and declined due to lack of support in others. As late as the 1960s, schools in Texas had what they called "Spanish detention," where students were kept after school for speaking Spanish in the classrooms or hallways. Prior to 1973, it was a crime in Texas for a teacher to teach in any language except English.

The civil rights movement of the 1950s and 1960s fueled changes and reform. From 1965 to 1966, the National Education Association conducted a survey of the Tucson, Arizona, schools. The results, published as *The Invisible Minority, Pero No Vencibles*, portrayed the depth of the exclusion of Spanish-speaking children in Arizona's schools. Civil rights groups protested policies like Spanish detention. In 1970, the LaRaza Unida Party organized school boycotts in Crystal City, Texas, demanding the development of new bilingual instruction. A Puerto Rican group, Aspira, sued the New York City public schools and obtained a consent decree guaranteeing the rights of Spanish-speaking students in New York. That same year, another advocacy group in San Francisco began the long process of demanding legal rights for Kinney Lau and 1,789 other Chinese-speaking students in that city.

Politicians soon followed. California governor Ronald Reagan signed legislation repealing the state's English-only school laws in 1967. In 1968, the U.S. Congress also passed Title VII of the Elementary and Secondary Education Act, providing federal funds to support bilingual education programs, to prepare teachers able to work in them, and to develop appropriate new curriculum. In 1970, the U.S. Office for Civil Rights informed school districts that they had an obligation under the Civil Rights Act to develop programs for students in need of English-language instruction and that they "must take affirmative steps to rectify the language deficiency in order to open its instructional program to these students." In 1971, Massachusetts enacted legislation in favor of bilingual education.

Finally, in 1974 in *Lau v. Nichols*, the U.S. Supreme Court ruled that San Francisco was wrong to claim that it did not discriminate against Chinese-speaking students because it offered them the same instruction as other students (though in this case they could not understand the instruction). The high court upheld the views of Shirley Hufstedler of the 9th Circuit, who wrote, "These Chinese

---

VIOLATION SLIP - SPANISH DETENTION

_____

(Student's name and classification)

Was speaking Spanish during school hours. This pupil must report to Spanish Detention in the Cafeteria on the assigned day. (The teacher reporting should place the date on this slip).

_____

(Dates to report)   (Teacher reporting)

Return this slip to Mr. _____
or Mr. _____ before 3:30 p.m.

As late as the mid-1960s, students received detention for being caught speaking Spanish in school.

Source: Richard Valencia: Chicano Students and the Courts

With the *Lau* decision, the U.S. Supreme Court made it clear that, although school districts might use any one of several different approaches to bilingual education, students who came to school not speaking English could not simply be allowed to languish in English-only classrooms, as had too often been the norm. In 1975, when U.S. Commissioner of Education Terrell Bell announced federal guidelines for implementing the *Lau* decision, the so-called Lau Remedies, the full force of the federal government was put behind effective bilingual instruction for all students.[8]

It may have seemed that the issue of bilingual education was settled in the United States. The federal budget for bilingual education was $45 million, which supported programs offering bilingual education in English and 26 languages including Russian, French, Portuguese, Cantonese, Pomo, Cree, Yup'ik, and Chamorro. Congress voted not only to expand the funding but also to support stronger programs in bilingual education "to the extent necessary to allow a child to progress effectively through the educational system."

children are not separated from their English-speaking classmates by state-erected walls of brick and mortar but the language barrier, which the state helps to maintain, insulates the children from their classmates as effectively as any physical bulwarks."[7]

However, as rapid and impressive as the legal victories of the 1960s and 1970s were, the offering of meaningful bilingual education varied greatly across the country and opposition to these programs emerged quickly. Within the Latino community, some leaders worried about a new

Lau v. Nichols

Under these state-imposed standards there is no equality of treatment merely by providing students with the same facilities, textbooks, teachers, and curriculum; for students who do not understand English are effectively foreclosed from any meaningful education.

Basic English skills are at the very core of what these public schools teach. Imposition of a requirement that before a child can effectively participate in the educational program he must already have acquired those basic skills is to make a mockery of public education. We know that those who do not understand English are certain to find their classroom experiences wholly incomprehensible and in no way meaningful.

… It seems obvious that the Chinese-speaking minority receives less benefit than the English-speaking majority from respondents' school system, which denies them a meaningful opportunity to participate in the educational program….

—U.S. Supreme Court ruling, *Lau v. Nichols*, 1974

form of bilingual segregation. Diego Castellanos wrote of the fears of some that "bilingual tracks" might be the new form of **de facto segregation**. Another scholar, Alfredo Mathew, feared that bilingual education could "become so insular and ingrown that it fosters a type of apartheid. . . ." Long-time civil rights scholar Gary Orfield wrote, "Without any serious national debate it seems that we have moved from a harsh assimilationist policy to a policy of linguistic and cultural separation." Even the programs designed to engage English-speaking and non-English-speaking students in two-way bilingual programs raised concerns, leading one Puerto Rican school administrator to lament, "The only ones that will emerge from the schools bilingual are the Anglo children. A natural language resource will be lost."

de facto segregation Segregation that occurs without legal sanction, often because of housing patterns.

At the same time, other critics with less initial sympathy to bilingual education were issuing much harsher statements. In 1974, Albert Shanker, the president of the American Federation of Teachers, wrote, "The American taxpayer, while recognizing the existence of cultural diversity, still wants the schools to be the basis of an American melting pot. . . . What these children need is intensive instruction in English so that they may, as soon as possible, function with other children in regular school programs."

In 1981, President Reagan said that he wanted teachers to be able to communicate with students who did not come to school speaking English: "But it is absolutely wrong and against American concepts to have a bilingual education program that is now openly admittedly dedicated to preserving their native language and never getting them adequate in English so they can go out into the job market and participate."[9]

BILINGUAL INSTRUCTION VERSUS AN ENGLISH-ONLY CURRICULUM

In the 1990s, more attacks on bilingual education emerged and several states passed laws demanding English immersion for all students. Bilingual programs became programs for "English language learners," and the goal of maintaining students' home languages receded as the focus became getting students to speak English as quickly as possible.[10] As the **Readings** at the end of this chapter show, the debate between those who want schools to strengthen bilingual students' ability to speak and read in their native languages as well as in English and those who feel that schools must teach students English as thoroughly and quickly as possible is alive and well today. As discussed in the Chapter 3 **Reading** by Marcelo Suárez-Orozco, whatever the outcome of the debates about the future of bilingual education, the United States is a nation—and especially a classroom—of immigrants, and with or without bilingual classes, teachers must teach many children who arrive in school with little, if any, English. But how do you best respond to these students? Do you help them maintain their first language while they learn English, or do you leave the first language to the parents while the school focuses on intensive English instruction?

Perhaps nowhere has the fight over an appropriate kind of bilingual education been more intense than in California. Already split almost evenly between European Americans and people of color, California is one of the most diverse states in the nation. In addition to people of African descent, most of whom speak English (although some recent immigrants are from the Caribbean and speak Spanish or Haitian Creole), California includes large numbers of Spanish-speaking citizens—recent and not-so-recent immigrants from Latin America—as well as a rapidly growing Asian population, including people who speak Chinese, Japanese, Vietnamese, Khmer, or one of a host of other languages.

Learning the Lingo: Bilingual Education

- **Bilingual education:** Many reformers began to use this term in the 1970s and continue to use it today. As the term implies, bi-lingual education programs stress maintaining the students' home language, offering students school instruction in that language while ensuring that the students learn English. The goal is to encourage students who come to school not speaking English to become truly proficient in two languages before they graduate. In some schools, "two-way bilingual programs" help students maintain their home language and learn English while helping students whose first language is English learn a foreign language.

- **English language immersion:** Advocates of English language immersion programs believe that it is the family's job to maintain the home language and that school should teach students English as quickly as possible so that they can be fully integrated into school life.

- **English as a second language:** As programs have shifted from maintaining both languages for students (true bilingual education) to a focus on helping students learn English as fast as possible, many educators have begun to use the lessons of foreign language instruction to develop more sophisticated programs to teach the English language to students who first learned to speak and write in another language.

- **Programs for English language learners (ELL):** Since some states (most notably California) have mandated English language immersion over bilingual education, educators have begun using the term "English language learners" rather than "bilingual students." These school programs focus on helping students learn the English language (at a faster or slower pace depending on local policy) rather than on maintaining two languages.

Since the *Lau* decision of 1974, California, which educates more students learning English than any other state, has had a variety of bilingual education programs. However, in 1998, most of these programs were curtailed significantly when California voters passed Proposition 227, which mandated that students who came to school in California not speaking English be placed in structured English immersion classes for a maximum of 1 year and then be transferred to regular classrooms conducted "overwhelmingly in English." The debate around Proposition 227 was intense. Advocates of the new law claimed that bilingual education segregated non-English-speaking students and limited their life chances by denying them the full opportunities of schooling. Opponents of the new law saw it as a racist effort to return to the old days when students who could not or did not learn English quickly enough were effectively forced out of school altogether.

Don Soifer, one of the supporters of Proposition 227, celebrated its victory: "Earlier this month, California voters soundly rejected bilingual education." From his perspective, a "bilingual establishment" was bent on preserving bilingual education programs even when their utility had long passed. Soifer contended that "children in bilingual programs generally learn English slower, later, and less effectively than their peers. The bilingual approach delays for years the time when students can graduate to 'mainstream' classrooms. Many children are in bilingual programs for five to seven years and do not even learn to write English until the fourth or fifth grade."[11]

Other Californians hold radically different views of Proposition 227. John Espinoza, a teacher in the Los Angeles Unified School District, believed that Los Angeles had developed an excellent program for English learners through its bilingual offerings until the new law effectively "ended bilingual education as we know it." According to Espinoza, "Proposition 227 will continue to wreck the educational opportunities for thousands of California's LEP [limited English proficiency] students. It is time for teachers to step forward, and dare we say, 'advocate' on behalf of the rights of LEP students."[12]

In spite of the intensity of the debates around Proposition 227, the impact has been less than either side predicted. In part, the language of the new law allowed

What do you think is a teacher's proper role in local, state, and national debates about the best way to educate students whose first language is not English? How would you participate in those debates, either now or in the future?

Join the Dialogue

A Growing Nation of ELL Students

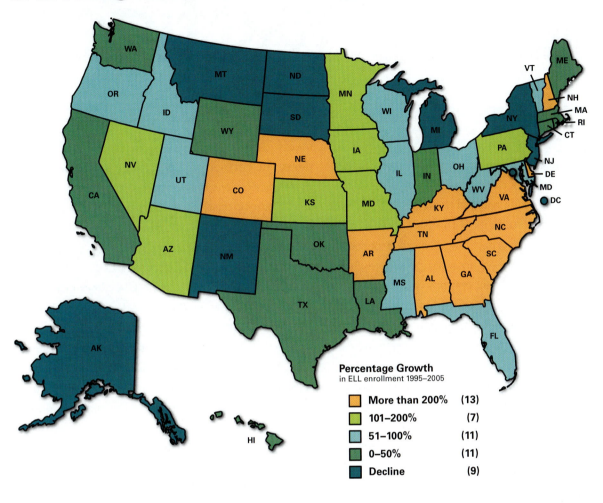

Percentage Growth
in ELL enrollment 1995–2005

- More than 200% (13)
- 101–200% (7)
- 51–100% (11)
- 0–50% (11)
- Decline (9)

Nationwide enrollments of English-language learners increased by 57 percent from 1995 to 2005. Public K-12 schools educated a total of 5.1 million ELL students in the 2005-06 school year. In 20 states, the size of the ELL population has at least doubled over this period, with the greatest percentage increases in Arkansas and South Carolina. However, the numbers of English-language learners declined in nine states.

Source: EPE Research Center, 2009. Analysis of data from the National Clearinghouse for English Language Acquisition and the U.S. Department of Education's Common Core of Data.

school districts and individual teachers considerable discretion. Saying that students should not "normally" be in English immersion for more than 1 year and that subsequent instruction had to be "overwhelmingly in English" allowed for a great deal of wiggle room. Almost a decade after the vote, a major study found very little evidence that the proposition's basic premise was correct. Students who needed to learn English when they came to school were doing slightly better on standardized tests, but they were also dropping out of school in higher numbers and graduating from high school in lower numbers.[13] New funding and a new focus on the needs of these students had clearly improved instruction in some schools, and some schools were making important strides. But a need remains for more resources and clearer policies across the state to serve all students.

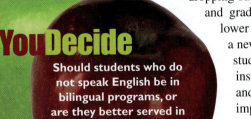

YouDecide

Should students who do not speak English be in bilingual programs, or are they better served in short-term programs that will help transition them into regular classrooms as quickly as possible?

Promising Practices

Three Tiers for English Learners

Because Valley High, an urban school in Sacramento [California] boasts such a diverse English learner population, they employ bilingual Spanish, Hmong, Chinese, Punjabi, and Hindi paraprofessionals to assist students with instruction in the content areas. The urban school has a 3 percent overall dropout rate—a noteworthy accomplishment considering that 62 percent of the students are eligible for free or reduced-price lunch and 26 percent are designated as English learners. Systematic use of data and personalized attention are key to Valley High's success. Through analysis of CST and CELDT (California state tests) scores, as well as feedback from teachers and feeder middle schools, each English learner is individually placed in the instructional program that best meets the student's needs. Valley High offers a tiered "EL Partnership" program with three levels of instruction: one for newcomer students, another set of "transitional" core courses for those English learners who have not yet attained the level of English fluency necessary to access college prep-level textbooks, and "SDAIE" core classes (which meet college entrance requirements). Teachers instructing classes at any of the three levels participate in a year-round professional learning program to ensure that they have the necessary knowledge and skills. Every incoming English learner sees a counselor and has a parent meeting to tailor the student's schedule to meet graduation requirements and aid English acquisition. Students with relatively low English fluency trade one elective for a second hour of ELD [English language development] class. Teachers are given the freedom and support to implement curricula to meet the needs of their diverse student population. Constant monitoring by the bilingual paraprofessionals, teachers, and administration ensures all students' progress is carefully tracked. Staff view this monitoring and support for English learners as integral to the results they are achieving. "Students do not fall through the cracks," notes EL Coordinator Linda Gonzalez.

Source: Reprinted from "How Are English Learners Faring under Proposition 227," by Thomas B. Parrish, Amy Merickel, María Perez, Robert Linquanti, Miguel Socías, and Angeline Spain, 2006, American Institutes for Research and WestEd, p. 12.

Race and Ethnicity of ELL Students

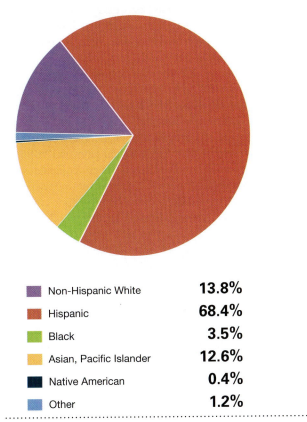

■ Non-Hispanic White	**13.8%**
■ Hispanic	**68.4%**
■ Black	**3.5%**
■ Asian, Pacific Islander	**12.6%**
■ Native American	**0.4%**
■ Other	**1.2%**

Most English-language learners from the ages of 5 to 17 are Hispanic, while almost 14 percent are white and 13 percent are of Asian or Pacific Islander descent.

Source: EPE Research Center, 2009. Analysis of the U.S. Census Bureau's American Community Survey (2005–2007).

Despite the research findings, voters in four other states have considered ballot initiatives requiring an end to bilingual instruction and a focus on English only. Initiatives passed in Arizona in 2000 and in Massachusetts in 2002 but were defeated in Colorado in 2002 and in Oregon in 2008. Nevertheless, proponents of more traditional approaches to bilingual education have found themselves on the defensive, and an increasing number of states refer to students in these programs as English language learners rather than as bilingual education students. This shift represents a clear change in the expectations for programs that serve students who come to school speaking a language other than English.[14]

Whatever one's own views on the debates about bilingual education, most of today's aspiring teachers are going to have students (sometimes many) who do not speak English, who still have not mastered the language, and who need substantial support to succeed in an English-speaking classroom, to say nothing of the other goal of bilingual education: maintaining students' home languages so that they can be successful bilingual citizens.[15]

In April 2009, the journal *Educational Leadership* devoted an entire issue to the best ways of supporting English language learners. Although the articles in that issue did not generate the heat of the earlier California, Arizona and Massachusetts debates, the educator-authors clearly had significantly different views on the best way to support these students. The **Readings** related to bilingual education in this chapter are taken from that issue. Orhan Agirdag, an educator in Belgium, cites the case of Europe, where many students cross borders and come to school speaking many different languages, in his discussion of the best ways to welcome all students in school while encouraging them to both maintain their home language and learn the language of their new home. Language, Agirdag insists, is part of many people's basic identity, and it is wrong to demean it in any way. He sees many advantages in encouraging students to both prize their native language and learn a second one. Such bilingualism allows students to maintain stronger ties with their family and community, and it fosters an adult society that is rich in linguistic ability. Although he does not disagree directly with Agirdag, professional consultant Kevin Clark focuses on making English immersion work, a necessity in California, Arizona, and Massachusetts, where it is illegal *not* to do so. Clark also believes that "active, direct, and explicit" instruction in English will help students master their new language—and succeed in the schools of their new community—much faster than any alternative.

You can certainly learn from both articles, and from the many advocates of differing perspectives on the issue, but at some point you will need to decide where you stand as an individual teacher. At the same time, you must find a way to survive, with integrity, even in a system that may have official policies with which you disagree intensely. Knowing how to be an effective teacher of students who are English language learners, sometimes in the very early stages of learning English, is one of the key challenges facing anyone entering the teaching profession today.

>> Special Needs: What Is the Best Education for Students with Disabilities?

In the last **Reading** in this chapter, Thomas Hehir, one of the foremost authorities on special education, asks, "What should the purpose of special education be?" He answers his own question by saying that "we can best frame the purpose of special education as minimizing the impact of disability and maximizing the opportunities for students with disabilities to participate in schooling and the community." In this answer, Hehir reflects the dominant thinking in the field of special education over the past few decades. He also makes it clear that this is easier said than done.

Hehir lists in his article many reasons why schools have a long way to go to reach the twin goals he outlines for special education—minimizing the impact of a disability and maximizing the opportunity for the student with the disability. Perhaps the most important reason, and certainly the most intriguing, is what he calls "ableism," society's pervasive negative attitude about disability. Until this ableism is addressed, especially by teachers and prospective teachers, there is little reason to hope for significant progress.

THE LEGAL FOUNDATION OF SPECIAL EDUCATION

Many teachers find that educating students with special needs is their primary calling, but *every teacher* needs a strong foundation in special education. Classrooms are becoming increasingly inclusive, which means that students with learning disabilities or physical limitations are educated alongside other students and special accommodations are made for the instructional needs of all students. As a result, someone prepared as a "general education" teacher of any grade can well expect to have students in class who need a wheelchair or a guide dog or an aide to get around, have attention-deficit/hyperactivity disorder (ADHD), are slower to learn certain concepts, or have a wide range of other mental or emotional impairments that make learning difficult for them and make including them in a well-integrated classroom a challenge for the unprepared teacher.[16]

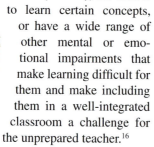

This didn't used to be the case. Throughout much of the nation's history, many students who had any of a number of different disabilities either were told to go home—that school was not for them—or were allowed to attend school but given no special services. Those who did attend school often fell further and further behind until dropping out seemed the only wise course. Massachusetts is today among the states offering the most services for students with special needs. One scholar has estimated, however, that in 1965 only 25% of the children potentially requiring special education in that state were enrolled in school. The majority of these students were simply excluded. As the civil rights movements of the 1950s and 1960s expanded to include not only African Americans and other people of color but also poor people of all races, women, people whose home language was other than English, and gays and lesbians, others came to demand their rights. These campaigns for full participation in American society were not separate movements. Disproportionate numbers of poor children, children of color, and non-English-speaking children had been classified as handicapped and were excluded from schools as having needs the schools could not meet. Parents and their advocates began to organize for change and for a legal mandate that every child deserved the best possible education.

Massachusetts was the first state to act when, in 1972, Chapter 766 of the state's General Laws stipulated that the schools of the state had to offer a free and appropriate education to every child. A little over 2 years later, in 1974, the U.S. Congress adopted a similar measure, Public Law 94-142, the Education for All Handicapped Children Act, which both recognized the breadth of the problem and mandated change.[17]

As a result of Public Law 94-142, the core responsibility of schools and school districts changed. Every child had to be given an education, and that education had to be equal to the education offered to other students and in "the least restrictive environment" possible. No child or youth could be turned away because the school or district lacked the skill or resources to provide the needed services. The funds made available by Congress as well as the specific demands and prohibitions contained in the text of this and subsequent national laws governing special education are quite specific in six major areas:

- **Zero reject.** Every school district must provide a "free appropriate public education to every child in the district." No exceptions are allowed no matter what the range or severity of the child's disabilities.

- **Nondiscriminatory assessment.** Since it had too often been the case that children of color and children who did not speak English were routinely misclassified, the law stipulates that special education decisions must be made by a multidisciplinary diagnostic team that includes the child's parents.

- **Least restrictive environment.** Certainly the most controversial aspect of the law, this provision says that, when possible, a child must be placed in a regular classroom in the nearest school and also that a continuum of other options should be available from in-school specialists to special residential schools.

- **Individualized education program.** Every child placed in a special education category must have his or her own individual education plan (IEP) that will provide information to all educational personnel and

safeguard the child's and the parents' rights to be sure that the original agreements about appropriate education are followed.

- **Parent participation.** Congress specifically mandated that parents be full partners in all stages of decision making, including curriculum and placements, thus giving special education parents a much greater say in their children's education than that held by parents of any other children.

- **Due process.** Every state and school district must have a review process that is seen as fair and impartial and that avoids the high cost of litigation in the courts.

With these provisions, Public Law 94-142 is clearly a bill of rights for students with disabilities. (Congress in 1990 changed the language from *handicapped* to *disabilities*.)

RESPONDING TO THE MANDATE

The same laws that provide for the needs of special education students have also stirred debates about the meaning of these rights. One set of debates has taken place primarily within the special education community itself. Understandably, parents want different kinds of educational placements and opportunities for their children. Some parents feel strongly that their special education children, even some with extensive and multiple disabilities, should remain in age-appropriate classrooms in a regular school. The call for inclusion is implied in the law itself, and many parents argue strongly against segregation of special needs youth in all but the most extreme cases. These parents often see separate schools as denying their disabled children essential social integration with their peers. They also worry that segregated classes will inevitably be seen as unequal.

Other parents argue almost exactly the opposite, that their special needs children either will not receive the necessary services in regular schools or will be made to feel far too uncomfortable by their less disabled peers and that they must be served in separate, often residential schools. Some parents argue that separate schools are "the least restrictive environment" for their children. Some deaf parents who

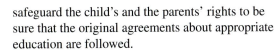

Public Law 94-142, Education for All Handicapped Children Act, 1975

The Congress finds that—

(1) there are more than eight million handicapped children in the United States today;

(2) the special educational needs of such children are not being fully met;

(3) more than half of the handicapped children in the United States do not receive appropriate educational services which would enable them to have full equality of opportunity;

(4) one million of the handicapped children in the United States are excluded entirely from the public school system and will not go through the educational process with their peers; there are many handicapped children throughout the United States participating in regular school programs whose handicaps prevent them from having a successful educational experience because their handicaps are undetected; ...

It is the purpose of this Act to assure that all handicapped children have available to them, ...a free appropriate public education which emphasizes special education and related services designed to meet their unique needs, to assure that the rights of handicapped children and their parents or guardians are protected, to assist States and localities to provide for the education of all handicapped children, and to assess and assure the effectiveness of efforts to educate handicapped children.

Did you know?

Approximately 17% of children have some type of developmental disability, including speech and language disorders, learning disabilities, or ADHD.

Me?

If I Were a Student in 1960. . .

Before the numerous legal actions and government mandates that changed educational opportunities for everyone, the classroom was a very different place. If you were a student 50 years ago, what opportunities might not have been available to you

- because of your gender?
- because of your race?
- because of a physical, mental, or learning disability?

Now change your circumstances and reconsider your options. For example, what restrictions or lack of educational opportunities might these people have faced?

- a female, Black high school student in Alabama
- a 5-year-old Latino boy starting kindergarten whose home language is Spanish
- a 14-year-old girl who just arrived in the United States with her family from Russia and who could not understand what her high school teachers were talking about
- a middle-schooler who has continually been reprimanded because he "can't sit still"
- a third-grade Chinese girl who uses a wheelchair

Do students today truly have educational equality? In what situations might students be at a disadvantage? Have you ever felt that educational opportunities were not available to you when they should have been?

---

contend that they and their deaf children are part of a distinct culture often join this category. Sometimes parents of gifted students agree. Still other groups of parents come to different conclusions about the most appropriate environment for their children. Since all parents wanting widely differing arrangements can claim that their choice for the schooling of their children is the least restrictive environment, and since federal law guarantees parents a significant say in the education of their children with disabilities, the issue can be exceedingly contentious.[18]

Another contentious area for special education has to do with the problem of inappropriate placements (the ten-

Did you know?

According to the National Institute of Mental Health, 2%–3% of children, or at least one child in a typical classroom, has ADHD. This represents about 2 million children in the United States; boys with ADHD outnumber girls with the diagnosis by 3 to 1.

Challenges of 5- to 15-year-olds with Disabilities

Mental	79%
Sensory	17%
Physical	17%
Self-Care	16%

(Percent equals more than 100% because some students deal with multiple challenges.)
Source: U.S. Census Bureau, Census 2000 Summary File 3.

dency in some places for special education to be a "dumping ground" for students whom the standard classrooms cannot easily accommodate), the cost of some placements, and the political clout that the laws give to special education parents. Parents have sometimes fought hard to have their children classified as in need of special education to get services for them, and some teachers have used the "special education" label to move disruptive students out of their classrooms. The result has been a growing number of children classified as "special needs" and a growing cost for their education. As early as 1993 in Massachusetts, where many of the first special education legal rights were enacted and 17% of students are classified as special needs (one of the highest percentages in the nation), a report prepared for a conservative foundation argued, "It simply is not fair to give absolute priority to the needs of 17 percent of the student body at the expense of the other 83 percent."[19]

More recently, commentators from a wide spectrum have made similar arguments. Ellen Guiney, executive director of the Boston Plan for Excellence, herself far from being a conservative critic of the schools, offers a far-reaching critique of the special education programs in her city and, by implication, the state of Massachusetts and the nation. She writes of the need to escape "the prevailing notion that special education is a place to put any student with learning or behavior problems; and secondly, the underlying premise that a heavy emphasis on implementing process measures, on meeting strict timelines, and on having teachers meet certification requirements will produce desired results."[20] Guiney and many fellow educators and reformers across the nation have come to have grave doubts that the results are worth the cost, or are fair to the students involved or to the majority of students in the schools.

In Guiney's view, special education programs in Boston and throughout the nation need to address evidence showing that there are

- too many students in special education, especially in substantially separate programs, and too many special education populations overrepresented by gender and race (Black and Hispanic students, especially males,

are overrepresented in special education overall and are greatly overrepresented in substantially separate classes for certain disability areas.)

- too many students in special education who have learning or behavioral difficulties, not disabilities
- too high costs for too few results

In her own research, Guiney found deep resentments among the special education students themselves. One told her, "Juvenile delinquency. That is what they treat us like. We're juveniles. And we're just a menace to society, so we have to be locked down here."

Guiney's solution also reflects the ideas of many other researchers: "Expand well-designed inclusion classrooms." Inclusive classrooms, they believe, offer the opportunity to bring children together rather than separate them, create integration rather than segregation, and end the sense of being "locked down" that too many special education students experience.

Inclusive classrooms require well prepared teachers. Often they require a team in which one teacher focuses on the whole class while a partner is free to focus on the needs of students with special needs, often one at a time. Inclusive classrooms are not a panacea. If a teacher is not prepared, inclusion can be a disaster. It often works best with more than one teacher and a relatively small group of students; it should not be used simply to save significant amounts of money over the cost of other options. To thrive, some students need to be in classes with others who have the same disabilities. As with most ideas in American education, what works for some students may not work well for others. Nevertheless, inclusive classrooms that serve the needs of a wide range of students are the most popular approach to responding to the needs of special education students today.

Connections

In Chapter 10, we discuss the debates over sorting and tracking students by ability levels.

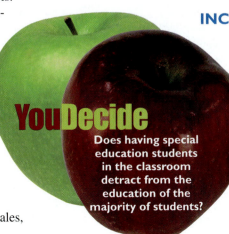

You Decide

Does having special education students in the classroom detract from the education of the majority of students?

INCLUSIVE CLASSROOMS

In the middle of these sometimes-heated debates, teachers must find their way and serve all their students. It is one thing for parents, advocates, and public officials to debate policy. It is something quite different for a teacher to face a class filled with students with widely diverse needs. From the 1960s onward, many observers have argued in favor of "inclusive classrooms" in which regular education and special

How is the "general education" classroom teacher affected by changes in special education?

"Many times the regular teacher has very limited support for included students. Most new teachers don't have a full understanding of the range of abilities they will see in a classroom. All of the students come to them with varying abilities, yet they are supposed to make sure all learn and do well on specific state tests. Today in special education, everything is data, data, data—but life is more than data."

—Deb Whitmore, special education teacher ■

education students are mixed together as the "least restrictive environment" in which all will learn most effectively. As special education researcher Robert Osgood says, during the past several decades, the ideal of inclusion has taken hold as a means to "break down distinctions between special and regular education in fundamental and dramatic ways." More recently, people worried about the burgeoning cost of special education have argued for inclusive classrooms, perhaps less on educational grounds than on the simple mathematics of the money saved when a student is moved from a special place-ment—often in a small class or a specialized, even residential school—to a regular classroom.[21]

Some school districts and some teachers have responded to the need to develop more inclusive classrooms by having classes cotaught by a regular teacher and a special education teacher. When two teachers not only teach together but also take the time to get to know each other well, they can build on each other's strengths and can more than double the benefit to their students that either one alone might offer. Coteaching is far from the only effective way to serve the needs of today's widely diverse and, it is hoped, inclusive classrooms. But it is an important attempt to answer the question of what a teacher is to do in light of the diversity of today's students.[22]

Moving an increasing number of students with disabilities into regular, inclusive classrooms can save money, but some of the most effective means of developing these

Learning the Lingo: Special Education

- **ARD (admission, review, and dismissal) committee:** Committee responsible for making the educational decisions for a student. The parents, or adult students, are among the members of the ARD committee.

- **IEP:** Individual education plan written by the ARD committee; describes the specific, individualized services that a student will receive from special education. Once finalized, this plan becomes a legal contract between the school and the student and his or her parents.

- **Inclusion:** Classes with both regular education students and those with disabilities who qualify for substantially separate classes, with additional staff to provide in-class support for the students with disabilities.

- **Residential school:** Separate schools that enroll special needs children for 24 hours a day and are usually attended by those who cannot obtain services in their community.

- **Resource room:** In-school services for students with disabilities who are in a regular education class but need specific additional support. Students go to a resource room for varying amounts of time each week, depending on need.

- **Substantially separate:** Classes for students with disabilities who have a particular impairment. Typically, these students are with other students only for noninstructional activities such as lunch.

Source: "Escaping from Old Ideas: Educating Students with Disabilities in the Boston Public Schools," by Ellen C. Guiney, Mary Ann Cohen, and Erika Moldow, in *A Decade of Urban School Reform: Persistence and Progress in the Boston Public Schools*, ed. S. Paul Reville with Celine Coggins, 2007, Harvard Education Press.

Teachable Moment

Gifted Students

Although most of the discussion about students with special needs focuses on those who with a physical, mental, or emotional disability that makes learning (or at least some forms of learning) difficult for them, gifted students (those who learn more quickly and who seem to surge ahead of their peers) may also require special attention.

Researcher Jennifer Stepanek makes the argument for special programs for gifted students, saying that although it is certainly true that all students can learn, "some students learn more quickly and are capable of higher level work than their age peers. Gifted students need different content and instruction in order to meet their needs." Many teachers are well aware that some of their students "get" a particular lesson much more quickly than others and that sometimes the students who learn most quickly end up being bored and disengaged in school as they wait for their classmates to catch up.

On the other hand, critics of gifted programs contend that the label "gifted" can too easily be applied to students who simply receive more home-based education and that the programs can often become another means of separating the haves and the have-nots. Critics note that many advocates of gifted education often count their own children among the gifted.

Although giftedness was once defined by a student's IQ (a single measure of intelligence), researchers now have doubts about IQ tests or any single measure. Howard Gardner's work on a person's "multiple intelligences" leads us to believe that some students may well be gifted in some areas but average, or even below average, in others. Giftedness does not come in one shape or size, and few, if any, young people are gifted in all areas.

Stepanek offers alternatives to the standard debates about inclusion versus separate classes for gifted students. She argues that, for gifted students, there may be times, such as when students are working on open-ended problem-solving activities, when heterogeneous or mixed groups are best, while at other times,

as when students are working on skill development or reviewing prior work, they do best in homogeneous groups with students of similar abilities.

QUESTIONS

- What do you think of Stepanek's assertion that "some students learn more quickly and are capable of higher level work than their age peers" and thus need special programs? What are the implications of this view for the development of inclusive classrooms and inclusive schools?

- Does it make sense to you, as Stepanek asserts, that heterogeneous groupings work well in some situations and that students should be separated by knowledge or ability into different groups, even different classes, at other times? Would you rather teach a diverse group of students or a mostly homogeneous group? Which is easier for the teacher? Which is better for the students?

Source: "The Inclusive Classroom: Meeting the Needs of Gifted Students," by Jennifer Stepanek, ERIC document 444306, retrieved June 9, 2009, from http://www.eric.ed.gov.

Teachable Moment

What Is Inclusion?

BY SHAFIK ASANTE

In 1955, the story of a brave and tired woman named Rosa Parks was put in front of this country's awareness. They say this woman had gotten tired, in fact, historically tired, of being denied equality. She wanted to be included in society in a full way, something which was denied people labeled as "Black" people! So Rosa Parks sat down on a bus in a section reserved for "White" people. When Rosa was told to go to "her place" at the back of the bus, she refused to move, was arrested, and history was challenged and changed. All of this happened because Rosa Parks was tired, historically tired of being excluded. She had sat down and thereby stood up for inclusion!

Another powerful cry for "inclusion" is being heard today. This new cry is being raised by people with unrecognized abilities (the so-called "disabled"). Many people whose abilities are regularly denied or ignored feel that society is not honoring the right to participate in society in a full way. Part of the call is for better accessibility, such as more wheelchair ramps, more signs and materials in Braille, community living, etc. The Americans with Disabilities Act represents an attempt to hear the "inclusion" cry. However, much more needs to be done, including a search for an acceptable definition and practice of inclusion. Across this country, a definition of inclusion is offered. It is generally accepted that "Inclusion" means inviting those who have been historically locked out to "come in." This well-intentioned meaning must be strengthened. A weakness of this definition is evident. Who has the authority or right to "invite" others in? And how did the "inviters" get in? Finally, who is doing the excluding? It is time we both recognize and accept that we are all born "in"! No one has the right to invite others in! It definitely becomes our responsibility as a society to remove all barriers which uphold exclusion since none of us

have the authority to "invite" others "in"! So what is inclusion? Inclusion is recognizing our universal "oneness" and interdependence. Inclusion is recognizing that we are "one" even though we are not the "same". The act of inclusion means fighting against exclusion and all of the social diseases exclusion gives birth to—i.e. racism, sexism, handicapism, etc. Fighting for inclusion also involves assuring that all support systems are available to those who need such support. Providing and maintaining support systems is a civic responsibility, not a favor. We were all born "in." Society will immediately improve at the point we honor this truth!!

Source: Reprinted from *When Spider Webs Unite,* Shafik Asante, n.d., Inclusion Press, http://www.inclusion.com/inclusion.html.

QUESTIONS

- How were Rosa Parks's experiences with inclusion (and exclusion) similar to those faced by people with special needs?
- What does the author mean when he says "we are all born 'in'?"

classrooms (such as coteaching) can be expensive to implement. For many students, the inclusive classroom provides a much better setting for their education, including their social development, than would a segregated setting. Inclusive classrooms can, indeed, be the least restrictive environment. With the right support in place—which often includes a special education expert, well-prepared teachers, and thoughtful accommodation to the students' needs—inclusive classrooms can be wonderfully engaging academic and social communities. But inclusive classrooms also make significant demands on teachers and on schools. When inclusion is done badly, or on the cheap, as is too often the case, the result can be failure for students. This can happen if teachers are not prepared or if an effective team is replaced by one lone teacher who is expected to educate everyone and who may simply be overwhelmed by the range of demands.

Anyone considering a career in teaching needs to develop significant expertise in the field of special education, regardless of the grade level or subject that person plans to teach. The inclusive classroom is the norm today, and an increasing number of teachers work as part of a team to provide the best educational services possible to a group of students. It is a norm in which the students sitting in a classroom today reflect diversities of academic abilities, physical abilities, and mental and physical health that were previously excluded from schools.

None of the debates presented in this chapter are going to be resolved soon. And no one entering the field of education should dare to ignore any of them. A teacher has a deep moral responsibility to teach, as effectively as is humanly possible, whatever group of young people ends up in front of her or him. But a teacher also has a role to play in helping shape the policies by which students are assigned to individual classrooms and the expectations that every teacher and school will have for all children.

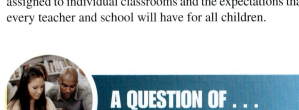

A QUESTION OF . . .

What was it like growing up with a disability?

"I grew up very 'mainstream.' I was one of the few disabled students—at least one of the few with a visible disability—in most of the schools I attended. I went to a huge high school in New York, and while there probably were other disabled students, I didn't see them or connect with them. I was very eager to not acknowledge my disability because there was such a stigma associated with it. So I was caught in a way—on the one hand I knew I was different and that I was going to have a different life than others, but on the other hand I was not eager to acknowledge such a stigmatized identity."[23]

—*Marilyn Rousso, President, Disabilities Unlimited Consulting Services* ■

REVIEW >>

- Who was traditionally left out of American schools?

  Prior to the 1960s and 1970s, school was not considered a necessity for everyone, as it is today. Girls, students who did not speak English, and students with various disabilities were often excluded from the full range of educational opportunities.

- What legal actions made school available for everyone?

  Fueled by the civil rights movement of the 1950s and 1960s, a number of key court cases and legislation opened to everyone the doors of education. The landmark Civil Rights Act of 1964 prohibited discrimination against students based on race, color, sex, or national origin. Title IX said that no one could be excluded, on the basis of his or her sex, from the benefits of any program in any school that received federal funds. The U.S. Supreme Court's decision in *Lau v. Nichols*, combined with the 1968 Bilingual Education Act, said that school districts could not ignore the needs of students who did not speak English. Finally, Section 503 of the Rehabilitation Act of 1973, followed by Public Law 94-142, the Education for All Handicapped Children Act, required that every child, in spite of any handicapping condition, receives a "free appropriate public education" designed specifically to meet his or her needs.

- What does it mean for schools to be gender fair?

  Some observers argue that, given the successes of the women's movement, education today should simply be blind to gender issues; others argue that gender-fair education means attend-

  ing quite specifically to the different learning styles and the different attitudes toward schooling and school success for boys and girls.

- What are the ongoing debates over bilingual education?

  Some people argue that, in today's world of expansive immigration, schools need programs of bilingual education that strengthen attachments to the home cultures and languages of the nation's diverse students while also engaging those students in successful mastery of English as a second language. Others argue, with equal commitment, that the only way to ensure the integration of all students into a common culture and a successful educational experience is to ensure that students arriving in U.S. schools are immersed in English as rapidly as possible.

- What is the best education for students with disabilities?

  Virtually no one would argue for a return to the "old days," when many students with physical, emotional, and mental "handicaps" were simply excluded from schools. But many observers today argue passionately that special education programs have grown too extensive, too bureaucratic, and too expensive. Others argue that the extensive and bureaucratic nature of the programs, linked with the financial investment in them, is the only guarantee that advances in services for special needs students will be preserved. In the case of special education, many educators also debate what sort of classroom environment most effectively serves students with different special needs.

What Does It Mean for Schools to Be Gender Fair?

From "WITH BOYS AND GIRLS IN MIND"

BY *MICHAEL GURIAN AND KATHY STEVENS*

The two articles that follow provide quite different perspectives on the issue of gender equity in the schools. Myra and David Sadker's groundbreaking 1994 book, *Failing at Fairness*, documented in great detail a reality that many educators knew well, even if others denied its existence—that schools traditionally treat boys and girls quite differently. Whether they believe boys simply need more attention, or because they know girls are more likely to be quiet and boys disruptive, or because they simply do not notice how they replicate the dominant culture, as Sadker and Sadker documented, teachers call on boys more than girls, spend more time attending to boys, and seem to favor boys in countless other ways. More recently, however, scholars and advocates have begun to argue that boys are the ones being short-changed in school today. For example, in January 2006, a *Newsweek* headline posed the following question: "The Boy Crisis. At every level of education, they're falling behind. What to do?"

In "With Boys and Girls in Mind," Michael Gurian and Kathy Stevens seek to document the reality that *Newsweek* was proclaiming, to give scientific reasons for it, and to provide important steps for educators who want to address "the boy crisis." However, in "The Truth about Boys and Girls," Sara Mead offers a biting critique of the work of Gurian and Stevens and others like them. She argues that "with few exceptions, American boys are scoring higher and achieving more than they ever have before. But girls have just improved their performance on some measures even faster." Mead insists that most evidence points to a narrowing of the academic gap between boys and girls rather than to a growing failure on the part of boys.

In addition to their value as different points of view in an ongoing debate, these articles provide a useful picture of the way scholars do their work and build on and argue with each other. Gurian and Stevens cite Sadker and Sadker's work and argue that it is time for another look at the issues. Mead in turn cites Gurian and Stevens' work and critiques their methodology as part of her argument that we should come to conclusions different from those advocated by Gurian and Stevens. Thus, these scholars keep up an ongoing dialogue and subject their own work, and that of their predecessors, to continuing review and improvement.

Something is awry in the way our culture handles the education needs of boys and girls. A smart 11-year-old boy gets low grades in school, fidgets and drifts off in class, and doesn't do his homework. A girl in middle school only uses the computer to instant-message her friends; when it comes to mastering more essential computer skills, she defers to the boys in the class.

Is contemporary education maliciously set against either males or females? We don't think so. But structurally and functionally, our schools fail to recognize and fulfill gender-specific needs. As one teacher wrote,

> For years I sensed that the girls and boys in my classrooms learn in gender-specific ways, but I didn't know enough to help each student reach full potential. I was trained in the idea that each student is an individual. But when I saw the PET scans of boys' and girls' brains, I saw how differently those brains are set up to learn. This gave me the missing component. I trained in male/female brain differences and was able to teach each individual child. Now, looking back, I'm amazed that teachers were never taught the differences between how girls and boys learn.

New positron emission tomography (PET) and MRI technologies enable us to look inside the brains of boys and girls, where we find structural and functional differences that profoundly affect human learning. These gender differences in the brain are corroborated in males and females throughout the world and do not differ significantly across cultures.

It's true that culture affects gender role, gender costume, and gender nuances—in Italy, for example, men cry more than they do in England—but role, costume, and nuance only affect some aspects of the learning brain of a child. New brain imaging technologies confirm that genetically templated brain patterning by gender plays a far larger role than we realized. Research into gender and education reveals a mismatch between many of our boys' and girls' learning brains and the institutions empowered to teach our children.

We will briefly explore some of the differences, because recognizing these differences can help us find solutions to many of the challenges that we experience in the classroom. Of course, generalized gender differences may not apply in every case.

The following are some of the characteristics of girls' brains:

- A girl's corpus callosum (the connecting bundle of tissues between hemispheres) is, on

Source: "With Boys and Girls in Mind," by Michael Gurian and Kathy Stevens, November 2004, *Educational Leadership, 62*, pp. 21–26.

average, larger than a boy's—up to 25 percent larger by adolescence. This enables more "cross talk" between hemispheres in the female brain.

- Girls have, in general, stronger neural connectors in their temporal lobes than boys have. These connectors lead to more sensually detailed memory storage, better listening skills, and better discrimination among the various tones of voice. This leads, among other things, to greater use of detail in writing assignments.
- The hippocampus (another memory storage area in the brain) is larger in girls than in boys, increasing girls' learning advantage, especially in the language arts.
- Girls' prefrontal cortex is generally more active than boys' and develops at earlier ages. For this reason, girls tend to make fewer impulsive decisions than boys do. Further, girls have more serotonin in the bloodstream and the brain, which makes them biochemically less impulsive.
- Girls generally use more cortical areas of their brains for verbal and emotive functioning. Boys tend to use more cortical areas of the brain for spatial and mechanical functioning (Moir & Jessel, 1989; Rich, 2000).

These "girl" brain qualities are the tip of the iceberg, yet they can immediately help teachers and parents understand why girls generally outperform boys in reading and writing from early childhood throughout life (Conlin, 2003). With more cortical areas devoted to verbal functioning, sensual memory, sitting still, listening, tonality, and mental cross talk, the complexities of reading and writing come easier, on the whole, to the female brain. In addition, the female brain experiences approximately 15 percent more blood flow, with this flow located in more centers of the brain at any given time (Marano, 2003). The female brain tends to drive itself toward stimulants—like reading and writing—that involve complex texture, tonality, and mental activity.

On the other hand, because so many cortical areas are used for verbal-emotive functioning, the female brain does not activate as many cortical areas as the male's does for abstract and physical-spatial functions, such as watching and manipulating objects that move through physical space and understanding abstract mechanical concepts (Moir & Jessel, 1989; Rich, 2000). This is one reason for many girls' discomfort with deep computer design language. Although some girls excel in these areas, more males than females gravitate toward physics, industrial engineering, and architecture. Children naturally gravitate toward activities that their brains experience as pleasurable—"pleasure" meaning in neural terms the richest personal stimulation. Girls and boys, within each neural web, tend to experience the richest personal stimulation somewhat differently.

The biological tendency toward female verbal-emotive functioning does not mean that girls or women should be left out of classes or careers that use spatial-mechan-ical skills. On the contrary: We raise these issues to call on our civilization to realize the differing natures of girls and boys and to teach each subject according to how the child's brain needs to learn it. On average, educators will need to provide girls with extra encouragement and gender-specific strategies to successfully engage them in spatial abstracts, including computer design.

What, then, are some of the qualities that are generally more characteristic of boys' brains?

Because boys' brains have more cortical areas dedicated to spatial-mechanical functioning, males use, on average, half the brain space that females use for verbal-emotive functioning. The cortical trend toward spatial-mechanical functioning makes many boys want to move objects through space, like balls, model airplanes, or just their arms and legs. Most boys, although not all of them, will experience words and feelings differently than girls do (Blum, 1997; Moir & Jessel, 1989).

Boys not only have less serotonin than girls have, but they also have less oxytocin, the primary human bonding chemical. This makes it more likely that they will be physically impulsive and less likely that they will neurally combat their natural impulsiveness to sit still and empathically chat with a friend (Moir & Jessel, 1989; Taylor, 2002).

Boys lateralize brain activity. Their brains not only operate with less blood flow than girls' brains, but they are also structured to compartmentalize learning. Thus, girls tend to multitask better than boys do, with fewer attention span problems and greater ability to make quick transitions between lessons (Havers, 1995).

The male brain is set to renew, recharge, and reorient itself by entering what neurologists call a rest state. The boy in the back of the classroom whose eyes are drifting toward sleep has entered a neural rest state. It is predominantly boys who drift off without completing assignments, who stop taking notes and fall asleep during a lecture, or who tap pencils or otherwise fidget in hopes of keeping themselves awake and learning. Females tend to recharge and reorient neural focus without rest states. Thus, a girl can be bored with a lesson, but she will nonetheless keep her eyes open, take notes, and perform relatively well. This is especially true when the teacher uses more words to teach a lesson instead of being spatial and diagrammatic. The more words a teacher uses, the more likely boys are to "zone out," or go into rest state. The male brain is better suited for symbols, abstractions, diagrams, pictures, and objects moving through space than for the monotony of words (Gurian, 2001).

These typical "boy" qualities in the brain help illustrate why boys generally learn higher math and physics more easily than most girls do when those subjects are taught abstractly on the chalkboard; why more boys than girls play video games that involve physical movement and even physical destruction; and why more boys than girls tend to get in trouble for impulsiveness, shows of boredom, and fidgeting as well as for their more generalized inability to listen, fulfill assignments, and learn in the verbal-emotive world of the contemporary classroom.

For a number of decades, most of our cultural sensitivity to issues of gender and learning came from advocacy groups that pointed out ways in which girls struggled in school. When David and Myra Sadker teamed with the American Association of University Women in the early 1990s, they found that girls were not called on as much as boys were, especially in middle school; that girls generally lagged in math/science testing; that boys dominated athletics; and that girls suffered drops in self-esteem as they entered middle and high school (AAUW, 1992). In large part because of this advocacy, our culture is attending to the issues that girls face in education.

At the same time, most teachers, parents, and other professionals involved in education know that it is mainly our boys who underperform in school. Since 1981, when the U.S. Department of Education began keeping complete statistics, we have seen that boys lag behind girls in most categories. The 2000 National Assessment of Educational Progress finds boys one and one-half years behind girls in reading/writing (National Center for Education Statistics, 2000). Girls are now only negligibly behind boys in math and science, areas in which boys have historically outperformed girls (Conlin, 2003).

Our boys are now losing frightening ground in school, and we must come to terms with it—not in a way that robs girls, but in a way that sustains our civilization and is as powerful as the lobby we have created to help girls. The following statistics for the United States illustrate these concerns:

- Boys earn 70 percent of Ds and Fs and fewer than half of the As.
- Boys account for two-thirds of learning disability diagnoses.
- Boys represent 90 percent of discipline referrals.
- Boys dominate such brain-related learning disorders as ADD/ADHD, with millions now medicated in schools.
- 80 percent of high school dropouts are male.
- Males make up fewer than 40 percent of college students (Gurian, 2001).

These statistics hold true around the world. The Organisation for Economic Co-operation and Development (OECD) recently released its three-year study of knowledge and skills of males and females in 35 industrialized countries (including the United States, Canada, the European countries, Australia, and Japan). Girls outperformed boys in every country. The

statistics that brought the male scores down most significantly were their reading/writing scores.

We have nearly closed the math/science gender gap in education for girls by using more verbal functioning—reading and written analysis—to teach such spatial-mechanical subjects as math, science, and computer science (Rubin, 2004; Sommers, 2000). We now need a new movement to alter classrooms to better suit boys' learning patterns if we are to deal with the gaps in grades, discipline, and reading/writing that threaten to close many boys out of college and out of success in life.

In 1996, the Gurian Institute, an organization that administers training in child development, education, and male/female brain differences, coined the phrase nature-based approach to call attention to the importance of basing human attachment and education strategies on research-driven biological understanding of human learning. We argued that to broadly base education and other social processes on anything other than human nature was to set up both girls and boys for unnecessary failure. The institute became especially interested in nature-based approaches to education when PET scans and MRIs of boys and girls revealed brains that were trying to learn similar lessons but in widely different ways and with varying success depending on the teaching method used. It became apparent that if teachers were trained in the differences in learning styles between boys and girls, they could profoundly improve education for all students.

Between 1998 and 2000, a pilot program at the University of Missouri—Kansas City involving gender training in six school districts elicited significant results. One school involved in the training, Edison Elementary, had previously tested at the bottom of 18 district elementary schools. Following gender training, it tested in the top five slots, sometimes coming in first or second. Statewide, Edison outscored schools in every subject area, sometimes doubling and tripling the number of students in top achievement levels. Instead of the usual large number of students at the bottom end of achievement testing, Edison now had only two students requiring state-mandated retesting. The school also experienced a drastic reduction in discipline problems.

Statewide training in Alabama has resulted in improved performance for boys in both academic and behavioral areas. Beaumont Middle School in Lexington, Kentucky, trains its teachers in male/female brain differences and teaches reading/writing, math, and science in separate-sex classrooms. After one year of this gender-specific experiment, girls' math and science scores and boys' Scholastic Reading Inventory (SRI) scores rose significantly.

Ultimately, teacher training in how the brain learns and how boys and girls tend to learn differently creates the will and intuition in teachers and schools to create nature-based classrooms (see "For Elementary Boys" and "For Elementary Girls" for strategies). In an elementary classroom designed to help boys learn, tables and chairs are arranged to provide ample space for each child to spread out and claim learning space. Boys tend to need more physical learning space than girls do. At a table, a boy's materials will be less organized and more widely dispersed. Best practice would suggest having a variety of seating options—some desks, some tables, an easy chair, and a rug area for sitting or lying on the floor. Such a classroom would allow for more movement and noise than a traditional classroom would. Even small amounts of movement can help some boys stay focused.

The teacher can use the blocks area to help boys expand their verbal skills. As the boys are building, a teacher might ask them to describe their buildings. Because of greater blood flow in the cerebellum—the "doing" center of the human brain—boys more easily verbalize what they are doing than what they are feeling. Their language will be richer in vocabulary and more expansive when they are engaged in a task.

An elementary classroom designed to help girls learn will provide lots of opportunities for girls to manipulate objects, build, design, and calculate, thus preparing them for the more rigorous spatial challenges that they will face in higher-level math and science courses. These classrooms will set up spatial lessons in groups that encourage discussion among learners. . . .

As educators, we've been somewhat intimidated in recent years by the complex nature of gender. Fortunately, we now have the PET and MRI technologies to view the brains of boys and girls. We now have the science to prove our intuition that tells us that boys and girls do indeed learn differently. And, even more powerful, we have a number of years of successful data that can help us effectively teach both boys and girls.

The task before us is to more deeply understand the gendered brains of our children. Then comes the practical application, with its sense of purpose and productivity, as we help each child learn from within his or her own mind.

For Elementary Boys

- Use beadwork and other manipulatives to promote fine motor development. Boys are behind girls in this area when they start school.
- Place books on shelves all around the room so boys get used to their omnipresence.
- Make lessons experiential and kinesthetic.
- Keep verbal instructions to no more than one minute.
- Personalize the student's desk, coat rack, and cubby to increase his sense of attachment.
- Use male mentors and role models, such as fathers, grandfathers, or other male volunteers.
- Let boys nurture one another through healthy aggression and direct empathy.

For Elementary Girls

- Play physical games to promote gross motor skills. Girls are behind boys in this area when they start school.
- Have portable/digital cameras around and take pictures of girls being successful at tasks.
- Use water and sand tables to promote science in a spatial venue.
- Use lots of puzzles to foster perceptual learning.
- Form working groups and teams to promote leadership roles and negotiation skills.
- Use manipulatives to teach math.
- Verbally encourage the hidden high energy of the quieter girls.

For a complete list of the references for this Reading, go to **www.mhhe.com/teach1e2010**.

From "THE TRUTH ABOUT BOYS AND GIRLS"

BY SARA MEAD

If you've been paying attention to the education news lately, you know that American boys are in crisis. After decades spent worrying about how schools "shortchange girls," the eyes of the nation's education commentariat are now fixed on how they shortchange boys. In 2006 alone, a *Newsweek* cover story, a major *New Republic* article, a long article in *Esquire*, a "Today" show segment, and numerous op-eds have informed the public that boys are falling behind girls in elementary and secondary school and are increasingly outnumbered on college campuses. A young man in Massachusetts filed a civil rights complaint with the U.S. Department of Education, arguing that his high school's homework and community service requirements discriminate against boys. A growth industry of experts is advising educators and policymakers how to make schools more "boy friendly" in an effort to reverse this slide.

It's a compelling story that seizes public attention with its "man bites dog" characteristics. It touches on Americans' deepest insecurities, ambivalences, and fears about changing gender roles and the "battle of the sexes." It troubles not only parents of boys, who fear their sons are falling behind, but also parents of girls, who fear boys' academic deficits will undermine their daughters' chances of finding suitable mates.

But the truth is far different from what these accounts suggest. The real story is not bad news about boys doing worse; it's good news about girls doing better.

In fact, with a few exceptions, American boys are scoring higher and achieving more than they ever have before. But girls have just improved their performance on some measures even faster. As a result, girls have narrowed or

Source: "The Truth About Boys and Girls," by Sara Mead, June 2006, *Education Sector*, www.educationsector.org.

even closed some academic gaps that previously favored boys, while other long-standing gaps that favored girls have widened, leading to the belief that boys are falling behind.

There's no doubt that some groups of boys—particularly Hispanic and black boys and boys from low-income homes—are in real trouble. But the predominant issues for them are race and class, not gender. Closing racial and economic gaps would help poor and minority boys more than closing gender gaps, and focusing on gender gaps may distract attention from the bigger problems facing these youngsters.

The hysteria about boys is partly a matter of perspective. While most of society has finally embraced the idea of equality for women, the idea that women might actually surpass men in some areas (even as they remain behind in others) seems hard for many people to swallow. Thus, boys are routinely characterized as "falling behind" even as they improve in absolute terms.

In addition, a dizzying array of so-called experts have seized on the boy crisis as a way to draw attention to their pet educational, cultural, or ideological issues. Some say that contemporary classrooms are too structured, suppressing boys' energetic natures and tendency to physical expression; others contend that boys need more structure and discipline in school. Some blame "misguided feminism" for boys' difficulties, while others argue that "myths" of masculinity have a crippling impact on boys.[1] Many of these theories have superficially plausible rationales that make them appealing to some parents, educators, and policymakers. But the evidence suggests that many of these ideas come up short.

Unfortunately, the current boy crisis hype and the debate around it are based more on hopes and fears than on evidence. This debate benefits neither boys nor girls, while distracting attention from more serious educational problems—such as large racial and economic achievement gaps—and practical ways to help both boys and girls succeed in school.

A New Crisis?

"The Boy Crisis. At every level of education, they're falling behind. What to do?"

—*Newsweek* cover headline, Jan. 30, 2006

Newsweek is not the only media outlet publishing stories that suggest boys' academic accomplishments and life opportunities are declining. But it's not true. Neither the facts reported in these articles nor data from other sources support the notion that boys' academic performance is falling. In fact, overall academic achievement and attainment for boys is higher than it has ever been. . . .

Reading

The most recent main NAEP assessment in reading, administered in 2005, does not support the notion that boys' academic achievement is falling. In fact, fourth-grade boys did better than they had done in both the previous NAEP reading assessment, administered in 2003, and the earliest comparable assessment, administered in 1992. Scores for both fourth- and eighth-grade boys have gone up and down over the past decade, but results suggest that the reading skills of fourth- and eighth-grade boys have improved since 1992.[2]

The picture is less clear for older boys. The 2003 and 2005 NAEP assessments included only fourth-and eighth-graders, so the most recent main NAEP data for 12th-graders dates back to 2002. On that assessment, 12th-grade boys did worse than they had in both the previous assessment, administered in 1998, and the first comparable assessment, administered in 1992. At the 12th-grade level, boys' achievement in reading does appear to have fallen during the 1990s and early 2000s.. . .[3]

Math

The picture for boys in math is less complicated. Boys of all ages and races are scoring as high—or higher—in math than ever before. From 1990 through 2005, boys in grades four and eight improved their performance steadily on the main NAEP, and they scored significantly better on the 2005 NAEP than in any previous year. Twelfth-graders have not taken the main NAEP in math since 2000. That year, 12th-grade boys did better than they had in 1990 and 1992, but worse than they had in 1996.[4]

Both 9- and 13-year-old boys improved gradually on the long-term NAEP since the 1980s (9-year-old boys' math performance did not improve in the 1970s). Seventeen-year-old boys' performance declined through the 1970s, rose in the 1980s, and remained relatively steady during the late 1990s and early 2000s.[5] As in reading, white boys score much better on the main NAEP in math than do black and Hispanic boys, but all three groups of boys are improving their math performance in the elementary and middle school grades.. . .[6]

Overall Long-Term Trends

A consistent trend emerges across these subjects: There have been no dramatic changes in the performance of boys in recent years, no evidence to indicate a boy crisis. Elementary-school-aged boys are improving their performance; middle school boys are either improving their performance or showing little change, depending on the subject; and high school boys' achievement is declining in most subjects (although it may be improving in math). These trends seem to be consistent across all racial subgroups of boys, despite the fact that white boys perform much better on these tests than do black and Hispanic boys.

Evidence of a decline in the performance of older boys is undoubtedly troubling. But the question to address is whether this is a problem for older boys or for older students generally. That can be best answered by looking at the flip side of the gender equation: achievement for girls. . . .

The Difference Between Boys and Girls

To the extent that tales of declining boy performance are grounded in real data, they're usually framed as a decline relative to girls. That's because, as described above, boy performance is generally staying the same or increasing in absolute terms.

But even relative to girls, the NAEP data for boys paints a complex picture. On the one hand, girls outperform boys in reading at all three grade levels assessed on the main NAEP. Gaps between girls and boys are smaller in fourth grade and get larger in eighth and 12th grades. Girls also outperform boys in writing at all grade levels.

In math, boys outperform girls at all grade levels, but only by a very small amount. Boys also outperform girls—again, very slightly—in science and by a slightly larger margin in geography. There are no significant gaps between male and female achievement on the NAEP in U.S. history. In general, girls outperform boys in reading and writing by greater margins than boys outperform girls in math, science, and geography.

But this is nothing new. Girls have scored better than boys in reading for as long as the long-term NAEP has been administered. And younger boys are actually catching up: The gap between boys and girls at age 9 has narrowed significantly since 1971—from 13 points to five points—even as both genders have significantly improved. Boy-girl gaps at age 13 haven't changed much since 1971—and neither has boys' or girls' achievement.

At age 17, gaps between boys and girls in reading are also not that much different from what they were in 1971, but they are significantly bigger than they were in the late 1980s, before achievement for both genders—and particularly boys—began to decline.

The picture in math is even murkier. On the first long-term NAEP assessment in 1973, 9- and 13- year-old girls actually scored better than boys in math, and they continued to do so throughout the 1970s. But as 9- and 13-year-olds of both genders improved their achievement in math during the 1980s and 1990s, boys *pulled ahead* of girls, opening up a small gender gap in math achievement that now favors boys. It's telling that even though younger boys are now doing better than girls on the long-term NAEP in math, when they once lagged behind, no one is talking about the emergence of a new "girl crisis" in elementary- and middle-school math.

Seventeen-year-old boys have always scored better than girls on the long-term NAEP in math, but boys' scores declined slightly more than girls' scores in the 1970s, and girls' scores have risen slightly more than those of boys since. As a result, older boys' advantage over girls in math has narrowed.

Overall, there has been no radical or recent decline in boys' performance relative to girls. Nor is there a clear overall trend—boys score higher in some areas, girls in others. . . .

The fact that achievement for older students is stagnant or declining for both boys and girls, to about the same degree, points to another important element of the boy crisis. The problem is most likely not that high schools need to be fixed to meet the needs of boys, but rather that they need to be fixed to meet the needs of *all* students, male and female. The need to accurately parse the influence of gender and other student categories is also acutely apparent when we examine the issues of race and income.

We Should Be Worried About Some Subgroups of Boys

There are groups of boys for whom "crisis" is not too strong a term. When racial and economic gaps combine with gender achievement gaps in reading, the result is disturbingly low achievement for poor, black, and Hispanic boys.

But the gaps between students of different races and classes are much larger than those for students of different genders—anywhere from two to five times as big, depending on the grade. The only exception is among 12th-grade boys, where the achievement gap between white girls and white boys in reading is the same size as the gap between white and black boys in reading and is larger than the gap between white and Hispanic boys. Overall, though, poor, black, and Hispanic boys would benefit far more from closing racial and economic achievement gaps than they would from closing gender gaps. While the gender gap picture is mixed, the racial gap picture is, unfortunately, clear across a wide range of academic subjects.

In addition to disadvantaged and minority boys, there are also reasons to be concerned about the substantial percentage of boys who have been diagnosed with disabilities. Boys make up two-thirds of students in special education—including 80 percent of those diagnosed with emotional disturbances or autism—and boys are two and a half times as likely as girls to be diagnosed with attention deficit hyperactivity disorder (ADHD).[7] The number of boys diagnosed with disabilities or ADHD has exploded in the past 30 years, presenting a challenge for schools and causing concern for parents. But the reasons for this growth are complicated, a mix of educational, social, and biological factors. Evidence suggests that school and family factors—such as poor reading instruction, increased awareness of and testing for disabilities, or over-diagnosis—may play a role in the increased rates of boys diagnosed with learning disabilities or emotional disturbance. But boys also have a higher incidence of organic disabilities, such as autism and orthopedic impairments, for which scientists don't currently have a completely satisfactory explanation. Further, while girls are less likely than boys to be diagnosed with most disabilities, the number of girls with disabilities has also grown rapidly in recent decades, meaning that this is not just a boy issue.

TABLE 1. Four-Year High School Graduation Rates by Race and Gender

	Male	Female
Asian	70%	73%
White	74%	79%
Hispanic	49%	58%
Black	48%	59%

Source: Jay P. Greene and Marcus Winters, *Leaving Boys Behind: Public High School Graduation Rates*, Manhattan Institute Civic Report No. 48, April 2006, http://www.manhattan-institute.org/html/cr_48.htm#05.

Moving Up and Moving On

Beyond achievement, there's the issue of attainment—student success in moving forward along the education pathway and ultimately earning credentials and degrees. There are undeniably some troubling numbers for boys in this area.

Boys are also more likely than girls to drop out of high school. Research by the Manhattan Institute found that only about 65 percent of boys who start high school graduate four years later, compared with 72 percent of girls. This gender gap cuts across all racial and ethnic groups, but it is the smallest for white and Asian students and much larger for black and Hispanic students. Still, the gaps between graduation rates for white and black or Hispanic students are much greater than gaps between rates for boys and girls of any race.[8] These statistics, particularly those for black and Hispanic males, are deeply troubling. There is some good news, though, because both men and women are slightly more likely to graduate from high school today than they were 30 years ago.[9]

The Source of the Boy Crisis: A Knowledge Deficit and a Surplus of Opportunism

It's clear that some gender differences in education are real, and there are some groups of disadvantaged boys in desperate need of help. But it's also clear that boys' overall educational achievement and attainment are not in decline—in fact, they have never been better. What accounts for the recent hysteria?

It's partly an issue of simple novelty. The contours of disadvantage in education and society at large have been clear for a long time—low-income, minority, and female people consistently fall short of their affluent, white, and male peers. The idea that historically privileged boys could be at risk, that boys could be shortchanged, has simply proved too deliciously counterintuitive and "newsworthy" for newspaper and magazine editors to resist.

The so-called boy crisis also feeds on a lack of solid information. Although there are a host of statistics about how boys and girls perform in school, we actually know very little about why these differences exist or how important they are. There are many things—including biological, developmental, cultural, and educational factors—that affect how boys and girls do in school. But untangling these

different influences is incredibly difficult. Research on the causes of gender differences is hobbled by the twin demons of educational research: lack of data and the difficulty of drawing causal connections among multiple, complex influences. Nor do we know what these differences mean for boys' and girls' future economic and other opportunities.

Yet this hasn't stopped a plethora of so-called experts—from pediatricians and philosophers to researchers and op-ed columnists—from weighing in with their views on the causes and likely effects of educational gender gaps. In fact, the lack of solid research evidence confirming or debunking any particular hypothesis has created fertile ground for all sorts of people to seize on the boy crisis to draw attention to their pet educational, cultural or ideological issues.

The problem, we are told, is that the structured traditional classroom doesn't accommodate boys' energetic nature and need for free motion—or it's that today's schools don't provide enough structure or discipline. It's that feminists have demonized typical boy behavior and focused educational resources on girls—or it's the "box" boys are placed in by our patriarchal society. It's that our schools' focus on collaborative learning fails to stimulate boys' natural competitiveness—or it's that the competitive pressures of standardized testing are pushing out the kind of relevant, hands-on work on which boys thrive.

The boy crisis offers a perfect opportunity for those seeking an excuse to advance ideological and educational agendas. Americans' continued ambivalence about evolving gender roles guarantees that stories of "boys in crisis" will capture public attention. The research base is internally contradictory, making it easy to find superficial support for a wide variety of explanations but difficult for the media and the public to evaluate the quality of evidence cited. Yet there is not sufficient evidence—or the right kind of evidence—available to draw firm conclusions. As a result, there is a sort of free market for theories about why boys are underperforming girls in school, with parents, educators, media, and the public choosing to give credence to the explanations that are the best marketed and that most appeal to their pre-existing preferences.

Unfortunately, this dynamic is not conducive to a thoughtful public debate about how boys and girls are doing in school or how to improve their performance. . . .

Dubious Theories and Old Agendas

Misapplying Brain Research to Education

"Girls have, in general, stronger neural connectors in their temporal lobes than boys have. These connectors lead to more sensually detailed memory storage, better listening skills, and better discrimination among the various tones of voice. This leads, among other things, to greater use of detail in writing assignments."

—Michael Gurian and Kathy Stevens, *Educational Leadership*, November 2004

This paragraph offers a classic example of how some practitioners misapply brain research to education and gender. For starters, "neural connectors" is not a scientific term—by the time the research evidence behind this claim gets to readers of this article, it is dramatically watered down and redigested from what the initial studies said.

But the real problem here is that Gurian and Stevens attempt to string together a series of cause-and-effect relationships for which no evidence exists. Yes, there is some evidence of greater interconnection between different parts of women's brains. Yes, some studies have found that women remember an array of objects better than men do and that they are better at hearing certain tones than men are. (It's also worth noting that most of these studies were conducted not with children but with adults). And some teachers may say that boys do not use detail in writing assignments. But there is no evidence causally linking any one of these things to another. Gurian and Stevens simply pick up two factoids and claim they must be related. They also ignore many other potential explanations for the behavior they describe, such as the possibility that boys use less detail because they are in a greater hurry than girls, or that they tend to read books that have less detailed description and therefore use less in their own writing.

It would be unfair to imply that these authors write about boys for purely self-serving motives—most of these men and women seem to be sincerely concerned about the welfare of our nation's boys. But the work in this field leaves one skeptical of the quality of research, information, and analysis that are shaping educators' and parents' beliefs and practices as they educate boys and girls. Perhaps most tellingly, ideas about how to make schools more "boy friendly" align suspiciously well with educational and ideological beliefs the individuals promoting them had long before boys were making national headlines. And some of these prescriptions are diametrically opposed to one another.

In other words, few of these commentators have anything new to say—the boy crisis has just given them a new opportunity to promote their old messages. . . .

For a complete list of the references for this Reading, go to www.mhhe.com/teach1e2010.

QUESTIONS

1. How could different groups of scholars disagree so completely when all claim that their work is based on solid research?

2. Think about schools where you have observed most recently. Can you find evidence that supports the arguments made in any or all of these articles? Think again, remembering the warning about the blinders most of us wear regarding these matters.

3. What do you think of the ways each article cites and then criticizes the previous one? To what degree have schools changed in the past decade, and to what degree do these authors simply reflect different philosophies?

What Are the Ongoing Debates over Bilingual Education?

From "ALL LANGUAGES WELCOMED HERE"

BY ORHAN AGIRDAG

The following two articles appeared in the same issue of *Educational Leadership* in April 2009. They certainly do not represent either end of the spectrum of opinions held within the bilingual education debate, in which some people argue strongly for equal emphasis on maintaining a student's first language while helping that student learn English and others focus almost exclusively on helping a student learn English as quickly as possible. Nevertheless a careful reading of the two articles points to important differences—hinted at in the titles—between the two articles.

This article by Orhan Agirdag (Ghent University in Belgium) reflects both his work among the many different linguistic groups of Europe and his analysis of the situation in the United States.

Have you ever received an unexpected phone call from a teacher who was deeply worried about the achievement of his language learners? Did you ever meet a principal who was desperately exploring ways to improve the relationship between her school and the parents of her language learners?

Indeed, not only in the United States, but also in various places around the world, educators are challenged by the difficulties of schooling language learners. One proposed solution has been bilingual instruction. Although a substantial body of research suggests that bilingual instruction is beneficial for language learners (Baker, 1996), other studies dispute these positive effects (Rossell, 2004). Even if we were certain about the purported benefits of this approach, schools often have difficulty implementing it.

For instance, it would not be feasible to provide bilingual instruction at a highly heterogeneous school in which students come from a great many linguistic backgrounds. With growing immigrant populations, this picture of linguistic diversity is becoming increasingly familiar to many educators. Schools can more easily implement bilingual instruction in relatively homogenous areas, such as the southwest region of the United States where large numbers of Spanish speakers live and where instruction in English and Spanish is feasible. It is less clear, however,

Source: "All Languages Welcomed Here," by Orhan Agirdag, April 2009, *Educational Leadership, 66*, pp. 20–25.

how to provide bilingual instruction in places where students speak dozens of languages.

Legal constraints can also hinder the implementation of bilingual education. In some countries (such as Turkey), the law only permits instruction in the official language. Other countries (such as Belgium) only allow bilingual instruction for language learners as an educational experiment. In addition, more and more countries are reducing the amount of existing bilingual instruction (Skutnabb-Kangas, 2000). For example, in 2004, the Netherlands stopped subsidizing almost all forms of bilingual instruction, which reduced the existing bilingual education to a few, mostly privately funded, programs.

Language Learning in Flanders

I conducted my study on the schooling of language learners in Flanders, which is located in the northern part of Belgium and has Dutch as its official language. After World War II, Flanders rapidly developed into a multicultural society, with a high number of immigrants coming from southern Europe, Turkey, and Morocco. Immigrant pupils, therefore, are often speakers of Turkish and Arabic, although their linguistic competence in Dutch is usually high. Nevertheless, one rarely uses the term *bilingual* in Dutch to refer to immigrants' linguistic backgrounds. Instead, the common expression is *linguistically different (anderstaligen)* or *linguistically deficient (taalachterstand)*.

To date, the educational achievements of second- and third-generation immigrants remain far behind those of their Dutch peers (Sierens, 2006). In fact, the educational inequality between immigrants and natives in Flanders is one of the highest among all countries in the Organization for Economic Cooperation and Development (OECD, 2006). Although such factors as differences in socioeconomic status and tracking in school can explain this inequality, immigrants' linguistic backgrounds are still perceived to be the main source of their learning difficulties.

There is no bilingual instruction in Belgium, even in the two official languages—Dutch and French (Manco & Crutzen, 1999). The overwhelming social pressure for Dutch monolingualism has also hindered the few experiments in bilingual Dutch/Turkish education. This focus on linguistic assimilation may be related to a far-right-wing presence in Flemish politics. The linguistic assimilation of immigrant children has become, according to the Flemish minister for education, the top priority of the equal opportunities policy in education (Blommaert & Van Avermaet, 2008).

Language and Identity

Even in the absence of bilingual instruction, language learners should have the right to feel at home in school. Cultural discontinuity between students' home-based and school-based experiences can have a negative effect on their academic performance, well-being, and sense of belonging at school. The larger the gap between these two experiences, the greater the disadvantage of cultural discontinuity (Gay, 2000).

When students have to leave their primary language at the school gates, they also leave a part of their cultural identity behind. As Cummins (2001) noted, "To reject a child's language in the school is to reject the child" (p. 19). Therefore, educators must try to close the gap between language learners' identities, which are intricately tied to language, and the school culture.

Teachers and administrators often express willingness to create a supportive learning environment for all students. However, they do not always command the tools necessary to realize such an environment. The literature about multilingual school settings is often of little help because the subject is highly complex and the arguments are more politicized than practical (Gersten, 1999). For many educators, the question of what they can realistically do remains unanswered.

To move toward a supportive school setting for all students, educators can create a linguistically plural learning environment, even without bilingual instruction. Plurilingualism in school—that is, making all students' languages visible and valuable—is advantageous for various reasons. The presence of students' home languages in school not only affirms language learners' identities, but also reduces linguistic barriers, opening doors for educators to build improved relationships with the learners' families and communities.

The recommendations that follow are based on my research in Belgium, but they are meaningful for educators in other countries as well. For this reason, I use the term *language learners* instead of *English language learners*.

Three Practices to Avoid

Insisting on a Monolingual Classroom

First, educators should strive to avoid *ethnocentric monolingualism*, that is, expressions of the superiority of one group's language over another (see Sue & Sue, 2008). Ethnocentric monolingualism is harmful, not only because it stigmatizes language learners, but also because it fails to recognize the value of various linguistic backgrounds.

One obvious expression of ethnocentric monolingualism is forbidding students to use their native language in school. In many schools, teachers may even formally punish students when they "catch them" speaking their home language with peers. School staff members and teachers may tend to use punitive practices because they often believe that speaking the home language slows the process of language learning, assuming it is in *competition* with the language that students are supposed to learn.

However, sociolinguistic research has found quite the reverse. Repeatedly, studies have shown that proficiency in the first language is positively related to proficiency in the second language (Cummins, 2000), suggesting that students' proficiency in their native language accelerates language learning. By extension, excluding students' home languages from the classroom does not assist them; rather, it may actually hinder their learning process.

Banning Home Languages Outside School

Another form of monolingual ethnocentrism is advising language learners to speak only in the majority school language outside school, such as at home with their parents and siblings. Educators may be unaware of the advantages that come with maintaining one's primary language. For example, speaking the native language provides students with better access to family and community networks, which function as social capital. Various studies have shown that family and community resources assist the educational progress of language learners (Portes & Rumbaut, 2001).

Restricting Praise to Second-Language Proficiency

Although it is crucial that language learners receive feedback as they make progress, educators should avoid praising only the students' new linguistic skills. Language learners might also be excellent musicians, outstanding athletes, or accomplished speakers of their home languages. If we want to promote their schooling, we should avoid reducing students to the sole status of language learners.

Five Practices to Adopt

The key element to promoting plurilingualism is to acknowledge and value language learners' linguistic backgrounds in close cooperation with both students and their parents.

Welcome Languages in the Classroom

Teachers should create an instructional climate that makes room for all students' languages. They can do this in different ways, such as by hanging posters on the wall that list significant words (such as *welcome*) in different languages.

Teachers can also reinforce plurilingualism in managing students' classroom behavior. For example, during my research I met a teacher who complained about the disruptive behavior of a Turkish-Belgian student in her class. Neither discipline nor praise seemed to improve his conduct. One day when I was observing in the classroom, I asked the boy, in Turkish, to be less noisy and to settle down and pay attention. This worked. Teachers can promote plurilingualism—and benefit, perhaps, from higher levels of student engagement—by learning a couple of key phrases, such as "Please quiet down" and "Nice job!" in languages that are commonly found in their classrooms.

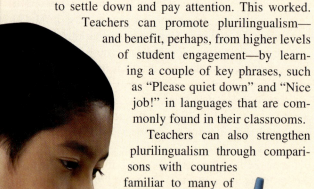

Teachers can also strengthen plurilingualism through comparisons with countries familiar to many of their immigrant students. For example, in geography, the teacher might compare the rather complicated linguistic situation of Belgium with that of Morocco, where Arabic and Berber are widely spoken.

Ask Students to Share Their Languages

Teachers should encourage students to bring their home languages into the classroom. For example, every day the teacher could ask a different student to share a significant word or sentence in his or her native language with the entire class. Both classmates and teacher could discuss this word or sentence: How does the student pronounce the word and what does he or she think about it? Afterwards, educators will notice that words like *friend* will have an effect on students' interactions beyond the classroom.

For example, at one of the schools in which I was doing research, I overheard Turkish-Belgian, Moroccan-Belgian, and Dutch pupils calling one another *kardas* on the school playground. *Kardas* is Turkish for *brother* or *friend*; it is often used to refer to friendly relationships with non-Turks. Now it has become a significant marker of interethnic friendship among pupils.

Have Students Help Their Peers

Teachers should encourage language learners from the same linguistic backgrounds to cooperate with one another to improve their progress. For instance, when a concept is unclear for a language learner, the teacher might call on another student from the same linguistic background to explain it. This is especially helpful when it comes to abstract concepts in math, such as *multiplication* or *mean*. After all, students often learn better from their peers than they do from their teacher.

Expand the School's Cultural Repertoire

School administrations should make the cultural repertoire of the school more plurilingual. Schools can easily do this by exposing students to subtitled movies, expanding the school's library of bilingual books and books written in different languages, providing materials in students' languages through the Internet, and helping students learn various songs in different languages.

One school in Antwerp reaches out to immigrant families by providing a welcoming message on the school Web site in 12 different languages. The message explains the school's system of communicating with parents using pictograms, which signal upcoming field trips, whether payment is required, and what their child should bring. The pictograms also indicate to parents when they are expected at school and for what reason.

Involve Parents

To realize an effective plurilingual learning environment, schools must involve students' parents. For example, teachers can call on parents to teach some aspects of their language to the whole class, including the teacher. In a French primary school, parents from more than eight different linguistic backgrounds taught students how to introduce themselves, count to 10, greet people, and say thank you in their languages (Helot & Young, 2002).

School-parent cooperation is crucial. Parental involvement in language learners' education often lags because of linguistic barriers. But when schools consider home languages not as obstacles but as assets, the "language wall" around the school breaks down.

A Word of Advice for Supporters

Supporters of plurilingualism tend to focus solely on policymakers and school administrators as they make arguments for plurilingual schools. The underlying assumption is that if they can convince policymakers and administrators to create a linguistically plural environment, language learners and their parents will welcome it with open arms. My research suggests that this may not be entirely true.

Language learners, their parents, and their teachers are not always passionate supporters of plurilingualism. The benefits of this approach are not always obvious to them, given that the broader society is often oriented toward monolingualism. Students may question why they should learn how to say *friend* in Arabic, for example, when they want to learn English instead. And parents may wonder why schools are presenting their children with languages other than the majority language.

Therefore, supporters of linguistic pluralism should clearly communicate why a linguistically diversified environment is preferable, because when language learners and parents are not convinced of the benefits of linguistic pluralism, their support for such projects will be weak. As a result, excellent projects on paper may fail dramatically in practice.

Learners and their parents should be aware of the benefits of plurilingualism—that it can close the gap between pupils' cultural identities and the school culture, reduce linguistic barriers, improve the school's relationship with parents and community members, and affirm rather than stigmatize language learners. Parent-teacher conferences and organizations, open houses, school newsletters, and Web sites are excellent channels for communicating this information.

Teachers should also understand these benefits because they often have to implement a heavy curriculum and, rightly, do not wish to devote time to something that may be of little help. Advocates of plurilingualism should clarify that a linguistically plural learning environment is not just based on a need for political correctness, but is rather a practice that actually facilitates language learning.

For a complete list of the references for this Reading, go to **www.mhhe.com/teach1e2010**.

From "THE CASE FOR STRUCTURED ENGLISH IMMERSION"

BY KEVIN CLARK

Kevin Clark is president of Clark Consulting and Training, which is based in California. He has worked with school districts to design programs for English language learners (ELLs) for 20 years.

When Arizona voters passed a ballot initiative in 2000 that required all English language learners to be educated through structured English immersion (SEI), the idea seemed simple enough: Teach students the English language quickly so they can do better in school. But as other states, districts, and schools that have contemplated an SEI program have learned, the devil is in the details. As it turns out, the simple goal to "teach English quickly" frequently evokes legal wrangling, emotion, and plain old demagoguery.

Few people would disagree that English language proficiency is necessary for academic success in U.S. schools. Less clear, however, is the optimal pathway for helping language-minority students master English. Conflicting ideologies, competing academic theories, and multiple metrics for comparing different approaches have rendered many schools, districts, and educators paralyzed by confusion. Bill Holden, principal of a California elementary school in which ELLs are three-fourths of the student population, told me, "At a certain point there were just so many mixed messages and contradictory directives and policies that we didn't really know what to do."

Despite the controversy, however, many schools in Arizona and other states have implemented structured English immersion or are in the process of doing so. As I have

worked with educators, school boards, and the Arizona English Language Learners Task Force to explore, design, and implement structured programs, a common theme emerges: These programs have the potential to accelerate ELLs' English language development and linguistic preparation for grade-level academic content.

Why Do Schools Implement Structured English Immersion?

Several factors usually account for school and district leaders' decisions to opt for structured English immersion. In three states (California, Arizona, and Massachusetts), the reason is straightforward: Laws passed through voter initiatives now require structured English immersion and restrict bilingual education.

Another factor is that most state student performance assessments are conducted in English, and schools or districts that miss targets face increased scrutiny and possible sanctions. This provides added incentive for schools to get students' English proficiency up to speed as soon as possible.

A third factor is the burgeoning subpopulation of ELL students who reach an intermediate level of English competence after a few years—and then stop making progress.

Source: "The Case for Structured English Immersion," by Kevin Clark, April 2009, *Educational Leadership, 66*, pp. 42–46.

These students (more than 60 percent of all ELLs in some districts, according to analyses I conducted for 15 districts) possess conversational English competence. But they lag in their ability to apply the rules, structures, and specialized vocabularies of English necessary for grade-level academic coursework; and their writing typically features an array of structural errors. My analyses showed that the typical intermediate-level ELL scores well below proficient on state-level tests in English language arts.

Some educators have acknowledged, in fact, that intermediate English competence is the logical outcome of their current practices and program designs. "Once we really analyzed our program for ELL students," one district superintendent told me, "we saw that we really didn't teach English to our students. We were teaching *in* English, but not really teaching English."

Confusion About Structured English Immersion

Keith Baker and Adriana de Kanter (1983) first coined the term *structured English immersion* (SEI) in a recommendation to schools to teach English to non-native speakers by using program characteristics from the successful French immersion programs in Canada. In 1991, J. David Ramirez and his colleagues conducted a voluminous study of ELL instructional programs and found that SEI programs shared two basic components: (1) teachers maximize instruction in English and (2) teachers use and teach English at a level appropriate to the abilities of the ELLs in the class (Ramirez, Yuen, & Ramey, 1991).

Since then, many people have taken a crack at defining structured English immersion. The definition presented to voters in Massachusetts was similar to those used in election materials in California and Arizona: "Nearly all classroom instruction is in English but with the curriculum and presentation designed for children who are learning the language" (Massachusetts Department of Education, 2003, p. 7).

But when Arizona's English Language Learner Task Force began meeting in late 2006, it found that few people seemed to know what SEI should look like. Many teachers, academics, and school administrators who testified before the task force had a negative view of the state-mandated approach. Presenters frequently confused SEI with *submersion*, the process of placing ELLs in regular classrooms that feature little or no instructional modifications and minimal instruction in the actual mechanics of English. Others viewed SEI as synonymous with specially designed academic instruc-

tion in English (SDAIE), also known as *sheltered* instruction, which features an array of strategies designed to help students of intermediate or higher proficiency access grade-level subject matter (Aha!, 2007).

Experience Fills in the Details

Notwithstanding the hodgepodge of definitions, mixed messages, and underlying emotions, educators have implemented structured English immersion programs at both the elementary and secondary levels. A framework for effective SEI is emerging that includes the following elements.

Significant amounts of the school day are dedicated to the explicit teaching of the English language, and students are grouped for this instruction according to their level of English proficiency. In Arizona, all ELLs must receive four hours of daily English language development. Other states and districts also provide large amounts of explicit instruction in English. For example, in Massachusetts, students at the lowest levels of English competence receive a minimum of two and one-half hours of daily English language development.

Grouping students for English-language instruction according to their English language ability is an important component of SEI because it enables teachers to effectively design language lessons. True beginners, for example, can benefit greatly from a direct lesson on common nouns, whereas intermediate students need to understand how subordinating conjunctions are used in academic writing.

The English language is the main content of SEI instruction. Academic content plays a supporting, but subordinate, role. The dominant focus is language itself: its rules, uses, forms, and application to daily school and nonschool situations and topics. The operant principle is that students must have a strong understanding of the English language before they can be expected to learn grade-level content.

Massachusetts, for example, tightly defines English language development instruction as "explicit, direct instruction about the English language intended to promote English language acquisition by LEP students and to help them 'catch up' to their student peers who are proficient in English" (Massachusetts Department of Education, 2006, p. 2).

Martin Ramirez, principal of a Yuba City, California, high school that has gained national attention for its SEI program, puts the language-content issue this way:

> We are charged with giving our ELLs a rigorous core content curriculum that is comparable to their English-speaking peers. But just putting them in a science course does not make it a rigorous curriculum. They will get access when they possess the language skills to be able to understand the content, and that is the role of our SEI program.

English is the language of instruction; students and teachers are expected to speak, read, and write in English. Accelerated language programs like SEI are based, in part, on the *comprehensible output* theory (Swain, 1985). This means that we cannot expect students to advance their language competence mainly through oral comprehension; instead, students get more proficient in English when they actually try to pro-

duce increasingly complex English language sentences. All materials and instruction in SEI programs are in English. For this reason, teachers and instructional support staff are not required to be able to speak a language other than English.

Although controversial, the limit on use of students' home languages keeps the goal of SEI programs clear. One administrator in an Idaho district summarized the rationale: "Unfortunately, our ELD classrooms in the past sometimes featured as much Spanish as English. It was just sending a very confusing message to students and staff."

Teachers use instructional methods that treat English as a foreign language. Structured English immersion programs reject the notion that teaching *in* English is the same as *teaching* English and that complex language skills can be learned through osmosis. SEI's foreign-language orientation calls for active, direct, and explicit instructional methods. Students have abundant opportunities to learn and produce new and more complex English language structures.

Students learn discrete English grammar skills. In SEI classrooms, teachers try to accelerate students' natural tendency to acquire language by providing grammatically focused lessons that raise students' conscious awareness of how English works while engaging them in relevant, age-appropriate learning tasks. Students are overtly taught English pronunciation and listening skills; word building; word-order rules; a wide range of vocabulary (synonyms, antonyms, survival vocabulary, academic word groups); and formulaic expressions not easily explained by grammar analysis ("There you go again"; "What's up with that?"). The overt teaching of verb tenses—almost nonexistent in most traditional public school English language development programs—is typically the anchor of many of these programs, accounting for up to one-fourth of the total instructional time.

Rigorous time lines are established for students to exit from the program. English language learners have little time to waste. While they are learning English, their English-proficient classmates continue to move ahead. For that reason, most SEI programs are designed to last one academic year. An SEI graduate should possess a foundational understanding of the mechanics, structure, and vocabulary of English that enables him or her to meaningfully access core content.

These SEI program graduates, however, are not finished learning English. Indeed, until students are reclassified as *fluent English proficient*, they are entitled to support services. In Yuba City, for example, when students exit the SEI program, they are enrolled in a mixture of sheltered and mainstream courses, including one period of advanced English language development. Federal law requires that students who have been reclassified be monitored for a two-year period.

Charting New Territory

Each of these program elements in some way runs counter to the assumptions and beliefs that have guided ELL program development throughout the last 30 years. In Arizona and elsewhere, advocates of structured English immersion face strong criticism from detractors who argue, among other things, that these programs are segregatory, experi-

mental, not based on research, nonculturally affirming, damaging to students' self-esteem, and perhaps even illegal (Adams, 2005; Combs, Evans, Fletcher, Parra, & Jiménez, 2005; Krashen, Rolstad, & MacSwan, 2007).

Proponents of SEI maintain that students can learn English faster than many theories suggest, that grouping students by language ability level is necessary for successful lesson design, and that the research support for immersion language-teaching methods and program design principles is solid (Arizona English Language Learners Task Force, 2007; Baker, 1998; Judson & Garcia-Dugan, 2004). As for the question of self-esteem, SEI advocates point out that ELLs are motivated by measurable success in learning the fundamentals of English, as well as by the improved reading comprehension, enhanced writing skills, and higher levels of achievement in core subjects that come from these enhanced language skills.

On the legal front, ballot initiatives requiring SEI programs have been found to comport with federal law. Under the federal framework, as articulated in *Castañeda v. Pickard* (1981), immersion programs are viewed as "sequential," in that their goal is to provide foundational English skills before students participate in a full range of academic content courses.

SEI Programs in Action

George Washington Elementary School in Madera, California, enrolls more than 500 English language learners in grades K–6. Located in the middle of a Spanish-dominant portion of a town in central California, the school was a magnet bilingual education site for decades—and unfortunately one of the lowest-achieving schools in the district. The school missed state and federal academic performance targets for years, and fewer than 3 percent of ELLs annually were reclassified as fully English proficient.

District data analyses showed that after the first full year of SEI program implementation, the school gained almost 30 points on state test metrics, and English language growth rates tripled in all grades, easily exceeding district and federal targets. The reclassification rate last year quadrupled to 12 percent. Perhaps most significant, almost 50 percent of the school's intermediate students advanced to the next level of proficiency or met the criteria for being fully English proficient. Before the SEI program, 70 percent of the school's ELL population regularly showed no English language growth—or even regressed—on the state's yearly English assessment.

Here's what an average day looks like for an ELL student at George Washington Elementary School:

- Pronunciation and listening skills, 20 minutes.
- Vocabulary, 30 minutes.
- Verb tense instruction, 20 minutes.
- Sentence structure, 20 minutes.
- Integrated grammar skills application, 20 minutes.
- English reading and writing, 60 minutes.
- Math (specially designed academic instruction in English), 40 minutes.
- Science, social science, P.E., 40 minutes.

At Yuba City High School in Northern California, almost half of the school's 450 ELLs test at intermediate or below on the state's language assessment. These students are enrolled in four periods of daily English language development courses: Conversational English and Content Area Vocabulary, English Grammar, English Reading, and English Writing. The school offers three levels for each course; students take an assessment every six weeks that could qualify them to move to the next level. Some students move so quickly that they exit the SEI program in less than a year. After the first year of Yuba City's SEI program, the proportion of students reclassified as fully English proficient tripled to 15 percent, nearly twice the state average.

Rethinking Assumptions and Beliefs

Not surprisingly, the decision to implement a structured English immersion program—whether by law or by choice—frequently brings about conflicts over ideology, pedagogy, and the very role of schooling for English language learners in a culturally and linguistically diverse society. Notwithstanding these challenges, an increasing number of schools, districts, and states across the country have seen that structured English immersion can help students gain the English language skills that are crucial for academic success and opportunities beyond school. As Adela Santa Cruz, director of the Office of English Language Acquisition Services for the Arizona Department of Education, said,

> We understand that implementing an SEI program requires some new ways of thinking and teaching, but once teachers and administrators come to understand SEI, they see it as a positive and effective vehicle for helping ELLs learn English much faster than we thought.

For a complete list of the references for this Reading, go to **www.mhhe.com/teach1e2010**.

QUESTIONS

1. If the authors of these two articles were advising a school on how to develop a program for students who arrive not speaking English (English language learners, as they are called today), how do you think they would differ in the recommendations they would make? In what ways might they make the same recommendations?

2. What is each author's strongest argument in favor of his own recommendations?

3. If you were in charge of a school or district, which author would you listen to? Could you draw from both?

What Is the Best Education for Students With Disabilities?

From "CONFRONTING ABLEISM"

BY THOMAS HEHIR

Thomas Hehir is widely known for his writing about special education. He is Professor of Practice and Director of the School Leadership Program at Harvard Graduate School of Education in Cambridge, Massachusetts.

When Ricky was born deaf, his parents were determined to raise him to function in the "normal" world. Ricky learned to read lips and was not taught American Sign Language. He felt comfortable within the secure world of his family, but when he entered his neighborhood school, he grew less confident as he struggled to understand what his classmates seemed to grasp so easily.

Susan, a child with dyslexia, entered kindergarten with curiosity about the world around her, a lively imagination, and a love of picture books. Although her school provided her with individual tutoring and other special education services, it also expected her to read grade-level texts at the same speed as her nondisabled peers. Susan fell further and further behind. By 6th grade, she hated school and avoided reading.

These two examples illustrate how society's pervasive negative attitude about disability—which I term *ableism*—often makes the world unwelcoming and inaccessible for people with disabilities. An ableist perspective asserts that it is preferable for a child to read print rather than Braille, walk rather than use a wheelchair, spell independently rather than use a spell-checker, read written text rather than listen to a book on tape, and hang out with nondisabled kids rather than with other disabled kids.

Certainly, given a human-made world designed with the nondisabled in mind, children with disabilities gain an advantage if they can perform like their nondisabled peers. A physically disabled child who receives the help he or she needs to walk can move more easily in a barrier-filled environment. A child with a mild hearing loss who has been given the amplification and speech therapy he or she needs may function well in a regular classroom.

But ableist assumptions become dysfunctional when the education and development services provided to disabled children focus on their disability to the exclusion of all else. From an early age, many people with disabilities encounter the view that disability is negative and tragic and that "overcoming" disability is the only valued result (Ferguson & Asch, 1989; Rousso, 1984).

In education, considerable evidence shows that unquestioned ableist assumptions are harming disabled students and contributing to unequal outcomes (see Allington & McGill-Franzen, 1989; Lyon et al., 2001). School time

Source: "Confronting Ableism," by Thomas Hehir, February 2007, *Educational Leadership, 64*(5), pp. 8–14. This article was adapted from Thomas Hehir's book, *New Directions in Special Education: Eliminating Ableism in Policy and Practice* (Cambridge: Harvard Education Press, 2005), pp. 13–64.

devoted to activities that focus on changing disability may take away from the time needed to learn academic material. In addition, academic deficits may be exacerbated by the ingrained prejudice against performing activities in "different" ways that might be more efficient for disabled people—such as reading Braille, using sign language, or using text-to-speech software to read.

The Purpose of Special Education

What should the purpose of special education be? In struggling with this issue, we can find guidance in the rich and varied narratives of people with disabilities and their families. Noteworthy among these narratives is the work of Adrienne Asch, a professor of bioethics at Yeshiva University in New York who is blind.

In her analysis of stories that adults with disabilities told about their childhood experiences (Ferguson & Asch, 1989), Asch identified common themes in their parents' and educators' responses to their disability. Some of the adults responded with excessive concern and sheltering. Others conveyed to children, through silence or denial, that nothing was "wrong." For example, one young woman with significant vision loss related that she was given no alternative but to use her limited vision even though this restriction caused her significant academic problems. Another common reaction was to make ill-conceived attempts to fix the disability. For example, Marilyn Rousso, an accomplished psychotherapist with cerebral palsy, recounts,

> My mother was quite concerned with the awkwardness of my walk. Not only did it periodically cause me to fall but it made me stand out, appear conspicuously different—which she feared would subject me to endless teasing and rejection. To some extent it did. She made numerous attempts over the years of my childhood to have me go to physical therapy and to practice walking "normally" at home. I vehemently refused her efforts. She could not understand why I would not walk straight. (1984, p. 9)

In recalling her own upbringing and education, Asch describes a more positive response to disability:

> I give my parents high marks. They did not deny that I was blind, and did not ask me to pretend that everything about my life was fine. They rarely sheltered. They worked to help me behave and look the way others did without giving me a sense that to be blind—"different"—was shameful. They fought for me to ensure that I lived as full a rich a life as I could. For them, and consequently for me, my blindness was a fact, not a tragedy. It affected them but did not dominate their lives. Nor did it dominate mine. (Ferguson & Asch, 1989, p. 118)

Asch's narrative and others (Biklen, 1992) suggest that we can best frame the purpose of special education as *minimizing the impact of disability and maximizing the opportunities for students with disabilities to participate* *in schooling and the community*. This framework assumes that most students with disabilities will be integrated into general education and educated within their natural community. It is consistent with the 1997 and 2004 reauthorizations of the Individuals with Disabilities Education Act (IDEA), which requires that individualized education program (IEP) teams address how the student will gain access to the curriculum and how the school will meet the unique needs that arise out of the student's disability. Finally, this framework embraces the diverse needs of students with various disabilities as well as the individual diversity found among students within each disability group.

Falling Short of the Goal

Minimizing the impact of disability does not mean making misguided attempts to "cure" disability but rather giving students the supports, skills, and opportunities needed to live as full a life as possible *with* their disability. Maximizing access requires that school practices recognize the right of students with disabilities to participate fully in the school community—not only in academic programs, but also in sports teams, choruses, clubs, and field trips. A look at common problems encountered by students with low-incidence disabilities, specific learning disabilities, and emotional disturbances illustrates that schools still have a long way to go in fulfilling the purpose of special education.

Students With Low-Incidence Disabilities

In Adrienne Asch's case, minimizing the impact of her blindness meant learning Braille, developing orientation and mobility skills, and having appropriate accommodations available that gave her access to education. Asch also points out that because of New Jersey's enlightened policies at the time, she could live at home and attend her local school, so she and her family were not required to disrupt their lives to receive the specialized services she needed.

Unfortunately, many students today with low-incidence disabilities like blindness and deafness are not afforded the opportunities that Asch had in the early 1950s. Parents sometimes face the choice of sending their children to a local school that is ill equipped to meet their needs or to a residential school with specialized services, thus disrupting normal family life. Parents should not be forced to make this Hobson's choice. Services can be brought to blind and deaf students in typical community settings, and most students can thrive in that environment (Wagner, Black-orby, Cameto, & Newman, 1993; Wagner & Cameto, 2004). It is up to policymakers to ensure that such services are available.

Students With Specific Learning Disabilities

Because students identified as having learning disabilities are such a large and growing portion of the school population, we might expect that these students would be less likely to be subjected to ableist practices. The available evidence, however, contradicts this assumption. Many students with dyslexia and other specific learning disabilities receive inappropriate instruction that exacerbates their disabilities. For example, instead of making taped books available to these students, many schools require those taught in regular classrooms to handle grade-level or higher text. Other schools do not allow students to use computers when taking exams, thus greatly diminishing some students' ability to produce acceptable written work.

The late disabilities advocate Ed Roberts had polio as a child, which left him dependent on an iron lung. He attended school from home in the 1960s with the assistance of a telephone link. When it was time for graduation, however, the school board planned to deny him a diploma because he had failed to meet the physical education requirement. His parents protested, and Ed eventually graduated (Shapiro, 1994).

We can hardly imagine this scenario happening today, given disability law and improved societal attitudes. Yet similar ableist assumptions are at work when schools routinely require students with learning disabilities to read print at grade level to gain access to the curriculum or to meet proficiency levels on high-stakes assessments. Assuming that there is only one "right" way to learn—or to walk, talk, paint, read, and write—is the root of fundamental inequities.

Seriously Emotionally Disturbed Students

Perhaps no group suffers from negative attitudes more than students who have been identified as having serious emotional disturbance (SED)—and no other subpopulation experiences poorer outcomes. Students with SED drop out of school at more than double the rate of nondisabled students. Only 15 percent pursue higher education, and approximately 50 percent are taught in segregated settings (U.S. Department of Education, 2003; Wagner & Cameto, 2004).

For large numbers of students with serious emotional disturbance, their IEPs are more likely to include inappropriate responses to control the most common symptom of their disability—acting-out behavior—than to provide the accommodations and support the students need to be successful in education. Only 50 percent of students with SED receive mental health services, only 30 percent receive social work services, and only 50 percent have behavior management appropriately addressed in their IEPs (Wagner & Cameto, 2004).

What *do* these students typically receive through special education? They are commonly placed in a special classroom or school with other students with similar disabilities (U.S. Department of Education, 2003)—often with an uncertified teacher.

Placing such students in separate classes without specific behavioral supports, counseling, or an expert teacher is unlikely to work. Substantial evidence indicates, however, that providing these students with appropriate supports and mental health services can significantly reduce disruptive behavior and improve their learning (Sugai, Sprague, Horner, & Walker, 2000). Such supports are most effective when provided within the context of effective schoolwide discipline approaches, such as the U.S. Department of Education's Positive Behavioral Interventions and Supports program (www.pbis.org). Schoolwide approaches also produce safer and better-run schools for all students.

Guidelines for Special Education Decision Making

The goal of minimizing the impact of disability and maximizing opportunities to participate suggests several guidelines for serving students with disabilities.

Recognize that diagnosis is important.

To minimize the impact of disability, parents and educators need a clear understanding of the nature of the student's disability. Clearly, to make good decisions for a 3rd grader who does not read well, we need to know whether the problem is related to mental retardation, dyslexia, attention difficulties, or some other source. The student with mental retardation may be performing up to his or her capacity, indicating that the current instructional approach is working well, whereas the student with attention problems may need targeted accommodations or carefully prescribed medication. The student with dyslexia may need a highly structured reading program provided by a teacher with specialized training.

Another example of the importance of careful diagnosis is the case of two vision-impaired students who are learning to read and have the same visual acuity level. Although both are functioning well at present with the support of large-print texts, one student's vision impairment is progressive. Detailed knowledge of the disability would guide the school in deciding that this student also needs to learn Braille to ensure his or her success in the future.

Consider family capacity and desires.

Good instructional decisions should take into account family capacity and desires. For example, the mother of an adolescent with Down syndrome, discussing her son's high school program, told me,

> I don't want the school wasting his time teaching him to cook or do laundry. I can teach him that! As a matter of fact, he is already a pretty good cook. I want him in band class.

Although learning independent living skills is important for many students, particularly those with mental retardation, learning to cook would be a waste of precious instructional time for this high schooler. His family was already doing a great job of minimizing the impact of his disability in this area.

Involve students with disabilities in education decisions when appropriate.

Students themselves play a crucial role in achieving better results. By involving students in decisions about their own education, we can gain important insights about the way they learn best, encourage them to take responsibility for their own education, and teach them to advocate for themselves as they move into higher education and employment. A focus on self-determination also helps students integrate their disability into their self-image in a natural, positive way (Ruosso, 1984). Self-determination is the opposite of the paternalism that has plagued the lives of so many people with disabilities.

Jorgenson (1997) provides practical suggestions about how to build self-determination, including involving students in important decisions regarding their education; transitioning students ages 18–21, particularly those not going on to postsecondary education, out of school settings to work and other typical adult settings; and integrating transition planning for students with disabilities into an inclusive process that helps students plan for their futures.

Encourage students to develop and use skills and modes of expression that are most effective for them.

Parents and educators naturally want children to have the ability to perform in a typical manner. But if instructional programs focus too much on this preference, many students with disabilities will miss education opportunities as schools disregard their more effective, disability-specific modes of learning and expression. Of course, deaf students who can read lips have a competitive advantage in a hearing world. However, research has long shown that most deaf children do not develop elaborate language through oral methods alone (Stuckless & Birch, 1966). Paradoxically, a deaf child who has developed language skills through learning American Sign Language from birth (or, more recently, through cochlear implants) may actually read lips better because he or she has developed a larger vocabulary.

Keep integration into the general education environment the priority.

IDEA's requirement that all students be educated in the least restrictive environment has resulted in significant positive change for students with disabilities. Research has shown that including students with disabilities in the general education environment improves academic achievement (Wagner et al., 1993). Inclusion also plays a central role in the integration of disabled people into all aspects of society, both by giving students the education they need to compete and by demonstrating to nondisabled students that disability is a natural aspect of life. For most students with disabilities, integration into regular classes with appropriate accommodations and support should be the norm.

Promote high standards.

The most damaging ableist assumption is the belief that people with disabilities are not intellectually capable. Therefore, although performance on a high-stakes test should not be the only means through which students with disabilities can demonstrate what they know and are able to do, the requirement to include students with disabilities in standards-based reform holds promise. Many in the disability community hope that this requirement will counter the low expectations that have plagued students with disabilities in the past.

To improve the likelihood that students with disabilities will be successful on high-stakes tests, schools should provide early intervention for those experiencing academic or behavioral difficulties, give all students access to the regular curriculum whenever possible, and carefully choose accommodations in both instruction and assessment so that these accommodations minimize the effects of the disability.

Employ concepts of universal design.

The principle of universal design first pertained to architecture; it called for public buildings to be designed so that people with disabilities would be able to use them. Buildings designed with this principle in mind, for example, would include ramps, automatic door opening devices, and fire alarm systems with lights activated for the deaf. Universal design allows for access without extra-ordinary means and is based on the assumption that disabled people are numerous and should be able to lead regular lives.

This principle has recently been applied to schooling and shows tremendous promise in minimizing the impact of disability and transforming the curriculum for all students. For example, Rose and Meyer (2002) have developed new multimedia curriculum materials that enable all kinds of students to gain access to information: students with physical disabilities can turn pages with the touch of a key; students with visual disabilities can expand the size of the print; students with learning disabilities can have words that they cannot decode read aloud to them.

Getting Past Ableism

The U.S. education system has made major strides in improving education opportunities for students with disabilities. More of these students are finishing high school than ever, and record numbers are moving on to employment and higher education (Wagner & Cameto, 2004). Much of this improvement has taken place because of the work of school leaders throughout the United States.

To continue and expand this progress, however, educators must recognize and challenge the ableist assumptions that still permeate the culture and guide much special education practice. Students with disabilities need carefully constructed, individual instructional programs that recognize the effects of their disability while creating opportunities for them to learn and fully participate in school and society.

For a complete list of the references for this Reading, go to **www.mhhe.com/teach1e2010**.

QUESTIONS

1. What do you think of Hehir's term *ableism*? Are schools guilty of this? Have you seen examples in your own schooling or in more recent observations? Do you think you have been an "ableist" at times?

2. If Asch is right that some parents and teachers overly shelter students with disabilities, while others insist that "nothing is wrong" and demand that these children act the same way as their nondisabled peers, is there a happy middle ground? Or is the search for a middle ground the wrong goal?

3. In the end, Hehir says, "Students with disabilities need carefully constructed, individual instructional programs that recognize the effects of their disability while creating opportunities for them to learn and fully participate in school and society." What would it take to prepare teachers to construct such programs? Is this realistic?

PHILOSOPHICAL AND PSYCHOLOGICAL
THEORIES

We teach so that others can learn. No one ever teaches just to teach or develops a curriculum for its own sake. Teaching is always (or always should be) done in the service of only one goal: student learning.

Given this obvious truism, that learning is the purpose of all education, it is surprising how little we know about how human beings really learn things. And most of what we do know about human learning is the result of very recent research. People have been teaching and learning for thousands of years, as long as there has been human life on this planet. Schools have been organized for hundreds of years to facilitate this process of teaching and learning for children and youth. Only in the past few decades, however, have scientists been able to conduct basic research on the human brain so that we have the beginning—and still only the beginning—of a true science of human learning. This chapter focuses on that science and the very human process of learning by addressing a key question for every teacher, "How will my students learn anything?"

Philosophers and psychologists differ substantially in their beliefs and ideas about how people learn. Nevertheless, to be a successful teacher, you must at least contemplate these ideas and come to some preliminary conclusions about your own stance. As researchers Morris L. Bigge and S. Samuel Shermis wisely note, "Everything teachers do is colored by the psychological theory they hold. Consequently, teachers who do not make use of a systematic body of theory in their day-by-day decisions are behaving blindly; little evidence of long-range rationale, purpose, or plan is observable in their teaching."[1] Of course, teachers may operate on the basis of unexamined theories or the folk wisdom of a school that often represents someone else's unexamined psychological theory. However, a true professional will grapple substantively with a range of theories of how children and adolescents learn and will come to his or her own informed conclusions, even if these conclusions are (as they should be) tentative and subject to change in light of new information and experience.

HOW DO CHILDREN LEARN?

FOCUS >>

- What have philosophers said about human learning?
- How have modern psychologists changed our way of thinking about learning?
- What is the link between brain research and day-to-day practice in schools?
- How can teachers and schools serve a range of learning styles?

This chapter has two key **Readings**. *How People Learn*, published by the prestigious National Academy of Sciences, represents the most cutting-edge research by psychologists and brain researchers on how human beings learn and what methods of teaching will be most effective with them. In the second **Reading**, psychologist Howard Gardner lists his eight—or nine—categories of human intelligence as well as reflects on how he came to see human intelligence in these multiple forms rather than as a single hierarchy of intelligence.

>> What Have Philosophers Said About Human Learning?

Since humans have been able to think about more than the necessities of survival, philosophers have pondered the meaning of education and specifically the roles of the teacher and the learner in the educational process. In this section, we look briefly at what a few selected philosophers have said about education through the centuries and how this philosophical thinking can influence what you do as a teacher.[2]

SOCRATES, 470–399 BCE

Socrates is often considered the earliest of the ancient Greek philosophers. Since Socrates himself wrote nothing, all that we know of him is through the writings of others, including his most famous student, Plato. Nevertheless, Socrates put an important stamp on education. What has become known as the Socratic dialogue emerged from this ancient philosopher's effort to lead his pupils to truth by continually asking them questions—questions that forced them to clarify their own views and deal with contradictions in their

own thinking. In the end, Socrates also believed that there were significant limits to human wisdom but that the search for truth through continued questioning and clarification was always worth it. According to Plato, Socrates once said of another supposedly wise man, "Well, although I do not suppose that either of us knows anything really beautiful and good, I am better off than he is—for he knows nothing, and thinks that he knows. I neither know nor think that I know. In this latter particular, then, I seem to have slightly the advantage of him."[3] Socrates's continued questioning brought him into conflict with the authorities in Athens, who accused him of corrupting the youth. After being tried and found guilty of "promoting dangerous ideas," Socrates was forced to drink poison made from the hemlock plant, the method of capital punishment in ancient Athens.

PLATO, 427–347 BCE

Although Plato studied with Socrates, he later came to different conclusions. If Socrates loved the questions, Plato wanted the answers. His goals for his students became much more specific—to help them move from a vague appreciation of the world to a clear understanding of objective realities that would help them understand what was good and how to lead ethical lives. In his most famous

Grand Avenue © United Features Syndicate, Inc.

example, Plato asked his listeners to "picture men dwelling in a sort of subterranean cavern. . .fettered from childhood, so that they remain in the same spot, able to look forward only. . .[with]. . .light from a fire burning higher up and at a distance behind them. . . ." The result of living in this cave was that these men could only see shadows, of themselves and of the world. They might argue all day long about the meaning of what they saw, but in the end, all the arguments were about shadows.

The educator's job was to drag the "occupants of the cave" into the light, which might be painful at first but which in time would allow them to see "things themselves, and from these he [sic] would go on to contemplate the appearance of the heavens and heaven itself." Having seen reality—and not the mere shadow of reality—students would never want to return to the cave, however painful the transition to light might be. The true educator facilitates just that transition, from the shadow of truth to real truth. Unlike many philosophers of education, ancient and modern, Plato also addressed the education of women, calling for the education of "female guardians" along with the "philosopher kings" who would lead society.[4]

ARISTOTLE, 384–322 BCE

A student of Plato, and perhaps the most famous Greek philosopher, Aristotle differed from Socrates and Plato in his focus not only on gaining a clear understanding of reality but also on using observation and data, not just argument, to gain that clarity. Aristotle also believed that every substance in the world had a nature (or potential) that it might or might not actualize. Just as an acorn could become a great oak (though most acorns would not), so could every human, if well educated, fulfill his potential as a reasonable and thoughtful person. As Aristotle wrote, "[F]or man, therefore, the life according to reason is best and pleasantest, since reason more than anything else *is* man." Further, he said, "Happiness extends, then, just so far as contemplation does, and those to whom contemplation more fully belongs are more truly happy." Such happiness, based on thoughtful contemplation, was the key to virtue in individual lives and in states, and it was the role of the educator to cultivate it in men. (Aristotle did mean men. He did not see such contemplation as the role of women.)[5]

JEAN-JACQUES ROUSSEAU, 1712–1778

One of the first modern philosophers, Jean-Jacques Rousseau was born in Switzerland, traveled widely in Europe, and lived much of his adult life in France. Although it may be hard to think of someone who was born three hundred years ago as "modern," Rousseau continues to be important in educational thinking. His ideas about education were rooted in his belief that, in each country, most people had far too little freedom because a small elite held the political power. On a smaller scale, he saw most schools as structured in a way that robbed young people of their freedom to think, create, and explore. Thus, as he looked at the world around him, Rousseau said, "Man is born free and everywhere he is in chains." Rousseau also discussed the education of women, though his ideal woman was supposed to be dependent on males and not quite so free of her chains. Recognizing that modern people cannot "return again to the forests to live among bears," Rousseau sought to develop a system of education that would foster human freedom. In his book *Emile*, he developed that system for an imaginary pupil, from birth to manhood. Emile's education started with "an incontestable principle that the first impulses of nature are always right. There is no original perversity in the human heart."

And if this is true, then the teacher's role is simply to allow Emile's—and every student's—inner goodness to appear. School should not make students dull through instruction in the lessons that some adults thought children should receive. Rather, Rousseau advocated helping students spend less time learning their lessons and more time living freely in the world so that through a range of experiences they might become both wise and happy. Rousseau's goal for a student was to become someone who "knows nothing by heart, he knows a great deal by experience." Such a student would come to love what he knows and therefore love himself and his world of freedom.[6]

JOHN DEWEY, 1859–1952

John Dewey was one of the most influential philosophers of education in the United States as well as the world. Often called "the father of progressive education," Dewey was as many times a critic of **progressive education** as he was its defender. Although Dewey wrote a great deal in the course of his long life, his core beliefs focused on a few key elements. Moving far beyond Rousseau's individualistic approach, Dewey wrote in *The School and Society* (1899), "We are apt to look at the school from an individualistic standpoint.... Yet the range of the outlook needs to be enlarged. What the best and wisest parent wants for his own child, that must the community want for all of its children." Like Rousseau, however, Dewey was critical of the boring nature of much traditional education in which the "subject-matter of education consists of bodies of information and skills that have been worked out in the past." As he continued in *Experience and Education* (1938), that traditional approach is one of imposition from above and from outside. Progressive education, Dewey said, was different:

> *To imposition from above is opposed expression and cultivation of individuality; to external discipline is opposed free activity; to learning from tests and teachers, learning through experience; to acquisition of isolated skills and techniques by drill, is opposed acquisition of them as means of attaining ends which make direct vital appeal; to preparation for a more or less*

progressive education An educational movement that began at the beginning of the twentieth century. Many progressive educators believe that schools should begin with the life experience of the child rather than with a preset curriculum (child-centered educators) and that the "real world" of experience provides a better focus than starting with abstract ideas.

Did you know?

One of the most-often quoted philosophers, Confucius (551–479 BCE) believed learning had nothing to do with intuition but resulted instead from long, careful study with a teacher (someone older and wiser) whose words and actions could be imitated. Confucius's succinct teaching style consisted of posing questions, citing passages from the classics, using analogies, and waiting for his students to arrive at the answers. According to Confucius, "He who learns but does not think is lost. He who thinks but does not learn is in great danger."

In Chapter 7, we discuss John Dewey and progressive education's goal of connecting curriculum with the current interests and experiences of young people.

Connections

remote future is opposed making the most of the opportunities of present life; to static aims and materials is opposed acquaintance with a changing world.

Finally, for Dewey, all this learning from experience—from the contemporary world of work and human activity—was also in the service of something larger. As Dewey said in *Democracy and Education* (1916), he was concerned with linking the "subject matter and method of education" with "the growth of democracy." For him, the two were always inextricably linked.[7]

MORTIMER ADLER, 1902–2001

Mortimer Adler agreed with Dewey about education's serving to broaden democracy, but he disagreed dramatically about the best kind of education to accomplish that goal. In *Paideia Proposal* (1982), he wrote, "'You propose,' the objectors may say, 'the same educational objectives for all the children.' Yes, that is precisely what we propose." Not only did he want the same objectives, he wanted the same course of study between kindergarten and the end of high school "with a satisfactory standard of accomplishment regardless of native ability, temperamental bent, or conscious preferences." To make exceptions by varying the curriculum according to individual student needs or interests was, Adler thought, to run a very grave risk of leaving some young people out of the democratic dialogue that was essential to a good society. Contrary to Dewey, Adler believed that great ideas had been developed over time, that a body of great works of literature embodied these ideas, and that this essential literature needed to be at the core of every young person's learning, if individuals were to have a good life and if free institutions were to be preserved in the larger society.[8]

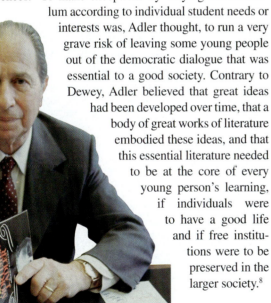

MAXINE GREENE, 1917–

In a recent interview, Maxine Greene said, "The only way to really awaken to life, awaken to the possibilities, is to be self-aware. I use the term wide-awakeness. . . . Without the ability to think about yourself, to reflect on your life, there's really no awareness, no consciousness." According to Greene, the purpose of education is to foster such an awareness or "awakeness," which is often done better through engagement with the arts than in a traditional classroom. Deeply concerned about the "prevailing cynicism" that characterizes "a world of fearful moral uncertainty," Greene calls on educators not to instruct in morals in any traditional way but rather to create significant encounters with works of art, with literature, and with life in ways that lead students to pose new questions, developing a new sense of moral urgency and passionate commitment to a better future for the human race.[9]

JANE ROLAND MARTIN, 1929–

Jane Roland Martin has focused on the fact that contemporary philosophers of education ignore the subject of women. In her book *Reclaiming a Conversation: The Ideal of the Educated Woman* (1985), Martin set out to change that situation. She insisted that "[i]n a society in which traits are genderized and socialization according to sex is commonplace, an educational philosophy that tries to ignore gender in the name of equality is self-defeating." Rather than ignoring gender, Martin seeks to raise the consciousness of women and men about the ways schooling has denigrated women and the work that is usually seen as "women's work," while building into the education expected for both women and men a greater respect for nurturing and an ethic of care. In attending to nurturing and caring as part of the core purpose of the curriculum, Martin argued, education could better serve "the full range of people's lives" and help all people address "the present perils to life on earth."[10]

BELL HOOKS, 1952–

A feminist scholar committed to a multicultural approach to education, bell hooks believes that for teachers who care about "the practice of freedom. . .there is an aspect of our vocation that is sacred." By this she means that such teachers must not only share information but also share in the intellectual and spiritual growth of their students and must come to see themselves as healers—of individual students and a broken world. To become such educators, hooks also insists that teachers

must transgress the traditional boundaries that define teaching. They must take on the overlooked issues of gender, race, and class, but also the erotic and the political. Doing so will involve educational acts of "political resistance," she says. But, hooks warns, "Teachers who care, who serve their students, are usually at odds with the environments wherein we teach."[11]

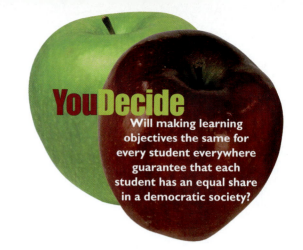

You Decide

Will making learning objectives the same for every student everywhere guarantee that each student has an equal share in a democratic society?

KWAME ANTHONY APPIAH, 1954–

According to Kwame Anthony Appiah, education should foster a kind of "rooted cosmopolitanism" in which students come to see themselves as citizens of the world (hence, becoming cosmopolitan) yet at the same time understand that they belong to a community and need to take responsibility for its destiny. More than some, Appiah worries about a kind of community identity that can separate men and women from other men and women and foster a cultural partiality that is dangerously divisive. He argues that a great respect for **individualism** that also focuses intensely on human rights—the individual

individualism Stresses self-reliance and independence of the individual apart from the society or group.

Did you know?

bell hooks is the pen name of Gloria Jean Watkins. Although she originally chose to author under her great-grandmother's name to avoid confusion with another Gloria Watkins in her community, the spirit of her defiant ancestor, known as a woman who was not afraid to speak her mind, gave her a "writer-identity that would challenge and subdue all impulses leading me away from speech into silence."

JOHN F. KENNEDY JR. FOR

rights of other free and independent humans—is both the key to building a better world and the best outcome of a truly liberal education.[12]

The list of important philosophers of education, or philosophers whose work has important implications for education, could go on and on. The descriptions offered here only hint at these philosophers' core ideas regarding teaching and learning. A much deeper look at their work is needed to understand the value of what they have to say to those of us who teach. After this cursory review, though, we need to ask, "What does this philosophy have to do with me as a teacher?"

You can probably be a very effective classroom teacher without ever having read Plato or Greene or any of the philosophers discussed here. But a teacher will have a less rich personal and intellectual life if he or she does not at least think about some of the major questions these philosophers have raised. There are few better ways to engage these questions than to read the work of some of the wise people who have thought about these questions, over the decades and over the centuries.

Many textbooks seek to put the different philosophers into different boxes: Maxine Greene represents **existentialism**, whereas Adler represents **essentialism**; Plato represents idealism, whereas Aristotle represents realism; and so on. The problem with these boxes is that they completely miss the rich complexity of these philosophers. Certainly, some fundamental disagreements exist among them. Greene is more than existentialism and Adler is more than essentialism, but Greene does worry about any effort to standardize education or to create a single set of standards, which for her are, by definition, far too confining of the human spirit. Adler, on the other hand, sees in standards and, indeed, in a single standardized curriculum for all students, the only key to a democratic education in which all people not only are created equal but also are allowed to be equal participants in a grand democratic dialogue that should be the outcome of effective schooling. Ironically, for all the philosophers' differences, that grand democratic dialogue is exactly the goal of their work, however different their proposed ways to get us there.

existentialism Stresses personal choice and responsibility while recognizing that human existence is wholly unexplainable and, perhaps, meaningless, in a chaotic universe.

essentialism Viewpoint in which groups of people, classified by race or population, share the same inherent essences (made up of characteristics or properties) that define the group and distinguish it from other communities.

>> How Have Modern Psychologists Changed Our Way of Thinking About Learning?

Some of the names and ideas presented in this section may be familiar to you, especially if you have already taken a basic psychology course. If so, this brief review will link these ideas directly to the classroom. Even if this is all new to you, you will likely revisit this material in more detail in future classes in child or adolescent development and, indeed, throughout your career as an educator. These scholars and the ideas they represent have helped shape the ways schools are organized and the ways in which teachers teach. A teacher who is not familiar with research in educational psychology and who is not able to place his or her own classroom practice in a clear theoretical construct can still be a good teacher. However, our schools need educational leaders who are "reflective practitioners," those who

Join the Dialogue

Imagine a roundtable discussion with philosophers such as Socrates, Plato, Aristotle, Jean-Jacques Rousseau, John Dewey, Mortimer Adler, Maxine Green, Jane Roland Martin, bell hooks, and Kwame Appiah. On which points do they agree? Where do they disagree? Where does one approach build on another's views? What do their different perspectives mean for the future of education?

Teachable Moment
Culture . . . Whose Culture?

When Mortimer Adler spoke about passing on the great ideas—the culture—that had been developed over centuries, he had a pretty clear idea of what culture that was. For Adler, and for many contemporary educators, the purpose of schooling is to induct students into a particular culture that has been developing in Europe and North America since the time of the Greek philosophers, but especially in the past few hundred years. Knowing this culture includes knowing the work of philosophers such as Socrates and Rousseau; great writers such as Shakespeare, Walt Whitman, John Steinbeck, and Robert Frost; great music from Bach to Beethoven to contemporary classical work; and so on.

Other philosophers have questioned whether inducting students into this "grand tradition" was either wise or good. When Rousseau said that he wanted a student who "knows nothing by heart, he knows a great deal by experience" or when Dewey objected to education which is "imposition from above," they were objecting to an education that, as they saw it, too often simply told students to learn the traditional literature and ideas by heart rather than engage with the ideas as they were relevant to their the lives and experiences.

In today's increasingly diverse world, more and more people are challenging the ideas that there is "one great culture" or "one grand narrative" that all students should learn. Jane Roland Martin is far from alone in noting how often women and women's ideas and experiences have been left out of what was called "culture." Historians like E. P. Thompson have insisted that history is not simply kings, presidents, and military leaders and that such history tends "to obscure the agency of working people, the degree to which they contributed, by conscious efforts, to the making of history."

With the increasing racial and ethnic diversity of American society, advocates of multicultural education have come to insist that there is not one culture that should be taught in schools but rather many cultures. The *multi* in multiculturalism is as important as the *culture*. Nearly all advocates of multiculturalism, though they differ greatly among themselves, insist that all students need to learn the literature and ideas of the African American experience—including the poems of Phillis Wheatley and Langston Hughes, the autobiographies of Frederick Douglass or Malcolm X, the novels of Zora Neale Hurston or Toni Morrison, and the music of Marian Anderson, Billie Holiday, Miles Davis, John Coltrane, Jimi Hendrix, or James Brown—as well as being exposed to works from the Latino (such as Carlos Fuentes or Gabriel Garcia Marquez), Asian (such as Amy Tan or Maxine Hong Kingston), and American Indian communities (Vine Deloria or the many collections of tribal legends now available)—every bit as much as they should be reading the works of White European and European American writers.

Ironically, the growing emphasis on a diversity of cultures has led some White students to think that other people have "culture" and that European Americans "have no culture." Of course, all people have culture—many different cultures—and part of the joy of living in today's diverse world is that all of us can be informed by, shaped by, and influenced by cultural developments that have come from many different eras and all corners of the globe, including the many communities that make up contemporary U.S. culture.

QUESTIONS

- Thinking back on your own experiences as a student, would you say your school mostly taught the "grand tradition" of literature and history based primarily on the works of European and European American males, or were diverse cultures and both genders represented in the curriculum?
- If you are a student of color, did you first learn of your own cultural history in school or elsewhere? If you are a White student, what do you know about your own cultural (ethnic or religious) roots? Where did you learn about your roots? Whatever your race and culture, does having a cultural identity matter to you?

know not only how to get things done in a classroom but also *why* certain things make sense to do at certain times, with certain groups of students, but perhaps not at other times or with other students.

JEAN PIAGET, 1896–1980

A Swiss psychologist, Jean Piaget focused on understanding the ways children think, reason, and learn. In the process, he wrote some of the most influential theories of child development. Piaget saw four basic stages, each with several substages, through which every child must move, and he believed that understanding these stages of development is key to effective education. Each stage represents a significantly different way of thinking and viewing the world. Children must move through the stages in a steady and gradual way that can be predicted with relative accuracy (for most healthy children) based on their chronological age. Piaget's stages of development are as follows:

- sensorimotor stage (ages 0 to 2 years)
- preoperational stage (ages 2 to 7 years)
- concrete operational stage (ages 7 to 11 years)
- formal operational stage (age 11 to adult)

In *The Moral Judgment of the Child*, Piaget illustrates these four stages by discussing a child's emerging sense of the rules for a game of marbles. For an infant in the sensorimotor stage, there is no game of marbles as such, for a game involves a level of interaction and a sense of other people that is beyond an infant. When a baby of 5 to 8 months is presented with something new, he or she will enjoy the touch and feel of the new object as well as the physical sensation of playing with it. According to Piaget, if you "give a baby a marble, it will explore its surface and consistency, but will at the same time use it as something to grasp, to suck, to rub against the sides of its cradle, and so on." At this stage, it is fascinating to watch an infant interact

with anything, inanimate or animate, but it would certainly make no sense to try to teach the infant the rules of any game. Such instruction would be absurdly beyond his or her stage of development.

The first stage does not last long, however. In the early years, certainly well before a child begins kindergarten or first grade, something Piaget calls "egocentrism" appears as a form of behavior between purely individual and socialized behavior. This as the "state of cooperation," in which individuals, recognizing each other as equals, can understand the difference between themselves and an inanimate object (such as a marble) and can enjoy having other children around them engaging in similar play with the marbles. At this stage, however, it is not reasonable to assume that the interaction will be governed by any external rules or that the children will focus on their interaction for long. Thus, in a game of marbles, a child who is 3 to 5 years old may do the things that one does when playing a game of marbles, but he or she is merely imitating what others do. The child may think he or she is playing the game, but the interaction with the other children is not really meaningful. So Piaget says, "He plays in an individualistic manner with material that is social. Such is egocentrism." Although the action has become social, the mental construct of the action, though it can be mistaken for social, is almost exclusively individual. This is the nature of the preoperational stage. Asking the child at this level to think in a more social way about a game or a lesson is simply courting frustration and failure.

By the time the marble-playing child has reached the third stage, around age 7 or, in many schools in the United States, at the transition into second or third grade and classes that assume basic literacy, the developmental stage is also changing significantly. The key change in moving to the third stage of development is a move from egocentric behavior to "the desire for mutual understanding." Up to this time, the child is happy with any success in the game of marbles no matter what success or failure other children may have. Now, with this transition, comes a desire to *win*, that is, to abide by the rules but at the same time acquire more marbles than the other children with whom the child is playing. As Piaget says, "The specific pleasure of the game thus ceases to be muscular and egocentric, and becomes social." At this stage, children insist on the adherence to common rules that lead to a conclusion that is accepted by all.

Finally, by age 10 or 11, the child has moved to what Piaget sees as the final stage of development, in which more formal reasoning develops and, in the marbles game example, the child's interest now moves beyond basic social aspects of the game and winning and losing to understanding the game and the rules that govern it. Piaget described observing a group of boys playing marbles who had reached this stage, "Not only do these children seek to cooperate, to 'fix things up,'. . .rather than play for themselves alone, but also—and this undoubtedly is something new—they seem to take a peculiar pleasure in anticipating all possible cases and in codifying them." Thus, throughout this fourth stage the dominating interest seems to be interest in the rules themselves. Children at this stage will make the game more complicated simply as a way to play with the rules as well as with the marbles. The politics of the game and the management of the game have come to replace the sheer interest in winning and the earlier kinesthetic sense of pleasure in the act of touching or moving the marbles.[13]

Piaget was not concerned with the implications of his research for the classroom or for teaching and learning. His objective was simply to describe children's thinking, not to improve it.[14] Nevertheless, his stages of development have some obvious implications for the way children learn. Many educators have spent the past half-century drawing out the details of what Piaget's stages of development mean for the classroom. If Piaget's stages analyze development correctly (which is certainly a subject of debate today), then it makes little sense to try to teach something before the child is ready to learn it, but it makes great sense to foster development and growth at the appropriate time. To return to the game of marbles, there would be little value in having kindergarten or first-grade students ponder the rules or possible changes in the rules of a game of marbles (or the rules of the classroom or the larger society), whereas the same discussion with a group of 10-year-olds in fifth or sixth grade might be extremely valuable. Knowing our students thus means knowing many aspects of their lives, including their developmental stages and what lessons they are or are not ready to learn and comprehend.

did, or, as he said, "We want to know why men behave as they do." With that knowledge, Skinner was sure that he could not only understand what people would do in similar circumstances but, by analyzing the causes of behavior, it would be possible to manipulate people so as to control their behavior in the future.[15] Skinner was convinced that there were rules of behavior every bit as clear as the rules of navigation and, if these rules were understood, humans could be guided through their lives as surely as winds and tides could be used to guide a sailing ship.

For Skinner, the most efficient ways for teachers to teach and students to learn was through what he called **"operant conditioning,"** or positive reinforcement. In experiments with pigeons, Skinner provided the rein-

> **operant conditioning** Use of positive or negative consequences to alter the responses and behavior of a student.

forcement with food; with children, he substituted praise for selecting the right answer or for engaging in the preferred action. Skinner did not have much patience with schooling that focused on students' learning through their own discovery or their own problem posing and problem solving. The purpose of schooling, he believed, was to transmit culture across the generations. Thus, although he noted that "[e]ducators have turned to discovery and creativity in an effort to interest their students," he believed it was much better to focus on "good contingencies of reinforcement [that] do that in a much more profitable way." Once a teacher had gotten a student to the right answer or the right action, the rest was fairly easy. The hard part involves getting people to behave in a certain way for the *first time* so that the behavior can be reinforced.[16] Once the desired behavior has been exhibited, praise and other positive reinforcement should easily make it replicable.

If human learning is simply a matter of responding positively to operant conditioning or positive reinforcement, then the implications for teaching are fairly obvious. It is the teacher's role to decide what behavior and knowledge the student should have, present it clearly, and provide much positive reinforcement for the student who adopts the knowledge, ideas, or actions.

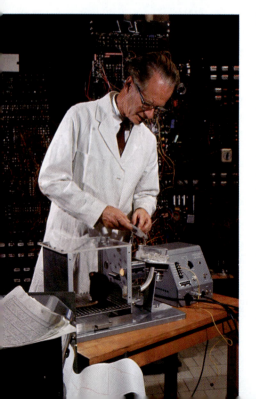

B. F. SKINNER, 1904–1990

The focus of B. F. Skinner's long and productive career as a psychologist was human behavior— how to understand it, predict it, and shape it. Because of his focus on behavior and actions, Skinner was much less interested in looking at brain activity or at emotions that were hard to measure. He wanted to know how to shape what people

LEV VYGOTSKY, 1896–1934

Lev Vygotsky's key work was done in the Soviet Union in the 1920s and 1930s, but it was the translation of his work into English in the 1960s and 1970s that made his influence on education in the United States significant. The developmental theory most closely associated with Vygotsky is what he called the "zone

Teachable Moment

Are You a Skinnerian?

No, it's not a term from the latest *Star Trek* movie. A "Skinnerian" is someone who practices the learning philosophy developed by B. F. Skinner. Skinner's operant conditioning was based on the premise that people would repeat positive behaviors if they received (and could look forward to) positive rewards.

Skinner believed there were five major obstacles to learning that called for five simple remedies:

Obstacle	Remedy
People have a fear of failure.	Give the learner immediate feedback.
The task is not broken down into small enough steps.	Break down the task into small steps.
Directions are lacking.	Repeat the directions as many times as possible.
The directions are not clear.	Work from the simplest to the most complex tasks.
Positive reinforcement is lacking.	Give positive reinforcement.

the teacher, and the student is treated as a relatively passive object to be led by immediate feedback and positive reinforcement to the end results that the teacher decides. Some observers feel this approach is better suited to helping rats learn how to run through a maze than to supporting young people in moving toward maturity.

Much research has confirmed Skinner's approach, especially regarding relatively straightforward tasks, such as learning how to ride a bike or how to sound out words as a first step toward reading. You may recall an instance when a teacher helped you learn something by breaking it down into smaller tasks and providing positive feedback.

Critics of Skinner, however, see his approach as too manipulative. All the decisions seem to rest with

QUESTIONS

- Following Skinner's philosophy, what kinds of lessons can best be delivered or broken down into a series of small steps? When might this approach get in the way of helping students cultivate a larger understanding of the issues?
- How important is positive reinforcement to you? When is the reward not as important as the process?

of proximal development"—the stage just beyond the child's current one, which, with proper input and support, the child can be expected to reach. In Vygotsky's words, this is "the distance between the actual developmental level as determined by independent problem solving and the level of potential development as determined through problem solving under adult guidance or in collaboration with more capable peers."[17] In a sense, Vygotsky saw the teacher's role as speeding up the movement from one of Piaget's developmental stages to the next. Like Piaget,

Vygotsky believed that certain developments needed to happen in order and the most that could be done was to move a child more quickly to the next level. A child certainly could not skip one stage and move on to the next.

Vygotsky's plea that educators should focus on this zone of development has two significant implications. The first relates to what American educators have come to call scaffolding. Scaffolding was developed by educators using Vygotsky's ideas with very young children. Parents and teachers know that young children will at first walk more confidently if someone holds their hand but later will walk with equal confidence without an adult hand in place. In the same way, children will learn when there are supports for learning. In time, those supports need to be removed for the child to truly "own" the learning. They will not learn if the supports are not removed eventually.

The idea of scaffolding has increasingly come to mean that more advanced students also need models and immediate feedback in the beginning, but in time that same modeling and feedback only gets in the way. In the beginning, as a student moves gingerly into the next zone of development, the support is essential. In time it is not. Scaffolding also means that little is learned the first time something is taught. It is by revisiting a subject, while also fostering greater and greater degrees of independent thinking about the subject, that a student comes to understands it. Perhaps an obvious example of scaffolding is represented by this chapter and, indeed by this book, which introduces a number of key topics to the aspiring teacher but does so under the assumption that the important discussions of how students learn and how teachers teach will be revisited multiple times in future courses.

Vygotsky's approach to children's learning has a second, perhaps even more essential, element. For Vygotsky, learning takes place in social interactions. The focus of teaching and learning is not the individual child's development but rather the constant give and take of children with each other and with more knowledgeable adults who can prod and support a child in moving to the next zone and then support him or her once there. Thus, he placed a heavy emphasis on problem solving under adult guidance or in collaboration with more capable peers. According to Vygotsky, human learning is always attained in social contexts, never simply alone. These social contexts extend from generation to generation as people not only learn about but also change a given culture, even as they pass it on to the next generation. The child does not reinvent the whole of its culture but rather emerges into active participa-

tion in that culture one step at a time in collaboration with teachers. In this way, Vygotsky differed dramatically from Skinner. As Vygotsky saw it, children are not simply candidates for being shaped in certain ways by rewards and punishments, like pigeons. They are unique in their need for social interactions that will help them develop and in time will help them shape the development of others.

JEROME BRUNER, 1915–

For decades, Jerome Bruner has been one of the most influential voices in educational psychology. Much more than Skinner, Bruner sees learning as an active process in which the learner has a key role, not merely responding to outside reinforcement but actively engaging in the process. Like Vygotsky, Bruner also sees learning as linking new information to what is previously known, not just previous information but also a previous "system of representation" that gives meaning and organization to ideas and information. Thus, according to Bruner, the interplay of the individual and the environment stimulates (or fails to stimulate) learning. Learning is neither gradual nor inevitable, but as Bruner says, "appears to be much more like a staircase with rather sharp risers, more a matter of spurts and rests." These growth spurts seem to take place when certain new capacities begin to develop in a child, but it is not just a matter of individual development. Some things in the external environment can slow down the growth process, whereas others can speed it up dramatically. Given this tendency for learning and growth to take place in fits and starts, good teachers will structure their classrooms to create environments that will move learning along at a healthy pace.[18]

Given Bruner's view of how children and youth learn, and of the key roles of the larger culture, the development of language, and of motivation in encouraging the spurts in growth, he recommends making the student an active partner in the learning process and engaging him or her in problem solving that requires "the exploration of alternatives." Learning is not a lone enterprise, and "[man] is not a naked ape but a culture-clothed human being, hopelessly ineffective without the prosthesis provided by culture. The very nature of his characteristics as a species provides a guide to appropriate pedagogy. . . ." Thus, in Bruner's view, the effective teacher will design lessons that are taught and learned in the appropriate sequence. In these lessons, learning builds on prior knowledge and the social context in which it is happening. The context needs to include not just the school but also what society wants students to

My Philosophy of Education

As an aspiring teacher, you may find it all too easy to say, "Just tell me what I need to know to be a good teacher—I don't need all this philosophy stuff." That may seem to make sense, given that the most important objective for a teacher is to be sure that the 20 to 30 or so young people in the classroom learn what they need to learn to be successful.

Such a "just the facts" (or skills) approach may work if you are training to become a plumber. However, if you only know what to do in class from one day to the next, you will be lost if you have a different group of students another year and have to adjust teaching methods. If you just learn the tricks of the trade, you will not be able to be an active player if the school decides to revise the curriculum and wants your involvement in developing not only a plan but also a rationale for the selected plan. As you advance throughout your career, it will be critical for you to develop your own personal philosophy and approach to teaching. This is not a going-through-the-motions kind of job—nor would you want it to be.

You will need to understand the philosophical and psychological underpinnings of the teaching practice and then determine which approaches resonate with your experiences. You may agree with Mortimer Adler that people have learned a basic body of knowledge over the centuries that must be passed on to the next generation in school. You may share Maxine Greene's belief that the most important thing schools can do is create an encounter with the arts, literature, and daily life that will lead students to develop their own sense of "awakeness" and moral courage. You may concur with Jean Piaget that we must help young people to move through a set of fairly standard developmental stages, or you may believe, as B. F. Skinner does, that a teacher should use incentives and rewards to get students to do what he or she has decided, in advance, is best for the students.

It is important to be able to articulate your own philosophy of education and your own understanding of psychology as the basis for the hundreds of daily decisions you must make in the classroom. You might not say, "I am doing this because I am a Piagetian [or a Skinnerian]," but you will be much more confident and consistent if you are clear on your own beliefs and how these beliefs are grounded in solid ideas.

QUESTIONS

- As you read the philosophers and psychologists in this chapter, which approaches seem to make more sense to you? Do certain approaches seem to apply in specific situations? How does knowing these approaches help provide a foundation for developing your own personal philosophy of education?

- As you begin teaching, how will your personal philosophy of education affect the decisions you make in the classroom? What if the philosophies of your school's administrators differ greatly from yours?

Teachable Moment

The Meaning of Constructivism

In their book *The Case for Constructivist Classrooms*, Jacqueline Grennon Brooks and Martin G. Brooks describe constructivism as "a process of making personal meaning." They note that the current political atmosphere is not always friendly to such a process since many people today are pressing for more direct instruction on the part of teachers and for more focus on the information to be learned on the part of students.

Nevertheless, Brooks and Brooks argue that the only education that really matters takes place when "students make their own meaning." In a constructivist classroom, a teacher "searches for students' understandings of concepts, and then structures opportunities for students to refine or revise these understandings by posing contradictions, presenting new information, asking questions, encouraging research, and/or engaging students in inquiries designed to challenge current concepts."

Brooks and Brooks describe five overarching principles that are evident in constructivist classrooms:

- *Teachers seek and value their students' points of view.* Teachers who consistently present the same material to all students simultaneously may not see students' individual perspectives on the material as being important and may even view them as interfering with the pace and direction of the lesson. In constructivist classrooms, students' perspectives provide the teacher with cues for subsequent lessons.
- *Classroom activities challenge students' suppositions.* All students, regardless of age, enter their classrooms with life experiences that have led them to presume certain truths about how their worlds work. Meaningful classroom experiences either support or contravene students' suppositions by either validating or transforming these truths.
- *Teachers pose problems of emerging relevance.* Relevance, meaning, and interest are not automatically embedded within subject areas or topics. Relevance emerges from the learner. Constructivist teachers, acknowledging the central role of the learner, structure classroom experiences that foster the creation of personal meaning.
- *Teachers build lessons around primary concepts and "big" ideas.* Too much curriculum is presented in small, disconnected parts and never woven into whole cloth by the learner. Students memorize the material needed to pass tests. Many students, even those with passing scores, are unable to apply the small parts in other contexts or to demonstrate understandings of how the parts relate to their wholes. Constructivist teachers often offer academic problems that challenge students to grapple first with the big ideas and discern for themselves, with mediation from the teacher, the parts that require more investigation.
- *Teachers assess student learning in the context of daily teaching.* Constructivist teachers don't view assessment of student learning as separate and distinct from the classroom's normal activities. Rather, assessment should be embedded directly into these recurrent activities.

Source: *The Case for Constructivist Classrooms*, by Jacqueline Grennon Brooks and Martin G. Brooks, 1999, Association for Supervision and Curriculum Development, 1999, pp. ix–x.

QUESTIONS

- As you think about your own experiences in school, were your teachers practicing constructivism, or were they presenting "the same material to all students simultaneously"? Or did they do some of both?
- If constructivism focuses so strongly on students' "making meaning" and on "relevance emerging from the learner," is there a danger that students will focus too much on themselves and not learn the things they need to learn in school? Is this part of the reason that, as Brooks and Brooks note, constructivism has many critics?

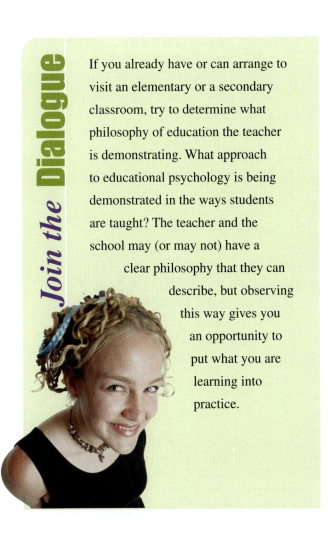

know. Teachers who understand this can provide optimal sequences of learning that will stimulate a series of intuitive leaps. This approach allows students to link new data with past experience and gives opportunities for confirmation checks before the new data are added to the learner's store of knowledge. According to Bruner, "[if] information is to be used effectively, it must be translated into the learner's way of attempting to solve a problem"; it is the teacher's role to help make that happen.[19]

>> What Is the Link Between Brain Research and Day-to-Day Practice in Schools?

In 1996, the National Academies, including the National Academy of Sciences and the National Research Council (organizations traditionally known for leading the nation's research in physics, chemistry, biology, and engineering), called together scientists in the field of psychology to look at a new set of scientific questions. These national leaders in American science decided the time was right to focus on

the schools and, specifically, to ask what the latest brain research tells us about how students learn. What began as a workshop on "The Science of Science Learning" quickly broadened to an effort to understand "the influence that cognitive science has on science and mathematics learning and teaching." The result was a publication, *How People Learn: Brain, Mind, Experience, and School*, which provides a core **Reading** for this chapter.[20]

How People Learn and similar studies represent a substantial new development in the use of basic research in psychology and the activity of the human brain to understand how human beings, especially young humans in school, go about the process of learning. Philosophers and psychologists, including those described earlier in this chapter, have been studying and speculating about these issues for a long time. Although much can be learned from their theories of how children learn, current science gives teachers a significantly more rigorous and scientific look at the learning process. The reports of that research enable us to reconsider effective teaching in new and exceedingly interesting ways.

We are still very early in the process of learning all that scientific research can tell us about the human brain and the learning process. Yet, significant results of studies like those reported in *How People Learn* shed new light on the age-old question facing teachers regarding how children learn what they learn. We now know much more about how the brain works. As the report says, research tells us that "both the developing and mature brain are structurally altered during learning. . . . Learning specific tasks appears to alter the specific regions of the brain appropriate to the task." Although teachers cannot observe the physical alterations in their students' brains that may take place while they are learning, teachers can see the results, especially if they know where to look.

Among the many conclusions of these studies are the following relevant findings about "how early **cognitive abilities** relate to learning":

> **cognitive abilities** An individual's ability to process, comprehend, store, and analyze information.

- Young children actively engage in making sense of their worlds. Research seems to say that Piaget was right about this. (See Piaget's game of marbles. At different stages, the children wanted to learn different aspects of the game as part of the process of making sense of their world.)

- Young children may lack a lot of knowledge, but they do have abilities to reason with the knowledge they do have (if it makes sense to them).

- Children require assistance for learning. Adults play a critical role in promoting children's curiosity and persistence by directing children's attention, structuring their experience, supporting their learning attempts, and regulating the complexity and difficulty of levels of information for them. (Recall Vygotsky's zones of proximal development.)

At the same time, research also points to other significant conclusions about learning and about teaching, including the following:

- People must achieve a threshold of initial learning and then build on that. It takes time to learn complex subject matter, and students need that time before they can be expected to demonstrate their understanding.

- Students develop a flexible understanding of when, where, why, and how to use their knowledge to solve new problems, if they first learn how to extract underlying themes and principles from their learning. Understanding how and when to put knowledge to use in different contexts is an important characteristic of expertise that takes time to develop.

Brain research can (and will) tell us much more, but the findings described here provide an important window into what the latest scientific studies of learning tell us, as teachers, about the most effective ways of teaching.

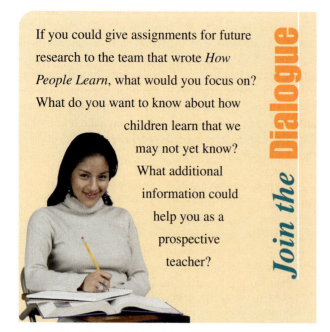

If you could give assignments for future research to the team that wrote *How People Learn*, what would you focus on? What do you want to know about how children learn that we may not yet know? What additional information could help you as a prospective teacher?

Join the Dialogue

Ironically, the results of the latest brain research tend to confirm the ideas of some earlier philosophers and contradict the ideas of others. As the authors of *How People Learn* conclude, "Traditional education has tended to emphasize memorization and mastery of text." But the latest research tells us that this approach does not work well for most students. When students begin to construct their own understanding of a topic—rather than memorizing someone else's views—and when students begin to be independent problem solvers, they learn not only the skills of problem solving but also the content of the ideas. For the first time, perhaps, the material seems relevant to the student and worth knowing—not because knowing the material will earn the student a good grade but because the information will help the student solve a problem he or she wants to solve.

>> How Can Teachers and Schools Serve a Range of Learning Styles?

Even in the seemingly most homogeneous classroom, many different learning styles will be represented. Too often, though, schools have been organized as if there was one right way to learn and those who did not learn in that way were somehow deficient. Today, many educators are acknowledging that people of different backgrounds—

Promising Practices

The Psychology of It

The American Psychological Association (APA) recently established a special task force to attempt to answer the question "What is the core knowledge from psychology that teachers need to know?" The task force, which includes 18 deans of colleges of education, began by identifying the core areas of psychology that are relevant to teacher preparation:

1. Learning theory: How do human beings learn what they learn?
2. Child/adolescent development: How does the age and developmental stage of a student impact what lessons can be taught effectively and how they should be presented?
3. Interpersonal communication and group interaction: How does what we now know about how groups operate, including elementary and secondary classroom groups, impact each of their members and what does this say about classroom management, and about how teachers should organize a class?
4. Assessment: What do we know about educational measurement that can help us evaluate student progress in the most meaningful ways?

The task force's mission is to determine ways for teachers to implement and apply this information in the classroom. Their goal is to

- build classroom *instructional strategies* that lead to student engagement and achievement
- develop effective *classroom management* strategies that lead to student self-regulation, engagement, and achievement

- recognize diversity of learners and address *individual differences* among students
- build successful relationships between home and school, targeting increased student *achievement and self-regulation*
- develop healthy *peer relationships* among students to improve classroom climate
- foster *healthy professional growth* for teachers

It is not typical for a major scientific organization, such as the APA, to spend so much time and energy asking how relevant their work is to classroom teachers, but the results could be significant for teachers inasmuch as they tell us more about child and adolescent development and the best ways to interact with and teach our students.

and different races, ethnic groups, and genders—may learn differently and, according to researchers like Howard Gardner, that there is no one kind of intelligence—no overall measure by which people may be smarter or less smart—but rather multiple modes of intelligence. We need to explore these issues as we consider how we can adjust schools and teaching to serve a range of learning styles.

RACE, ETHNICITY, CLASS, CULTURE, GENDER, AND LEARNING

Looking carefully at issues faced by Hispanic students in schools in the United States, Eugene E. Garcia, the author of *Hispanic Education in the United States*, notes the challenge that some students face, given the cultural differences between their schools and their own communities:

> *Schools attempt to assimilate minority students to mainstream values without considering the potential ramifications of doing so. When the values of the home and community are incongruent with the values of the school, minority children may experience confusion, stress, and adjustment problems that ultimately result in low self-esteem and poor academic performance. Hispanic students who do achieve may be viewed as assimilating and run the risk of being accused of "selling out" or "becoming a coconut" by their Hispanic peers. Peer rejection can be very damaging for racial and ethnic minority youth for whom the need for peer affiliation is very strong.*[21]

Many other scholars have come to similar conclusions. Yet far too often schools are conducted as if such issues—confusion, stress, adjustment problems, and fear of success—were all individual problems to be addressed in counseling or through better motivation rather than being structural problems embedded in the very fabric of institutional education in the United States.

Victoria Purcell-Gates, a professor of literacy at Michigan State University, tells of a disturbing experience she had while visiting an elementary school in a midwestern city:

> *A fourth-grade teacher grinned up at me knowingly as she condemned a young mother: "I knew she was ignorant just as soon as she opened her mouth!" This teacher was referring to the fact that Jenny, the mother of Donny, one of her students, spoke in a southern mountain dialect, a dialect that is often used to characterize poor whites known variously as "hillbillies," "hicks," or "ridgerunners."*

Connections

Recall Lisa Delpit's discussion of the ways schools can fail "other people's children," in Chapter 3.

Purcell-Gates concludes that unless the school directly engages with Donny and his mother and the many students like him, school will not do anything to cross "the cavernous and uncrossable ravine that seems to lie between children of poverty. . .and their full potentials as literate beings." Engaging with Donny does not mean treating him just like every other fourth grader in the school; Donny may need some support that other students do not need. It also does not mean placing the blame on him or his mother or making the kind of snap judgments his teacher made. It does mean understanding that Donny needs very explicit instruction so that he will come to understand that he needs, in his own way, to be bilingual (even if in his case he needs to be bilingual between two different forms of English)—to honor and appreciate his home language and to have the skill to "code switch" and speak another language in school and larger public arenas including the world of work. To fail to give the Donnys of this world the clear explanations that they need, to pretend to treat them like every other student, is to fail to be their teacher.[22]

A generation of feminist scholars also has found that traditional classrooms can be very unwelcoming places for girls and young women. Looking specifically at the study of mathematics, researcher Diana B. Erchick notes that, in math classes, women often find that they "fit the model of the silent learner who believes that authorities rarely tell you why something is as it is." Silencing students who not only need more explanation of why things are as they are, but who also desire to link their thoughts and feelings, is a recipe for failure. The research also shows that a mathematics program that is taught in a more student-centered way and in which the work is clearly connected to larger issues can be much more effective for women students.[23]

In all these cases—the Latino students and other students of color of both genders, poor and easily marginalized White students, and women of all races and ethnicities—the challenge to learning is cultural, not biological. Yet, in ignoring these powerful, socially constructed realities that have a dramatic impact on how different people learn and comprehend, schools do a substantial disservice to the majority of their students.

YouDecide

Do students of different races, ethnicities, or genders learn differently?

PORTRAIT OF AN EDUCATOR

Carol Gilligan

Carol Gilligan was an associate professor at the Graduate School of Education at Harvard in the 1970s, teaching and writing about young people's psychological and moral development, when she started to see a pattern that others had ignored. Looking at interviews she and her colleagues had conducted, she noticed that "the women's voices sounded distinct." Gilligan discovered that the recurrent problems in interpreting women's development were due to the repeated exclusion of women from the

Source: *In a Different Voice: Psychological Theory and Women's Development*, by Carol Gilligan, 1982, Harvard University Press, p. 1.

critical theory-building studies in psychological research. In her groundbreaking book, *In a Different Voice: Psychological Theory and Women's Development*, Gilligan noted that nearly all major psychologists up to her time, from Freud to Piaget, had studied White, middle-class men and boys and then generalized their findings into supposedly "universal" rules of child and adult human development.

For example, most psychologists, including Gilligan's mentor Lawrence Kohlberg, saw increasing individual separation from families and groups as an essential element in maturing. However, Gilligan found that for women, connections to family and community mattered much more, not because they were failing to mature but because maturity meant something different for them.

Following Gilligan's lead, more scholars began to ask similar questions about other groups of people who were excluded from the prime focus of most psychologists up to the 1980s, including poor people, African Americans, Latinos, and Asians and those who did not fit the scientific definition of "normal," which had too often meant European American middle-class males. At a moment in history when historians, sociologists, and educators were demanding a more multicultural approach to *what* was being taught in school—adding the voices and experiences of many different people to the school curriculum—Gilligan's research added the demand that educators pay much more careful attention to *who* was being taught. If different people learn and develop differently, at least in part because of their gender, race, ethnicity, and class backgrounds, then teachers have a responsibility to avoid seeking to fit all students into a single developmental mode. Rather, they need to respond to the needs of a very diverse group of learners who may gather in their classroom—a more difficult but ultimately a much more rewarding assignment.

"NORMAL" LEARNING

Although it is essential to consider the impact of culture, gender, and other such variables on the ways students learn, such appreciation for social differences is only the beginning of our understanding of the wonderful diversity of learning styles represented in every classroom. In his insightful book *Schools That Learn*, Peter Senge reports:

A QUESTION OF . . .

What is a major challenge in teaching today?

"Number one is meeting the needs of all the different learners in the classroom and being able to differentiate instruction to help each child reach his or her individual benchmarks."

—*Lori Talish, first-grade teacher*

Recently, a teacher commented to me that she had eighteen kids in her class and fifteen had different sorts of "learning problems." What is the real meaning of this comment? For the teacher, I believe it was an expression of frustration, a plaintive acknowledgment that she could not provide all that her kids required. But what does it mean when three-quarters of the kids in a class are "abnormal"? Does it not say something about how normal is defined?

Until we develop much more elastic and engaging understandings of the meaning of "normal" or the meaning of "learning," we are doomed to a cycle of failure, for ourselves and for our students. We will forever be plagued with the frustrations of the teacher who reported her problems to Senge. Although Senge has an appreciation for the ways a diversity of students can overwhelm a teacher, he also makes an important point: something is profoundly wrong with the definition of what constitutes a "normal student" or normal success in today's schools.

In fact, Senge believes that one of the major reasons we are not able to think more creatively about how students learn, and how best to construct schools that will encourage learning is that we are stuck in an industrial model of education in which the school is seen as a factory designed to turn out uniform parts. According to Senge, these industrial-age or factory-model assumptions about learning include the following:

1. **Children are deficient and schools fix them**. Children are often taught in school that they *don't* know how to do something, such as paint, sing, or do mathematics. Rather than help them, schools simply label them as "deficient" and reinforce a sense of "I can't do that."

2. **Learning takes place in the head, not in the body as a whole**. Schools are too often organized as if children are disembodied minds, ignoring the growing and restless bodies that these minds are placed in. Students are expected to learn a plethora of facts and figures, regardless of the relevance to their lives as they experience them as young people.

3. **Everyone learns—or should learn—in the same way**. Too often schools are organized as if all students learn best through hearing—rather than touch—and by passively listening rather than through activities. Students will either inherently already learn in that fashion or adapt to these expectations if they are to succeed.

4. **Learning takes place in the classroom, not in the world**. The school's curriculum is the only thing that matters. The experiences of the students—at home, at play, and in other activities—add nothing to their "real" education.

5. **There are smart kids and dumb kids**. Schools still too often sort and track students. Some who thrive in one kind of learning are called "smart," and too many others are discarded as not really up to meeting academic standards.

Senge notes that these five assumptions are in some sense stereotypical and that most educators would disagree with them in principle. Nevertheless, he notes, "the system seems to embody these assumptions, and everyone acts as if they were correct—even if they would prefer to act differently."

The challenge for a teacher is to create, as much as possible in the context of a system that is often beyond one's control, a very different kind of learning experience for the students in the classroom. Such efforts will never be perfect. However, partial success is far better, for the teacher and for her or his students, than accommodating a structure that is educationally wrong. Even worse is an approach to education that allows one's work to be shaped by unexamined assumptions that may be operating in a particular school but that are completely at odds with one's own beliefs and values.[24]

GARDNER'S MULTIPLE INTELLIGENCES

In Senge's discussion of these misleading industrial-age approaches to education, he also notes that substantial groundbreaking research undercuts these all-too-easy assumptions and, in fact, points to the reality that many different young people, and adults, have many different learning styles, different ways of knowing things, and different modes of intelligence and expertise. No one has explored the different forms of human intelligence and expertise more deeply than Harvard professor Howard Gardner.

Becoming disenchanted with what had been, at least for most of the twentieth century, a general understanding of intelligence as a single, even measurable, amount, Gardner said, "Dating back a century to the time of the French psychologist Alfred Binet (1857–1911), psychologists believe that there is a single intelligence, often called 'g' for general intelligence; we are born with that intelligence; our intelligence comes from our biological parents and, as a result, intelligence is not significantly alterable; we psychologists can tell you how smart you are. . . ." But such a view, however widespread among psychologists in the scientific community, did not work when Gardner looked around at the world of real, live human beings. According to Gardner, individuals have different human faculties and their strength (or weakness) in one intellectual area simply does not predict whether they will be strong or weak in some other area.

Gardner's "multiple lenses on the mind" consists of eight forms of intelligence, (now sometimes expanded to nine):

1. linguistic intelligence
2. logical mathematical intelligence
3. musical intelligence
4. spatial intelligence
5. bodily-kinesthetic intelligence
6. interpersonal intelligence (understanding of other persons)
7. intrapersonal intelligence (understanding oneself)
8. naturalist intelligence (the capacity to make distinctions in nature—"between one plant and another, among animals, clouds, mountains, and the like")

Gardner also describes what "may be a ninth or existential intelligence." According to Gardner, this is the "'intelligence of big questions.' When children ask about the size of the universe, when adults ponder death, love, conflict, the future of the planet, they are engaging in existential issues."

All humans, he says, have these eight or nine intelligences, and no two of us have them in exactly the same mix. That is what makes us both human and interesting. However, this newer, more complex understanding of intelligence has made intelligence much more difficult to

What About Me?

Smart in So Many Ways

Consider what interests you or what you believe you are good at doing. Put a check mark on the line next to the statement that is most often true for you:

Linguistic

"word smart"

I like to:
___ tell stories
___ read
___ talk and express
myself clearly
___ persuade, argue
or negotiate
___ teach or discuss topics
with others
___ write

Logical / Mathematical

"logic smart"

I like to:
___ use logic to
solve problems
___ explore mathematics
___ explore science
___ observe and question
how things work
___ figure out how to
fix things

Musical

"music smart"

I like to:
___ use rhythms
___ respond to music
___ sing
___ recognize and
remember melodies
and chords
___ use songs to help
me remember
___ relax with music

Spatial

"picture smart"

I like to:
___ draw or sketch
___ visualize
___ add color
___ build models
___ create illustrations
___ use space and
spatial relationships

Bodily–Kinesthetic

"body smart"

I like to:
___ experience physical
movement
___ act things out
___ use note cards and
models to learn
___ work with others
___ touch and feel material
___ be active and enjoy
sports

Intrapersonal

"self smart"

I like to:
___ be independent and
work on my own
___ reflect on ideas
___ read and contemplate
new thoughts
___ go off and think
through a situation
alone
___ be self-disciplined and
set individual goals
___ make sense through
personal experiences
and inner expression

Interpersonal

"people smart"

I like to:
___ inspire and
lead others
___ learn through
discussions
___ work with a group
of people
___ "read" other
people
___ hear another
person's point
of view
___ be compassionate
and helpful

Naturalist

"outdoor smart"

I like to:
___ be outdoors
___ camp and hike
___ work in the earth
___ collect samples
___ take field trips
___ appreciate nature

QUESTIONS

- What are your strongest areas of "intelligence" (that is, which columns have the most check marks)?
- Does this result coincide with strengths required in the career you have chosen?
- How will you respond to students whose greatest strengths are like yours?
- How will you respond to students whose strengths are quite different from yours?

Source: Reprinted from *Peak Performance: Success in College and Beyond*, 7th edition, by Sharon K. Ferrett, 2010, McGraw-Hill.

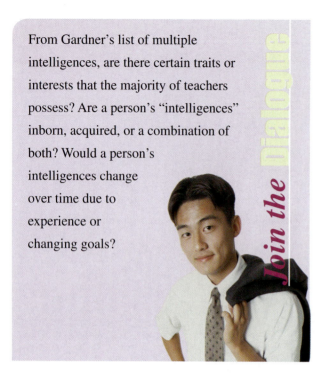

measure. No longer could a single test or a single number (an intelligence quotient, or IQ) define a human as smart or not so smart. No one paper-and-pencil test could provide for the now much more complex analysis of intelligence needed to understand each human being. Instead, Gardner looked to other measures, including brain research (which shows us where in the brain different sorts of mental activity happen) and anthropology (which tells us what different societies have valued at different times in history).[25]

SEE, LISTEN, MOVE

Are you a reader, a listener, or a doer? Everyone has his or her own preferred learning style, which may (or may not) correlate with different types of intelligence. Academic success comes with knowing not only your preference but also how to incorporate other styles to enhance learning (that is, how to think outside the box—or at least outside your comfort zone). The three primary learning styles are as follows:

- visual learners: people who remember what they see better than they remember what they hear; who learn from charts and pictures; and who find reading very informative, often more so than listening to a lecture

- auditory learners: people who remember what they hear better than what they see and who listen well to lectures and instructions, as well as to music and telephone conversations

- kinesthetic learners: people who learn best from hands-on activities; who need to touch, build, and develop models in order to learn something; and for whom the physical act of writing something down or making a model or a collection is the best form of learning[26]

Traditional schooling—in which teachers talk and students listen—has favored auditory learners over either visual or kinesthetic learners. Although schools are changing and finding better ways to include all learners, they are still essentially auditory places. In much the same way that schools have favored linguistic and logical mathematical intelligence over other forms of intelligence, they have too often favored one learning style over others. But knowing more about multiple forms of intelligence and multiple learning styles can help make a teacher *much* more effective. Rather than labeling a student whose strength is in linguistic areas as smarter than a student whose strength may be in musical or interpersonal areas, and rather than labeling a student whose learning style is auditory as a better student than one who learns best kinesthetically, today's teachers have the challenge of learning more about their students and then tailoring their teaching to reach students with many different forms of intelligence and many different learning styles. It is no easy task, but it will dramatically improve the success and happiness of all students.

At this point, if we revisit Senge's assumptions about how schools are organized, we clearly see the "truth" regarding how schools *should* be organized—in both the kinds of learning that they value and in their day-to-day practices:

1. **All children bring strengths as well as weaknesses to school**. No child starts out at "zero," with the school's role as the oh-so-powerful overseer who puts the student on the "right path."

2. **Learning involves the entire body**. It involves what we feel and how we interact with the information—both physically and mentally.

3. **Different people learn in different ways and at different paces**. As you have just read, the past fifty years have seen groundbreaking research on child development, on learning styles, and on the nature of the learning process. Clearly, an extraordinary variety of learning styles and preferences are to be found in our classrooms. A "one-size-fits-all" approach to teaching simply does not work.

4. **Students' real-life experiences play a major role in their total learning**. Genuine learning occurs in the context of our lives as we relate new information to past experiences and as we challenge and connect external dialogues to lessons in the classroom.

5. **Different students will excel in different educational settings**. The more opportunities students have to be challenged and inspired, rather than relegated to distinctions of "superior" or "inferior," the more likely they are to embrace learning and attempt new experiences.

We have a long way to go to make the structure of our schools and our own classrooms fit what we know about

Visit a school and observe a classroom with Senge's five industrial-age assumptions in hand. How many of these assumptions do you see in practice at the school or in the classroom? What might be done to improve this specific situation so that students and teachers can break out of the industrial model of education?

Join the Dialogue

real learning and real success for the majority of students—students who are, in their own way, just as normal as those who succeed in the more traditional structures.

One of the enduring problems of education is that the gap between theory and practice is typically vast. Scientists and educational researchers often make great and important discoveries, but they also fail to write or speak about these discoveries in ways that are accessible to teachers. Teachers' lives are so busy with planning lessons, grading papers, and keeping up with the day-to-day demands of teaching that reading basic research, even if it were written in more accessible ways, seems virtually impossible. Yet this gap must be narrowed. Teachers need and want to know things that will help them be successful, and few things are more worth knowing than how the children in their classrooms go about learning. Basic research tells us so much about these young minds. Finding ways to read, ponder, and use this research is the challenge every teacher must tackle.

REVIEW >>

- **What have philosophers said about human learning?**

  For hundreds of years, philosophers have debated how people learn as well as the best methods for facilitating the learning process. Rarely have philosophers agreed completely, although their approaches often have similar points or build upon each others' foundations, such as the early philosophers Socrates, Plato, and Aristotle, whose teacher-to-student-becomes-teacher relationships built on each predecessor's philosophy. "Modern" philosophers, such as Rousseau, Dewey, Adler, Greene, Martin, hooks, and Appiah, have each in his or her own way developed and influenced current thinking on teacher-student interactions that create optimal learning for all students.

- **How have modern psychologists changed our way of thinking about learning?**

  As with the philosophers, psychologists over the past 100 years have researched human learning and teaching with varying results. Piaget proposed the four levels of development through which a student must systematically progress before attempting subsequent learning. Skinner looked beyond the learning process itself at how to shape the process into desired results. According to Skinner's operant conditioning approach, immediate feedback and positive reinforcement produce the end results the teacher desires. A more student-driven approach, Vygotsky's "zone of proximal development" described the stage, just beyond the child's current one, that the child can be expected to reach with proper input and support. Like Vygotsky, Bruner also sees learning as linking new information to what is previously known. The student must be an active partner in the learning process, engaging in problem solving and the exploration of alternatives.

- **What is the link between brain research and day-to-day practice in schools?**

  Although research on the brain and the learning process is still relatively new, reports such as *How People Learn* have provided significant information on how children learn and the ramifications of this information for teachers.

- **How can teachers and schools serve a range of learning styles?**

  Students learn in many different ways. Effective learning occurs when we look at how individuals learn best rather than when we follow a traditional, industrial model of education, in which teachers are dictators of information and students are receptacles for that information (as described by Senge). Issues such as ethnicity and gender can play a role, as well as learning preferences for receiving and associating information. Howard Gardner's work supports the belief that we all possess a variety of intelligences, reflecting our strengths as individuals, which should be embraced in the learning process.

What Is the Link Between Brain Research and Day-to-Day Practice in Schools?

From *HOW PEOPLE LEARN: BRAIN, MIND, EXPERIENCE, AND SCHOOL*

BY JOHN D. BRANSFORD, ANN L. BROWN, AND RODNEY R. COCKING

For as long as humans have tried to teach things to each other, from the most basic survival lessons to the most complex theories about how the universe works, people have speculated about how they themselves and other people learn. Only recently have scientists in psychology and related fields been able to do the kind of basic research that offers a new scientific understanding about how human beings actually do learn, and therefore about the most effective ways for other human beings—called teachers—to teach. In the past decade, the National Academy of Sciences, the nation's most prestigious organization of scholars, has commissioned important studies on the way the brain works and the ways people learn. The material presented here is an excerpt from the introduction to one of these studies. Anyone aspiring to be a teacher will gain a great deal by reading the entire How People Learn text and other studies that are sure to follow. This research is still in its infancy, and corrections and new conclusions are bound to come out in the years ahead. Nevertheless, this reading gives an overview of the current state of our knowledge about the human brain and human learning.

The essence of matter, the origins of the universe, the nature of the human mind—these are the profound questions that have engaged thinkers through the centuries. Until quite recently, understanding the mind—and the thinking and learning that the mind makes possible—has remained an elusive quest, in part because of a lack of powerful research tools. Today, the world is in the midst of an extraordinary outpouring of scientific work on the mind and brain, on the processes of thinking and learning, on the neural processes that occur during thought and learning, and on the development of competence.

The revolution in the study of the mind that has occurred in the last three or four decades has important implications for education. As we illustrate, a new theory of learning is coming into focus that leads to very different approaches to the design of curriculum, teaching, and assessment than those often found in schools today. Equally important, the growth of inter-disciplinary inquiries and new kinds of scientific collaborations have begun to make the path from basic research to educational practice somewhat more visible, if not yet easy to travel. Thirty years ago, educators paid little attention to the work of cognitive scientists, and researchers in the nascent field of cognitive science worked far removed from classrooms. Today, cognitive researchers are spending more time working with teachers, testing and refining their theories in real classrooms where they can see how different settings and classroom interactions influence applications of their theories.

What is perhaps currently most striking is the variety of research approaches and techniques that have been developed and ways in which evidence from many different branches of science are beginning to converge. The story we can now tell about learning is far richer than ever before, and it promises to evolve dramatically in the next generation. For example:

- Research from cognitive psychology has increased understanding of the nature of competent performance and the principles of knowledge organization that underlie people's abilities to solve problems in a wide variety of areas, including mathematics, science, literature, social studies, and history.
- Developmental researchers have shown that young children understand a great deal about basic principles of biology and physical causality, about number, narrative, and personal intent, and that these capabilities make it possible to create innovative curricula that introduce important concepts for advanced reasoning at early ages.
- Research on learning and transfer has uncovered important principles for structuring learning experiences that enable people to use what they have learned in new settings.
- Work in social psychology, cognitive psychology, and anthropology is making clear that all learning takes place in settings that have particular sets of cultural and social norms and expectations and that these settings influence learning and transfer in powerful ways.
- Neuroscience is beginning to provide evidence for many principles of learning that have emerged from laboratory research, and it is showing how learning changes the physical structure of the brain and, with it, the functional organization of the brain.

Source: "Learning: From Speculation to Science," by John D. Bransford, Ann L. Brown, and Rodney R. Cocking, editors, 2000, *How People Learn: Brain, Mind, Experience, and School*, National Academies Press, pp. 3–27.

- Collaborative studies of the design and evaluation of learning environments, among cognitive and developmental psychologists and educators, are yielding new knowledge about the nature of learning and teaching as it takes place in a variety of settings. In addition, researchers are discovering ways to learn from the "wisdom of practice" that comes from successful teachers who can share their expertise.
- Emerging technologies are leading to the development of many new opportunities to guide and enhance learning that were unimagined even a few years ago.

All of these developments in the study of learning have led to an era of new relevance of science to practice. In short, investment in basic research is paying off in practical applications. These developments in understanding of how humans learn have particular significance in light of changes in what is expected of the nation's educational systems.

In the early part of the twentieth century, education focused on the acquisition of literacy skills: simple reading, writing, and calculating. It was not the general rule for educational systems to train people to think and read critically, to express themselves clearly and persuasively, to solve complex problems in science and mathematics. Now, at the end of the century, these aspects of high literacy are required of almost everyone in order to successfully negotiate the complexities of contemporary life. The skill demands for work have increased dramatically, as has the need for organizations and workers to change in response to competitive workplace pressures. Thoughtful participation in the democratic process has also become increasingly complicated as the locus of attention has shifted from local to national and global concerns.

Above all, information and knowledge are growing at a far more rapid rate than ever before in the history of humankind. As Nobel laureate Herbert Simon wisely stated, the meaning of "knowing" has shifted from being able to remember and repeat information to being able to find and use it (Simon, 1996). More than ever, the sheer magnitude of human knowledge renders its coverage by education an impossibility; rather, the goal of education is better conceived as helping students develop the intellectual tools and learning strategies needed to acquire the knowledge that allows people to think productively about history, science and technology, social phenomena, mathematics, and the arts. Fundamental understanding about subjects, including how to frame and ask meaningful questions about various subject areas, contributes to individuals' more basic understanding of principles of learning that can assist them in becoming self-sustaining, lifelong learners.

Learning With Understanding

One of the hallmarks of the new science of learning is its emphasis on learning with understanding. Intuitively, understanding is good, but it has been difficult to study from a scientific perspective. At the same time, students often have limited opportunities to understand or make sense of topics because many curricula have emphasized memory rather than understanding. Textbooks are filled with facts that students are expected to memorize, and most tests assess students' abilities to remember the facts. When studying about veins and arteries, for example, students may be expected to remember that arteries are thicker than veins, more elastic, and carry blood from the heart; veins carry blood back to the heart. A test item for this information may look like the following:

1. Arteries
   a. Are more elastic than veins
   b. Carry blood that is pumped from the heart
   c. Are less elastic than veins
   d. Both a and b
   e. Both b and c

The new science of learning does not deny that facts are important for thinking and problem solving. Research on expertise in areas such as chess, history, science, and mathematics demonstrate that experts' abilities to think and solve problems depend strongly on a rich body of knowledge about subject matter (e.g., Chase and Simon, 1973; Chi et al., 1981; deGroot, 1965). However, the research also shows clearly that "usable knowledge" is not the same as a mere list of disconnected facts. Experts' knowledge is connected and organized around important concepts (e.g., Newton's second law of motion); it is "conditionalized" to specify the contexts in which it is applicable; it supports understanding and transfer (to other contexts) rather than only the ability to remember.

For example, people who are knowledgeable about veins and arteries know more than the facts noted above: they also understand why veins and arteries have particular properties. They know that blood pumped from the heart exits in spurts and that the elasticity of the arteries helps accommodate pressure changes. They know that blood from the heart needs to move upward (to the brain) as well as downward and that the elasticity of an artery permits it to function as a one-way valve that closes at the end of each spurt and prevents the blood from flowing backward. Because they understand relationships between the structure and function of veins and arteries, knowledgeable individuals are more likely to be able to use what they have learned to solve novel problems—to show evidence of transfer. For example, imagine being asked to design an artificial artery—would it have to be elastic? Why or why not? An understanding of reasons for the properties of arteries suggests that elasticity may not be necessary—perhaps the problem can be solved by creating a conduit that is strong enough to handle the pressure of spurts from the heart and also function as a one-way valve. An understanding of veins and arteries does not guarantee an answer to this design question, but it does support thinking about alternatives that are not readily available if one only memorizes facts (Bransford and Stein, 1993).

Pre-Existing Knowledge

An emphasis on understanding leads to one of the primary characteristics of the new science of learning: its focus on the processes of knowing (e.g., Piaget, 1978; Vygotsky, 1978). Humans are viewed as goal-directed agents who actively seek information. They come to formal education with a range of prior knowledge, skills, beliefs, and concepts that significantly influence what they notice about the environment and how they organize and interpret it. This, in turn, affects their abilities to remember, reason, solve problems, and acquire new knowledge.

Even young infants are active learners who bring a point of view to the learning setting. The world they enter is not a "booming, buzzing confusion" (James, 1890), where every stimulus is equally salient. Instead, an infant's brain gives precedence to certain kinds of information: language, basic concepts of number, physical properties, and the movement of animate and inanimate objects. In the most general sense, the contemporary view of learning is that people construct new knowledge and understandings based on what they already know and believe (e.g., Cobb, 1994; Piaget,1952, 1973a,b, 1977, 1978; Vygotsky, 1962, 1978). A classic children's book illustrates this point; see Box 1.

A logical extension of the view that new knowledge must be constructed from existing knowledge is that teachers need to pay attention to the incomplete understandings, the false beliefs, and the naive renditions of concepts that learners bring with them to a given subject. Teachers then need to build on these ideas in ways that help each student achieve a more mature understanding. If students' initial ideas and beliefs are ignored, the understandings that they develop can be very different from what the teacher intends.

Consider the challenge of working with children who believe that the earth is flat and attempting to help them understand that it is spherical. When told it is round, children picture the earth as a pancake rather than as a sphere (Vosniadou and Brewer, 1989). If they are then told that it is round like a sphere, they interpret the new information about a spherical earth within their flat-earth view by picturing a pancake-like flat surface inside or on top of a sphere, with humans standing on top of the pancake.

The children's construction of their new understandings has been guided by a model of the earth that helped them explain how they could stand or walk upon its surface, and a spherical earth did not fit their mental model. Like *Fish Is Fish*, everything the children heard was incorporated into that preexisting view.

Fish Is Fish is relevant not only for young children, but for learners of all ages. For example, college students often have developed beliefs about physical and biological phenomena that fit their experiences but do not fit scientific accounts of these phenomena. These preconceptions must be addressed in order for them to change their beliefs (e.g., Confrey, 1990; Mestre, 1994; Minstrell, 1989; Redish, 1996).

A common misconception regarding "constructivist" theories of knowing (that existing knowledge is used to build new knowledge) is that teachers should never tell students anything directly but, instead, should always allow them to construct knowledge for themselves. This perspective confuses a theory of pedagogy (teaching) with a theory of knowing. Constructivists assume that all knowledge is constructed from previous knowledge, irrespective of how one is taught (e.g., Cobb, 1994)—even listening to a lecture involves active attempts to construct new knowledge. *Fish Is Fish* (Lionni, 1970) and attempts to teach children that the earth is round (Vosniadou and Brewer, 1989) show why simply providing lectures frequently does not work. Nevertheless, there are times, usually after people have first grappled with issues on their own, that "teaching by telling" can work extremely well (e.g., Schwartz and Bransford, 1998). However, teachers still need to pay attention to students' interpretations and provide guidance when necessary.

BOX 1 *Fish Is Fish*

Fish Is Fish (Lionni, 1970) describes a fish who is keenly interested in learning about what happens on land, but the fish cannot explore land because it can only breathe in water. It befriends a tadpole who grows into a frog and eventually goes out onto the land. The frog returns to the pond a few weeks later and reports on what he has seen. The frog describes all kinds of things like birds, cows, and people. The book shows pictures of the fish's representations of each of these descriptions: each is a fish-like form that is slightly adapted to accommodate the frog's descriptions—people are imagined to be fish who walk on their tailfins, birds are fish with wings, cows are fish with udders. This tale illustrates both the creative opportunities and dangers inherent in the fact that people construct new knowledge based on their current knowledge.

There is a good deal of evidence that learning is enhanced when teachers pay attention to the knowledge and beliefs that learners bring to a learning task, use this knowledge as a starting point for new instruction, and monitor students' changing conceptions as instruction proceeds. For example, sixth graders in a suburban school who were given inquiry-based physics instruction were shown to do better on conceptual physics problems than eleventh and twelfth grade physics students taught by conventional methods in the same school system. A second study comparing seventh–ninth grade urban students with the eleventh and twelfth grade suburban physics students again showed that the younger students, taught by the inquiry-based approach, had a better grasp of the fundamental principles of physics (White and Frederickson, 1997, 1998). New curricula for young children have also demonstrated results that are extremely promising: for example, a new approach to teaching geometry helped second-grade children learn to represent and visualize three-dimensional forms in ways that exceeded the skills of a comparison group of undergraduate students at a leading university (Lehrer and Chazan, 1998). Similarly, young children have been taught to demonstrate powerful forms of early geometry generalizations (Lehrer and Chazan, 1998) and generalizations about science (Schauble et al., 1995; Warren and Rosebery, 1996).

Active Learning

New developments in the science of learning also emphasize the importance of helping people take control of their own learning. Since understanding is viewed as important, people must learn to recognize when they understand and when they need more information. What strategies might they use to assess whether they understand someone else's meaning? What kinds of evidence do they need in order to believe particular claims? How can they build their own theories of phenomena and test them effectively?

Many important activities that support active learning have been studied under the heading of "metacognition." Metacognition refers to people's abilities to predict their performances on various tasks (e.g., how well they will be able to remember various stimuli) and to monitor their current levels of mastery and understanding (e.g., Brown, 1975; Flavell, 1973). Teaching practices congruent with a metacognitive approach to learning include those that focus on sensemaking, self-assessment, and reflection on what worked and what needs improving. These practices have been shown to increase the degree to which students transfer their learning to new settings and events (e.g., Palincsar and Brown, 1984; Scardamalia et al., 1984; Schoenfeld, 1983, 1985, 1991).

Imagine three teachers whose practices affect whether students learn to take control of their own learning (Scardamalia and Bereiter, 1991). Teacher A's goal is to get the students to produce work; this is accomplished by supervising and overseeing the quantity and quality of the work done by the students. The focus is on activities, which could be anything from old-style workbook activities to the trendiest of space-age projects. Teacher B assumes responsibility for what the students are learning as they carry out their activities. Teacher C does this as well, but with the added objective of continually turning more of the learning process over to the students. Walking into a classroom, you cannot immediately tell these three kinds of teachers apart. One of the things you might see is the students working in groups to produce videos or multimedia presentations. The teacher is likely to be found going from group to group, checking how things are going and responding to requests. Over the course of a few days, however, differences between Teacher A and Teacher B would become evident. Teacher A's focus is entirely on the production process and its products—whether the students are engaged, whether everyone is getting fair treatment, and whether they are turning out good pieces of work. Teacher B attends to all of this as well, but Teacher B is also attending to what the students are learning from the experience and is taking steps to ensure that the students are processing content and not just dealing with show. To see a difference between Teachers B and C, however, you might need to go back into the history of the media production project. What brought it about in the first place? Was it conceived from the start as a learning activity, or did it emerge from the students' own knowledge building efforts? In one striking example of a Teacher C classroom, the students had been studying cockroaches and had learned so much from their reading and observation that they wanted to share it with the rest of the school; the production of a video came about to achieve that purpose (Lamon et al., 1997).

The differences in what might seem to be the same learning activity are thus quite profound. In Teacher A's classroom, the students are learning something of media production, but the media production may very well be getting in the way of learning anything else. In Teacher B's classroom, the teacher is working to ensure that the original educational purposes of the activity are met, that it does not deteriorate into a mere media production exercise. In Teacher C's classroom, the media production is continuous with and a direct outgrowth of the learning that is embodied in the media production. The greater part of Teacher C's work has been done before the idea of a media production even comes up, and it remains only to help the students keep sight of their purposes as they carry out the project.

These hypothetical teachers—A, B, and C—are abstract models that of course fit real teachers only partly, and more on some days than others. Nevertheless, they provide important glimpses of connections between goals for learning and teaching practices that can affect students' abilities to accomplish these goals.

Key Findings

1. Students come to the classroom with preconceptions about how the world works. If their initial understanding is not engaged, they may fail to grasp

the new concepts and information that are taught, or they may learn them for purposes of a test but revert to their preconceptions outside the classroom.

2. To develop competence in an area of inquiry, students must: (a) have a deep foundation of factual knowledge, (b) understand facts and ideas in the context of a conceptual framework, and (c) organize knowledge in ways that facilitate retrieval and application.

3. A "metacognitive" approach to instruction can help students learn to take control of their own learning by defining learning goals and monitoring their progress in achieving them.

Implications for Teaching

The three core learning principles described above, simple though they seem, have profound implications for the enterprise of teaching and teacher preparation.

1. *Teachers must draw out and work with the preexisting understandings that their students bring with them.* This requires that:

   - The model of the child as an empty vessel to be filled with knowledge provided by the teacher must be replaced. Instead, the teacher must actively inquire into students' thinking, creating classroom tasks and conditions under which student thinking can be revealed. Students' initial conceptions then provide the foundation on which the more formal understanding of the subject matter is built.
   - The roles for assessment must be expanded beyond the traditional concept of testing. The use of frequent formative assessment helps make students' thinking visible to themselves, their peers, and their teacher. This provides feedback that can guide modification and refinement in thinking. Given the goal of learning with understanding, assessments must tap understanding rather than merely the ability to repeat facts or perform isolated skills.
   - Schools of education must provide beginning teachers with opportunities to learn: (a) to recognize predictable preconceptions of students that make the mastery of particular subject matter challenging, (b) to draw out preconceptions that are not predictable, and (c) to work with preconceptions so that children build on them, challenge them and, when appropriate, replace them.

2. *Teachers must teach some subject matter in depth, providing many examples in which the same concept is at work and providing a firm foundation of factual knowledge.* This requires that:

   - Superficial coverage of all topics in a subject area must be replaced with in-depth coverage of fewer topics that allows key concepts in that discipline to be understood. The goal of coverage need not be abandoned entirely, of course. But there must be a sufficient number of cases of in-depth study to allow students to grasp the defining concepts in specific domains within a discipline. Moreover, in-depth study in a domain often requires that ideas be carried beyond a single school year before students can make the transition from informal to formal ideas. This will require active coordination of the curriculum across school years.
   - Teachers must come to teaching with the experience of in-depth study of the subject area themselves. Before a teacher can develop powerful pedagogical tools, he or she must be familiar with the progress of inquiry and the terms of discourse in the discipline, as well as understand the relationship between information and the concepts that help organize that information in the discipline. But equally important, the teacher must have a grasp of the growth and development of students' thinking about these concepts. The latter will be essential to developing teaching expertise, but not expertise in the discipline. It may therefore require courses, or course supplements, that are designed specifically for teachers.
   - Assessment for purposes of accountability (e.g., statewide assessments) must test deep understanding rather than surface knowledge. Assessment tools are often the standard by which teachers are held accountable. A teacher is put in a bind if she or he is asked to teach for deep conceptual understanding, but in doing so produces students who perform more poorly on standardized tests.

Unless new assessment tools are aligned with new approaches to teaching, the latter are unlikely to muster support among the schools and their constituent parents. This goal is as important as it is difficult to achieve. The format of standardized tests can encourage measurement of factual knowledge rather than conceptual understanding, but it also facilitates objective scoring. Measuring depth of understanding can pose challenges for objectivity. Much work needs to be done to minimize the trade-off between assessing depth and assessing objectively.

3. *The teaching of metacognitive skills should be integrated into the curriculum in a variety of subject areas.* Because metacognition often takes the form of an internal dialogue, many students may be unaware of its importance unless the processes are explicitly emphasized by teachers. An emphasis on metacognition needs to accompany instruction in each of the disciplines, because the type of monitoring required will vary. In history, for example, the student might be asking himself, "who wrote this document, and how does that affect the interpretation of events," whereas in physics the student might be monitoring her understanding of the underlying physical principle at work.

- Integration of metacognitive instruction with discipline-based learning can enhance student achievement and develop in students the ability to learn independently. It should be consciously incorporated into curricula across disciplines and age levels.
- Developing strong metacognitive strategies and learning to teach those strategies in a classroom environment should be standard features of the curriculum in schools of education.

Evidence from research indicates that when these three principles are incorporated into teaching, student achievement improves. For example, the Thinker Tools Curriculum for teaching physics in an interactive computer environment focuses on fundamental physical concepts and properties, allowing students to test their preconceptions in model building and experimentation activities. The program includes an "inquiry cycle" that helps students monitor where they are in the inquiry process. The program asks for students' reflective assessments and allows them to review the assessments of their fellow students. In one study, sixth graders in a suburban school who were taught physics using Thinker Tools performed better at solving conceptual physics problems than did eleventh and twelfth grade physics students in the same school system taught by conventional methods. A second study comparing urban students in grades 7 to 9 with suburban students in grades 11 and 12 again showed that the younger students taught by the inquiry-based approach had a superior grasp of the fundamental principles of physics (White and Frederickson, 1997, 1998).

Bringing Order to Chaos

A benefit of focusing on how people learn is that it helps bring order to a seeming cacophony of choices. Consider the many possible teaching strategies that are debated in education circles and the media. Figure 1.1 depicts them in diagram format: lecture-based teaching, text-based teaching, inquiry-based teaching, technology-enhanced teaching, teaching organized around individuals versus cooperative groups, and so forth. Are some of these teaching techniques better than others? Is lecturing a poor way to teach, as many seem to claim? Is cooperative learning effective? Do attempts to use computers (technology-enhanced teaching) help achievement or hurt it?

This volume suggests that these are the wrong questions. Asking which teaching technique is best is analogous to asking which tool is best—a hammer, a screwdriver, a knife, or pliers. In teaching as in carpentry, the selection of tools depends on the task at hand and the materials one is working with. Books and lectures *can* be wonderfully efficient modes of transmitting new information for learning, exciting the imagination, and honing students' critical faculties—but one would choose other kinds of activities to elicit from students their preconceptions and level of understanding, or to help them see the power of using meta-cognitive strategies to monitor their learning. Hands-on experiments *can* be a powerful way to ground emergent knowledge, but they do not alone evoke the underlying conceptual understandings that aid generalization. There is no universal best teaching practice.

If, instead, the point of departure is a core set of learning principles, then the selection of teaching strategies (mediated, of course, by subject matter, grade level, and desired outcome) can be purposeful. The many possibilities then become a rich set of opportunities from which a teacher constructs an instructional program rather than a chaos of competing alternatives.

Focusing on how people learn also will help teachers move beyond either-or dichotomies that have plagued the field of education. One such issue is whether schools should emphasize "the basics" or teach thinking and problem-solving skills. This volume shows that both are necessary. Students' abilities to acquire organized sets of facts and skills are actually enhanced when they are connected to meaningful problem-solving activities, and when students are helped to understand why, when, and how those facts and skills are relevant. And attempts to teach thinking skills without a strong base of factual knowledge do not promote problem-solving ability or support transfer to new situations.

Designing Classroom Environments

Chapter 6 of this volume proposes a framework to help guide the design and evaluation of environments that can optimize learning. Drawing heavily on the three principles discussed above, it posits four interrelated attributes of learning environments that need cultivation.

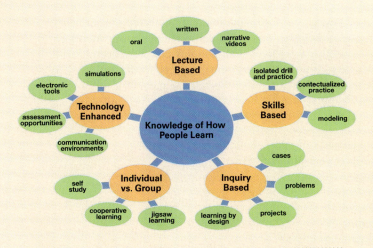

Figure 1.1 With knowledge of how people learn, teachers can choose more purposefully among techniques to accomplish specific goals.

1. **Schools and classrooms must be learner centered.** Teachers must pay close attention to the knowledge, skills, and attitudes that learners bring into the classroom. This incorporates the preconceptions regarding subject matter already discussed, but it also includes a broader understanding of the learner. For example:

   - Cultural differences can affect students' comfort level in working collaboratively versus individually, and they are reflected in the background knowledge students bring to a new learning situation (Moll et al., 1993).

   - Students' theories of what it means to be intelligent can affect their performance. Research shows that students who think that intelligence is a fixed entity are more likely to be performance oriented than learning oriented—they want to look good rather than risk making mistakes while learning. These students are especially likely to bail out when tasks become difficult. In contrast, students who think that intelligence is malleable are more willing to struggle with challenging tasks; they are more comfortable with risk (Dweck, 1989; Dweck and Legget, 1988).

   Teachers in learner-centered classrooms also pay close attention to the individual progress of each student and devise tasks that are appropriate. Learner-centered teachers present students with "just manageable difficulties"—that is, challenging enough to maintain engagement, but not so difficult as to lead to discouragement. They must therefore have an understanding of their students' knowledge, skill levels, and interests (Duckworth, 1987).

2. **To provide a knowledge-centered classroom environment, attention must be given to what is taught (information, subject matter), why it is taught (understanding), and what competence or** *mastery looks like.* As mentioned above, research discussed in the following chapters shows clearly that expertise involves well-organized knowledge that supports understanding, and that learning with understanding is important for the development of expertise because it makes new learning easier (i.e., supports transfer).

   Learning with understanding is often harder to accomplish than simply memorizing, and it takes more time. Many curricula fail to support learning with understanding because they present too many disconnected facts in too short a time—the "mile wide, inch deep" problem. Tests often reinforce memorizing rather than understanding. The knowledge-centered environment provides the necessary depth of study, assessing student understanding rather than factual memory. It incorporates the teaching of meta-cognitive strategies that further facilitate future learning.

   Knowledge-centered environments also look beyond engagement as the primary index of successful teaching (Prawaf et al., 1992). Students' interest or engagement in a task is clearly important. Nevertheless, it does not guarantee that students will acquire the kinds of knowledge that will support new learning. There are important differences between tasks and projects that encourage hands-on doing and those that encourage doing with understanding; the knowledge-centered environment emphasizes the latter (Greeno, 1991).

3. *Formative assessments—ongoing assessments designed to make students' thinking visible to both teachers and students—are essential. They permit the teacher to grasp the students' preconceptions, understand where the students are in the "developmental corridor" from informal to formal thinking, and design instruction accordingly. In the assessment-centered classroom environment, formative assessments help both teachers and students monitor progress.*

   An important feature of assessments in these classrooms is that they be learner-friendly: they are not the Friday quiz for which information is memorized the night before, and for which the student is given a grade that ranks him or her with respect to classmates. Rather, these assessments should provide students with opportunities to revise and improve their thinking (Vye et al., 1998b), help students see their own progress over the course of weeks or months, and help teachers identify problems that need to be remedied (problems that may not be visible without the assessments). For example, a high school class studying the principles of democracy might be given a scenario in which a colony of people have just settled on the moon and must establish a government. Proposals from students of the defining features of such a government, as well as discussion of the problems they foresee in its establishment, can reveal to both teachers and students areas in which student thinking is more and less advanced. The exercise is less a test than an indicator of where inquiry and instruction should focus.

4. *Learning is influenced in fundamental ways by the context in which it takes place. A community-centered approach requires the development of norms for the classroom and school, as well as connections to the outside world, that support core learning values.*

The norms established in the classroom have strong effects on students' achievement. In some schools, the norms could be expressed as "don't get caught not knowing something." Others encourage academic risk-taking and opportunities to make mistakes, obtain feedback, and revise. Clearly, if students are to reveal their preconceptions about a subject matter, their questions, and their progress toward understanding, the norms of the school must support their doing so.

Teachers must attend to designing classroom activities and helping students organize their work in ways that promote the kind of intellectual camaraderie and the attitudes toward learning that build a sense of community. In such a community, students might help one another solve problems by building on each other's knowledge, asking questions to clarify explanations, and suggesting avenues that would move the group toward its goal (Brown and Campione, 1994). Both cooperation in problem solving (Evans, 1989; Newstead and Evans, 1995) and argumentation (Goldman, 1994; Habermas, 1990; Kuhn, 1991; Moshman, 1995a, 1995b; Salmon and Zeitz, 1995; Youniss and Damon, 1992) among students in such an intellectual community enhance cognitive development.

Teachers must be enabled and encouraged to establish a community of learners among themselves (Lave and Wegner, 1991). These communities can build a sense of comfort with questioning rather than knowing the answer and can develop a model of creating new ideas that build on the contributions of individual members. They can engender a sense of the excitement of learning that is then transferred to the classroom, conferring a sense of ownership of new

Figure 1.2 Students spend only 14 percent of their lives in school.

ideas as they apply to theory and practice. Not least, schools need to develop ways to link classroom learning to other aspects of students' lives. Engendering parent support for the core learning principles and parent involvement in the learning process is of utmost importance (Moll, 1990; 1986a, 1986b).

Figure 1.2 shows the percentage of time, during a calendar year, that students in a large school district spent in school. If one-third of their time outside school (not counting sleeping) is spent watching television, then students apparently spend more hours per year watching television than attending school. A focus only on the hours that students currently spend in school overlooks the many opportunities for guided learning in other settings.

Applying the Design Framework to Adult Learning

The design framework summarized above assumes that the learners are children, but the principles apply to adult learning as well. This point is particularly important because incorporating the principles in this volume into educational practice will require a good deal of adult learning. Many approaches to teaching adults consistently violate principles for optimizing learning. Professional development programs for teachers, for example, frequently:

- *Are not learner centered*. Rather than ask teachers where they need help, they are simply expected to attend prearranged workshops.

- *Are not knowledge centered*. Teachers may simply be introduced to a new technique (like cooperative learning) without being given the opportunity to understand why, when, where, and how it might be valuable to them. Especially important is the need to integrate the structure of activities with the content of the curriculum that is taught.

- *Are not assessment centered*. In order for teachers to change their practices, they need opportunities to try things out in their classrooms and then receive feedback. Most professional development opportunities do not provide such feedback. Moreover, they tend to focus on change in teaching practice as the goal, but they neglect to develop in teachers the capacity to judge successful transfer of the technique to the classroom or its effects on student achievement.

- *Are not community centered*. Many professional development opportunities are conducted in isolation. Opportunities for continued contact and support as teachers incorporate new ideas into their teaching are limited, yet the rapid spread of Internet access provides a ready means of maintaining such contact if appropriately designed tools and services are available. The principles of learning and their implications for designing learning environments apply equally to child and adult learning. They provide a lens through which current practice can be viewed with respect to K-12 teaching *and* with respect to preparation of teachers in the research and development agenda. The principles are relevant as well when we consider other groups, such as policy makers and the public, whose learning is also required for educational practice to change.

QUESTIONS

1. As you think about the schools you attended and those you have observed more recently, to what degree does the teaching reflect what these authors call the "latest scientific thinking" about how people learn? Did the teaching build on pre-existing knowledge? Were the students encouraged to be active or passive learners?

2. As you read the *Fish Is a Fish* example, ask yourself if you have ever had an experience like the fish did, such as a time when you completely misunderstood something because you were hearing the story through an inappropriate filter. Try to think of specific examples.

3. Does this research mean a teacher should never give direct instruction to students? In light of the theories presented here, when might traditional "teaching by telling" be appropriate? When might it be inappropriate?

4. Late in the article, the authors say, "There is no universal best teaching practice." Why do you think they say that? Do you agree or disagree with their conclusion? Are there universally worst teaching practices?

How Can Teachers and Schools Serve a Range of Learning Styles?

From "MULTIPLE LENSES ON THE MIND"

BY HOWARD GARDNER

One of the nation's most respected educational psychologists, Howard Gardner is a professor at the Harvard Graduate School of Education. He has written dozens of books and articles, and his primary contribution to our thinking about education—the notion that there is not one but many forms of intelligence—has significant implications for every teacher. His work frees us from the traditional belief that some students are smarter than others on any single scale and calls on all teachers to cultivate the rich differences in learning styles and in basic intelligence that can be found in any classroom.

Let me provide a few contextual remarks. First of all, as a young person, the child of refugees from Nazi Germany, I had been a good student and a serious musician. When I began to study 'real' psychology, I was intrigued by the fact that the arts were rarely mentioned in serious psychology circles. To have a mind was to be a scientist, or at least to think scientifically; many psychologists were ex-engineers or suffered from physics envy; the last thing that they wanted to do was to be seen as artistic 'softies.' Early on, I decided that I wanted to illuminate the nature of artistic thinking. Also, I was particularly interested in issues of creativity— how does a person conjure up something new, whether it is a sonnet, a symphony, a sketch, or a scientific theory?

My First Studies

For the first ten years of my professional career, I studied how the mind develops in children and how it breaks down under conditions of brain damage. As you may know, the single most important thing about a brain lesion is where the damage is. If one is right handed, and suffers injury in the middle areas of the left hemisphere, one is likely to become aphasic—to have a major disturbance of one's language facilities. But if you suffer injury to the right hemisphere, your language will be ostensibly fine, but,

Source: "Multiple Lenses on the Mind," by Howard Gardner, paper presented at the ExpoGestion Conference, Bogotá, Colombia, May 25, 2005. For a fuller explanation of Gardner's theories of multiple intelligences, see *Intelligence Reframed*, by Howard Gardner, 1999, Basic Books.

depending on the location and depth of the lesion, you are likely to be impaired in musical cognition, spatial cognition, and/or your understanding of other people.

With normal and gifted children and with brain damaged adults, I studied how human beings deal with various kinds of symbols. As I've already mentioned, I had a particular interest in the arts. And so I studied the development and breakdown of musical abilities, graphic abilities, metaphoric and narrative capacities, and other abilities crucial in the arts. Of course, when you look at these abilities, you necessarily encounter nonartistic capacities as well—mastery of ordinary language, calculation, understanding of other persons, and the like.

At the time that my studies began, I had been a convinced Piagetian—I believed that logical-mathematical thought was the center of all cognition. I believed that children passed through a series of qualitatively different stages, and that their mental world gets remade, whenever they enter the next stage. I believed that cognitive development is completed by the middle of adolescence, at the latest. And I never thought at all about intelligence tests.

I still think that Piaget is the greatest student of the development of the mind. Every student of cognitive development owes an incalculable debt to Piaget. And yet, with the benefit of hindsight, I can see that during that decade, I gradually lost my Piagetian religion. By 1980, I believed that there were a series of relatively independent cognitive capacities of which logical-mathematical thought was only one. I believed that stages were much looser than Piaget had envisioned, and, more importantly, that one's sophistication with one kind of mental representation did not predict one's sophistication with other mental representations. I believed that cognitive development continues well past adolescence, and that various cognitive capacities—like creativity, leadership, and the ability to change the minds of other persons—remain to be illuminated, despite Piaget's remarkable achievements. Finally, I had become deeply estranged from standard intelligence (IQ) testing.

The Organization of the Mind

In the West, a certain view of mind has held sway for a century. Dating back a century to the time of the French psychologist Alfred Binet, psychologists believe that there is a single intelligence, often called 'g' for general intelligence; we are born with that intelligence; our intelligence comes from our biological parents and, as a result, intelligence is not significantly alterable; we psychologists can tell you how smart you are—traditionally, by giving you an IQ test, more recently, by examining the shape of your brain waves, perhaps ultimately, by looking at a chip on which your genes are encoded.

My research in cognitive development and cognitive breakdown convinced me that this traditional view of intellect is not tenable. Individuals have different human faculties and their strength (or weakness) in one intellectual sphere simply does not predict whether a particular individual will be strong or weak in some other intellectual component. I developed a definition of intelligence—a biopsychological information-processing capacity to solve problems or fashion products that are valued in at least one community and culture. I think of the intelligences as a set of relatively independent computers. One computer deals with language, a second with spatial information, a third with information about other people.

But how to figure out what is the right set of computers? I came up with a set of eight criteria of what counts as an intelligence. Unlike most approaches to intelligence, the criteria were not dependent on results of a paper and pencil test. Rather I looked at criteria from neurology: which brain regions mediate particular skills; anthropology—which abilities have been valued in different cultures across history and pre-history; special populations, such as prodigies, savants, and individuals with learning disabilities. All these individual have jagged intellectual profiles, ones not easily explained if one believes in a single 'general intelligence.'

Ultimately I came up with a list of eight, possibly nine intelligences. I will mention each, and then give examples of individuals or roles that stand out in that particular intelligence:

1. Linguistic intelligence—the intelligence of a writer, orator, journalist.
2. Logical mathematical intelligence—the intelligence of a logician, mathematician, scientist—Piaget thought that he was studying all of intelligence, but he was really focusing on this particular intelligence.

Most tests of intelligence focus on logical and linguistic intelligence. They do a pretty good job at predicting success in school—but not nearly as good a job as last year's grades! My goal is not to denigrate these traditional *scholastic* intelligences, but rather to give equal attention to other intellectual faculties.

3. Musical intelligence. The capacity to create, perform, and appreciate music. Some people call this a talent. That is fine, so long as you recognize that being good with words or with numbers is also a talent. What I cannot accept is that linguistic facility is deemed intelligence, while skill with music or with other persons is *merely* a talent.
4. Spatial intelligence. The capacity to form mental imagery of the world—the large world of the aviator or navigator, or the more local world of the chess player or the surgeon—and to manipulate those mental images.
5. Bodily-kinesthetic intelligence. The capacity to solve problems or fashion products using your whole body, or parts of your body, like your hands or mouth. This intelligence is exhibited by athletes, dancers, actors, craftspersons, and, again, surgeons.

The next two intelligences have to do with the world of human beings.

6. Interpersonal intelligence involves the understanding of other persons—how to interact with them, how to motivate them, how to understand their personalities, etc. This skill is obviously important for people in business, teachers, clinicians, and those involved in politics or religion.

7. Intrapersonal intelligence is the capacity to understand oneself—one's strengths, weaknesses, desires, fears. Access to one's emotional life is important for intrapersonal intelligence.

Whether or not you have heard of multiple intelligence theory, you have certainly heard of emotional intelligence. What Daniel Goleman means by emotional intelligence is similar to what I mean by the personal intelligences.

8. Naturalist intelligence involves the capacity to make consequential distinctions in nature—between one plant and another, among animals, clouds, mountains, and the like. Scientist Charles Darwin had naturalist intelligence in abundance. Most of us no longer use our naturalist intelligence to survive in the jungle or the forest. But it is likely that our entire consumer culture is based on our naturalist capacity to differentiate one car make from another, one sneaker from another, and the like.

9. I have speculated that there may be a ninth or existential intelligence. I call this the 'intelligence of big questions.' When children ask about the size of the universe, when adults ponder death, love, conflict, the future of the planet, they are engaging in existential issues. My hesitation in declaring a full blown existential intelligence stems from my uncertainty about whether certain regions of the brain are dedicated to the contemplation of issues that are too vast or too infinitesimal to be perceived. And so, recalling a famous Fellini movie, I speak of 8 1/2 intelligences.

So there you have it, my list of the multiple intelligences. Even if my approach is correct, I am sure that I have not identified all of the intelligences and that I have not described them perfectly. I am equally confident that each intelligence itself has separable components. But I am not interested in proving the existence of 8 or 9 intelligences, or 40–50 sub-intelligences, in particular. I am trying to make the case that we have a multiplicity of intelligences, each relatively independent of the others. From this claim—that we possess eight or nine relatively autonomous intellectual computers—three interesting claims follow.

a. All of us have these 8 or 9 intelligences, that is what makes us human beings, cognitively speaking. Rats might have more spatial intelligence, hummingbirds might have more musical intelligences, but we are the species that exhibits these particular intelligences. And that is important to know—whether you are a teacher, a businessman, or a parent.

b. No two individuals have exactly the same profile of intelligences, not even identical twins. And so whether you are a teacher, business person or parent, you may assume that every person's profile differs from yours, and from every other person, even clones of one another.

c. Having an intelligence does not mean that you will behave morally or intelligently. Intelligences are simply computers that can be put to work. But you can use your interpersonal intelligence for moral purposes—like Nelson Mandela—or for immoral purposes, like Slobodan Milosevic. By the same token, you might have a computer that works very well, and yet use it very stupidly. A mathematically-talented person might prove an important new theorem, but she might also waste her time multiplying ever bigger figures in her head.

The theory of multiple intelligences has aroused enormous interest among educators, and in many parts of the world. But that is a story for another occasion.

QUESTIONS

1. Think about yourself as you read Gardner's list of different kinds of intelligence. In what ways are you most intelligent? In what ways are you least intelligent?

2. If Gardner is correct that there are many different kinds of intelligence, why do so many people still categorize some people as "smart" or "gifted" and others as "stupid" or "slow?"

3. How different would schools be if they were designed to cultivate all forms of intelligence? What would happen to tests and grades?

4. In this essay, Gardner talks about how his own life experience, as well as his academic study, helped him to form the ideas that made him famous. How do your experiences and your studies mix in your life? How do you think they mix in the lives of students in school today or for those who will be in your classroom tomorrow?

6

CURRICULUM AND STANDARDS

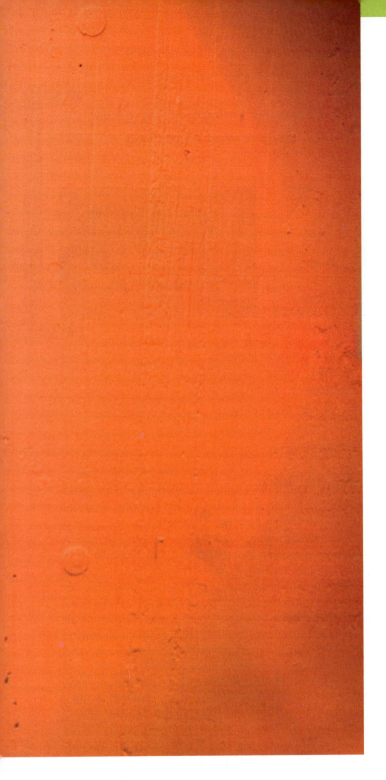

What will I teach?" is a standard question asked by anyone considering a career in teaching, whether you will be teaching elementary, middle, or high school. How will you know what to teach your students? Who determines what they need to learn? How much freedom will you have, and how much will you have to follow a plan that has been developed elsewhere? All of these questions lead to a discussion of the *curriculum*—the content of what is taught in school.

As we explore the topic of curriculum, we will discover that there are many debates going on in the United States about what *should* be taught in school today. Some educators believe that a multicultural approach is essential whereas others believe that such an approach separates people from one another. Some educators believe that high and clear national standards for what should be taught are the key to creating effective schools in today's complex world. Others view the same standards as an undemocratic imposition that "crushes the life" out of school. We will examine these ongoing debates and look at what teachers can—and cannot—do to influence the content of the curriculum, especially when many other forces are seeking to shape the curriculum and the way it is implemented in the classrooms.

The **Readings** for this chapter reflect the lively debates taking place in the curriculum arena today. Three pairs of essays present the perspectives of educators who disagree sharply with each other. In the first **Reading**, Sonia Nieto, a widely respected leader in the multicultural education movement, lays out the case for multicultural education. Paired with this essay is a response by noted historian Arthur M. Schlesinger, Jr., who argues that multicultural education is factually wrong in the material it emphasizes and deeply divisive for society. Next are two essays in which longtime school principal and educator-author Deborah Meier argues against the current standards movement, and school board member and author Abigail Thernstrom argues that the exact same standards are absolutely essential to achieving the educational equity that is so important to Meier. Finally, in response to the question "How do different curricula reflect different philosophies of education?" well-known author E. D. Hirsch, Jr.,

WHAT WILL I TEACH?

- What is curriculum? Why teach *this* and not *that*?
- What are some of the current debates about multicultural education?
- Do the standards address what students need to know?
- How do different curricula reflect different views of the purpose of education?

argues in favor of a common core of knowledge that must be presented in the curriculum of every school. Teacher and writer Bob Peterson counters that such a common core curriculum is deeply flawed because it reflects values that are not the right ones for a school to foster and, even if the values were better, it represents an imposition that stifles teacher and student creativity. Regarding what should be taught in the schools today, there are few (if any) areas in which the authors of these pieces would agree—but they do encourage you to think critically and creatively about the matter.

» What Is Curriculum? Why Teach *This* and Not *That*?

DEFINING CURRICULUM

"Debates over what is basic to the curriculum are also debates over identity," says William Pinar, one of the nation's leading curriculum theorists. In deciding what should be taught in school as well as what can be "skipped," educators make powerful decisions about how they want their students to experience and understand the world around them and their place in it. Schools cannot teach everything. Teachers; school leaders; local, state, and federal officials; and many others are always asking, "What knowledge is most important for our students at this moment in their lives?" They are continually picking and choosing and making hard decisions. These decisions determine what gets taught in school—what the curriculum includes and what it excludes.[1]

On one level, the answer to the question "What is curriculum?" is a simple one. Curriculum is the "stuff" that is taught in school. Students have their textbooks and readers and other supplemental literature, some published in hard copy and a great deal more on the Internet and in digital format. In addition, teachers have their guidebooks, supplemental materials, and directives from the school district and the state. All of this material is part of the formal curriculum. Students and teachers also receive informal messages about what they are supposed to be studying and learning, from school policies and from the culture in which they live. For example, when the state says that students will be tested in language arts and mathematics but not in science and social studies, it has set the school curriculum every bit as much as when a publisher includes some material in a textbook and leaves out other information.

One cannot look at the materials of the curriculum apart from the human beings who use those materials. Science educator Meredith Houle, building on the work of J. T. Remillard, describes multiple forms of curriculum. First, she says, we must look at the *participatory relationship* between the written curriculum, which is often handed down from some higher authority, and the teacher who decides to, or is told to, use the curriculum. In the course of this relationship between curriculum and teacher, when the teacher designs a specific lesson plan to use the curriculum on a certain day in a certain classroom context, the *planned curriculum* comes into existence. Finally, the *enacted curriculum* represents what really happens in a classroom as a teacher seeks to

Components of the Teacher-Curriculum Relationship

Teacher → **Participatory Relationship** → Curriculum

Planned Curriculum

Enacted Curriculum

Source: From "Examining Key Concepts in Research on Teachers' Use of Mathematics Curricula." *Review of Educational Research, 75* (2): 211-246 by Janine Remillard, © 2005 by Sage Publications Inc.

put plans into practice. Remillard reminds educators that the curriculum will be modified as it is co-constructed by teachers and students in a particular context. These elements—the materials, the planning on how to use them by the teacher, and the reality of what takes place in the classroom—are equally part of what we mean when we use the word *curriculum*.[2]

THE GOALS OF THE CURRICULUM

One of the twentieth century's most influential educators, Ralph Tyler, proposed in 1950 what came to be known as the "Tyler rationale," four questions that should be asked before developing a curriculum:

1. What educational purposes should the school seek to attain?
2. What educational experiences can be provided that are likely to attain these purposes?
3. How can these educational experiences be effectively organized?
4. How can we determine whether these purposes are being attained?[3]

Tyler's questions have a fundamental logic. At their most basic, the questions ask the teacher to determine the goals of any given lesson, what steps should be taken to accomplish the goals, and finally, and most important, how the teacher knows the student learned what the teacher set out to teach him or her.

Many teachers shorten this list of questions to only two: (1) What sorts of experiences should I arrange for my class? and (2) How should I organize my students to move through

these experiences? You may feel reasonably well prepared to face the classroom if you know what activities you are going to do with your students and how you are going to organize their day. However, this simplified version of Tyler's questions leaves out perhaps the most important questions. As Tyler noted, it is essential to start at the beginning, "If we are to study an educational program systematically and intelligently we must first be sure as to the educational objectives aimed at."[4] If you, as a teacher, do not know what your long-term goal is and what you want to accomplish, not just in a given day but over the course of weeks and months with a group of students, and if you do not, to use more current language, have clear standards for what your students should learn, school can easily degenerate into busy work, into one thing after another, without long-term meaning or purpose. As Pinar noted, thinking about the curriculum is really asking questions about identity—national identity and individual identity—and not merely questions like "What do I do on Monday?" If such larger questions are not asked, you can come to the end of the term and realize that your students may or may not have learned a whole range of vaguely interesting facts and ideas, but they will not have had an education.

At the other end of the spectrum is the question of *evaluation*. Teachers can teach with great skill and enthusiasm and still find that some or all of their students fail to learn what their teachers thought they were teaching. Evaluation is, therefore, not merely a matter of giving the students grades. Indeed, the primary question of evaluation in curricular matters is not "Did the student succeed in learning?" but "Did the teacher succeed in teaching?" Sometimes it takes many different teaching methods and many different structured experiences before all the

Connections

In Chapter 7, we further explore evaluation and assessment and the teacher's role in the process.

A QUESTION OF . . .

How do you approach curriculum development?

"With empathy. I attempt to see every lesson through the lens of my students. As I write curriculum and lesson plans and present concepts, I'm perceiving the lessons through the eyes of a fourth grader. The question that goes through my mind is, 'How can I engage each student?' When I see the world fresh, I'm enthusiastic about learning and so are my students."

—*Sarah Pennisi, fourth grade student teacher* ■

Teachable Moment

Project-Based Learning

Project-based learning (PBL) is one of the latest curricular developments to be implemented in many schools around the United States. It is not a new concept. A century ago, John Dewey's colleague William Heard Kilpatrick advocated what he called the "Project Method," in which students learned by class projects. More recently, psychologists have argued that new research shows that most young people learn more by doing than just hearing. At the same time, society's shift from an industrial economy to one based on communications technology has meant that schools need more than ever to foster the social, interactive aspects of education.

These developments have pointed many educators in the direction of PBL. Of course, PBL means different things to different people, and the quality of implementation can vary widely. Overall, however, PBL calls on the teacher to develop a hands-on class project that will encourage students to learn a lesson that traditionally might have been taught through direct instruction and textbook reading. Examples of PBL might include the following:

- A social studies teacher asks students to design a student government association for a school. In the process, they study how governments, including the government of the United States, have been formed in the past and learn about the inevitable compromises of the legislative process—in a school or the U.S. Congress.
- A mathematics teacher has students develop a business plan for a venture they might launch in the school. They study the concepts of profit and loss, profit margin, and break-even point (which can be determined through either a spreadsheet or an algebraic equation).
- A science teacher asks students to design an energy-efficient house. They analyze different renewable energy sources, including how much energy wind turbines or solar panels generate in comparison with traditional sources of energy.

Source: This material was informed by *Project Based Learning Handbook: A Guide to Standards Focused Project Based Learning for Middle and High School Teachers*, by T. Markham, J. Larmer, and J. Ravit, 2003, Buck Institute of Education, retrieved July 26, 2009, from http://www.bie.org/index.php/site/PBL/pbl_handbook/.

PBL requires teachers to be very clear about the learning outcomes they want to achieve, and they need to avoid "project-itis," in which the project itself takes over the students' time and energy and learning goals are marginalized.

When PBL is done successfully, teachers report that, among other things, it

- overcomes the divide between learning information and applying it
- helps students learn new things while also developing their ability to solve problems, communicate with others, and manage their own time
- connects learning to the real world and therefore helps students see learning as a something to do throughout their lives
- relates education to both future careers and responsible citizenship
- breaks down the divisions between different **academic disciplines**

Although research on the effectiveness of PBL is in the early stages, a fairly clear consensus agrees that PBL is at least as effective as traditional instruction and sometimes is much more effective. PBL may appeal to many students who are not engaged in traditional academic pursuits, a significant issue among both disadvantaged and privileged students. This sort of disengagement is a significant contributor to the enormous dropout rate among high school students. Even many high-achieving students say that they are bored in school, and PBL engages them in ways that traditional classes do not. PBL helps students learn new material because they are motivated to solve a problem posed in their project. It also can help them be successful in traditional standardized forms of testing if the projects have been organized so that the ideas and concepts learned by doing the project relate to clear goals and learning outcome expectations.

QUESTIONS

- Were you assigned "projects" in school? Do you remember what you learned from them, or just the fact that you participated?
- Think about teaching in your area of interest. Can you design a project that would help students learn something that you think is especially important for them to know?

academic disciplines Areas of study, such as mathematics, science, or English, that can be divided into subdisciplines, such as algebra, physics, and literature.

students in a class will "get" the content of a lesson. But the wise teacher is constantly evaluating his or her work. To separate evaluation from curriculum is to disregard the fundamental question of outcomes without which goals may never be met and experiences may never work.[5]

Although the so-called Tyler rationale has been used widely for over fifty years, it has not been without its critics. Stanford professor Elliot Eisner was one of many to raise significant challenges. Eisner found Tyler's approach to be useful and rational, but he also found it seriously flawed, especially in fields like the arts, where student creativity is as important as student mastery of existing knowledge. Eisner said that clear objectives in curriculum design could easily mask the extent to which the same curriculum might lead to different outcomes in different contexts. (Recall Houle's emphasis on the interaction of curriculum materials, teachers, and students.) He also worried that overly rigid curriculum design could turn quickly into equally rigid systems of evaluation in which the entire purpose of education would be reduced to the most simplistic level and thoughtful judgment by student and teacher would take a back seat to the quest for "right answers." These warnings are serious and as useful as a rational approach to curriculum development and implementation can be.[6]

DIFFERENT APPROACHES TO CURRICULUM

Herbert M. Kliebard, a leading historian of curriculum, describes four different schools of thought that have battled for control of the curriculum in U.S. schools:

- The *humanist* group believes that the traditional academic disciplines (history, English, mathematics, and the sciences, joined by other fields of study) represent the core of what should be taught to all students. Humanists believe that exercise of the mind in such study develops the ability to think rationally and could serve as a solid foundation for the future.

- A second group, *developmentalists*, believe that young people have widely disparate native abilities and that the curriculum should therefore be differentiated by developmental stage as well as by ability, sorting some for a college education and professional life and many more for much lower level careers.

- A third group, who came to be known as *social efficiency educators*, want to eliminate waste in education—waste of time and waste of money—by focusing schools on preparing students to fit with the needs of the national economy. They believe that scientific research and rigorous testing yield a scientifically based curriculum.

- Finally, a group of educators known as *social meliorists*, or *social constructionists*, believe that the school curriculum should prepare students who could build a more just and democratic social order. Though this group has often represented a minority view, at certain times (such as during the Great Depression of the 1930s and the civil rights movement of the 1950s and 1960s), the voices of social meliorists helped define the purpose of schooling in the United States.[7]

Kliebard notes that no one of these approaches has been dominant for long and that advocates of all four argue with each other as much today as they did a hundred years ago. Since the 1960s, some of the focus and some of the names have changed, but the battles have continued. E. D. Hirsch, Jr., whose views are included in one of the **Readings** and who argues for a return to what he sees as the "basics," shares a humanist trust in the traditional academic disciplines as a key to successful schooling. Bob Peterson, an elementary school teacher from Milwaukee, Wisconsin, challenges Hirsch's back-to-basics views in the **Readings** and could probably be classified most closely with the *social meliorists*. Although Peterson makes clear his appreciation that Hirsch "raises the issue of unequal access to knowledge and literature in our **stratified society**," he also sees Hirsch's proposals as making the inequity much worse. Hirsch and Peterson

stratified society Privileges and benefits are dispersed according to a socially constructed value system wherein some people and groups are considered subordinate to those that are more elite or entitled.

are not the first to argue about these issues—and they will certainly not be the last.

Although educators have fought and argued at national meetings, in local school boards, within faculty meetings of teacher education programs, and at the smallest gathering of teachers engaged in curriculum planning, no one school of thought has ever won. And no one perspective is likely to have a permanent victory. There are too many deep-seated debates about the nature and purpose of education in the United States for the question of the best curriculum to be resolved. Quite different approaches to the curriculum have had their moments of supremacy and of decline. Some have merged into indistinct coalitions, and some have been on the verge of disappearing, only to rise again as social conditions changed and schools were asked to respond to differing local or national conditions.

As Kliebard concludes, "in the end, what became the American curriculum was not the result of any decisive victory by any of the contending parties, but a loose, largely unarticulated, and not very tidy compromise."[8] Navigating that "not very tidy compromise" is the challenge facing every classroom teacher. Almost any curricular decision that can be made, by a state or federal agency or an individual teacher, is bound to elicit praise from some and hostility from others. In this situation, the more informed the teacher is, the more successful his or her voyage will be.

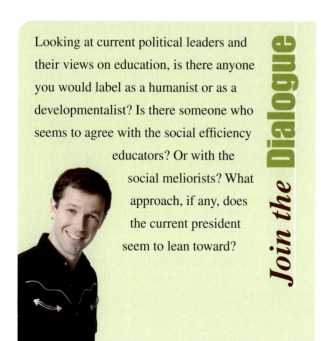

Join the Dialogue

Looking at current political leaders and their views on education, is there anyone you would label as a humanist or as a developmentalist? Is there someone who seems to agree with the social efficiency educators? Or with the social meliorists? What approach, if any, does the current president seem to lean toward?

THE HIDDEN CURRICULUM

Historian and long-time school leader Larry Cuban notes that when we talk about the curriculum of a school, we must always address at least two different but nevertheless linked curricula: "The *official* curriculum (what subject matter, skills, and values authorities expect teachers to teach) and the *taught* curriculum (what teachers believe about content and its presentation and what they actually do)."[9] In other words, what are teachers expected to teach *and* what do they actually teach—by their words, actions, procedures, and so on?

The official curriculum is usually stated in ways that reflect what citizens of a community—or at least those citizens with the most powerful voices—believe every child should know by the time they finish school. The official curriculum typically includes basic skills and values, such as democracy and fair play. It also includes content knowledge—such as the ability to read, write, and count; probably some knowledge of the community's and the nation's history and culture; and likely much more.

Yet communities, and those in authority in a given school or community, may also have a "hidden curriculum"—lessons that were taught very effectively though no one in the school acknowledged the fact. For example, half a century ago, schools in many parts of the United States were legally segregated by race. No one said that the purpose was to teach inferiority to some students and superiority to others, but that was as effectively a part of the curriculum as any other more overtly stated values. Racism was taught every day as students passed each other on the way to different schools, and it was repeated in classrooms as one group of students used new textbooks and another got the hand-me-downs.

Within individual classrooms, what teachers believe and what they do can differ radically. A teacher can deeply want to engage a class and make learning exciting, but he or she may succeed or may fail. Virtually all studies of teachers' interactions with male and female students come to the same conclusion—teachers call on boys much more often than they call on girls, and much more than they think they differentiate. A teacher who values and talks about gender equity may easily teach the opposite without realizing it. Both teachings are a real part of the curriculum—what gets taught and what gets learned. Teachers must always be on the lookout for the hidden curriculum they and other teachers and school leaders are teaching to the students at the same time they are thoughtfully and carefully teaching the subject matter and skills that are part of the school's formal curriculum.[10]

>> What Are Some of the Current Debates About Multicultural Education?

Few debates in the area of curriculum have generated as much discussion as the topic of **multicultural education**. Multicultural education has had many supporters—some of whom advocate quite different things from each other. Multicultural education has also had powerful critics who also disagree among themselves.

> **multicultural education**
> Curriculum that embraces and incorporates the wide spectrum of human variations, such as those that exist with ethnicity, gender, religion, and physical and mental abilities, into its core content.

These debates among and between these advocates and critics of multicultural education reveal a great deal about not only what they want taught, or not taught, but also the widely differing beliefs about the purpose of schooling and the national identity that these diverse voices support. If Pinar is right that debates about curriculum are also debates about identity, then the battles over multicultural education represent significantly different versions of the national identity that different educators want the schools to teach.

James Banks, considered by many to be the "father of multicultural education," describes the origins of a movement that has transformed the curriculum of many, though certainly not all, schools in the United States in the past half-century. "Multicultural education," Banks says,

> *grew out of the ferment of the civil rights movement of the 1960s. During this decade, African Americans embarked on a quest for their rights that was unprecedented in the United States. A major goal of the civil rights movement of the 1960s was to eliminate discrimination in public accommodations, housing, employment,*

Hidden in Plain Sight

The hidden curriculum is essentially all those lessons that you learned at school even though they weren't part of the official curriculum. It may be that no one *taught* them per se, but somehow everyone learned these lessons or they were expected to if they were going to fit in and be accepted. These are the messages students receive that often deal with attitudes, values, beliefs, and behavior. These messages can both complement and contradict each other as well as the official curriculum. The hidden curriculum at one school can be very different from that found at another school.

Check off the elements of the hidden curriculum that you have witnessed or experienced as a student:

Hidden Curriculum	I've Witnessed or Experienced
Same person is always picked first to lead a task.	
Teacher calls on one gender more than the other.	
Teacher is consistently more pleasant and accommodating to certain students.	
Students must sit in specific groups or designated locations at lunch, such as by gender, in a corner, etc.	
Textbooks are new, clean, and from current copyright years or are in bad condition (torn, taped up, dirty) and are dated.	
Not enough materials for everyone—some students must share.	
Students are tested on certain subjects more than on others.	
Certain subjects are always scheduled during peak alertness hours.	
Certain subjects are always scheduled right after lunch.	
Some specific accomplishments receive more visibility than others (such as sports, music, etc.).	
Students in certain school activities receive special privileges, are exempt from responsibilities, or are viewed in a positive light.	
Students in certain school activities are considered to be inferior or perceived negatively.	
The same classes or coursework gets cancelled, postponed, or abbreviated in favor of other assignments or school functions.	
The school building is in terrific condition, or it is shabby and not well kept up.	
The same or similar students are voted into positions of recognition (such as prom queen, student government).	
Other:	
Other:	
Other:	
Other:	
Other:	

Rethinking Our Schools

Rethinking Schools is a quarterly magazine, an organization, and a Web site (www.rethinking schools.org), and it is one of the most valuable resources that any teacher, or aspiring teacher, can utilize. The curriculum resources they offer can be a gold mine of material for teachers—especially new teachers—who want to teach well. According to the organization's mission statement, *Rethinking Schools* is "committed to equity and to the vision that public education is central to the creation of a humane, caring, multiracial democracy." Examples of their newest publications include the following:

- *Teaching for Joy and Justice*
- *Rethinking Multicultural Education*
- *Unlearning "Indian" Stereotypes*
- *Rethinking Early Childhood Education*

Rethinking Schools began in 1986 when a group of Milwaukee, Wisconsin, area teachers began talking about not only how to improve what went on in their own classrooms but also how to help shape the **education reform movements** in the country. What began as a local community of teachers has become an important resource for educators across the country. When the group that founded *Rethinking Schools* first gathered, they were concerned about the curriculum, including the hidden curriculum, in many of the textbooks they were asked to use, about the impact of testing on quality teaching, and more broadly about a kind of joylessness that they found in too many schools. These issues remain at the core of their work and, while they attempt to have an impact on national policy, they also seek to provide resources to classroom teachers who want to teach well.

Behind *Rethinking Schools* is a group of teachers who believe that schools need to do more than produce tomorrow's workers. Schools need to be places where students and teachers gather to talk, play, and work together in the present and begin to model a different society for the future. They help teachers who want to apply these same principles in what they teach and the way that they teach.

education reform movements Widespread public or professional movements based on new theories, data, beliefs, or strategies meant to change the education system for the better. Goals often address the development of better-achieving students or cost reduction in schools.

QUESTIONS

- What responsibility do teachers, especially beginning teachers, have to read journals like *Rethinking Schools* that will give them new ideas?

- What responsibility do teachers have to share their ideas with others and to try to shape the national dialogue about education reform as well as to succeed in their own classrooms? How will you participate in this dialogue and through what avenues? Information-sharing Web sites? Blogs? Professional journals? Conferences?

PORTRAIT OF AN EDUCATOR

Jerrold Zacharias

During World War II, Jerrold Zacharias was a member of the team of American physicists at the Los Alamos Laboratory in New Mexico, where the first atomic bomb was developed. At the end of the war, Zacharias joined the faculty at the Massachusetts Institute of Technology. It was here at MIT that he became deeply concerned with what he saw as the poor quality of physics instruction in American schools.

In 1956, Zacharias assembled the Physical Science Study Committee (PSCC), which was a team of high school teachers of physics as well as college faculty. Their mission: to develop a completely new high school physics curriculum. Instead of having students read textbooks and memorize information, Zacharias

and his team wanted the high school physics course to focus on observation and experiments so that students would start to think like scientists. The work of the PSCC received an enormous boost in 1957 when the Soviet Union launched Sputnik, the first space satellite. In the midst of the Cold War, U.S. leaders were deeply concerned that the Russians' ability to launch a space satellite before the United States meant that the nation was falling behind in science. One result was major new spending by the National Science Foundation on elementary and secondary math and science curricular materials aimed to improve students' general understanding of science and to produce many more top-flight scientists and engineers.

Because of Zacharias's foresight, the PSCC was well positioned to be a leader in the emerging field of science education. In time, the PSCC, under Zacharias's leadership, produced important new science curriculum materials, including films, books for teachers, and textbooks for students. The high school textbook *PSCC Physics*, written by another MIT professor, Francis Friedman, was eventually translated into 17 languages.

In the 1960s, Zacharias and his colleagues expanded their work to focus on elementary school science through the Elementary Science Study (ESS) developed at the Education Development Center, Inc. (EDC) in Newton, Massachusetts. The result of this later work was a new curriculum, *Insights: An Elementary Hands-on Inquiry Science Curriculum*, developed by Zacharias and educators at the EDC that helped transform elementary science education.

The original focus of the PSCC and the ESS was to shift the physics curriculum—and eventually all high school and elementary school science education—from textbooks to experiments and observations. In time, the impact of the PSCC stretched far beyond physics. Increasingly, all of the science courses at American high schools shifted from a textbook focus to a lab focus, and the goal became more interesting courses that fostered a much deeper understanding of the scientific disciplines. Although too few American students study science with sufficient depth and rigor, the science curriculum in the United States has been transformed by the work of Jerrold Zacharias and his professor and teacher colleagues.

Sources: "Physics at MIT: From Bell's Phonautograph to Technology Enhanced Active Learning," by Anthony P. French, 2005, *MIT Physics Annual*, retrieved June 22, 2009, from http://web.mit.edu/physics/alumniandfridnds/physicsatmit_05_french.pdf; and "Insights: An Elementary Hands-on Inquiry Science Curriculum," by Karen Worth, 2007, *Forum on Education of the American Physical Society*, retrieved June 21, 2009, from www.aps.org/units/fed/newsleters/summer2007/worth.html.

and education. The consequence of the civil rights movement had a significant influence on educational institutions as ethnic groups—first African Americans and then other groups— demanded that the schools and other educational institutions reform curricula to reflect their experiences, histories, cultures, and perspectives.[11]

An example of these roots of multicultural education can be found in the **Readings** for this chapter, as Sonia Nieto locates her commitment to the field in her own experience growing up in Brooklyn, New York, during the 1940s and speaking only Spanish when she entered the first grade. Like many of her peers, Nieto assumed that her sense of being different meant that there was something wrong with her. She wanted to ensure that the next generation of students would not have this sense that something was wrong with them. Nieto also defines multicultural education as affecting not just the curriculum but also all aspects of the life of a school. She

sees multicultural education as being part of a larger school reform effort as well as being a movement that challenges racism and advocates for ethnic, linguistic, religious, economic, and gender pluralism. It affects the culture of the schools where it is adopted as well as the school's curriculum and the pedagogy (how the curriculum is taught).[12] In this view, multicultural education becomes the philosophy at the heart of the school—a philosophy with a clear sense of the kind of identity that schools should foster and a clear sense of mission based in a social meliorist approach to the curriculum.

Once launched, the movement for multicultural education led educators to look carefully at the content of the curriculum, to see whose stories were told and whose were excluded. Banks notes,

When feminists (people who work for the political, social, and economic equality of the sexes) looked at educational institutions, they noted problems similar to those identified by ethnic groups of color.

Textbooks and curricula were dominated by men; women were largely invisible. Feminists pointed out that history textbooks were dominated by political and military history—areas in which men had been the main participants. Social and family history and the history of labor and ordinary people were largely ignored. Feminists pushed for the revision of textbooks to include more history about the important roles of women in the development of the nation and the world.[13]

The origins of the movement for a multicultural curriculum in the schools are important to understand. Multicultural education was not born because a group of curriculum experts were trying to come up with the next big idea for what should be taught. On the contrary, the pressure to change the curriculum of American schools came from outside the schools—from movements to include the nation's full diversity, especially people of color and women, in all aspects of national life. Once again, a curricular debate was

You Decide

Does multicultural education undermine a sense of national identity for American students?

also a debate about identity. To understand the importance of multicultural education, simply open a textbook that was used in schools in the 1950s and early 1960s. Virtually all Americans were White, and almost all important actions involved men. Women were included but, with few exceptions, were passive bystanders. African Americans, Latino Americans, and Asian Americans were virtually invisible, not only in history books, but also in literature and in the examples used in mathematics and the sciences. From learning to read by following the stories of Dick and Jane—two White children who lived in the suburbs with their dog Spot—to high school history books that told of America's "discovery" by Europeans as if the land had been uninhabited, to science texts that told of the exploits of European American males, the identity taught in these texts was of a White, mostly middle class, male-dominated nation. The much more inclusive story of the nation's history, literature, science, and culture that is told in most schools today is vastly different from that of decades not long gone.

As it has developed over recent decades, the movement for a more multicultural curriculum has become increasingly sophisticated. Not surprisingly, the movement has also experienced resistance. Some people, including the historian Arthur Schlesinger, Jr., argue that there is a danger of multicultural education pushing out what they see as the main story line. Thus, as he discusses in one of the **Readings** for this chapter, Schlesinger sees the call for multicultural education as an "attack on the common American identity." Others argue that there is simply no time to cover all of the material that multicultural education demands or for teachers to learn so many different stories. Such critics see in multicultural education the perhaps-unintended result that history and other subjects become an unintelligible muddle in which so much information is presented that no story line makes any sense.

Even more troublesome to some critics is the concern that respect for multiple cultures can quickly become a kind of "value-free" education. In the article, "The Pitfalls of Multicultural Education," Albert Shanker, former president of the American Federation of Teachers, attacked the movement, asking with scorn:

> *Do we really want them to "respect and accept" the "values, beliefs, and attitudes" of other people, no matter what they are? Do we want them to respect and accept the beliefs that led Chinese leaders to massacre dissenting students in Tiananmen Square?[14]*

Others who may not be as hostile to the whole idea as Shanker still see multicultural education as perhaps important for classrooms in which there are many students

Did you know?

Dick and Jane

Between the 1930s and the 1960s, the *Dick and Jane* series of readers was used in teaching 85,000,000 children to read—approximately 80% of all first graders. The series was conceived in 1927 by Zerna Sharp, who believed that children would read better if they identified with the characters in the illustrations and read words that sounded familiar. The first African American main characters didn't appear until 1965 in *Now We Read*. The series was discontinued in 1970.

of color but virtually irrelevant for segregated European American classrooms. Still others say that although multicultural education is fine for history teachers, it has nothing to do with those who teach science or mathematics.[15]

cultural assumptions Underlying beliefs that are themselves part of a culture and that influence how a culture behaves and reacts to certain populations or behaviors.

Banks sees multicultural education as "a broad concept with several different and important dimensions." He lists five areas that need to be given careful attention in any effective program of multicultural education:

1. **Content integration.** Teachers should include, for example, the stories of American Indians, Africans, Asians, as well as European immigrants in the story of the United States and the lives of women as well as men. Stories from diverse cultures should be used in word problems in a math class or in science experiments.

2. **The knowledge construction process.** This is more difficult and requires teachers and eventually their students to look at the ways certain dominant **cultural assumptions** are included in the curriculum. It involves asking students, for example, "Why do you think so many of the famous scientists are male?" or "Why did it take more than two hundred years for the country to elect anyone other than a White male as president?"

3. **Prejudice reduction.** It is not easy to grow up in the United States without inheriting a whole mix of racial and gender stereotypes. Banks would argue that directly challenging this sort of built-in prejudice is also part of a teacher's job.

4. **An equity pedagogy.** For example, many teachers find that students from upper-class families initially do better in school than students from poor families, that boys are more likely to talk in class, and that some students are easily marginalized if they belong to an underrepresented racial group in a class. Banks would argue that a teacher should pay special attention to ensure that the poor children get the academic support they need to do as well as their better-off peers, that classes need to be structured so that girls are led to speak as much as boys, and that every student is incorporated into the culture of the classroom.

5. **An empowering school culture.** Multicultural education does not stop at the classroom door. How teachers of different races interact in the lunchroom and in curriculum planning meetings, how the school sorts its students, and if the building feels welcoming are all part of building a multicultural school culture.

In outlining this wide range of goals for what multicultural education should accomplish in the transformation of

Join the Dialogue

Can you recall a teacher who reflected a multicultural approach to his or her teaching? What did the teacher say or do that you then (or just now) recognized as representing a multicultural curriculum? How did you and other students react—positively or negatively?

schools and the larger society, Banks understands that different people understand multicultural education in different ways. There is no one-size-fits-all definition. Indeed, he notes,

Connections

In Chapter 10, we look at the impact of sorting and tracking students.

practicing educators use the term multicultural education to describe a wide variety of programs and practices related to educational equity, women, ethnic groups, language minorities, low-income groups, and people with disabilities. In one school district, multicultural education may mean a curriculum that incorporates the experiences of ethnic groups of color; in another, a program may include the experiences of both ethnic groups and women. In a third school district, this term may be used. . . to mean a total school reform effort designed to increase educational equity for a range of cultural, ethnic, and economic groups.

Given the elastic nature of the term, it is also important for everyone to develop his or her own clear definition.

Banks also recognizes how lofty the goals are and how very difficult the challenge is. He notes that, "Multicultural education is a continuing process because the idealized goals it tries to actualize—such as educational equality and the eradication of all forms of discrimination—can never be fully achieved in human society." Nevertheless it is a movement of powerful ethical force with practical meanings that no aspiring teacher can ignore.[16]

Teachable Moment

A Mission of Multiculturalism

Following is the mission statement from the Amherst Regional Public Schools in Massachusetts, along with their policy statement that outlines their commitment to becoming a multicultural school system:

The mission of our schools is to provide all students with a high quality education that enables them to be contributing members of a multiethnic, multicultural, pluralistic society. We seek to create an environment that achieves equity for all students and ensures that each student is a successful learner, is fully respected, and learns to respect others.

Diversity is a strength because it challenges every student, every teacher, and every person in the school system to understand, respect, and value the differences among us. In the four towns that comprise the school district, more than thirty languages are spoken in the homes of our students and nearly 30% of the entire student body belongs to the ALANA (African American, Latino, Asian, and Native American) population. In every elementary school classroom there is at least one student who is learning English as a new language—from the nearly 300 students who receive instruction in English as a Second Language, to those enrolled in Transitional Bilingual Educational programs, which teach academic subjects in the native language until the ability to learn English is acquired. Creating a diverse school community that reflects the community at large includes addressing racism and other forms of discrimination in the classroom to help students understand the nature and com-plexity of a multicultural society. But diversity isn't something that can be forgotten when the bell rings at the end of the school day. All of our schools are devoted to promoting equity in all aspects of education, inside the classroom and out. The commitment to equity is demonstrated by having set specific goals for Becoming a Multicultural School System (BAMSS). These explicit goals call for equity in hiring, establishment of a multicultural curriculum, and attention to the needs of each and every student.

Source: Amherst Regional Public Schools, "A Commitment to Equity" and "Mission Statement," retrieved July 6, 2009, from www.arps.org.

QUESTIONS

- Ask yourself, "Would I want to teach in a district with as clear and explicit a commitment to diversity as Amherst, Massachusetts?" Would this make the district appealing to you? Unappealing? Or is it irrelevant?
- Can schools succeed if their mission is to "provide all students with a high quality education?" Is this standard too high?

>> Do the Standards Address What Students Need to Know?

HISTORICALLY SPEAKING: THE STANDARDS MOVEMENT

As a new school year began in September 1989, President George H. W. Bush and the nation's governors, led by their co-chair Bill Clinton of Arkansas, met for an "Education Summit" and began the process of creating a set of National Education Goals that could guide both federal and local education efforts.[17] In his January 1990 State of the Union address, President Bush presented these goals to a joint session of Congress. Four years later, Clinton, who by then had succeeded Bush as president, presented the same goals as legislation to Congress, resulting in the passage of the *Goals 2000: Educate America Act* that expanded the role of the federal panel designated to implement the goals.

Presidents Bill Clinton and George H. W. Bush were involved in crafting the original Goals 2000, precursor to No Child Left Behind.

In deference to the American tradition of **local autonomy** in education, both Bush (a Republican) and Clinton (a Democrat) insisted that not only implementation but also the design of specific policies and curricula would remain at the local level. Goals 2000 did not mean a national curriculum for the United States (although a national curriculum is the norm in many other countries). The role of the national movement was to build support, provide modest funds, and most of all outline the long-term goals themselves.

Unlike later legislation, Goals 2000 was hardly likely to stir significant debate. Who in 1990 could oppose the proposition that by the year 2000,

- All children in America will start school ready to learn.
- The high school graduation rate will increase to at least 90%.
- American students will. . .[have] demonstrated competency in challenging subject matter. . .so they

may be prepared for responsible citizenship, further learning, and productive employment in our modern economy.

- American students will be the first in the world in science and mathematics achievement.
- Every adult American will be literate and will possess the knowledge and skills necessary to compete in a global economy and exercise the rights and responsibilities of citizenship.
- Every school in America will be free of drugs and violence and will offer a disciplined environment conducive to learning.

The year 2000 came and went without any of the goals having been met. But the movement toward higher expectations and standards for the schools was not without substantial long-term impact on the curriculum of the nation's schools. The national **standards movement** did not spring forth from the minds of presidents and governors. Many people trace the current standards movement to the surprise appearance of a major federal report, *A Nation at Risk*, in 1983. A number of reports had appeared, all of which called for a much better school system, with much higher standards, for all American children. But among the reports, *A Nation at Risk* received by far the most attention

> **local autonomy** The ability of local school districts, state governments, or even individual schools and classroom teachers (rather than higher-level authorities in the state or federal government) to retain control over laws and policies affecting their citizens.
>
> **standards movement** A push to make educational institutions and sometimes individual teachers and students accountable for students' academic performance; often measured by means of standardized testing and evaluations.

Did you know?

China, India, and Singapore have national standards for the English language, as well as their native languages.

Goals 2000, American Education Act

Goal for 2000: 90% graduate high school

Where we're at today: 71% graduate high school. That number drops to 53% in 19 of 50 biggest U.S. cities.

Goal for 2000: #1 in Math and Science

Where we're at today: #24 in Math; **#17** in Science.

Goal for 2000: Every adult will be literate.

Where we're at today: 47 million American adults are functionally illiterate.

Do you think Goals 2000 were realistic, attainable goals at the time they were drafted?

with its ringing call to action that warned, "Our Nation is at risk. Our once unchallenged preeminence in commerce, industry, science, and technological innovation is being

A QUESTION OF . . .

How has your job changed since you began teaching?

"Starting at kindergarten, so much as changed. It used to be more about the basics—knowing their letters, counting, etc. What we teach kids now in kindergarten used to be taught in first grade. The expectations are for younger and younger kids to learn more and more."

—*Andrea Mackoff, first grade teacher* ■

overtaken by competitors throughout the world. . . ." The report went on to describe what it called "a rising tide of mediocrity that threatens our very future as a Nation and a people." This rising tide meant that students in other nations were doing much better than many of those in the United States and that the "mediocre educational performance" of the schools was undermining the nation's competitive edge and national security.[18] With these dire warnings, the report received an extraordinary level of response.

Some observers viewed *A Nation at Risk* as a badly needed educational call to arms. Others saw it as overblown but a good way to raise public attention and funding for schools. Still others saw it as a direct attack on the educational equity movements of the 1960s that had brought so many previously excluded students—disabled students, students who did not speak English, and students who were excluded from many aspects of schooling because of their race, ethnicity, or gender—into the mainstream of education by the 1980s. But no one ignored the report and its call for much higher standards for what should be expected of schools, teachers, and students.[19]

While many scholars see the standards movement as originating in the conservative reform efforts of the 1980s, others insist that, in fact, the standards movement was born out of an earlier, substantial commitment to educational equity. For example, Edmund Gordon and Cynthia McCallister argue that *Brown* v. *Board of Education* ended racial segregation in the nation's schools in the name of equality and one cannot guarantee equality without some standards against which to measure it. To those who hold this view, standards are the key to equity or, as McCallister says, "Determinations of equity are impossible absent a set of standards against which to evaluate a particular condition. . . . The standards provide a set of criteria against which educational justice is determined."[20] Whether as a criterion for judging equity and justice or as a means of ensuring the nation's competitive advantage, after the mid-1980s, the standards movement was here to stay.

Throughout the 1980s, while debates about *A Nation at Risk* dominated the headlines, the National Council of Teachers of Mathematics (NCTM), a U.S. and Canadian organization of mathematics teachers, had been working to create the *Curriculum and Evaluation Standards for School Mathematics* that was published in 1989 and that has served as the model for a whole range of standards reports issued for the sciences, English, social studies, history, and other fields. The NCTM standards were the first discipline-specific standards for the schools, and they provided a solid foundation for the standards movement. NCTM added further detail to their standards with a 1991 publication that described effective mathematics teaching and a 1995 document on assessment in mathematics. Finally, in the late 1990s, NCTM appointed a new commission to revise and update all their recommendations, which resulted in a new *Principles and Standards for School Mathematics*, published in 2000. Unlike the vague Goals 2000, the NCTM standards

To some people, taking a standardized test ranks up there with going to the dentist. Think about your own experience with standardized tests and respond to the following questions:

- Do you remember taking standardized tests (tests prepared by the district or state rather than your own teacher) when you were in school?
- How did you feel about these tests? Scared? Prepared? Bored?
- Did your teacher give you hints—or tell you directly—about how he or she felt about them? Hostile? Concerned?
- How did you do on the tests?
- Most aspiring teachers tend to do well on standardized tests. Why do you think this is true? Do good test-takers make good teachers?

were clear and specific on what U.S. students should know about math. Leaders in other fields followed the model as they created their own standards.[21]

While NCTM and other organizations of teachers worked on standards in their areas, the National Education Goals Panel was created as a joint federal and state effort that took over the process of encouraging the development of national standards in virtually every field. Ultimately, the panel also took on an unexpected role of refereeing the fierce debates that some of the standards generated, most notably in history, between those who held radically different interpretations of the history of the peoples of the United States. The standards debates, as with the earlier battles about multicultural education, once again came down to the fundamental question of identity—the national and personal identities that different groups of people thought the public schools should foster. As educational historian Jonathan Zimmerman has said of these "cultural wars," "at stake was nothing less than the nation's definition of itself."[22] The debate about the history standards has been so fierce that none have ever been approved at the federal level and (to the chagrin of many textbook publishers) many states have different—and conflicting—standards for the way the nation's story should be taught.

You Decide

Should the United States have a national curriculum that all students will learn, or should different states, districts, and individual teachers decide the curriculum for their schools and classrooms?

At the same time, a number of private foundations encouraged the development of "high standards, high expectations," in all schools. By supporting intensive reform efforts in certain schools, these foundations seek to provide models for the whole national campaign.

Goals 2000 and the standards movement were not without their critics. The opposition has usually come from two perspectives. On the one hand, experienced educators have asked the tough questions: Who is going to provide the resources to meet these goals? What kinds of policies are needed in terms of family leave, Head Start, and expanded kindergarten programs to ensure that "all children in America will start school ready to learn?" What kinds of resources—for retraining teachers, for providing curriculum, and for offering other incentives—will it take to increase the high school graduation rate to 90%? And what is the point of goals that have no meaningful resources behind them?

From another perspective, any effort at national goals is seen as a step toward a national curriculum and national control of education, something to be opposed fiercely. Although a Republican president launched the national standards movement, the Republicans in Congress in the 1990s promised to "strengthen the rights of parents to protect their children against education programs that undermine the values taught in the home,"[23] and this included a

Teachable Moment
It All Adds Up

Following is an excerpt from the NCTM *Principles and Standards for School Mathematics*:

We live in a mathematical world. Whenever we decide on a purchase, choose an insurance or health plan, or use a spreadsheet, we rely on mathematical understanding. The World Wide Web, CD-ROMs, and other media disseminate vast quantities of quantitative information. The level of mathematical thinking and problem solving needed in the workplace has increased dramatically.

In such a world, those who understand and can do mathematics will have opportunities that others do not. Mathematical competence opens doors to productive futures. A lack of mathematical competence closes those doors.

Students have different abilities, needs, and interests. Yet everyone needs to be able to use mathematics in his or her personal life, in the workplace, and in further study. All students deserve an opportunity to understand the power and beauty of mathematics. Students need to learn a new set of mathematics basics that enable them to compute fluently and to solve problems creatively and resourcefully.

This vision of mathematics teaching and learning is not the reality in the majority of classrooms, schools, and districts. Today, many students are not learning the mathematics they need. In some instances, students do not have the opportunity to learn significant mathematics. In others, students lack commitment or are not engaged by existing curricula.

Attaining the vision laid out in Principles and Standards *will not be easy, but the task is critically important. We must provide our students with the best mathematics education possible, one that enables them to fulfill personal ambitions and career goals in an ever changing world.*

Source: "Introduction" to *Principles and Standards for School Mathematics, Standards 2000 Project*, by the National Council of Teachers of Mathematics, 2000, retrieved September 10, 2009, from http://standards.nctm.org/document/chapter1/index.htm.

QUESTIONS

- Is it true that "those who understand and can do mathematics will have opportunities that others do not?" Is math that important? Can some people get along just fine with very limited math knowledge?
- Is the situation today as bad as the authors of this document claim?

---

deep distrust of what was by then a Democratic president's Goals 2000 agenda.

Looking back on a decade of work and debate around national educational standards, Marge Scherer, one of the editors of *Educational Leadership*, the journal of the Association for Supervision and Curriculum Development, wrote that "high and rigorous academic standards are:

- A way to establish what all students need to know and be able to do;
- A result of a public and political outcry for increased accountability in schools;
- Not yet well implemented in most schools, although not for want of trying;

- Fraught with challenges and difficulties, but still an opportunity to raise the achievement of all;
- A bipartisan reform that offers a common ground on which advocates of good education can unite."[24]

The ambivalence in Scherer's comments, that standards provide a good baseline, that they are not yet well implemented, and that they are fraught with difficulty but provide an important opportunity, represents an accurate reflection of the views of many educators.

Although many states adopted tough standards throughout the 1990s, it was the federal No Child Left Behind Act (NCLB), enacted by Congress in 2001, that dramatically raised the profile of educational standards. Now every state was expected to have standards in most core areas of the curriculum and to test students on an annual basis to ensure that they were meeting the standards. Also, the test scores had to be disaggregated (that is, examined according to different categories of students—by gender and race, for example) so that the public could see the progress being made by girls as well as boys and by students of different ethnic groups, not just the progress of the ever-elusive "average student." Schools that failed to make "adequate yearly progress" became subject to a range of sanctions, including greater freedom for parents to remove their children, and eventually closure.

In Chapter 11, we discuss in further detail the debates and the politics surrounding No Child Left Behind.

Connections

NCLB has created some of the fiercest educational debate the country has ever seen. While much of the debate centers on the tests used to measure progress, the standards are the core of what counts as progress.[25]

SURVIVING AND THRIVING AS A TEACHER IN THE MIDST OF THE STANDARDS DEBATES

That heated debate exists about any national standards of what should be taught in schools should come as no surprise, even if the standards were not accompanied by tough testing measures. Not only has the United States traditionally trusted states and often local schools and districts to set the appropriate standards for their students, but also, as scholar Michael Apple reminds us, "In a society driven by social tensions and by increasingly larger inequalities, schools will not be immune from—and in fact may participate in recreating—these inequalities. If this is true of education in general, it is equally true of attempts to reform it."[27]

Education professor Christine Sleeter provides a helpful way of looking at some of the current, confusing debates about educational standards. Like a long line of advocates for educational equity, Sleeter insists that culturally relevant standards are essential to measuring meaningful progress in achieving equity. "But," she warns, "efforts to offer all children an intellectually rich curriculum have become conflated with standardizing what everyone should know, thereby reducing the diverse funds of knowledge with which next generations have awareness or familiarity. *High standards* and *standardization* are not the same thing yet they have been treated as if they were." For Sleeter, standards refer to a clear public measure of quality—what do the students need to know? Standardization on the other hand is an unnecessary rigidity in defining the particular ways that teachers are supposed to meet the standards.[28]

Two professional development experts, Deborah E. Burns and Jeanne H. Purcell, who have spent many years working with teachers to help them survive in an increasingly standards-based world, describe how important they believe it is to engage teachers in a discussion of the standards and in the multiple ways that the standards can be met. Reporting on their work with teachers in three Rhode Island school districts, Burns and Purcell had asked teachers to look at the standards from multiple perspectives. One teacher suddenly saw options that had not been apparent before and exclaimed, "Now I see how I can make my learning outcomes more challenging for my students. I need to incorporate all types of learning for students, not just facts." Another said, "I could teach this piece of knowledge from six different perspectives. It's just a matter of deciding what to pick for my particular group of students within the time frame." When teachers come to see their essential role in the standards movement as being in the key position of moving from general goals to specific learning outcomes, then they will have the opportunity not only to discuss the standards but also "to own them, breathe life into them, and incorporate them into the curriculum."[29]

A national debate is ongoing about whether current educational standards allow for the kind of teacher empowerment that Burns and Purcell advocate. In one of the **Readings** for this chapter, Deborah Meier, who has long advocated high standards developed at the school level but who has fought against the imposition of standards by those outside the schools, and Abigail Thernstrom, an equally longtime advocate for tough state standards and state-mandated accountability systems, debate which approach is best for schools and especially for those students often left behind in schooling. For Meier, the standards movement, "even in the hands of sincere allies of children" is "fundamentally misguided," because it "undermines the capacity of schools to instruct by example in the qualities of mind that schools in a democracy should be fostering in kids. . . ." Thus, Meier sees no

Teachable Moment

On a Need-to-Know (and Be-Able-to-Do) Basis

What does a teacher *need to know* and *be able to do*? This question is often heard in discussions about the standards. But what do aspiring teachers really "need to know" and "be able to do" before they enter a classroom for the first time? The answer to this question generates heated debate. Linda Darling-Hammond, one of the major voices for reform, writes a great deal about this topic. In *A Good Teacher in Every Classroom: Preparing the Highly Qualified Teachers Our Children Deserve*, Darling-Hammond and co-author Joan Baratz-Snowden write:[26]

Specifying what teachers need to know and be able to do is not a simple task. As is true with all professions—including medicine, the law, and the clergy—there is no one right way to behave as a teacher. Some effective teachers are charismatic whereas others are more retiring. Some are emotional and some are reserved. Some appear stern while others appear more nurturing. There are many different ways that professionals can vary and still be highly effective. Within this variation, however, there are common practices that draw on shared understanding of how to foster student learning. These include:

- *Knowledge of learners and how they learn and develop within social contexts.*
- *Understanding of the subject matter and skills to be taught in light of the social purposes of education.*
- *Understanding of teaching in light of the content and learners to be taught, as informed by assessment and supported by a productive classroom environment.*

Teaching is complex and the various kinds of knowledge about teaching, learning, and subject matter are interdependent. As professionals, teachers make a commitment to learn what they need to know to help all students succeed. A professional teacher can no longer naively assert, "I taught a great lesson, but nobody 'got it'." Teaching, as John Dewey once remarked, is like selling commodities—they are not sold if nobody buys them. And a teacher has not taught if no one learns. The vision of professional

Preparing Teachers for a Changing World

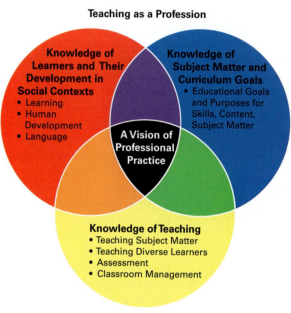

Teaching as a Profession

Knowledge of Learners and Their Development in Social Contexts
- Learning
- Human Development
- Language

Knowledge of Subject Matter and Curriculum Goals
- Educational Goals and Purposes for Skills, Content, Subject Matter

A Vision of Professional Practice

Knowledge of Teaching
- Teaching Subject Matter
- Teaching Diverse Learners
- Assessment
- Classroom Management

Learning in a Democracy

Source: "A Good Teacher in Every Classroom: Preparing the Highly Qualified Teachers Our Children Deserve," by Linda Darling-Hammond and Joan Baratz-Snowden, 2007, *Educational Horizons*, 85, pp. 111–132.

teaching depicted in the illustration connects teaching with student learning and requires that teachers be able to point to evidence of that learning. It also requires that teachers be mindful of what it means to educate students within a democracy so that, as citizens, they can participate fully in political, civic, and economic life.

QUESTIONS

- What are the things that you most want to know and what are the skills you think you need to have before you complete your own teacher preparation program?
- Can it ever happen that a teacher might teach a "great lesson," but no one (or not all students) would learn from it? Isn't it putting a great deal of pressure on teachers to say that they need to be judged by what their students learn rather than on what they teach? Is that fair?

way that Burns and Purcell's goal of having teachers own and breathe life into the standards can be accomplished. Thernstrom looks at the same standards and sees them as "new demands [that] are driving better instruction" and as a way to deliver "a vital message: no excuses." Standards, Thernstrom says, are key to school success for all students.

>> How Do Different Curricula Reflect Different Views of the Purpose of Education?

The final set of **Readings** for this chapter give graphic examples of the ways that two different educators with quite different philosophies of education approach the curriculum. E. D. Hirsch, Jr., one of the nation's best-known curriculum advocates, has developed something he calls the "core knowledge curriculum." Hirsch answers the "What will I teach?" question very specifically: "teach this core knowledge." Hirsch understands that the debate can go on forever about what core knowledge is of most importance. He is clear "not to claim that the content we recommend is better than some other well-thought-out core. . . . But one must make a start." And having a core of knowledge avoids what Hirsch sees as the too-common situation in which there is no agreement at all about what knowledge is most important.

Bob Peterson, another highly regarded teacher, has serious problems with Hirsch's curriculum model. Peterson has multiple complaints about the core knowledge curriculum: it "misdiagnoses what ails American education," it defines knowledge in such a way that small bits of information or facts pass for understanding, and it "focuses almost exclusively on contributions and perspectives of mainstream European Americans." (Recall the debates about multicultural education earlier in this chapter.) In the end, Hirsch and Peterson have different goals for what students will learn in school, they seek to foster different senses of identity in their students, and thus they answer the question of what to teach quite differently.

It is one thing to sit in class and debate the merits of Hirsch's or Peterson's or Meier's and Thernstrom's views (and that debate is important to developing an informed understanding of the current status of curriculum debates in the United States). It is quite a different matter to find ways to survive and thrive as a teacher in schools that are increasingly dominated by state and national standards—to "own them, breathe life into them." This goal may be difficult to achieve, but no teacher today can ignore the standards.

The standards, and the state tests that measure them, have had a huge impact on schools and specifically on teachers and principals. In too many places the standards and the tests have come to be viewed as an impossible barrier that drives everything else out of the school day and takes the life out of teaching. However, the kind of

data that the tests provide can help schools break through the tendency to have low expectations for all students and instead focus on just what it will take to help every student succeed. A lot depends on the nature of the standards and the tests, but a lot also depends on the approach individual educators take to using them.

Of course, no educator wants to be seen as opposing high standards. No one advocates for mediocrity. Nevertheless, the standards debate is a complex one for all of us. Who sets the standards? Who measures progress toward meeting the standards? How much freedom and flexibility should an individual classroom teacher have in deciding the standards to be met and the means of meeting them? These debates are alive and well in every classroom, school board, and legislative hall in the United States today, and it is here that today's and tomorrow's curriculum is being defined.

Vito Perrone, a longtime teacher (and teacher of teachers) summarizes the current situation and its cost:

In too many school systems teachers are not expected to make significant decisions about what to teach. And the decisions that are open to them often have fairly rigid boundaries. Elaborate curriculum guides with detailed objectives organized around subject fields and extending to the sequence of topics to be taught are not uncommon, leaving little room for the personal interest or invention of teachers or students.

Perrone makes it clear that he thinks allowing this situation to continue is a mistake. "Learning in such schools invariably gets reduced to small pieces of knowledge ordered by a predetermined sequence with considerable stress placed on coverage." To move from mere coverage to creating the kinds of intellectually challenging communities—for students and for teachers—that schools ought to be, Perrone argues, is the challenge facing teachers today. Like others, Perrone also asserts a teacher's right, indeed duty, to be active in helping to create intellectually challenging communities in schools.[30]

Advocates of higher and more specific standards will argue with Perrone that, although the standards set out the basic outline of what teachers are expected to teach, many teachers still have significant room to incorporate their personal interests or to be inventive. The key is to use the standards as a launching pad, not as a rigid formula. Schools and school districts have embraced the standards in different ways, from mandating approaches like direct instruction (a model of implementing the reading standards that scripts virtually every word a teacher says) to encouraging much more open-ended arrangements that use resources like the NCTM standards and examples as a starting point for teacher-led curricular planning.[31]

Part of asserting one's right and duty to help shape the curriculum involves returning to the Tyler rationale discussed at the beginning of the chapter. Whatever the mandates of their schools, individual teachers, as well as curriculum leaders and school boards, must ask the same basic questions about

Teachable Moment
What *Doesn't* Get Taught?

As many schools are allocating more time for math and reading to address recent standards and the testing that goes with them, instructional time and attention is being diverted from other traditional areas within the curriculum, such as social studies, music, art, physical education, and oftentimes the sciences—even lunch. In one study, more than 60% of schools report that they have decreased the amount of time devoted to subjects not specified for testing under federal law so that they could emphasize reading and math. In some cases, certain subjects were skipped altogether to double math or reading time.

Given the pressure that teachers and school administrators feel to raise their test scores in core areas, it is not surprising that more and more hours in the school day would be devoted to the subjects that are being tested. Many observers are pleased that schools are now devoting this time to reading and mathematics so that more students have a better chance of gaining real mastery in these fields. However, the focus on a few core subjects is not without its cost, which some critics say is very high.

According to Susan Griffin, executive director of the National Council for the Social Studies, "We're hearing that social studies is almost disappearing in the elementary schools. In this global economy and very complex world, if students aren't prepared, how are they going to make good decisions?" Even at the high school level, the study of U.S. history, world history, and other subjects that fall under social studies, as well as the arts, are often getting far less time

and attention than they did a decade or two ago. If schools are supposed to prepare well-rounded citizens who understand the world historically and aesthetically, and if other aspects of student's lives, including their health and the growing obesity epidemic, are to be addressed, something is going to have to give or change. This is an issue that educators and policy makers will continue to address carefully in the next few years.

QUESTIONS

- When you were in high school, how much attention was given to social studies or the arts? Did you feel that some subjects were "privileged" because of the tests that were given at your school?
- Can you construct arguments for as well as against focusing the school curriculum on only a few subjects and leaving others aside?

Source: "Study: NCLB Leads to Cuts for Some Subjects," by Michelle R. Davis, April 5, 2006, *Education Week*; and "Effects of NCLB's Focus on Reading and Math," by Anne C. Lewis, April 2008, *Education Digest*.

The Principal Objective in Florida

Paul George, a professor of education at the University of Florida, describes how school leaders in Florida found ways not only to live with but also to use standards to create educational success for their students. Based on a careful look at the work of 50 principals in Florida, George concluded that the best of them aim for success in the following ways:

- **Set urgent goals.** Principals know that they have to make identifiable progress almost immediately.
- **Engage school personnel.** School leaders know that they cannot succeed without the support and trust of the school's teachers and other administrators. Principals often begin by developing cohesiveness and commitment among a small group of school and teacher leaders.
- **Use school achievement data.** Florida's principals have become data-driven organizational leaders. In the most effective schools, skilled analysis of student achievement data has become a crucial step in breaking through the barriers of low achievement and low expectations.
- **Strengthening professional development.** Inservice education was once a casual affair, but a new sense of urgency has transformed its focus to training that will lead directly to improved test scores. The biggest change is an intense interest in developing higher-order thinking skills.
- **Align the curriculum.** For better or worse, many schools openly declare that they review every activity in terms of how much of an impact it has on the state assessment. School leaders spend much time monitoring and coaching for effective curriculum alignment. At one school, counselors examined students' schedules to determine whether each student was taking a sufficiently rigorous program and rescheduled many students into more demanding courses.
- **Increase time for academics.** One of the most typical, and perhaps least desirable, methods for increasing the amount of time devoted to tested subjects is to decrease the amount of time usually available for subjects that are not currently tested. In many schools, exploratory curriculum and guidance programs have been replaced by basic academic courses. Science and social studies may suffer.
- **Choose instructional materials to support standards.** Schools use a mix of state-produced, commercial, and local curriculum materials targeted to improving achievement, focusing on those designed for new state standards and state test preparation.
- **Build interdisciplinary teams.** The interdisciplinary teams that have grown in middle schools throughout the United States encourage collaboration among teachers and a more careful focus on small groups of students.
- **Promote the test.** Many schools target public relations efforts at students, teachers, and parents to persuade them of the importance of the standards and the state test, often using special incentives to motivate students toward improved performance.
- **Redefine school leadership.** Florida principals now see themselves as instructional leaders; everything else is viewed as an irritating distraction from this responsibility.

QUESTIONS

- Is it realistic for principals to "see themselves as instructional leaders" and view everything else as an irritating distraction? What happens when an angry parent shows up, or the boiler in the building breaks, or the district demands budget cuts?
- If you were teaching in a Florida school led by a principal who held to these goals, which ones of them would help you, which ones would make life more difficult, and which would not matter at all?

Source: "A+ Accountability in Florida?" by Paul S. George, September 2001, Educational Leadership 59 (1), pp. 23–32.

the curriculum. Recall that Tyler asked teachers to focus on four questions: What is the purpose? What experiences attain the purposes? How can these experiences be organized? and How can we determine whether the purposes are being attained?

In Chapter 11, we explore in more detail the state and national movement toward standards-based testing.

Connections

To a much larger degree than at any time in history, the first of Tyler's questions is being determined at the national and state levels. Although standards do not always do so directly, they dictate much of the purpose of contemporary education. Nevertheless, individual teachers can add their own sense of purpose to their classrooms. The next two questions, regarding the development and organization of student experiences, leave much room for teacher involvement in most situations. In extreme cases, such as with direct instruction, all questions of experience and organization are answered, but most teachers find themselves in situations closer to those described by Burns and Purcell. With the right time and planning, they can design and craft their own classes in response to their students' individual needs.

It is in the arena of Tyler's last point—determining if the standards have been met—that some of the greatest controversy arises today. Nearly every state now has state-level tests, many of which a student must pass in order to graduate. Teachers and principals, as well as students, are evaluated based on how well students do on these tests. The temptation to "teach to the test" is certainly significant today. Among the most pressing questions currently is whether such pressures will foster more creativity on the part of teachers to help their students achieve well, or whether the pressures will simply move most teachers toward a mindless conformity to preplanned "test prep" instruction.

Returning once again to William Pinar's statement that "[d]ebates over what is basic to the curriculum are also debates over identity," we know that teachers will be able to ask not only "What will I teach?" but also "What sort of identity am I trying to foster in my students?" and "What sense of themselves and what sense of place in a national identity am I developing when I select the stories to use to teach a first grader to read or a middle school student to engage with algebra or a high school senior to think about advanced study in the sciences, world history, and the best way to prepare for college and life beyond?" The day-to-day questions of curriculum are best framed in the answer to these much larger questions.

REVIEW >>

- **What is curriculum? Why teach *this* and not *that*?**

  The total curriculum (that is, the "stuff" that gets taught in school) comprises both the official curriculum, which is planned course content, as well as the hidden curriculum, which involves all the messages that students receive about their education. Debates over the structure of curriculum and a teacher's ability to affect it have been ongoing for many years. The Tyler rationale is a model that outlines the overall objectives of curriculum development and looks beyond simply planning and executing lessons to the educational purposes and subsequent evaluation. Primarily four schools of thought (humanists, developmentalists, social efficiency educators, and social meliorists) have and continue to dominate the discussion of curriculum in the United States.

- **What are some of the current debates about multicultural education?**

  Multicultural education has many advocates (who often disagree with each other) as well as many opponents (who likewise disagree). Often referred to as the "father of multicultural education," James Banks outlined critical areas that must be given attention in any effective program of multicultural education: (1) content integration, (2) the knowledge construction process, (3) prejudice reduction, (4) an equity pedagogy, and (5) an empowering school culture. Critics of multicultural education cite a variety of concerns, including loss of students' perceived national identity, issues with a "value-free" education, and unfair expectation on teachers to learn and address a plethora of cultural nuances.

- **Do the standards address what students need to know?**

  For decades, curriculum standards have been the subject of heated debate at the state and federal levels. The standards debate has come up repeatedly as part of efforts to clarify who has the authority to determine what content should be delivered in the schools: during the civil rights movement, in terms of equity in education; with the publication of *A Nation at Risk*, which called for a better school system; after the unveiling of Goals 2000, which enumerated high ideals for our nation's education system; and with passage of the No Child Left Behind Act, which required states to have standards in most core areas of the curriculum and annually test students' proficiency. As decisions are made about what to cover, and whether it should be mandated at some level, there are ramifications for what is *not* going to be covered and for the accountability of many participants, including teachers, students, and administrators.

- **How do different curricula reflect different views of the purpose of education?**

  Pinar's assertion that the debates regarding curriculum are really debates about identity comes full circle when we review the various philosophies of curriculum, such as Hirsch's core knowledge curriculum, which contends that curriculum must start somewhere or at least at a core of knowledge all should be expected to learn. Critics claim that such an approach limits the perspectives delivered in the classroom. These types of debates—about identity, perspectives, and knowledge—are central to the ongoing standards and curriculum discussion.

What Are Some of the Current Debates About Multicultural Education?

From *AFFIRMING DIVERSITY*

BY SONIA NIETO

In this selection, Sonia Nieto, from the University of Massachusetts at Amherst, provides a clear definition and a compelling case for the importance of multicultural education based on both her scholarly research and her personal autobiography.

Multicultural education cannot be understood in a vacuum but rather must be seen in its personal, social, historical, and political context. Assuming that multicultural education is "the answer" to school failure is simplistic at best, for it overlooks important social and educational issues that affect the daily lives of students. Educational failure is too complex and knotty an issue to be "fixed" by any single program or approach. However, if broadly conceptualized and implemented, multicultural education can have a substantive and positive impact on the educational experience of most students. That is the thesis of this book.

I have come to this understanding as a result of many experiences, including my childhood and my life as a student, teacher, researcher, and parent. As a young child growing up in Brooklyn, New York, during the 1940's, I was able to experience firsthand the influence that poverty, discrimination, and the perception of one's culture and language as inferior can have. Speaking only Spanish when I entered the first grade, I was immediately confronted with the arduous task of learning a second language while my already quite developed native language was all but ignored. Some forty years later, I still recall the frustration of groping for words I did not know to express thoughts I could very capably say in Spanish. Equally vivid are memories of some teachers' expectations that because of our language and cultural differences, my classmates and I would not do well in school. This explains my fourth-grade teacher's response when mine was the only hand to go up when she asked if anybody in the class wanted to go to college. "Well, that's O.K." she said, "because we always need people to clean toilets."

I also recall teachers' perceptions that there was something wrong with speaking a language other than English. "Is there anybody in this class who started school without speaking English?" my tenth-grade homeroom teacher asked loudly, filling out one of the endless forms that teachers are handed by the central office. By this time, my family had moved to what was at the time a working-class and primarily European American neighborhood. My class-

mates looked in hushed silence as I, the only Puerto Rican in the class, raised my hand timidly. "Are you in a special English class?" he asked in front of the entire class. "Yes," I said, "I'm in Honors English." Although there is nothing wrong with being in a special class for English as a second language (ESL), I felt fortunate that I was able to respond in this way. I had learned to feel somewhat ashamed of speaking Spanish and wanted to make it very clear that I was intelligent in spite of it. Many students in similar circumstances who are in bilingual and ESL classes feel guilty and inferior to their peers.

Those first experiences with society's responses to cultural differences did not, of course, convince me that something was wrong with the responses. Rather, I assumed, as many of my peers did, that there was something wrong with us. We learned to feel ashamed of who we were, how we spoke, what we ate, and everything else that was "different" about us. "Please," I would beg my mother, "make us hamburgers and hot dogs for dinner." Luckily, she never paid attention and kept right on cooking rice, beans, platanos, and all those other good foods that we grew up with. She and my father also continued speaking Spanish to us, in spite of our teachers' pleas to speak to us only in English. And so, alongside the messages at school and in the streets that being Puerto Rican was not something to be proud of, we learned to keep on being who we were. As the case studies point out, these conflicting messages are still being given to many young people.

Immigration is not a phenomenon of the past. In fact, the experience of immigration is still fresh in the minds of a great many people in our country. It is an experience that begins anew every day that planes land, ships reach out our shores, and people make their way on foot to our borders. Many of the students in our schools, even if they themselves are not immigrants, have parents or grandparents who were. The United States is thus not only a nation of immigrants as seen in some idealized and romanticized past; it is also a living nation of immigrants even today.

The pain and alienation of the immigrant experience, however, have rarely been confronted in our

Source: *Affirming Diversity*, by Sonia Nieto, 1992, Longman.

schools. This experience includes the forced immigration of enslaved Africans and the colonization of American Indians and Mexicans from within. Because schools have traditionally perceived their role to be that of an assimilating agent, the isolation and rejection that come hand in hand with immigration and colonization have simply been left at the schoolhouse door. Curriculum and pedagogy, rather than using the lived experiences of students as a foundation, have been based on what can be described as an alien and imposed reality. The rich experiences of millions of our students, their parents, grandparents, and neighbors have been kept strangely quiet. Although we almost all have an immigrant past, very few of us know or even acknowledge it.

What the research reported in this book suggests to me is that we need to make this history visible by making it part of the curriculum, instruction, and educational experience in general. Whether through the words of Manuel, who claims that he cannot be an American because it would mean forsaking his Cape Verdean background, or those of Vanessa, who knows nothing about her European American past and even feels uncomfortable discussing it, it has become clear that the immigrant experience is an important point of departure for beginning our journey into multicultural education. This journey needs to begin with teachers, who themselves are frequently unaware of or uncomfortable with their own ethnicity. By going through a process of reeducation about their own backgrounds, their families' pain, and their rich legacy of stories, teachers can lay the groundwork for students to reclaim their own histories and voices.

As an adult, I have come to the conclusion that no child should have to go through the painful dilemma of choosing between family and school and of what inevitably becomes a choice between belonging and succeeding. The costs for going through such an experience are high indeed, from becoming a "cultural schizophrenic" to developing doubts about one's self-worth and dignity.

Some Assumptions

It is necessary to clarify a number of assumptions embedded in the text. The first concerns who is included in multicultural education. My perspective is that multicultural education is for everyone regardless of ethnicity, race, language, social class, religion, gender or sexual preference. My framework for multicultural education is thus a very broad and inclusive one. Nevertheless, although I refer in the text to many kinds of differences, I am particularly concerned with race, ethnicity, and language. These are the major issues that provide a lens through which I view multicultural

education. This perspective is probably based on a number of reasons, not the least of which is my own experience. Another reason concerns the very history of multicultural education. A direct outgrowth of the civil rights movement, multicultural and bilingual education was developed as a response to inequality in education based on racism, ethnocentrism, and language discrimination. Although I believe it is imperative to include other differences, for me it is necessary to approach an understanding of multicultural education with a firm grounding in these three areas.

This brings up another dilemma related to inclusion. It is easier for some educators to embrace a very inclusive and comprehensive framework of multicultural education because they have a hard time facing racism. They may prefer to deal with issues of class, exceptionality, or religious diversity because, for them, these factors may be easier to confront. Racism is an excruciatingly difficult issue for most of us. Given our history of exclusion and discrimination, this is not surprising. Nevertheless, I believe it is only through a thorough investigation of discrimination based on race and other differences related to it that we can understand the genesis as well as the rationale for multicultural education. I will also refer to gender, social class, and exceptionality because these areas provide other important lenses with which to view inequality in education. However, because no one book can possibly give all of these issues the central importance they deserve, I have chosen to focus on race, ethnicity, and language.

Another assumption that guides this book is that teachers should not be singled out as the villains in the failure of so many students. Although some teachers do indeed bear the responsibility for having low expectations, being racist and elitist in their interactions with students and parents, and providing educational environments that discourage many students from learning, most do not do so consciously. Most teachers are sincerely concerned about their students and want very much to provide the best education they can. Nevertheless, they are often at the mercy of decisions made by others far removed from the classroom. In addition, they

have little to do with developing the policies and practices in operation in their schools and frequently do not even question them.

Teachers are also the products of educational systems that have a history of racism, exclusion, and debilitating pedagogy. As such, they put into practice what they themselves have been subjected to and thus perpetuate structures that may be harmful to many of their students. Furthermore, the disempowerment felt by so many teachers is a palpable force in many schools. Finally, schools cannot be separated from communities or from our society in general. Oppressive forces that limit opportunities in the schools are a reflection of such forces in the society at large. Thus, the purpose of this book is not to point a finger but to provide a forum for reflection and discussion so that teachers take responsibility for their actions, challenge the actions of schools and society that affect their students' education, and help effect positive change.

From THE DISUNITING OF AMERICA

BY ARTHUR M. SCHLESINGER, JR.

Although many educators have rallied to the cause of multicultural education, others have become increasingly critical. Few issues have cut so deeply to the core questions of the nature and purpose of schooling and the fundamental nature of the American story as multicultural education. Arthur M. Schlesinger, Jr., advisor to President John F. Kennedy and well-known liberal icon, surprised many with the vehemence of his attack on multicultural education. For Schlesinger, multiculturalism can quickly lead to division and separation. As he makes clear, he wants none of it.

The attack on the common American identity is the culmination of the cult of ethnicity. That attack was mounted in the first instance by European Americans of non-British origin ("unmeltable ethnics") against the British foundations of American culture; then, latterly and massively, by Americans of non-European origin against the European foundations of that culture. . . . And the non-Europeans, or at least their self-appointed spokesmen, bring with them a resentment, in some cases a hatred, of Europe and the West provoked by generations of Western colonialism, racism, condescension, contempt, and cruel exploitation. . . .

Is Europe really the root of all evil? The crimes of Europe against lesser breeds without the law (not to mention even worse crimes—Hitlerism and Stalinism—against other Europeans) are famous. But these crimes do not alter other facts of history: that Europe was the birthplace of the United States of America, that European ideas and culture formed the republic, that the United States is an extension of European civilization, and that nearly 80 percent of Americans are of European descent.

When Irving Howe, hardly a notorious conservative, dared write, "The Bible, Homer, Plato, Sophocles, Shakespeare are central to our culture," an outraged reader ("having graduated this past year from Amherst") wrote, "Where on Howe's list is the *Quran*, the *Gita*, Confucius, and other central cultural artifacts of the peoples of our nation?" No one can doubt the importance of these works

nor the influence they have had on other societies. But on American society? It may be too bad that dead white European males have played so large a role in shaping our culture. But that's the way it is. One cannot erase history.

These humdrum historical facts, and not some dastardly imperialist conspiracy, explain the Eurocentric slant in American schools. Would anyone seriously argue that teachers should conceal the European origins of American civilization? or that schools should educate the 20 percent and ignore the 80 percent? Of course the 20 percent and their contributions should be integrated into the curriculum too, which is the point of cultural pluralism.

But self-styled "multiculturalists" are very often ethnocentric separatists who see little in the Western heritage beyond Western crimes. The Western tradition, in this view, is inherently racist, sexist, "classist," hegemonic; irredeemably repressive, irredeemably oppressive. The spread of Western power. Thus the popularity of European classical music around the world—and, one supposes, of American jazz and rock too—is evidence not of wide appeal but of "the pattern of imperialism, in which the conquered culture adopts that of the conqueror." . . .

Is the Western tradition a bar to progress and a curse on humanity? Would it really do America and the world good to get rid of the European legacy?

No doubt Europe has done terrible things, not least to itself. But what culture has not? History, said Edward Gibbon,

Source: The Disuniting of America: Reflections on a Multicultural Society, by Arthur M. Schlesinger, Jr., 1991, Whittle Direct Books, pp. 70–83.

is little more than the register of the crimes, follies, and misfortunes of mankind. The sins of the West are no worse than the sins of Asia or of the Middle East or of Africa.

There remains, however, a crucial difference between the Western tradition and the others. The crimes of the West have produced their own antidotes. They have provoked great movements to end slavery, to raise the status of women, to abolish torture, to combat racism, to defend freedom of inquiry and expression, to advance personal liberty and human rights.

Whatever the particular crimes of Europe, that continent is also the source—the *unique* source—of those liberating ideas of individual liberty, political democracy, the rule of law, human rights, and cultural freedom that constitute our most precious legacy and to which most of the world today aspires. These are *European* ideas, not Asian, nor African, nor Middle Eastern ideas, except by adoption.

The freedoms of inquiry and of artistic creation, for example, are Western values. Consider the differing reactions to the case of Salman Rushdie: what the West saw as an intolerable attack on individual freedom the Middle East saw a proper punishment for an evildoer who had violated the mores of his group. Individualism itself is looked on with abhorrence and dread by collectivist cultures in which loyalty to the group overrides personal goals—cultures that, social scientists say, comprise about 70 percent of the world's population.

There is surely no reason for Western civilization to have guilt trips laid on it by champions of cultures based on despotism, superstition, tribalism, and fanaticism. In this regard the Afrocentrists are especially absurd. The West needs no lectures on the superior virtue of those "sun people" who sustained slavery until Western imperialism abolished it (and, it is reported, sustain it to this day in Mauritania and the Sudan), who still keep women in subjection and cut off their clitorises, who carry out racial persecutions not only against Indians and other Asians but against fellow Africans from the wrong tribes, who show themselves either incapable of operating a democracy or ideologically hostile to the democratic idea, and who in their tyrannies and massacres, their Idi Amins and Boukassas, have stamped with utmost brutality on human rights. . . .

The genius of America lies in its capacity to forge a single nation from peoples of remarkably diverse racial, religious, and ethnic origins. It has done so because democratic principles provide both the philosophical bond of union and practical experience in civic participation. The American creed envisages a nation composed of individuals making their own choices and accountable to themselves, not a nation based on inviolable ethnic communities. . . .

Americans of whatever origin should take pride in the distinctive inheritance to which they have all contributed, as other nations take pride in their distinctive inheritances.

Belief in one's own culture does not require disdain for other cultures. But one step at a time: no culture can hope to ingest other cultures all at once, certainly not before it ingests its own. As we begin to master our own culture, then we can explore the world. . . .

Above all, history can give a sense of national identity. We don't have to believe that our values are absolutely better than the next fellow's or the next country's, but we have no doubt that they are better *for us*, reared as we are—and are worth living by and worth dying for. For our values are not matters of whim and happenstance. History has given them to us. They are anchored in our national experience, in our great national documents, in our national heroes, our folkways, traditions, and standards. People with a different history will have differing values. But we believe that our own are better for us. They work for us; and, for that reason, we live and die by them. . . .

The American identity will never be fixed and final; it will always be in the making. Changes in the population have always brought changes in the national ethos and will continue to do so; but not, one must hope, at the expense of national integration. The question America confronts as a pluralistic society is how to vindicate cherished cultures and traditions without breaking the bonds of cohesion—common ideals, common political institutions, common language, common culture, common fate—that hold the republic together.

Our task is to combine due appreciation of the splendid diversity of the nation with due emphasis on the great unifying Western ideas of individual freedom, political democracy, and human rights. These are the ideas that define the American nationality—and that today empower people of all continents, races, and creeds.

"What then is the American, this new man? . . . Here individuals of all nations are melted into a new race of men." Still a good answer—still the best hope.

1. Clearly, Schlesinger and Nieto represent very different perspectives on the value of multicultural curricula in the schools. Whose argument do you find more compelling?

2. Nieto placed much of her approach in her personal experience as an immigrant. What would Schlesinger say to her on that issue?

3. Why does Schlesinger take such a hard line in his attack on multicultural education? What does he fear will happen to education and to society if a multicultural perspective becomes strong? How do you respond to his concerns?

Do the Standards Address What Students Need to Know?

From *WILL STANDARDS SAVE PUBLIC EDUCATION?*

BY DEBORAH MEIER AND ABIGAIL THERNSTROM

No one has been a stronger critic of the standards movement, and especially the standardized testing that often accompanies standards-based reforms, than Deborah Meier. Now teaching at New York University, Meier began her career as a kindergarten teacher in Chicago, founded the Central Park East schools in New York, served as principal of the Mission Hill School in Boston for a decade, and is the author of numerous books on education—all of which are infused with her indefatigable commitment to listening to the voices of children and to teaching them democratic values. In a short volume, *Will Standards Save Public Education?*, Meier first outlines her own critique of the standards movement and standardized testing and then invites many of her critics, some gentle, some harsh, to respond. Anyone interested in this critical debate should take the time to read the whole book. These excerpts outline a small part of the debate between Meier and one of her sharpest critics—and one of the strongest defenders of the standards movement, including standardized testing—Abigail Thernstrom, then a member of the Massachusetts state Board of Education and a longtime advocate for tough content-based standards for schools.

Meier

I know how advocates of the movement to standardize standards will respond [to this critique of the standards movement]: "Good reform ideas can always be misused. Our proposals are designed to help kids save public education, and ensure equity."

I disagree. Even in the hands of sincere allies of children, equity, and public education, the current push for far greater standardization than we've ever previously attempted is fundamentally misguided. It will not help to develop young minds, contribute to a robust democratic life, or aid the most vulnerable of our fellow citizens. By shifting the locus of authority to outside bodies, it undermines the capacity of schools to instruct by example in the qualities of mind that schools in a democracy should be fostering in kids—responsibility for one's own ideas, tolerance for the ideas of others, and a capacity to negotiate differences. Standardization instead turns teachers and parents into the local instruments of externally imposed expert judgment. It thus decreases the chances that young people will grow up in the midst of adults who are making hard decisions and exercising mature judgment in the face of disagreements. And it squeezes out those schools and educators that seek to show alternate possibilities, explore other paths. . . .

In brief, our hope lies in schools that are more personal, compelling, and attractive than the Internet or TV, where youngsters can keep company with interesting and powerful adults who are in turn in alliance with the students' families and local institutions. We need to surround kids with adults who know and care for our children, who have opinions and are accustomed to expressing them publicly, and who know how to reach reasonable collective decisions in the face of disagreement. That means increasing the local decision making, and simultaneously decreasing the size and bureaucratic complexity of schools. Correspondingly, the worst thing we can do is to turn teachers and schools into vehicles for implementing externally imposed standards.

Thernstrom

[T]he reforms that Deborah Meier scorns have been inspired, first and foremost, by concern for highly disadvantaged kids, who for so long have been educationally neglected. And already in Massachusetts the new demands are driving better instruction. For instance, for years Boston promoted students who had not mastered the most basic reading and math skills; the district is now talking about strategies to teach reading to those who arrive in high school functionally illiterate. It's running a catch-up summer school. Many districts are placing new emphasis on early intervention to rescue children already behind by second grade; some are running summer workshops in content areas for teachers; others are adding more reading and writing to their curricula, since the tests ask open-ended questions that assess the student's ability to understand complex material and organize a short essay.

The demand for academic rigor is changing teaching in the tony suburbs too. But it's not the kids in Lexington

Source: "Educating a Democracy," by Deborah Meier, and "No Excuses," by Abigail Thernstrom, in *Will Standards Save Public Education?* edited by Deborah Meier, 2000, Beacon Press, pp. 4–5, 19–20, 35–36.

and Concord who will gain the most from the new stress on solid skills and a basic knowledge of core subjects. Deborah Meier wants different standards for advantaged and disadvantaged children. Instead, the state is delivering a vital message: no excuses. Kids can come from low-income, one-parent families, or from chaotic neighborhoods. The color of their skin may be a few shades darker than that of an Irish Catholic. But in the classroom, it doesn't matter. They can still be expected to acquire the knowledge and skills they will need to hold down decent jobs in today's economy. And knowledge and skills are the road to true equality.

Low expectations are demeaning and patronizing, and let's not kid ourselves about the basic economic picture.

QUESTIONS

1. Since both Meier and Thernstrom frame their approach to the standards movement out of concern for poor students and students of color, how could they differ so much in their answer to the question of what kind of education offers the most promising opportunity for traditionally marginalized students?

2. Although the debate between Meier and Thernstrom is about curriculum standards, do you see larger issues reflected here?

3. Who, in the end, do you find most convincing? Would you propose yet another way?

How Do Different Curricula Reflect Different Views of the Purpose of Education?

The two authors whose work is presented here—E. D. Hirsh, Jr., and Bob Peterson—could not differ more radically in their answer to the question "What should schools teach?" and by extension "How should they teach it?" You must dig further, however, to find the differences and similarities in their answer to the question Pinar asks about the core identity (for individuals and a nation) embedded in their different approaches to the curriculum. It is important to read these two articles with reference to each other. Although Hirsch and Peterson hardly represent all of the many different perspectives on curriculum, viewing these two articles as a debate about two different philosophies of education is an invitation to join the debate yourself.

From "THE CORE KNOWLEDGE CURRICULUM—WHAT'S BEHIND ITS SUCCESS?"

BY E. D. HIRSCH, JR.

E. D. Hirsch, Jr. is one of the most well-known curriculum reformers in the United States today. With the publication of his 1987 book *Cultural Literacy: What Every American Needs to Know,* Hirsch in a dramatic way joined the battles about what schools should teach. In that and subsequent books, and in the work of the Core Knowledge Foundation, which Hirsch founded, he advocates forcefully that there is a core knowledge—a common set of information—that every American should know. Some people agree with Hirsch, some disagree, but few can ignore his ideas and their impact on schools.

The Mohegan School, in the South Bronx, is surrounded by the evidence of urban blight: trash, abandoned cars, crack houses. The students, mostly Latino or African-American, all qualify for free lunch. This public school is located in the innermost inner city.

Mohegan's talented principal, Jeffrey Litt, wrote to me that "the richness of the curriculum is of particular importance" to his students because their educational experience, like that of "most poverty-stricken and educationally underserved students, was limited to remedial activities." Since adopting the Core Knowledge curriculum, however, Mohegan's students are engaged in the integrated and coherent topics like: Ancient Egypt, Greece, and Rome; the Industrial Revolution; limericks, haiku, and poetry; Rembrandt, Monet, and Michelangelo; Beethoven and Mozart; the Underground Railroad; the Trail of Tears; *Brown v. Board of Education*; the Mexican Revolution; photosynthesis; medieval African empires; the Bill of Rights; eco-

systems; women's suffrage; the Harlem Renaissance—and many more.

The Philosophy Behind Core Knowledge

In addition to offering compelling subject matter, the Core Knowledge guidelines for elementary schools are far more specific than those issued by most school districts. Instead of vague outcomes such as "First graders will be introduced to map skills," the geography section of the *Core Knowledge Sequence* specifies that 1st graders will learn the meaning of "east," "west," "north," and "south" and locate on a map the equator, the Atlantic and Pacific Oceans, the seven continents, the United States, Mexico, Canada, and Central America.

Our aim in providing specific grade-by-grade guidelines—developed after several years of research, consultation, consensus-building, and field-testing—is *not* to claim that the content we recommend is better than

Source: "The Core Knowledge Curriculum—What's Behind Its Success?" by E. D. Hirsch, Jr., 1993, *Educational Leadership* 50 (8).

some other well-thought-out core. No specific guidelines could plausibly claim to be the Platonic ideal. But one must make a start. To get beyond the talking stage, we created the best specific guidelines we could.

Nor is it our aim to specify everything that American schoolchildren should learn (the Core Knowledge guidelines are meant to constitute about 50 percent of a school's curriculum, thus leaving the other half to be tailored to a district, school, or classroom). Rather, our point is that a core of shared knowledge, grade by grade, is needed to achieve excellence and fairness in elementary education.

International studies have shown that *any* school that puts into practice a similarly challenging and specific program will provide a more effective and fair education than one that lacks such commonality of content in each grade. High-performing systems such as those in France, Sweden, Japan, and West Germany bear out this principle. It was our intent to test whether in rural, urban, and suburban settings of the United States we would find what other nations have already discovered.

Certainly the finding that a school-wide core sequence greatly enhances achievement *for all* is supported at the Mohegan School. Disciplinary problems there are down; teacher and student attendance are up, as are scores on standardized tests. Some of the teachers have even transferred their own children to the school, and some parents have taken their children out of private schools to send them to Mohegan. Similar results are being reported at some 65 schools across the nation that are taking steps to integrate the Core Knowledge guidelines into their curriculums.

In the broadcast feature about the Mohegan School, I was especially interested to hear 5th grade teacher Evelyn Hernandez say that Core Knowledge "tremendously increased the students' ability to question." In other words, based on that teacher's classroom experience, *a coherent approach to specific content enhances students' critical thinking and higher-order thinking skills.*

I emphasize this point because a standard objection to teaching specific content is that critical thinking suffers when a teacher emphasizes "mere information." Yet Core Knowledge teachers across the nation report that a coherent focus on content leads to higher-order thinking skills more securely than any other approach they know, including attempts to inculcate such skills directly. As an added benefit, children acquire knowledge that they will find useful not just in next year's classroom but for the rest of their lives.

Why Core Knowledge Works

Here are some of the research findings that explain the correlation between a coherent, specific approach to knowledge and the development of higher-order skills.

Learning can be fun, but is nonetheless cumulative and sometimes arduous. The dream of inventing methods to streamline the time-consuming activity of learning is as old as the hills. In antiquity it was already an old story.

Proclus records an anecdote about an encounter between Euclid the inventor of geometry, and King Ptolemy I of Egypt (276–196 B.C.), who was impatiently trying to follow Euclid's *Elements* step by laborious step. Exasperated, the king demanded a faster, easier way to learn geometry—to which Euclid gave the famous, and still true, reply: "There is no royal road to geometry." . . .

Because modern classrooms cannot effectively deliver completely individualized instruction, effective education requires grade-by-grade shared knowledge. When an individual child "gets" what is being taught in a classroom, it is like someone understands a joke. A click occurs. If you have the requisite background knowledge, you will get the joke, but if you don't, you will remain puzzled until somebody explains the knowledge that was taken for granted. Similarly, a classroom of 25 to 35 children can move forward as a group only when *all* the children have the knowledge that is necessary to "getting" the next step in learning. . . .

Just as learning is cumulative, so are learning deficits. As they begin 1st grade, American student are not far behind beginners in other developed nations. But as they progress, their achievement falls farther and farther behind. This widening gap is the subject of one of the most important recent books on American education, *The Learning Gap* by Stevenson and Stigler.

This progressively widening gap closely parallels what happens *within* American elementary schools between advantaged and disadvantaged children. As the two groups progress from grades 1–6, the achievement gap grows ever larger and is almost never overcome. The reasons for the parallels between the two kinds of gaps—the learning gap and the fairness gap—are similar.

In both cases, the widening gap represents the cumulative effective of learning deficits. Although a few talented and motivated children may overcome this ever-increasing handicap, most do not. The rift grows ever wider in adult life. The basic causes of this permanent deficit, apart from motivational ones, are cognitive. Learning builds upon learning in cumulative ways, and lack of learning in the early grades usually has, in comparative terms, a negatively cumulative effect. . . .

High academic skill is based upon broad general knowledge. Someone once asked Boris Goldovsky how he could play the piano so brilliantly with such small hands. His memorable reply was: "Where in the world did you get the idea that we play the piano with our hands?"

It's the same with reading: we don't read just with our eyes. By 7th grade, according to the epoch-making research of Thomas Sticht, most children, even those who read badly, have already attained the purely technical proficiency they need. Their reading and their listening show the same rate and level of comprehension; thus the mechanics of reading are not the limiting factor. What is mainly lacking in poor readers is a broad, ready vocabulary. But broad vocabulary means broad knowledge, because to know a lot of words you have to know a lot of things. Thus, broad general knowledge is an essential requisite to superior reading skill and indirectly related to the skills that accompany it.

Superior reading skill is known to be highly correlated with most other academic skills, including the ability to write well, learn rapidly, solve problems, and think critically. To concentrate on reading is therefore to focus implicitly on a whole range of educational issues.

It is sometimes claimed (but not backed up with research) that knowledge changes so rapidly in our fast-changing world that we need not get bogged down with "mere information." A corollary to the argument is that because information quickly becomes obsolete, it is more important to learn "accessing" skills (how to look things up or how to use a calculator) than to learn "mere facts." . . .

In fact, the opposite inference should be drawn from our fast-changing world. The fundamentals of science change very slowly; those of elementary math hardly at all. The famous names of geography and history (the "leaves" of that knowledge tree) change faster, but not root and branch from year to year. A wide range of this stable, fundamental knowledge is the key to rapid adaptation and the learning of new skills. It is precisely *because* the needs of a modern economy are so changeable that one needs broad general knowledge in order to flourish. Only high literacy (which implies broad general knowledge) provides the flexibility to learn new things fast. The only known route to broad general knowledge for all is for a nation's schools to provide all students with a substantial, solid core of knowledge.

Common content leads to higher school morale, as well as better teaching and learning. At every Core Knowledge school, a sense of community and common purpose have knit people together. Clear content guidelines have encouraged those who teach at the same grade level to collaborate in creating effective lesson plans and schoolwide activities. Similarly, a clear sense of purpose has encouraged cooperation among grades as well. Because the *Core Knowledge Sequence* makes no requirements about *how* the specified knowledge should be presented, individual schools and teachers have great scope for independence and creativity. Site-based governance is the order of the day at Core Knowledge schools—but with definite aims, and thus a clear sense of communal purpose.

The Myth of the Existing Curriculum

Much of the public currently assumes that each elementary school already follows a schoolwide curriculum. Yet frustrated parents continually write the Core Knowledge Foundation to complain that principals are not able to tell them with any explicitness what their child will be learning during the year. Memorably, a mother of identical twins wrote that because her children had been placed in different classrooms, they were learning completely different things.

Such curricular incoherence, typical of elementary education in the United States today, places enormous burdens on teachers. Because they must cope with such diversity of preparation at each subsequent grade level, teachers find it almost impossible to create learning communities in their classrooms. Stevenson and Stigler rightly conclude that the most significant diversity faced by our schools is *not* cultural diversity but, rather, diversity of academic preparation. To achieve excellence and fairness for all, an elementary school must follow a coherent sequence of solid, specific content.

QUESTIONS

1. What does E. D. Hirsch, Jr., believe to be the most basic things that every child in the United States needs to know? Do you agree?

2. Reflect on the schools you attended and any in which you have observed. Do you think they have a core curriculum, either that proposed by Hirsch or another? Or are they examples of places Hirsch describes as having only a "mythical curriculum?"

3. If the elementary school you attended became a Core Knowledge school, would it be better or worse than it was when you were there?

Bob Peterson is a longtime elementary school teacher who teaches a bilingual fifth-grade class at La Escuela Fratney in Milwaukee, Wisconsin. He is also an editor of and regular contributor to the education journal *Rethinking Schools*, in which this piece appeared originally.

Hirsch's "cultural literacy" project is problematic on a number of levels. First, Hirsch misdiagnoses what ails American education, arguing that a lack of emphasis on "content" has left our children "culturally illiterate." Second, he defines knowledge in a way that equates learning with memorizing and teaching with the transmission of information. Third, his definition of "core knowledge" attempts to institutionalize a curriculum that focuses almost exclusively on contributions and perspectives of mainstream European Americans—albeit with a slight nod toward a more multicultural perspective. In this regard, he is smart enough to try to co-opt what he can't defeat.

Hirsch also makes some valuable points, however. He raises the issue of unequal access to knowledge and literature in our stratified society. And he argues that schools have a responsibility to ensure that all members of society have sufficient "intergenerational" knowledge so they can participate in the economic and political affairs of our nation. That his solution to these problems is off base does not negate the validity of this concern for equity.

Hirsch's Growing Popularity

E. D. Hirsch is a professor of English at the University of Virginia. His big splash on the educational scene came in 1987 with the publication of *Cultural Literacy: What Every American Needs to Know*. Combining theoretical analysis with entertaining anecdotes about illiteracy and a list of 5,000 things that "culturally literate" Americans need to know, Hirsch's book climbed to the top of the *New York Times* best-selling list. . . .

In critiquing Hirsch, it is essential to note that the debate over his views is part of a broader controversy in American society sparked by shifting demographics, the civil rights and feminist movements, increased immigration by people of color, and the changing global economy and rising prominence of Asia, Africa, and Latin America.

Source: "What Should Children Learn?: A Teacher Looks at E. D. Hirsch," by Bob Peterson, 1995, in *Rethinking Schools: An Agenda for Change*, edited by David Levine, Robert Lowe, Bob Peterson, and Rita Tenorio, New Press, pp. 74–88.

As historian Ronald Takaki, author of *A Different Mirror*, has noted: "What is fueling this debate over our national identity and the content of our curriculum is America's intensifying racial crisis."

In response, Hirsch, [Allan] Bloom, [William] Bennett, and others have "attempted to create an ideological consensus around the return to traditional knowledge," according to Michael Apple, University of Wisconsin professor of education. They believe that the "'great books' and 'great ideas' of the 'Western tradition' will preserve democracy. . . increase student achievement and discipline, increase our international competitiveness, and ultimately reduce unemployment and poverty."

This "return to tradition" perspective contrasts sharply with those who in recent decades have pushed for a more inclusive definition of American culture and school curriculum. For instance, Theresa Perry and James Fraser point out in their book *Freedom's Plow: Teaching in the Multicultural Classroom*, "If there is to be democracy in the 21st century, it must be multiracial/multicultural democracy. . . . The debate is about the United States of America, and what its definitive values and identity will be in the next century."

The debate over Hirsch, then, is about far more than culture and education; it strikes at the core of our vision of this country's future. The irony is that Hirsch, in his attempt to define the twenty-first century American identity, relies on educational methods and content that dominated the nineteenth century.

Hirsch and Culture

My criticism of Hirsch's perspective fall into two categories: his definition of "national culture" and his definition of knowledge.

Hirsch writes about a "single national culture" that all literate people share. He argues that middle-class children acquire mainstream literate culture "by daily encounters with other literate persons" and that "disadvantaged" children don't. Schools, he argues, should provide an "antidote to [the] deprivation" of "disadvantaged" children by making "the essential information more readily available." As he writes in *Cultural Literacy*, "We will be able to achieve a just and prosperous society only when our schools ensure that everyone commands enough shared background knowledge to be able to communicate effectively with everyone else."

Hirsch admits that multicultural education is "valuable in itself" but then goes on to add an all-important caveat that it "should not be allowed to supplant or interfere with our schools' responsibility to ensure our children's mastery of American literate culture." Equal access to culture is an undeniably worthwhile concern and Hirsch's care for equity should be commended. But a deeper look at his assumptions and limitations reveals that implementation of his ideas would more likely marginalize instead of enfranchise those students Hirsch says he wishes to help.

There are several related issues here involving complex questions of culture in a changing society. One needs to look not just at Hirsch's rhetoric of concern, but also at his definition of "traditional culture," his neglect of "nonmainstream" cultural histories and traditions, and his dismissal of the need to teach children to think critically.

First of all, what is Hirsch asking children to learn? After reading eight books by Hirsch it is clear that his view of "American literate culture" is overwhelmingly European-American based. Moreover, while he talks about the "classless character of cultural literacy" he virtually ignores the history, tradition, and literature of and about the working class and other marginalized groups and their conflicts with dominant society. He knows better than to dismiss the contributions of women completely, but recognizes them in a way that doesn't question the status quo. . . .

Hirsch and Knowledge

The only conceivable way that a teacher could "cover" the amount of material prescribed by the Core Knowledge Foundation in the suggested time is if one defined learning as superficial acquaintance with "facts"—elevating word recognition to the status of knowledge. Although the *Core Knowledge Sequence* says it is "not a list of facts to be memorized," practical realities will push in that direction.

In analyzing Hirsch's books, it's clear that his definition of knowledge is synonymous with a superficial familiarity with facts and relies on rote memorization and the acquisition of disconnected bits of information. In fact, Hirsch himself admits that his lists will almost certainly lead to "the trivialization of cultural information." Moreover, it is likely that Hirsch's "core knowledge" curriculum might serve as fertile ground for a new crop of standardized tests that rely on "facts" rather than knowledge.

In an age where technological advances have led to what is uniformly acknowledged to be an "information glut," Hirsch stands firmly in a nineteenth century approach and boldly states that "only a few hundred pages of information stand between the literate and illiterate, between dependence and autonomy." And in many cases, Hirsch implies, it's not necessary to understand *why* something is important; one must just know that it *is* important.

When meeting with college-level English teachers from the National Council of Teachers of English and the Modern Language Association in 1987, Hirsch was criticized for the "narrowing of national culture" and the teaching of small bits of information. "A telling moment came when he [Hirsch] said it wasn't so important to read Shakespeare or see performances of the plays themselves—plot summaries or 'Lamb's Tales' would do fine," according to Peter Elbow, a professor of English at the University of Massachusetts at Amherst. Ultimately, Hirsch's emphasis on the transmissions of disconnected facts—what he calls "core knowledge"—directly contrasts with the need for students to think analyze, critique, and understand their world.

Even if the facts that Hirsch promoted were completely multicultural, his approach would be flawed by his definition of knowledge. Students need more than facts. They need to understand the relationships between "facts" and whose interests certain "facts" serve. They need to question the validity of the "facts," to ask questions such as "why" and "how." They need to know how to find information, to solve problems, to express themselves in oral and written language so their opinions can be shared with, and have an influence on, broader society. It is only through such an approach that students can construct their own beliefs, their own knowledge.

In his sections on the American Revolution and the Constitution, for example, Hirsch essentially dismisses as irrelevant the pro-slavery, antiwoman assumptions of our Founding Fathers. No mention is made that about 40 percent of the delegates to the Constitutional Convention were slave owners, that Washington himself had slaves, and that in 1779 he ordered that U.S. troops launch an expedition against the Iroquois Confederacy and seek the "total destruction and devastation and the capture of as many persons of every age and sex as possible. . . ."

Hirsch and Teaching

Embedded in Hirsch's viewpoint on culture and knowledge is his approach to teaching. First, rather than calling upon students to study less but understand more, he advocates a more-the-merrier approach—regardless of whether children understand what is presented to them. Second, he distorts the relationship between content and skills, criticizing what he claims are current emphases on "mental skills," "learning-to-learn skills," and "critical thinking skills."

On the issue of more versus less, good teaching requires a precarious balance between exposing students to lots of information and studying a few topics in depth. While Hirsch alludes to this balance, ultimately he advocates pumping as much information as possible into students. This stands in sharp contrast to the fine work of many teachers—whether in groups such as the Coalition of Essential Schools or as part of national curriculum groups such as the National Council of Teachers of English—who hold that "less is more" and encourage in-depth projects by students.

The question of content versus skills is a bit more complicated. Hirsch emphasizes content over skills largely on the grounds that students will understand what they read only if they have sufficient "relevant prior knowledge." Likewise, he argues that broader thinking skills also depend on a wealth of "relevant knowledge."

Like any good teacher, Hirsch recognizes that there is an important relationship between content and skills. No good teacher would deny the importance of prior knowledge in the educational process or that adults have important information to share with children. Hirsch, however, distorts this relationship by overemphasizing content to the degree that the teaching of skills all but disappears from the curriculum.

Despite Hirsch's rhetoric of giving children what they need to seek meaning from reading, his prescriptions make it likely that reading will become a mechanical process dependent on calling up what one has memorized. . . . The problem is not that students don't get the "core knowledge" and facts that Hirsch holds dear. Rather, the problem is that they are being bombarded with thousands of bits of disconnected information and rarely write, discuss, or read things that are meaningful to their lives.

For kids in my class who briefly read Hirsch's article on high mountains, or for the hundreds of thousands of others who are daily bombarded with facts either through Hirsch's series or one of several basal programs, the issue is not whether they will be able to recall 50, 500, or even 5,000 core facts. The issue is whether they will be in classrooms where they are respected and challenged—not only to understand the world but to develop the cross-cultural perspectives, critical skills, and moral courage needed to deal with the very racial, gender, class, and ecological problems that their tomorrow will bring.

QUESTIONS

1. As you read Peterson's critique of Hirsch, which author's argument did you find most compelling?

2. Peterson criticizes Hirsch in several different ways. You may agree with Peterson on some of these issues and with Hirsch on others. What is your view on the debate about "national culture?" What is your view on the debate about core knowledge? What is your view on the debate about the nature of good teaching?

3. In this article, Peterson says that Hirsch's approach "directly contrasts with the need for students to think analyze, critique, and understand their world," yet in Hirsch's own piece, he says that his approach is the best one for facilitating just such analysis and critique and understanding. How do you account for this difference? Which author do you think offers the best way to help students to understand their world?

4. As you read what Peterson says about "Hirsch and Knowledge," think about James Banks's discussion of multicultural education. How would Banks respond to these articles?

7

MOTIVATING, MA
AND ASSESSING

Now that we've examined the diversity of today's students, the insights of learning theory, and the nature of the curriculum, we will focus on how to put it together: on pedagogy. It is one thing to gain a solid intellectual understanding of what social scientists can tell us about today's students, what psychologists can tell us about learning theory, and what curriculum theorists can tell us about curriculum development, but it is quite another thing to pull it all together as an effective teacher of *real* students in a *real* classroom. In this chapter, we discuss various viewpoints on motivating students, keeping a classroom under control, and providing fair and accurate assessment of a student's progress.

All teachers worry about whether their students will be interested in what they have to teach. The first **Reading** for this chapter, from *I Won't Learn From You!* by well-known educator Herbert Kohl, addresses that concern directly. Kohl reminds us that there can be a difference between a student's having trouble learning a lesson because the material is either too difficult or is not being presented effectively and what Kohl calls "willed not-learning." As Kohl describes it, in willed not-learning the student makes a conscious decision that, in a given set of circumstances, the cost and consequences of learning are too high or too negative, and so the student expends substantial energy in not-learning. Kohl describes two significant examples of willed not-learning, one from his own life and one from that of a student. In both cases, the individuals had important short-term reasons for not learning, but the costs of not-learning were also, in the long term, extremely high.

The second **Reading** comes from a book written many decades ago by John Dewey, in which he argues that the most effective teachers link the lessons taught in class to the life experiences of their students. It is not that teachers *substitute* life experience for the lessons but rather that they help students make connections so that what is being taught in class and what is being experienced out of class are linked to each other.

Whether they call it "control" or "discipline" or "classroom management," new (and not-so-new) teachers are always concerned about keeping order in the classroom, the subject of the second part of this chapter. The **Reading** from Harvard psychologist Ross W. Greene's book *Lost at School* gives clear examples of what can go wrong when teachers and other school leaders fail to develop clear and consistent

NAGING, HOW WILL I TEACH?

FOCUS >>

- How will I motivate my students?
- How will I control my classroom?
- How will I assess my students in a fair and meaningful way?

long-term plans for helping students stay engaged in school. He offers specific recommendations for an approach that helps ensure a healthy learning community.

Finally, the chapter addresses assessment—ways in which teachers and higher authorities evaluate students. Teachers are being told increasingly that clear and concrete evaluation rubrics are the key to fair and effective evaluation of students. The last **Reading** for the chapter provides a detailed rubric used by one New York City high school. Such rubrics are becoming more common in schools across the country, and gaining familiarity with them is important.

>> How Will I Motivate My Students?

One of the reasons teaching can be such hard work is that teachers get caught up in the pressure to "cover the curriculum," abandoning their responsibility to make learning interesting and relevant. They worry (often with justification) about how they will be judged, especially by how their students score on certain external tests. They are not always sure how to stay in charge of a classroom full of energetic young people. Teachers sometimes forget that one of their essential responsibilities is to make learning interesting and engaging for their students, to find ways to connect what students must learn to be successful in life with the students' own interests and life experiences *right now*.

Who has not been bored in school? Who has not wondered what the point of any lesson might be? Who has not practically (or actually) fallen asleep as a teacher droned on and on about a topic that might have been of interest to the person who developed the curriculum in a faraway state office but that does not seem interesting to the teacher and is obviously of no interest to the students? Happily, this is far from the whole picture. There are magical moments in classrooms, when the curriculum, teachers' and students' passion for knowing, and the life experiences on which most real learning builds all come together.

The problem of making the curriculum interesting and relevant to students and their teachers is not a new one. Well over a century ago, the reform movement known as pro-

gressive education was born in large part to overcome the terrible boredom experienced in school. Although the movement has many facets, finding better ways to engage students in their school experience was an important goal for many progressives. No one advocated this focus on student interests more than the philosopher John Dewey.

Connections

Recall the discussions of progressive education and its impact on the teaching profession in Chapter 1 and of John Dewey's philosophy in Chapter 5.

Teachable Moment
Keeping It Fresh

As a teacher, you will have some days when you feel more like an entertainer, tap dancing on your desk to keep your students' attention. If only you could find a way to rap the periodic table or phrase the scientific method like a cleaned-up version of a Dane Cook joke, then maybe your students would be more interested in what you have to tell them.

Educators Barry Perlman and Lee McCann contend that an effective presentation begins with the teacher's attitude about the material. If you're disinterested in the topic you are teaching, then your students will recognize that quickly and will more than likely adopt an equally unenthusiastic view. So, rather than finding ways to cleverly rhyme "fluorine" and "chlorine", Perlman and McCann recommend you try the following:

- Put yourself in your students' shoes (or desks) as if this is the first time you've heard the material you plan to deliver. What are your expectations of what you'll be hearing? What would "grab" you or confuse you?
- After you have taught for awhile, pretend you are teaching today's class for the first time. Remember the excitement, anticipation, satisfaction, appreciation, and revelation you felt when you first taught it.
- Think of ways you can "mix it up" by talking from various areas in the classroom, using visuals including the chalkboard, PowerPoint, or video clips, and finding creative ways to physically involve students in the discussion.

- If you were a colleague critiquing your performance in the classroom, what would you advise or think about today's class period? What would be its strengths and weaknesses?

Perlman and McCann also suggest that sometimes to get your "mojo" back, you have to take a quick break. Go outside, even if just to walk around your building for a few minutes. It is amazing how seeing things from a different physical perspective changes your mood. "If you have energy," they say, "you will bring it to your students."

Source: Modified from *Preparing for a Class Session*, by Baron Perlman and Lee I. McCann, April 2007, Association for Psychological Science, http://www.psychologicalscience.org/observer/getArticle.cfm?id=2155.

QUESTIONS

- Are there certain topics you dread having to teach? Do you have this negative attitude because you don't feel comfortable with the content or how to relay it to students? Are there other reasons?
- Think of a class presentation you sat in this week. Was the instructor genuinely enthusiastic about the material, or did it seem like he or she was just "going through the motions?" Even if the presentation was good, how could the instructor "mix it up" the next time?

Arne Duncan, President Barack Obama's choice for Secretary of Education, is a 1982 graduate of the University of Chicago Laboratory Schools, founded by John Dewey.

Throughout a long life, Dewey advocated finding ways to connect what happened in school to the "real life" of students so that they would invest more in their learning and take more away from what happened during the school day. Dewey wanted to change school from being a world where only teachers were active and students were passive (and often bored) and create an educational place in which students and teachers engaged in a mutual effort to understand the world. In the short book *Experience and Education*, a selection of which is included in the **Readings** for this chapter, Dewey described the difference between what he called traditional education and the progressive education with which his name has long been associated. Traditional education, Dewey said, assumes that "[t]he subject-matter of education consists of bodies of information and of skills that have been worked out in the past; therefore the chief business of the school is to transmit them to the new generation." This basic assumption accounts for much of the structure of schooling, as Dewey observed it a century ago and as many of us observe it today. So, he says, in these traditional schools, "the subject-matter as well as standards of proper conduct are handed down from the past, the attitude of pupils must, upon the whole, be one of docility, receptivity, and obedience."

Connections

Recall the discussion of Paulo Freire in Chapter 1 and his plea to replace "banking" in education with open dialogue.

Progressive education for Dewey had a different starting point. According to Dewey, "The traditional scheme is, in essence, one of imposition from above and from outside. It imposes adult standards, subject matter, and methods upon those who are only growing slowly toward maturity. Consequently, they must be imposed; even though good teachers will use devices of art to cover up the imposition so as to relieve it of obviously brutal features." Such imposition not only leads many students to disengage from school, it also leads more than a few to rebel in ways that undermine the effective management of a class. According to Dewey, the only way for schools to avoid the disconnect and brutality of traditional education is to connect the curriculum with the current interests and experiences of young people.

Many observers have misinterpreted Dewey and other progressive educators to imply that they were opposed to content. In fact, Dewey himself was deeply critical of those who became so focused on the individual child and his or her experience that they forgot that the purpose of schooling was to *teach* that child something that was new and beyond the child's experience. However,

YouDecide

If a student is bored and disengaged in class, is it the teacher's fault for not finding the right way to reach the student or the student's fault for not trying hard enough, or both?

PORTRAIT OF AN EDUCATOR

Leonard Covello

Leonard Covello was—and still is—a legendary educator for many New Yorkers.[3] He was the principal of Benjamin Franklin High School in East Harlem in New York City from the time he founded the school in 1934 to 1956. Born in Italy, Covello came to New York's East Harlem when he was nine. He dropped out of high school, eventually returned, graduated from Columbia University, and earned a Ph.D. at New York University. Though deeply loyal to his Italian community, and somewhat disillusioned with his own educational experience in New York and at Columbia, Covello found his true calling as a teacher. From 1914 to 1934, with a short break for service in the U.S. Army, Covello taught at De Witt Clinton High School in New York and also developed his own ideas of what a true community-based high school should look like, building on many of the ideas that had been in circulation among progressive educators for half a century, but also taking them in his own direction.

When Covello was given the chance to open a new high school for boys in the ethnically diverse immigrant community of East Harlem in 1934, he sought to create a school that was

Source: Leonard Covello with Guido D'Agostino, *The Heart Is the Teacher* (New York: McGraw-Hill, 1958), p. 182; Michael C. Johanek and John L. Puckett, *Leonard Covello and the Making of Benjamin Franklin High School* (Philadelphia: Temple University Press, 2007), p. 137; and Paula S. Fass, *Outside In: Minorities and the Transformation of American Education* (New York: Oxford University Press, 1989), p. 57.

intimately tied to, rather than cut off from, the surrounding community. In his autobiography, *The Heart Is the Teacher*, Covello wrote, "What was in the back of my mind was a neighborhood school which would be the educational, civic, and social center of the community. We wanted to go beyond the traditional subject-centered and the current child-centered school to the community-centered school." Covello was making important distinctions. He wanted students to learn so that they would succeed in life, but he thought the traditional subject-specific approach to teaching and learning bored students and cut learning off from their own experience. He was also critical of the individualistic approach that some progressive educators had taken with their version of child-centered pedagogy. His approach to academic work sounded very much like what would later be called problem-based education. For example, a Covello syllabus said, "Each student will be asked to select a problem and follow it through the field of American literature…each group will report to the class at stated intervals on the results of and the inferences to be drawn from their reading." At the same time, Paula Fass, author of one of the major studies of Covello's work said, "[H]is efforts were praised by contemporaries and have remained a model of cultural contact aimed at alleviation of the conflicts between the school and the local community within which it was often an alien presence."

For Covello, the key to managing and motivating a group of students (in his case, young boys, many of whom were immigrants or the children of immigrants from Italy as well as Africa, the West Indies, Ireland, Germany, Austria, Poland, and later increasingly from Puerto Rico, and many other parts of the world) was to make the school a community—their community—and to organize the school so that students used it as a base to address and help resolve problems in their own home communities. This was more than civic engagement. It was involving students, and the whole school, in discovering the underlying causes of community problems and finding ways to bring about real change. With such a focus, Covello believed, students would achieve academically, be much easier to manage (for they were self-managing), and make real contributions to their home community, not just in the future but while they were students.

After he retired his principal position in 1956, Covello stayed active in education. He worked closely with the Commonwealth of Puerto Rico in its efforts to help Puerto Rican immigrants adjust to their new life in New York City. And he served as an informal advisor to a group of parents and civil rights advocates who were seeking much greater community control of the large New York City school system during the 1960s. He died in Italy in 1982 at the age of ninety-five, after a decade of work helping to reform education in Sicily.

Dewey did argue that the only way to teach the new was to connect it to what the student already knew (often based on out-of-school experiences) and on what the student *wanted* to know. Only in this way, he said, could the child come to "own" the knowledge and have it be interesting enough to remember or connected enough to be of use.[2]

Another contemporary advocate of a progressive approach to schooling, Vito Perrone, has his own list of ways of "teaching for understanding." For Perrone and his

colleagues who helped create this approach, the goal is to link the curriculum (what the larger society believes students need to know to be effective in the adult world), with the interests of students as thoughtful individuals (not mere receptacles for knowledge). The word *connected* appears a great deal in the writing of these proponents of teaching for understanding. The curriculum needs to be *connected* to the interests of the students. And the assessment system needs to be *connected* to an ongoing feedback loop to students and teachers regarding the depth of their understanding of the issues under consideration. Thus, Perrone calls for schools in which

- the students help select the specific books and articles to read or plays to produce after the teacher has outlined some clear goals.
- the students also have time to think for themselves and decide what Perrone calls "a particular direction" and topic to which they can make a personal commitment based on their own previous interests (often interests from outside of the class).
- teachers believe that they also have something to learn from their students and respect the opinions and experiences of their students, but they also bring their own passions and experiences to the class.
- students gain "expertness" from presenting their work to an audience that will expect high standards and from participating in the world outside of school through letters, service learning, and other work with those beyond the school's walls.

In such classrooms there has to be a lot of flexibility. Teachers need a clear plan, but they also need to be open to where the energy of the class will lead. Perrone concludes, "If we were to act on such understandings, students' experiences in schools would be much different, far more productive." After all, he insists, "It may seem obvious that our teaching should be directed toward understanding, that being able to give back information on a Friday test, too often the typical fare, is not sufficient."[4]

The discussion about teaching for understanding or engaging student experience in school life is not an either-or divide. After all, no one advocates "teaching for confusion," and no educators believe the classroom should be a boring place cut off from the larger world or the interests of students. The debates are ones of degree. When does a focus on student interest get in the way of serious attention to things that students *need* to learn to be successful in later schooling or adult life? When does the student's role in defining content get in the way of the teacher's responsibility to bring expert knowledge—his or her own and that of the textbooks—to the class? The same approaches that can at one moment make a classroom come alive can, if used incorrectly, also make it deadly dull. The challenge for every teacher is to be sure that their students' experience is engaging and linked to understanding, the "real world," and academic success.

What About Me?

What's My Motivation?

What motivates you in the classroom? Do certain types of teaching—or teachers—engage you more than others? What turns you off or puts you to sleep? Put a check mark by the statements that best reflect your learning style:

_____ I like to listen to a good lecture.

_____ I do my best work when I am in a small group with other students.

_____ I do my best work when I am left alone to research a project.

_____ I'd rather learn the material from a text rather than a lecture.

_____ I need to try something myself in order to really learn it, rather than just listening.

_____ I need to develop or find a picture or graph in order to make sense of an idea.

_____ I write a response or summarize in order to know that I understand something.

_____ I take careful notes and find them useful in preparing for a test.

_____ I easily get bored in class.

_____ I prefer it when my instructors use visual supports or PowerPoint presentations.

Other: _____

Other: _____

Other: _____

How you would describe the characteristics of your best teacher and your worst teacher? What aspects of your best teacher kept you motivated?

Remember: not all of your students will be like you. Some things that work for you as a student will not work for some of the students in your classroom. Be ready to try new ways of teaching and learning to create a motivating atmosphere in your classroom.

Teachable Moment

Motivated Inside and Out

Every day we experience positive motivation, which is the drive toward a goal or something we wish to obtain. We also deal with negative motivation, which steers us away from punishment or unpleasant consequences. In the classroom, students may say that the latter—negative motivation (such as fear of failing a test or class or being reprimanded for missing school or not doing their work or paying attention)—is what drives them more than positive motivation. Even adults dealing with daily stressors (and teachers, dealing with the demands from students, administrators, parents, lesson plans, standardized tests, and so on) may often feel like they are working to avoid the "bad" that can happen rather than focusing on the good.

Motivation comes from two sources: internal (intrinsic), which means your inner drive to achieve, and external (extrinsic), which is the motivation that comes from others, such as parents, partners, spouses, and teachers (which can be both positive and negative). Ultimately, intrinsic motivation is what leads us to success. In the long run, you must be motivated for your own reasons, not others', if you are going to succeed. The same goes for your students, which means that finding ways to tap into their intrinsic motivation is much more effective than even the best extrinsic motivation.

As a teacher, you have an enormous power to use both positive and negative motivation with your students. How you use that power will not only affect how your students respond in class but also how they view their learning experience and ultimately grow as individuals.

QUESTIONS

- In your experience as a student, do you recall more the positive or the negative motivation you received from your teachers?
- What can a teacher do to help students create intrinsic motivation (that is, wanting success for themselves and their personal satisfaction) rather than relying too much on extrinsic motivation?

>> How Will I Control My Classroom?

I recently accompanied a group of first-year graduate education students on a visit to a nearby high school. Like most aspiring teachers, they were especially concerned about discipline and **classroom management**. One of them asked a high school senior at the school we were visiting, "What should a teacher do when a classroom is out of control?" The senior, wise perhaps beyond his years, responded, "No classroom starts out out-of-control."

A classroom that is "out of control" is a miserable place for students and teachers. It is also a place where no learning or

> **classroom management** Maintenance of a classroom community focused on learning, which includes discipline for disruptive students and systems of encouragement for all students.

Promising Practices

The Jigsaw

The "jigsaw" has been designed by educators as a means of motivating students by making them not only learners, but also researchers, and teachers to each other. In the jigsaw, the class is divided into small groups. Each group is given a different assignment that is essential to the larger lesson of the day. For example, one group might research the habitat of lions and another group researches how they reproduce and rear their young. Then the groups reassemble so that each new group has one member of the old groups. That member is then responsible for teaching the new group the information that his or her group researched previously. In this example, the habitat group members would become the experts on the lion's habitat and then the new groups would each contain one habitat expert, one reproductive expert, and so on. In the second round, the expert in each group would be responsible for teaching the whole group about his or her area of expertise.

The idea of a jigsaw was developed in Austin, Texas, as a way to mix students across racial lines after the public schools had been integrated. It has been used subsequently to allow different students to read different parts of a long text, do research on different topics on the Internet, and the like. In many cases, a jigsaw can turn a class of passive and disinterested students into highly motivated team members who want to be the experts who teach others as much or more than they want to learn from others. As the teacher steps out of center-stage and hands the responsibility for learning and teaching to the group, students' motivation can soar if the project is well conceived and carefully organized.

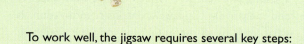

To work well, the jigsaw requires several key steps:

- The teacher needs to be clear on the purpose of the overall activity and organize the "research" groups of three to five students to ensure a good mix.
- Participants in each group are then given time to read, do Internet research, or otherwise prepare to be the class experts in their particular area. They also need time to make notes and carefully prepare the presentations they will each make to other class members.
- After the groups are reconfigured, it is essential that each of the second groups has at least one of the experts in each area of the lesson. The groups then need time to share what each member has learned so that the whole group gets all parts of the lesson.
- Finally, jigsawing works best when students have ample time to write about and to share, as a class, how they experienced the exercise—both what they learned and how they liked the experience.

Source: The Power of Protocols: An Educator's Guide to Better Practice, 2nd edition, by Joseph P. McDonald, Nancy Mohr, Alan Dichter, and Elizabeth C. McDonald, 2007, Teachers College Press, pp. 34–36.

understanding or engagement is going on. It is not likely to be a place where many assessments, internal or external, show much progress. The Brazilian educator Paulo Freire describes a scene that may be all too familiar:

> I remember myself as an adolescent, and how much it hurt me to see the disrespect that one of our teachers left himself open to, being the object of abuse by most of the students because he had no way of imposing order on the class. His class was the second of the morning, and already beaten down, he came into the room where the young people with a mean streak waited to punish and mistreat him. On finishing this travesty of the class, he could not turn his back to the students and walk to the door. The boisterous jeers would fall on him, heavy and arresting, and this must have petrified him. From the corner of the room where I sat I saw him, pale, belittled, shrinking toward the door. He would open it quickly and disappear, wrapped in his unsustaining weakness.[5]

Although this particular memory comes from a different generation and a different country, the scene plays itself out in classroom after classroom in every place and time. None of us wants to be the beaten-down teacher who Freire describes. Thus, a number of scholars have attempted to provide answers to our questions and fears about classroom management.

ZERO TOLERANCE

One approach to student discipline has come to be known as the "**zero-tolerance** policy." In response to the concerns of many teachers, parents, and community groups about what seem to be out-of-control classrooms, many school systems have

zero tolerance Strict adherence to a set of rules and punishment for all infractions even the most minor ones.

adopted tough discipline codes that say essentially "one strike and you're out." A student who breaks certain rules, who gets into an argument with a teacher, or who threatens a student or teacher is expelled on the spot. One advocate of tough classroom management is Lee Canter. Canter's book, *Back to School With Assertive Discipline*, and the Canter approach have been the basis for many professional development programs and seminars for teachers. Canter starts with some basic assumptions about the central role of discipline, saying, "[Y]ou need to get all of your students on *your* behavior track. Students need to know exactly what is expected of them." Once students know the rules, they must also be taught the consequences of breaking the rules. Students need to be taught to be responsible for their actions and understand that the choice is theirs: to follow the rules of the classroom and enjoy the rewards or to disregard the rules and accept the consequences. It is important to note here that the rewards are at least as important as the punishments and consequences. Canter contends that the "positive reinforcement system is the single most important tool you have to help students shape appropriate behaviors."[6]

Canter's approach may seem similar to that of B. F. Skinner, whose view of how learning can be fostered was discussed in Chapter 5. Like Skinner, Canter believes that the behavior of children can be controlled through the right use of stimuli—the rewards and punishments that Canter discusses. Like Skinner, Canter strongly implies that once students are taught the rules and especially the positive success that goes with following the rules, most of the rest will be easy. For aspiring teachers, indeed for many veteran teachers, this may make a great deal of sense, resulting in more orderly classrooms and more effective learning.

But as with Skinner, many educators are quite critical of Canter and others who seem to adopt a behaviorist approach to discipline. Landon E. Beyer raises significant concerns

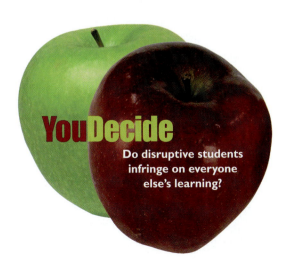

You Decide
Do disruptive students infringe on everyone else's learning?

Did you know?

More than 200,000 school children are paddled, spanked, or subjected to other physical punishment each year. Nineteen percent are students with disabilities. Although 30 states prohibit corporal punishment in public schools, the other 20 allow it in some form.

about "the nearly wholesale embrace of **behavioral psychology** as the basis for mainstream approaches to classroom discipline," because, as he sees it, the result is that "students become people whose interests and backgrounds are largely ignored, needing to be coaxed or cajoled to do the right thing, and punished if they do not; people who need to be kept 'on-task,' where that 'task' is created and imposed on them by others; people requiring surveillance and monitoring and who may need to be kept in line by informants since they cannot be trusted." Beyer argues for a different approach, not because he naively believes that all students will automatically behave, but because he believes that "teachers can, and should, bring students into the classroom decision-making process in ways that respect students potential autonomy and political identity, as well as their awareness of their own and larger worlds." If the purpose of schooling is among other things to prepare democratic citizens, isn't it counterproductive to organize classrooms in which the agency of students,

behavioral psychology Belief that people's actions, thoughts, and feelings are considered behaviors and, as such, can be influenced by outside stimuli from the broader environment or by the direct intervention of an educator.

Did you know?

More than 90% of U.S. schools have violence prevention programs. Urban schools are more likely than rural schools to use student-to-student or adult-to-student methods of violence prevention, such as individual attention, mentoring, tutoring, or coaching of students. More than 2,100 students were expelled in the 2003–2004 school year for possessing a firearm at school.

the ability to participate in democratic give and take, and the ability to see teaching and learning as moral callings is undermined by the structure of the relationships?[7]

ESTABLISHING EXPECTATIONS

An alternative approach to classroom management is offered by education professor Barbara McEwan. McEwan, who has conducted many workshops for teachers on effective classroom management, is wary of any set of rules or "tricks of the trade" that will ensure a well-managed class. She believes that only thoughtful decision making creates a classroom climate that is conducive to learning while at the same time helping to create the future citizens that a democratic society needs. She worries that a too-tightly managed classroom can be profoundly undemocratic. Thus, she asks,

If only the most quiet, docile, dependent behaviors are seen as worthy of reward, what behaviors then can we reasonably expect students to exhibit when they reach the age of majority? Even more alarming is that classrooms that depend on extrinsic methods of behavioral control typically spawn peer rejection and distrust as a natural outcome of some students being punished more often, others being rewarded more often.

McEwan insists that there is no one-size-fits-all answer and that democracy must be crafted one classroom at a time, but she advises every teacher to consider some basic questions:

- What expectations have been discussed with my students that will lead to a classroom climate that supports the needs of all members?
- If I did not discuss expectations at the beginning of the year, what is the most important to focus on now?
- Will all students have some input into how the expectations are established?
- Will the expectations be presented in ways that are accessible to all learning styles, not just auditory learners?
- Are the expectations too high for some students?
- Are the expectations too low for some students?
- If so, what adjustments need to be made to be equitable?

According to McEwan, "Working toward a democratic classroom requires an integration of all decisions, with the definitive goals being the security and self-esteem of every student." There will always be those who say that such an approach is too "touchy-feely" and will result in chaotic classrooms. In the end, McEwan and many other educators insist that although an appropriate level of teacher control is essential, too much teacher-centered control will subvert both the short-term goal of having students engaged in learning and the longer-term goal of preparing democratic citizens.[8]

Join the **Dialogue**

Arrange to observe a teacher in a classroom in a school near you. As you prepare for the visit, look at Vito Perrone's list of ways to develop and maintain a productive classroom. Attempt to record which of Perrone's "rules" the teacher followed and which he or she did not. However, be careful not to judge. Do you think the teacher you observed would agree, for the most part, with Perrone, or did he or she have a different philosophy for developing and maintaining a productive classroom? If you have the opportunity, ask the teacher.

TEACHER BEHAVIORS IN THE CLASSROOM

Vito Perrone says, "I don't particularly like the terms *classroom management* and *discipline. . . . Developing and maintaining productive classrooms* seems more appropriate, more useful as a formulation. It creates a more positive discourse." Nevertheless, Perrone understands the importance of the topic—to the teacher's well-being as well as to the creation of a healthy atmosphere for student learning. Because of the topic's importance, Perrone has also spent time discussing it with generations of aspiring teachers whom he has taught. Together they have come up with their own list of principles for developing and maintaining productive classrooms:

- **Be well prepared for each day.** Being well prepared starts with having a very clear goal or purpose in mind for each lesson and then being sure that the materials are ready, the technology works, and the class time has been planned out.

- **Use challenging ideas and materials.** It is difficult to maintain students' interest if the ideas under examination (the questions being posed and the materials being used) don't cause students to wonder, or if they make little connection to students' interests and the world.

- **Be reasonably consistent.** While absolute consistency is a false goal, students need to have a reasonably clear sense that the rules of the classroom will not change, that their work will be assessed by the same rules that were used the day before, and that when teacher and student come to an agreement, it will "stick."

- **Be clear about what really matters.** It makes little sense to expend energy lamenting all the things we believe our students should have learned before they ended up with us. If high-quality work matters, then we have to make sure the students know what high-quality work looks like and turn all our efforts toward helping them reach that high-quality work.

- **Show respect for the students.** Students know when they are being respected and seen as persons capable of achieving and being responsible. When students are resistant to teachers and the content, the resistance typically has its base in feelings of disrespect, which leads, not surprisingly, to students' disrespect of teachers.

- **Know the students.** Obviously this means knowing more than the students' names (though that is terribly important). It means knowing their interests, what they care about, the ideas that motivate them, and how they will likely respond to different situations.

- **Be physically present.** Teachers need to be present when their students arrive, greeting them and acknowledging their presence.

A QUESTION OF . . .

What advice would you give a new teacher?

"Make sure you are prepared each day to do something. If you do not have a lesson, the students will run all over you. Basically, you need to be able to control a class of students so that their time with you is spent learning. And mean what you say—if you tell someone to sit down or you will write them up, then you better do it. They need to be able to trust your word in all areas."

—*Jennifer Seal, high school advanced placement teacher*

Teachable Moment
Equal Expectations

Being culturally aware is critical to any teacher who wants to have a classroom management style that is fair, equitable, and antiracist. Gloria Ladson-Billings, one of the best-known researchers about effective education, tells the story of observing a classroom of kindergarten and first-grade students. Four children sitting at a table—three White students and one African American student—are working on an assignment to write a sentence that describes their weekend. When asked about what she did on the weekend, the African American girl responds, "Oh, nuttin'." Moments later, she walks away from the table and from the assignment altogether. When the teacher asks the now-wandering student, "Would you like to try writing your sentence today, Shannon?" the student simply shakes her head no. The teacher seems to shrug it off, saying, "That's okay. Maybe you'll feel like writing tomorrow." For Ladson-Billings, this is clearly not okay. The teacher has given the child "permission to fail," when what she desperately needs is a "demand to succeed." There are multiple ways to make the demand, but the demand must be made, for all students, no matter their race, gender, or excuse.[10]

Researchers Pedro A. Noguera and Jean Yonemura Wing tell an equally disturbing story of a different sort. Talking with a recent African American graduate of Berkeley (California) High School, they heard him relay an incident of arriving at class with a friend just after the bell had rung and being told, "You guys gotta be here when the bell rings, you gotta go to OCS [on-campus suspension]. Go." However, as the two African American boys walked to their suspension, two White girls arrived at the same classroom, even later, to be greeted with "Hurry up, hurry up, you're about to miss the assignment." The racism of the encounter was not lost on the student. Noguera and Wing noted,

A closer look at the Berkeley High School discipline system reveals countless stories in which students— the majority of whom are African American—are removed from spaces of learning and placed into spaces of punishment. Their stories reveal an approach to discipline that focuses on separating "bad" kids from "good" kids, while ignoring the racial implications of the practice. Meanwhile, the need to find ways to reengage students with learning, especially those who are most frequently punished, is rarely considered.[11]

In both instances, the racism of the situation was immediately apparent to the outside observer, but not to the teacher. It is difficult to observe one's own actions, especially in times of stress, and yet such self-critique is essential if a teacher is to be effective. Classroom management (or discipline) can easily and with the best of intentions fall into "separating the bad kids from the good kids" on racial or other ethnic or gender lines. Doing so fails to engage students in learning, which is an essential component not only of an effective system of education but also, indeed, of effective discipline itself. It requires a self-reflective educator to manage the process well.

QUESTIONS

- If you were Shannon's teacher, or if you were the teacher in the high school in Berkeley, how do you think you would have handled the situation? How would having read this case study affect the way you might handle a future Shannon or a group of high school boys?
- Both Ladson-Billings and Noguera believe that race had a lot to do with the way the teacher acted in each situation, even though one teacher was especially easy on a student and another was especially tough. What do you think?

Take a careful look at the approaches to managing a successful classroom advocated by Lee Canter, Barbara McEwan, Vito Perrone and Ross Greene. Then think about the schools you attended. Did the teachers you had seem to reflect any of their views, or a mixture, or none of them? Think about classes where you may be observing now. Do the teachers reflect one approach to discipline, a mix, or none of them? Finally, think about the classroom you may soon have as a teacher. Whose approach do you find most helpful? Least helpful?

In the end, Perrone, like any good educator, knows that "[a]ll of us have some difficult days, when things don't go as well as we would like, when we feel discouraged, sometimes angry at the behavior of our students." Teaching is a career that demands we stay resilient, keep coming back to our core values, and keep reminding ourselves that our students do want to learn and that "they desire self-efficacy and respect, and that we must not ever quit on them."[9]

In his book *Lost at School: Why Our Kids With Behavioral Challenges Are Falling Through the Cracks and How We Can Help Them*, Harvard psychologist Ross W. Greene proposes a new approach to classroom discipline that he calls "collaborative problem solving." Greene begins his approach to student discipline with the assumption that when a student acts out in class, it is for a very simple reason—the student has an unsolved problem and "acting out" (that is, creating a confrontation with the teacher) is a result of that problem. For example, the student may be embarrassed because he or she cannot do a particular assignment. The student may have difficulty getting along with other students. The student (and this is certainly true of many students) may simply find sitting for the required amount of time to be a challenge. Whatever the unsolved problem, Greene says the key to discipline is to develop a collaborative relationship with the young person to *solve* the problem. Threatening punishments or saying that the school has "zero tolerance" will not do anything to improve a situation with a student who just does not understand an assignment. The student won't gain understanding from the threats. Threatening punishment when a student is already angry with another student or the teacher will not reduce the anger. And threatening punishment when a student desperately needs to move around is not likely to work as a long-term solution, even if it buys a few uneasy moments of stoicism. Taking the time to find a win-win solution, to engage in collaborative problem solving with a student, will accomplish much more.

Linda Darling-Hammond, a longtime teacher educator, describes a study in which she compared the overall effectiveness of teachers she considered well prepared with those she considered ill prepared. The results were eye-opening. The ill-prepared teachers all said that while they had the motivation, they did not have the skill or as one said, "I wasn't equipped to deal with it, and I had no idea." On the other hand, the well-equipped teachers knew how to use what they had learned—about student diversity, about curriculum, about child development—and put it together in a way that allowed them to engage in careful planning and come to school each day fully prepared: "I'm miles ahead of other first-year teachers. There are five other first-year teachers here this year. I am more confident. I had a plan for where I was trying to go. The others spent more time filling days. I knew what I was doing and why—from the beginning."

Having a plan, which also means taking the time to develop that plan, and knowing what one wants to accomplish with a group of students, is key to effective classroom management and direction. It is also, as we will see, a key to dealing with the ever-expanding role of assessment in the lives of students and teachers.

>> How Will I Assess My Students in a Fair and Meaningful Way?

Assessment takes place in many forms and at many levels. Every effective teacher is continually asking, "How are my students doing?" "Are they individually and as a class understanding the material I am presenting?" "How can I be more effective with them?" Beyond these day-to-day assessments,

> **assessment** Informal or formal documentation of the particular skills, knowledge, and academic progress of a student or group of students.

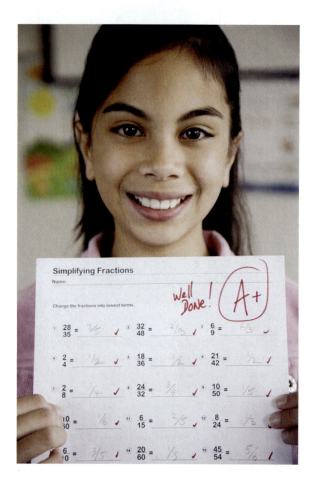

Simplifying Fractions

Name: _____

Well Done! (A+)

Change the fractions into lowest terms.

teachers are expected to give grades. Whether they are the traditional A/B/C/D/F or pass/fail, or a new and more creative approach, students expect grades, parents expect grades, and school administrators expect teachers to give grades. Far beyond anything an individual teacher does, states and

In Chapter 11, we discuss in detail the latest ramifications of the No Child Left Behind Act.

Connections

the federal government are increasingly mandating more and more tests. Some states now have so-called high-stakes tests that students must pass in order to proceed to the next grade or to receive a diploma. With passage of the No Child Left Behind Act (NCLB) in 2001, the federal government demands that every state test its students every year and that not only students, but also teachers, schools, and school districts, be measured by the results. Finally, the National Assessment of Educational Progress and other national and international measures assess how much students are learning and how their mastery of material compares to that of students in other classrooms in other places near and far. Teachers today face more pressures around more kinds of assessment than any previous generation of educators. Knowing how to teach—fostering student learn-

ing and engagement and success in such an environment—is critical to being a successful educator.

CLASSROOM-LEVEL ASSESSMENT

Good teachers are continually scanning the room to see who is paying attention, who seems to understand the material, and who is having trouble. Teachers also learn to double-check their initial assessments. Sometimes a student who seems completely "tuned out" is in fact deeply engaged in a conversation or a lesson. Similarly, some students have learned how to "fake it" and may not really understand or may not even be listening despite the thoughtful look planted on their faces.

To test their initial impressions and to gather more substantive feedback, teachers use multiple forms of assessment: giving students quizzes and longer examinations and assignments, anywhere from the drawings of a first grader to the reports and term papers of high school students. Increasingly, many schools are also asking for student portfolios (summaries of a student's work over a grading period or a year) that can show progress and mastery of material, however slowly gained, and that allow students to demonstrate their best work for assessment. Good teachers are generally wary of too much focus on tests as the sole measure of student learning, yet most teachers and most school systems require tests as one type of assessment.

Once a teacher has asked for written work, such as a quiz, a paper, or any project, he or she has an immediate obligation to assess that work. Students need feedback in a timely way if they are to learn from their work. They also need detailed and timely responses. Getting work back weeks after it was submitted is simply not useful to a student. "Good work" or "needs revision" written in red across the top of a paper is not sufficient feedback to enable a student to make sense of the evaluation. Many teachers also allow students to revise work, to take comments and suggestions seriously, and to try to do better. No professional writer, whether a newspaper reporter writing for an immediate deadline or the author of a novel or a textbook with a long-term contract, ever assumes that the first draft will be the final draft. It is interesting that, although most adults expect their written work to be edited, revised, and edited again, we do not always give students the same opportunity.

The evaluation of student work needs to be fair and needs to be perceived as fair by all students. Students often ask each other, "What'd she [or he] give you?" but the question implies that grades, especially positive grades, are dispensed by some sort of all-knowing benevolent, or mean-spirited, authority figure. In an effort to make grading fairer and to make the system of grading more transparent, many schools and individual teachers are now developing their own detailed grading **rubrics**. (The rubric used at New Design High School in New York City is included in the **Readings** for this chapter.) Most rubrics

rubric Chart with outlined criteria levels for a project or course, which allows students and teachers to know the expectations and makes grading easier, less subjective, and fairer.

Teachable Moment

Bloom's Taxonomy

Many educators use Bloom's Taxonomy as a way to understand different levels of teaching strategies and of assessments used to evaluate student learning. In 1956, psychologist Benjamin Bloom led a group of educational psychologists who studied the kinds of questions elementary and secondary students were asked on tests and in class. They developed a six-level classification of test questions that quickly came to be known as Bloom's Taxonomy.

The lowest level of questions, knowledge, gets by far the most attention in school. Many exam questions are at the simpler (and perhaps more boring) level than the more advanced questions that require students to move from learning and memorizing information to using that information to think creatively for themselves. Bloom and his colleagues found that over 95% of test questions that students are asked are at the knowledge level. Sadly, little has changed since that time, although as a result of Bloom's work, teachers and test makers are certainly attempting to use class assignments, in-class tests, and state-mandated high-stakes tests to probe students at increasingly advanced levels.

Examples of the kinds of questions that might be asked in the six categories include the following:

- **Knowledge.** When was the American Revolution fought? What is the name of the current model of the cell membrane?

- **Comprehension.** How did developments in the North American colonies in the 1760s and 1770s lead to the American Revolution? What is the purpose of the cell membrane?

- **Application.** How is the American Revolution related to the French Revolution and the Haitian Revolution? Demonstrate how the cell membrane regulates what comes in and leaves the cell.

- **Analysis.** What are some examples of the different motives of different people who participated in the American Revolution on the American and on the British sides? Differentiate between the functions of each part of the cell membrane.

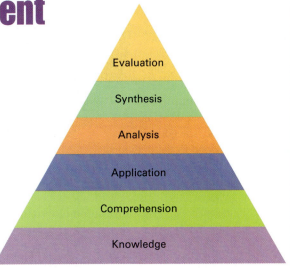

- **Synthesis.** In addition to those listed in your textbook, can you think of other reasons that residents of British North America might have been ready for a revolution in the 1770s? If you had been advising the British Parliament, what might you have predicted when the Stamp Act passed? How would a rigid cell membrane structure affect how the cell itself functions?

- **Evaluation.** Different historians give different reasons for the causes of the American Revolution. Describe the reasoning of two differing historians and then give your own analysis. Do you agree more with one, or is there a third reason that you prefer? Based on your knowledge of the cell, defend or criticize the theory that the disease cystic fibrosis affects the endoplasmic reticulum.

QUESTIONS

- As you think about your own experience as a student, were you asked mostly knowledge-level questions on tests or did the tests cover many different levels on Bloom's chart?
- Pick a content area other than the ones given in the examples here and develop a set of six questions for the levels in Bloom's Taxonomy.

follow a similar pattern, beginning with a clear set of standards and then asking, for each standard, how well the student is doing. For example, a rubric might allow a teacher to indicate whether a student is "exceeding the standard," "meeting the standard," "approaching the standard," "emerging," or if there is simply "no evidence." The categories may or may not correspond to the traditional A/B/C/D/F grading system. But whether the standards are translated into letters or numbers, students who are graded with a rubric know in much greater detail what the teacher thinks they have accomplished and where their work has fallen short or needs revision. The process of grading is much more transparent. It is perceived as fairer because it is fairer. And students have much more information about what needs to be done to improve.

The best rubrics, like those from New Design, assess student work in multiple areas, such as personal responsibility, social responsibility, critical and creative thinking, content knowledge and skills, communication, and the like. Some students easily do well in some areas and need much more effort in others. It is important to reward and recognize success while insisting that success in some areas may not be sufficient if students cannot do minimally acceptable work in other areas. A clear rubric allows a teacher to assess the work across multiple domains and do so in a way that is transparent to the students, parents, and other teachers.

The school in which you teach will probably have its own rubric, but the more familiar you are with rubrics, the more effectively you can use them to make your own judgments about what is working and what is not working for students.

HIGH-STAKES ASSESSMENTS

Since passage of NCLB in 2001, the debate about high-stakes assessments has become intense among teachers. The stakes are high for individual students because they may not be promoted to the next grade or allowed to graduate if they do not pass the tests. Of course, much of the debate is not new. A decade before the passage of NCLB or the widespread use of high-stakes testing, Terry Meier, a professor at Wheelock College, spoke for many when she said, "No phenomenon poses a greater threat to educational equity, and ultimately to the quality of education in this country, than the escalating use of standardized achievement tests."[12]

Recall the discussion of Howard Gardner's theory of multiple intelligences in Chapter 6.

Connections

YouDecide

Does a greater emphasis on assessment challenge students and teachers to focus on the results of their effort?

Despite the critique, advocates of standardized tests and tougher forms of accountability such as high-stakes tests have been winning the political argument in recent years. There are many advocates for higher levels of accountability—for students, teachers, and school districts—than has been typical of American education in the past. It is far too simplistic to say that all educators fall into one of two camps—pro-test or anti-test or pro–high stakes or anti–high stakes. Many observers take many different reasoned positions along the spectrum.

Some favor tough assessments of individuals and districts on a regular basis and over many subject areas, some favor a minimal level of test-demonstrated competence for graduation, and some favor using standardized tests only to evaluate schools but not individual students or teachers. Yet others oppose all such use of standardized testing because they see huge flaws in the tests, grave inequity in almost any system of implementation, or feel that alternative means of assessment provide a clearer and fairer picture of student, teacher, and school district achievement. Yet in the middle of all these debates, individual teachers need to develop their own clear views *and* find ways to survive and thrive even when their views are not the ones being implemented in their school, their district, or the nation.

Researchers Martin R. West and Paul E. Peterson describe what they see as a slowly emerging consensus among one group of political leaders and educators in favor of much tougher forms of accountability than have existed in the past:

> *The accountability movement has its origins in long-standing efforts to measure cognitive aptitude and ability. It is premised on the notion that standardized tests can and do measure an important dimension of educational quality. Such a position is increasingly uncontroversial, as evidence mounts that student achievement as measured by standardized tests is strongly associated with both individual and aggregate economic success.*[13]

Many others would say that no such consensus exists and that, indeed, any effort to measure student achievement by standardized tests is, at best, highly controversial. For all the controversy, however, standardized tests are a major part of the educational landscape for teachers today.

Debates about standards and accountability and the testing that often accompanies these movements are among the most intense in education today. But as West and Peterson point out, while educators may be debating these issues, an accountability movement based primarily on standardized test scores has gained many supporters, especially in many state legislatures, the U.S. Congress, and among the last three presidents. And legislatures, Congress, and presidents do make state and national law. These advocates of accountability argue that, without tests to measure student achievement and without accountability for failure to measure up, there is simply no seriousness about the quality of education in the United States.

Linda Darling-Hammond takes a different approach to the questions of accountability, standardized tests, and high-stakes tests. While hardly opposed to accountability (Darling-Hammond played a critical role in raising the standards and accountability measures for schools of education), she has grave reservations about the current accountability movement as institutionalized in federal law. Darling-Hammond sees much to admire in the goals of NCLB "to raise the achievement levels of all students, especially underperforming groups, and to close the achievement gap that parallels race and class distinctions," but she worries about the gap between goals and reality. Thus she notes, "The proliferating nicknames emerging as this intrusive legislation

YouDecide

Is the current emphasis on testing students driving all the spontaneity and fun out of school?

plays out across the country give a sense of some of the anger, bewilderment, and confusion left in its wake: 'No Child Left Untested,' 'No School Board Left Standing,' and 'No Child's Behind Left' are just a few of them." She worries that the law's impact will be almost the opposite of its goals; that "the law threatens to increase the growing dropout and pushout rates for students of color, ultimately reducing access to education for these students rather than enhancing it," and that it will lead states and districts to change their assessment and accountability systems, replacing "instructionally rich, improvement-oriented systems with more rote-oriented punishment-driven approaches."

For Darling-Hammond and many other critics, there are several interlocking problems with NCLB. The law fails to address "the enormous inequality in the provision of education offered in the United States" and "mistakes measuring schools for fixing them." For critics like Darling-Hammond, there is too much testing and too little fixing. Annual test score goals are called "adequate yearly

Learning the Lingo: Assessment

- **Standardized achievement tests:** A test is "standardized" when the same test is given to many students across a school district or state with clear right and wrong answers. A standardized test, as such, may or may not have anything to do with individual students' academic success.

- **The accountability movement:** The current accountability movement is a combination of (1) clear standards; (2) tests that measure whether students meet the standards; and (3) specific penalties, for students, teachers, or schools, for failure to meet the standards. The penalties may include not allowing an individual student to graduate or closing or reorganizing a school in which large numbers of students fail a given test.

- **High-stakes tests:** This is one specific form of accountability in which a state or district requires students to pass a specific test in order to move on to the next grade or receive a diploma. The stakes are high for individual students in this case, as opposed to other forms of accountability that apply more to schools and districts. NCLB does not specifically require high-stakes tests, but some states have implemented them since the act passed (if not before).

- **Formal assessments:** The simplest definition of a formal assessment is a test designed by someone other than the teacher. Students in most schools are given many tests to assess how well they have mastered specific skills or bodies of knowledge (criterion-referenced tests) or how they compare with their peers in other schools, districts, states, and even other countries (norm-referenced tests). Formal assessments are used in many states to determine if students are ready to be promoted or to receive a high school diploma.

- **Informal assessments:** Teachers are continually assessing the progress of each of their students—scanning the class for who seems to be learning the material, paying attention to writing samples, reading and grading homework, and in the case of science classes, looking at student's success, or lack of success, in the lab. Increasingly many educators are paying careful attention to students' written work, using it not only to assess overall achievement but also to determine where students are demonstrating mastery, where students may be having difficulty, and what sorts of mistakes students may be making that can lead to future lessons being planned to address specific areas.

Teachable Moment

Authentic Assessment

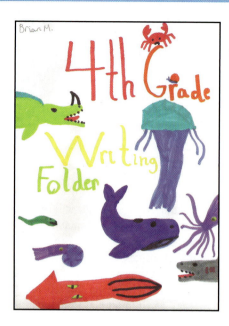

Experts in the field of special education have been especially concerned that high-stakes tests are fundamentally discriminatory toward students with special needs, even if accommodations, such as increased time to take the tests, are made for these students. Also, many educators, including those who are sympathetic to mandated testing and even high-stakes tests, believe that these tests should be *one of* the means rather than *the only* means of assessing student achievement. Due to these concerns, a new approach to assessment that adds much more detail and nuance to the evaluation of individual students has emerged: authentic assessment.

Authentic assessment is a much more comprehensive evaluation process. Among the hallmarks of authentic assessment are the following:

- Teachers are asked to collect examples of student work almost every day and to use that work to show whether a student is making progress on an ongoing basis (rather than in the one-time snapshot allowed by any test). This evaluation of student progress can also be used to measure whether the student is at the beginning, developing, or proficient level of specific state-mandated goals and standards.
- Teachers are also asked to construct specific assignments of increasing difficulty, linked to specific state curriculum standards that will allow students to demonstrate growing expertise. Such curriculum-based assessment links gradual progress to high long-term expectations for students.
- Students are asked to develop a portfolio of their work. Portfolios allow students to show some of their best work and allow for continuous assessment not just throughout one school year but also from year to year.
- In addition to collecting materials with which to assess their students, teachers are asked to make direct observations of students while they are at work. How are they behaving in class? What sorts of teaching methods seem to work best for each student? What daily routines foster learning?

- Teachers also need to speak with other people in the lives of their students, including other teachers, parents, and community members.

Such complex measures of student work can sometimes be seen as "soft" to the advocates of state-mandated testing. However, in the hands of expert teachers who link the evaluation of student work, portfolios, and observations to high standards and to the state standards for student progress, they can allow teachers and administrators to analyze student achievement more thoroughly and accurately as well as to design much more sophisticated approaches to supporting students who seem to be in academic trouble.

QUESTIONS

- Have you had the opportunity to look at portfolios of student work or otherwise examine examples of the work that students have handed in during their time in school? If so, did you see signs of progress over time? Whether or not you have done so, what are some of the things you might look for as a teacher that would tell you a student was making progress, based on an examination of their written work?

- If you were using a version of authentic assessment in your classroom and an administrator or parent said, "I only care about the student's test scores," how would you respond? How would you defend your practice? Where would you compromise?

progress," and schools whose test scores (for the whole student body and for specific subgroups) do not meet the goals are subject to sanctions that include notification of parents, opportunities for students to transfer out, and ultimately closure. As she says, all of this is based on NCLB's theory of action "that low-quality schools will be motivated to change if they are identified and shamed, and that their students will be better served if given other educational options."

See Chapter 11 for conflicting views on No Child Left Behind.

Connections

In states that have moved the farthest in NCLB implementation, making the standardized tests a truly high-stakes graduation requirement, the impact on the dropout rate has been dramatic. In Massachusetts, 71% of African American students graduated the year before the tests became a graduation requirement, but only 59.5% did so the next year. For Latino students the rate went from 54% to 45%, and for Asian students it dropped from 89% to 81%.

Monty Neill, who leads a national research center that focuses on the shortcomings of many standardized tests, summarizes the critique of the accountability and assessment aspects of NCLB:

The one-size-fits-all assessment requirements—annual testing in reading and math and periodic testing in science—and the accountability provisions attached to them are rigid, harmful, and ultimately unworkable. They will promote bad educational practices and deform curricula in significant ways. In the end, they will lower, not raise, standards for most students. For example, the assessment requirements will lead to further devaluing of non-tested subjects like social studies, music, and art. NCLB focuses on large-scale testing, which is a poor tool for diagnosing individual students' needs and for assessing higher-order learning. The provisions of the law are turning large number of schools, particularly those serving low-income children, into test-prep programs. The testing regime punishes the teachers who choose to work in the nation's most underresourced schools and fosters the inaccurate view that most of the nation's public schools are failing.[14]

To Neill, as well as Darling-Hammond, much of what is being done in the nation's schools today in the name of assessment deserves a failing grade itself.

A group of scholars is emerging today who take yet a different approach to the issue of high-stakes standardized tests. Although they do not like them, these educators have shifted their focus from opposition to the tests, as such, to finding ways to support teachers, who must still work in

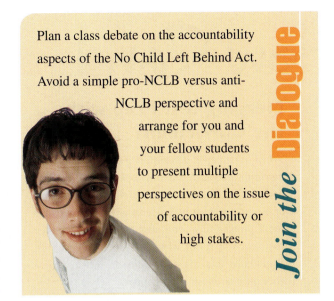

Plan a class debate on the accountability aspects of the No Child Left Behind Act. Avoid a simple pro-NCLB versus anti-NCLB perspective and arrange for you and your fellow students to present multiple perspectives on the issue of accountability or high stakes.

Join the **Dialogue**

schools that are increasingly dominated by the tests. In this context, Arthur Costigan begins the first chapter of *Teaching Language Arts in a Test Driven Era* by saying, "This book is about how to engage in best practices in Language Arts instruction in an educational era which is increasingly driven by high stakes tests and increased accountability." Costigan is opposed to these tests, but he also understands the reality of teachers' lives and has come to believe that something close to what Vito Perrone calls "teaching for understanding" will not only engage students more deeply in their own learning but also, in the end, give them a mastery of material that will serve them well on the tests themselves. Thus Costigan says,

I would like to point out, however, that the more involved students are with the real issues of contemporary society, the more their writing is likely to be rich, engaging, and, yes, even free from errors. I am not being naïve when I point out that doing real writing has a way of eliminating errors and making students pay attention to communicating the best way that they can, if only because they begin caring what they write, rather than adhering to imposed formulas.

This is not naïveté, but serious accommodation to the reality of today's world.[15]

Another author, Judith McVarish, says much the same thing of the elementary mathematics curriculum. McVarish is also highly critical of the current high-stakes standardized tests, but she also believes that teachers can find the right balance between test preparation and truly engaging instruction. McVarish makes it clear that she is opposed to "drill and kill" test prep, not only because it is a diversion from meaningful learning but also because it can be bad test prep. Instead, McVarish calls for a balance that focuses on the interests of children but also links those

How Can I Make a Difference?

Merging Test Prep with the Curriculum

When I first began administering state test preparation in my language arts classes, I found it incredibly boring. It felt so formulaic, and rarely did the stories or prompts engage my students or interest me. As a result, grading their work was as torturous as their completion of it. But, when I began embedding test preparation into the curriculum, the whole experience became much more positive.

Test prep can provide an opening for teaching a wide range of topics and integrating new activities into classroom lessons. For example, I recently found that it provided me with a unique opportunity for integrating character education into the curriculum. I hoped to have students explore common character traits of humanitarians, but I couldn't easily fit the lesson into the state curriculum content standards. I could, however, justify it as test prep. I gave each student a biography of a different Nobel Laureate, for which they completed reading comprehension questions and a lengthy open-ended response that they shared with the class. For the persuasive writing prompt, I used editorials and provocative topics of interest to my students. I also found that students could help create fun speculative writing prompts or bring in their favorite song lyrics for the explanatory writing prompts. The possibilities for merging test preparation with your current curriculum are endless when you start thinking creatively.

The amount of time spent on test prep has not decreased; however, it is hidden. As the test nears, I hear students ask, "Are we going to prepare for the test at all?" illustrating that the preparation material has fit organically into the coursework. And after the exams, I have yet to hear a student say they did not feel prepared.

—Deirdra Grode, seventh- and eighth-grade social studies and language arts teacher
2008 ASCD Outstanding Young Educator Award winner

QUESTIONS

- Have you ever heard a teacher complain that test prep was taking up too much class time? How do you think that teacher would respond to Grode's idea of hiding test prep within regular class lessons?
- Is Grode being realistic? Do you think this approach to test prep will work for students and teachers? Why or why not?

Source: "Taking a Creative Approach to Test Prep," by Deirdra Grode, July 2009, *Education Update* Vol. 51, No. 7. Copyright © 2009 by Association for Supervision and Curriculum Development, http://www.ascd.org/publications/newsletters/education_update/jul09/vol51/num07/In_the_Classroom_with_Deirdra_Grode.aspx.

interests to material that they must know to succeed in today's schools. So she says, "[T]hough maintaining such a balance is not an easy task, I believe we can provide rich learning environments for students and still prepare them for taking standardized tests that have enormous, long-term implications." But, she insists, "The trick is to keep the power priority in proper alignment." This "trick" has been forgotten by far too many in today's world, but it is one that is essential to the successful teacher of the next generation.[16]

REVIEW >>

- **How will I motivate my students?**

  No child comes to school as a blank slate. Some students, as those described by Kohl, come to school with very good reasons for not wanting to learn certain things. All students arrive, as John Dewey and the progressive education movement suggest, with many experiences of life outside of the school building. Vito Perrone advocates "teaching for understanding," which links curriculum with the interests of students as thoughtful individuals. The wise teacher will find ways to address students' reasons for not learning and the experiences that students bring with them to make what happens in school more interesting and more productive for all concerned.

- **How will I control my classroom?**

  The management of a classroom requires more than making it an interesting and engaging place, although that is an essential starting point. A variety of philosophies exist regarding how to manage a classroom, including zero tolerance, establishing clear expectations, and being prepared and consistent in your actions in the classroom. Greene's "collaborative problem solving"

  begins with the assumption that when a student acts out in class, it is because the student has an unsolved problem that needs to be addressed. In all situations, planning is key, and classrooms need to be places where the structures and rules are clear and where the values of a democratic society are modeled.

- **How will I assess my students in a fair and meaningful way?**

  Teachers have a responsibility to continually assess what learning is taking place in their classrooms. Assessment takes many forms, including informal assessments (such as scanning the classroom and asking questions to see if students are grasping the material) as well as formal assessments, such as high-stakes tests. Teachers have many options to ensure fair and accurate assessment, such as using a rubric that provides clear feedback to students and their parents regarding progress and areas for improvement. The accountability movement and the impact of standards and high-stakes tests generate heated discussion, especially regarding fairness for all groups of students.

How Will I Motivate My Students?

From *I WON'T LEARN FROM YOU!*

BY HERBERT KOHL

Herbert Kohl began his teaching career in New York City in the 1960s. More than four decades later, he remains as committed as ever to the success of all the students with whom he comes in contact. His essay from the *Discipline of Hope* was one of the **Readings** for Chapter 1. Here Kohl describes a situation faced by too many teachers too many times: willed refusal to learn. As Kohl explains, "willed refusal to learn" is something quite different from sheer stubbornness or inability to learn. It is a conscious decision to "not-learn" a particular body of knowledge. Kohl insists that teachers will make progress only if they understand and respect such decisions on the part of students even as they fulfill their responsibility to be sure that all students learn the things they need to know to function successfully in the modern world.

Years ago, one of my fifth-grade students told me that his grandfather Wilfredo wouldn't learn to speak English. He said that no matter how hard you tried to teach him, Wilfredo ignored whatever words you tried to teach and forced you to speak to him in Spanish. When I got to know his grandfather I asked, in Spanish, whether I could teach him English, and he told me unambiguously that he did not want to learn. He was frightened, he said, that his grandchildren would never learn Spanish if he gave in like the rest of the adults and spoke English with the children. Then, he said, they would not know who they were. At the end of our conversation he repeated adamantly that nothing could make him learn to speak English, that families and cultures could not survive if the children lost their parents' language, and finally that learning what others wanted you to learn can sometimes destroy you.

When I discussed Wilfredo's reflections with several friends, they interpreted his remarks as a cover-up of either his fear of trying to learn English or his failure to do so. These explanations, however, show a lack of respect for Wilfredo's ability to judge what is appropriate learning for himself and for his grandchildren. By attributing failure to Wilfredo and by refusing to acknowledge the loss his family would experience through not knowing Spanish, they turned a cultural problem into a personal psychological problem: they turned willed refusal to learn into failure to learn.

I've thought a lot about Wilfredo's conscious refusal to learn English and have great sympathy for his decision. I grew up in a partially bilingual family, in a house shared by my parents, born in New York City, and my grandparents, born in the Yiddish-speaking Polish part of the Jewish settlements in Eastern Europe called the Pale. I know what it is to face the problem of not-learning and the dissolution of culture. In addition, I have encountered willed not-learning throughout my thirty years of teaching and believe that such not-learning is often and disas-

trously mistaken for failure to learn or the inability to learn.

Learning how to not-learn is an intellectual and social challenge; sometimes you have to work very hard at it. It consists of an active, often ingenious, willful rejection of even the most compassionate and well-designed teaching. It subverts attempts at remediation as much as it rejects learning in the first place. It was through insight into my own not-learning that I began to understand the inner world of students who chose to not-learn what I wanted to teach. Over the years I've come to side with them in their refusal to be molded by a hostile society and have come to look upon not-learning as positive and healthy in many situations.

Before looking in detail at some of my students' not-learning and the intricate ways in which it was part of their self-respect and identity, I want to share one of my own early ventures into not-learning and self-definition. I cannot speak Yiddish, though I have had opportunities to learn from the time I was born. My father's parents spoke Yiddish most of the time and since my family lived downstairs from them in a two-family house for fourteen of my first seventeen years, my failure to learn wasn't from lack of exposure. My father speaks both Yiddish and English and never indicated that he wouldn't teach me Yiddish. Nor did he ever try to coerce me to learn the language, so I never had educational traumas associated with learning Yiddish. My mother and her family had everything to do with it. They didn't speak Yiddish at all. Learning Yiddish meant being party to conversations that excluded my mother. I didn't reject my grandparents and their language. It's just that I didn't want to be included in conversations unless my mother was also included. In solidarity with her, I learned how to not-learn Yiddish.

There was Yiddish to be heard everywhere in my environment, except at public school: on the streets, at home in every store. Learning to not-learn Yiddish meant that I had to forget Yiddish words as soon as I heard them. When words stuck in my head I had to refuse to associate the sounds with any meaning. If someone told a story in Yiddish, I had to talk to myself quietly in English or hum to myself. If a relative greeted me in Yiddish I responded with the uncomprehending look I had rehearsed for those occasions. I also remember learning to concentrate on the component sounds of words and thus shut out the speaker's meaning or intent. In doing so, I allowed myself to be satisfied with understanding the emotional flow of a conversation without knowing what people were saying. I was doing just the reverse of what beginning readers are expected to do—read words and understand meanings instead of getting stuck on particular letters and the sounds they make. In effect, I used phonics to obliterate meaning. . . .

In the course of my teaching career I have seen children choose to not-learn many different skills, ideas, attitudes, opinions, and values. At first I confused not-learning with failing. When I had youngsters in my classes who were substantially "behind" in reading, I assumed that they had failed to learn how to read. Therefore I looked for the sources of their failure in the reading programs they were exposed to, in their relationships with teachers and other adults in authority, and in the social and economic conditions of their lives. I assumed that something went wrong when they faced a written text, that either they made errors they didn't know how to correct or they were the victims of bad teaching.

Other causes of failure I searched for were mismatches between the students' language and the language of the schools or between the students' experiences and the kind of experience presupposed by their teachers or the reading texts. In all of these cases I assumed that my students had failed at something they had tried to do. Sometimes I was correct, and then it was easy to figure out a strategy to help them avoid old errors and learn, free of failure. But there were many cases I came upon where obviously intelligent students were beyond success or failure when it came to reading or other school-related learning. They had consciously placed themselves outside the entire system that was trying to coerce or seduce them into learning and spent all their time and energy in the classroom devising ways of not-learning, short-circuiting the business of failure altogether. They were engaged in a struggle of wills with authority, and what seemed to be at stake for them was nothing less than their pride and integrity. Most of them did not believe that they were failures or that they were inferior to students who succeeded on the schools' terms, and they were easy to distinguish from the wounded self-effacing students who wanted to learn but had not been able to do so.

I remember one student, Barry, who was in one of my combined kindergarten/first-grade classes in Berkeley in the 1970s. He had been held back in the first grade by his previous teacher for being uncooperative, defiant, and "not ready for the demands of second grade." He was sent to my class because it was multi-age graded, and the principal hoped I could get him to catch up and go on with other students his age by the end of the year. Barry was confident and cocky but not rude. From his comments in class it was clear that he was quite sensitive and intelligent. The other students in the class respected him as the best fighter and athlete in class, and as a skilled and funny storyteller.

During the first week of school, one of the students mentioned to me that their last year's teacher had been afraid of Barry. I've seen a number of cases where white teachers treat very young African American boys as if they were seventeen, over six feet tall, addicted to drugs and menacing. Barry was a victim of that manifestation of racism. He had evidently been given the run of the school the previous year—had been allowed to wander the halls at will, refuse participation in group activities, and avoid any semblance of academic work. Consequently he fell behind and was not promoted from first to second grade.

The first time I asked Barry to sit down and read with me he threw a temper tantrum and called me all kinds of names. We never got near a book. I had to relate to his behavior, not his reading. There was no way for me to discover the level of his skills or his knowledge of how reading works. I tried to get him to read a few more times and watched his responses to me very carefully. His tantrums clearly were manufactured on the spot. They were a strategy of not-reading. He never got close enough to a book to have failed to learn how to read.

The year before, this response had the effect he wanted. He was let alone and, as a bonus, gained status in the eyes of the other children as being someone teachers feared. Not-reading, as tragic as it might become in his future, was very successful for him as a kindergartner. My job as a teacher was to get him to feel more empowered by reading than by practicing his active not-learning to read.

I developed a strategy of empowerment for Barry and didn't even bother to think about remediation. I was convinced he could learn to read perfectly well if he assented to learn how to read. The strategy was simple and involved a calculated risk. I decided to force him to read with me and then make it appear to other members of the class that he could read well, and that his past resistance was just a game he controlled. The goal was to have him show me up in class, as if his past failure was a joke he was playing on us all, and have him display to the entire class a reading ability he didn't know he had.

I prepared myself for a bit of drama. One Monday afternoon I asked Barry to come read with me. Naturally, all the other students stopped what they were doing and waited for the show. They wanted to see if Barry would be able to not-read one more time. He looked at me, then turned around and walked away. I picked up a book, went over to him, gently but firmly sat him down in a chair, and sat down myself. Before he could throw the inevitable tantrum I opened the book and said, "Here's the page you have to read. It says, 'This is a bug. This is a jug. This is a bug in the jug.' Now read it to me." He started to squirm and put his hands over his eyes. Only I could see a sly grin forming as he sneaked a look at the book. I had given him the answers, told him exactly what he had to do to show me and the rest of the class that he knew how to read all along. It was his decision: to go on playing his not-learning game or accept my face-saving gift and open up the possibility of learning to read. I offered him the possibility of entering into a teacher/learning relationship with me without forcing him to give up any of his status, and fortunately he accepted the gift. He mumbled, "This is a bug, this is a jug, this is a bug in a jug," then tossed the book on the floor, and, turning to one of the other children, said defiantly, "See, I told you I already know how to read."

This ritual battle was repeated all week and into the next, subsiding slowly as he felt that the game was no longer necessary and that he was figuring out the relationship of letters to sounds, words, and meanings. After a while, reading became just another one of the things that Barry did in class. I never did any remedial teaching or treated him as a failed reader. In fact, I was able to reach him by acknowledging his choice to not-learn and by tricking him out of it. However, if he had refused assent, there is no way I could have forced him to learn to read. That was a very important lesson to me. It helped me understand the essential role that will and free choice play in learning, and it taught me the importance of considering people's stance towards learning in the larger context of the choices they make as they create lives and identities for themselves. . . .

1. Have you ever consciously (or unconsciously) decided to "not-learn" in the way that Kohl describes?

2. Think about students you have known: fellow students when you were in elementary or high school, those in your college program, or students in schools where you may have observed. Have you ever seen willful "not-learning" going on? How was it handled—as stubbornness, as a learning disability, or as not-learning?

3. At one point in the article, Kohl says of educators that "they turned a cultural problem into a personal psychological problem." Have you seen examples of that in the schools where you have observed?

4. If teachers took Kohl's assertion seriously that sometimes there are good reasons for not-learning, how do you think it would affect the structure of schools and the practice of teaching?

5. Is there ever a time when you would support a student in a decision to not-learn?

From *EXPERIENCE AND EDUCATION*

BY JOHN DEWEY

John Dewey (1859–1952) has arguably been the most influential philosopher of education in the history of the United States. In the early years of the twentieth century, Dewey did more than anyone else to create what he called a new philosophy of education. At the very beginning of the century, Dewey helped found and lead the "laboratory school" at the University of Chicago, where many so-called progressive ideas were developed and tested. After his move to Columbia University in New York City, Dewey published his most famous book, *Democracy and Education*, in 1916. He continued to write about philosophy, education, and a number of related fields and, in 1938, he published *Experience and Education*, summarizing again many of his ideas about the way young people learn and how the schools might much more effectively foster and direct that learning process. The excerpt that follows is a limited selection from Dewey's short but important book.

Mankind likes to think in terms of extreme opposites. It is given to formulating its beliefs in terms of *Either-Ors*, between which it recognizes no intermediate possibilities. When forced to recognize that the extremes cannot be acted upon, it is still inclined to hold that they are all right in theory but that when it comes to practical matters circumstances compel us to compromise. Educational philosophy is no exception. . . .

At present, the opposition, so far as practical affairs of the school are concerned, tends to take the form of contrast between traditional and progressive education. If the underlying ideas of the former are formulated broadly, without the qualifications required for accurate statement, they are found to be about as follows: The subject-matter of education consists of bodies of information and of skills that have been worked out in the past; therefore the chief business of

Source: Experience and Education, by John Dewey, 1997 (originally published 1938), Touchstone.

238

the school is to transmit them to the new generation. In the past, there have also been developing standards and rules of conduct; moral training consists in forming habits of action in conformity with these rules and standards. Finally, the general pattern of school organization (by which I mean the relations of pupils to one another and to the teachers) constitutes the school a kind of institution sharply marked off from other social institutions. Call up in imagination the ordinary school-room, its time schedules, schemes of classification, of examination and promotion, of rules of order, and I think you will grasp what is meant by "pattern of organization." If you then contrast this scene with what goes on in the family, for example, you will appreciate what is meant by the school being a kind of institution sharply marked off from any other form of social organization.

The three characteristics just mentioned fix the aims and methods of instruction and discipline. The main purpose or objective is to prepare the young for future responsibilities and for success in life, by means of acquisition of the organized bodies of information and prepared forms of skill which comprehend the material of instruction. Since the subject-matter as well as standards of proper conduct are handed down from the past, the attitude of pupils must, upon the whole, be one of docility, receptivity, and obedience. Books, especially textbooks, are the chief representatives of the lore and wisdom of the past, while teachers are the organs through which pupils are brought into effective connection with the material. Teachers are the agents through which knowledge and skills are communicated and rules of conduct enforced.

I have not made this brief summary for the purpose of criticizing the underlying philosophy. The rise of what is called new education and progressive schools is of itself a product of discontent with traditional education. In effect it is a criticism of the latter. When the implied criticism is made explicit it reads somewhat as follows: The traditional scheme is, in essence, one of imposition from above and from outside. It imposes adult standards, subject matter, and methods upon those who are only growing slowly toward maturity. The gap is so great that the required subject-matter, the methods of learning and of behaving are foreign to the existing capacities of the young. They are beyond the reach of the experience the young learners already possess. Consequently, they must be imposed; even though good teachers will use devices of art to cover up the imposition so as to relieve it of obviously brutal features.

But the gulf between the mature or adult products and the experience and abilities of the young is so wide that the very situation forbids much active participation by pupils in the development of what is taught. Theirs is to do—and learn, as it was the part of the six hundred to do and die. Learning here means acquisition of what already is incorporated in books and in the heads of the elders. Moreover, that which is taught is thought of as essentially static. It is taught as a finished product, with little regard either to the ways in which it was originally built up or to changes that will surely occur in the future. It is to a large extent the cultural product of societies that assumed the future would be much like the past, and yet it is used as educational food in a society where change is the rule, not the exception.

If one attempts to formulate the philosophy of education implicit in the practices of the new education, we may, I think, discover certain common principles amid the variety of progressive schools now existing. To imposition from above is opposed expression and cultivation of individuality; to external discipline is opposed free activity; to learning from texts and teachers, learning through experience; to acquisition of isolated skills and techniques by drill, is opposed acquisition of them as means of attaining ends which make direct vital appeal; to preparation for a more or less remote future is opposed making the most of the opportunities of present life; to static aims and materials is opposed acquaintance with a changing world. . . .

It is at this point that the reference made earlier to *Either-Or* philosophies becomes particularly pertinent. The general philosophy of the new education may be sound, and yet the difference in abstract principles will not decide the way in which the moral and intellectual preference involved shall be worked out in practice. There is always the danger in a new movement that in rejecting the aims and methods of that which it would supplant, it may develop its principles negatively rather than positively and constructively. Then it takes its clew in practice from that which is rejected instead of from the constructive development of its own philosophy. . . .

When external authority is rejected, it does not follow that all authority should be rejected, but rather that there is need to search for a more effective source of authority. Because the older education imposed the knowledge, methods, and the rules of conduct of the mature person upon the young, it does not follow, except on the basis of the extreme *Either-Or* philosophy, that the knowledge and skill of the mature person has no directive value for the experience of the immature. On the contrary, basing education upon personal experience may mean more multiplied and more intimate contacts between the mature and the immature than ever existed in the traditional school, and consequently more, rather than less, guidance by others. The problem, then, is: how these contacts can be established without violating the principle of learning through personal experience. The solution of this problem requires a well thought-out philosophy of the social factors that operate in the constitution of individual experience.

What is indicated in the foregoing remarks is that the general principles of the new education do not of themselves solve any of the problems of the actual or practical conduct and management of progressive schools. Rather, they set new problems which have to be worked out on the basis of a new philosophy of experience. The problems are not even recognized, to say nothing of being solved, when it is assumed that it suffices to reject the ideas and practices of the old education and then go to the opposite extreme. Yet I am sure that you will appreciate what is meant when I say that many of the newer schools tend to make little or nothing of organized subject-matter of study; to proceed as if any form of direction and guidance by adults were an invasion of individual freedom, and as if the idea that education should be concerned with the present and future meant that acquaintance with the past has little or no role to play in education. . . .

It is not too much to say that an educational philosophy which professes to be based on the idea of freedom may become as dogmatic as ever was the traditional education which is reacted against. For any theory and set of practices is dogmatic which is not based upon critical examination of its own underlying principles. Let us say that the new education emphasizes the freedom of the learner. Very well. A problem is now set. What does freedom mean and what are the conditions under which it is capable of realization? Let us say that the kind of external imposition which was so common in the traditional school limited rather than promoted the intellectual and moral development of the young. Again, very well. Recognition of this serious defect sets a problem. Just what is the role of the teacher and of books in promoting the educational development of the immature? Admit the traditional education employed as the subject-matter for study facts and ideas so bound up with the past as to give little help in dealing with the issues of the present and future. Very well. Now we have the problem of discovering the connection which actually exists *within* experience between the achievements of the past and the issues of the present. We have the problem of ascertaining how acquaintance with the past may be translated into a potent instrumentality for dealing effectively with the future. We may reject knowledge of the past as the *end* of education and thereby only emphasize its importance as a *means*. When we do that we have a problem that is new in the story of education: How shall the young become acquainted with the past in such a way that the acquaintance is a potent agent in appreciation of the living present?

Criteria of Experience

Growth or growing as developing, not only physically but intellectually and morally, is one exemplification of the principle of continuity. The objection made is that growth might take many different directions: a man, for example, who starts out on a career of burglary may grow in that direction, and by practice may grow into a highly expert burglar. Hence it is argued that "growth" is not enough; we must also specify the direction in which growth takes place, the end towards

which it tends. Before, however, we decide that the objection is conclusive we must analyze the case a little further.

That a man may grow in efficiency as a burglar, as a gangster, or as a corrupt politician, cannot be doubted. But from the standpoint of growth the question is whether growth in this direction promotes or retards growth in general. Does this form of growth create conditions for further growth or does it set up conditions that shut off the person who has grown in this particular direction from the occasions, stimuli, and opportunities for continuing growth in new directions? What is the effect of growth in a special direction upon the attitudes and habits which alone open up avenues for development in other lines? I shall leave you to answer these questions, saying simply that when and only when development in a particular line conduces to continuing growth does it answer to the criterion of education as growing. For the conception is one that must find universal and not specialized limited application.

In a word, we live from birth to death in a world of persons and things which in large measure is what it is because of what has been done and transmitted from previous human activities. When this fact is ignored, experience is treated as if it were something which goes on exclusively inside an individual's body and mind. It ought not to be necessary to say that experience does not occur in a vacuum. There are sources outside an individual which give rise to experience. It is constantly fed from these springs. No one would question that a child in a slum tenement has a different experience from that of a child in a cultured home; that the country lad has a different kind of experience from the city boy, or a boy on the seashore one different from the lad who is brought up on inland prairies. Ordinarily we take such facts for granted as too commonplace to record. But when their educational import is recognized, they indicate the second way in which the educator can direct the experience of the young without engaging in imposition. A primary responsibility of educators is that they not only be aware of the general principle of the shaping of actual experience by environing conditions, but that they also recognize in the concrete what surroundings are conducive to having experiences that lead to growth. Above all, they should know how to utilize the surroundings, physical and social, that exist so as to extract from them all that they have to contribute to building up experiences that are worth while.

Traditional education did not have to face this problem; it could systematically dodge this responsibility. The school environment of desks, blackboards, a small school yard, was supposed to suffice. There was no demand that the teacher should become intimately acquainted with the conditions of the local community, physical, historical, economic, occupational, etc., in order to utilize them as educational resources. A system of education based upon the necessary connection of education with experience must, on the contrary, if faithful to its principle, take these things constantly into account. This tax upon the educator is another reason why progressive education is more difficult to carry on than was ever the traditional system.

1. When Dewey asks the reader to "call up in imagination the ordinary school-room...," he was writing in 1938. Was the school you attended more like the one Dewey described as ordinary, or did it represent what he called "the new education?" What about classrooms you have observed more recently?

2. What do you think of Dewey's critique of "the new education?"

3. Although Dewey's views have been among the most influential of any writer in the field of education, their impact on classroom practice has been much more limited. How do you account for that difference?

4. Think back to the **Readings** from E. D. Hirsch and Bob Peterson in Chapter 6 regarding curriculum. What would Hirsch and Peterson think of Dewey? What would Dewey think of them? Try to note points of both agreement and disagreement in each case.

How Will I Control My Class?

From *LOST AT SCHOOL: WHY OUR KIDS WITH BEHAVIORAL CHALLENGES ARE FALLING THROUGH THE CRACKS AND HOW WE CAN HELP THEM*

BY ROSS W. GREENE

Ross Greene is a clinical psychologist at Harvard University and the Massachusetts General Hospital. His book *The Explosive Child* focuses on responding to the needs of individual children who are unusually angry and unable to control their anger. In *Lost at School*, Greene turns his attention to whole classrooms—to the young people who sometimes disrupt them, to the teachers who try to manage them and teach in them, and to the parents, community leaders, and school authorities who worry about them and ultimately are responsible for them. Greene seeks a third way between a zero-tolerance policy that punishes every infraction, whether or not the punishment accomplishes change, and a classroom in which anything goes and where the lack of control means that little or no learning takes place. He believes, and provides significant evidence, that a classroom in which teachers and students engage in collaborative problem solving can be an emotionally healthy and academically rigorous atmosphere in which real learning and real healing take place.

The wasted human potential is tragic. In so many schools, kids with social, emotional, and behavioral challenges are still poorly understood and treated in a way that is completely at odds with what is now known about how they came to be challenging in the first place. The frustration and desperation felt by teachers and parents is palpable. Many teachers continue to experience enormous stress related to classroom behavior problems and from dealing with parents, and do not receive the support they need to help their challenging students. Half of teachers leave the profession within their first four years, and kids with behavioral challenges and their parents are cited as one of the major reasons. Parents know there's trouble at school, know they're being blamed, feel their kids are being misunderstood and mistreated, but feel powerless to make things better and are discouraged and put off by their interactions with school personnel.

School discipline is broken. Not surprisingly, tightening the vise grip hasn't worked. A task force of the American Psychological Association has recently concluded that zero-tolerance policies, which were intended to reduce violence and behavior problems in our schools, have instead achieved the opposite effect. A review of ten years of research found that these policies have not only failed to make schools safe or more effective in handling student behavior, but have actually increased behavior problems and dropout rates. Yet public elementary and secondary schools in the United States continue to dole out a whopping 110,000 expulsions and 3 million suspensions each year, along with countless tens of millions of detentions.

Behind the statistics, behind each expulsion, suspension, and detention, are human beings—kids, teachers, parents—doing the best they can with the tools they have. Dramatic changes are needed to help them. And my experience suggests that these changes won't be as painful and difficult as many fear. We cannot keep doing things the way we always have and continue losing kids on a scale that is truly astounding. This book is about doing things a different way.

It was early October, and the students in Mrs. Lori Woods' sixth-grade class were hard at work on a social studies assignment. There was, however, one clear exception, a boy named Joey. Mrs. Woods had already had a few difficult moments with Joey, especially at times when he refused to work on class assignments. That Joey was clearly not working on his social studies project was an irritation; that he was now distracting two other kids pressed Mrs. Woods into action. She walked over to Joey's table.

"Joey, is there a problem?" Mrs. Woods whispered. "Because you're bothering the students around you."

Joey looked up at his teacher. "I don't know what to do."

"Joey, the instructions are on the board. How can you not know what to do?"

Two kids seated near Joey snickered.

Source: Lost at School: Why Our Kids With Behavioral Challenges Are Falling Through the Cracks and How We Can Help Them, by Ross W. Greene, 2008, Scribner, pp. xi–xiii, 1–3, 5–8, 37, 49, 52–57, 72–74.

"Because I don't!"

Now most of the other kids were watching.

"Back to work everyone," said Mrs. Woods. She turned her attention back to Joey. "Joey, let's talk about it at my desk so we don't disturb your classmates." She began walking toward the front of the room, but Joey didn't budge. Mrs. Woods turned back around.

"Joey, come up to my desk. Please."

"No way," Joey said under his breath, but loudly enough to once again draw the attention of his classmates.

"Excuse me?"

Joey's face reddened. "I'm not coming up to your desk."

The entire class was now riveted, awaiting the teacher's response.

"Joey, if you don't come up to my desk now, I'll have to send you to the office."

"I'm not going there, either."

"Joey, *now*!"

"No way."

Mrs. Woods walked over to one of the students near the front door of the classroom. "Taylor, please go to the office and tell Mrs. Westbrook that I have a problem in our classroom and that we need Mr. Middleton to come immediately." Mrs. Woods hoped that the threatened arrival of the assistant principal might persuade Joey to rethink his stance.

Taylor dutifully jumped out of her seat and ran to the office. Mrs. Woods walked to the doorway of the classroom and turned to address the rest of her students. "I don't want to have to say this again: Get back to work."

"What's up?" asked Mr. Middleton when he arrived, a little out of breath. Mr. Middleton had been an assistant principal for twelve years (a science teacher for sixteen years before that), and was known among the faculty as a congenial, even-keeled man who was probably miscast as the school's primary disciplinarian.

"Joey was disrupting the class so I told him to come up to my desk and he refused. Then I told him that he had to go to the office and he refused. So there he sits." Mrs. Woods motioned in Joey's direction.

Mr. Middleton looked over his glasses into the classroom. "Let's see what I can do."

Mr. Middleton walked over to Joey, leaned down, and spoke softly. "Joey, I understand we have a problem. Why don't we talk about it in my office?"

Joey exploded. He jumped out of his seat, his head hitting Mr. Middleton in the jaw. "*I'm not going to the freaking office!*" he screamed and ran toward the door. The other kids gasped. Stunned by the blow to his jaw, Mr. Middleton grasped vainly at Joey. Joey pushed Mrs. Woods out of the way, screaming, "I hate your guts!" As he passed Taylor's desk, he blurted, "I'm going to kill you!" Taylor recoiled as Joey ran out of the classroom. He ran down the hallway to the front of the school and out of the building with Mr. Middleton giving chase. As Mr.

Middleton ran past the main office, he yelled to Mrs. Westbrook, the secretary, "Get Mrs. Galvin!" Mrs. Westbrook hurried into the principal's office and told Mrs. Galvin, the school principal, that Joey had just run out of the building with Mr. Middleton in his wake. Mrs. Galvin bolted out of her office to assist in the chase. Mr. Sizemore, one of the physical education instructors, heard the commotion from the copy room and sprinted after Joey as well. . . .

What are we going to do about Joey?

More than ever, that's the big question. Because there sure are a lot of Joeys out there. Kids who can't seem to function in a classroom, have a hard time getting along with other kids, don't seem to respect authority, aren't responding to the school discipline program. Kids whose problems don't get better. Sometimes we read about them in the newspaper and see them on TV, especially if they hurt someone badly enough or are led out of the school in handcuffs. The stakes are high. When we don't help the Joeys, we lose them.

How are we going to help Mrs. Woods? Another big question. Mrs. Woods' classroom is full of kids with all kinds of academic, behavioral, emotional, and social challenges. She'd like nothing better than to be able to give all of them the help they need. She's put a lot of time and energy into helping her challenging students over the years, but often hasn't had much to show for her efforts. As a minimum, she needs some way of making sure the challenging kids in her class don't disrupt the learning of the other kids. But she also has high-stakes testing to worry about, lessons to plan, countless meetings to attend, and the latest school system initiatives to digest and implement, so she's pressed for time as it is. When we don't help Mrs. Woods, we lose her, too. . . .

The premise of this book is that kids with behavioral challenges lack important thinking skills, an idea supported by research in the neurosciences over the past thirty years on kids who are aggressive and have difficulty getting along with people and those diagnosed with ADHD, mood and anxiety disorders, oppositional defiant disorder, conduct disorder, and language-processing disorders. The thinking skills involved aren't in the traditional academic domains—reading, writing, and arithmetic—but rather in domains such as regulating one's emotions, considering the outcomes of one's actions before one acts, understanding how one's behavior is affecting other people, having the words to let people know something's bothering you, and responding to changes in plans in a flexible manner. In other words, these kids have a *developmental delay*, a learning disability of sorts. In the same way that kids who are delayed in reading are having difficulty mastering the skills required for becoming proficient in reading, challenging kids are having difficulty mastering the skills required for becoming proficient in handling life's social, emotional, and behavioral challenges.

How do we help kids who have traditional developmental delays? First we assess the factors that are inter-

Answer: Challenging kids aren't challenging every minute. They're challenging sometimes, under certain conditions, usually when the environment is demanding skills they aren't able to muster or presenting problems they aren't able to solve. As you've read, lagging skills are the *why* of challenging behavior. Unsolved problems are the *who*, *what*, *where*, and *when* of challenging behavior and help adults pinpoint the specific circumstances or conditions under which a kid's challenging behavior is most likely to occur.

So if a kid is having difficulty in his interactions with a particular classmate (a "who") or teacher (another "who"), and those interactions are setting the stage for challenging behavior, then getting along with that particular classmate or teacher is an unsolved problem. If a kid is having difficulties with a particular assignment (a "what"), and those difficulties are setting the stage for challenging behavior, then difficulty with that assignment is an unsolved problem. Difficulties on the school bus, in the cafeteria, or in the hallway (all "where" and "when") are also unsolved problems. If the kid could resolve these problems in an adaptive manner, he would.

I use the terms "unsolved problems," "triggers," "circumstances," "antecedents," and "situations" interchangeably throughout the book. They all refer to the same thing. I like "unsolved problems" best, though, because it unambiguously tells us that there's a problem the child is having difficulty solving on his own. . . .

Lesson Plans

There are basically three options for handling unmet expectations. I call these options plans, as in Plan A, Plan B, and Plan C.

Plan A is when adults *impose their will* in response to an unmet expectation. Plan A is far and away the most popular way adults handle problems or unmet expectations with kids, and not only in schools. Often, Plan A implies the preferred option, but not in this book. . . .

Plan C involves *dropping an expectation completely*, at least temporarily. At first glance, Plan C may sound like "giving in," but, as you'll read below, that's not the case. . . .

Plan B refers to *Collaborative Problem Solving*, in which the child and adult are engaged in a process of *resolving a problem or unmet expectation in a realistic and mutually satisfactory manner*. As you'll soon discover, this is the Plan with the greatest potential for durably solving the problems and teaching the lagging skills giving rise to kids' social, emotional, and behavioral challenges in a way that is fair, respectful, humane, and effective. As you may have guessed, Plan B is what the rest of this book is about. . . .

Plan B involves Collaborative Problem Solving. Plan B helps adults clarify and understand a child's concerns about or perspectives on a particular problem, be it excessive badgering of other kids, refusing to work, pencil sharpening, incomplete homework, or class disruptions. Plan B also helps the kid understand the adult's concerns about the problem. And Plan B helps adults and kids work together toward

---

fering with skill acquisition and then provide specialized instruction to teach them the skills they're lacking in increments they can handle. When you treat challenging kids as if they have a developmental delay and apply the same compassion and approach you would use with any other learning disability, they do a lot better. Continue treating them as if they're unmotivated, manipulative, attention-seeking, limit-testing. . . continue relying heavily on consequences to address their difficulties, well, they often don't do better. That's because consequences don't teach kids the thinking skills they lack or solve the problems that set the stage for their challenging behavior. Why have we been so zealously overapplying consequences to kids with behavioral challenges? Because we didn't realize they had a developmental delay. . . .

Now back to our original questions: What are we going to do about Joey? And how are we going to help Mrs. Woods and Ms. Lowell [Joey's mother]?

Just as we would with any other developmental delay, we're going *to help Mrs. Woods and Ms. Lowell figure out what skills Joey is lacking and teach them to him. And we're going to help them figure out what (unsolved) problems are setting the stage for Joey's challenging behavior and help him solve them.*

No, it's not going to be easy, and it's definitely going to take time. Helping kids with behavioral challenges is never easy and is always time-consuming. But intervening in ways that aren't working is always harder and more time-consuming than intervening in ways that are working. . . .

Q & A

Question: I'm not quite clear about what you mean by "unsolved problems." Can you explain further?

mutually satisfactory solutions so that both parties' concerns are addressed, the problem gets solved, and, as will become clear, as we move forward, lagging skills get taught.

Is the kid going to need help for the rest of his life? Actually, the reason you're helping him now is so he won't need your help for the rest of his life.

This next part is important. There are two ways to use Plan B: *Emergency B* and *Proactive B*. When I first describe Plan B, it's common for adults to come to the erroneous conclusion that the best time to use Plan B is at the precise moment when a kid is beginning to show signs of challenging behavior. That's Emergency Plan B, and the timing is actually not the best because the kid may already be upset or heated up and because, if you're a teacher, you've got a lot of other things going on in your classroom at that moment. Few of us do our clearest thinking, resolve difficult problems, and learn new skills when we're already upset, so crisis *management* is not your best long-term strategy. You'll go much further with crisis *prevention*. As I mentioned earlier, because challenging behavior tends to be highly predictable, you don't have to wait until a kid is in the midst of a challenging episode to try to solve the problem that caused the episode. The goal is to get the problem solved or the skill taught *proactively*—before it comes up again. That's Proactive Plan B.

When Mrs. Woods threatened to send Joey to the assistant principal because he wouldn't come up to her desk, that was Plan A. Could she have used Emergency Plan B instead? Yes, and Emergency Plan B would have worked out a lot better for Mrs. Woods, Mr. Middleton, Joey, and the other kids in the class. But if Mrs. Woods had previously observed that Joey became confused on assignments and was easily embarrassed in front of his classmates, then Proactive Plan B would have been even better. Will anarchy ensue in Mrs. Woods' classroom if she doesn't use Plan A? No, it won't.

By the way, there's another reason to be using Plan B instead of Plan A: If you want to help a kid, you're going to need a helping relationship to accomplish the mission. Time and time again, research (and practical experience) has shown that the most reliable factor leading people to change—by far—is the relationship they have with the person helping them change. And while you may have thought that helping is the sole domain of professional helpers—medical doctors, mental health professionals, clergy, and the like—educators often find themselves in a position to help kids who are in distress.

Why would kids need the help of a teacher on nonacademic problems? Because, either in their own eyes or the eyes of others, they are involved in problem situations they are not handling well. What is the goal of the helping relationship? To help kids not only better manage a given problem, but to apply the learning to sorting out other problems and to preventing problems from occurring in the first place. Helping provides kids with tools to become more effective self-helpers and more responsible "agents of change" in their own lives.

As noted by Dr. Gerald Egan, author of *The Skilled Helper: A Problem-Management and Opportunity-Development Approach to Helping*, helping is messy. Helping is a working alliance, a two-way collaborative process, and a two-person team effort. Helping is not something that teachers do to kids; rather, it is a process that teachers and kids work through together.

In trying to forge a helping relationship with a challenging kid, it can be useful to think about the qualities you'd seek in someone you were hoping could help you. Are you seeking someone who cares? Whom you feel you can trust? Who takes the time to listen to you? Who asks the right questions and truly tries to understand your concerns? Who has the wisdom and know-how to help in ways that are effective and durable? Who involves you in the process?

Plan B is a relationship-building process. Plan A pushes kids away.

Q & A

Question: Doesn't helping kids with behavioral challenges take a lot of time?

Answer: Yes, helping, especially the kind that involves teaching skills and solving problems durably, takes time. But perpetually dealing with kids' challenges in ways that aren't working takes much more time. And don't forget, Proactive Plan B is taking place at opportune moments, not under emergency conditions.

Question: Like when? Don't forget, I have twenty-five kids in my class. I'm the only one in there, and I have a bunch of kids who are on special education programs and need my attention.

Answer: Most teachers find that Proactive Plan B can be done during the times they're devoting individual attention to other student problems (for instance, academic challenges), such as before school, after school, during recess, or during lunch; whenever there's an opportunity to take five or ten minutes to help a kid. You'll probably want to devote your initial Plan B efforts to helping the kids whose challenges are most severe and who are disrupting the classroom process the most. Then move on to the rest of the kids who need Plan B. You're devoting a lot of time to the kids with behavioral challenges already. While Plan B takes a little extra time and planning up front, my experience is that it dramatically reduces the amount of time you're spending on challenging behavior overall. . . .

Question: So when Mrs. Woods let Joey know that she wanted him to get back to work and stop disturbing his classmates, that wasn't Plan A?

Answer: No, that was Mrs. Woods reminding Joey of her expectations. She moved into Plan A in imposing her will when her expectation remained unmet. But the most important point is that Joey's difficulty getting started on assignments was a predictable problem, and one that would have been possible to clarify and address proactively. . . .

Question: Is it safe to assume that you're not too enthusiastic about zero-tolerance policies?

Answer: As noted in the Introduction, I believe zero-tolerance policies are a great example of a very fascinating and counterproductive human tendency to add more Plan A when it's clear Plan A isn't getting the job done. . . .

Let's Get It Started

If you're feeling like you don't know much about how to do Plan B yet, don't despair; you're about to find out. So far, what you know about Plan B is that it's one of three ways adults handle problems with kids, and that it's quite different from the usual ways. You also know that, depending on your timing, there are two forms of Plan B. Proactive B is used well before a challenging behavior occurs yet again, and is made possible by the fact that challenging episodes tend to be highly predictable. Emergency B is used in the midst of a challenging episode. . . .

- Goal #1: Pursue unmet expectations and ensure that your concerns about a given kid's challenges are addressed.

  If a kid is doing something you wish he wasn't—for example, interfering with the learning of his classmates, calling out without raising his hand, treating other kids in an unkind manner or making classmates feel unsafe—or not doing something you wish he was, such as not working on a given assignment, failing to complete homework, or not working cooperatively with the kids in his group, you have unmet expectations to pursue and to be addressed.

- Goal #2: Solve the problem precipitating a child's challenging episodes in a collaborative, mutually satisfactory, and durable fashion.

  Most kids with behavioral challenges have five or six unsolved problems that are routinely precipitating their challenging episodes. The goal is to resolve them one by one so that, after a period of time, they aren't causing challenging episodes anymore. But the collaborative and mutually satisfactory elements are crucial. As you've already read, solutions that don't stand the test of time usually fall flat because they fail to identify and resolve the concerns of both parties.

- Goal #3: Teach the kid the skills he's lacking.

  The more adults use Plan B to solve problems, the more practice and help kids receive with a lot

of the skills they're lacking. Plan B helps kids think about, identify, and articulate the concerns that are precipitating challenging behavior; take into account situational factors and others' perspectives; move off of their original solutions; generate alternative solutions; consider whether those solutions are realistic and mutually satisfactory; and talk about problems without going over the edge— all things kids with behavioral challenges may not be very good at. Plan B doesn't teach these skills in one repetition, it takes multiple reps (as it does with any new skill).

- Goal #4: Reduce challenging behavior.

  In helping adults better understand challenging behavior, solve problems durably and collaboratively, and identify and teach lagging thinking skills, challenging behavior will be reduced. The work is often slow and messy. There's no way around that. CPS is not a quick fix. Of course, you don't fix a reading disability in a week, either. In fact, find a challenging kid people are trying to fix quickly and you'll see a challenging kid it's taking a very long time to fix. There's no cookie cutter, either. The approach must be tailored to the needs of each individual child to whom it is being applied.

- Goal #5: Create a helping relationship.

  Why be adversarial, why be the enemy, when you and the kid can be on the same team? In creating a process that helps you and the kid collaborate on solutions that will address each others' concerns, Plan B facilities a helping relationship. The kid comes to feel that you actually care about his concerns, that you feel his concerns are legitimate. He realizes that you're going to listen to him, try to understand him, and make sure that his concerns are addressed. He knows you're not mad, that he's not in trouble, that you're not going to tell him what to do. He begins to trust you, to rely on you. . . as a helper. . . .[17]

How Will I Assess My Students in a Fair and Meaningful Way?

NEW DESIGN HIGH SCHOOL COMMUNITY HABITS RUBRIC

New Design High School is one of many new small high schools that have been created in the past decade as part of a national effort to break up large and seemingly impersonal comprehensive high schools into small learning communities in which faculty and students can get to know each other as they focus on a unique approach to a high-quality education. As New Design was being launched, the faculty created the following detailed rubric for evaluating student work. The rubric illustrates well another movement in contemporary education, one that allows students and teachers much more detailed discussion of both the fairness and rationale for any grading system while spelling out the criteria for assessment. As you read this document, you will see that it lays out clear criteria for exceeding, meeting, or failing to meet a long list of goals that the school has for its students. These lists allow teachers to recognize that a student may be exceeding expectations in one area and may be far from meeting them in another. It also allows a teacher to explain to a student or a parent exactly where the student stands and what steps need to be taken for a student to meet or exceed all of the many expectations that the school rightly holds for its students and graduates.

HABIT 1: PERSONAL RESPONSIBILITY

	Exceeding the Standard	Meeting the Standard	Approaching the Standard	Emerging	No Evidence
Be Punctual *Attendance*	Student is always present, on time, and fully prepared to begin with his/her materials.	Student is usually present, on time, and fully prepared to begin with his/her materials.	Student is sometimes tardy and/or missing some materials, but is able to complete most required tasks.	Student frequently struggles to complete required tasks because of his/her attendance and/or lack of materials.	
Prepare and Produce *Student Work*	Student completes work that reflects a great deal of effort and goes beyond requirements in quality.	Student completes work that represents the student's potential and effort. All requirements of the task(s) are met.	Student completes work that approaches the student's potential and reflects some effort. Requirements of the task(s) are met, though at a basic level.	Student completes minimal work and shows little effort. Many requirements of the task(s) are unmet.	
Personal Growth	Student consistently and independently challenges her/himself as an independent thinker. Even without teacher prompting, student creates a plan of action, and follows through.	Student identifies challenges and takes risks to change her/his attitudes and habits to become an independent thinker. Student creates plan of action. Student follows through with plan to meet goals.	Student identifies challenges and is open to changing her/his attitudes and habits to become an independent thinker. Student creates plan of action, but sometimes struggles to follow through.	Student identifies challenges and is open to changing her/his attitudes and habits to become an independent thinker. Student creates plan of action, but rarely follows through.	

HABIT 2: SOCIAL RESPONSIBILITY

	Exceeding the Standard	Meeting the Standard	Approaching the Standard	Emerging	No Evidence
Professionalism *Behavior*	Student not only follows professionalism guidelines, but also consistently encourages others to act more professionally.	Student follows professionalism guidelines, helping to create a positive learning environment that helps both her/him and other students to excel.	Student mostly follows professionalism guidelines, but needs reminders every now and then in order to help her/him excel academically.	Student struggles and needs constant reminders of the professionalism guidelines. Lack of professionalism detracts from the learning environment.	

Source: New Design High School Community Habits Rubric, distributed to all teachers at New Design High School, New York City.

HABIT 3: CRITICAL AND CREATIVE THINKING

	Exceeding the Standard	Meeting the Standard	Approaching the Standard	Emerging	No Evidence
Define Problems *Asking questions*	Student is able to evaluate a situation and ask insightful questions that lead to defining his/her own problem.	Student defines the problem and poses questions that help clarify the problem.	Student defines some parts of the problem and poses questions that address the problem.	Student attempts but struggles to define the problem or pose questions that address the problem.	
Predict *Hypothesize Estimate Infer*	Student uses imagination, experiences and observations to make multiple logical predictions.	Student uses available experiences and observations to make a logical prediction.	Student uses limited experiences and observations to make a partial prediction.	Student uses limited experiences and observations to offer an illogical prediction.	
Talk to the Text	Student engages with the text: questions and comments are very detailed and reflect a deep understanding of the text.	Student "talks to the text" in order to further her/his understanding of the text.	Student somewhat "talks to the text," but more commentary in the margins is needed in order to further her/his understanding of the text.	Student minimally "talks to the text." Comments reflect little understanding of the text.	
Investigate *Gather Evidence*	Student gathers detailed, well-chosen evidence. Student's explanation reflects thorough thinking about the question.	Student gathers well-chosen evidence. Student's explanation reflects his/her thinking about the question.	Student gathers some evidence; attention is not paid to the quality of the evidence. It is difficult for student to explain how evidence addresses the question.	Student needs to gather more evidence in order to address the question.	
Analyze *Analyze Synthesize Justify Imagine Create*	Student creates a thorough and original analysis of the evidence to answer the question and prove her/his argument.	Student thoroughly analyzes evidence to answer the question and prove her/his argument.	Student analyzes evidence, but needs to be more thorough in order to more fully answer the question and prove her/his argument.	Student summarizes but fails to analyze evidence, therefore not proving her/his argument.	
Revise *Seek Other Perspectives Revise Work*	Student revisits the problem/question and reevaluates her/his answer. Detailed revisions are made to clarify and deepen original thinking.	Student clarifies thinking and alters ideas when necessary to better explain his/her answer to the question/problem.	Student clarifies some thinking and addresses some concerns with the work. More revision is needed.	Student makes minimal revisions to work.	

HABIT 4: APPLICATION OF KNOWLEDGE IN SUBJECT AREA
TO BE CREATED BY EACH SUBJECT AREA
Hold Content and Skills Constant

	Exceeding the Standard	Meeting the Standard	Approaching the Standard	Emerging	No Evidence
Understand Content *Curriculum Standards (what to know)*	Student shows extensive knowledge of key concepts and content.	Student shows solid understanding of key concepts and content. Student applies content knowledge appropriately.	Student shows some understanding of key concepts and content.	Student shows limited understanding of key concepts and content.	
Demonstrate Content Area Skills *Skills Specific to the Discipline (what to do)*	Student demonstrates sophisticated mastery of required skills, going beyond the requirements of the assignment.	Student demonstrates proficient mastery of required skills and is able to independently apply them when needed.	Student demonstrates beginning mastery of skills and attempts to apply them independently when needed.	Student demonstrates little mastery of skills and makes few attempts to apply them independently.	

HABIT 5: COMMUNICATION

	Exceeding the Standard	Meeting the Standard	Approaching the Standard	Emerging	No Evidence
Communicate Key Idea *Thesis Summary*	Student communicates main idea clearly. Main idea is thoughtful and detailed.	Student communicates main idea clearly. Main idea uses specific details.	Student communicates main idea. Main idea needs more detail.	Student needs to develop and clarify main idea.	
Organize Thoughts *Outline/Graphic Organizer Essay/Project Organization*	Student organizes thoughts clearly throughout work; details build upon each other in order to best support main idea.	Student organizes thoughts clearly and places details in appropriate sections in order to support main idea.	Student attempts to organize thoughts clearly, but details need to be reorganized in order to support main idea.	Student uses minimal organization in work.	
Writing Mechanics	Student work has no grammatical/spelling errors.	Student work has few grammatical/spelling errors.	Student work is understandable despite grammatical/spelling errors.	Student work is difficult to understand due to grammatical/spelling errors.	
Present Ideas Orally	Student's eloquence and passion come across with his/her eye contact, body language, diction, voice volume, and tone.	Student uses appropriate eye contact, body language, diction, voice volume, and tone throughout presentation.	Student at times uses appropriate eye contact, body language, diction, voice volume and/or tone.	Student minimally attempts to use appropriate eye contact, body language, diction, voice volume and/or tone.	
Present Ideas Visually *Artwork Poster Graph/Table*	Student presents key ideas in vivid, clear, and unique manner.	Student presents key ideas in vivid, clear manner.	Student presents key ideas.	Student needs to clarify the key ideas to present and determine how best to present those ideas.	

1. As far as you know, has a teacher ever used a rubric like this to assess your work? If so, did the use of a rubric make the assessment seem more or less fair?

2. Can you imagine using a rubric like this in grading your students? Would it make your life easier, or is it too complicated?

3. If you were going to use a rubric like the New Design High School one, what changes would you want to make? What would you want to be sure remained unchanged?

8

TECHNOLOGY
HOW IS IT CHANGING

S chools and classrooms are extraordinarily stable places, changing little in their physical set-up over decades. If you were to compare the average classroom today—elementary, middle, or high school—with those of 20 or even 50 years ago, you would see surprisingly little change. However, the school of today does have a new tool: the computer. Computers were not available to any schools prior to 1975, when the first microcomputer was developed. By 1999, 95 percent of schools and 63 percent of classrooms had not only a computer but also Internet access, enabling use of the World Wide Web as an instructional and research tool.

Today some schools provide laptops to their students, and large numbers of students have computers at home as well as cell phones in their pockets that allow them to send and receive an amazing amount of information. We are not far from reaching a goal set by President Bill Clinton in his 1996 State of the Union address: a computer with Internet access in every classroom. We certainly have a generation of students wired to the world in ways that no former generation could have imagined.[1]

Although some teachers and a few schools have used the power of modern computers and access to the Web to fundamentally transform the way learning and teaching takes place in the modern classroom, many other teachers tend to use technology, if they use it at all, in the same ways they use traditional, text-based materials.

Today's students, by contrast, have grown up with technology. They have likely spent more time playing video and computer games than reading. Such students come to school with radically different expectations than their predecessors, assuming that, like the rest of their lives, education should be fast paced, well connected to the larger world, and experiential rather than plodding, isolated, or text based. Such a situation, on the edge of what some observers see as a fundamental transformation of not only education but also the nature of knowledge, is fraught with both possibility and peril for all teachers. For those just entering teaching who, like their students but unlike their older teacher peers, have grown up with technology, the challenges to rethink the work of the teaching profession are significant.[2]

OUR SCHOOLS?

FOCUS >>

- How is technology transforming today's schools—or at least some of them?
- Are we on the edge of a wonderful new era, or is there a downside to all this technology?
- What is the digital divide, and how does it affect my teaching?
- How can I use technology to improve my teaching?

The **Readings** for this chapter will help us explore some of these questions. In the first Reading, journalist Matt L. Ottinger reports on the way technology has been used to completely transform every aspect of one small rural high school in north central Indiana. All entering students begin their school days with a specific problem and then work in teams with their classmates and their teachers, using the amazing reach of technology to solve the problem, whether it is a problem in science, social studies, or mathematics. In the second **Reading**, another journalist, Linda Starr, describes the work of Bernie Dodge, one of the leading advocates of the use of technology to change school from a place where "teachers teach and students learn" (mostly by memorizing to prepare for a test) to one where students and teachers work together to solve problems and engage with the larger world of ideas. Finally, in the last **Reading**, Kathleen Kennedy Manzo offers further advice to teachers on how to use the technology available today and how to engage their sometimes-reluctant colleagues to dive in to the world of technology in today's classrooms.

>> How Is Technology Transforming Today's Schools—Or at Least Some of Them?

As we move further from an industrial age into an information age, we find more and more examples of the use of technology in individual classrooms and sometimes entire schools. If the industrial-era school too often taught students to be passive, information-age schools must help all students take charge of their own education and become problem solvers able to use the incredible resources available to even the most isolated schools. The fact that such schooling is *much* more interesting to students and often much more engaging to their teachers is a valuable byproduct that is transforming schooling and every aspect of the world in which schools are operating.

In the midst of an era of extraordinary change—in the economy, in communications, in all aspects of society—teachers are being asked to rethink every aspect of what it means for teachers to teach and students to learn. Technol-

ogy brings opportunities—and challenges—to this generation of teachers as has not occurred perhaps since the inven-

Technology Users

Teens who say they are average to heavy users of:

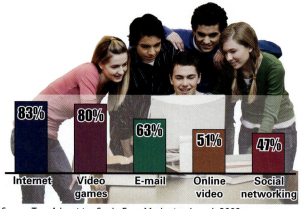

| Internet | Video games | E-mail | Online video | Social networking |
| 83% | 80% | 63% | 51% | 47% |

Source: Teen Advertising Study, Fuse Marketing, June 1, 2009, www .fusemarketing.com.

tion of the printing press. This chapter examines what this shift in thinking can mean for teachers and schools, as well as some of the promises and pitfalls of the new technology.

NEW TECH HIGH SCHOOLS

New Tech High School in Rochester, Indiana, sits in a small rural town in north central Indiana amidst some of the richest farmland in the country. You would not necessarily expect to find there what some are calling the future of American schools. The New Tech high school movement began in Napa, California, in 1996 as an effort to connect student learning to the reality of the changing nature of the job market. At the New Tech schools, students study world history by doing research and producing a video about a specific problem in the world today that can be addressed through a better understanding of history and geography. They learn biology by developing a video on genetics for their parents or on biodiversity and the water cycle for the community. The goal of New Tech is to use project-based, group learning to generate discussion and problem-solving skills in the classroom. The project method, which was so much a part of progressive-era classroom reforms a century ago, seems to have emerged again at a time when many educators want to make sure that learning engages students in ways that fit the new kinds of jobs available in a global economy.[3]

Connections

Recall the discussion of project-based learning in Chapter 6.

More than 30 schools in eight states have adopted the New Tech model, and the state of Indiana has been especially active in promoting it. Although most of Indiana's New Tech schools are in urban Indianapolis, the rural Rochester school district had a new superintendent and a new principal who were anxious to reinvent their schools. They determined that their high school dropout rate was too high and that their students, who came to school with a much more sophisticated sense of the world than their predecessors, needed a different kind of high school experience. If you visit a classroom at New Tech High School, you will notice there is very little "teacher talk." However, the shift to the New Tech model is not always easy. One veteran, now an enthusiastic supporter of the model, said, "Teachers have to come out of their comfort zones. In a traditional class, there's a lot of quiet and it's mostly the teacher talking." In the New Tech model, one sees clusters of young people working on projects, deeply engaged with each other and with the source of most of the information they seek—the Internet. In this setting, teachers become coaches, rather than instructors, putting into action an approach that many discuss but few actually see.

A QUESTION OF . . .

How has technology impacted teaching?

"Technology has become the foundation of most high school classrooms. Teachers utilize everything from PowerPoint to electronic grading systems to make teaching more efficient. In the end, those who benefit the most from the integration of technology in the classroom are the students and parents."

–Joshua Ball, high school geography teacher ■

Critics of the New Tech model wonder about the quality of the information that students are receiving. They fear that crucial aspects of what one should learn in high school are simply missed by the focus on depth over breadth. They may also worry that the almost-exclusive focus on group work disadvantages students who learn best alone. Although the debate is sure to continue, New Tech schools demonstrate one model of an entire school—and structure of schooling—transformed by technology.

WEBQUEST

Bernie Dodge of San Diego State University has become something of an educational technology guru with his invention of WebQuest, a method for doing significant student-led research using the World Wide Web. Dodge defines WebQuest as "an inquiry-oriented activity in which some or all of the information that learners interact with comes from resources on the Internet."

In the interview included with the **Readings** for this chapter, Dodge describes a time early in his development of the WebQuest method—in which students are given

Join the Dialogue

Individually, or as a group within your class, design your ideal school of the future. What will be the place of technology? What sort of technology will be in use? What limitations will be placed on the technology? What will be the place of teachers? Of textbooks? Of students?

Promising Practices

Laptops for Everyone

In rural Snow Hill, North Carolina, the Greene County Public Schools have bridged the digital divide and then some, more than tripling the college-going rate among their high school students in just 6 years, due in large part to their use of technology.

In 2003, the school district launched its Informational Age Technology for Every Child initiative, known as iTECH. Though Greene County schools operate in a small, low-wealth county, the school district boldly committed to the iTECH program, which gave every middle and high school student a laptop computer. According to the district Web site, "The school system recognized the enormity and expense of this technology undertaking but believed the investment of time and money was necessary in order to fulfill its mission: to offer its students a challenging curriculum that prepares them for the 21st century."

Yet no one was deluded into thinking that the laptops alone would make a difference. "Technology is much more than equipment," said Dr. Pat Mac-Neill, assistant superintendent of Greene County Public Schools. "We are committed to using our laptops and infrastructure to deliver engaging, effective curriculum that is rigorous and relevant to all students."

In the first year of the initiative, end-of-course scores rose from 67% to 78%. The long-range impacts have been even more impressive: when the iTECH program began, 26% of Greene Central High School students were college bound. In 2009, the college-going rate increased to 94%. Dr. MacNeill says dropout and teen-pregnancy rates have fallen as well.

Dr. MacNeill sees the technology not as the solution, but as a facilitator. She says the technology program has made the students "more engaged, more active in their learning" and made school "more purposeful and relevant to them."

Sources: "Critical Balance in a Culture of Change," Greene County Public Schools, http://www.gcsedu.org/site_res_view_template.aspx?id=41a06954 -2646-471a-be66-138ca7482fcf; "Pioneering One-to-One Laptop District Selects Carnegie Learning Math Curricula for Core Classroom Instruction," http://www.reuters.com/article/pressRelease/idUS204561+28-Jul-2009 +BW20090728; "An Apple for Your Teacher," Anne Marie Chaker, July 22, 2009, *Wall Street Journal*, http://online.wsj.com/article/SB10001424052970204900904 574304140278264598.html.

assignments that require them to use information found only on the Internet—when he was attempting to transform a classroom for aspiring teachers into one where technology played a larger role. Through "Treasure Hunts" and other activities, students were required to do online research in real time during classes as well as outside of class. Dodge described his own role after giving the students an assignment and letting them loose to do their own research. Instead of standing in front of the room talking at the students, he walked around the room "listening to the buzz of conversations" as students helped each other and were forced, by the assignment, to work as a group and to come to group decisions. He realized quickly that the life of the class was much richer than anything he had seen

Did you know?

Online learning, or distance learning, is gaining popularity at the high school level. In Alabama, students in all of the state's 371 high schools are able to take courses not offered at their schools through a **distance-learning program** that uses online and interactive video conferencing technology to link classrooms and offer coursework, including advanced placement and foreign languages, to students in schools where those courses may not be available. Alabama also introduced a requirement that, starting in 2009, all incoming freshmen must take at least one distance-learning class during their 4 years of high school.[4] What distance-learning options does your state offer? At the high school level? At the elementary school level?

distance-learning program Courses or workshops in which the teacher and student are not physically together and interact through alternative methods; presently, these courses are conducted almost entirely on the Internet.

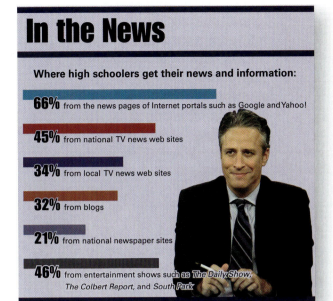

In the News

Where high schoolers get their news and information:

66% from the news pages of Internet portals such as Google and Yahoo!

45% from national TV news web sites

34% from local TV news web sites

32% from blogs

21% from national newspaper sites

46% from entertainment shows such as *The Daily Show*, *The Colbert Report*, and *South Park*

Source: "Teens Tune into News on the Internet," September 22, 2006, press release, Knight Foundation, www.knightfoundation.org.

before in his own teaching. Students were asking more complex questions and thinking more seriously about their work. He loved what he saw and was determined to build on the experience. For Dodge, this was the beginning of a new way to teach teachers and to encourage them to teach their students.

There are many parallels between WebQuest and what happens at New Tech High School and in other classrooms that have embraced the power of technology to transform learning environments. The primary focus of learning moves from teacher talk (which is linked to passive student listening) to greater, direct activity on the part of the students. Advocates for this use of technology contend that it puts more responsibility on the learners themselves. However, this is hardly a form of teaching that exempts the teacher. A good teacher who is using WebQuest or who is

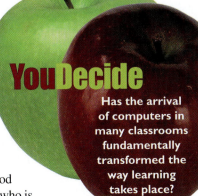

You Decide

Has the arrival of computers in many classrooms fundamentally transformed the way learning takes place?

working at a New Tech school spends a lot of time defining specific research problems that will generate the kind of student research and learning needed for their curricular goals as well as developing the right list of resources and sites that will help students accomplish those goals.

New Tech schools and WebQuest are just two examples on a long list of teachers, schools, and curricula that have been fundamentally transformed because they embraced technology, not only as a tool for teaching but also as an organizational structure for schooling and, indeed, for understanding the nature of knowledge. At its best, technology can change the classroom from a place where teachers teach and students learn—mostly passively—to a place where students take the lead, organizing their learning, studying, and researching in ways that are meaningful to them, and producing meaningful work instead of absorbing the work of others. When teachers choose this approach to education, students take on a different identity as learners. They usually have much more confidence in their work—for it is *their* work—and they feel a sense of ownership of the outcomes that they cannot gain through listening, reading, and preparing to report the information back on a test. At its worst, however, technology can be far less—as humdrum as the worst traditional form of education and as distracting as the constant chatter of too many cell phone conversations. Many educators are not sure whether the huge introduction of technology into schools has been as good as its proponents argue, or as bad as its detractors fear. It is to these arguments that we now turn.

>> Are We on the Edge of a Wonderful New Era, or Is There a Downside to All This Technology?

SEYMOUR PAPERT: ADVOCATE EXTRAORDINAIRE

No one has been a stronger advocate for the use of computers in education than Seymour Papert. Since the 1970s, Papert, who teaches at the Massachusetts Institute of Technology, has embraced the use of computer-based technology in the schools and has urged others to do the same. Papert notes what many have observed, "Across the world children have entered a passionate and enduring love affair with the computer. What they do with computers is as varied as their activities. . . . [T]he love affair involves more than the desire to do things with computers. It also has an element of possessiveness and, most importantly, of assertion of intellectual identity."

Given this "love affair," which extends to other digital media, it continues to frustrate Papert that so many schools seem to do so little with computers despite examples such as New Tech High or WebQuest. Although computers can now be found in many classrooms, Papert notes that what goes on in most classrooms today is essentially the same as what went on a century ago—teachers teach and students learn. The computers, if they are there at all, sit on the sidelines. They may be used to do traditional assignments, or to practice drill exercises, but the possibilities they offer are barely explored. All that changes, however, when students go home. Outside of school, Papert realized, students were spending hours playing computer games, tracking information, keeping in touch with each other. . .not because

they had been assigned to do so but because they wanted to. The creativity he saw, compared to the lack of creativity in many school assignments, was amazing.

Imagining a visit by teachers from the 19th century, Papert asks what the visitors would see when today's children leave school, arrive at home, and turn on their computers:

> While the technology itself might first catch the eye of our visitors, they would in time, being teachers, be struck by the level of intellectual effort that the children were putting into this activity and the level of learning that was taking place, a level that seemed far beyond that which had taken place just a few hours earlier in school. The most open and honest of our time-traveling teachers might well observe that never before had they seen so much being learned in such a confined space and in so short a time.

Some observers might argue with Papert about the value of what is being learned from this interaction with computers, but few would disagree with his basic notion that this generation's love affair with technology remains somewhat incomprehensible to their elders.[5]

Researchers at the Education Development Center report that teachers are using technology in a variety of ways. For many, the computer is an ideal way to prepare lessons, communicate with each other and with parents, and keep records and grades. A National Center for Educational Statistics survey conducted in 2000–2001 found that teachers ranked a computer with e-mail access as their top technological need followed by a telephone, reference materials on CD-ROM, and computer access for their students.

A small but growing number of teachers make far greater use of the new technologies. These more extensive users may be younger teachers who have grown up with the new technology themselves, or they may be teachers like Thelma, whom Papert describes. Thelma, a fifth-grade teacher in New York City, never thought of herself as a "technology person." As a teacher, she had brought hamsters, plants, and posters into her classroom, so why not computers? But unlike the hamsters, plants, and posters, the computers fundamentally changed the nature of the teaching and learning process for Thelma's students. Papert described what he saw in Thelma's classroom:

> Even now I can close my eyes and see a 1981 scene in a fifth-grade classroom in a New York City public school. Two worlds seemed to coexist in one room: At one end, a teacher, Thelma, was giving a "lesson" at the blackboard; at the other, a cluster of students was working with two computers. The computer group ran into a problem and sent someone to "ask the teacher." Thelma said, "Maybe Bill can help"—and continued her lesson without missing a beat, quite unperturbed by the fact that Bill had now joined the ranks of students who weren't even pretending to listen to her.
>
> The front and back of the room were separated by much more than a difference between the technology

of the computer and the technology of the blackboard. A far greater difference marked the children's relationship with what they were doing. In the front, they were following someone else's agenda; in the back, they were following their own.[6]

Two decades before WebQuest or the growth of New Tech, Papert used almost the same words to describe the divide between places where an old technology fosters a teacher-centered learning agenda and places where new technologies foster student-centered agendas. The split has only grown since then.

Papert, like others before him, deeply dislikes the fact that traditional schooling "has an inherent tendency to infantilize children by placing them in a position of having to do as they are told, to occupy themselves with work dictated by someone else and that, moreover, has no intrinsic value—schoolwork is done only because the designer of a curriculum decided that doing the work would shape the doer into a desirable form." He wants something radically different "because I am convinced that the best learning takes place when the learner takes charge." But he also believes that the new technologies make it possible to implement these changes to a degree previously unimagined. Today, children can truly start with their curiosity, seek to understand new ideas, and discover new knowledge as they seek to answer questions of their own asking.

Papert describes what he sees as two camps into which he believes most educators fall. On the one hand are the "Schoolers"—people who believe that schools can certainly be improved by making the current situation better. They may use computers to keep records or communicate, but they are not interested in fundamental change. When the conversation turns to mega-change, "[m]any become indignant" and say, "Tell us how to use your computers to solve some of the many immediate practical problems we have." On the other side are "Yearners," who are frustrated by the many institutional impediments to change and who have a vision of something quite different and more intellectually engaging for students and teachers. Some Yearners operate as a "sort of fifth column within School itself: Large numbers of teachers manage to create within the walls of their own classrooms oases of learning profoundly at odds with the education philosophy publicly espoused by their administrators." Papert saw the Yearners as a "minority who have not yet been able to loosen the hold of the educational establishment on how children are taught."[7]

More recent studies of teachers' attitudes toward computer use in the classroom confirm Papert's views of a divide among educators. However, these studies also point to ways that technology itself is helping to create different attitudes about its use. Perhaps technology helps create more Yearners, even as Yearners help foster the use of new technology. One study of teacher technology use in rural Texas found that "higher users of technology had a more favorable attitude toward change, were more able to cope with uncertainty and risk, less fatalistic, and had higher levels of motivation, more social participation, and greater exposure to communication channels." In other words, those who used computers and related technology enough to become comfortable with it also found themselves using the technology in increasingly creative ways that fostered a more favorable attitude.

School districts have not done all they can to foster the kind of positive view that some teachers exhibit. The federal Office of Technology Assessment found that, although school districts are spending an increasing amount of money on computer hardware and software, they spend relatively little on training. Clearly those who lack sophisticated technological skills are not likely to take the risks of fundamentally rethinking their classroom practice, even if they will use computers for e-mail communication or as sophisticated typewriters.[8] If the new technology is to fulfill the promise that some visionaries see for it—a promise that could dramatically improve the education of every student in the United States—then school districts are going to have to do much more to foster computer use and computer literacy among all teachers.

Who's Blogging?

- About **50%** of all blogs are authored by teenagers
- **35%** of all online teen girls blog
- **20%** of online teen boys blog
- **31%** of high school students post comments on blogs or online columns at least once a week
- **Two-thirds** of teenage bloggers provide their age and first name; **60%** offer their location and contact information; and **20%** divulge their full name

Sources: 2003 study by the Perseus Development Corp; "Teenage Use of Blogs Tops Internet Activity," by Justin Broglio, October 26, 2005, North Lake Tahoe Bonanza, http://www.tahoebonanza.com/article/20051026/News/110260007; Children's Digital Media Center at Georgetown University.

Of course, many new teachers and aspiring teachers (possibly including you) who have grown up with computers will enter the teaching profession with a level of technological mastery unimaginable to their senior colleagues and principals. However, being comfortable with the technology is only a first step. Knowing how to use it to foster serious student learning is a different matter.

Papert wrote in 1993, "Large numbers of children see the computer as 'theirs'—as something that belongs to them, to their generation." Many of the children he described are now adults, and some of those adults are becoming teachers. They bring with them a confidence of their own skill with what Papert calls the "Knowledge Machines" that will likely transform schools, no matter what administrators, more senior teachers, professional developers, or policy makers do or fail to do.

NEIL POSTMAN: DISSENTER

Not everyone believes this "revolution" is a good thing. Neil Postman has spoken with great urgency of the need for educators to stop and ask where the introduction of computer-based technology is taking us as a society and specifically as teachers. In his book *Technopoly: The Surrender of Culture to Technology*, Postman says, "We need to know in what ways it is altering our conception of learning, and how in conjunction with television, it undermines the old idea of school." Many, including Papert, agree that the computer is fundamentally undermining older ideas of

Tweens and Technology

How kids ages 7–12 spend their media time:

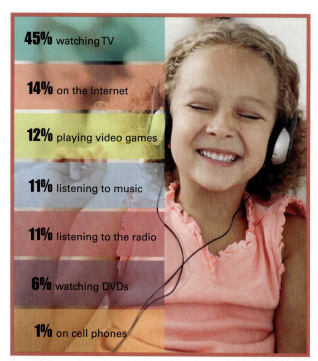

45% watching TV

14% on the Internet

12% playing video games

11% listening to music

11% listening to the radio

6% watching DVDs

1% on cell phones

Source: Solutions Research Group for YTV, 2007.

school. Postman differs, however, because he is not sure that this is such a good thing.

Postman's view of the new technology is clearly negative. He sees it undermining the very fabric not only of schooling but also of culture as we have known it. Postman makes two basic points about the impact of computer-based technology on education: (1) The impact is far more profound than most people, including most proponents of computers in the classroom, have even dared think; and (2) this impact is undermining many values that we hold dear, including values about the importance of education.

Ironically, given their starkly different views of the positive or negative impact of computers, Postman sounds very much like Papert when he talks about the total impact of computers on schools and society. Postman insists,

> A new technology does not add or subtract something. It changes everything. In the year 1500, fifty years after the printing press was invented, we did not have old Europe plus the printing press. We had a different Europe. After television, the United States was not America plus television; television gave a new coloration to every political campaign, to every home, to every school, to every church, to every industry.

Postman believes that the very culture into which the new technology has been embedded becomes a different culture. People have access to different information, they think about things in different ways, and they value different ideas—all because of the impact of the new technology.

Certainly it is true that the invention of printing in medieval Europe put books into the hands of a great many people who had never even held a book and, therefore, never had any reason to learn to read. Because of television, people today have access to global events and close-up knowledge of national and world leaders in a way that previous generations could not possibly imagine. However, as a result of television, many observers worry about a decline in reading (when television brings information so much more quickly and in such rich and colorful detail),

Teachable Moment

Virtual Bullying

As Internet access becomes more universal and **social media sites** continue to grow in popularity, concerns about Internet safety grow as well. An incident that raised the profile of this serious issue is the tragic story of Megan Meier, a 13-year-old student in Missouri who committed suicide after she was "cyberbullied."

In 2006, Meier befriended someone she thought was a boy who was interested in her on MySpace. According to Megan's mother, Tina Meier, after about a month of friendly online interaction, Megan received a message from "Josh" saying, "I don't know if I want to be friends with you any longer because I hear you're not nice to your friends."

Around the same time, Megan told her mother that someone using Josh's account was posting cruel things about her online. Not long after these incidents, Megan, who had a history of depression, hanged herself.

The story gained national attention, largely because of the truth that was revealed several weeks after Megan's death: "Josh" never existed. A neighborhood mother had created Josh's MySpace profile and corresponded with Megan, allegedly to gain Megan's trust and learn what Megan was saying about her daughter.

This story may seem like an extreme case, but according to one report, nearly half of all teenagers report they have been the victim of cyberattacks. Everything from text messaging to e-mail can be used to bully victims. Some people create Web sites dedicated solely to harassment.

Nancy Willard, executive director of the Center for Safe and Responsible Internet Use, defines cyberbullying as "being cruel to others by sending or posting harmful material or engaging in other forms of social aggression using the Internet or other digital tech-

social media sites
Internet websites constructed through user-generated content, participation, and social interaction.

nologies." She identifies several forms that cyberbullying can take:

- Flaming. Online fights using electronic messages with angry and vulgar language.
- Harassment. Repeatedly sending nasty, mean, and insulting messages.
- Denigration. "Dissing" someone online. Sending or posting gossip or rumors about a person to damage his or her reputation or friendships.
- Impersonation. Pretending to be someone else and sending or posting material to get that person in trouble or to endanger that person or to damage that person's reputation or friendships.
- Outing. Sharing someone's secrets or embarrassing information or images online.
- Trickery. Talking someone into revealing secrets or embarrassing information, and then sharing it online.
- Exclusion. Intentionally and cruelly excluding someone from an online group.
- Cyberstalking. Repeated, intense harassment and denigration that includes threats or creates significant fear.

Bullying among school-age children is nothing new, of course. What's different about bullying online is that it's tougher for teachers to see, which makes it tougher for them to take action. However, teachers can now access many online resources to help them identify the signs and talk with students and parents about how to prevent cyberbullying and other online safety concerns.

QUESTIONS

- If you heard that a student was bullying another online, how would you handle it? Or, if you have been bullied online, how did you handle it?
- How might you talk with your students about Internet safety and cyberbullying in your classroom? Is it a teacher's responsibility to do so?

Sources: "Parents: Cyber Bullying Led to Teen's Suicide," ABC News, November 19, 2007, http://abcnews.go.com/GMA/Story?id=3882520&page=1; "Educator's Guide to Cyberbullying and Cyberthreats," by Nancy Willard, April 2007, http://www.cyberbully.org/cyberbully/docs/cbcteducator.pdf.

in imagination (since television does the imaginative work for us), in face-to-face community (since television connects us to the world but tends to encourage us to stay at home rather than meet with our neighbors or participate in community activities), and in our view of our ability to shape the world (since television makes us passive consumers rather than active agents).

LARRY CUBAN: A WORD OF CAUTION

Postman and Papert both claim that schools as we know them cannot survive the impact of computer technology and the changes in learning styles and worldwide connectivity that they bring, but others are not so sure. In his book *Teachers and Machines*, Larry Cuban reminds us that nearly a century ago, in 1913, the inventor Thomas Edison predicted, "[S]cholars will soon be instructed through the eye. It is possible to touch every branch of human knowledge with the motion picture." In 1922, Edison said, "I believe that the motion picture is destined to revolutionize our educational system and that in a few years it will supplant largely, if not entirely, the use of textbooks." Cuban wonders if people like both Papert and Postman, for all their differences, are wrong. Maybe they, like Edison a century before, are overestimating things and perhaps, once again, the changes will not be as great as proponents or detractors expect.

Cuban is cautious about predictions of sweeping changes in schools. He describes what he sees as a standard response to proposals to introduce new technologies:

> *Reformers, more often than not, were foundation executives, educational administrators, and wholesalers who saw solutions to school problems in swift technological advances. Not long after each innovation was introduced came academic studies to demonstrate the effectiveness of the particular teacher aid as compared to conventional instruction. Invariably, the mechanical or electronic device proved as effective as a teacher in conveying information to students. Marring the general favor and scientific credibility enjoyed by the innovation, however, would be scattered complaints from teachers or classroom observers about the logistics of use, technical imperfections, incompatibility with current programs, or similar concerns. At a later point, surveys would document teacher use of the particular tool as disappointingly infrequent. Such surveys would unleash mild to harsh criticism of administrators who left costly machines in closets to gather cobwebs, or stinging rebukes of narrow-minded, stubborn teachers reluctant to use learning tools that studies had shown to be academically effective. . . . Few scholars, policy makers, or practitioners ever questioned the claims of boosters or even asked whether the technology should be introduced.*

For many who have observed schools over many years, this description remains haunting.[9]

>> What Is the Digital Divide, and How Does It Affect My Teaching?

In describing his own enthusiasm for the New Tech High School model, one of Indiana's business leaders says, "Our mission here is to bridge the digital divide."[10] The term *digital divide* is often used in discussions of educational technology. According to a 2007 report, "Though an exact definition remains elusive, the term 'digital divide' generally refers to the disconnect that occurs between those with access to technology and those without, while recognizing the myriad factors that can have an impact on that inequity."

Many critics of the use of computers in schools do not share all of Postman's fears, even if they do not embrace all of Papert's enthusiasm. Nevertheless, these critics see some much more immediate problems with the way in which computers are used in school, even if they are as enthusiastic as Dodge or Papert about the potential of the new technologies to transform learning. These critics see schools in which European American students have much more access to computers—and much more interesting assignments on the computers—than are available to most students of color. They see wealthy schools having more computers and dramatically better computer instruction than schools that serve poor students. And they see a built-in bias, in favor of boys over girls, in the way that computers are used in schools and in the computer games students use at home. All these inequities are part of the digital divide.

Speaking at the 2007 conference of the International Society for Technology in Education, Sylvia G. Rousseau, of the University of Southern California, said, "As much as I admire technology. . .it has a mixed history in the way it has impacted our lives." Rousseau and many others believe that contemporary technology—television, video games, the

In My Room

What kids ages 6–14 have in their bedrooms:

69% have TVs
49% have Video gaming systems
46% have VCRs
37% have DVD players
35% have Cable/satellite
24% have Computers
18% have Internet access

Source: U.S. Multicultural Kids Study 2005, Nickelodeon and Cultural Access Group.

PORTRAIT OF AN EDUCATOR

Sherry Turkle

Sherry Turkle is the Abby Rockefeller Mauzé Professor of the Social Studies of Science and Technology at the Massachusetts Institute of Technology, where she also directs the MIT Initiative on Technology and Self. A sociologist and a licensed clinical psychologist, Turkle has focused much of her research on the way people relate to technology, on the way that relationship can change the way people think, and on the problem of computer addiction. She has become a leading voice in helping teachers understand what happens when computers become a large part of the lives of their students.

Turkle is cautiously enthusiastic about the impact of technology on education. She consistently reminds us that the new technologies available today not only provide us with new information and can be used to teach in new ways, but they also fundamentally affect the way we think:

> Some thinkers argue that the new opacity is empowering, enabling anyone to use the most sophisticated technological tools and to experiment with simulation in complex and creative ways. But it is also true that our tools carry the message that they are beyond our understanding. It is possible that in daily life, epistemic opacity can lead to **passivity**.

Source: "How Computers Change the Way We Think," by Sherry Turkle, January 30, 2004, *Chronicle of Higher Education.*

I first became aware of that possibility in the early 1990s, when the first generation of complex simulation games were introduced and immediately became popular for home as well as school use. SimLife teaches the principles of evolution by getting children involved in the development of complex ecosystems; in that sense it is an extraordinary learning tool. During one session in which I played SimLife with Tim, a 13-year-old, the screen before us flashed a message: "Your orgot is being eaten up." "What's an orgot?" I asked. Tim didn't know. "I just ignore that," he said confidently. "You don't need to know that kind of stuff to play."

For me, that story serves as a cautionary tale. **Computer simulations** enable their users to think about complex phenomena as dynamic, evolving systems. But they also accustom us to manipulating systems whose core assumptions we may not understand and that may not be true.

> **passivity** A lack of initiative and inactivity or the too-easy acceptance of the ideas and opinions of others; many observers worry that computers, like television, increase the easy acceptance of outside ideas and opinions with little resistance or thought.
>
> **computer simulations** Representation and imitation of real-world activities by computer programs.

In her book *The Second Self: Computers and the Human Spirit*, Turkle uses Jean Piaget's approach to child development to examine how children learn about computers and how this affects their minds. Additionally, she has written numerous books and articles on the relationship of technology and education (including the topic of cyberbullying) while also directing a research center at MIT with a similar focus. She is a featured media commentator on the effects of technology for CNN, NBC, ABC, and National Public Radio, including appearances on programs such as *Nightline* and *20/20*.

As an educator who has spent her career studying the social and psychological impact of technology, Turkle has much to say to every teacher who wants to expand the use of technology in the classroom and to understand students who have grown up in a world of omnipresent technology that was unimaginable only a few years ago.

World Wide Web—all reinforce a cultural construct of race, class, and gender that undermines the achievement of some children while fostering the dominance of others. When low-income students use computers, if they use them, to foster drilling while more privileged children use the same computers to construct new knowledge, or when the computers used in most classrooms open to a desktop screen that most middle-class children find familiar but children who have spent more time in rural fields or urban streets do not, then, as Rousseau says, "The issue isn't all technology, yet in this day, it has everything to do with technology."[11]

The digital divide has several aspects. First, significant differences exist in what technology is available to whom. A 2003 report from the National Center for Education Statistics found that 70.7% of public high school students used a computer at home. However, if we disaggregate this number by race, a different picture emerges: 81.4% of European American students used computers at home, but only 44.2% of African American students and 49.1% of Latino students did so. Two decades after computer use became widespread in schools and at home, students are still "digitally divided" in terms of what experiences they bring to school with them.

Nevertheless, schools substantially narrowed the divide in terms of in-school computer use during the 1990s. A total of 88% of public high school students aged 15 or older reported using computers in school. In this setting, the racial divide

My Tech Autobiography

Answer the following questions about your early experiences with technology:

- How old were you when you first used a computer?
- Was it at home or school (or elsewhere)?
- Was it to play a game or something else?
- Who taught you how to use it?
- Did you have computers in your classroom and/or in a computer lab?
- Did your school teach you how to use computer technology to build on knowledge you already had, or were your computer knowledge and your school knowledge kept separate for some period of time?

Compare your answers with those of classmates. Did they have similar experiences?

receded significantly: 89.2% of European American students, 89.0% of African American students, and 83.8% of Latino students used computers in their classrooms. Recall for example that Rochester, Indiana, chose to embrace the New Tech model specifically because the district's leaders wanted to respond effectively to growing poverty in their part of rural America. Statistics do not necessarily tell us all we would like to know about how computers are used in classrooms, nor do they communicate the full impact of the wide differential in home use, but schools seem to be making substantial gains in closing what has been a yawning digital divide.[12]

Second, even as schools were successful in narrowing the digital divide in terms of overall computer use, race and class still seem to play a significant role in determining *how* computers are used in schools. A survey conducted for the Educational Testing Service (ETS) in 1998 found that the complaint voiced by University of Wisconsin professor Michael Apple in the 1980s, that "[t]here is evidence of class-, race-, and gender-based differences in computer use," was still very true at the end of the 1990s. In the ETS study, European American students reported using computers primarily for simulations and applications—that is for self-directed and engaging research—31% of the time and almost exactly the same amount of time for drill and practice, 30%. By contrast, African American students reported using computers in school only 14% of the time for simulations and applications, whereas they used them for drill and practice 52% of the time. The same study found that students in Title I schools (those serving students whose families live in poverty) used computers for simulations and applications only 13% of the time, whereas students in schools that did not receive Title I funds reported spending 30% of their time on these more creative activities.[13]

Third, significant (and often unexamined) deep cultural assumptions are built into technology. In many cases, boys seem to take to computers more quickly than girls, perhaps because of an early introduction to computer games. A study from 2000 that looked at girls and technology reported,

Girls have specific criticisms of the violence in current games as well as the general sense that they would be more interested in games that allowed them to create rather than destroy. When given the opportunity to describe their "ideal" computer

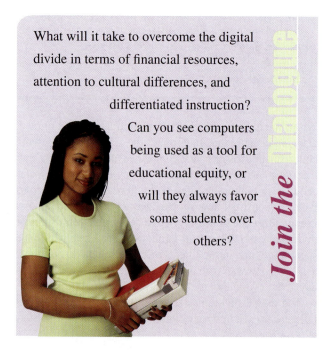

What will it take to overcome the digital divide in terms of financial resources, attention to cultural differences, and differentiated instruction? Can you see computers being used as a tool for educational equity, or will they always favor some students over others?

Join the Dialogue

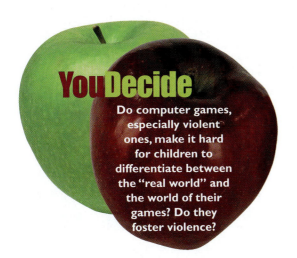

You Decide

Do computer games, especially violent ones, make it hard for children to differentiate between the "real world" and the world of their games? Do they foster violence?

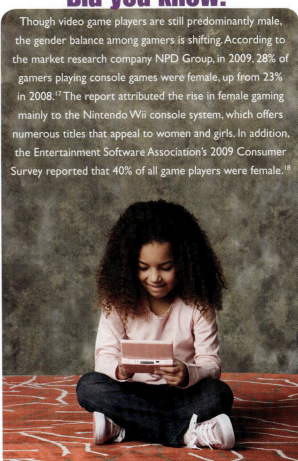

Did you know?

Though video game players are still predominantly male, the gender balance among gamers is shifting. According to the market research company NPD Group, in 2009, 28% of gamers playing console games were female, up from 23% in 2008.[17] The report attributed the rise in female gaming mainly to the Nintendo Wii console system, which offers numerous titles that appeal to women and girls. In addition, the Entertainment Software Association's 2009 Consumer Survey reported that 40% of all game players were female.[18]

game, they talk about how they would value games that involve simulation and identity play. They would appreciate opportunities to "work through" real-life problems in the simulated world of the screen. Many describe games that would allow them to swap identity or face struggles they have yet to encounter.[14]

Another report expressed concern over the gender balance and gender roles represented in video games. Researchers analyzed 1,716 characters in video games and found that, of these, male human characters totaled 1,106 (64%), whereas female human characters numbered only 283 (17%). They also found that half of all female characters "were props or bystanders," meaning they did not

engage in any action or provide useful resources, "while male characters were predominantly competitors."[15]

Tony Scott, who has spent many years working on ways to use computers effectively in classrooms, and his colleagues are among those who expand on these questions of culture in computers and video games. To what degree, they ask, do computers impose one specific set of cultural norms on students who, because of gender, ethnicity, or simply differing values, do not want that set of (perhaps unexamined but very powerful) cultural norms? According to Scott and his colleagues,

There is a fact, not often enough acknowledged, that computer hardware carries cultural content: Computers can be adapted to work in Spanish, but they are designed in English. . .the menu structure, the design of icons, and the styles of problem decomposition and solution together construct the **computer-human interface**. *So whatever communicative process can be created within and between ethnic minorities, insofar as they are mediated by computer, they are also mediated by Anglo culture.*[16]

> **computer-human interface** Point of contact and interaction between human and computer.

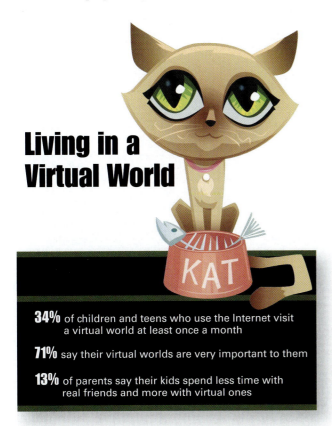

Living in a Virtual World

34% of children and teens who use the Internet visit a virtual world at least once a month

71% say their virtual worlds are very important to them

13% of parents say their kids spend less time with real friends and more with virtual ones

Sources: University of California-Irvine, Center for the Digital Future of University of Southern California, Media Research Lab of Iowa State University, Just Kid Inc.

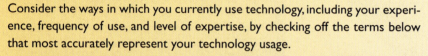

What About Me?

Techno-Savvy

Consider the ways in which you currently use technology, including your experience, frequency of use, and level of expertise, by checking off the terms below that most accurately represent your technology usage.

Technology	Internet	E-mail	Cell Phone	Texting	Blogging
Experience	__ None	__ None	__ None	__ None	__ None
	__ Less than a year	__ Less than a year	__ Less than a year	__ Less than a year	__ Less than a year
	__ 1–3 years	__ 1–3 years	__ 1–3 years	__ 1–3 years	__ 1–3 years
	__ 4–8 years	__ 4–8 years	__ 4–8 years	__ 4–8 years	__ 4–8 years
	__ 9+ years	__ 9+ years	__ 9+ years	__ 9+ years	__ 9+ years
Frequency of Use	__ Daily	__ Daily	__ Daily	__ Daily	__ Daily
	__ Weekly	__ Weekly	__ Weekly	__ Weekly	__ Weekly
	__ Monthly	__ Monthly	__ Monthly	__ Monthly	__ Monthly
	__ Rarely	__ Rarely	__ Rarely	__ Rarely	__ Rarely
Expertise	__ A lot to learn	__ A lot to learn	__ A lot to learn	__ A lot to learn	__ A lot to learn
	__ Feel comfortable	__ Feel comfortable	__ Feel comfortable	__ Feel comfortable	__ Feel comfortable
	__ Knowledgeable	__ Knowledgeable	__ Knowledgeable	__ Knowledgeable	__ Knowledgeable
	__ Have taught to others	__ Have taught to others	__ Have taught to others	__ Have taught to others	__ Have taught to others

Technology	Social Media (Facebook, MySpace)	Twitter	Video Games	Digital Camera	Digital Video
Experience	__ None	__ None	__ None	__ None	__ None
	__ Less than a year	__ Less than a year	__ Less than a year	__ Less than a year	__ Less than a year
	__ 1–3 years	__ 1–3 years	__ 1–3 years	__ 1–3 years	__ 1–3 years
	__ 4–8 years	__ 4–8 years	__ 4–8 years	__ 4–8 years	__ 4–8 years
	__ 9+ years	__ 9+ years	__ 9+ years	__ 9+ years	__ 9+ years
Frequency of Use	__ Daily	__ Daily	__ Daily	__ Daily	__ Daily
	__ Weekly	__ Weekly	__ Weekly	__ Weekly	__ Weekly
	__ Monthly	__ Monthly	__ Monthly	__ Monthly	__ Monthly
	__ Rarely	__ Rarely	__ Rarely	__ Rarely	__ Rarely
Expertise	__ A lot to learn	__ A lot to learn	__ A lot to learn	__ A lot to learn	__ A lot to learn
	__ Feel comfortable	__ Feel comfortable	__ Feel comfortable	__ Feel comfortable	__ Feel comfortable
	__ Knowledgeable	__ Knowledgeable	__ Knowledgeable	__ Knowledgeable	__ Knowledgeable
	__ Have taught to others	__ Have taught to others	__ Have taught to others	__ Have taught to others	__ Have taught to others

- How much time do you spend each day using technology (including cell phone usage, the Internet, and the like) for personal, educational, and work-related purposes? Would you consider any of that wasted time?
- Which of these technologies do you think will be valuable to you in the classroom? In addition to those you have already taught others, which would you feel comfortable teaching?

What Teens Are Doing Online

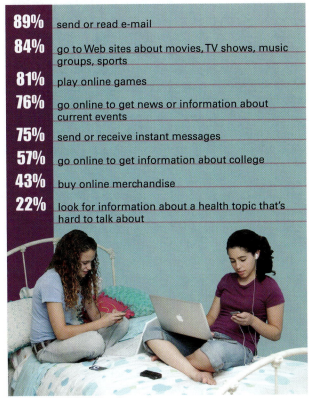

89%	send or read e-mail
84%	go to Web sites about movies, TV shows, music groups, sports
81%	play online games
76%	go online to get news or information about current events
75%	send or receive instant messages
57%	go online to get information about college
43%	buy online merchandise
22%	look for information about a health topic that's hard to talk about

Sources: University of California-Irvine, Center for the Digital Future of University of Southern California, Media Research Lab of Iowa State University, Just Kid Inc.

If the computers that are appearing in more and more American classrooms reflect the dominance of one set of cultural assumptions, is it any wonder that some students, who for whatever reason do not share those assumptions, feel excluded?

>> How Can I Use Technology to Improve My Teaching?

Gwen Solomon and Lynne Schrum, two advocates for the positive inclusion of computer technology in the class-room, suggest six steps that educators need to take to har-ness technology and, especially, the World Wide Web for learning in the best ways possible:

- First, we must recognize that the Web provides ways to address standards and acquire information that students need, and it expands their opportunities to learn.

- Second, we must recognize that many free, high-quality resources are available online. These primary sources, interactive games, simulations, and other

Tweens on the Phone

Of kids ages 7–12

35%	own cell phones
20%	text message
58%	download or watch TV on their phones
35%	play music on their phones

Source: "Kids on the Go: Mobile Usage by U.S. Teens and Tweens," The Nielsen Company, December 2007.

materials optimize the investment we've already made in equipment and infrastructure.

- Third, to reach true classroom integration, we have to invest in professional development that will enhance teacher comprehension and comfort with what the Web offers.

- Fourth, we have to link Web-based activities with **standards-based curricula** and topics needed for tests. All eyes are on test results, so we should use technology to help prepare students to think—in all ways possible.

> **standards-based curricula**
> Curricula centered around the standards, which are used as the guide for instruction and for student evaluation.

- Fifth, we have to prepare future educators to integrate technology as easily as previous generations used textbooks and chalkboards.

- Sixth, we must involve parents and community members in understanding the value of using Web-based activities for student learning, as well as engage them in dialogue about educational goals and values.[19]

Ways to Incorporate Technology into Your Classroom

Internet: Start each day or week with a news story from a relevant content area. Research and track data that changes regularly, such as temperature, rainfall, gas prices, or the stock market.

Digital video: Document classroom processes, such as how to set up and clean lab equiptment. Have students research, script, and record a "newscast" of a current or historical event.

E-mail: Have the class write and send an e-mail to an expert or an author, asking for his or her opinion or insight on a topic you are studying.

Spreadsheets and Databases: Use data students have collected to build charts, graphs, or tables.

Word processing: Publish a student-produced class "newspaper" or newsletter.

These straightforward recommendations provide an important entry into a discussion of what schools and individual teachers can and should do in a world in which the Web, the Internet, and the computer itself increasingly dominate many aspects of learning and of culture. Whether they are using the Web, using computers to approach learning in new ways, or using other forms of technology such as graphing calculators, students often become much more deeply engaged in learning and more enthusiastic about school work when new forms of technology allow them to take charge of their education.

At a 2008 meeting of teachers and technology consultants (described in the last **Reading** for this chapter), teachers and former teachers talked of struggling with ways to use some of the new technology that no previous generation of teachers could have imagined. Reporting on the Silver Springs, Maryland, meeting, Kathleen Kennedy Manzo noted, "The teachers and technology consultants at an institute here almost make it look easy to integrate streaming video, social networking tools, and Internet resources into everyday classroom lessons." For those who embrace the technology, the opportunities seem endless. Even the omnipresent cell phones that students carry can be turned to educational purposes rather than being seen as only a problem or a distraction from the purpose of schooling.

The introduction of technology into a school can take time. A professional development facilitator from Pennsylvania advised teachers to "start small." Another former teacher turned technology trainer in Oregon said, "We want to show teachers how they can use technology to deliver standards-based lessons, and it doesn't have to take over their classroom." Being realistic, this teacher was saying, included understanding that for all the enthusiasm that computer technology can generate, teachers need to remember that their students still need to pass the standards-based examinations. This may not be the complete rethinking of schooling that Papert or the New Tech High School advocates want, but it is a blend that might work for many teachers.

Did you know?

According to an August 2009 report from Common Sense Media, 51% of teens check social networking sites more than once a day (22% do it more than 10 times a day), 28% have shared personal information on a social media site that they normally would not have shared in public, 39% have posted something they regretted, and 54% have joined an online community or a Facebook or MySpace group in support of a cause. Though many parents are worried about social media, according to the report, 75% of parents say the Internet helps their child's academic performance.[20]

Teachable Moment

Using Podcasting in the Classroom

A few years ago, the idea that students could write, create, and broadcast an audio or video program might have seemed far-fetched. Today, thanks to podcasting, this possibility is as close at hand as your classroom computer.

Podcasting is something of a catch-all phrase, and its meaning is often confused: you don't need an iPod to make one, hear one, or see one; and the focused audiences of most podcasts usually wouldn't qualify as *broad*casting. Ultimately, a podcast is a downloadable, shareable audio or video recording, and because anyone with the right equipment can now make a podcast, this relatively new media format can serve as a great tool for students to develop several valuable skills.

Teacher Allisyn Levy explains, "A classic mantra of teaching is that the best way to internalize something you've learned is to teach it to someone else. By recording students as a form of documenting their learning, I can give them an authentic audience with whom to share their knowledge."

Although students likely will get most excited about using the technology and recording themselves, the key learning component comes in their preparation and scripting of the podcast. Based on the subject matter, students can work independently on the script or can work in teams. There is no length constraint to a podcast, but you might want to put a time constraint on it, to challenge your students to give serious thought to the most important parts of the lesson that they want to share. Teams work well here, as students must discuss and ultimately agree on what they think is most important to include, how to sequence the information, and how to talk about each of the topics.

Once the script is developed, a new learning component takes place, as students must work together

Source: "Creating Classroom Podcasts," by Allisyn Levy, n.d., Teachers Network, http://www.teachersnetwork.org/NTNY/nychelp/technology/podcast.htm.

to record the podcast. (In terms of the technical components of recording a podcast, many different approaches and technologies are available. Your classroom computer may already have the necessary resources: If not, check with your technology support administrator to be sure you have all the tools you need.) Levy suggests, "Have students take turns being the 'audio engineer' and record themselves. This is a great way for them to hear their own mistakes or the quality of their voice, fluency, etc., and be self-motivated to improve."

After the podcasts are complete, you can play them for the class, put them on a Web site, burn a CD so that each student has a copy of the entire class's work, play them for parents, and so on. There are many options, all of which are more likely to engage and inspire students than a standard poster or book report.

QUESTIONS

- Have you listened to or watched a podcast? Made your own? What has been your experience with this technology? What benefits do you see in using it in the classroom?
- With which subjects or topics might podcasting work well as an educational tool? What benefits can you envision from incorporating podcasting with these lessons?

Teachable Moment

The Cell Phone: Turning It Into a Teaching Tool

What would happen if instead of silencing or confiscating cell phones in the classroom, teachers encouraged students to use them?

Hall Davidson, the director of the Discovery Educator Network, wants teachers to realize the potential power the instruments hold for enlivening lessons and engaging students in the content they are learning.

Most cell phones, Mr. Davidson points out, have a number of features that schools once paid thousands of dollars for as separate devices—camera, videorecorder, GPS, text messaging, music player. What's more, many students, even in low-income areas, own one.

At a weeklong workshop for a corps of teachers who have become leaders in using instructional technology, Mr. Davidson gave a glimpse of what might be coming to a classroom near you.

"Are we going to ignore a device that does all this stuff?" Mr. Davidson asked the group of about 60 teachers at a workshop held this summer at the Discovery Communications headquarters here.

Students, for example, can do first-person interviews with a cell phone, with audio or video that can be posted to school wikis, collaborative Web sites, to enhance their reports and projects. They can receive class assignments and start their research using Web features on their phones. And they can record themselves practicing musical instruments, or a foreign language, and send the recordings to their teachers.

Teachers can also make good use of cell phones, Mr. Davidson says. In just a few seconds, each student can take part in polls posted by the teacher that ask students' opinions on topics related to lessons or procedures. Videos outlining instructions and lessons for substitute teachers can be recorded and sent by cell phone. When language is a potential communication barrier between parents and teachers, messages can be translated into other languages before they are sent.

While many of the potential applications are not quite ready for prime time, Mr. Davidson thinks that within a year or so they will be, but only if educators see their potential and figure out how to integrate the technology well.

Source: Reprinted from "The Cellphone: Turning It Into a Teaching Tool," by Kathleen Kennedy Manzo, September 10, 2008, *Education Week*, 28(3), pp. 10–11.

Workshop participants expressed enthusiasm for the idea, but with reservations. Although use of cell phones is widespread, many students still do not have them. And those who do may have older models, with fewer features, or have limits on the number of calls and text messages they can send and receive.

Students also need to control impulses to interact with friends by phone during class. Moreover, school policies are often at odds with using the phones as part of instruction. "I think that with the use of a specific plan and guidelines for the use of cell phones, there is no way to ignore the possibility of their use in the classroom," Rachel Yurk, a sixth grade teacher in New Berlin, Wisconsin, who attended the workshop, said by e-mail. "What will be hard is getting these policies in place and anticipating all the ways that kids will use and even abuse them."

New York City, for example, has taken a hard line with its 2-year-old ban on cell phones. Two years ago, the district angered parents and students when it confiscated thousands of cell phones, which officials argued were distracting students from learning. But some teachers say it is time for schools to move into the 21st century. "Gone are the days when we told kids they could only use a pencil in math. Now, we use markers, glue sticks, computer applications, and many other items not deemed 'worthy' of math years ago," Howard J. Martin, an Austin, Texas, teacher and information-technology facilitator wrote in an e-mail. "Any tool that we train students to use responsibly should be considered if proper use shows some benefit to our kids."

QUESTIONS

- Do you believe that using a cell phone in class can be as helpful as the article implies?
- Are schools right, such as the case in New York City, in banning cell phones entirely?

That's Not Fair (Use)

Before the Internet, students who wanted to plagiarize a source at least had to type the material from the original source into their paper. Now, with copying and pasting, the Internet makes it ridiculously easy to claim others' work as one's own—and statistics suggest that students are not hesitating to plagiarize. According to a 2008 survey of teens by the Josephson Institute Center for Youth Ethics, "More than one in three (36 percent) said they used the Internet to plagiarize an assignment. In 2006 the figure was 33 percent."

Although more than a third of teens admitted to plagiarism using the Internet, even more are likely committing plagiarism without realizing it. George M. Bodner, who serves on the Ethics Committee of the American Chemical Society, suggests that "[c]onfusion about what constitutes plagiarism—not malicious intent—is the leading cause of plagiarism at the graduate school level." If graduate students conducting research are confused about what constitutes plagiarism and what is considered fair use, it is easy to see how not all middle or high school students would be clear on the matter.

To help set your students on the right path, it is important that you become educated about plagiarism and fair use. "Fair use" means that it is legal and ethical to use a direct quote from the Internet or another source, including a book, in something you claim as your own work. According to the U.S. Copyright Office, fair use is limited to the following: "quotation of excerpts in a review or criticism for purposes of illustration or comment; quotation of short passages in a scholarly or technical work, for illustration or clarification of the author's observations; use in a parody of some of the content of the work parodied; summary of an address or article, with brief quotations," and similar use. Even when the quotation is within the fair use guidelines, it is essential to give a reference through a footnote or other indication that these words were written by someone other than yourself.

Despite the laws in place, students may still not be clear—and it is certainly not safe to assume that they understand the rules and expectations regarding plagiarism. As a teacher, you have the opportunity not only to enforce the rules of plagiarism but also to use the discussion of plagiarism as way to challenge your students to consider issues of ethics and fairness. When a student's writing suddenly becomes "too good," there may be reason to suspect plagiarism has occurred. Although many college-level instructors use online services to check for plagiarism, this method is not as common for lower grades, which means that plagiarism is sometimes hard to catch, especially with so many sources of information available today. The key is to develop a sense of ethical responsibility within students so that they understand plagiarism is not acceptable.

The Internet offers numerous resources that you can use to become educated on this issue, and many conferences and lectures are dedicated to the topic as well. In addition, many schools are adopting honor codes and ethics policies to deal with these issues and to encourage ethical behavior; but these work only if students first understand them and then internalize them. By learning more and involving your students in the conversation, you can take a stand against plagiarism.

Sources: "The Ethics of American Youth—2008 summary," by Josephson Institute Center for Youth Ethics, http://charactercounts .org/programs/reportcard/; "Fair Use," U.S. Copyright Office, revised May 2009, http://www.copyright.gov/fls/fl102.html.

QUESTIONS

- Have you ever been uncertain about how or whether to cite a source, or if the way you paraphrased something was enough to avoid plagiarism? If so, how did you handle that situation? Would you handle it the same way now? Why or why not?
- Do you feel informed enough to discuss issues of plagiarism and fair use with your students? If not, what do you need to learn to be sufficiently informed and to feel comfortable talking about it?

Many teachers have adopted a positive stance toward the new technologies and believe that they will only improve what goes on in their classrooms. The 30 New Tech schools across the country, and others like them that have made new technologies the core of the school structure, may be unique, but they are hardly alone. Many examples can be found in which classrooms and curricula have been fundamentally rethought because of the technology that is now so widely available and popular with so many students.

Researchers Peter H. Kahn, Jr., and Batya Friedman describe the work of one teacher in an otherwise traditional high school who fundamentally transformed the education of a group of students by the use of educational computing practices. The changes moved the classroom "toward student participation, cooperation, and interest, and a school culture that is imbued with using computer technology to foster democratization."

Harvey, the teacher who Kahn and Friedman observed, supported the development of a student-led Computer Center User Society, which decided the policies and rules of that class's computer program. When the students were put in charge of their learning, everything else in the class changed—not only because they had greatly expanded access to computers but because they could decide how to use the computers to enhance their education. Arriving at the computer center on Sunday morning to get some work done, Harvey found that the students, each of whom had a key to the center, were already there and, indeed, he could not find a free terminal.

As Kahn and Friedman say, "Many people believe that for students to learn, teachers must instruct, by which it is meant that learning depends on a teacher who correctly sequences curriculum content, drills students on correct performance, corrects mistakes, and then tests for achievement." Of course, traditional schools may incorporate "a few sideways embraces of critical thinking and cognition. But if push comes to shove. . . . Back to basics." But the class they describe is fundamentally different.

Technology makes possible some pretty clear characteristics of this classroom. Kahn and Friedman sound like many others when they say,

> *Educational computing can be enhanced by software designs which shift more of the control over technology, and responsibility for learning, back on the student.* Interactive Physics II *(Baszucki, 1992), for example, allows the user to access a large number of physical components (springs, ropes, blocks, and disks) and properties (forces and gravity) to model and investigate two-dimensional physical systems. Through such construction kits, the user engages actively in a design, received immediate data by which to judge its success, and then is positioned to rework a better design, and thus continue the generative process.*

It is no wonder that many of today's students, who have grown up with computer games from their earliest years, find such learning opportunities not only more engaging

and exciting but also much more reflective of "real world" learning.[21]

In their 2005 study of the use of digital resources by science and mathematics teachers, Katherine Hanson and Bethany Carlson (researchers from the Education Development Center in Newton, Massachusetts) found overwhelmingly positive responses to technology. Some of the most enthusiastic comments were about the impact of Web resources on a teacher's own curriculum planning. Hanson and Carlson heard things like, "some of the techniques discussed on the web and the motion videos on some of the topics help in giving me insights into handling a particular topic with greater depth," and "I don't have to reinvent the wheel. I can stay up-to-date easily. No zillion trips to the library. . . . [I] can collaborate with colleagues who aren't in my area. . . . I can learn new topics easily without taking a class or going to a conference."

Teachers in the study found that the new technologies gave them significant new ways to connect with their students and to help their students learn much more. They reflect, "[The Web] allows my students to arrive at conclusions on their own as opposed to listening to me lecture," or "Web-based resources provide more universal access for multiple audiences. . . . [The Web] also presents information that addresses audiences that do not learn from conventional classroom instructional strategies by presenting 'the picture' of an idea in a dynamic way. This facilitates abstraction for many learners (of all ages)."

Hanson and Carlson found that neither age nor years of professional experience were significant variables. Of the 12 teachers who used the Internet the most, six had 15–37 years of teaching experience. It also seemed to make little difference whether teachers were from urban, suburban, or rural schools. If anything, teachers in schools that were more isolated in other ways had a greater enthusiasm for what the new technologies made possible. One teacher in a rural school in the South reported, "We are isolated, resource-shy. The kids have a **myopic** view of the world here. There's not a lot of impact from the outside. The Web opens

myopic Unable to see the full scope of things.

Teachable Moment
Stealing Ideas From Technology

Many people, educators included, dismiss video games as mindless entertainment, a waste of time, or the main reason kids don't play outside enough. Recently, some games, such as the *Grand Theft Auto* series, have come under attack for being something much worse—negative influences that send dangerous messages about crime, violence, and race.

Whether such games are any more or less of a bad influence on children than violent movies or music that glorifies sex and drugs will continue to be debated. But no amount of furor or outrage will decrease their popularity. In fact, such responses will probably just increase it. As a result, students in your classroom are likely to play these games and to have passionate opinions in the debate about them.

You may expect to hear arguments in defense of video games from game players (and game developers), but you might be surprised to learn that video games are gaining defenders in the halls of academia, too. In "Open-Ended Video Games: A Model for Developing Learning for the Interactive Age," Kurt Squire of the University of Wisconsin-Madison examines "how players make meanings around depictions and race in the game…and how game experiences become models-to-think-within players' lives."

Squire recounts interviews with several young players of *Grand Theft Auto: San Andreas* and finds that "different kids from different social groups" had quite different perspectives on the issues of "race, class, and violence in their game play."

The typical player of open-ended games like those in the *Grand Theft Auto* series will invest more than 100 hours to learn and master the game. Hoping that students will invest similar time outside of school to learn and master the subjects you are teaching them might sound like wishful thinking, but this passion for technology—whether video games, cell phones, iPods, or the Internet—can be an avenue for classroom learning. The key is to find ways to connect that passion to the curriculum.

As Squire points out, "A number of educators and critics have raised valid concerns that what players learn from games is not the properties of complex systems, but simple [tricks and techniques], such as always keep two spearmen in every city." However, as a teacher, you are in a position to leverage the knowledge students already have from games and other technologies into stronger learning experiences in the subjects you teach.

QUESTIONS

- What knowledge and experience have you gained through your personal use of technology that has complemented your classroom learning? How did you develop that knowledge? How did you make the connection?
- What is your own opinion of games like *Grand Theft Auto*? Do you agree with the critics? Whatever your views, can you imagine using these video games or others as a basis for classroom discussion, or are they best left outside of the school curriculum?

Source: "Open-Ended Video Games: A Model for Developing Learning for the Interactive Age," by Kurt Squire, in *The Ecology of Games: Connecting Youth, Games, and Learning*, edited by Katie Salen, 2008, The John D. and Catherine T. MacArthur Foundation Series on Digital Media and Learning, MIT Press, pp. 167–198.

A Web of Learning Tools

Recent years have seen an explosion in the number of learning tools available on the Internet. These are of a few of the ones that have become popular with teachers:[22]

- **http://www.gcast.com:** enables students to share their knowledge and creativity in a podcast, a downloadable radio show

- **http://www.shidonni.com:** lets students create their own characters and animate their own stories with them

- **http://www.mathplayground.com:** provides a place for elementary and middle school students to practice math skills and play logic games

- **http://play.ekoloko.com:** gives students a virtual world in which they can interact and work on solving problems together

- **http://www.sciencecomics.uwe.ac.uk:** offers comics, games, and teacher resources about science

doors for kids to see applications of what I teach—fuel cell, power plants, wastewater treatment. It's a resource for visual learners." An urban teacher reported, "The Web opens up the world to them, gives them a wealth of information." Finally, a suburban teacher commented on the benefits of technology: "You can bring such a variety of REAL information [that is] more engaging for students than made up examples in books."

Of course, not all teachers share the same enthusiasm for the impact of the Web on classrooms as those who spoke to Hanson and Carlson. Even among that group of teach-

ers, there were many complaints: lack of time, difficulty of accessing quality data, the need for much more sophisticated professional development, and so on. Nevertheless, these professionals were not about to turn their backs on the new technologies. On the contrary, they wanted more and better technology. One teacher was proud of what already existed in his school, "We have computers that hook up to the TV. . . . Kids often use Learn Star. It can be displayed on TV and they play against one another." But this teacher also wants much more: "I'm interested in my students using microscopes, capturing images, making measurements." The changes that these teachers describe represent significant steps away from traditional passivity and toward an active, learner-in-charge education that most educators see as the ideal.

In this chapter we have seen examples of teachers and students "owning" their education when technology is used well in schools—not just as a skill to be mastered but as a tool to connect with the extraordinary resources of the modern world. However, most proponents of an expanded use of computer technology in schools will admit that, at times, something important can be lost. If intensive use of computers can widen the resources available to students and their teachers, they can also narrow the focus of activities and miss a sense of order and mastery that some older curricula afforded.

As with many of the topics discussed in this book, a new or aspiring teacher needs to consider the impact of technology on the classroom from multiple angles. Straightforward questions can be asked: How will I use the new technology that is available to me and how will it affect my classroom? What can I learn from others that will help me be a better teacher? Will technology change schools and the work of teachers beyond recognition? Is this a good thing or a bad thing, or a little bit of both? Or is the truth somewhat closer to the arguments of Larry Cuban, who wonders if the current predictions about technology will suffer the same fate as Thomas Edison's 1922 prediction that the motion picture would supplant textbooks and teachers? Finally, do I want to support the changes that seem to be looming, or do I have a professional responsibility to oppose them if I think they are leading in the wrong direction?

Whatever you decide about these issues, it is as true of technology as it is of the impact of high-stakes testing or the arguments about how best to ensure that no child is left behind: Teachers are not mere recipients of the impact of these social forces on schools. Rather, they are shaping these social forces in their own classrooms, and they will play a major role in deciding if technology has a positive, negative, or largely insignificant impact on schools, students, and other teachers in the decades to come.

How Can I Make a Difference?

Our Techno World

We often embrace new technologies so quickly and so thoroughly that, soon after their introduction, we can't imagine our lives without them. Things we take for granted today—making a phone call from almost anywhere without searching for a pay phone or needing a quarter, sending a note or a photo anywhere in the world in an instant without an envelope or a stamp, carrying our entire music collection in our pocket, looking up almost any piece of information without an encyclopedia or even a library, and shopping in an endless mall of stores around the globe from the comfort of our home—would have sounded like crazy dreams just a few decades ago.

As a teacher who has experienced tectonic technological shifts within your own lifetime, you will have a perspective on the impact of current technologies that your students most likely lack. Think for a moment about the technology available today that did not exist when you were in elementary school (or, for that matter, the technology available today that did not exist when your *parents* were in elementary school), and you will appreciate the speed and power of change when it comes to technology.

By helping your students take a step back and think about the technologies they take for granted, you can broaden their outlook while examining a wide range of issues related to technology. A conversation about the circumstances that led to a technological breakthrough can help your students to understand how technology can change society and can spark a discussion about problem solving. An examination of the impact of a specific technology can lead to new understanding about cultural shifts and societal resistance to change. Challenging students to consider intriguing hypothetical scenarios (How would the Constitutional Congress of 1787 have been different if the framers had had cell phones? How would their lives be different today if the Internet didn't exist?) can challenge their assumptions about how they use technology, help them appreciate perspectives other than their own, and inspire creative thinking.

It is impossible to say what new technologies your students will see in their lifetimes, but no matter what technology emerges in the years to come, it will most definitely shape their world. That's why it is critical that they learn to appreciate the role of technology in their lives while they're in school. The more they understand about how and why technology is developed, as well as how and why it affects society and culture, the more prepared they will be to adapt to technological change and thrive on it—and even, perhaps, to help discover and harness new technologies themselves.

QUESTIONS

- What technology that did not exist when you were in elementary school has had the greatest impact on your life? How has it changed your life and your outlook on the world? Do you think students who have always known this technology are spoiled? Why or why not?

- Think of and describe an exercise that would help students reflect on how they use technology. What would be the objective of the exercise? How would you measure whether the exercise was effective?

REVIEW >>

- How is technology transforming today's schools—or at least some of them?

  The appearance of technology has caused teachers to rethink every aspect of what it means for teachers to teach and students to learn. Many educators, such as those involved in the New Tech schools and WebQuest, are embracing technology and implementing it in ways that will allow students to take charge of their own learning, follow their own interests, and be connected to a wider world of research, information, and people, even if other educators are ignoring the technological revolution that is taking place.

- Are we on the edge of a wonderful new era, or is there a downside to all this technology?

  Several conversations are happening regarding the impact of technology in schools. On one level, theorists like Seymour Papert and Neil Postman debate large-scale societal questions such as "Should we introduce computers and other related technology into our schools at all?" and "What will be the benefits, and costs, if we do or do not do so?" Theorists such as Larry Cuban believe that the effect of tech-

nology may not be as great as some would predict. In spite of the debates, technology is playing an increasing role in many schools today.

- What is the digital divide, and how does it affect my teaching?

  Not everyone has the physical access to technology or the skill or opportunity to take full advantage of it, especially those in lower-income areas. Also, boys have traditionally been more involved than girls in activities such as gaming and thus have had more experiences with technology. However, that is changing as boys and girls spend more time using all aspects of technology on a daily basis.

- How can I use technology to improve my teaching?

  Connections to a larger world of research and to a global conversation are at the fingertips of teachers and their students. Teachers who use this technology to create a place of inspired learning—rather than for old-fashioned drills—will be comfortable enough with the technology to test its limits. They will also be able to engage in an ongoing conversation with their students, who are developing their own technological expertise outside of school at a fast clip.

How Is Technology Transforming Today's Schools—Or at Least Some of Them?

From "NEW TECH HIGH: EDUCATION REFORM COMES TO INDIANA CLASSROOMS"

BY MATT L. OTTINGER

As this article from the Indianapolis Chamber of Commerce magazine indicates, the Indiana business community and at least some teachers and educational leaders appear to have great enthusiasm for this new approach, which not only uses technology in the classroom but also makes technology the center of the entire curriculum. Although many schools use technology for some lessons and projects, this article describes a school that is fundamentally changing every aspect of the curriculum, teacher work, and student learning.

When the powers-that-be in Rochester Community School Corporation (RCSC) decided to adopt the revolutionary, project-based New Tech High model, they were undoubtedly taking a risk. After all, implementing a new educational paradigm, retraining teachers and adopting new technology are initiatives that could cost several million dollars, according to RCSC Superintendent Debra Howe, Ph.D.

"Transforming our high school is an economic development issue," Howe says. "We're trying to retrofit a 1960s building for a 2007 world, so it's going to cost. . . . Change in general is difficult, but everyone needs to be looking out for what's best for our kids."

The building Howe described is Rochester High School, which now hosts over 600 students. The New Tech model was implemented this year in just the freshman class, with its 166 students, and will be progressively used in each freshman class for the next four years, at which point the entire building will be a New Tech High School.

The program, now in 30 schools in eight different states, is also being adopted in varying degrees this year at Arsenal Tech and Decatur Central high schools in Indianapolis. Implementation in additional school corporations is scheduled for the 2008–2009 academic year.

What's so new about New Tech?

New Tech High originated in Napa, California in 1996. The idea was initiated by businesspeople in the community who had visions of a workforce trained in the ways of the New Economy—employees properly prepared for a world of advanced technology and the practicality of functioning in a business environment. New Tech utilizes project-based, group learning to generate discussion and problem-solving skills in the classroom, and the technology allows students to put their creations to the test.

According to the New Tech Foundation's web site, "instead of plugging their knowledge into fill-in bubbles on Scantron sheets at finals time, students present tech-based projects about the subject at hand. You won't find simple book reports at New Tech High—you're likely to see a detailed web site with original graphics and links to related sites, or a beautifully designed PowerPoint presentation combining digital photography and original text."

New Tech also consists of more college level courses, which Howe describes as giving students an important, early connection to higher education that they haven't had in the past.

Teachers become students

With New Tech, there is little room for fear of change or a reactionary attitude from teachers. Rochester High School teacher Dan McCarthy, a 28-year classroom veteran, is welcoming the new program with open arms—although he's not naïve to the challenges it presents.

"Teachers have to come out of their comfort zones," notes McCarthy, an English teacher who has had to expand his knowledge of geography in order to teach his new Global Perspectives class. "In a traditional class, there's a lot of quiet and it's mostly the teacher talking. But it's not really productive in terms of engagement."

To become acquainted with the new model, all affected educators in Indiana had to job shadow teachers in California, so it was a learning experience for more than just students. However, McCarthy concedes that students have also had to modify their thinking to a large degree.

"I think it's been a challenge, especially for our most talented students, to adopt a new way of thinking," he says. "But I think it also benefits them the most. I'd always felt guilty about holding back above average students. Teaching to tests like the ISTEP always put a cap on those kids, but now there are no limits."

McCarthy explains the practicality of New Tech as being a critical component.

Source: "New Tech High: Education Reform Comes to Indiana Classrooms," Indiana Chamber of Commerce, November/December 2007, *BizVoice*, pp. 72–76.

Readings

"Students should never be asking why we're doing something in this program, because it's all real world scenarios," he offers. "There's a lot more rigor here, but it's more useful."

Group approach

According to McCarthy, some parents have been concerned that there is too much focus on group work. However, he noted that about 75% of the evaluations are on an individual basis, and students can even be fired from particular groups for not living up to their responsibilities. The challenge then becomes how to reintegrate those students into the system.

One project in McCarthy's class includes students drafting a real estate proposal

and presentation to people who might consider relocating to the Rochester area, highlighting its demographic makeup, history and even relevant issues currently facing its county government. Meanwhile, just down the hall, biology teacher Amy Blackburn has her students developing a movie presentation on biodiversity and the water cycle. One movie from each class will be shown on the local cable channel.

Before each project, students draft personal contracts outlining their goals and contributions, and are evaluated according to how they live up to those agreements. Projects are also outlined on rubrics, which provide detail of every objective of every assignment.

Nate Basham, a 15-year-old freshman at Rochester High, welcomes the challenge of the New Tech model and sees a definite benefit.

"I like the business concepts," he says. "We have to find a lot of information, develop our computer skills and learn to present in front of people. We have to give presentations all the time."

Basham also describes how the longer-term projects could present a time management crisis if a student lacks in preparation.

"We have to keep up with rubrics in every class, which can be hard," he contends. "But I know this will help me a lot more than just reading right out of a book. The multiple projects make it harder to prepare, but it will help me learn time management skills. It's all very doable if you just try."

It's that ongoing effort that educators hope will keep students engaged over the long haul. McCarthy has already seen a benefit in this regard.

"One problem I had before was kids sleeping in class," McCarthy quips. "I've always taken that as an insult and a sign of complete withdrawal. Now, nobody has their head down."

In with the new

The New Tech model was first introduced in Indiana in November 2005 at a conference titled "Indiana's Future: Economic Development and the High School Connection." At the Indianapolis conference, governors from around the nation, as well as leaders from the United Kingdom and China, convened to discuss 26 new change models for American high schools.

After New Tech was chosen for selected Indiana schools, plans were put in place to implement the system. Aiding in this transition has been Nancy Sutton, senior fellow for state leadership development for the University of Indianapolis' Center for Excellence in Leadership of Learning (CELL) program. Sutton is former director of the Small High Schools network in Colorado and had worked on projects with the Bill & Melinda Gates Foundation, which has donated millions of dollars to New Tech High School.

"Rochester had a support system in the community to put this in place and there's a lot of national support, so it's a great fit," Sutton reports. "Implementing this is all about change management. That's something businesses understand, but schools don't always."

Sutton explains the transition has been a byproduct of public universities, schools and businesses working together. One such business organization that has had a hand in the

New Tech revolution is TechPoint. Not only has the association offered its time and resources toward the New Tech conversion, the TechPoint Foundation invested $150,000 in July toward the new curriculum at Arsenal Tech.

At a "New Economy, New Rules" presentation in Indianapolis in September, TechPoint Foundation board chairman Mike Simmons discussed why the move is imperative to local schools.

"Our mission here is to bridge the digital divide," he told the assembled audience. "In this form of project-based learning, the class looks more like a lab than a traditional classroom." Simmons also described the impression the students in Napa and Sacramento, California made on him when he traveled there for a New Tech site visit. "I was shocked at the professional maturity of the kids. I could see the pride they took in their classroom."

Simmons believes the true measure of success will not be as quantifiable as in the past, but will be gauged, at least in part, by enthusiasm.

"Instead of worrying about ISTEP scores going up a few points, a key indicator will be getting kids to want to go to school," he surmises. "In California, attendance and graduation rates have significantly increased."

Business at hand

At the heart of the matter lies New Tech's perceived ability to enhance the business community by producing a more skilled and dynamic workforce. According to the Rochester school board, that was paramount in the decision to choose New Tech.

"We listened to what the Rochester area business community needed as characteristics in employees," says Donald Meyer, president of the Rochester Community School Corporation board. "Those needs turned out to be qualities and life skills that would assist students in school and in the decades following."

Perhaps it's those qualities that have motivated many Rochester businesses to partner with the school system and become actively involved in the paradigm shift.

"It is true that a whole lot of kids are already familiar with technology, but New Tech will expose more kids, to better technology, who otherwise wouldn't have access to it," details Alan Terrell, president of Rochester Telephone Company, Inc. "However, I think there's a good chance that collaborative problem solving will be more valuable than the technology involved. The abilities to communicate effectively, problem solve, and deal with conflict resolution are most important in business because that's exactly what takes place every day."

Terrell explains that while his company has not had difficulty finding qualified staff since he has few vacant positions and the jobs are usually higher paying than the average, an uneducated workforce has been a concern in Rochester in the past.

The Rochester school corporation has partnered with state colleges and local businesses in efforts to develop connections through student internships, job shadowing, and by raising money in the community. Howe describes her hope to raise $30,000 within the local community as a means to demonstrate local support when applying for grants.

These partnerships and exposure to businesses will likely prove critical, since the workforce in the Rochester area has shown a need for improved preparation. According to the 2000 census, 32% of 19 to 24-year-olds in Fulton County did not have a high school diploma, and only 4% had bachelor's degrees or higher.

At the September presentation, David Shane, president and CEO of LDI Ltd. in Indianapolis and a former senior advisor to Gov. Mitch Daniels on education issues, offered that New Tech will act as a preventative measure against perpetuating antiquated educational strategies as the business world evolves.

"The world still seeks capital, and technology is a changing world," he said. "There's a saying that if your job can be subjected to an algorithm, it probably will be in the near future."

Shane stated that nine out of 10 jobs disappear because of technology.

"What do we do with all the people who lose their jobs to machines?" he asked. "We have to teach people to run those machines."

Perhaps it will ultimately be the collective educational machine in Indiana that benefits most from this new model. Or maybe it won't live up to the billing, eventually prompting educators to revert back to a more traditional, rigid style of teaching in the future.

But if New Tech works as Howe, the Rochester school board, and the entire community hope, and it eventually permeates Indiana's instructional landscape, one wonders if tie-dye shirts, fine wine and Reggie Miller may have to settle on becoming the next-best gifts California has ever introduced to the Hoosier state.

QUESTIONS

1. Would you like to teach at a New Tech High School? Why or why not?

2. Do you think you would have done better or worse in high school if you had attended a New Tech High? How would you have liked the emphasis on group work? The focus on projects?

3. Can you think of some things that would be lost for students or teachers in the New Tech model?

4. Can you think of some things that would be gained for students or teachers in the New Tech model?

From "MEET BERNIE DODGE—THE FRANK LLOYD WRIGHT OF LEARNING ENVIRONMENTS!"

BY LINDA STARR

Bernie Dodge, a professor at San Diego State University, has become a national leader—some say a kind of guru—for the use of technology in school classrooms. His signature approach to educational technology, WebQuest, can be researched further at webquest.org.

Why were WebQuests developed? Why should teachers use them? What does the future hold for educational technology? WebQuest creator Bernie Dodge answers those questions and more.

Bernie Dodge, a professor of educational technology at San Diego State University, has been cited by eSchool News as one of the nation's top 30 educational technology innovators. Probably best known as the creator of the WebQuest model for technology integration, Dodge is also the author of a number of educational software packages for children and technology tools for educators.

This week, Dodge shares with *Education World* readers his thoughts about WebQuests—and about the future of educational technology.

Education World: What drew you to the field of educational technology—at a time when it wasn't even a field yet?

Bernie Dodge: Hey. . . My hair has more salt than pepper, but I'm not *that* old! Ed Tech as a field has been around in some form since the 1960s—or even earlier. I was drawn to it because it seemed like a perfect blend of my backgrounds in engineering and teaching. My first job after teaching math in the Peace Corps was at my alma mater, Worcester Polytechnic Institute, helping faculty develop innovative off-campus learning projects. As part of that experience, I thought about getting into educational television production. I liked the idea of being both planful and creative about helping people learn. That drew me to the instructional technology doctoral program at Syracuse University. I dropped my Sesame Street career goal quickly when I saw the bigger picture of becoming an architect of learning environments, and that led directly to my job on the faculty at San Diego State University.

EW: Would you describe briefly how and why you developed the WebQuest model? Did you start with a goal? a need? an inspiration?

Dodge: It started with a course I was teaching for second-semester student teachers. I wanted them to learn about an educational simulation called Archaeotype, but I didn't have a copy of the software or the means to show it. So instead, I put together an experience in which they worked in groups attacking a pile of different information sources about Archaeotype that I had lined up: a few pages of an evaluation report on the project, a few Web sites that described the software and the constructivist philosophy behind it, a virtual chat with one of the developers in New York, and a room-based videoconference with a teacher who had tested the program. The task was to divvy up these sources, integrate the information, and decide whether, and how, the Archaeotype program could be used at the inner-city school at which they were student teaching.

EW: Was the lesson successful?

Dodge: It was great! Having done my part ahead of time by organizing the resources, I had to speak very little during the two hours they worked on it. I enjoyed walking around and helping where necessary and listening to the buzz of conversations as students pooled their notes and tried to come to a decision. The things they were talking about were much deeper and more multifaceted than I had ever heard from them. That evening I realized that this was a different way to teach—and that I loved it!

EW: How long did it take you to develop the WebQuest format?

Dodge: A few weeks later—pretty much all in one sitting—I put together a template, set up in the same way I had done the Archaeotype lesson: introduce the situation, list some information resources, give them a task that required grappling with the information, lay out the steps on what to do with the information, and then bring it to a conclusion. I used a search engine to look around for various names to give this way of teaching and soon settled on "WebQuest." At that time (February 1995), there were no pages with that word to be found. My students used my template to create their own interdisciplinary lessons. Soon after, Tom March used the structure to develop Searching for China, as part of his work for Pacific Bell's Education First initiative. I wrote "Some Thoughts About WebQuests", an article for a distance education newsletter, and suddenly the idea began to catch on. That is how it all began.

EW: In the Overview section of The WebQuest Page, you define a WebQuest as "an inquiry-oriented activity in which some or all of the information that learners interact with comes from resources on the Internet." Based on that definition, can't many other online activities, including Treasure Hunts and Subject Samplers, also be classified as WebQuests?

Dodge: I have to say that I'm not a big fan of Treasure Hunts or Subject Samplers, because sometimes I put myself in the shoes of some cantankerous school board member peeking into a lab and seeing what goes on there. It isn't easy to justify the expense of all that hardware, training, and infrastructure when most of what the kids are doing is merely reading pages on a screen and answering low-level questions about them.

EW: What elements or features do you see as distinguishing WebQuests from other Web-based activities?

Dodge: The key idea that distinguishes WebQuests from other Web-based experiences is this: A WebQuest is built around an engaging and doable task that elicits higher order thinking of some kind. It's about *doing* something with information. The thinking can be creative or critical, and involve problem solving, judgment, analysis, or synthesis. The task has to be more than simply answering questions or regurgitating what's on the screen. Ideally, the task is a scaled down version of something that adults do on the job, outside school walls.

EW: It's been said that teachers will integrate technology into the curriculum only if they can see how it will benefit themselves and their students. How do WebQuests benefit students?

Dodge: There are lots of worthwhile things to do with the Web in schools, and WebQuests are just one possibility. WebQuests lend themselves particularly well to topics that require higher-level thinking and tasks with many possible end results. Other forms of interactive lessons are applicable to other parts of the curriculum. The benefit to using WebQuests, once you have identified the right place to try one, is that it puts more responsibility on the learners

themselves. That's a key benefit to the learners, because ideally they'll be getting some scaffolded practice at making sense of new information, parsing data that comes from something other than a textbook, accommodating the opinions of others, and organizing themselves and each other to produce something to be proud of.

EW: How do WebQuests benefit teachers?

Dodge: All teachers want to see that kind of student growth, so the benefit to them is seeing the center of gravity of the room move to where the kids are. If you've done the work of preparing a good WebQuest ahead of time (or selecting one made by someone else), you have a more gratifying day, by working with individuals and small groups as a coach rather than having to keep all those eyes on you as the only source of data in the room. Of course, as with all constructivist teaching, there may well be a mismatch between what's learned in a WebQuest and what's measured on standardized tests. Talented teachers are finding ways to hit both targets—but it's not easy.

EW: What knowledge and/or skills does a teacher need to create a WebQuest?

Dodge: Several things are needed: some technical, some pedagogical. First, teachers need to be able to create Web pages, which is a useful skill to have anyway—and one that gets easier every year. Second, teachers need to know where to find things on the Web, so getting deeply familiar with a good search engine like AltaVista or Google is a must. The rest has more to do with being a good teacher. Crafting an engaging assignment is something seasoned

teachers can do in their sleep, and it's a critical part of designing a successful WebQuest. Finding a task that forces thinking about content is at the heart of the WebQuest. Without that, it's just another Web page. Finally, even though roles are not absolutely essential in a WebQuest, I find that it helps if teachers have more than superficial knowledge about cooperative learning strategies. Creating situations that force students to depend on one another is one of those things that distinguish great WebQuests from merely good ones.

EW: Is there a tool available to help teachers evaluate the WebQuests they create or use or to help administrators and parents evaluate the WebQuests students are involved in?

Dodge: Rubrics are great for evaluating complex performances, and creating a WebQuest is certainly one of those. With the help of some excellent staff developers at San Diego Unified School District, I've put together "A Rubric for Evaluating WebQuests". It allows teachers to assign a score to a given WebQuest and provides specific, formative feedback for the designer.

EW: What are your favorite WebQuests? What elements or features make them especially worthwhile and enjoyable?

Dodge: My list of favorites changes all the time. Let me focus on a few that are both exemplary and not overwhelming to teachers thinking about getting into WebQuest design.

At conferences I always show Cynthia Matzat's Radio Days because it's so elegantly simple. It draws kids into the 1930s and '40s by having them create a radio play complete with sound effects and ads. It makes great use of the Web by making all those old sound clips instantly available and provides the right balance of structure and freedom so that every team's production will be unique. Cynthia recently told me that the plays created by the kids are actually broadcast on their local radio station.

Another one I like is Journey Into the Unknown: A WebQuest on the Lewis and Clark Expedition, designed by Missy Lanza, Samantha Levin, and Molly Decker, students at the University of Richmond. It draws kids into learning about Lewis and Clark by giving them the task of creating a board game about it. That is the kind of task that students will see as an engaging challenge, yet doing it well requires mastering the facts and structure of the story.

Finally, any list of my favorites has to include Hello Dolly, by Keith Nuthall. Keith steeps his students in several conflicting viewpoints on the topic of cloning and guides them to a discussion (and, ideally, a consensus) on what our government's policy should be about regulating cloning. I like this one because it brings into the classroom an issue that adults are grappling with right now. The experience of seeing the complexity of the issue and honoring the strongly expressed views of classmates seems like terrific practice for tomorrow's voters.

EW: What kinds of Web-based learning activities do you see teachers using in the future?

Dodge: Even though going wireless is just the next natural step in the evolution of computers, it has the potential for making a radical difference in the way we teach. Imagine having a number of flat pads with touchscreens no bigger than a standard notepad scattered around the classroom. At first, the devices will need a stylus for input, but in two years, they will start to be voice activated.

EW: How will those devices affect teaching?

Dodge: When such devices are common, teachers can bring the Web (and thus the world) to where the kids are, rather than forcing them to move to a desktop computer or a lab.

It will allow educators to take better advantage of teachable moments. When a question comes up in class discussion, the teacher can deputize a student to look it up and bring back the answer while the topic is still in play. Teachers can integrate the Web with other media more seamlessly and put learners together around tables, rather than letting the computer dictate how groups are arranged. Once a few of these things get into the hands of creative teachers, we are going to see a lot of new teaching ideas bloom.

EW: Do you see a time when Web-based learning will replace text-based learning?

Dodge: There will always be paper-based books, but I think at some point in this decade it will make economic sense to distribute textbooks in purely digital form. Once there's a light, durable, wireless appliance that's cheap enough, schools will be able to assemble the best parts of what each publisher has to offer and download whatever parts are needed, as they are needed. That means that the information will probably be much more up-to-date and supplemented by access to human tutors and a community of other learners. That all takes money, of course, so let's hope that the economy continues to perk along nicely and that taxpayers see the value of putting more resources into schools.

QUESTIONS

1. Dodge describes his enjoyment at "walking around and helping where necessary and listening to the buzz of conversation. . . ." Is this what you would consider teaching? Would you want to teach the way Dodge describes?

2. As a teacher, would you want to use WebQuest in your classroom? Do you think you have the skill to do so now?

3. What do you think of Dodge's critique of "Treasure Hunts" or technology that is used merely to help kids in "reading pages on a screen and answering low-level questions about them"? What does Dodge's answer say about the many different ways that technology can be used in a classroom?

4. What would those concerned about the digital divide or critics like Postman want to ask Dodge in a similar interview? Can you imagine how Dodge would respond?

How Can I Use Technology to Improve My Teaching?

From "NETWORKING TEACHERS COAXING COLLEAGUES TO USE TECHNOLOGY"

BY KATHLEEN KENNEDY MANZO

Education Week is the premier national newspaper in the United States for those who want to follow current trends in K–12 education. Covering everything from the impact of state and national elections on schools to the impact of the latest hurricane or the latest research or, in this case, the latest gathering of teachers, *Ed Week* is the source many education professionals depend on to keep them up to date.

The teachers and technology consultants at an institute here almost make it look easy to integrate streaming video, social-networking tools, and Internet resources into everyday classroom lessons.

Like the digital haiku poems students can create using a single image, a music clip, and some simple text. Or the interactive map of a Civil War battlefield with links to historical photos and accounts of events at the site. Then there are the cellphone applications for conducting instant classroom polls or communicating with students about assignments.

"We want to show teachers how they can use technology to deliver standards-based lessons, and it doesn't have to take over their classroom," said Jennifer Gingerich, a former teacher who demonstrated how moviemaking applications can be used to bolster language arts, social studies, and science lessons.

For Ms. Gingerich, a technology trainer in Oregon, and many of the educators attending the Discovery Educator Network institute this summer, letting teachers see how technology tools can be used to generate practical activities for students can win over even reluctant colleagues and spark them to update their instruction.

"On my own, it was very difficult getting started using technology in my classroom, but when I started reaching out to other people, it wasn't so overwhelming," said Heather Sullivan, a teacher and technology facilitator at Manalapan High School in Freehold, N.J. "If you can convince teachers to let you show them a few strategies, and they see that it is doable and can be fun, you start to win them over."

She and other educators are doing just that in live sessions held around the country, in hundreds of webinars and videoconferences, on blogs and social-networking sites, and even in virtual meetings in Second Life, a parallel universe online.

As a leader of the New Jersey network, Ms. Sullivan can offer guidance and resources to teachers in her district and throughout her state, as well as stay up to date on technology-based teaching strategies through participation on the Discovery Educator Network's national leadership council.

The network, called DEN, was organized by Discovery Education, a division of the media company Discovery Communications. DEN aims to expand the use of instructional technology through professional development for teachers. It offers regular live and online conferences—hundreds of webinars, blogs, meetings, and workshops, all of which help explain and show how various devices and applications work and ways to adapt them to the curriculum.

In the Second Life version of the network, an Internet-based virtual meeting, teachers can attend weekly workshops, hear expert speakers, view software demonstrations,

Source: "Networking Teachers Coaxing Colleagues To Use Technology," by Kathleen Kennedy Manzo, September 10, 2008, *Education Week*, 28(3), pp. 10–11.

or have impromptu discussions about instruction, all via their personalized digital characters, or avatars.

Twenty state affiliates hold their own professional development sessions, both online and live, and share resources on their DEN Web pages.

The national network helps Discovery Education provide support to schools and districts that buy its products and services. Although membership in DEN is free to any teacher, more resources are available to customers, who spend $1,500 to $2,000 a year or more for the rights to download streaming video—video accessed through the Web—from Discovery's archives of some 80,000 clips. But while many of the workshops and webinars might be viewed as promotional—such as those that offer product demonstrations—a number of them address broad or targeted issues related to teaching with technology.

One webinar last May, for example, presented tips for producing podcasts. Other such online seminars demonstrated moviemaking techniques, test-prep strategies, and a technology primer for teachers. Most of the webinars attract fewer than 100 participants, according to Discovery Education officials, but one featuring the producer of Planet Earth, a film series by Discovery Communications, drew more than 1,200 viewers.

Many of the webinars, as well as state-level events, are generated by network members and not related specifically to Discovery products. Twenty state councils were founded by teachers who joined the national network, and their members generally plan and run their own events and Web pages.

All the training programs are designed with academic standards and curriculum requirements for related subjects in mind, according to Scott Kinney, who manages professional-development programs for Discovery Education.

"We don't want [our product] to be this thing over in a corner that's nice to have but doesn't get used effectively," said Mr. Kinney, a former school administrator. "We want to be an integral part of teaching and learning. So we work a lot on content and on how to build capacity and support implementation."

Unleashing Passion

That's where teachers like Jennifer Dorman come in. Ms. Dorman, like some two dozen other educators here, has been invited to professional-development sessions by Discovery Education because of her skill at demystifying educational technology for her peers in and beyond Pennsylvania's Central Bucks school district. She has become an expert on social-networking outlets, or online groups of people with personal or professional connections, which she uses to foster relationships among educators throughout the country and abroad.

"Technology allows you to connect with teachers all over the world," she told participants at the institute. "Many teachers are interested in building a professional network, but they just don't know where to go. There are all these ways to find people you are compatible with and can help you with your teaching challenges."

Ms. Dorman does just that for hundreds of teachers through her blog and a wiki space she uses to share Web resources, lesson ideas, and online workshops, as well as general technology tips.

"We have a user group that's very passionate about the product," said Mr. Kinney. "But we want to bring everybody up [to a higher level of technology usage]. So we try to find one or two passionate teachers in each school. We then support the heck out of those teachers, because when they stand up in front of their colleagues and share what they've learned, it's that much more powerful."

It is often those teachers who have the kind of advice their colleagues can use right away, and the best understanding of local curricular and policy issues that might help or hinder technology use.

For teachers in the Central Bucks district, where Ms. Dorman is a professional-development facilitator, a new technology-integration plan has helped boost demand for her kind of assistance. This past summer, the 20,000-student district offered several hundred workshops on specific technology topics, or featuring technology-based instructional approaches in various subject areas.

But Ms. Dorman's advice for teachers is to start small.

She points them to a few simple tools, like wikis, YouTube, or RSS aggregators—which provide news updates from Web sites—and helps teachers weave them into class lessons.

Simple is often the message that Ms. Gingerich, the technology trainer, also has for the Oregon teachers she works with.

For her filmmaking demonstration, she points to free applications she got off the Internet, such as Photo Story or Movie Maker. She suggests teachers plan the lesson around a curricular goal and teach technical skills—such as selecting and loading photos, creating titles or text, incorporating sound, and editing the film—in quick, separate lessons.

"You can't give up three months of the curriculum to make a movie. I use four classes, and the movie is finished," Ms. Gingerich said. "It's a research and writing activity, not a technology activity."

It was advice like that that drew Teryl Magee into DEN a few years ago. When she found out her district near Knoxville, Tenn., subscribed to Discovery's streaming-video program, she started participating in the online and live workshops to learn how to use the resources in her 4th grade classroom. She now organizes state-level DEN events that introduce teachers to computer-based instructional materials. She also contributed to the DEN Earth and Space Virtual Project, a six-week webinar series on lessons related to planets and space missions.

"Fortunately or unfortunately, the [state and district academic] standards have to take center stage in my teaching," Ms. Magee said. "But the technology gives you a level of creativity, and it keeps [the students] engaged."

QUESTIONS

1. The technology advocates described here take a much more step-by-step approach to introducing technology to classrooms than New Tech High, WebQuest, or Papert. Does this step-by-step approach make sense? Would it appeal to you?

2. As you read the article, who do you identify with: the passionate users, the teachers in the middle, or those who do not attend conferences like this at all because they reject using technology in their classrooms?

3. The teachers in this article are from every level—elementary, middle, and high school. Does technology work equally well at all levels of schooling?

9

PROFESSIONAL ISSUES

WHO WILL INFLUENCE MY CAREER?

Virtually every student in a teacher preparation program has spent at least 12 years in school—observing teachers closely. As Dan Lortie noted in his classic sociological study, *Schoolteacher*, "Teaching is unusual in that those who decide to enter it have had exceptional opportunity to observe members of the occupation at work; unlike most occupations today, the activities of teachers are not shielded from youngsters." In this way, teaching is quite different from almost any other profession where people may not feel that they know as much about what people actually *do* when they go to work. Almost everyone who has been a student believes they know what teachers do.

However, the true picture is much more complicated. Although some parts of a teacher's work are visible to students, other aspects—such as the rules and regulations that affect teachers; the salaries they are paid; and their interactions with colleagues, conversations with parents, meetings with supervisors, and participation in a teacher union or other organizations—can be hidden almost completely from students.[1] In this chapter, we seek to gain a better understanding of the daily life of teachers, especially those aspects that are not readily visible to their students.

The **Readings** for this chapter focus on two of the chapter's main topics—teacher unions and the people who impact a teacher's workday, for better and for worse. "Why Teachers Should Organize" is from a speech given more than 100 years ago by Chicago teacher union leader Margaret Haley. In that speech, Haley laid out the rationale for having teacher unions and the importance of having organizations that give teachers a voice and protect their rights. A century later, Rochester, New York, teacher union president Adam Urbanski looks at the situation facing teacher unions in his article "TURNing Unions Around." He focuses on the changes unions need to make if they are to be a positive force in their second century of existence.

The second set of **Readings** describes some of the many personal relationships that are part of any teacher's work life. In a humorous story, "The Desecration of Studs Terkel: Fighting Censorship and Self-Censorship," Portland, Oregon, teacher Bill Bigelow describes how he

285

FOCUS >>

- Historically speaking: How has teacher work changed—for better or worse?
- How much do teachers get paid?
- What is tenure?
- Will I join a union?
- Why is professional development important?
- Who are the people who impact a teacher's workday?

got into trouble with one school administrator, how other teachers and union leaders supported him, and ultimately how he found a different school with a different administrator a much more appealing place to work. Finally, in an exchange of letters entitled "Two Teachers of Letters," Claire Fox, who was about to become a teacher, wrote to her favorite teacher, Margaret Treece Metzger, asking advice about the rewards and pitfalls of teaching and received a long, thoughtful response outlining the good and the bad and most of all the incredible rewards of a long career as a classroom teacher.

>> Historically Speaking: How Has Teacher Work Changed—For Better or Worse?

In 1904, Margaret Haley, a Chicago teacher, stood in front of the National Education Association (NEA) to give one of the major speeches at their annual meeting. Haley was not an especially welcome speaker. At the beginning of the twentieth century, the NEA was not the teacher-controlled organization that it is now. When Haley spoke, the NEA was dominated by the male elite of education—superintendents and college professors—who had little interest in hearing from an upstart woman from Chicago who had organized a union to challenge the policies and **prerogatives** of the male administrators and school board members who ran the Chicago schools.

prerogatives Powers or privileges associated with a certain rank in a profession.

In her speech, Haley did not mince words about what she thought needed to happen to make schools better places for teachers and their students. Haley said that teachers needed to organize teacher unions to take charge of their own profession: "Nowhere in the United States today does the public school, as a branch of the public service, receive from the public either the moral or financial sup-

port needed to enable it properly to perform its important function in the social organism." These conditions, Haley told the NEA, meant that teaching could not be effective until changes were made, and the key to making the necessary changes was the creation of new organizations—unions of teachers modeled on the nation's growing labor unions—that would challenge the current unfair conditions in which teachers worked. Haley described these unhappy conditions very specifically:

1. *"Greatly increased cost of living."* Haley wanted a raise for all teachers everywhere.
2. *"Insecurity of tenure of office and lack of provision for old age."* Haley wanted tenure that would provide job security to protect teachers from getting fired if their political party lost the next election. She also wanted a retirement pension system for teachers.
3. *"Overwork in overcrowded schoolrooms."* Haley wanted smaller class size. The norm in many cities like Chicago was fifty or sixty students in a class. Teachers needed time to engage with individual students and time to think.
4. *"And, lastly, lack of recognition of the teacher as an educator in the school system, due to the increased tendency toward 'factoryizing education,' making the teacher an automaton, a mere factory hand. . . ."* She was tired of being a cog in a wheel and tired of an educational system in which school

boards and high-level administrators, mostly men like the people in her audience, made all the decisions while the teachers, mostly women, were expected to carry out the decisions without ever thinking or using their own creativity or professional judgment in teaching.[2]

The problems Haley described were very real then, and many of these problems still exist today. Yet it is hard for today's teachers, for whom classes of 25 or 30 students can be a real handful, to imagine classes of 50 or 60 students. When Haley spoke a century ago, teachers had no job security. In rural areas (which was still most of the country), they had to conform to the whims of the local school board, which often set the hour by which they had to be home in the evening and listed the things they could, and could not, do in their free time. In the nation's big cities, teaching was usually a patronage job, given to a voter (or the voter's daughter) in return for political favors and was forever revocable if the favors did not continue or if a different political faction or party came to power.

In 1896, Amelia Allison described in the *Atlantic Monthly* the political reality teachers faced, reporting the words of an anonymous teacher who described what happened when her father found himself at odds with one of the political parties in her city: "As our district was likely to have a close contest, it was suggested that my father be 'whipped into line.' The only lash that he could be made to feel, they thought, was a threat to remove me." The threat was made but also rebuffed. Happily for this teacher, the party that made the threats lost the election, and she con-

Rules for Teachers in 1915

1. You will not marry during the term of your contract.
2. You are not to keep company with men.
3. You must be home between the hours of 8 pm and 6 am unless at a school function.
4. You may not loiter downtown in any of the ice cream stores.
5. You may not travel beyond the city limits unless you have permission of the chairman of the school board.
6. You may not ride in carriages or automobiles with any man except your father or brother.
7. You may not smoke cigarettes.
8. You may not dress in bright colors.
9. You may under no circumstances dye your hair.
10. You must wear at least 2 petticoats.
11. Your dresses may not be any shorter than 2 inches above the ankles.
12. To keep the classroom neat and clean you must sweep the floor once a day, scrub the floor with hot soapy water once a week, clean the blackboards once a day, and start the fire at 7 am to have the school warm by 8 am when the scholars arrive.

Source: New Hampshire Historical Society

tinued in her position. It was hardly the kind of job security to inspire confidence or a long-term commitment to the profession.[3]

Slowly these things did change, although none have changed completely. The points of Haley's speech sound all too familiar a century after it was given. But significant victories have been achieved in the intervening decades, and by almost any standard, teachers' work lives are better today.

Margaret Haley

>> How Much Do Teachers Get Paid?

An exhaustive study of teacher salaries conducted by the American Federation of Teachers in 2007 indicated that the average teacher's salary in the United States was $51,009. The average starting salary was $35,284. However, averages tell only part of the story. No one actually gets paid an "average" salary. Teacher salaries vary greatly depending on the state and district where one is employed. Part of the salary difference is due to cost-of-living differences around the nation. The median list price of a home in 2009 was $150,000 in El Paso, Texas, and $829,000 in San Francisco, California. As a result, San Francisco teachers need a much higher salary than El Paso teachers just to have a decent place to live. In addition to living costs, however, part of the difference in teacher salaries in different cities and regions is due to the success of teacher unions and associations in bargaining for higher salaries for their members. In 2007, the highest salaries were paid in California, with an average of $63,640,

Did you know?

Comparing teacher salaries by state is tricky business. In addition to the average salary, you have to consider cost of living, benefits, and your own lifestyle when deciding where to live and teach. Teachers in California are among the highest paid, but California is one of the most expensive places in the country to live. The average salary in South Dakota is the lowest, but that state ranks significantly higher than California in affordability. Some of the best-ranked states, in terms of cost of living compared to average salary, are Illinois, Delaware, and Georgia. The worst are Vermont, New Hampshire, and Hawaii.

Teachers' Salaries

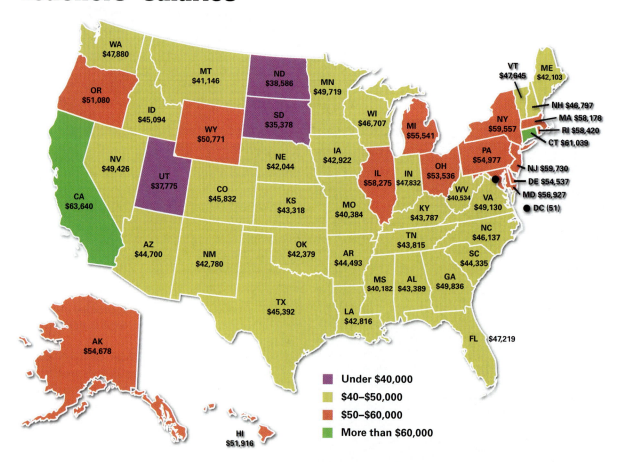

Source: American Federation of Teachers, "Survey and Analysis of Teacher Salary Trends 2005" (Washington, DC: American Federation of Teachers, AFL-CIO, 2007), p. 24.]

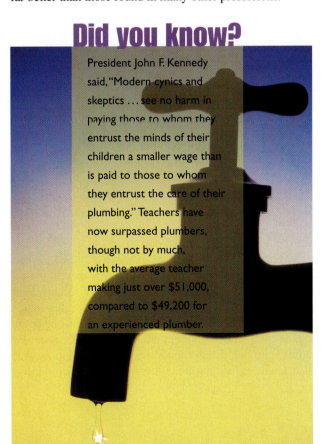
and the lowest in South Dakota, with a statewide average of $35,378. The starting salaries in these two states were $38,875 in California and $26,988 in South Dakota.

Another way to evaluate compensation is to compare salaries of teachers with those of other professionals. In 2005, accountants, for example, had a national average salary of $63,180, architects an average of $73,650, and computer software engineers in systems software an average of $90,780. Some occupations were ranked below the teacher average of $51,009, including medical and public health social workers ($46,320) and athletic trainers ($40,720). If salary is your major consideration, then teaching is clearly not the most desirable profession. However, teacher salaries are not the terrible national embarrassment that they were not all that long ago. The substantial benefits offered to teachers in terms of health care, pensions, and job security are often far better than those found in many other professions.

Average Teacher Pay Versus Comparable Professions*

*Comparable Professions with a bachelor's degree

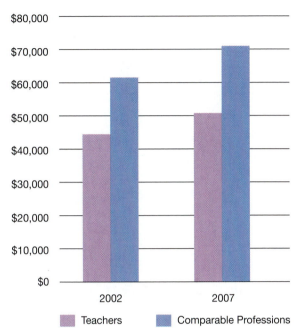

Teachers | Comparable Professions

Source: American Federation of Teachers, "Survey and Analysis of Teacher Salary Trends 2005" (Washington, DC: American Federation of Teachers, AFL-CIO, 2007), p. 20.]

Teachers, teacher unions, and many other people concerned about equity in education have spent the last century doing something about low and unfair teacher salaries. Soon after Haley spoke, women teachers in New York City began a campaign for "equal pay for equal work" for female and male teachers doing the same job. Up to this time, most school districts had two pay scales: one rate for women and a different, significantly higher rate for men holding the same positions. The female teachers rebelled, and by the 1920s in most major cities the old gender-based pay scales were abolished, though to this day men are more often promoted to the highest-paying administrative positions than women.

In addition to gender discrimination, teacher salaries were often unequal for teachers of different races. Well into the 1930s and 1940s, states and school districts that claimed to offer "*separate but equal*" schooling to White and Black students had two different pay scales for White and Back teachers. A White teacher with the same level of preparation and **seniority** could receive as much as 40 percent

> **seniority** A ranking method that often grants employees promotions and other privileges (and protects employees from layoffs) based on the amount of time an employee has been at the company.

Average Beginning Teacher Salaries by Region

Legend: Midwest, Northeast, South, West

Source: Survey and Analysis of Teacher Salary Trends 2007, American Federation of Teachers, 2008.

ground, being recognized as the official bargaining agents for teachers in many school districts in the 1960s and 1970s. Once they were recognized officially, teacher unions immediately began their own negotiations with school boards, demanding contracts that stipulated salaries (significantly higher salaries than in the past), schedules for raises, improved benefits, and better working conditions.

Another area of compensation that many people don't consider as they start their careers is what kind of financial security they will have once they leave the profession (that is, with a pension or retirement fund). As many people learned all too painfully in the economic downturn that started in 2008, retirement planning is important for everyone no matter what your age. Campaigns for retirement pensions for teachers began in the 1920s and expanded rapidly in the 1960s and 1970s. By now, teachers have better pension systems than do most professionals. Although the current economic climate is causing more people—teachers included—to work later in their careers than they had planned, teachers in most states (and each state's requirements are different) are typically eligible to receive full pension benefits after 30 or 35 years of service, regardless of age. Because these pension plans are funded through government retirement funds, unlike many private retirement plans (such as a company's 401k), they are more stable and offer a guaranteed source of retirement income.

>> What Is Tenure?

Tenure is the right of a teacher to keep his or her job subject to good behavior. It is a significant right that nearly all teachers have today. Tenure is usually awarded after a relatively short probationary period, often 3 years. (College professors, by contrast, usually have to wait 7 years before being considered for tenure.) This is a far cry from the days when teaching jobs were awarded, and could be lost, based on political favoritism. Today, discussions of teacher tenure have shifted from concerns about protection from political interference to an issue of ensuring continued excellence. Some observers worry that teachers have too much job security and that it is difficult to get rid of a teacher who has become ineffective. Others argue that tenure continues to protect teachers, as professionals, from the whims of administrators or rapidly shifting political currents. Although there are heated debates about the advantages and disadvantages of the kind of job security that tenure offers teachers, virtually no one is proposing

more than a Black teacher doing the same work. Among those who suffered from the two-tier salary schedule was Norma Marshall, a teacher in Baltimore, Maryland, and the mother of future U.S. Supreme Court Justice Thurgood Marshall. One of the younger Marshall's first cases as a civil rights lawyer for the NAACP was a 1937 challenge to Maryland's two-tier salary schedule. In a series of subsequent cases in the 1930s and 1940s, Marshall and the NAACP won a legal mandate for equal salaries for Black and White teachers a decade before their more direct assault on "separate but equal" that led to the *Brown* v. *Board of Education* decision in 1954.[5]

In addition to ending unequal salaries based on gender or race, teachers banded together to advocate for across-the-board raises for all teachers. In 1961, the federal government formally recognized the right of teachers to join unions. In the decade that followed, teacher unions gained

Teachable Moment

Unexpected Raise

In 1967, teachers in the United States were paid an average of $6,830 per year. Once inflation is controlled for, this salary is equal to $42,399 in 2007 dollars. In the four decades spanning 1967 and 2007, teacher salaries rose to $51,009. During this period, teachers gained $8,610 in buying power, or $215 per year. But some years were better than others. The worst periods came during the economic slowdowns of the 1970s and the very start of the 1980s. Two of the best periods came in the prosperous years immediately following the expansion of collective bargaining in the 1960s and in the recovery from the recession of the early 1980s. In each of these time periods, real salaries for teachers went up more than 2 percent annually.[6] Between 1984 and 1989, teachers saw a real increase in mean salary that averaged $1,039 per year. This is more in just 5 years than the total increase in the average teacher salary from 1995 to 2005.

In stark contrast to the preceding 10 years, the average teacher salary jumped from $47,602 in 2005 to $51,009 in 2007, or $3,407 (4.5%). This is three times more than the increase in teachers' pay during the 1995–2005 period and the largest single increase since 1991. The growth was even higher for beginning teachers, up 6.2% to an average of $35,284. After 3 years of lagging behind increases in inflation, teachers' salaries finally exceeded the inflation rate. (The news was not as positive for **charter school** teachers, whose annual average salary is $41,106—nearly $10,000 less than that for traditional public school teachers.)

When the American Federation of Teachers reported salary statistics in 2005, their conclusion was "teachers need a raise." In 2007, their conclusion was a cautious "and they got one." However, during this time period, the U.S. economy was at an all-time high, with the stock market hitting its highest point ever in October 2007. It has experienced volatile fluctuation since then, however, dropping to half of its peak just 14 months later. Since salaries—and job opportunities—in teaching have mimicked the ups and downs of the economy, teachers' salaries might once again experience little to no growth in the coming years.

charter school
Differentiated from public and private schools in that they are given greater autonomy from the rules and regulations of the school district but are not allowed to charge tuition. In exchange, "charters" present the school's goals and systems of accountability—if stated goals are not reached.

Source: "Survey and Analysis of Teacher Salary Trends 2005," by American Federation of Teachers, 2007, pp. 2–3, 13.

Increases in Teacher Pay

Source: Survey and Analysis of Teacher Salary Trends 2007, American Federation of Teachers, 2008.

QUESTIONS

- How important is salary to you in considering a career in teaching?
- Considering recent raises, are teachers now paid fairly? If not, what should they do about it? What arguments might convince a school board or a state legislature to provide more funds for teacher salaries?

a return to the job insecurity that teachers faced a century ago. Today, however, many people, including many teachers, are advocating tougher standards for awarding tenure as well as streamlined procedures for removing ineffective teachers. An increasing number of teachers are saying that they cannot afford to have their own reputations undermined by others who cannot or will not pull their own weight.

YouDecide

Does tenure allow underperforming teachers to keep their jobs?

>> Will I Join a Union?

Much has changed since Margaret Haley stood in front of the National Education Association in 1904 and called on teachers to get organized to fight for better salaries and improved working conditions. Schools are flexible institutions. They have changed over the years, sometimes for the better and sometimes for the worse. One of the most important forces for improving schools has been teachers. Sometimes working alone, sometimes in small informal groups, and sometimes in larger district and national asso-

ciations and unions, teachers have changed schools dramatically. They will continue to do so as a new generation takes its place within the profession.

Decades of work by Haley and thousands of other teachers resulted in the creation of unions and associations of teachers across the United States, especially in large cities, during the early years of the twentieth century. The National Education Association, which had greeted Haley with such limited enthusiasm in 1904, was transformed slowly from an organization led and controlled by administrators and college faculty into a teacher-led and teacher membership association that increasingly took on the identity of a union. At the same time, the American Federation of Teachers, which began with Haley's organizing efforts in Chicago, became a powerful union for teachers, especially teachers in some of the nation's largest cities that also had a strong history of labor union strength.

The NEA has 3.2 million members today, including teachers from the kindergarten to university levels, and it serves as the bargaining agent for teachers in 14,000 communities across the United States. The AFT has 1.3 million members, including K–12 teachers, **paraprofessionals**, and others working in schools and related fields. The two national unions no longer compete but instead work closely together toward what their leaders see as

> **paraprofessionals** In the education system, workers—usually teacher aides or assistant teachers—who do not hold the state-required teacher certification but work alongside and assist primary teachers.

common goals. Today, most teachers in the United States are union members, and teacher unions are a large and powerful force in the lives of teachers, in schools, and in local, state, and federal policy.[7]

As Adam Urbanski, himself the president of a teacher union, notes in one of the **Readings** for this chapter, there has been a danger that, as teacher unions become more and more like other industrial unions, focused on salaries, benefits, pensions, and work rules, they will lose sight of other professional concerns about the quality of schooling that also matter to their members. There is no question that teacher unions have done a great deal to improve the lives of teachers over the past half-century. As important as the hard-won union gains in salaries, health care, and pensions were, unions have also been the primary source of protection for teachers from unreasonable decisions by administrators and school boards. Nearly all teachers in the United States are protected today by tenure and union contracts, as none were a century ago. The protection offered by tenure and union contracts is still far from absolute, but it is much greater than that experienced by past generations of

Did you know?

In most school districts in the United States, teachers must join a teacher union when they accept a teaching job; thus, every teacher in the district is a union member by virtue of accepting a job there. These "closed shop" districts and states can have important advantages for teachers. When every teacher in the district is a member of the union, it can draw on a broad base of union dues to grow in strength and present a united front when fighting for benefits, not only for salaries but also for health and retirement benefits and rules about working conditions. On the other hand, a teacher who disagrees with the union or does not like the idea of being a union member cannot quit the union without quitting his or her job. In "open shop" districts and states, such as New Mexico, union membership must be voluntary. Twenty-two states, including Nevada and Texas, have enacted "right-to-work" laws, which guarantee employees the right to decide for themselves whether to join a union. These states still have teacher unions, sometimes strong ones, but they are limited in their reach and impact. Not surprisingly, teacher salaries and benefit packages are higher in "closed shop" states.

Source: "Right to Work States," National Right to Work Legal Defense Foundation, Inc., http://www.nrtw.org/rtws.htm.

What About Me?

Union Pros and Cons

What is the personal impact of joining a teacher's union? Place a check mark next to each item that makes a difference to you.

Pro		Con	
Unions try to negotiate the most beneficial contracts for all teachers in the district.		Negotiations between the school board and union can lead to deep tensions. Individual teachers cannot negotiate their own level of pay.	
Tenure offers a high level of job protection and due process rights if the administration seeks to fire you.		Tenure makes it difficult at times to discharge underperforming teachers.	
Unions provide professional networking services.		Many teachers do not want to become concerned with the politics associated with unions.	
Unions give teachers a national voice to argue for things such as better pay and working conditions.		Because of the large number of members, unions can become powerful political machines.	
Many unions offer liability insurance to their members, which may cover attorney fees, assault, damages, and personal injury.		Union members may not be able to shop for their own personal health insurance.	
Unions provide professional development seminars, conferences, and workshops.		Unions may resist education reform to protect jobs.	
Unions may offer discounts to their members on things such as travel, lodging, and entertainment.		Members must pay annual dues.	
Unions have won long term-benefits for teachers in terms of salary and job benefits.		Unions may no longer be necessary, and teachers are unlikely to lose the benefits they have won through unions.	
Unions have and continue to enhance the professional status of teachers.		It might seem "unprofessional" to join a union, and union membership might lower the professional status of teachers.	

How Can I Make a Difference?

Become an Advocate for Your Teaching

For a very shy second grader, as I was, Mrs. Grant could be a little frightening. This boisterous, full-of-energy teacher was nothing like the other teachers who taught a more "traditional" curriculum—the ones I was most comfortable with. For those teachers, I could stay in my seat, finish my work, get my A's, and go home. In Mrs. Grant's class, those kinds of days were the exceptions, not the norm.

Mrs. Grant wanted us to be informed consumers, so she erected an in-class grocery store where we learned to manage employees, select healthy food and stay within a budget, and pay (and make change) accurately. She wanted us to be activists, and we lobbied our state legislature to anoint the lady bug the state bug of Iowa, including a massive letter-writing campaign, development of a bill, hand-made buttons and bumper stickers, a trip to the state legislature, and a class visit from our state representative. We even made front-page news of the Des Moines Register!

She also wanted us to be caring, social, and collaborative people and continually had us pair up with other students, although never the same person. (I'll never forget the time she caught me pairing up with the same boy twice in a row. She definitely knew how to command your attention when you didn't follow the rules!) I'm sure to some of the parents, Mrs. Grant was a little "over the top." With her non-traditional approach to teaching (especially for 1972 standards), how could she prove to them that she was covering the basic material required for second grade? I'm sure that wasn't easy, and I wonder if that was even her intent. But for a shy 7-year-old, who ended up on the front page of the newspaper with her congressman, Mrs. Grant was exactly what we needed.

—Personal story

In today's era of accountability, it may not be as easy to design your lessons exactly the way you want. In some schools and school districts, teachers have little flexibility to teach material beyond what is prescribed by authorities. However, the situation could be the exact opposite in a school just down the street, where teachers might have lots of flexibility, especially if they can find ways to connect their own lessons to the state standards. (One can imagine, for example, that the students in the preceding story might do better than the average class of second graders on any test of mathematics or on social studies.)

When bringing new ideas into the classroom, make sure you have the support of everybody involved—students, coworkers, parents, and administrators. New ideas and ways of teaching can seem intimidating for some, but if you become proactive by explaining and sharing your style with the community, you are much more likely to have their support. Even if you don't have everyone's support, at least they won't be surprised.

Talk to parents early on and often. Send them letters explaining your classroom organization and why you are confident your style works in helping students learn what they need to know. Try to speak at community events, providing a glimpse into the classroom, and plan events or publications outside of the classroom. Invite administrators into the classroom and show them student work. Form idea exchanges with fellow teachers. Creating change takes time and energy, but with the right attitude and constant communication, you can provide your students with a more suitable learning experience. A longer list of advocacy ideas, specifically for English teachers but with ideas applicable for all disciplines, can be found at http://www.ncte.org/magazine/advocacyideas.

QUESTIONS

- Can you think of any times in your life when you were taught by a teacher in an innovative way? Does this experience now stand out to you as a special memory? How did your parents or guardians react when they heard about this approach?
- What happens when you believe you can teach material in a better way but your ideas are not welcomed by administrators or parents? Think about a plan of action you might design in such a situation.

teachers. The story of Bill Bigelow's experiences as a first-year teacher (in the **Readings**) offers one example of both the significance and the limits of this kind of protection.

Today, there are more arguments about teacher unions than about most other topics in education. Some observers argue that, although unions may once have served an essential purpose, today they are only a barrier to further progress in education reform. Proponents of these views see unions as protecting mediocre teachers and making it far too hard to dismiss incompetent ones. They see the sometimes-rigid work rules required by teacher union contracts as stifling innovation and creative leadership. They argue that an employer-employee relationship built on the model of factory work is inappropriate to today's service-oriented professionals.

On the other hand, many people want to protect teacher unions just as they are. After all, they argue, unions have forced teacher salaries to their current levels and the salaries are still too low and rising far too slowly. These union advocates say that much more needs to be done to bargain for quality pay for teachers. Although teachers have protections, they can still lose their jobs because of political views or philosophical differences with ever-changing administrative agendas. If the unions do not protect teachers, these advocates for traditional **unionism** argue, who will? And if teachers are not protected, who will want to enter the profession, and how many children will suffer because of the loss of good people?

> **unionism** Advocacy and support for unions.

A growing number of people seek a new way of viewing the place of teacher unions, and Adam Urbanski is among the most articulate of them. Urbanski argues that teacher unions in America "must be reformed." He is certainly not making this argument as an opponent of unions. On the contrary, Urbanski has spent most of his life as a union member and many years as the president of the teacher union in Rochester, New York. But he is also a realist who knows that "unless it is voices from within the teacher union movement who are driving the call for reforms, there is a great risk that the voices from outside would be viewed as hostile 'bashing.'" Although Urbanski can bargain with as much toughness as any union leader to protect salaries and other benefits, he can also—perhaps with special effectiveness because of his background—call for fundamental change in the role of teacher unions today. He wants to work closely with parents. He wants to see continual improvement in the quality of teaching and the standards for teachers, and he wants unions to take the lead in promoting excellence rather than protecting mediocrity. He wants, above all, to

see "better learning and higher achievement for America's children." He believes that unions must make this their top priority, even more important than their own appropriate self-interest in salaries and working conditions.

>> Why Is Professional Development Important?

Teachers, often working closely with administrators, parents, and community organizations as well as their own unions and in more informal gatherings, are addressing many of the problems that have long plagued the profession. In 2002, Dan Lortie looked at the changes in teachers' lives that had taken place since his book *Schoolteacher* was published in 1975. He saw two especially significant changes:

> **professional development** Lectures, group exercises, or other activities that provide skills and knowledge pertaining to the profession, for both career development and advancement.

- **Professional development**—activity focused on helping experienced as well as beginning teachers to strengthen their teaching capabilities—has had remarkable growth. Not long ago, school districts rejected plans to spend time and money on staff development, arguing that this was the responsibility of state agencies, and that it made little sense to invest in teachers who might move away. Today, we find an increasing focus on such undertakings at the local level.

- There is an increased emphasis on teachers analyzing their tasks and the choices they make in the course of their working day. "Reflective practice" describes the process in which teachers think longer and harder about what they do and work to guide their activities accordingly.

Teachers know they are never finished learning. However strong their initial preparation, there is always more to learn—about what to teach and how to teach.[8]

Teacher professional development has also gotten much better in most places. Teachers once viewed nearly all professional development days as a time to listen to an "expert" selected by the district who might have no idea of the day-to-day realities of a specific group of teachers. Today, professional development often consists of much higher level activity, often conducted by and among a specific group of teachers with topics and leaders selected by teachers. Teachers today spend much more time talking to each other, comparing "what

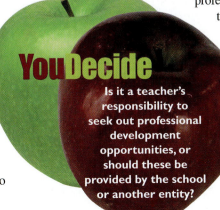

YouDecide

Is it a teacher's responsibility to seek out professional development opportunities, or should these be provided by the school or another entity?

works," and looking carefully at specific examples of student work to see how they might more effectively help students improve while also treating students more equitably. Teachers have sought increasingly to become what best-selling author Donald Schon calls a "reflective practitioner": someone who continually thinks about one's professional work, discusses it with fellow professionals, and uses that thinking and those conversations to improve practice—one's own and that of one's colleagues. In other words, teaching today is a much more intellectually rigorous and engaging profession than it has ever been.

>> Who Are the People Who Impact a Teacher's Workday?

In 2004 and 2005, a survey asked 800 American teachers, "What are the biggest challenges you face in your work?"

The researchers involved in the survey were careful to query a wide range of teachers and to talk with teachers in more prosperous schools as well as teachers from schools serving low-income children. The answers will probably not surprise those who are more familiar with what happens during a teacher's day. Almost a third of the teachers overall, and slightly more than that among the teachers in the low-income schools, listed "communicating with parents" as their most significant challenge. Interestingly, "maintaining order and discipline" and "preparing students for testing" were seen as the biggest challenges by only one-fifth or less of the teachers. Given that school administrators and school system structures are in many ways responsible for issues of resources and also for "needed guidance and support," one can conclude that teachers' relationships with parents and with those in authority in school districts are challenges, perhaps greater challenges than their dealing with students and certainly greater than dealing with their peers (other teachers).

As a teacher, you must find ways to relate to the many people who will hold administrative authority over you, as well as the many other people—perhaps parents, most of all—who can be not only your allies but also your most critical opponents. How will you interact with the various people who have authority in your professional life? When should you stand your ground, and when should you compromise? When is it best to go it alone, and when should you reach out? When and how can you make a wide range of alliances and build the friendships you need? These are essential questions for you to consider as you strive to make connections with the people inside and outside of the classroom who will impact your teaching.

FELLOW TEACHERS

Although the days of the one-room schoolhouse are long gone, many teachers still come to work, close their classroom doors, focus on their students, and then go home

Connections

The topics of maintaining order and discipline and preparing students for testing were explored in Chapter 7.

The Biggest Challenges Faced by Teachers				
	Elementary School	Secondary School	Schools With Less Than 50% Low-Income Students	Schools With 50% or More Low-Income Students
Base Number of Teachers: 800	501	270	362	422
Communicating with parents: 31%	31%	30%	24%	40%
Getting sufficient resources and materials: 22%	21%	24%	25%	19%
Maintaining order and discipline in the classroom: 20%	17%	23%	20%	20%
Preparing students for testing: 14%	16%	13%	17%	11%
Getting needed guidance and support: 9%	11%	7%	10%	8%
No answer: 3%	4%	3%	5%	2%

Source: *The MetLife Survey of the American Teacher,* by Dana Markow and Suzanne Martin, 2005, Harris Interactive, p. 8.

again. This isolation can give teachers a certain freedom. Indeed, some revel in the fact that "when you close your classroom door, no one really knows what you do." But the isolation can also be painful and ultimately self-defeating.

In her study of teacher work, Susan Moore Johnson found teachers split on the question of how isolated they were. Some teachers felt very isolated from colleagues, reporting that no one else in their school knew what or how they taught. One teacher commented, "I am isolated. I do what I want when I want to do it, and how I want to do it." A teacher of English language learners had given up on many aspects of the school, saying, "I tend to isolate myself. I was at a school that had a lot of problems with discipline. But I found that I could just have my own little world and control that." A high school social studies teacher generalized, "Teachers are isolated people. They don't know what others are doing. Things that work for them, they keep them year after year. You don't have time to sit down and discuss with each other from different areas. As small as this school basically is, I don't know all the people who are here."

Johnson reported that the majority of teachers she interviewed did not want such intense isolation. Many longed for more collaboration, including one who said, "I think that we could learn from each other. We really could." Another teacher was happy with the links with immediate colleagues in one department but noted that, "if there's isolation, it's from the rest of the building." Still, Johnson concluded that teachers agreed "virtually unanimously that the threat of isolation was ever present" but also that "the benefits of collegial interaction were many."

A QUESTION OF . . .

How does collaboration improve your curriculum?

"A teacher I worked with told me, 'One night at about 7 o'clock I was still working on a curriculum unit for *Sarah, Plain and Tall*, and I realized that all over the city other teachers were probably also developing lessons for the same book. It just didn't make sense.' And it doesn't. Establish a community of people who develop curriculum together. The work not only goes faster, but it's usually better because you have someone to talk through your ideas with."

—*Linda Christensen, former language arts coordinator for the Portland (Oregon) Public Schools; editor of the journal* Rethinking Schools; *and author of* Reading, Writing, and Rising Up: Teaching About Social Justice and the Power of the Written Word[10]

Today, many schools are moving to reduce the level of isolation and create more collegial working conditions. One suburban elementary teacher Johnson interviewed painted a very different picture than other teachers:

We're just not individuals coming to work. We work together for the kids; we work together as colleagues, too. If I have an idea, I can go to people and say, "I think this might work with what you're doing." We communicate as far as what we do in our classrooms. I get a lot of support from the teachers here.

Others reported similar arrangements from which they gained a great deal. Some found opportunities to team teach and one noted, "We really work together. All lesson plans are planned together so that we try to give all eighth graders the same education." Another junior high school teacher reported that the department was the place where teachers came together, noting, "We're in constant contact with each other. Everybody knows what everybody else is doing and gets ideas from each other." Another reported that her principal encouraged collaboration in which teachers not only shared lesson plans but "[w]e have a system where we can go into each other's classrooms—any classroom in the school up to grade four—and observe other teachers."

Although isolation can sometimes be appealing, as no one wants to have every move scrutinized, most educators conclude that it is a recipe for failure. As a teacher, especially a novice teacher, you need to have many mentors and to learn from, and also teach, other adults. One teacher Johnson interviewed remarked that "teaching's a lot more

Teachable Moment
Finding Support

A teacher's job isn't just performed in front of a classroom. Grading assignments, planning lessons, writing letters of reference, meeting with parents, and attending extracurricular events, such as sporting events or dances, take up a large portion of a teacher's working hours. The advent of technology has given teachers a new resource as they find ways to perform this work, as teacher unions and associations and school districts are encouraging teachers to share ideas and materials on the Internet. Using technology gives teachers innovative ideas that have been proven to work in a classroom setting, and it shortens the number of hours spent working outside of the classroom as teachers learn from each other.

One of the greatest strengths of the Internet is that it enables teachers to share lesson plans—and many Web sites provide this service for free. Teachers.net allows users to share lesson plans on their Web site, which currently has over 4,000 individual lesson and classroom ideas posted. Some Web sites cater to specific subjects, such as Mathforum.org, which offers math lesson plans. Among the many other resources offered through Web sites are worksheets, science experiments, and videos.

teachers.net℠

In addition, teachers interact and talk with other teachers all over the country in Web site forums organized specifically for teachers. Some of these include Teacherlingo.com and TheTeachersCorner.net. At these sites, teachers can share stories of both success and failure, ask for advice, and build a professional and social network.

QUESTIONS

- Can you think of other Web sites or outside resources that connect teachers and allow them to exchange ideas? Have you participated in any of these exchanges? (If not, try one.)
- How important is it for teachers to share thoughts and ideas with other teachers? Does this end up taking more time, or does it save time?

---

than just sitting in a classroom and teaching kids. . . . If you just do that you're going to be burned out real quick." Beyond survival, many of the teachers with whom she spoke made it clear that only through collaboration could teachers be a force for change in their schools:

If we get our act together, and we want something to happen, we can make it happen for the most part, within the confines of what a school will allow. If we choose to pick an issue, that issue has to be addressed. If there is no universal feeling towards it, then it doesn't get addressed.

Like other citizens, teachers are limited in what they can do alone. But no school or school leader can ignore a group of teachers who are clear, focused, and well organized. Not only will those teachers have a better

sense of support, but they will be more able to make the school a better place for themselves and their students.[9]

ADMINISTRATORS

The acclaimed author Frank McCourt begins his account of his years as a teacher in the New York City public schools with the words, "On the first day of my teaching career, I was almost fired for eating the sandwich of a high school boy." McCourt proceeds to tell the story of his very first class, which began with a small-scale fight in which one student threw his sandwich bag at another and a much larger fight was about to begin. He describes his first response:

I came from behind my desk and made the first sound of my teaching career:

"Hey." Four years of higher education at New York University and all I could think of was Hey.

But that was not enough to head off the incipient fight. Neither was McCourt's command to "[s]top throwing sandwiches," especially since the sandwich had already been thrown and laid there on the floor between the students. "Professors of education at New York University never lectured on how to handle flying-sandwich situations." But novice though he was, McCourt was also clear that "[t]hey had to recognize I was boss, that I was tough, that I'd take none of their shit." So McCourt decided to eat the sandwich and flipped the paper cover into the trash basket. The class cheered, and he had them. The dramatic move had succeeded. Except for one thing.

My students smiled till they saw the principal's face framed in the door window. Bushy black eyebrows halfway up his forehead shaped a question. He opened the door and beckoned me out. A word, Mr. McCourt?

The word, of course, was "I'm sure you understand, Mr. McCourt, it isn't seemly to have teachers eating their lunch at nine A.M. in their classrooms in the presence of these boys and girls." No asking about the situation. No hearing McCourt's early-morning triumph of classroom management. Rules were rules and administrators were there to enforce them. McCourt's career began with both a success with students and a failure with administrators. As you read McCourt's book *Teacher Man,* you sense that both events marked his career for the next 30 years.[11]

School administration today is complex, with an extraordinary range of superintendents, deputy superintendents, principals, vice principals, and specialized teachers all interacting with classroom teachers on a regular basis. These positions were created for important reasons: to allow teachers to spend their time focused on students instead of on other matters and to represent the diverse needs and aspirations of democratic communities that expect many different things from schools. Teachers would say this happens with varying success and not always due to the support or involvement of their administrators (and sometimes in spite of it).

Another teacher, Bill Bigelow, tells a similar story in the **Readings** for this chapter. During Bigelow's first year of teaching in Portland, Oregon, a parent had complained about a student assignment, and when the vice principal of the school looked at the assignment, he too found the work "negative" and perhaps obscene, even though Bigelow had assigned a reading from an official text in use in the school. As you read Bigelow's article you will see that, like McCourt, he got off with a warning and a compromise.

Bigelow also discusses a range of ways in which teachers can find support as well as censure. For Bigelow, the first support came from Thurston Ohman, his union representative, who assured him, "You haven't done anything wrong," and "If they try to come after you in some way, the union will back you 100%." Bigelow also reflects on

how rare the intrusions of people like his meddling vice principal really are. He notes that "in my experience, the intrusions of the Lloyd Dixons of the world are exceptions. . . . [W]e have an enormous amount of freedom." (Sometimes that isolation is not all a bad thing!) Even as Bigelow tells the story of his run-in with Lloyd Dixon, he reflects on other administrators who "were extraordinarily supportive and even enthusiastic about livelier, risk-taking teaching." He mentions Shirley Glick, who "offered nothing but encouragement" and notes that the reality of life as a teacher is that "[t]he Lloyd Dixons of the world exist, but so do the Shirley Glicks."

Finally, Bigelow reflects thoughtfully on what he might have done to reach out to the parent who first made the complaint and to other parents whom he came—too slowly he admits—to see as allies rather than as censors. A great deal has been written about the characteristics of effective schools that seem to stand out for their success with students, including students from different racial and ethnic backgrounds, genders, and economic status. Nearly all of this literature, known logically as "effective school literature," points to one variable above others in the recipe for success: strong, consistent, and inspired leadership. Thus, the principal who can sometimes be seen by teachers as the "evil administrator" may, in fact, be the key to the success of the whole school's approach to its students. Of course, this is not always the case. True tyrants are not strong and inspired and consistent leaders, and true leaders see a key part of their work as inspiring their team—the teachers and other educators who interact on a day-to-day basis with students. Teachers need to understand that teachers and administrators have different work lives, interact with different people, and may sometimes come into conflicts in which neither side should be seen automatically as right or wrong.[12]

In *The Good High School,* a series of case studies of the character and culture of effective high schools, Sara

PORTRAIT OF AN EDUCATOR

Deborah Meier

Born in 1931, Deborah Meier counts as her early teaching jobs kindergarten and Head Start positions in Chicago, Philadelphia, and New York. In 1985, she accepted an invitation to found a new school: Central Park East Secondary School in East Harlem. Under Meier's leadership, Central Park East Secondary School became a model in which both teachers and students have a meaningful voice in all aspects of the school. As Meier designed the school, her role as an administrator was drastically different from what she had experienced in other schools. Faculty decisions were generally made by consensus rather than by administrative order. Student work was evaluated by portfolios in which students selected and put their best work forward. Students also had a significant voice in decisions affecting the school. More than 90% of the students at Central Park East Secondary School went on to college, mostly to 4-year schools.

In 1997, Meier moved to Boston and brought the same philosophy of democratic education, including active teacher, student, and community participation, to the Mission Hill School, a public K–8 school that she founded and led (until 2005) in the low-income Roxbury community of Boston.

A school administrator, Meier was also an early and active union member and supporter of the union movement in education and of the democracy within unions. In a recent interview, Meier reiterated her far-reaching critique of the current focus on standards, testing, and accountability that is supported strongly by the U.S. Department of Education under President Barack Obama, as it was under President George W. Bush. For her, these top-down measures undermine the fundamental fabric of democracy on which public schools rest and that they were originally designed to support. Meier gave voice to a different image of education, saying,

> I am in favor of reinvigorating the democratic underpinnings of our nation—which include the ideal of local control, respect and trust for ordinary citizens, and on and on—rather than seeking to "race to the top" by cutting schools off from their roots—their community. If any institution needed to remain close to those who are most affected, it is our public schools, because of their subtle influence on the mindset of future citizens. Yet we act as if this were not true.

When asked if, in spite of the current popularity of the standards and accountability, Meier is still an optimist, she responded,

> Most days I am! Teaching has reinforced my belief in human possibility. I have rarely met a 5-year-old whose intellectual capacity did not astound me. We need schools that challenge this curiosity for all our children and for the adults who keep company with them. There is a natural thirst for fairness, as well as for wonderment, curiosity and even empathy that suggests that we will keep trying to become a better world. Losing now and then is not the end of the journey. (But, on occasion, I want it RIGHT NOW, while I'm still around—which may be a bit less likely.)[15]

A prolific author, Meier continues to actively teach and write, including a blog for *Education Week*.

Lawrence Lightfoot looked carefully at the kind of leadership that allowed these schools to be effective, or as she called them "good." According to Lightfoot, "The tone and culture of schools is said to be defined by the vision and purposeful action of the principal. He is said to be the person who must inspire the commitment and energies of his faculty; the respect, if not the admiration of his students; and the trust of the parents." Lightfoot is also clear in using the word "his." The image of a school administrator in much of the effective school literature, such as Lightfoot's, seems very male—a father figure or a general or a coach, an image of "steely objectivity, rationality, and erect posture." Further examination points to a more complex image:

Part of the goodness of these schools, I think, has to do with the redefinition of leadership. In all cases, the caricatures are empty and misleading. . . . The redefinition includes softer images that are based on nurturance given and received by the leader; based on relationships and affiliations as central dimensions of the exercise of power; and based on a subtle integration of personal qualities traditionally attached to male and female images.

This is, perhaps, a model of leadership closer to Bigelow's Shirley Glick than to Lloyd Dixon. As a teacher, you'll definitely want to join a community led by someone closer to Glick than Dixon.[13] In my own career as a teacher—from fourth grade in New York City to various colleges and universities in Massachusetts and New York—I have also found more than my share of Lloyd Dixons and Shirley Glicks, though I am happy to report that the Glicks outnumbered the Dixons by a substantial margin.

Sonia Nieto tells of a teacher who responded to Nieto's question "What keeps you going?" by saying, "My principal. I have the most wonderful principal in the world. I wouldn't want her job for anything in the world, but I thank God (and her) every day that she does it. She creates a climate in our school that allows me to teach and grow the way I do."[14] A good principal can make all the difference in making teaching happy and productive work.

PARENTS AND COMMUNITY MEMBERS

Children and adolescents do not come to school as blank slates, and they do not view themselves only, or even primarily, as students. They are daughters, sons, siblings, and sometimes even aunts, uncles, and parents themselves—all living in many different family arrangements. They live in communities and walk and ride down urban sidewalks or suburban streets or country lanes and meet other children and adults. They may be active in a religious community or in youth or adult organizations. They may also be in a gang or in a host of other destructive **social networks**. Teachers' lives are going to be affected directly and indirectly by all these networks of relationships that children bring to school with them. The most successful teachers know this and do everything they can to connect with other adults in their student's lives.

social networks Groups of people who are linked for various reasons, such as beliefs, behaviors, or personal similarities.

Teachers need to tap in to as many sources of support as possible, among parents and other community leaders. Bill Bigelow, who wished that he had reached out to parents earlier in his career, advises,

> Put down roots in the school community—go to students' games or performances; sit next to your kids' parents. Learn all you can about the community your school serves. Call parents; make them your allies. Especially call them to praise their kids and learn more about them.[16]

Ohio parent activist Lola Glover recommends reaching out and doing so quickly. She says that one of the biggest mistakes teachers make is not being in touch with parents until there's a problem:

> And most parents don't want to hear the problem. If you start off that way with a parent, it will take some real doing to get on the right foot with them again.
> It's not going to be easy to build an alliance

with 30 parents, so start with one or two. Get those parents to be your liaisons. Let them know how much you care and what you are trying to accomplish in the classroom.

> I am convinced that if students begin to see parents and people in their community and their schools working together, a lot of things would change. First of all, the kids' attitudes would change. Right now, kids' attitudes have not changed about school because they don't see any connection between home and school. They do not see any real efforts being made by either side to come together for the purpose of improving their schools or educational outcomes.

While building these kinds of alliances is never easy, Glover also insists, "I know we'll never find the answer if we keep this division between us."[17] Welcoming family and the community into schools is not easy and there is no clear-cut way to do so. However, teachers and schools that cut themselves off from their students' families and communities risk a level of alienation that will defeat any other efforts they make.

At the same time, communities can be too intrusive. Some parents, especially in more prosperous communities, can become "helicopter parents," hovering over their children and their children's teachers at every moment. Some level of isolation from family and especially from less healthful

Connections

Recall the discussion in Chapter 2 regarding the need for teachers to see their students as young people whose lives are lived in the midst of a web of important relationships.

community invasion is essential. Thus, Sara Lawrence Lightfoot observes another characteristic of good schools:

> *I do believe that good schools balance the pulls of connection to community against the contrary forces of separation from it. Administrators at Kennedy [a public high school in the Bronx, one of New York City's poorest neighborhoods] vividly portray their roles as a "balancing act." They walk the treacherous "tightrope" between closed and open doors, between autonomy and **symbiosis**. Schools need to provide asylum for adolescents from the rugged demands of outside life at the same time that they must always be interactive with it.[18]*

symbiosis A sustained relationship between two people or two groups of people that is mutually beneficial.

The effective teacher lives her or his working life somewhere on that tightrope.

DON'T GO IT ALONE

If there is a key theme to this chapter, it is very simple: Don't try to go it alone. Relationships with administrators, fellow teachers, unions and their leadership, parents, and community representatives are not always easy, but they are essential. This advice contradicts some popular images of the successful teacher as a kind of "lone ranger." Over several generations, numerous teacher autobiographies and other accounts tell of the lone teacher who stood up to the administration and the community in the name of the kids and succeeded against all odds. These can be inspiring stories, and they can remind us of just how important our work is. They can also be dangerous. Teaching is heroic work, but it is not generally the heroism of the lone individual as much as it is the heroism of the community of teachers.

One recent version of the lone-ranger hero teacher is Erin Gruwell. In her book *The Freedom Writers Diary* (which was made into a movie, *Freedom Writers*, starring Hilary Swank and Patrick Dempsey), Gruwell describes how she is able to turn things around in spite of all the odds. As a young, White

teacher who initially has difficulty connecting to her deeply disengaged Asian, African American, and Latino students, Gruwell tells of how she finally made the connection and together with her "freedom writers" created new stories of overcoming oppression. It is an inspiring story. However, it is also one that has irritated many teachers.

In a review for *Rethinking Schools*, Chela Delgado named the problem that many teachers had with this and similar stories: "[I]t's a movie about a white savior." This is a dangerous role model for any teacher to follow. On the one hand, Delgado appreciates the movie's major theme, saying, "There is something deeply worthwhile about Ms. G attempting to connect the oppression of her own people to the oppression experienced by her students." However, she says, the problem "isn't so much the kind of cookie-cutter stereotyping that we see in Hollywood's white-teacher-as-savior genre," but "it's the highly individualistic nature of these stereotypes." (Remember, Margaret Haley did not call on teachers to stand up to the system alone but to join with others.) Delgado is also deeply troubled by the depiction of race in *Freedom Writers* and similar stories. They are nearly all the story of the White teacher "saving" children of color. In this case, "[t]here is a marked absence of black and Latino adults." Thus, Delgado concludes, "Don't be fooled into thinking the short-lived triumph of one savior in one classroom is enough." Only larger alliances—across traditional dividing lines of race, class, and gender, but also among many teachers and many non-teacher allies—will bring the kind of changes in teachers' work lives and in the structures of schooling that are needed if teaching is to be as rewarding a profession as it can be and if all the nation's children are to get the education they deserve.[19]

STUDENTS

Class Size Many classrooms remain overcrowded, but 50 students per class is no longer the norm. However, multiple studies and debates have long surrounded the effects of smaller class sizes for students. Research has been used to prove arguments from both camps—that smaller classes translate into higher-achieving students or that smaller classes don't make a difference or even, in some cases, negatively affect student achievement. Current research still stands divided on the issue, which makes class size a heated legislative and policy issue for administrators, educators, and parents—all of whom believe themselves to be correct in their opinions on the matter.

Tennessee's Project STAR (Student/Teacher Achievement Ratio) was a pioneering study on the issue of smaller classes. The 4-year study beginning in 1985 has been called "one of the most important educational investigations ever carried out" by Harvard professor Frederick Mosteller. Incomplete scientific evidence of the time led legislators to doubt the impact of smaller classes for students; thus, the study used a comprehensive scientific-based approach to track student achievement. The study tracked students in elementary school because the foundation for all future schoolwork is laid there.

Actress Hilary Swank and Erin Gruwell.

Promising Practices

Gateway to the Future

The vow that high school students will be able to complete 2 years of college coursework while completing their 4 years of high school is bold. At Dayton Early College Academy (DECA), however, a combination of rigorous study and exceptional faculty support make this a reality. Through the support of the University of Dayton and KnowledgeWorks, DECA maintains a level of autonomy from the school district and can make choices that are most beneficial for the school. The school is governed by a board of directors, but the administrative decisions are made largely by those most affected by the decisions—the teachers. This approach has, therefore, created a nurturing, close-knit environment in which students remain the primary focus.

One of the most distinguishing features of DECA's model is the school's insistence on personalized support. Before the school year, two teachers sit down with each student and the student's parents to discuss the student's goals, strengths, and weaknesses, in order to form a "personalized learning plan." Students aren't graded in the traditional sense, but rather, they are required

to progress through a sequence of six gateways to graduation. Meetings are held consistently throughout the year to assess each student's improvements and to develop new goals. Students can begin taking college classes tuition-free as soon as their second year.

With all-encompassing support that relies on input and direction from all those connected with the student—teachers, parents, and staff—DECA fulfills the promise of 2 years of college completed by high school graduation. In its first year, the school admitted 95 ninth graders and had a waiting list of over 200 students. It has since expanded to accommodate freshmen through seniors.

Sources: Rethinking High School: Five Profiles of Innovative Models for Student Success, by Tracy A. Huebner and Grace Calisi Corbett, 2005, WestEd, http://www.wested.org/online_pubs/gates.profiles.pdf; and Dayton Early College Academy Web site, http://daytonearlycollege.org.

Join the Dialogue

If possible, spend a full day—or at least as much time as possible—in a classroom, observing all the people with whom the teacher comes into contact. Note the interactions with the children. Note which adults come into the room—either in person or through various announcements. Who does the teacher talk to at lunch? After school? Ask the teacher about his or her most important interactions, and create a "portrait" of that one teacher on one day. (Note, however, that no one day is "typical" of a teacher's life, but a detailed picture of one day can add significant insight to your understanding of teachers' lives.)

Researchers found no differences in test scores for fifth-grade students who attended smaller classes while in third grade.

With current budget cuts, many school districts are increasing class sizes. Having larger classes may be the only way these schools can avoid cutting arts funding or after-school activities. As school funding continues to be trimmed, schools will have to make difficult decisions for their students and—obviously—not everybody is going to be happy about it.[20]

The Reason We Teach For all the relationships that are important for teachers, Judy Logan, in reflecting on her own long and successful career as a teacher in San Francisco, reminds us which relationships are the most important to any teacher— those with the students. Teachers spend far more work time with students than with all adults combined. More important, students are the point of all the work that goes on in schools (a reality that is sometimes forgotten by adults, who can be too busy and too overwhelmed by the many demands of the job). Thus, Logan writes,

Being student-centered doesn't mean that I am against parents or colleagues or administrators. It does mean I can sometimes treat the adolescent as the adult whom the parent does not yet see, the colleague may be still trying to control, the administrator may view as a threat ("What do you mean you don't want to salute the flag!"). . . . While I have many enriching and affectionate relationships with colleagues, parents, and

STAR compared over 6,000 students from inner-city, rural, urban, and suburban school locations. Students were tested in three class environments: small classes with 13–17 students, a control group of classes with 22–26 students, and a group of classes (with 22–26 students) that had both a teacher and a full-time teacher aide working with the students. At the end of the study, STAR found that students in the smaller classes scored the highest on the Stanford Achievement Test (SAT) and the criterion-referenced Basic Skills First Test (BSF), across all geographic locations and grade levels. Inner-city small classes made the greatest gains on the SAT scores, whereas small classes in rural schools had the highest SAT and BSF scores. Teachers claimed that they were able to more effectively identify student needs and could provide more individual attention to students with smaller classes.

Other proponents of smaller class size have cited the decreased workload on teachers, which reduces the risk of teacher burnout. Consider that a composition teacher, with a class of 25 students, will spend at least 8 hours reading, analyzing, and responding to each assigned paper if he or she spends 20 minutes on each one. If that same teacher has 125 students, which can be the case in secondary environments with multiple classes, the teacher will need almost 42 hours to respond to papers with the same level of consideration!

On the opposite side of the debate, many researchers have found evidence that class size has little to no impact on student achievement, claiming that teacher quality is far more influential. A 2003 study in Louisiana found that as "the percentage of highly certified teachers in a district increased, so did the district's performance score," whereas class size seemed to have no effect on student performance, positive or negative. Often when states implement policies to create smaller classes, they must hire more teachers, many of whom are younger, inexperienced teachers. As a 2002 study found, a 1996 law mandating smaller classes in California meant that 28,000 new teachers had to be hired, though many lacked experience or credentials. More experienced teachers went to new openings in wealthier areas, leaving low-income schools with inexperienced teachers.

Join the **Dialogue**

What are your thoughts about smaller class sizes? What are the positives and the negatives? If you were in charge of a school's budget, would you choose to enlarge classes to save money before cutting other programs? Why?

administrators (my best friends are teachers), my deepest relationships are with my students.[21]

Being student-centered does not mean forgetting about the other adults in the school or in our lives, but it does mean keeping our "eyes on the prize" and not being diverted from the real point of teaching.

REVIEW >>

- **Historically speaking: How has teacher work changed—for better or worse?**

  In 1904, Chicago educator Margaret Haley made the plea for teachers to be better paid and to have job security, a retirement plan, more manageable class sizes, and more say in the curriculum and decision-making process. Today, although teachers still face many hurdles, there have been great improvements in each of these areas.

- **How much do teachers get paid?**

  The latest data from the American Federation of Teachers indicates that U.S. teachers make an average of just over $51,000. However, this value fluctuates widely based on geography, and cost-of-living must be taken into account. Although teachers' salaries were flat for many years, the average salary took an unexpected spike in 2006–2007, outpacing many other comparable jobs and the inflation rate. In addition to salaries, teachers generally have pension plans that are more dependable than the average worker's 401k and that can be accessed at an earlier age (depending on years of service).

- **What is tenure?**

  Tenure is the right of a teacher to keep his or her job subject to good behavior. It is usually awarded after a relatively short probationary period, often 3 years.

- **Will I join a union?**

  Most teachers are required to join their local union once they accept a teaching position. During the past 100 years, teacher unions have fought hard to improve teachers' benefits and working conditions. There is great debate today as to whether unions are still needed and if their influence positively affects teachers' current concerns.

- **Why is professional development important?**

  Teachers must continually look for ways to improve their "craft," learning from experts in various areas of curriculum and class management as well as from each other. Individual teachers are encouraged not only to participate in professional development but also to find ways to lead the discussion of a variety of topics.

- **Who are the people who impact a teacher's workday?**

  When a recent survey asked teachers to list their biggest challenges, a majority of the answers involved relationships, especially interactions with parents. Every teacher must find successful ways to communicate with fellow teachers, administrators, parents, and their students, taking advantage of any opportunity to collaborate and build supportive networks. Debates are ongoing regarding class size and what impact, if any, it has on student achievement. The most important relationships are with the students, who are the real reason for teaching.

Will I Join a Union?

From "WHY TEACHERS SHOULD ORGANIZE"

BY MARGARET HALEY

Margaret Haley's 1904 speech to the National Education Association described the conditions faced by far too many teachers a century ago. It also reflects Haley's hopes and demands for change and her belief that a better type of schooling could be achieved through a public investment in teachers.

Nowhere in the United States today does the public school, as a branch of the public service, receive from the public either the moral or financial support needed to enable it properly to perform its important function in the social organism. The conditions which are militating most strongly against efficient teaching, and which existing organizations of the kind under discussion here are directing their energies toward changing briefly stated are the following:

- Greatly increased cost of living, together with constant demands for higher standards of scholarship and professional attainments and culture, to be met with practically stationary and wholly inadequate teachers' salaries.
- Insecurity of tenure of office and lack of provision for old age.
- Overwork in overcrowded schoolrooms, exhausting both in mind and body.
- And, lastly, lack of recognition of the teacher as an educator in the school system, due to the increased tendency toward "factoryizing education," making the teacher an automation, a mere factory hand, whose duty it is to carry out mechanically and unquestioningly the ideas and orders of those clothed with the authority of position, and who may or may not know the needs of the children or how to minister to them.

The individuality of the teacher and her power of initiative are thus destroyed, and the result is courses of study, regulations and equipment which the teachers have had no voice in selecting, which often have no relation to the children's needs, and which prove a hindrance instead of a help in teaching. . . .

Two ideals are struggling for supremacy in American life today: one the industrial ideal, dominating thru the supremacy of commercialism, which subordinates the worker to the products and the machine; the other, the ideal of democracy, the ideal of the educators, which places humanity above all machines, and demands that all activity shall be the expression of life. If this ideal of the educators cannot be carried over into the industrial field, then the ideal of industrialism will be carried over into the school. Those two ideals can no more continue to exist in American life than our nation could have continued half slave and half free. If the school cannot bring joy to the work of the world, the joy must go out of its own life, and work in the school as in the factory will become drudgery.

Source: "Why Teachers Should Organize," by Margaret Haley, *National Education Association Addresses and Proceedings*, 1904, pp. 145–152.

From "TURNING UNIONS AROUND"

BY ADAM URBANSKI

Adam Urbanski, the longtime leader of the Rochester, New York, Teachers' Association, as well as a vice president of the American Federation of Teachers, is also a leader of a network of unions that he helped to create: the Teacher Union Reform Network. TURN, as he describes in this article, is committed to dramatically expanding the roles and responsibilities of teacher unions. Urbanski has become one of the leading voices for reform in education in the United States today and for including teacher unions as a key partner in the reform effort. Equally critical of some of the traditional teacher union activities and of those who oppose teacher unions, Urbanski has, through TURN and his own prolific work as a reformer, sought to help carve out a different approach to the place of teacher unions in the twenty-first century educational picture.

Teacher unions in America must be reformed. This can best happen if teacher unionists themselves recognize not only the need for change but also that it is in the enlightened self-interest of their unions to welcome the next logical stage in their unions' evolution.

Certainly, forces and threats from the outside can play a role. In fact, much hinges on the capacity of teacher union leaders to understand the changing environment and to interpret it for their members. Such a proactive mode would ensure that the changes are not merely a begrudging accommodation but rather a purposeful fulfillment of our own vision for our institution and our members. But unless it is voices from within the teacher union movement who are driving the call for reforms, there is a great risk that the voices from outside would be viewed as hostile "bashing." So it does matter a great deal who is calling for teacher union reform. In a sense, unions are more likely to change if the unionists are *agents* of reform. Ironically, if unionists do not become agents of reform, they will remain *targets* of reform.

A persuasive case for teacher union reform can only be made in a manner that is sensitive to the experience and culture of these unions. This, after all, is not a matter of abandoning what teacher unions are; instead, this is a matter of building on the foundation that has been laid.

The industrial union model that emerged from years of struggling for parity with management was a good match for the industrial-style school organization. It mirrored the institution in which the teachers' unions existed, and the effectiveness of this approach brought it both legitimacy and loyalty.

Indeed, industrial unionism served teachers well. It helped them to achieve middle class status and to launch college and university-fueled professional careers for their children. It has also improved the terms and conditions under which teachers worked and, in many instances, it democratized the workplace.

Recognizing all this as an important foundation for building the next stage of teacher unionism is indispensable. Whatever is to become part of the "new unionism" must be built on the essential commitments of what teacher unions have always stood for and must always retain: a commitment to democratic dynamics, fairness and due process, self determination, unity without unanimity, social justice, and valuing the dignity of all work and workers.

Why Change

There is no reason to believe that reforming unions would prove any less difficult than reforming schools and education. Nonetheless, teacher unions must change in tandem with the changes that are so obviously needed in schools and in education. Reinventing both is necessary for maintaining public support and confidence in the institution of public education. Just like today's schools, unions today are more like yesterday than they've ever been before. They still expend most of their energy and resources on defending a very small minority of troubled members, they still define their mission narrowly to bread-and-butter issues, and they still confine themselves to reacting to management's actions and provocations.

Change is inevitable, and only growth is optional. And while it is possible to change without improving, it is not possible to improve without change. So it is futile to agonize over whether or not to change. The choice is only whether the changes will be the kind that truly improve our institutions and increase the chances that more students will learn. The strong unions that we've built, therefore, must now help deliver a more genuine profession for teachers and more effective schools for all students. This won't be easy. Even in states where collective bargaining does exist, professional issues are either outside the scope of collective bargaining or, at best, are "permissive" items of bargaining. Thus, the collective voice of teachers is often muzzled on the very matters that can best assure

Source: "TURNing Unions Around" by Adam Urbanski, *Contemporary Education*, 69 (Summer 1998).

improvements in the education industry and engender public confidence in schools. Our colleagues in higher education did achieve the right to negotiate professional issues and thus to maintain their professional status. That pattern was unfortunately denied to elementary and secondary levels. In essence, teachers have a so-called "profession," while the professionals have little or no voice in professional matters.

Precisely because there is a connection between what teachers do collectively and what they are professionally, the scope of collective bargaining must be expanded to permit negotiations on professional, pedagogical, and instructional issues. As it happens, this is a good fit with what new teachers now expect from their union: to invest no less in meeting their professional needs (access to new knowledge; professional development; opportunities to plan, design and implement new programs; opportunities for continuous learning) than in the traditional union priorities such as contract negotiations, grievance processing, health, and other benefits. But teacher unions have additional reasons to seek union reform and school reform: to help diminish the isolation among teachers thus improving collaboration, communication debate, and learning about reform; to encourage initiative from teachers and their unions, taking the lead with reform and promoting the kind of initiative that make sense to the practitioners in education; to help ensure that reform goes beyond rhetoric; to increase prospects and pathways for translating good ideas into practical local reality; and to create, articulate and actualize our own vision for our unions, our profession, and our schools.

A Vision for the (Near) Future

What might be the vision that teachers and teacher unionists wish for themselves in the foreseeable future? Here is a glimpse of what might be possible only a few years hence:

Instead of two major teachers' unions, there is now one merged organization that acts not only as an advocate for all of America's educators but also as a lobby for all of their students. Features of industrial unionism have yielded to changes that offer the promise of making public education more effective. The scope of collective bargaining has been extended to include negotiations on professional issues in addition to wages, benefits, and working conditions. The union now promotes such practices and dynamics as peer review, differentiated staffing and pay, public school choice, professional accountability, the transfer of teachers based on criteria other than seniority alone, and the involvement of parents, students, and peers in teacher evaluations.

The union now not only considers itself the voice of teachers, it sees its role as giving voice to teachers. It now spends as much energy and resources on the professional needs of its members as it does on collective bargaining, contract enforcement, economic benefits, and other basic traditional union functions. Recognizing that the welfare of the union and its members hinges on the effectiveness of the profession and industry within which it exists, the teachers' union has formalized its commitment to reform.

This new teachers' union considers unionism and professionalism as complementary and not mutually exclusive. It helps its members become agents of reform rather than the passive targets of reform; it views the negotiated contract as the floor and not the ceiling for what union members are willing to do for students; and it acts as the guardian of professional and educational standards.

Rhetoric Into Reality

Any vision is only a pipe dream unless created twice: first in the mind and then in the real world. But whatever we can envision we can also achieve, and some have already begun to build tomorrow today.

In Rochester, for example, the teachers union learned over the last decade and a half that the more the teachers union promotes educational reforms and professionalism, the stronger and more credible the union becomes. We have also learned that the stronger the union becomes, the more it is able to promote the needed changes in education. Through collaboration and a willingness to re-think traditional postures, the union achieved a substantial number of changes:

- Negotiated a school-based planning process that involves teachers, parents and high school students, and school administrators in making decisions about each school's instructional program.
- Altered the traditional teacher evaluation process by developing the Performance Assessment Review for Teachers (PART)–a portfolio-based system that includes peer evaluations and parallels the principles and criteria of the National Board for Professional Teaching Standards.
- Negotiated a "professional day" provision that eliminates the teachers' dismissal time so that the teachers' workday ends when the teachers' professional responsibilities (as determined by the teachers) are completed.
- Introduced aspects of pay for knowledge, skills and additional service into the teacher compensation system.
- Negotiated an annual Classroom Resource Fund to support effective school practices and to invest in what works for student learning.
- Initiated and published a pedagogical journal that features articles by teachers and paraprofessionals themselves.
- Supported public school choice as a way to empower parents and students while providing additional incentives to schools.
- Negotiated the Career in Teaching Program that includes differentiated staffing and differentiated pay.
- Developed "lead teacher" positions for accomplished teachers who assume additional responsibilities and roles in exchange for additional pay and a different job description.
- Negotiated a formal role for teachers in the annual evaluation of their supervisors and other administrators.

- Negotiated a role for parents in the teacher evaluation process.
- Designed and negotiated an internship program for new teachers and a peer intervention plan for tenured teachers experiencing difficulty with their classroom teaching.
- Adjusted teacher seniority provisions for teacher assignments and transfers.
- Initiated and continues to support a homework hotline for students to help them with homework and school-related matters.

By placing a premium and a priority on what we are *for*, not just what we are *against*, we began to bridge the gap between unionism and professionalism. And although this has been a rocky and scenic route, we remain determined to continue on this path in collaboration with school management when we can and alone when we must. Along the way, we have found it necessary to promote "creative insubordination" and "reform without permission" during periods of hostile and anti-union school management postures. . . .

Conclusions

In his last speech to the AFT Convention in 1996, the late AFT President Albert Shanker reminded the assembled teacher unionists that "It is no less the responsibility of a teachers' union to preserve public education than to negotiate good contracts." To achieve this, teacher unions will have to change their traditional orientation. They will have to seek not only the job-related interests of their members but also the success of the education industry. They will have to recognize that teachers will do well only if their students do well and that no community would long toler-

ate teachers doing well while students do not. Thus, school productivity must become central to the mission of teacher unions, too. Real change is real hard and takes real time. But it can be done; it's just that it can't be done easily. Along the way there will be false starts, wrong turns and negative findings. And pain. But the pain is in itself evidence that the changes are real.

We can succeed if we are passionate about change and commit for the long haul. But to do that, we first must instigate among our colleagues a revolution of rising expectations and create a vision that inspires others to aspire to more. Then we must do the hard work that is unavoidable when the agenda is so ambitious. When we succeed, we will have built a more genuine teaching profession for ourselves and more effective schools for all of our students. And the new teacher unions can lead the way.

Who Are the People Who Impact a Teacher's Workday?

From "THE DESECRATION OF STUDS TERKEL: FIGHTING CENSORSHIP AND SELF-CENSORSHIP"

BY BILL BIGELOW

Bill Bigelow has had a long and successful career as a classroom teacher in Portland, Oregon, and also as an editor of *Rethinking Schools*. The following account of Bigelow's experience with difficult supervisors and parents during his first year of teaching is from an article he wrote for a *Rethinking Schools* publication.

It began with a call that I was to report to the vice-principal's office as soon as possible. The voice at the other end indicated that it was urgent.

I was a first-year teacher at Grant High School in Portland, Oregon. The call gave me the creeps. From the moment we met I'd felt that Lloyd Dixon, the curriculum VP, could look deep into my soul—and that he didn't like what he saw. Whenever we passed in the hall he smiled at me thinly, but with a glance that said "I've got your number Bigelow." He had a drawl that reminded me of the Oklahoma highway patrolman who gleefully arrested me in 1971 for not carrying my draft card.

It was my first year as a teacher. And I must confess, my classroom difficulties made me a tad paranoid.

Dixon's secretary ushered me into his office when I arrived. "It seems we have a problem, Bill," he said. He paused to look at me to make sure I was duly appreciative of the serious nature of the meeting. "The mother of a student of yours, Dorothy Jennings, called to say that you had given her smutty material, a book that discusses oral sex. What's the story?"

I explained to the vice-principal that the "smutty" material was Studs Terkel's *Working*, a book that includes interviews with dozens of people—auto workers, hotel clerks,

Source: "The Desecration of Studs Terkel: Fighting Censorship and Self-Censorship," by Bill Bigelow, in Kelley Dawson Salas, Rita Tenorio, Stephanie Walters, and Dale Weiss, eds., *The New Teacher Book: Finding Purpose, Balance, and Hope During Your First Years in the Classroom*, 2004, pp. 123–126.

washroom attendants, musicians—who describe what they do for a living and how they feel about it. I told him that it was a text the school had purchased and that I issued it to my ninth graders for some in-class reading during our career education study.

"Well, Bill, Dorothy apparently took the book home. And her mother's upset because of a section Dorothy read her about a prostitute, where she describes having oral sex."

I told him that I had not assigned that chapter and that students didn't have permission to take the books home, as I taught two sections of the class but had only 35 copies of the book. I didn't mention that indeed I had considered using the chapter, "Roberta Victor, Hooker," because it was filled with insights about sexism, law, and hypocrisy. (The alleged oral sex description was a brief reference in a long interview.)

Dixon ordered me to bring him a copy of *Working* so that he could read the passages I assigned, and to meet with him the next day. "You should be aware that I regard this as a serious situation," he said. And with that, New Teacher was waved out the door.

I went to see my friend Tom McKenna, a member of a support group I'd helped organize among teachers in the area. Tom suggested I talk with our union rep. My visit with Thurston Ohman, a big-hearted man with an easy from-the-belly laugh was a revelation. "You haven't done anything wrong," he assured me. "If they try to come after you in some way, the union will back you 100%."

Solidarity

It was a delicious moment, and I realized how utterly alone I'd felt up until that point. Ironically, in my history classes and my freshman social studies classes we'd recently studied the rise of labor unions, but until that instant I'd never personally been a beneficiary of the "injury to one is an injury to all" solidarity.

Buoyed by my talk with Ohman, I returned to VP Dixon's office the next day. He wasn't worried about Mrs. Jennings anymore. But he was still upset. "Bill, I read over the pieces you assigned. Very interesting. Pretty negative stuff. My daughter is an airline stewardess. She doesn't feel like the gal in that book.

"Do you know that the reading on the auto worker uses the s-word five times and the f-word once?"

"The s-word?" I asked.

"Yes. On pages 258, 259, 261, and twice on page 262. The f-word is used on page 265."

I didn't want to laugh, but I didn't know what to say. His complaint was about an interview with Gary Bryner, president of the United Auto Workers local at the Lordstown, Ohio, General Motors plant. Given Mr. Dixon's comment about his daughter, I had a hunch that his ire was aimed more at Bryner's "negative" critique of the plant's deadening working conditions and his descriptions of workers' resistance than

at his occasional use of s- and f-words. But this wasn't the time or place to argue politics. "I guess I didn't realize, Mr. Dixon."

"No. Well, Bill, here's what I'd like you to do. Get a black marker and every time this gentleman uses the s- and f-words, darken them so students won't be exposed to that kind of language. Will you do that for me, Bill?"

I know some people would have fought it. Had it not been my first year as a teacher—a temporary teacher, no less—I would have fought. Instead I made one of those compromises that we're not proud of, but that we make so we can live to fight another day. After school, marker in hand, I cleansed Gary Bryner of his foul language—in all 35 copies of *Working*.

Twenty-some years later, the censored books are still in circulation in Portland high schools.

I offer this instance of curricular interference as a way of acknowledging that administrative repression can be a factor in limiting the inventiveness of a new teacher. But in my experience, the intrusions of the Lloyd Dixons of the world are exceptions that prove the rule. And the rule is that we have an enormous amount of freedom.

Even as a first-year teacher the Jennings affair was my only brush with administrative censure. I frequently brought in controversial guest speakers, films, and additional readings. It was 1978-79, the year of Three Mile Island, the final months of the Sandinista revolution in Nicaragua, and a growing awareness of the injustices of South African apartheid. In class, we study all of these.

No doubt, it's important for individuals early in their teaching careers, as well as those of us further along, to make an assessment of the political context in which we work. After all, if we lose our job, we don't do anyone any good. But generally, I believe that the most powerful agent of censorship lives in our own heads, and we almost always have more freedom than we use. The great Brazilian educator Paulo Freire once wrote that in schools we should attempt to fill up all the political space we're given. But we rarely do.

That said, a few years ago a school district in an affluent Portland suburb terminated a good friend of mine at the completion of her third year of probation, spouting nonsense about her failure to teach critical thinking skills and the like. The obvious irony for those of us at her hearing was that she was fired precisely because she was successful at teaching her students to think critically. She had the misfortune of being one of the only non-tenured teachers in a progressive, pedagogically adventurous social studies department during the rise of the ferociously conservative Oregon Citizens Alliance. The political environment had shifted to the right; it was sacrificial lamb time.

It's worth mentioning that during my first years at Jefferson High School, following my year at Grant, I was gifted with supervising vice-principals who were extraordinarily supportive and even enthusiastic about livelier, risk-taking teaching. Shirley Glick was one of several VPs who offered nothing but encouragement as I felt my way toward a more critical and multicultural curriculum. The Lloyd Dixons of the world exist, but so do the Shirley Glicks.

Incidentally, I never met Mrs. Jennings. But she left her mark. For a long time I subconsciously imagined a Mrs. Jennings sitting at every student's home, hoping for a chance to chew me out for some teaching crime I'd committed: "You snake, why'd you use that book/film/article/poem with my innocent child?"

In my imagination, parents were potential opponents, not allies, and I avoided calling them to talk about their children or what I was trying to teach. This neglect was a bad habit to fall into. Even from a narrow classroom management standpoint, my failure to call moms, dads, or grandparents from time to time made my quest for classroom order a lonely campaign. Parents could have exerted a bit of pressure on the home front. But they also could have told me something about their son or daughter, offered a fuller portrait than what I saw in my daily slice of 47 minutes.

And that would likely have made me a more effective teacher.

QUESTIONS

1. What do you think of Bigelow's decision to make "one of those compromises that we're not proud of"? Would you have made the same compromise or handled things differently?

2. Bigelow says that for most teachers "the most powerful agent of censorship lives in our own heads." Do you agree? Can you think of examples, in your own life or among teachers you have known or observed, when such self-censorship was a reality?

3. Could Bigelow have found a better way to relate to Mr. Dixon? To Dorothy Jennings's mother? To Dorothy herself?

4. What do you think of Bigelow's self-criticism at the end of the article about the way he related to parents early in his own career? Do parents make for more effective teaching? How? How not?

From "TWO TEACHERS OF LETTERS"

BY MARGARET TREECE METZGER AND CLAIRE FOX

This chapter focused on the question "What will my life be like as a teacher?" In the exchange of letters that follows, two teachers reflect on their lives in the profession. One is a young teacher about to begin her first job. The response is from a senior teacher who, for all her reservations, has arrived at a clear answer to the question of whether teaching is right for her.

Spring 1984

Dear Mrs. Metzger,

I am writing to you as a former student who has just graduated from Brown University and who is considering teaching English next year. I remember you as a compelling and demanding teacher who seemed to enjoy her job. At the moment, you are the only person I know who would support my career choice. Almost everyone else is disparaging about teaching in public schools.

I am told that I did not have to go to Brown University to become a teacher. I am told that teaching is a "wonderful thing to do until you decide what you really want to do with your life". I am told that it is "nice" that I'm going to be a teacher. Why does it seem that the decision to teach in our society is analogous with the decision to stunt one's growth, to opt out intellectually in favor of long summers off?

But teaching matters. I know that. You mattered to me, and others teachers mattered to me. I enjoyed student teaching and I look forward to next year. I have imaginary dialogues with the students in my mind. I hear myself articulating my policy on borderline grades, explaining why I keep switching chairs from circles to rows as I flounder in my efforts to decide what's best, or laughing with the students as I struggle to overcome saying "okay" too often when I lecture. But I wonder how much teaching is actually an ego trip, a ploy to be liked, accepted, and respected by a group of people who have limited say in the matter. I also know the humiliation of a student's glare. I know there will be problems, yet I cannot deny the tremendous sense of worth I felt as a student teacher when students offered me their respect and when students worked hard and were proud of their effort.

I wonder where I would get this sense of worthiness if I were to work in a New York advertising firm or as an engineer at Bell Labs. And yet, going to work for a big corporation—whether in an advertising firm, a bank, or a publishing house—impresses me. It would seem "real," "grown up," as teaching never will. Nobody would tell me that being an engineer is "nice" or a wonderful way to figure out what I "really want to do".

For graduation, my mother and sister gave me a beautiful sleek attaché case. My reaction was twofold. First, I realized it would never be large enough to carry the load of an English teacher, and second, I realized that, should I ever decide to leave teaching, it would be perfect for the real world of professional writers and young executives.

Source: "Two Teachers of Letters," by Margaret Treece Metzger and Claire Fox, 1986, *Harvard Educational Review*, 56:4, pp. 349–354.

My mother doesn't want me to go into teaching. She is afraid I will get "stuck," that my efforts will not be appreciated or rewarded, and that I will not meet men. When I called home from Minneapolis after a long, productive, and exhilarating day interviewing at schools, my mother congratulated me and suggested that I spend the evening putting together a second resume—a writing resume—before I forgot everything else I know how to do. She suggested I spend the following day visiting television studios scouting for writing jobs, "just in case."

And my mother has been in public education for almost 20 years! Granted, when she entered Boston College in 1952, she had to choose between teaching and nursing. I, however, have chosen to teach from among many options available to me as a Brown graduate with a strong liberal arts degree.

I write to you, Mrs. Metzger, because you were the first person to excite me about the processes of writing and because your integrity in the classroom has long been an influence on me—and on my decision to teach. You mattered. I am turning to you because you are a professional; and you continue to choose teaching after eighteen years. I welcome any advice, comments, or solace you could offer me.

Sincerely,
Claire Fox

Spring 1984
Dear Claire,
I admire your courage to consider teaching. Your friends and relatives are not alone in their negative opinions about teaching. I'm sure you read the claim in the President's Commission on Education that education is a national disgrace. *Newsweek*'s September 1984 cover showed a teacher in a dunce cap with the headline, "Why Teachers Fail—How to Make Them Better." NBC ran a three-hour special on education—an expose of inadequate schools. At least four blue ribbon studies have concluded that teacher education is inadequate, that the pay is the lowest of all professions, that schools have deplorable management, and that the job is full of meaningless paperwork.

I know that much of the criticism is valid. However, the reports sensationalize and do not tell the whole truth. I appreciate your letter because you are giving me a chance to defend a profession I love.

Claire, I look forward to teaching. By mid-August I start planning lessons and dreaming about classrooms. I also wonder whether I'll have the energy to start again with new classes. Yet after September gets underway, I wake up in the morning expecting to have fun at work. I know that teaching well is a worthwhile use of my life. I know my work is significant.

I am almost forty years old and I am happier in my job than anyone I know. That's saying a lot. My husband, who enjoys his work, has routine days when he comes home and says: "Nothing much happened today—just meetings." I never have routine days. When I am in the classroom, I usually am having a wonderful time.

I also hate this job. In March I wanted to quit because of the relentlessness of dealing with one hundred antsy adolescents day after day. I lose patience with adolescent issues: I think I'll screech if I have to listen to one more adolescent self obsession. I am physically exhausted every Friday. The filth in our school is an aesthetic insult. The unending petty politics drain me. Often I feel undermined on small issues by a school system that supports me well on academic freedom.

Like all jobs, teaching has inherent stresses. As you know from student teaching, you must know how to discipline a roomful of adolescents: you need to have a sense of purpose about what you are teaching; you need to cope with the exhaustion, and, as an English teacher you must get the paper grading under control. I am always saddened by the number of excellent teachers who leave teaching because they think these difficult problems are unsolvable.

A curious irony exists. I am never bored at work, yet my days are shockingly routine. I can tell you exactly what I have done every school day for the past eighteen years at 10:15 in the morning (homeroom attendance), and I suspect I will do the same for the next twenty years. The structure of the school day has changed little since education moved out of the one room schoolhouse. All teachers get tired of the monotonous routine of bookkeeping, make-up assignments, twenty minute lunches, and study hall duties. I identify with J. Alfred Prufrock when he says, "I have measured out my life with coffee spoons." My own life has been measured out in student papers. At a conservative estimate I've graded over 30,000—a mind-boggling statistic which makes me feel like a very dull person indeed.

The monotony of my schedule is mirrored in the monotony of my paycheck. No matter how well or poorly I teach, I will be paid at the same amount. There is absolutely no monetary reward for good performance, or any recognition of professional growth or acquired expertise. My pay depends on how long I've taught and my level of education. I work in a school district in which I cannot afford to live. I am alternately sad and angry about my pay. To the outside world, it seems I am doing exactly the same job I did in 1966—same title, same working conditions, same pay scale (except that my buying power is 8 percent less than it was when I earned $5,400 on my first job). To most people I am "just a teacher."

But that is the outside reality. The interior world of the teacher is quite different. Although you have to come to some terms with the outward flatness of the career, I want to assure you that teachers grow and change. So little research has been done on stage development of teachers that the literature recognizes only three categories—intern, novice, and veteran. This is laughably over-simplified. There is life after student teaching; there is growth after the first year. You will some day solve many problems that seem insurmountable during your exhilarating student teaching and your debilitating first year.

Sometimes I am aware of my growth as a teacher, and I realize that finally, after all these years, I am confident in the classroom. On the very, very best days, when classes sing, I am able to operate on many levels during a single class; I integrate logistics, pedagogy, curriculum, group dynamics, individuals needs, and my own philosophy. I feel generous and good-natured toward my students, and I am challenged by classroom issues. But on bad days, I feel like a total failure. Students attack my most vulnerable points. I feel overwhelmed by paperwork. I ache from exhaustion. I dream about going to Aruba, but I go to the next class.

I keep going because I am intellectually stimulated. I enjoy literature, and I assign books I love and books I want to read. I expect class discussions and student papers to give me new insights into literature. As you may remember, I tell students that in exchange for my hard work, they should keep me interested and they should teach me. They do.

To me, teaching poses questions worthy of a lifetime of thoughts. I want to think about what the great writers are saying. I want to think about how people learn. I want to think about the values we are passing on to the next generation. I am particularly interested in teaching thinking. I love to teach writing. I am working now on teaching writing as a tool for thinking. Questions about teaching are like puzzles to me; I can spend hours theorizing and then use my classroom as a laboratory.

I am also intellectually challenged by pedagogical problems. I have learned to follow the bizarre questions or the "wrong questions." Some questions reveal chasms of ignorance. For example, "Where is Jesus' body?" or "Before movies were in color, wasn't the world dull just being in black and white?" Sometimes students make shocking statements which demand careful responses: "All athletic girls are lesbians" or "Sexually abused toddlers probably really enjoy sex." And every year, new students require new teaching skills—Cambodian boat children who have never been in school and are illiterate even in their own language, or handicapped children such as a deaf Israeli girl who is trying to learn English without being able to hear it.

And then there are all the difficult, "normal" situations: students and parents who are "entitled," hostile, emotionally needy, or indifferent; students who live in chaotic homes, who are academically pressured, who have serious drug and alcohol problems. The list goes on and on. No school of education prepared me for the "Hill Street Blues" intensity and chaos of public schools. I received my combat training from other teachers, from myself, and mostly from the students. You will too.

Sometimes I think I can't do it all. I don't want to be bitter or a martyr, so I am careful to take care of myself. I put flowers on my desk to offset the dreariness of an old school building. I leave school several times a week to run errands or to take a walk in order to feel less trapped.

Other teachers take courses at local colleges, join committees of adults, talk in the teachers' lounge, or play with computers. In order to give to others, teachers must nurture themselves.

Ultimately, teaching is nurturing. The teacher enters a giving relationship with strangers, and then the teacher's needs must give way to students' needs. I want to work on my own writing; instead I work on students' writing. My days are spent encouraging young people's growth. I watch my students move beyond me, thinking and writing better than I have ever done. I send them to colleges I could never afford. And I must strive to be proud, not jealous, of them. I must learn generosity of heart.

I am a more compassionate person because I have known teachers and students. I think differently about handicaps because I worked with Guy, who is quadriplegic from a rugby accident. Refugee problems have a human face because I've heard Nazmul tell stories about refugee camps in Bangladesh, and I've heard Merhdad tell about escaping from Iran, hidden in a camel's baggage. I have seen the school social worker given suicidal students his home phone number, telling them to call anytime. I have seen administrators bend the rules to help individual students through personal crises. Every day I hear stories of courage and generosity. I admire other teachers.

Facing every new class is an act of courage and optimism. Years ago, the courage required was fairly primitive. I needed courage to discipline my classes, to get them into line, to motivate them to work. But now I need a deeper courage. I look at each new class and know that I must let each of these young people into my life in some significant way. The issue is one of heart. Can I open my heart to two hundred more adolescent strangers each year? Put bluntly, can I be that loving?

I hope to love my students so well that it doesn't even matter whether they like me. I want to love them in the way I love my own son—full of respect and awe for who they are, full of wanting their growth, full of wonder at what it means to lead and to follow the next generation.

Claire, when you consider a life's work, consider not just what you will take to the task, but what it will give to you. Which job will give self-respect and challenge? Which job will enlarge you and give you in abundance? Which job will teach you lessons of the heart?

With deep respect,
Margaret Metzger

QUESTIONS

1. Can you identify with the questions Claire Fox is asking at the beginning of this exchange of letters?

2. Do you know a teacher like Mrs. Metzger? Someone to whom you can ask similar questions? Someone who equally loves teaching?

3. Can you imagine yourself as a Mrs. Metzger some day? How do you think you would then answer Claire Fox's questions?

10

LEGAL, ETHICAL, AND ECONOMIC
RESPONSIBILITIES

E ducators and political leaders talk about "leveling the playing field," or ensuring that "no child is left behind." The issue of fairness seems to be a high priority for just about everyone. Determining what is fair, however, is a much more difficult proposition. What seems fair to one person can seem very unfair to another. Actions that address an unfair situation for some can create unfairness—or be perceived to create unfairness—for others. And actions that can seem neutral or innocent to one person can be deeply troubling to another. Every teacher has a professional responsibility to seek to be fair—to every student, to colleagues, and in the school policies that they advocate—but doing so is neither simple nor free of pitfalls.

Fairness can be a difficult and often elusive concept in American education. Some failures of fairness are due to deep structural problems in the education system (perhaps most of all the financial arrangements for supporting public schools and the pervasiveness of deep-seated racism and other forms of **institutionalized inequity**). Some failures are due to our tendency to overlook inequities that are right in front of us. Yet other aspects of education

> **institutionalized inequity** Embedded practice of injustice and inequality that permeates a society and is often unseen; quite different from inequity that results from individual decisions.

that are seen as unfair to some represent the triumph of someone else's definition of educational justice. Some unfairness is due to the desires of those with privilege to maintain their privilege, some to simple oversight, and some to honest differences of opinion about what is best for children. Few failures are due to teachers' deliberate decisions to be unfair.

In this chapter, we look carefully at some of the areas in which schools are failing at fairness, including why school funding isn't equal, how students are treated differently by perceived ability, why students drop out or their performance lags behind others, and what situations teachers will either face (or cause) that challenge their ethical commitments to their students, their peers, and their profession. In this chapter, we have two goals: (1) to understand the larger social issues that lead schools to operate as they do, and (2) to consider the ways in

HOW CAN WE MAKE OUR CLASSROOMS FAIR?

FOCUS >>

- Why is school funding unequal?
- Why do schools sort and track students?
- Why do students drop out before completing high school?
- Why is there an achievement gap?
- How do teachers sometimes get themselves into trouble?

which teachers, individually and in groups, can be fair, or as fair as possible, in the way they carry out their work.

A number of **Readings** help us to engage these issues. The first essay, by Stan Karp, provides an overview of the current state of school funding. By looking specifically at court-mandated efforts in the state of New Jersey, Karp helps us understand what has and has not changed in efforts to make the funding of schools fairer, especially for students living in relatively poor school districts. In the next two **Readings**, Jeannie Oakes and Tom Loveless, two well-known researchers in the field, present radically different interpretations of what current research tells us about the impact of tracking and ability grouping on the long-term academic achievement of students and the fairness of the decisions to track, or not to track, them. Finally, the essay "Why Are All the Black Kids Sitting Together in the Cafeteria?" by Beverly Daniel Tatum engages us in a discussion of what we should do to ensure fairness to all students.

>> Why Is School Funding Unequal?

It costs money to operate schools. Teachers need to be paid, buildings need to be maintained, and supplies need to be purchased. If some schools have significantly more money than other schools, many observers wonder how that could possibly be fair. School funding in every state except Hawaii has traditionally been based primarily on the local property tax base, which means that wealthier communities that have a much higher tax base per pupil can have a huge advantage over poor districts that have far fewer funds available. In part to remedy inequities between districts, states have been financing more of the cost of running schools from state-generated revenues. In many states today, the state puts as much money into schools as local communities do, though this too varies significantly. In 1970, some states provided as little as 10% of school funds for their districts. By 2000, the lowest state contribution was 20%. Many states more than matched local revenues, and some provided as much as 80% of the cost of local

school operations. During these same years, the percentage of a local **school district**'s funds that come from the federal government has stayed at around 10%.[1]

In 1961, the California Supreme Court ruled that a system of school finance "which invidiously discriminates among students on the basis of wealth violates the equal protection guaranty of the state constitution."[2] Many hoped that the result of California's *Serrano v. Priest* decision could be meaningful change in the distribution of school funds in California and a national movement in the same direction. Neither development took place, however.

> **school district** State-designated authority that administers primary and secondary schools in an established geographic boundary.

In California, a combination of legislative inaction and legal challenges slowed the implementation of the *Serrano* decision to a crawl. The optimism generated by *Serrano* came to a halt in 1973 when the U.S. Supreme Court ruled 5–4 in a Texas case, *San Antonio School District v. Rodriguez*, that unequal school financing based on differences in property tax receipts could not be challenged, at least not

in the federal courts. Speaking for the Court's majority, Justice Lewis Powell wrote,

The argument here is not that children in districts having relatively low assessable property values are receiving no public education; rather, it is that they are receiving a poorer quality education than that available to children in districts having more assessable wealth. Apart from the unsettled and disputed question whether the quality of education may be determined by the amount of money expended for it, a sufficient answer to appellees' argument is that, at least where wealth is involved, the Equal Protection clause does not require absolute equality or precisely equal advantages.

Where the Money Goes*

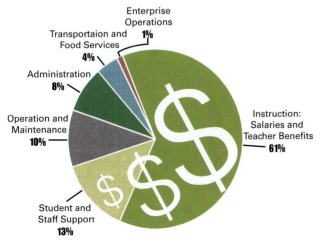

Source: Center for Education Statistics.   *Nationally per student

How Much Is Spent on Education?

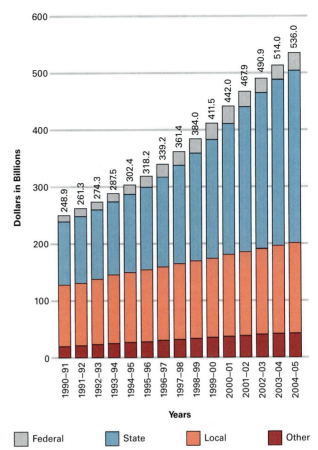

Source: NCES, "Common Core of Data," surveys and unpublished data.

This graph shows that federal funding for Title I, which provides grants to help disadvantaged children, rose from under $3 billion in 1980 to more than $7 billion in 2000 and nearly $14 billion in 2005.

In this opinion, Justice Powell offered two of the major arguments that have continued to be used in this debate: differences are not necessarily unfair as long as everyone gets a minimum education, and it is not clear that more money buys more quality education. Finally, Powell added a third argument that, coming from the Supreme Court, more or less closed the debate. He wrote, "Education, of course, is not among the rights afforded explicit protection under our Federal Constitution. Nor do we find any basis for saying it is implicitly so protected." Given that decision, further discussion of any federal role in fiscal equity in education seemed pointless.

Not everyone on the Court agreed with the majority; it was, after all, a 5–4 decision. As happened so often during the succeeding decades, Justice Thurgood Marshall spoke in a powerful dissent:

The Court today decides, in effect, that a State may constitutionally vary the quality of education which it offers its children in accordance with the amount of taxable wealth located in the school districts within which they reside. The majority's

decision represents an abrupt departure from the mainstream of recent state and federal court decisions concerning the unconstitutionality of state educational financing schemes dependent upon taxable local wealth. More unfortunately, though, the majority's holding can only be seen as a retreat from our historic commitment to equality of educational opportunity and as unsupportable acquiescence in a system which deprives children in their earliest years of the chance to reach their full potential as citizens.

Marshall, the lead attorney in winning the pivotal *Brown v. Board of Education* case, had a very different read of the U.S. Constitution than some of the other justices. For him, "[t]he fundamental importance of education is amply indicated by the prior decisions of this Court, by the unique status accorded to public education by our society, and by the close relationship between education and some of our most basic constitutional values."[3]

The result of the *Rodriguez* decision was that gross inequities continued to be the rule in terms of spending on pupils in different school districts around the nation, even in school districts that were geographically close to each other. Indeed, for the past 30 years, some of the greatest inequities have been between cities and suburbs in the same metropolitan area. Although the Supreme Court's 1973 decision closed the door on federal appeals related to schools' dependence on property taxes, the story was far from over. Many state constitutions said much more about education and educational equity than the federal constitution. If Justice Powell

was right, and education was not a right afforded by the federal constitution, it was certainly a right afforded in almost every state constitution.

As Stan Karp reports in the **Readings** for this chapter, since the *Rodriguez* decision, 40 out of the 50 state supreme courts have heard school finance cases, and in about half the cases, the courts decided that, one way or another, over-reliance on property taxes represented an unconstitutional (per the state constitution) inequity in school finance. However, as Karp also notes, winning a court case and bringing about change can be two different things. Equalizing the funding is of little help if the total funding for schools in the state is inadequate or shrinking.

Although the nation's schoolchildren are becoming much more racially diverse, the majority of voters are largely European American. Thus, a vote for more school funding is a vote to educate "other people's children," given that the majority of voters in many places do not have school-aged children. Thus, in the case of California, although the state did assume an increasing proportion of the cost of school funding, which equalized funding to some extent, the state also came up with less and less money overall. The result, as Karp notes, is that although in the 1960s California was fifth in the nation in per-pupil spending and a model for many educational reforms, by the 1990s the state was 30th out of the 50 states in school spending, and teachers and students were suffering. Clearly, equalization alone was not the solution.[4]

In rejecting the *Rodriguez* case, Justice Powell made it a point to say that there was still what he called the "unsettled and disputed question whether the quality of education may be determined by the amount of money expended for it." Many observers still debate that question. In his review of a number of recent books on school reform, *New Yorker* contributor James Traub captured one perspective:

And where many liberals, including [Jonathan] Kozol, go wrong is in overestimating the importance of school spending. Of course, schools should have a decent physical plant, books that aren't falling apart, computers, and so on, but per-pupil spending, [James] Coleman noted, has virtually no correlation with school success.[5]

On the other hand, many people wonder why such an argument is made about schooling but not about other aspects of society. The late U.S. senator Paul Wellstone made this point eloquently:

We need to rebuild our crumbling school buildings. I have asked senators during a floor debate how well they would do if we had no air conditioning during

YouDecide

What should be a school district's primary source of funding—local, state, or federal government?

Join the Dialogue

In his dissent in the *Rodriguez* case, Supreme Court Justice Thurgood Marshall wrote that allowing unequal school funding across districts to continue represents "a retreat from our historic commitment to equality of educational opportunity and as unsupportable acquiescence in a system which deprives children in their earliest years of the chance to reach their full potential as citizens." Do you agree? Is money that important to a good education?

the hot Washington summers, if the heating was inadequate during the winters, if the toilets didn't work, if the copy and fax machines were broken, if there was no e-mail, if the roof leaked during rainstorms, if the building was decrepit, rather than majestic. "These are the conditions facing millions of schoolchildren," I shouted on the floor of the Senate. "What kind of message do we send these children? We are telling them that we don't value or care about them."

Wellstone was specific about what he suspected was at least one of the causes of much of the inequity. Looking at Connecticut, one of the states that spends the most on its schools, Wellstone found that school systems across the state spent an average of $147.68 per student per year on textbooks and instructional supplies. In Hartford, the amount was $77, only 52% of the statewide average. Hartford school enrollment was more than 92% minority, whereas nearby towns such as Avon, East Granby, and Wethersfield were less than 5% minority. "Perhaps, certain children," he said, "are getting an especially strong dose of the 'we don't value or care about them' message."[6]

Join the Dialogue

A big percentage of a school district's funding comes from the local tax base. As property values have plummeted recently—more than 20% in many areas—the amount of property taxes collected is also going down. How can local school districts plan for a possible shortfall in funding? Should funding be coming from other sources to make up the difference? How might teachers be affected in terms of their salaries and in the classroom?

In some states, educators, parents, and their political allies have sought legislative support or have turned to the courts to ensure better funding for the schools. Believing that money makes a difference in the quality of education, they have sought to create a minimum base of funding that must be available to every school in their state. Increasingly, these advocates have started to campaign for what they call "adequacy" in school funding. It does not matter to them if all schools are funded equally if the amount of funding is not sufficient. However, many observers today are less worried than those from a generation before about ensuring total equality in school funding. But they do want to be sure that, through political campaigns, legislative votes, or court decisions, every school has adequate funding to provide their students with a quality basic education.

In New York, the final resolution of a long-contended suit by the Campaign for Fiscal Equity will eventually add millions of dollars to the budgets of the New York City schools. In New Jersey, as Karp describes in the **Readings**, the state supreme court came up with a clear definition of "adequacy." Assuming that the state's wealthiest districts were not wasting money, the Supreme Court of New Jersey, after years of inaction by governors and legislatures, defined adequacy as the average of the amount spent on education by the state's 130 richest districts (out of a total of 600 districts). The court then added additional funds for poor districts to cover full-day kindergarten, tutoring, and other needs. The results were dramatic. Since the new funds became available, "over 40,000 3- and 4-year-olds now attend high-quality, full-day pre-K and kindergarten programs. The math and language test score gap between urban and suburban fourth graders has been cut in half. New Jersey boasts the highest high school graduation rates in the country, including the highest rates for African American and Hispanic students. . . ." Clearly, money has made a real and measurable difference.

Karp concludes that more is yet to be done. Although New Jersey has more money for the poorest districts, some

Teachable Moment

School Funding

Despite 30 years of campaigns to equalize school funding, the most prosperous districts in some states spend a great deal more money on schools than do poor districts. In other states, legislative decisions or court orders have led to significant equalization in school funding, giving students in very poor cities the same level of education as students in very rich districts. For example, for the 2005–2006 school year,[7]

In Illinois,

- The city of Chicago spent $9,282 per pupil per year on education.
- Two of the most prosperous suburbs, Niles Township and New Trier, spent $16,470 and $17,184, respectively, per pupil.

In New York,

- New York City spent $15,539 per pupil per year.
- Two poor districts in upstate New York, Lancaster Central and North Syracuse, spent $10,020 and $11,183, respectively, per pupil.
- Two prosperous Long Island suburbs, Manhasset and Great Neck, spent $23,210 and $23,521, respectively.

In New Jersey (where the *Abbott* case, discussed in the first **Reading**, led the state to seek to equalize funding),

Students Entering High School Who Are Proficient on Eighth-Grade Exams:

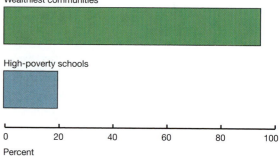

Wealthiest communities

High-poverty schools

Percent

- Camden, an old industrial city with a limited tax base, spent $20,077.
- Princeton, a university town in the middle of the state with many resources, spent $18,146.
- Two other towns not covered in the court order, Harrison Township and Point Pleasant, spent $9,696 and $10,630, respectively.

QUESTIONS

- What does equal educational opportunity or fairness mean if only half as much is spent on a child who goes to school in the city of Chicago as another child who goes to school only a few miles north, in Niles Township or New Trier?
- How would you propose to handle the disparities noted here? Or do they matter?

"I'M HOME EARLY. DUE TO BUDGET CUTS, THE SCHOOL DISTRICT IS LAYING OFF STUDENTS."

© www.CartoonStock.com

of those in the middle are still suffering. Between No Child Left Behind and a fast-changing economy, the nation's expectations for schools are changing. However, clear steps toward fairness in school spending have been made in some places, and these can be a model for others, if there is a will to do so. As Karp concludes, "Beneath the legal briefs, the legislative jargon. . .lie two central questions: Will we provide schools with the resources they need to make high-quality education possible, and will we provide those resources to all children, or only some children?"[8]

Another recent report, "Funding Student Learning: How to Align Education Resources With Student Learning Goals," notes that as important as the amount of money spent is the way it is spent. The authors describe "a finance system not capable of supporting high levels of student learning: not designed for it, not operated in order to accomplish it,

Teachable Moment

From "Equity, Adequacy, and the Evolving State Role in Education Finance"

SEAN P. CORCORAN AND WILLIAM N. EVANS

All fifty state constitutions mandate a statewide system of public education, charging state governments with providing a "thorough and efficient system of free public schools" (or similar language). State legislatures fulfill this obligation by establishing compulsory schooling laws, curriculum standards, and institutions governing the formation and operation of school districts. Despite constitutional goals, states historically played only a minor role in the *financing* of public schools, leaving the funding and day-to-day management of schools in the hands of local governments.

This long-standing devolution of **fiscal responsibility** to local school districts all but dissolved over the past century. State aid in the form of flat grants and "minimum foundation" programs became common practice in the first half of the century; later, legal challenges to state school finance systems led to far-reaching reforms that further expanded the fiscal responsibilities of the states.... These challenges originated as "equity" suits that sought to break the link between local property wealth and school resources. [See Stan Karp's **Reading** in this chapter] A later wave of litigation instead sought "adequacy" in school expenditure, as defined by the level of spending necessary to reach some performance standard. Despite the disparate objectives of these challenges, the result was more often than not an increased state role in school funding....

> **fiscal responsibility** Using available resources in a responsible and effective manner, balancing income and expenditures, and maintaining transparency in finances.

The national trend in state funding masks considerable variation across states in aid to local school districts. In 1970, for example, the fraction of school revenues from state sources varied across states from a low of 10–18 percent in New Hampshire, South Dakota, and Nebraska to a high of 60–70 percent in New Mexico, Alaska, and Delaware.... By 2001, the variation across states in the state share was much smaller, ranging from lows of 20–35 percent to a high of nearly 80 percent. Almost every state increased its share of public school revenues over this period, with Florida, Texas, and Pennsylvania being notable exceptions. Generally speaking, increases in the state share appear to reflect increases in state spending on education rather than declines in local revenues.

Explanations for this dramatic shift in fiscal responsibility for public schools from local to state can be found in part in a series of legislative and court-mandated reforms to state finance systems that originated in California's *Serrano I* ruling (1971) and continue to this day. These reforms arose initially in response to inequities generated by reliance on local property taxes for school funding, but in recent years have been driven by concerns over the adequacy of funding for public education, in particular the funding of education for students from disadvantaged backgrounds.

Pressure to reform state school funding originated in state legislatures and—more frequently—in the courts. At last count, litigants had challenged the constitutionality of state school finance systems in all but five states.

QUESTIONS

- Do you know how schools are financed in the state where you live or where you want to teach? Can you think of reasons why a teacher might want to know such information?
- Is it fair for states to step in when local communities traditionally raised the funds for their schools? By contrast, is it fair for children who live in a poor community to attend schools that are less well funded than the schools serving other children in a wealthier community?

Source: Reprinted from "Equity, Adequacy, and the Evolving State Role in Education Finance," by Sean P. Corcoran and William N. Evans, in Helen F. Ladd and Edward B. Fiske, eds., 2007, *Handbook of Research in Educational Finance and Policy,* Routledge.

not transparent enough to understand it, not accountable for it." The key is not only, or not even necessarily, more money but better ways to link the way school budgets are prepared and administered with the outcomes that educators seek in terms of effective programs for all students.[9]

>> Why Do Schools Sort and Track Students?

In the United States, the purpose of public education has never been completely clear. On the one hand, throughout history many observers have said that the fundamental purpose of public education in a democratic society, as ours aspires to be, is to ensure that everyone has a solid basic education. According to the recent federal legislation, the goal is "no child left behind." If education is really meant to be structured so that no one is left behind, then the standard of fairness—inclusion and equity to an increasingly high standard—seems pretty clear.

However, even a casual examination of the structure of schooling illuminates a second, and sometimes contradictory, purpose. According to educator Joel Spring, "schools are meant to be 'the sorting machine'," selecting some students for high levels of academic achievement and social, political, and economic leadership; others to be the middle managers; and still others to be the failures who, because of the perceived **meritocratic** nature of schooling, say, "I have only myself to blame." If schools are inevitably the sorting machine, then the definition of fairness changes dramatically. Instead of ensuring success for all, schools must determine who succeeds and who fails without tipping the balance because of gender, race, wealth, or a hundred other ways by which the larger society privileges some and marginalizes others. If schools truly are sorting machines, then those who have power and position will use their status to ensure that their children are among the winners.[10]

meritocratic Reward system based on a person's ability or talent, rather than social status.

tracking Educational practice of dividing students into different "tracks" based on perceived academic ability or achievement, with higher tracks given more challenging work.

Debates about fairness often come to a head around issues of **tracking** and ability grouping in schools. Many schools in the United States have traditionally encouraged various forms of tracking. Elementary school teachers have long divided students into different groups, such as the "Redbirds" and "Bluebirds" that Jeannie Oakes and Tom Loveless discuss in the **Readings** for this chapter. Of course, although teachers pretended that these were simply different groups, students nearly always knew which group was for the strong readers and which group was for "dummies." (Indeed, in my own experience as a fourth-grade teacher, the children were much better than the teachers at remembering which color was code for the "smarter" kids.)

Since their creation in the 19th century, American high schools have usually had different tracks for students based on both ability and perceived future plans. (Too often, those in authority made these decisions about ability and appropriate future plans based on students' race, class, or gender.) In 1892, when less than 10% of all youth ages 14 to 17 even attended high school, the National Education Association appointed a prestigious group of educators known as the Committee of Ten, chaired by the president of Harvard University, Charles W. Eliot, to make recommendations about the best curriculum for the nation's emerging high schools. Under Eliot's leadership, the committee issued a report in 1893 that said that, although there might be different courses of study depending on students' interests, there could be no distinction between curriculum for the college bound and for those preparing for "life" (that is, those planning to work directly after high school). The Committee of Ten insisted that preparation for college, whether or not one attended, was preparation for life.

Although many praised the committee's report, many others attacked it, none more than G. Stanley Hall, perhaps the nation's most famous developmental psychologist at the time. For Hall, the Committee of Ten's report was filled with fallacies, especially the notion that all students should be taught in the same way and to the same extent regardless of "probable destination." To Hall, this recommendation flew in the face of the reality that students varied greatly in their abilities and included a "great army of incapables, shading down to those who should be in schools for the dullards or subnormal children."

Connections

Recall the Chapter 1 discussion of how and why high schools were developed.

At about the same time, W. E. B. Du Bois, the first African American to earn a Ph.D. at Harvard, famously attacked the system of vocational education for African Americans that had been developed after Reconstruction in the segregated South under the leadership of Booker T. Washington. In Du Bois's view, Washington and his White supporters had made a terrible bargain, creating a system of education for the newly freed slaves that condemned them to a permanent form of second-class citizenship, a kind of across-the-board tracking of all African Americans. Thus, in 1902, Du Bois wrote, "Industrial schools must beware of placing undue emphasis on the 'practical' character of their work. . . . The ideals of education, whether men are taught to teach or to plow, to weave or to write must not be allowed to sink to sordid utilitarianism. Education must keep broad ideals before it, and never forget that it is dealing with Souls and not with Dollars."

During the same decade, Jane Addams and other feminists were, as previously noted, challenging an educational system that offered boys higher-order thinking skills in preparation for higher-level professional work but condemned girls to classes in cooking and sewing.

Between 1910 and 1917, a growing chorus of educators argued for federal legislation (which eventually became the Smith-Hughes Act of 1917) that would create separate high school programs for job-skill training for a large subset of the adolescent population who were not to be college bound. The educational philosopher John Dewey vigorously attacked the plan for vocational education, insisting that "[t]he dominant vocation of all human beings at all times is living—intellectual and moral growth. . . . To predetermine some future occupation for which education is to be a strict preparation is to injure the possibility of present development." David Snedden, commissioner of education in Massachusetts and one of the architects of vocational education, found Dewey's attack "discouraging" and indeed "incredible" since arranging for "greater productive capacity" for these students headed for the world of work would only make their lives better, even if it also limited their future life choices.

In the end, Hall, Washington, Snedden, and their allies won and Eliot, Du Bois, Addams, and Dewey lost. High schools throughout most of the 20th century were highly tracked places where students were sorted early into quite separate vocational, general, and college prep tracks. As elementary schools became increasingly preparatory for high school, in contrast to the earlier common schools offering a rudimentary education to all, they too took on many aspects of a tracked system, preparing their students at earlier years to fit into one of the tracks that the high schools offered.

Connections

In Chapter 4 we discussed how girls and women have been and still are treated differently in education.

In the 1980s, researchers and advocates began to develop a significant body of literature that showed a negative impact of tracking on those students slotted for the lower tracks while showing that the most advanced students also benefitted from an untracked school. Suddenly, a new consensus seemed to have emerged. Throughout the 1980s and 1990s, few voices were raised in favor of tracking, yet the vast majority of schools remain tracked. Researchers had achieved something of a consensus, but many teachers simply did not believe research that contradicted the only way they had ever seen schools organized, and many parents worried that detracking would hurt their children who were in more advanced tracks.[11]

In her book *Crossing the Tracks: How "Untracking" Can Save America's Schools*, Anne Wheelock directly challenges the folk wisdom that tracking is essential for well-managed, effective schools. In her survey of schools from Massachusetts to California, Wheelock describes both the political context and the pedagogical methods of untracking. She found educators in many places who understood why parents and teachers believed that tracking was best for all students but who also worked to change both the perceptions and the reality within their schools. A principal from Kentucky whom Wheelock interviewed told her that the first essential move to untracking a school was to give parents the guarantee that their child is not going to be harmed. "Parents ask, 'Can you be sure my child is not going to be worse off?' I can say 'She won't be worse off, and we hope she will be better off.'"[12] This process, like all democratic processes, takes time. Parents needed to know that they have a real voice and are not simply being consulted after the fact.

According to Wheelock, the schools that implemented **heterogeneous groupings** gained significant pedagogical opportunities. She insists that eliminating tracking only works when there is a "climate of high expectations and participatory learning for all," when there is support for "teachers' readiness for change and willingness to take risks," and when there is a "rich, high-level curriculum that reflects the goal of preparing students for a multiplicity of productive adult roles."[13] In a foreword to Wheelock's book, Jeannie Oakes elaborates on the themes she had explored earlier in *Keeping Track* (see the **Readings** for this chapter). The battle over tracking, according to Oakes, is really symbolic of a larger struggle over the purpose of education. Thus, she argues,

> **heterogeneous groupings** Group of students mixed by ability or needs to discourage tracking.

Another norm that bolsters and legitimizes tracking is the American emphasis on competition and individualism over cooperation and the good of the community—a norm suggesting that "good" education is a scarce commodity available only to a few winners. Although the American system of public

To Track or Not to Track

While researchers debate the interpretation of their studies, and school boards, superintendents, and principals set district and school policy, teachers have to make day-to-day decisions about how students are tracked or not tracked. Oftentimes significant decisions about tracking and ability grouping are made by individual teachers. Jessie Singer describes her decision early in her first year as a teacher at Cleveland High School in Portland, Oregon, not to follow the well-meaning advice of a senior colleague to "just make it through the year" and wait until another day to ask larger questions. Instead, in addition to her teaching, Singer decided to look at her school "with the eyes of an anthropologist gathering data." What she found were disturbing questions. When she asked, "Who is represented and honored in the school?" she found that the answers led to other questions about how students were separated by social class, gender, or race.

When Singer started asking questions directly of students and teachers, she gathered significant new evidence. Heather, a sophomore in a "regular" class cried when she was asked about college preparation and wrote, "My counselor told me my freshmen year that I was not college material. She said I am a regular student and should just hope to get through the next four years. Why are you making me write a college essay when I am not headed there?" Deanna, a fellow teacher said, "I feel like I am tracked in our department because I am not an honors teacher. I'm seen as just a regular teacher and my kids don't matter." If both teachers and students were feeling that many of them didn't matter because of the system of tracking, something needed to be done.

Singer also felt that her very "newness" allowed her to ask questions that others couldn't. Thus, in one department meeting, she asked her senior colleagues to consider, "Who is honored here?" She thought, "As a new teacher, I had an advantage. I felt I had a kind of permission to share my observations as a naïve and new agent." The conversations were still difficult. One teacher said, "My regular students are lazy and hard to deal with." But another asked, "What does it say about us as educators if we are only feeling successful with an already successful group of kids?"

In the end, Singer's questions, backed up by her research and the support that she had cultivated, led the department to untrack the ninth grade. She was pleased to report:

We decided that all students should begin their time at Cleveland High School with an opportunity to be seen equally—without pre-assigned labels. As a result of this work, freshmen classes now represent the true population of our school with equal numbers of boys and girls, students from different neighborhoods, and diverse backgrounds. A colleague in my department who was initially resistant to the idea of untracking, walked into my classroom and said, "I love teaching my freshmen classes. In all my years of teaching this age group these classes are more engaged and more fun to teach than any I have taught before."

Quite an accomplishment for a first-year teacher who started out just asking questions! Of course, not every teacher is going to be as fortunate as Singer. She was in a place where questions were allowed if not always encouraged. She quickly found colleagues, in her school and beyond, so that her efforts were not isolated. As a result of her questions and her beliefs, she was able to develop a clear agenda and move quickly.

QUESTIONS

- How do you think you would respond if, as a new teacher, a senior colleague told you to stop asking so many questions and "just make it through the year"?
- Is this story of Jessie Singer's experience realistic? Can you imagine playing a similar role in your first year as a teacher?

Source: "Getting Students Off Track," by Jessie Singer, 2004, in *The New Teacher Book*, Rethinking Schools, pp. 210–216.

education was designed to promote the common good and to prepare children for participation in a democratic society, more recent emphasis has been placed on what a graduate can "get out" of schooling in terms of income, power, or status.[14]

As we noted at the beginning of this section, the American system of education has always been torn between promoting the common good and selecting and nurturing a few winners who will be the leaders—and prime beneficiaries—of the society. Tracking is an ideal means of accomplishing the latter goal, for it identifies differences early and builds on them throughout schooling. A different model is needed, however, if the other goal—the democratic goal—is to be central.

Much more recently a new group of scholars (Tom Loveless, whose article is in the **Readings**, is an example), have begun to question the detracking agenda. Although Loveless would not argue for a return to the rigid tracking favored by G. Stanley Hall or David Snedden, and he decries the ways in which tracking has too often mirrored race and class divides in the past, he and others do favor something like the system of tracking that exists in the majority of schools today. Loveless contends that tracking today is based on a combination of teacher recommendations, student grades, test scores, parental preference, and even students' own views. He sees important virtues in a system that for high-achieving students offers "tracked classes with an accelerated or enriched curriculum" that "are superior to heterogeneously grouped classes." Oakes, on the other hand, sees major pitfalls in this same flexibility, which she believes can quickly shade into a vagueness that gives preference to a privileged few students.

YouDecide
Is there a specific scenario in which students benefit from tracking?

guidance at the high school itself. I simply turned in my books at the school office and went away. That's all there was to it. No one spoke to me. No one asked me why I was leaving or discussed my problems with me.

As he celebrated that day with his friends, Covello wondered aloud if anyone at the school cared if he ever came back. A friend responded, "Come back? Does a jailbird wanna get back to prison?" Sadly, both the friend's response and the attitude of those long-ago school authorities at Morris High School has been repeated many times since then.[15]

Today, students still get bored with school, and some still view school as a kind of prison. Students still slip between the cracks and school administrators may be as indifferent as those at Covello's school. However, a century ago, more than 90% of high school students followed the road Covello took that day: they dropped out well before graduating. Today, around 70% of high school students do graduate. A century ago, few people, including teachers and administrators, worried about the dropout rate. High school was for a minority, and plenty of jobs in the industrial economy did not require a diploma. Today, attitudes and opportunities have changed dramati-

Connections
Leonard Covello's impact on education is discussed in "Portrait of an Educator" in Chapter 7.

>> Why Do Students Drop Out Before Completing High School?

Just over a century ago, Leonard Covello, a young high school student at Morris High School in New York City, decided to drop out. Unlike many dropouts, Covello eventually returned and went on to a career as one of New York City's most respected high school principals. But in 1905, he was bored with school and saw no connection between what he was studying and any future he envisioned for himself. He remembered the day well:

What stands foremost in my mind concerning this decision was the indifference and the lack of

Did you know?
About 1.2 million students drop out of school each year, or about 2,500 each day. Of the 50 largest U.S. cities, 17 have high school graduation rates lower than 50%. The lowest graduation rates are in Detroit, Indianapolis, and Cleveland. Philadelphia, Tucson, and Kansas City (Missouri) have improved the most in graduation rates. The United States is ranked 10th in the world in high school graduation rates.

Teachable Moment
Getting Kids to School

Regular attendance obviously plays an important role in student success. Once a student starts getting behind, dropping out becomes a less painful option than trying to catch up. In many school districts, just getting students to show up to class is half the battle. The St. Louis Public Schools district has always grappled with getting students to attend on the first day of school. For the 2009–2010 school year, new leaders began tackling the problem by starting a campaign of attendance more than a month before the buses rolled.

Top administrators visited area churches, urging congregants to get their children to class. Hundreds of volunteers canvassed neighborhoods to hand out back-to-school fliers. The district even blasted all 25,000 students with a phone message, prerecorded by St. Louis Rams linebacker Chris Draft, and held a first-day drawing to give 500 students two tickets each to a St. Louis Rams game.

The results? Board president Rick Sullivan said that many schools reported calmer, less chaotic classrooms, and their numbers were better than expected.

However, for the entire district, Superintendent Kelvin Adams reported that an estimated 19,632 students came on the first day, or about 80% of those enrolled—roughly the same as the previous year.

Source: "Some First-day Kinks to Iron Out for St. Louis Schools," by David Hunn, August 21, 2009, *St. Louis Dispatch*, http://www.stltoday.com/stltoday/news/stories.nsf/education/story/853ACC5544A0C1C38625761900133A8E?OpenDocument.

QUESTIONS

- Why do you think some districts find it so hard to get students to come to school? Can you imagine a school in which 20% of the students simply did not show up on the first day, or any day? If you were a leader in this or a similar school or district, what would you do?

- Did you ever consider skipping school? What made you attend day after day? Why do you think what worked for you might not work for some young people?

Did you know?

The average high school dropout earns $19,000 a year, compared to $28,000 for a high school graduate with no higher education.

cally. Schools are held accountable for their dropout rates, and most teachers and administrators will do all they can to keep students in school. School systems develop programs to encourage those who have left to return and complete their education. Today's postindustrial economy offers few opportunities for those who lack a high school diploma or proficiency in reading, writing, and mathematics.

As we saw in Chapters 3 and 4, with passage of the Education for All Handicapped Children Act in 1975, most *legal* barriers to the full inclusion of all children in the nation's classrooms had finally fallen. However, cultural barriers can be more difficult to challenge than legal ones. Students who feel or are made to feel unwelcome will drop out or, perhaps more accurately, will be pushed out by failures, conscious and unconscious, on the part of schools to create the kinds of educational communities that truly leave no child behind.

Just as the Supreme Court's 1954 *Brown v. Board of Education* decision did not end racial segregation in schools, the federal legislation of the 1970s did not end other forms of exclusion. Well-known historians of education David Tyack and Elisabeth Hansot use the example of African Americans to explore the many forms of discrimination that continue in the schools:

> Beyond the bias built into law and clear policy, blacks also faced a more amorphous and less conscious kind of discrimination, which became labeled "institutional racism." Blacks found that civil rights laws did not dismantle many of the attitudinal, economic, and institutional hurdles they faced. In public education, civil rights groups targeted a number of forms of institutional racism: the omission of blacks and the use of negative stereotypes of African-Americans in textbooks; biased behavior of teachers toward people of color, arguably all the more potent in its impact when unconscious; the use of racially unfair tests; bias in counseling; the failure to appoint and advance black employees; and the tracking of blacks into slow lanes or dead-end vocational programs that blocked them from further education or white-collar jobs.[16]

These more amorphous but often more powerful forms of discrimination continue in schools to this day, and they apply to African Americans and other people of color, girls of all races and ethnic groups, and also to many other young people never formally discriminated against or excluded, as well as to those whose exclusion or second-class status was officially ended in the 1950s, 1960s, and 1970s.

Researcher Michelle Fine spent the 1984–1985 school year in another New York City high school asking herself—and the students, teachers, and administrators—why the majority of students still dropped out of that particular school prior to graduation. Fine listened carefully to their stories, including these:

> Diana (a seventeen-year-old dropout): My mother has lupus. She's dying and those doctors are killing her. Nobody speaks English good in my family, and she wants me there. My brothers and sisters, they little and need me. . . .

> Broderick (a sixteen-year-old dropout): Where else am I gonna make this money, even with a diploma?

Dropouts Among 16 to 24-year-olds

	Native-born						Foreign-born					
Race/ethnicity	White	Black	Hispanic	Asian	Pacific Islander	American Indian/Alaska Native	White	Black	Hispanic	Asian	Pacific Islander	American Indian/Alaska Native
Percent	6	12	11	2	6	15	5	8	34	4	12	1

Source: U.S. Department of Commerce, Census Bureau, American Community Survey (ACS), 2007.

Teachable Moment
Tracking the Dropout Rate

No one knows for sure how many students drop out before completing high school. Students move or transfer to different schools, districts do not want to acknowledge the depth of the dropout problem, and few informed observers trust the official **dropout rate** announced by any school district.

Nevertheless, some pretty convincing evidence indicates that the dropout rate is growing in the United States, especially in many of the largest cities. Despite significant efforts to reduce the dropout rate in New York City, for example, one study estimated that the percentage of students who did not finish high school had grown from 17.5% in 2000 to 21% in 2007. Perhaps most worrisome is that the greatest growth in dropout numbers came from ninth graders, who were dropping out in much larger numbers in 2007 than they had in 2000. These statistics generate several debates, including the following:

> **dropout rate** Number or percentage of students who enter school but do not graduate, often calculated on the basis of those who enter ninth grade but do not finish twelfth grade.

- The New York City Department of Education estimated that 74% of all of the students "discharged" from the city's high schools (meaning students who left a city high school before graduating for any reason) were moving to a district outside of the city, yet researchers found no census data to indicate that so many adolescents were moving out of New York.
- The Department of Education also reported that 2,084 students in the class of 2007 transferred to parochial schools, whereas only 821 had done so in 2004. But parochial school enrollment did not show such an increase over those years.
- Researchers also found that many more African American and Latino students left the schools than White or Asian students, and many more boys than girls, numbers that would not make much sense if the majority who left were simply moving elsewhere.

Source: "Number of Students Leaving School Early Continues to Increase, Study Says," by Jennifer Medina, *New York Times*, April 30, 2009.

Tracking Early Departures

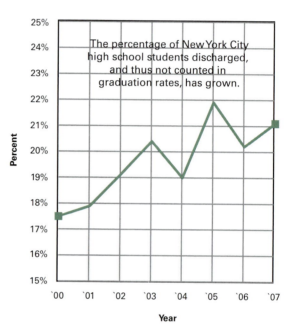

Source: "High School Discharges Revisited," Jennifer L. Jennings and Leonie Haimson.

The honest answer is that no one knows exactly how many students actually drop out in New York City—as opposed to moving, transferring, or otherwise continuing their high school careers elsewhere. The same holds true for most other districts in the United States.

If more students are dropping out of school today than did so ten years ago, they are dropping out in a society and an economy that offers them far less opportunity for a fulfilling life than any previous generation of non-high school graduates faced.

QUESTIONS

- Why do you think it is so hard to get accurate data about the dropout rate? Can you think of reasons the numbers would be hard to find? Who might benefit by not knowing the actual numbers or by having the numbers appear smaller than they really are?
- If you could make one policy that might reduce the dropout rate, what would it be? Is implementing your policy realistic?

I know it's a risk. I just got out of Spofford [juvenile facility]. I worry about how my mother feels 'bout it. . . . Sometimes I feel it's immoral, when I sold Angel Dust to a pregnant girl. Won't do that again. But you can't have a heart up here. . . . If I don't give it to her, someone will.

Fine summarized the reasons for dropping out that she heard from Diana, Broderick, and too many others, saying that *dropout* really is not the right word—exclusion from the school would be a better one. At her school, Fine found that exclusion happens,

- "when my Momma comes and they show her no respect" . . .

- When national suspension and expulsion rates double for Black and Latino students compared with those for white (non-Latino) students.

- Inside the fifteen-year-old history book introduced by a white teacher to her African-American student body with the following apology: "This book is not too good on Blacks."

- It existed in a literature class in which "good reading" signified the whiteness and usually the maleness of the authors, or a social studies class in which culture got defined as "what the Puritans and Pilgrims gave us," spoken to a group of African-American and Latino blank-looking faces.

- Exclusion was being held back in grade because you missed classes January through March, nursing your grandmother back to health after coronary surgery.

- It was feeling confused in class, but "embarrassed to ask for help."

- Exclusion was also being absent for five days and never being missed, or hearing that a diploma will bring you success, but knowing that your mother, uncle, and brothers, all graduates, can't find work.

Fine's list goes on. It includes students recruited to jobs or for-profit schools that turn out to be dead ends. It includes students who are continually silenced in school and demand the right to tell the truth about "racism; of an economy that declares itself prosperous while many live in poverty, sickness, and substandard (or no) housing; of an ideology of education as the Great Equalizer when there's little evidence; and of the secrets of sexism that claim the bodies and minds of their mothers, sisters, aunts, and themselves." The result of these realities is that in the school Fine studied, not that long ago, out of a student body of 3,200, only 200 students graduated in June 1985, and 70% of those who start ninth grade do not ever graduate. Across the United States, 25%–30% of all the nation's fifth graders never make it to a high school diploma.[18]

How much has changed in the 20 years since Fine completed her study? The answer is a great deal and not very much. Many cities, including New York, have instituted multiple pathways to encourage students in danger of dropping out to obtain their high school diploma by a different route. In 2006, the City of New York offered a complex array of options, including afternoon and evening high schools for students who wanted to work full time, learning-to-work programs that blend high school classes with in-depth job readiness, transfer high schools that offer rigorous academic programs for overage students who want to try again, and GED (General Education Diploma) programs.

At the same time, increasingly rigorous standards and tests have discouraged some students, especially those who were already behind academically and who, with the new standards, come to feel that they will never make it. Students who never bothered to start high school are rarely counted as dropouts, and some who simply stop showing up are listed as having moved when in fact they have dropped out but never notified the school. In 2006, official New York Department of Education reports said that, overall, nearly 140,000 New York youths ages 16–21 were off-track for their age cohort or had already dropped out of school, and about half of all incoming high school freshmen become overage and behind schedule during high school.[19]

How Can I Make a Difference?

What Can We Do About the Dropout Problem?

If the United States is to be a truly democratic society, the dropout rate needs to be addressed. In a new report from Jobs for the Future and the Everyone Graduates Center, *Graduating America: Meeting the Challenge of Low Graduation-Rate High Schools,* the report's authors, Cheryl Almeida, Robert Balfanz, Joanna Hornig Fox, Janet Santos, and Adria Steinberg, outline the current situation and provide specific recommendations for change:

> In his first major address to Congress, President Barack Obama envisioned a country where dropping out "is no longer an option." He linked improving high school graduation rates to restoring the nation's economic and political standing in the world.
>
> Since then, federal officials and educators have focused on transforming or replacing the 2,000 high schools that produce more than half of U.S. dropouts. No longer can these failing schools, which routinely graduate fewer than two-thirds of their students, "go it alone." Substantially increasing the number of young people who earn a high school diploma and are ready for college will require effective partnerships among the federal government, states, communities, and school districts.
>
> The timing could hardly be better. The American Recovery and Reinvestment Act (ARRA) is pumping billions of dollars into turning around low-performing schools and has laid important groundwork for different levels and branches of government to work together.
>
> Despite the temptation to quickly scale up interventions that have made an impact in a few places, it would be a waste of precious resources to do so without carefully analyzing the conditions that make success possible. Too often, good ideas are applied in the wrong places. And no single approach—or particular combination of federal, state, and local participation—will work for every low graduation-rate high school.
>
> While high schools with low graduation rates have developed in every state and many communities across the country, they are concentrated in a subset of 17 states that produce approximately 70 percent of the nation's dropouts. These states, which are the focus of this report, are by no means homogeneous. Some are densely populated; others are not. Nearly half have raised their graduation rates, while rates remain stagnant or have worsened in others. These 17 states are the "make or break" places on the road to reaching the President's goal of making America once again first in the world in educational attainment.
>
> **Recommendations for Immediate Federal Action:** The federal government has a once-in-a-generation opportunity to stimulate significant progress in solving the nation's graduation crisis. Leaders in policy and practice must seize the moment and plan thoughtful approaches to using federal ARRA and other funding to help turn around failing high schools. In particular, federal officials should rethink how they can most effectively target resources to tackle the challenges posed by the high schools that produce most of the nation's dropouts....

>> Why Is There an Achievement Gap?

In 2004, educator Jacqueline Jordan Irvine reflected on the current state of American education and the two factors that were her greatest disappointments after a career focused on improving the schools: the increase in segregation in schools, and the continuing decline in the school achievement of African American and Latino students. For Irvine, as disturbing as the stubborn continuity, even growth, of segregation might be, the more significant issue is the **achievement gap** between students of different races shown in test scores on most standardized examinations. Children of color are not being taught in ways that help them achieve at the same level as White students. Irvine continues,

> achievement gap Lower educational scores for populations of students based on gender, race/ethnicity, or socioeconomic status; most prevalent between students of color and White students.

> *This test-score gap is revealed in the fact that white students, on average, score 20 to 30 points higher than their black and Hispanic peers. But*

Recommendation: The ARRA should require states applying for Race to the Top funding to identify their lowest graduation-rate high schools and to analyze the concentration and spread of these high schools, as well as other relevant school, student, and contextual factors in the selection of strategies.

Recommendation: No single strategy or approach will work for all states, districts, and schools. Capacity-building and technical-assistance efforts need to be flexible enough to allow those with the capacity to lead to do so, which will sometimes be the state and other times the district or school, often in concert with reform organizations. Federal and state leaders can use a variety of approaches to build capacity. For example, they can support community-led efforts to raise the graduation rate through a community investment fund, similar to a fund mandated in the 2009 Edward M. Kennedy Serve America Act.

Recommendation: Transforming or replacing all of the nation's low graduation-rate high schools will require investment in new school designs, as well as growing and spreading models that are effective for the low-income students who predominate in failing schools, including the substantial percentage of students who are not on track to graduate. More is known now than ever before about what works for this group of young people. Promising results are emerging from new small schools and programs that put them back on track to graduation. The federal government can provide incentives for states to reallocate resources and encourage innovators to expand the supply of such designs and models.

Recommendation: The whole nation suffers from the failure of high schools in Florida, California, and other large states. Like the financial services giant AIG, they are simply too big to fail. And many communities in states such as South Carolina and Michigan, where industry has left, may be too fragile to recover on their own. Graduation Bonds, similar to the Recovery Bonds mandated in the ARRA, could go a long way toward providing needed seed capital to enable districts to transform or replace low graduation-rate high schools and to develop new options for dropouts.

In Conclusion: In order to make progress, our nation's leaders and the public must get beyond the myth that "nothing works," that low graduation-rate schools cannot be transformed or replaced successfully. The growing knowledge base of promising strategies, combined with a more concerted effort to match reforms to the circumstances where they are most likely to succeed, can go a long way in helping the nation reach the president's goal of once again being the first in the world in the percentage of our young people who complete high school and earn a postsecondary credential as well.

Source: *Graduating America: Meeting the Challenge of Low Graduation-Rate High Schools,* by Robert Balfanz, Cheryl Almeida, Adria Steinberg, Janet Santos, and Joanna Hornig Fox, July 2009, Jobs for the Future, www.jff.org.

QUESTIONS

- Can you imagine teaching in one of the high-drop-out-rate schools identified in this report? If you found yourself in such a school, are there things you, as a teacher, could do while waiting for state and federal action?
- The report recommends that federal and state leaders "can support community-led efforts to raise the graduation rate through a community investment fund." If you were to receive such funds, can you imagine designing a new high school that would address the needs of students in danger of dropping out?

the importance of the discrepancy becomes even more apparent when considering what a 30-point difference means for the average black or Hispanic student. Seventeen-year-old black and Hispanic students have skills in reading, mathematics, and science that are similar to those of a 13-year-old white student.

These realities, with varying specificity, are true North and South, urban and rural, and also in integrated suburban schools. While some of the achievement gap can be explained by gaps in income (as if that is in itself an accept-

able explanation), it is also true that African American and Latino children perform less well in school even when compared with Whites of the same economic and social class.[20]

Beverly Daniel Tatum offers a partial explanation of the pervasiveness of racism that accounts for some of these differences. In her

Connections

Recall the Chapter 3 discussion of continued segregation in the schools.

PORTRAIT OF AN EDUCATOR

Marian Wright Edelman

Marian Wright Edelman was born in 1939 in South Carolina and grew up as the daughter of a Baptist minister in the segregated South. As a lawyer and education advocate, she became a national voice, sometimes a national conscience, for fairness and a more ethical approach to the education of all of the nation's children. Edelman remembers lessons of her childhood fondly and they have affected the direction of her life work as an educator. In her book *The Measure of Our Success*, she wrote,

> *The adults in our churches and community made children feel valued and important. They took time and paid attention to us. They struggled to find ways to keep us busy. And while life was often hard and resources scarce, we always knew who we were and that the measure of our worth was inside our heads and hearts and not outside in our possessions or on our backs.*

After attending Spelman College and Yale Law School, Edelman was the first African American woman admitted to the Mississippi Bar. She directed the NAACP Legal Defense and Education Fund office in Jackson, Mississippi, during the height of the civil rights movement in the 1960s.

Edelman later moved to Washington, D.C., and in 1973 she founded the Children's Defense Fund. She has been its president for more than three decades. Edelman described the work of the Children's Defense Fund, saying, "We are most interested in helping those children in American society who have the least." Since 1973, Edelman has had a nonstop schedule: testifying before Congress, drafting and lobbying for legislation that supports education and helps children, speaking to education groups, and finding ways to rally the widest possible coalition of people who will care about poor children "either because they will feel good that they have done the right thing at a not-too-great cost or because they will realize that their own economic or social interest is also served."

The Children's Defense Fund web site describes the organization as "the foremost national proponent of policies and programs that provide children with the resources they need to succeed." These include advocacy for stronger policies that support families, help prevent teen pregnancy, provide jobs, and shift national resources from a military buildup to education programs that serve all of the nation's children. Increasingly, the Children's Defense Fund is focused on providing health care for all Americans, especially children, as an essential foundation to an effective education while continuing to support legislation and financing for better schools. Much of what came to be known as the child advocacy movement began at the Children's Defense Fund. For Edelman, the civil rights movement and her long campaign for better education and social services for all children, especially poor and marginalized children, are one continuous movement.

Sources: Marian Wright Edelman, The Measure of Our Success: A Letter to My Children and Yours (Boston: Beacon Press, 1992), p. 5; and Marian Wright Edelman, Families in Peril: An Agenda for Social Change (Cambridge: Harvard University Press, 1987), p. ix.

Achievement Gap

Blacks and Hispanics score (on average) 21 to 32 points lower than Whites on tests by the National Assessment of Educational Progress (NAEP).

Reading

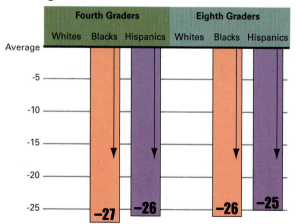

Mathematics

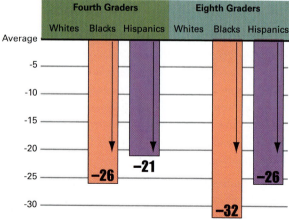

Source: U.S. Department of Education, National Center for Education Statistics, National Assessment of Educational Progress (NAEP), various years, 1990–2007 Reading and Mathematics Assessments, NAEP Data Explorer.

book *Why Are All the Black Kids Sitting Together in the Cafeteria? And Other Conversations About Race*, a selection from which is included in the **Readings** for this chapter, Tatum identifies a question that many teachers, especially many European American teachers, often ask each other: If integration is the goal, why do so many kids of color voluntarily segregate themselves in school, especially in high school? It is a very real and important question and deserves our attention. So, too, does the obvious reality that Tatum notes: "Conversely, it could be pointed out that there are many groups of White students sitting together as well, though people rarely comment about that."[21]

The question of self-segregation allows Tatum to look at not only some of the reasons for this choice on the part of many African American adolescents but also the social pain

that leads to it. As her son David enters adolescence, Tatum asks, "Do the women hold their purses a little tighter, maybe even cross the street to avoid him? Does he hear the sound of automatic door locks on cars as he passes by? Is he being followed around by the security guards at the local mall?"[22] Given the likely answers to these questions, it is no wonder, Tatum concludes, that African American adolescents are likely to self-segregate. Finding others with whom they can share these experiences, with some degree of safety, becomes terribly important in adolescence.

Perhaps educator Asa Hiliard said it best. Surveying a wide range of efforts to make schools, especially urban schools serving poor students and student of color, more effective, he concluded, "There are literally hundreds of other examples that document excellent achievement in urban schools.

Promising Practices

STEM Education

Historically, girls and students of color have scored lower in areas such as math and technology, creating a disadvantage when it comes to going to college or entering a workforce that is increasingly technology oriented. Across the board, Americans have not done well in science or mathematics in comparison to students from many other countries. The Obama administration's education reform includes efforts to focus attention on these disciplines by implementing expanded STEM (science, technology, engineering, and math) programs.

Although science and math are typically covered in a high school curriculum, the areas of technology and engineering are often overlooked and do not have learning or content standards as there are for math or science. When Arne Duncan, Secretary of Education, was superintendent of Chicago's schools in 2006–2007, the public school district fostered study in STEM disciplines by implementing collaborations among K–12 schools, universities, and private organizations. Secondary teachers attended supplementary courses at colleges to keep themselves up-to-date with current research in their subject areas. Students attended after-school clubs created in partnership with local museums and community groups that focused on

science and math. In another out-of-the-classroom-and-into-the-real-world move, students were paired with STEM professionals in internship programs.

With an expanded STEM emphasis in American schools, and more effective approaches to instruction, experts hope that all American students will become competitive in a global market. For more information on the project, visit www.stemedcoalition.org.

Source: "Momentum Building on STEM Education," by Laura Devaney, August 14, 2009, eSchool News, http://www.eschoolnews.com/news/top-news/index.cfm?i=60180

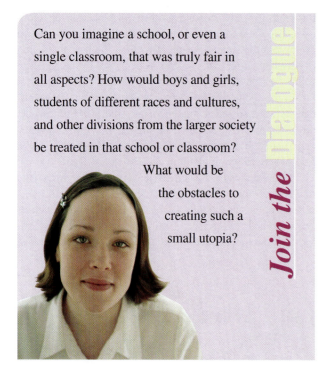

Results like those would be typical *if we had the will to see it happen.*"[23] Having the will to make change happen is essential to making schools fairer places for everyone.

In discussing the issues of fairness and unfairness in American education, it is important to note how rapidly things can change, sometimes for the better, sometimes for the worse, and sometimes just differently. In a particularly perceptive study of urban youth, *Identity & Inner-City Youth: Beyond Ethnicity and Gender,* Shirley Brice Heath and Milbrey W. McLaughlin noted that the experience of race and ethnicity at the beginning of the 21st century is different from what it was in the 1950s and 1960s, when many of the images related to these issues were created by the civil rights movement. Thus, they assert that policy makers (and teachers) can be thrown off balance if they retain "images from the 1960s of proud, protesting, largely homogeneous [African American] urban ghetto communities." The reality, these researchers assert, is that many of today's urban youth do not live in a community of one ethnic group, such as African American or Latino, but "what they see today are different groups continually moving in and out of their housing project and neighborhoods." The result is that "for today's youth, ethnicity comprises not the primary identity but an additional 'layer of identity.'"

Heath and McLaughlin found that gender roles had also changed and, if anything mattered, more than in previous decades among today's poor urban youth. Their interviews with city youth led them to conclude that "lived experiences every day told the young that their gender mattered as much as if not more than their ethnicity." In many poor urban neighborhoods today, something that "amounted to a dual society" has developed. Young women and young

men have taken on very specific—and very different—social roles. The young person that steps out of role is courting disaster. At the same time "many of the institutions that had lent social control for sustained family life in past generations, such as churches and gender-segregated religious clubs, no longer endured in inner cities."[24]

In the midst of the ever-changing reality faced by many of today's young people, teachers have a special responsibility to understand what is affecting their students' lives and then move from understanding to action. As Pedro Noguera reminds us in the **Readings** for Chapter 11, teachers cannot fix all of the social, cultural, and economic forces that make life hard and discouraging for too many young people today. But teachers can—and must—be people who offer young people hope. In the midst of an unfair and unjust world, teachers can help create classrooms and schools that, as Heath and McLaughlin say, give "visible and ongoing voice to a conception of youth as a resource to be developed and as persons of value to themselves and to society."[25] Students are not victims to be felt sorry for, but persons of value with unique strengths and needs.

Not only are students' lived experiences of ethnicity and gender changing constantly, but also the meaning of fairness is changing. Some forms of unfairness have been eliminated. State legislatures no longer pass laws mandating the legal segregation of schools by race. School districts no longer (for the most part) segregate girls and boys, requiring girls to focus on home economics while the boys learn industrial arts. High school dropout rates for all students, and especially for African American students, are not what they were in 1950. Many forms of once-common racist and sexist language are not tolerated and are illegal in many schools. Victories have been won. In some ways, schools are manifestly fairer places than they were 20, 30, or 50 years ago. Some observers see this as a sign of inevitable progress and hope that the remaining forms of unfairness will also decline in due course. Others are not so sure and worry that as some forms of unfairness and discrimination disappear, new forms—sometimes more insidious forms because they come from unexpected quarters—may begin to emerge.

>> How Do Teachers Sometimes Get Themselves Into Trouble?

Although the primary focus of this chapter is fairness toward students—in the classroom and in the nation—teachers are also expected to be fair and ethical in their relationships with each other and with their employer, the school district. In *Tough Choices for Teachers: Ethical Challenges in Today's Schools and Classrooms,* Robert Infantino and Rebecca Wilke explore a wide range of **ethical dilemmas** that teachers can encounter, including when it is permissible to use school supplies, what sort of stance

Teachable Moment

Spelling Out Discrimination and Sexual Harassment

School districts have explicit guidelines regarding inappropriate or unlawful conduct on the part of employees and students. Following are excerpts from the St. Charles (Missouri) R-VI School District Board of Education's "Prohibition Against Illegal Discrimination and Harassment" policy that is distributed to employees, parents, and students:

General Rule:

The St. Charles R-VI School District Board of Education is committed to maintaining a workplace and educational environment that is free from illegal discrimination or harassment in admission or access to, or treatment or employment in, its programs, activities, and facilities. Discrimination or harassment against employees, students or others on the basis of race, color, religion, sex, national origin, ancestry, disability, age, or any other characteristic protected by law is strictly prohibited in accordance with the law. The St. Charles R-VI School District is an equal opportunity employer. Students, employees, and others will not be disciplined for speech in circumstances where it is protected by law. The Board also prohibits:

1. Retaliatory actions based on making complaints of prohibited discrimination or harassment or based on participation in an investigation, formal proceeding or informal resolution concerning prohibited discrimination or harassment.
2. Aiding, abetting, inciting, compelling, or coercing discrimination or harassment.
3. Discrimination or harassment against any person because of such person's association with a person protected from discrimination or harassment due to one or more of the above-stated characteristics.

All employees, students, and visitors must immediately report to the district for investigation any incident or behavior that could constitute illegal discrimination or harassment.

Additional Prohibited Behavior

Behavior that is not unlawful or does not rise to the level of illegal discrimination of harassment might still be unacceptable for the workplace or the educational environment. Demeaning or otherwise harmful actions are prohibited, particularly if directed at personal characteristics including, but not limited to, socioeconomic level, sexual orientation, or perceived sexual orientation.

Additionally, the policy spells out behaviors that could constitute sexual harassment:
1. Sexual advances and requests or pressure of any kind for sexual favors, activities, or contact.
2. Conditioning grades, promotions, rewards or privileges on submission to sexual favors, activities or contact.
3. Punishing or reprimanding persons who refuse to comply with sexual requests, activities or contact.
4. Graffiti, name calling, slurs, jokes, gestures of communications, or a sexual nature based on sex.
5. Physical contact or touching of a sexual nature, including touching of intimate parts and sexually motivated or inappropriate patting, pinching, or rubbing.

QUESTIONS

- Why do you think school districts issue statements like this? What might have happened that would lead a district to send such explicit rules to teachers, parents and students?
- If you were a teacher, would you find a policy like this to be reassuring (because you were protected) or a type of bureaucratic interference (because there are so many rules to follow)?

Source: "Prohibition Against Illegal Discrimination and Harassment," St. Charles, Missouri R-VI School District Board of Education, 2009.

ethical dilemma Problem for which no solution presents itself that is morally or ethically clear and acceptable in the circumstances.

to take toward grading and letters of reference, and the inevitable questions about a teacher's social life in and out of school.[26] Infantino and Wilke offer a series of snapshots of the kinds of ethical dilemmas that new as well as experienced teachers can easily find themselves facing:

- A newly-minted social studies teacher has been asked by "Marcos" to write a letter of support for his college application. The problem is that Marcos is not working very hard and has been difficult in class. But he begs for the letter. A senior colleague says, "Just write a nice letter—you can skip some of the details." But while the new teacher certainly wants to support all of her students and does not want to keep one of them out of college, she also has grave reservations about sending off a vague letter which in the end fails to tell the truth about either the student's academic work or his behavior in class.

- A department chair is leading a search committee that includes one first-year teacher for a new hire in the department. In the midst of the committee's review of three strong candidates, one veteran teacher said, "You know, an African American male really would not fit in that well here. After all, we have so few students of color, and most don't even graduate." The committee then turns to the newest member. How should she respond?

- A first-year elementary teacher attends a faculty meeting where the group is told that things are disappearing from the school supply closet. Later she runs into one of the senior teachers walking down the hall with an armload of paper and other supplies. She looks shocked but the veteran says, "What's wrong?" and she continues "now you know when to sneak down here and get a few things when you need them. It's all for the good of the kids, right?" Is it, the novice wonders, for the good of the kids or is it old-fashioned theft?

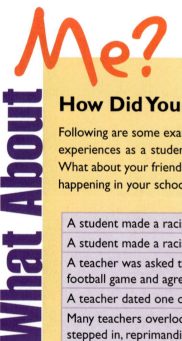

How Did Your Teachers Respond?

Following are some examples of common ethical issues that teachers face daily in a classroom. Regarding your own experiences as a student, have you ever been aware of one of your teachers taking any of the following actions? What about your friends' teachers? Put a check mark next to each example that you have heard about or witnessed happening in your school.

A student made a racial slur and the teacher promptly reprimanded the offending student.	
A student made a racial slur and was ignored by the teacher.	
A teacher was asked to boost a student's grade so that the student could play at next week's football game and agreed, providing the athlete with make-up work and extra credit opportunities.	
A teacher dated one of his or her students.	
Many teachers overlooked the frequent bullying of a particular student until one teacher stepped in, reprimanding the bullies and providing help to the bullied student.	
A teacher posted a bulletin board, showed a video, or created a lesson that subsequently got the teacher in trouble with administration.	
A teacher had clear favorites in the classroom and often rewarded those students undeservedly and punished students he or she didn't like.	
A teacher dated one of his or her administrators or fellow teachers.	
A teacher was asked to boost a student's grade so that the student could play at next week's football game and disagreed, eventually taking a position at another school.	
A teacher frequently stole supplies from the school.	
A teacher led a group of students in protesting for a change to faulty school policy or curriculum.	

- A new teacher is told by very influential parents that she needs to change a student's grade. The wealthy father is clear, "Matthew has always been a straight A student, and now he has a B+ in your class. This is simply unacceptable." The teacher stands her ground but wonders if the administration will back her up or even if she wants to stay in a profession with such pressures.

- A first-year teacher tells her close friend who is a teacher at a different school, "I really, really blew it! You know that cute boyfriend I was telling you about? Well, I didn't tell you everything. First of all, he's the assistant principal at the school here and, oh my gosh, I hate to even say it, but he's. . .he's also married!"[27]

These stories represent very real and immediate ethical dilemmas, and almost every teacher is going to face one if not multiple versions of these and others. Oftentimes, the "right" decision or action is far from clear. In a school where the supplies are kept from the students, is it wrong to grab supplies when the administration isn't looking and use them for the good of the kids? If a student is having a bad year, does a college admission office need to know that? If two consenting adults who happen to be on the same faculty are attracted to each other, is that anyone else's business?

Some ethical issues are crystal clear. One of my colleagues begins the orientation for new student teachers with the warning, "And don't date your students." Student teachers and recent college graduates may be close in age and attracted to their high school students, but crossing that student-teacher boundary is unacceptable in all circumstances (and more than likely illegal). However, many a teacher has engaged in what started as innocent behavior, from a mild flirtation with a colleague to a pat on a student's back, only to later find himself or herself in deep trouble, accused of improper behavior or even sexual harassment. Such accusations are not always fair, but it is important to be cautious in interactions with students and colleagues to avoid even the perception of improper behavior. (In the last example from Infantino and Wilke, the new teacher was fired. The tenured administrator she was dating was simply reprimanded.)

Also, teachers hear racist, sexist, and homophobic comments and need to decide how to respond in the moment. Agreeing, as one of the teachers in the above examples was asked to do (or appeared to be expected to do), with a racist decision is just plain wrong.

Teachers will always need to balance many competing pressures—from administrators, parents, and students—within the confines of the economic environment in which they do their jobs and given the availability of resources: The reality is that schools are not always fair places, and some observers may ask, "Why rock the boat?" However, it is a teacher's responsibility to address injustices and create an environment that benefits all students equally. Kelly Dawson Salas, a fourth-grade teacher in Milwaukee, Wisconsin, describes ways that teachers can directly attack unfairness when they see it:

> Teachers can be agents of change. We shouldn't accept the idea that we don't have the power to do anything in the situation. Even if you don't see yourself as a political person or someone with control over what you're doing, in reality you're making thousands of political decisions every day. Not intervening when a student makes a racist comment is a political decision. Teaching from textbooks that emphasize only the European-American experience is another one. Those are political decisions that hurt students. You can also make choices that help students—choose to intervene when you hear a homophobic slur, choose to find books that represent the experiences of many different kinds of people, etc.[28]

Start small, perhaps, but in these and a hundred other ways, teachers are better situated than anyone else in this society to begin to slowly but specifically undo the great unfairness that has infected education, and so much else in our world, for far too long.

A QUESTION OF . . .

How can a teacher inadvertently get in trouble?

"As a male teacher, I think that there is always a slight paranoia in the back of my mind when dealing with female students in the classroom. I can look back and remember fifteen years ago when I was in school and it was not uncommon for male teachers to place a single hand on the back of a female student who was having issues in class to make her feel more comfortable. Now I am afraid of accidentally brushing against a female student because of what the consequences might be. I am not encouraged to cite a female on dress code violations because that insinuates that I was 'looking.'"

—*Eric Steele, high school history teacher* ▪

REVIEW >>

- Why is school funding unequal?

  In many school districts, a significant amount of financial support comes from the local tax base. In wealthier areas, more education dollars are generated and thus the funding per student may be much higher, offering students more resources and attracting better teachers with better pay. To offset this difference, state funding has increased, although federal funds have historically remained around 10%. There have been legal challenges to this system, but the Supreme Court ruled in *San Antonio School District v. Rodriguez* that unequal school financing based on differences in property tax receipts could not be challenged in federal courts, though state courts have sometimes ruled that there must be greater equity between districts.

- Why do schools sort and track students?

  In many schools, students are put on tracks based on ability and perceived future plans, which is too often decided by those in authority based on students' race, class, or gender. Over time, due to challenges to the process and its implications, tracking was refocused more on a student's ability (or lack thereof), as students with like abilities are grouped together. Supporters of both sides of the tracking debate

believe their approach benefits students the most and provides them with the focus they need to succeed.

- Why do students drop out before completing high school?

  Approximately 30% of U.S. students leave school before they complete high school. Students drop out for various reasons, including boredom, family issues, societal pressures, and a feeling of not belonging.

- Why is there an achievement gap?

  Research shows that students of color lag behind others in test scores and academic achievement. Among the reasons that researchers offer for this gap is an underlying racism that continues to permeate society. This can lead to low expectations for students of color and can too often involve a mismatch between students' cultural assumptions and those of teachers and schools.

- How do teachers sometimes get themselves into trouble?

  Teachers have an ethical, professional, and legal commitment not only to their students but also to their colleagues and employers. Teachers will often face complex situations and ethical dilemmas that will test their character and challenge their ability to "do the right thing," even if they believe they are being treated unfairly.

Why Is School Funding Unequal?

From MONEY, SCHOOLS, AND JUSTICE

BY STAN KARP

Stan Karp is a longtime public school teacher in New Jersey who also writes regularly for *Rethinking Schools*.

For the past 30 years, battles over school funding have been clogging the nation's courts. Ever since the U.S. Supreme Court declared in 1973 (*San Antonio v. Rodriguez*) that education was not a fundamental right protected by the U.S. Constitution, equity advocates have fought a state-by-state battle against the "savage inequalities" of school finance systems that provide sharply different levels of education to students from different class, race, and community backgrounds.

Typically, inequities have been traced to wide gaps in per-pupil spending and to finance systems that rely heavily on unequal property tax bases to fund schools. More recently, "adequacy" cases have focused on the gap between what school funding systems provide and what state and federal education standards (including the No Child Left Behind Law) demand of schools. In many ways school funding systems simply mirror—and reproduce—the inequality we see all around us.

Although the details are complicated, the heart of the matter is simple: Our schools don't get enough money, and the money they do get is not distributed fairly. Beneath the legal briefs, the legislative jargon, and the complex formulas that dominate debate over school finance, lie two central questions: Will we provide schools with the resources they need to make high-quality education possible, and will we provide those resources to all children, or only some children? The answer we give will go a long way toward determining whether our society's future will be one of democratic promise or deepening division.

Since the early 1970s, more than 40 state high courts have issued decisions in school finance cases. About half declared existing funding systems illegal or inadequate and mandated a variety of corrective measures.

But as New Jersey's Education Law Center has pointed out, "Law books are filled with wonderful paper victories which have never been implemented." While glaring disparities in school funding may persuade judges to order reform, it's been difficult to prevent governors and state legislators from limiting the impact of court orders. Restrained by separation-of-powers concerns and a conservative political climate, most courts have given states wide latitude to proceed with half measures and evasive action.

In some states, tentative steps toward equity taken under court pressure have been thwarted by the rising tide of anti-tax populism. California is a prime example. The state's 1972 Serrano decision was one of the first rulings that required a state to correct massive inequities among districts in educational services. Some efforts were made to equalize spending by revising aid formulas and transferring some property tax revenues from wealthier to poorer districts. But these efforts were derailed by Proposition 13, a 1978 ballot initiative that capped property taxes in one of the opening rounds in the "tax revolt" that came to shape local, state, and federal tax policy in the '80s and '90s (and which, despite promises of relief to hard-pressed taxpayers, has succeeded primarily in swelling government budget deficits, starving public services, and redirecting wealth upward). As a result, California was forced to assume a greater share of local school spending, which did lead to a degree of greater "equity" among districts. But there was also a dramatic decline in spending on schools in California relative to other states. In the '60s, California was fifth in per-pupil spending; by the end of the '90s it was 30th, well below the national average. Class size in California grew to among the highest in the nation. Because of Proposition 13 and its offspring, support for California schools tended toward "equalization" at a level that kept them in a state of perpetual budgetary crisis.

The property tax issue is both a root problem and, in some ways, a distraction from the core issues of adequacy and equity. Local property taxes still supply about 43 percent of all school funds. State support varies, but on average provides about 49 percent. The federal government's share of education spending, despite the huge impact of federal policies like NCLB, is still only about 8 percent.

Since the distribution of property in the United States has never been more unequal, and since many communities have never been more segregated by race and class, it's inevitable that schools heavily dependent on property taxes will be unequal. In fact, with more than 16,000 separate school districts, the reliance on property taxes functions as a sorting mechanism for class and race privilege, and allows pockets of "elite schooling" to exist within the public system. Any real chance of increasing and redistributing education resources requires fundamentally

Source: "Money, Schools, and Justice," by Stan Karp, 2007, *Rethinking Schools* 21:4, pp. 27–30.

changing the connection between school spending and local property taxes.

In some ways, relying on local property taxes serves the agenda of the conservative forces that dominate state and local governments. When local communities must assume growing fiscal burdens for schools by more heavily taxing local residential and commercial property, it creates a strong budgetary pressure for austerity. When school budgets are presented like sacrificial lambs to hard-pressed local taxpayers (who never get to vote on tax abatements for real estate developers or whether the Defense Department should build another aircraft carrier), the budget process is driven not by what schools and children need, but by how to keep the tax rate flat. When only a fraction of the local population has children in the schools, and an even smaller fraction usually votes on budget referendums, you have a system that works well to undercut quality education and keep communities divided. The reliance on property tax funding for schools, then, works at one level to protect privilege and at another as a vise to squeeze local budgets.

Nevertheless, there are growing efforts to find alternatives sparked by court orders, heavy local tax burdens, and the ongoing national debate about education reform. One set of fiscal reforms is geared to redistributing property tax revenues from richer districts to poorer ones. Another seeks to replace property taxes with other taxes—often sales taxes—and have the state assume a larger fraction of overall school spending. Still another set of proposals involves redefining state aid formulas so that fewer funds go to districts as "flat grants" and more through "foundation formulas," which guarantee a base level of funding for each student and are calculated in ways that promote greater equalization.

The problem is that no particular financial mechanism, in itself, guarantees either equity or quality in education. It's true that relying on some taxes, like property and sales taxes, tends to be regressive, while progressive income and corporate taxes are fairer ways to raise revenues. But choosing a particular funding mechanism does not assure that adequate funds will be available. A number of states have adopted new formulas promising better funding, only to see them cut once the higher costs became clear. If the underlying motivation is a desire to cut taxes or hold down educational spending, rather than to promote quality and equity, it may not matter what fiscal mechanism is chosen to do the job.

Another response has been to try to define what an "adequate" education means, and then peg funding formulas to the cost of providing it. Here again, debate persists over what level of educational services the state is obligated to provide for all.

This tension is reflected in New Jersey's *Abbott* decisions, which are arguably the most progressive rulings for poor urban schools in the history of school finance cases. The case takes its name from an alphabetical list of families who sued the state on behalf of their children, and initially it covered familiar territory. The New Jersey Supreme Court ruled that the state's system of school funding, which relies heavily on unequal property tax bases in nearly 600 separate districts, denied children in urban areas equal access to the "thorough and efficient" education guaranteed by the state's constitution. The Education Law Center documented gross inequality and pressing need in urban districts, and the court established unequivocally that it was the state's obligation to redress this inequality.

Where *Abbott* really blazed new ground was in the standard it set for this equity mandate. Throughout long years of litigation, the court repeatedly pressed the state to define the essential elements of a "thorough and efficient" education. Repeatedly, successive state administrations avoided this request, fearing that a generous definition would obligate them to provide such resources to poor districts, while a low estimate would require explaining why the state's most successful districts were spending much more (a gap that would call attention to the very inequality the court was seeking to address).

The state tried changing the subject from "money" to "standards." It adopted "core curriculum content standards" and argued that if all districts implemented these standards, all students would receive an equally adequate education. Essentially, the Court responded: nice try, but no sale. Standards may be helpful in defining educational expectations and outcomes, it argued, but they are not a substitute for the programs, staff, and resources needed to reach them. When the court looked closely at the funding formula passed by the state legislature to support the new standards, the numbers looked suspiciously like political calculations designed to keep state school aid at or near existing levels without redressing the record of inequality the court had before it.

Frustrated by the state's evasions, the New Jersey high court ultimately devised its own formula. It took as its equity standard the level of spending in the state's richest and most successful school districts. Arguing, plausibly, that these districts obviously knew what it took for kids to succeed educationally, the court ordered the state to raise per pupil spending in the poorest urban districts to the average level of the 130 richest. And citing deeper social problems and the cumulative effects of concentrated poverty, the court ordered "supplemental funding" in poor districts for programs like full-day pre-K, summer school and tutoring, above and beyond parity for regular educational programs. *Abbott* remains "the first decision in the history of school finance reform to establish an equality standard for the allocation of education resources to poor urban children." Moreover, the court's decision was phrased in striking language that made clear the implications of the social problems it was addressing. "The fact is that a large part of our society is disintegrating, so large a part that it cannot help but affect the rest. Everyone's future is at stake, and not just the poor's," it wrote.

This extraordinary decision opened up a new era of reform in New Jersey's urban districts. While unending battles over implementation and budgetary issues continue, there has also been significant progress since *Abbott* funding started to flow in the late 1990s. Over 40,000 3- and 4-year-olds now attend high-quality, full-day pre-K and kindergarten programs. The math and language test score gap between urban and suburban 4th graders has been cut in half. New Jersey boasts the highest high school graduation rates in the country, including the highest rates for African American and Hispanic students, though significant gaps among groups and communities remain.

But while *Abbott* brought long overdue equity to the 31 poor urban districts that were parties to the case, it did not fix the state's overall school finance system. More than 400 "middle districts" remain squeezed by property tax formulas and perpetual state budget crisis. Poor rural districts and surrounding "Abbott rim" districts have had little success gaining access to the same levels of funding.

In fact, New Jersey's experience underscores the contradiction between equity goals and school funding systems based on local property taxes. The state is among the highest spenders on education and has the best funding levels for poor schools. But it ranks 41st out of 50 states in the total share of local school costs picked up at the state level: about 40 percent. Because the *Abbott* mandates directed a larger portion of this state aid to the poorest districts, suburban and rural districts were pitted in competition for an increasingly inadequate pool of state funds. State aid to non-*Abbott* districts has remained flat for five years, making them more dependent than ever on raising local property taxes, which are now the highest in the nation. Unless New Jersey adopts a new school funding formula that significantly increases state share and reduces reliance on local property taxes, sustaining both the *Abbott* commitments and the state's status as a leader in educational achievement will be increasingly difficult.

Almost monthly, a prominent academic or government agency issues a report claiming that public education is vitally important to some aspect of our nation's future from global competitiveness to national security to multicultural harmony. But the main prerequisite for improving this critical social institution is a funding system that provides excellent schooling for all kids through sustainable and fair tax policies. This means moving away from systems that rely on local property taxes and toward regional, state, and federal funding sources.

To really make good on promises of educational equity and excellence will take tens of billions of dollars over many years, the kind of sums that have been poured into the military for decades. In 2005–06, total K-12 education spending in the U.S. was about $500 billion. The most recently proposed military budget for FY2008 is $622 billion. Public and private reports have documented a need for more than $300 billion in construction and renovation of K–12 facilities (costs that are generally not included in the per-pupil expenditures that are the focus of most equalization efforts). And putting aside for the moment the many dubious aspects of the No Child Left Behind act, studies indicate that to even approach NCLB's fanciful goal of 100 percent proficiency for all students on state tests by 2014 would require an annual increase in school spending of about $130 billion above current levels, about ten times the current size of Title I, the largest federal education program.

Only a national effort to reform social spending and tax policies can generate such resources: That means public campaigns to put new state and federal tax policies behind the nation's lofty educational rhetoric. It also means broader public efforts to reorder the nation's social priorities. That, after all, is what excellence and equity in school funding is ultimately all about.

QUESTIONS

1. Does Karp give you satisfactory evidence to help resolve the debate about whether more money makes a difference in the quality of schools? What additional information would be helpful to you in answering such questions?

2. Given his views, why isn't Karp happier about the New Jersey Supreme Court's decision? What more does he want done?

3. Imagine yourself as an urban, a suburban, or a rural teacher in New Jersey. What would you think of the outcome of the *Abbott* case and its impact on your school and your students? Would a similar case have an impact on the schools with which you are most familiar?

4. Karp says, "the heart of the matter is simple: Our schools don't get enough money, and the money they do get is not distributed fairly." Are those issues two sides of the same coin, or are they two quite different and, sometimes, contradictory issues?

Why Do Schools Sort and Track Students?

From "THE TRACKING WARS"

BY JEANNIE S. OAKES

Jeannie S. Oakes is director of education and scholarship at the Ford Foundation in New York City. Prior to 2008, she was professor of education and director of the Institute for Democracy, Education, and Access at the University of California–Los Angeles. Since the publication of her book *Keeping Track: How Schools Structure Inequality* in 1985, she has emerged as one of the nation's leading critics of tracking and ability grouping in public school classrooms, and her research has been cited by many who are successfully detracking schools. In "The Tracking Wars," she looks back on the many debates and the significant research of the past 20 years—much of it fostered by Oakes's 1985 book. Her conclusion is that, although much has changed, the pervasiveness of tracking, now sometimes called ability grouping, and its negative impact on students continue to be a reality in many schools.

Much has changed over the past twenty years, but much remains the same. Academic standards and test-based accountability, ideas only germinating in 1985, now dominate American schooling. Market mechanisms for improving schools—choice and competition, relief from regulation, a focus on bottom-line outcomes, and straightforward privatization—that were pretty marginal in 1985 now sit at the center of the school reform stage. Equity remains a prominent value, but its framing has shifted dramatically. Desegregation has been supplanted for the most part by a high-stakes, "no excuses" agenda composed of reforms that push all schools, however segregated by race or social class, to have all students meet challenging academic standards, with "no child left behind."

These new directions in American schooling seem profoundly incompatible with practices that sort students into classrooms where they experience strikingly different and unequal resources, opportunities, and expectations. Nevertheless, tracking remains firmly entrenched in American schools. That tracking persists is not the result of inattention: neither is it for a lack of effective alternatives.

In the years since *Keeping Track* was published, tracking has reached educators', researchers', and the public's attention on several levels. More than ever before, Americans know that tracking exists; that students' assignments to various classes are not random, unstructured happenings; that this nearly ubiquitous schooling practice has been designed and implemented to achieve some purposeful end; and that tracking cannot be ignored in thoughtful examinations of schooling. Tracking is now more often understood as an active intervention in the lives of children—a willful practice chosen by policymakers and educators. Following close behind this increased awareness has been intense scrutiny to determine whether tracking actually accomplishes the educational purposes it purports to accomplish, and whether it is consistent with the democratic goals of schooling.

The answers to these questions have troubled many progressive policymakers, educators, and public commentators on educational quality and equity. Concerned that tracking violates a social justice standard that assures individuals and groups equitable access to educational resources and opportunities, many have argued that tracking is inconsistent with the American dream of schooling that provides every child an equal chance to succeed. Reformers around the nation moved to detrack schools. These progressives were joined by an unlikely set of allies: widely read conservative academics such as Diane Ravitch and Mortimer Adler, who argued that tracking's differentiated curriculum is antithetical to schooling's goal of ensuring that all students learn the traditional Western canon.

At the same time, however, tracking's defenders have charged that the research jury is still out, that any problem with tracking can be fixed without dismantling it, and that, if policymakers and schools move toward detracking too fast and unadvisedly, they place educational excellence at risk. Some claim that inequalities associated with tracking are gone, and that today's grouping is free of the problems of earlier times. The characterization of this debate as "the tracking wars" is not my own, but I can hardly disagree with it; it aptly describes the intensity of the responses and interactions among the critics and advocates of tracking and detracking. . . .

By the end of the 1980s, concerns about tracking had entered the popular discourse and influenced public policy goals. Harsh judgments about tracking's effects were reported in the popular media, including such articles as "Is Your Child Being Tracked for Failure?" (*Better Homes and Gardens*), "The Label That Sticks" (*U.S. News and World Report*), and "Tracked to Fail" (*Psychology Today*). Leading policy groups made recommendations for eliminating or at least curtailing tracking practices, and many school reformers took action.

The National Governors' Association, for example, proposed eliminating tracking as a strategy for meeting the ambitious national education goals they had set in 1989. The governors saw tracking as a major impediment to their goal of educating all students to demonstrate mastery of challenging subject matter, so that the United States would be first in the world in science and mathematics achievement on tests taken at the completion of grades four, eight, and twelve. The NAACP Legal Defense Fund, the ACLU, and the Children's Defense Fund all raised tracking as a second-generation segregation issue. And the U.S. Department of

Source: "The Tracking Wars," by Jeannie Oakes, in *Keeping Track: How Schools Structure Inequality*, 2nd ed., 2005, Yale University Press, pp. 214–221, 226–227, 229–231, 236–237.

Education's Civil Rights Division targeted tracking as critical in determining racially mixed schools' compliance with Title VI regulations. Educator groups also adopted antitracking policy positions. At its national convention in 1990, the National Education Association recommended (albeit cautiously) that schools abandon conventional tracking practices. Several of the major subject matter organizations of teachers—the National Council for the Social Studies, the National Council of Teachers of English, the National Council of Mathematics Educators—all went on record as saying that tracking posed serious barriers to high-quality and equitable teaching and learning. Some state education agencies, including those in California and Massachusetts, declared that tracking should be eliminated, at least prior to senior high school. . . .

At the same time these policy initiatives were beginning, courts began to take a more intense look at tracking. In Rockford, Illinois; San Jose, California; New Castle County (Wilmington), Delaware; Woodland Hills, Pennsylvania; and Augusta, Arkansas, plaintiffs in school desegregation cases charged that the districts' tracking undermined desegregation because it resegregated minority and white students within schools. In 1994, the federal magistrate and judge in Rockford found, based in large part on analysis of its tracking practices, that the district engaged in racial discrimination. The same year, the federal judge in Arkansas ordered that the district cease its use of ability grouping by class. . . .

Other detracking efforts were very much homegrown. For example, an innovative San Diego high school English teacher, Mary Catherine Swanson, noticed that when her mostly white school became more diverse owing to an attendance boundary change, the school's tracking system relegated most of the newcomers to low-track classes. Outraged, Swanson created AVID (Advanced via Individual Determination), a scheme that placed supposed unqualified students into college-track classes and provided them with a support course in which they learned study skills and received academic tutoring. AVID has now expanded to schools across the nation. . . .

Objections to detracking were immediate and loud, often undermining the potential for reasoned dialogue about legitimate concerns that detracking would compromise the education received by the most academically able students. Such concerns could not be addressed in environments in which detracking was instantly assumed to be an assault on opportunities for high achievers. It wasn't so much that anybody questioned the findings of inequality (at least at first); rather the implications of heterogeneity were so totally unacceptable that thoughtful discussion was often derailed with caricatures and scenarios of doom. The loudest and most highly organized objections came from educators who specialized in "gifted and talented" education. Separate programs were the cornerstone of their practice and theory, and they feared, probably correctly, that calls for detracking placed those programs at risk. Supported by powerful par-

ent advocacy groups, the gifted-education community soon came out swinging.

The arguments ran the gamut, asserting that gifted students were as far from the norm and as "needy" of separate learning environments as low-IQ students; ridiculing the idea of mixed-ability classrooms by comparing them to a varsity football team that accepts everyone who wants to play, regardless of skills; warning that detracking would place "our nation's most precious resource" (gifted students) at risk; and suggesting that average and below-average students feel better if they are not confronted each day by the intellectual superiority of their gifted peers. These arguments were bolstered by "research reviews" purporting to show that students, particularly gifted students, should be kept in separate homogeneous classes. Most shrewdly, opponents of detracking quickly defined tracking out of existence. As long as there was a theoretical possibility that a student's track might change, they contended, assignments to low or high classes was simply an educational determination more properly called ability grouping. Conceding that the narrower, rigid tracking may well be bad, they distanced those critiques from "ability-grouped classes." High-ability groups, they concluded, are not discriminatory, even though minority students may be underrepresented in them. "Flexible groupings," particularly as applied to elementary classrooms, became the key definitional defense. . . .

The Research Battleground: Scientific Uncertainty or Solid Evidence?

Does Tracking Create Unequal Opportunity?

Working with a team of research colleagues at RAND and with the support of the National Science Foundation, I examined the relationship of race, social class, and tracking to students' opportunities to learn science and mathematics in a national sample of six thousand classrooms in twelve hundred schools. Survey data from school principals and from mathematics and science teachers allowed us to examine differences between schools and within schools. The results, which we ended up calling *Multiplying Inequalities*, were striking. Differences in opportunities to learn science and mathematics resulted from the combined effects of disparities between tracks within schools and differences among schools' tracking practices. Consistent with the data reported in *Keeping Track*, high-track classes consistently offered richer learning opportunities and more resources, including more highly qualified teachers, than low-track classes.

At the grossest level, we found that senior high school tracking shapes the number and type of academic courses students take. Low-track students are seldom required to take as many math and science classes as high-track students, and they rarely do. Additionally, those not preparing for college take advanced classes only rarely. In every aspect of what makes for a quality education, kids in lower-

343

track classes typically get less than those in higher tracks and gifted programs.

At all levels of schooling, low-track math and science courses offered less demanding topics and skills, while high-track classes typically included more complex material and more thinking and problem-solving tasks. Teachers of low-ability classes also placed considerably less emphasis than teachers of high-track classes on more general learning goals, such as having students become interested in science and mathematics, acquire basic concepts and principles, and develop an inquiry approach to science and a problem-solving orientation to mathematics. The ability to meet such goals does not depend on students' prior academic achievement

or skill levels. Researchers and educators increasingly see reaching these goals as possible for all but seriously impaired students, and policymakers increasingly describe them as essential for all students. Nevertheless, those teaching low-tracked classes typically reported these goals as less important for their students. Additional research is consistent with these findings of clear track-related differences in students' access to knowledge. . . .

Is Tracking Discriminatory?

Are the racial patterns fair? We certainly can argue that they are not fair, given that the differences in the quality of what students experience constrain rather than expand the opportunities of students in low-track classes and that African Americans and Latinos suffer these constraints more often than other students. . . .

My conclusion is that race itself does indeed influence track placements, Latinos and African Americans being more likely than whites and Asian students to be placed in low-track classes. Although the lower average of achievement of Latinos and African Americans certainly "explains" (in a statistical sense) much of the disproportionate assignment of these students to lower-track classes, we also find significant and disturbing evidence of racial bias. . . .

Certainly, these patterns reflected very real differences in minority and white students' previous learning opportunities and their effects on academic preparation. Yet these associations with students' prior achievement do not demonstrate that the schools in our study made fair and racially neutral assignments. In fact, students' race or ethnicity was often important in *determining* the probability of participating in college preparatory math and English, over and above their measured achievement. . . .

Does Tracking Affect Students' Schooling Outcomes?

The best new evidence from the past twenty years adds to *Keeping Track*'s claim that tracking fails to foster the outcomes schools value—academic excellence and educational equity. Tracking is particularly inconsistent with today's national goals of having all students meet high academic standards and leaving no child behind. There is little disagreement that grouping affects students' schooling outcomes with exactly the opposite effect. Nobody today makes evidence-based claims that students in low-track classes benefit from tracking. Incontrovertibly, tracking widens the inequality among students in what they learn in school; students in high-track classes learn more than students in low-track classes. In today's rhetoric, tracking systematically leaves children not in the high track behind. The widening gap is associated with obvious and measurable advantages that allow high-track students to reach their "potential" and disadvantages that depress the achievement of low-track students.

However, the research on the relationship between tracking and students' schooling outcomes is complicated. Researchers' answer to the question of whether tracking affects outcomes depends on their definition of tracking, the outcomes they are interested in, the specific formulation of their research questions, and their research methods. Since achievement test scores are the most frequently studied outcome, let's begin there: the research on tracking and ability grouping consistently finds that the achievement gap between students in high- and low-classes groups grows over time.

My colleagues and I found this differential effect of tracking on students' measured achievement in the Match-making studies of three comprehensive high schools as well as in our studies of tracking in San Jose [California], Rockford [Illinois], Wilmington [Delaware], and Woodland Hills [Pennsylvania]. In all of these schools, high-track placement led to achievement gains, and low-track placement had negative effects. Students in lower-level courses consistently demonstrated lesser gains in achievement than their comparably scoring peers in high-level courses. These results were consistent across achievement levels: whether students began with relatively high or relatively low achievement, those placed in lower-level courses showed smaller gains (or greater losses) over time than similarly situated students placed in higher-level courses. . . .

From "THE TRACKING AND ABILITY GROUPING DEBATE"

BY TOM LOVELESS

Tom Loveless is one of a small but growing group of researchers who have begun to challenge Oakes's research. Where Oakes sees a continuing problem, Loveless sees progress in eliminating the negative impact of old-style tracking and a new kind of tracking that fosters excellence in both high-level and low-level students. He is a senior fellow at the Brookings Institution, and the essay reprinted here was first published in *The Fordham Report*, a regular publication of the conservative Fordham Foundation. As is clear from these two articles, Loveless and Oakes disagree strongly on the impact of tracking, especially in today's educational climate.

What Is Tracking?

Thirty years ago, the terms "ability grouping" and "tracking" were used to identify two distinct approaches to grouping students.

Ability grouping referred to the formation of small, homogeneous groups within elementary school classrooms, usually for reading instruction. Children of approximately the same level of reading proficiency would be grouped for reading instruction, perhaps into "redbirds" and "bluebirds."

Tracking referred to a practice in which high schools tested students, typically with both achievement and IQ tests, and used these scores to place their students into separate curricular tracks, or "streams," as they are called in Europe. . . .

Writers now use the terms "tracking" and "ability grouping" interchangeably. One hears, for example, that "tracking begins in kindergarten. . . ."

Tracking in High Schools

High school systems have changed significantly from the college-general-vocational tracks of yore. They are still distinguished by a hierarchy of coursework, especially in mathematics and English, but two and three track systems and mixed systems with both tracked and heterogeneous classes are prevalent. Typically, students are grouped independently from subject to subject. A student who is a poor reader but strong in mathematics and science, for example, can progress to advanced placement (AP) courses in calculus or physics. The independence of subjects is not pure, however. The vagaries of scheduling may still allow a student's placement in one subject to influence placement in another, and the mere existence of prerequisites can't help but link a student's present and past track levels. Nevertheless, it is more accurate to think of today's tracks as multiple pathways through different disciplines than as a single road winding through the full high school curriculum.

These tracks have diminished their preoccupation with students' destinations, most notably with deciding who will be prepared for college and who will be prepared for work. The honors track remains focused on college preparation to be sure, but, invariably, middle and low tracks also declare preparation for college as goals. With enrollment in vocational courses in steep decline, the focus of low tracks has shifted toward academic remediation. . . . Classroom studies indicate that low tracks continue to dwell on basic skills, featuring a dull curriculum and inordinate amounts of drill and practice. But such curricular banality may be caused by the lack of interesting materials or good instructional strategies for addressing stubborn learning problems, especially problems persisting into the high school years. Despite remedial students' academic deficiencies, counselors frequently point low track students toward community colleges. The bottom line is that all high school tracks may lead to colleges, albeit to dramatically different types of institutions.

Another change is that the high track has become more accessible. When principals are asked how they assign students to tracks, they report that completion of prerequisite courses, course grades, and teacher recommendations are the chief criteria, not scores on standardized tests. Parent and student requests are also factored into track placement. More than 80% of schools allow students to elect their course level provided prerequisites have been met, and many schools offer a waiver option for parents who insist, despite the school's recommendation, that their child enroll in a high track class. A degree of self-tracking exists today that was unheard of decades ago. . . .

The Research

In the last two decades, researchers have . . . analyzed large national surveys to evaluate tracking. High School and Beyond (HSB) is a study that began with tenth graders in 1980. The National Educational Longitudinal Study (NELS) started with eighth graders in 1988. These two studies followed tens of thousands of students through school, recording their academic achievement, courses taken, and attitudes toward school. The students' transcripts were analyzed, and their teachers and parents were interviewed. The two massive databases have sustained a steady stream of research on tracking.

Three findings stand out. High track students in HSB learn more than low track students, even with prior achievement and other pertinent influences on achievement statistically controlled. Not surprising, perhaps, but what's staggering is the magnitude of the difference. On average, the high track advantage outweighs even the achievement difference between the student who stays in school until the senior year and the student who drops out.

The second major finding is that race and tracking are only weakly related. Once test scores are taken into account in

Source: "The Tracking and Ability Grouping Debate," by Tom Loveless, *Fordham Report* (August 1998), reprinted in Evans, ed., *Taking Sides*, pp. 194–202.

NELS, a student's race has no bearing on track assignments. In fact, African-American students enjoy a 10% advantage over white students in being assigned to the high track. This contradicts the charge that tracking is racist. Considered in tandem with the high track advantage just described, it also suggests that abolishing high tracks would disproportionately penalize African-American students, especially high achieving African-American students. Moreover, NELS shows that achievement differences between African-American and white students are fully formed by the end of eighth grade. The race gap reaches its widest point right after elementary and middle school, when students have experienced ability grouping in its mildest forms. The gap remains unchanged in high school, when tracking between classes is most pronounced.

Third, NELS identifies apparent risks in detracking. Low-achieving students seem to learn more in heterogeneous math classes, while high and average achieving students suffer achievement losses—and their combined losses outweigh the low achievers' gains. In terms of specific courses, eighth graders of all ability levels learn more when they take algebra in tracked classes rather than heterogeneously grouped classes. For survey courses in eighth grade math, heterogeneous classes are better for low achieving students than tracked classes.

These last findings are important because we don't know very much about academic achievement in heterogeneous classes. When the campaign against tracking picked up steam in the late 1980s, tracking was essentially universal. Untracked schools didn't exist in sufficient numbers to evaluate whether abandoning tracking for a full regimen of mixed ability classes actually works. The NELS studies that attempt to evaluate detracked classes, which thus far have been restricted to mathematics, point toward a possible gain for low achieving students and a possible loss for average and above average students, but these findings should be regarded as tentative.

To summarize what we know about ability grouping, tracking, and achievement: The elementary school practices of both within-class and cross-grade ability grouping are supported by research. The tracking research is more ambiguous but not without a few concrete findings.

Assigning students to separate classes by ability and providing them with the same curriculum has no effect on achievement, positive or negative, and the neutral effect holds for high, middle, and low achievers. When the curriculum is altered, tracking appears to benefit high ability students. Heterogeneous classes appear to benefit low ability students but may depress the achievement of average and high achieving students.

Fosters Race and Class Segregation?

Critics charge that tracking perpetuates race and class segregation by disproportionately assigning minority and poor children to low tracks and white, wealthy children to high tracks. When it comes to race, the disparities are real, but, as just noted, they vanish when students' prior achievement is considered. A small class effect remains, however. Students from poor families are more likely to be assigned to low tracks than wealthier students with identical achievement scores. This could be due to class discrimination, different amounts of parental influence on track assignments, or other unmeasured factors.

The issue ultimately goes back to whether tracking is educationally sound. Those who complain of tracking's segregative impact do not usually attack bilingual or Title I programs for promoting ethnic and class segregation, no doubt because they see these programs as benefiting students. If low tracks remedied educational problems, the charge of segregation would probably dissipate. Does tracking harm black students? A telling study conducted by the Public Agenda Foundation found that "opposition to heterogeneous grouping is as strong among African-American parents as among white parents, and support for it is generally weak." If tracking harms African-American students, one would not expect these sentiments.

Why Is There an Achievement Gap?

From "WHY ARE ALL THE BLACK KIDS SITTING TOGETHER IN THE CAFETERIA?

BY BEVERLY DANIEL TATUM

Trained as a clinical psychologist, Beverly Daniel Tatum is now the president of Spelman College, a historically black women's college in Atlanta, Georgia. Tatum spent much of her career as a professor and then dean of Mount Holyoke College, a women's college in Massachusetts. While at Mount Holyoke, Tatum received national attention for her book *Why Are All the Black Kids Sitting Together in the Cafeteria? And Other Conversations About Race*, which was first published in 1997 and then revised in 2003. Taking as her starting point a question about seeming self-segregation on the part of Black students that many White educators who work in racially integrated schools ask themselves—sometimes quietly and sometimes more openly—Tatum explored the way many African American students living in integrated communities come to understand themselves and their relationships to their White peer students and White teachers.

The Early Years: "Is my skin brown because I drink chocolate milk?"

Think of your earliest race-related memory. How old were you? When I ask adults in my workshops this question, they call out a range of ages: "Three," "Five," "Eight," "Thirteen," "Twenty." Sometimes they talk in small groups about what they remember. At first they hesitate to speak, but then the stories come flooding forward, each person's memory triggering another's.

Some are stories of curiosity, as when a light-skinned child wonders why a dark-skinned person's palms are so much lighter than the backs of their hands. Some are stories of fear and avoidance, communicated verbally or nonverbally by parents, as when one White woman describes her mother nervously telling her to roll up the windows and lock the doors as they drove through a Black community. Some are stories of active bigotry, transmitted casually from one generation to the next through the use of racial slurs and ethnic jokes. Some are stories of confusing mixed messages, as when a White man remembers the Black maid who was "just like family" but was not allowed to eat from the family dishes or use the upstairs bathroom. Some are stories of terror, as when a Black woman remembers being chased home from school by a German shepherd, deliberately set loose by its White owner as she passed by. I will often ask audience members, "What do you remember? Something someone said or did? A name-calling incident? An act of discrimination? A casual observation of skin color differences? Were you the observer or the object of observation?" . . .

Like many African Americans, I have many race-related memories, beginning when I was quite small. I remember being about three years old when I had an argument with an African American playmate. He said I was "black." "No I'm not," I said, "I'm tan." I now see that we were both right. I am black, a person of African descent, but tan is surely a more accurate description of my light brown skin than black is. As a three-year-old child who knew her colors, I was prepared to stand my ground. As an adult looking back on this incident, I wonder if I had also

begun to recognize, even at three, that in some circles it was better to be tan than to be black. Had I already started internalizing racist messages?

Questions and confusion about racial issues begin early. Though adults often talk about the "colorblindness" of children, the fact is that children as young as three do notice physical differences such as skin color, hair texture, and the shape of one's facial features. Certainly preschoolers talk about what they see, and often they do it in ways that make parents uncomfortable. How should we respond when they do? . . .

The first conversation of this type I remember occurred when my oldest son, Jonathan, was enrolled in a day care center where he was one of few children of color, and the only Black child in his class. One day, as we drove home from the day care center, Jonathan said, "Eddie says my skin is brown because I drink too much chocolate milk. Is that true?" Eddie was a White three-year-old in Jonathan's class who, like David, had observed a physical difference and was now searching for an explanation.

"No," I replied, "your skin is brown because you have something in your skin called melanin. Melanin is very important because it helps protect your skin from the sun. Eddie has melanin in his skin, too. Remember when Eddie went to Florida on vacation and came back showing everybody his tan? It was the melanin in his skin that made it get darker. Everybody has melanin, you know. But some people have more than others. At your school, you are the kid with the most!"

Jonathan seemed to understand the idea and smiled at the thought that he was the child with the most of something. I talked more about how much I liked the color of his pecan-colored skin, how it was a perfect blend of my light-brown skin and his father's dark-brown complexion. I wanted to affirm who Jonathan was, a handsome brown-skinned child. I wanted to counter the implication of Eddie's question— that there was perhaps something wrong with brown skin, the result of "too much" chocolate milk. . . .

Jonathan's questions and comments, like David's and Eddie's, were not unusual for a child of his age. Preschool children are very focused on outward appearances, and skin color is the racial feature they are most likely to comment

Source: *Why Are All the Black Kids Sitting Together in the Cafeteria? And Other Conversations About Race*, by Beverly Daniel Tatum, 2003, Basic Books, pp. 31–74.

on. I felt good about my ability as a parent to respond to Jonathan's questions. (I was, after all, teaching courses on the psychology of racism and child development. I was not caught completely off guard!) But I wondered about Jonathan's classmates. What about Eddie, the boy with the chocolate milk theory? Had anyone set him straight?

In fact, Eddie's question, "Is your skin brown because you drink too much chocolate milk?" represented a good attempt to make sense of a curious phenomenon that he was observing. All the kids in the class had light skin except for Jonathan. Why was Jonathon's skin different? It didn't seem to be dirt—Jonathan washed his hands before lunch like all the other children did, and there was no change. He did often have chocolate milk in his lunch box—maybe that was it. Eddie's reasoning was first-rate for a three-year-old. The fact that he was asking about Jonathan's skin, rather than speculating about his own, reflected that he had already internalized "Whiteness" as the norm, which it was in that school. His question did not reflect prejudice in an adult sense, but it did reveal confusion. His theory was flawed, and he needed some help.

I decided to ask a staff member how she and the other preschool teachers were handling children's questions about racial differences. She smiled and said, "It really hasn't come up." I was amazed. I knew it had come up; after all, Jonathan had reported the conversations to me. How was it that she had not noticed?

Maybe it was easy not to notice. Maybe these conversations among three-year-olds had taken place at the lunch table or in the sand box, away from the hearing of adults. I suspect too, that there may have been some selective inattention on the part of the staff. When children make comments to which we don't know how to respond, it may be easier simply not to hear what has just been said or to let it slip from our consciousness and memory. Then we don't have to respond, because it "hasn't come up."

Many adults do not know how to respond when children make race-related observations. Imagine this scenario. A White mother and preschool child are shopping in the grocery store. They pass a Black woman and child, and the White child says loudly, "Mommy, look at that girl! Why is she so dirty?" (Confusing dark skin with dirt is a common misconception among White preschool children.) The White mother, embarrassed by her child's comment, responds quickly with a "Ssh!"

An appropriate response might have been: "Honey, that little girl is not dirty. Her skin is as clean as yours. It's just a different color. Just like we have different hair color, people have different skin colors." If the child still seemed interested, the explanation of melanin could be added. Perhaps afraid of saying the wrong thing, however, many parents don't offer an explanation. They stop at "Ssh," silencing the child but not responding to the question or the reasoning underlying it. Children who have been silenced often enough learn not to talk about race publicly. Their questions don't go away, they just go unasked.

I see the legacy of this silencing in my psychology of racism classes. My students have learned that there is a taboo against talking about race, especially in racially mixed settings, and creating enough safety in the class to overcome that taboo is the first challenge for me as an instructor. But the evidence of the internalized taboo is apparent long before children reach college.

When addressing parent groups, I often hear from White parents who tell me with pride that their children are "colorblind." Usually the parent offers as evidence a story of a friendship with a child of color whose race or ethnicity has never been mentioned to the parent. For example, a father reported that his eight-year-old daughter had been talking very enthusiastically about a friend she had made at school. One day when he picked his daughter up from school, he asked her to point out her new friend. Trying to point her out of a large group of children on the play ground, his daughter elaborately described what the child was wearing. She never said she was the only Black girl in the group. Her father was pleased that she had not, a sign of her colorblindness. I wondered if, rather than a sign of colorblindness, it was a sign that she had learned not to be so impolite as to mention someone's race.

My White college students sometimes refer to someone as Black in hushed tones, sometimes whispering the word as though it were a secret or a potentially scandalous identification. When I detect this behavior, I like to point it out, saying it is not an insult to identify a Black person as Black. Of course, sometimes one's racial group membership is irrelevant to the conversation, and then there is no need to mention it. But when it is relevant, as when pointing out the only Black girl in a crowd, we should not be afraid to say so. . . .

Identity Development in Adolescence: "Why are all the Black kids sitting together in the cafeteria?"

Walk into any racially mixed high school cafeteria at lunch time and you will instantly notice that in the sea of adolescent faces, there is an identifiable group of Black students sitting together. Conversely, it could be pointed out that there are many groups of White student sitting together as well, though people rarely comment about that. The question on the tip of everyone's tongue is "Why are the Black kids sitting together?" Principals want to know, teachers want to know, White students want to know, the Black students who aren't sitting at the table want to know.

How does it happen that so many Black teenagers end up at the same cafeteria table? They don't start out there. If you walk into racially mixed elementary schools, you will often see young children of diverse racial backgrounds playing with one another, sitting at the snack table together, crossing racial boundaries with an ease uncommon in adolescence. Moving from elementary school to middle school (often at sixth or seventh grade) means interacting with new children from different neighborhoods than before, and a certain degree of clustering by race might therefore be expected, presuming that children who are familiar with one another would form groups. But even in schools where the same children stay together from kindergarten through eighth grade, racial grouping begins by the sixth or seventh grade. What happens?

One thing that happens is puberty. As children enter adolescence, they begin to explore the question of identity, asking "Who am I? Who can I be?" in ways they have not done before. For Black youth, asking "Who am I?" includes thinking about "Who am I ethnically and/or racially? What does it mean to be Black?"

As I write this, I can hear the voice of a White woman who asked me, "Well, all adolescents struggle with questions of identity. They all become more self-conscious about their appearance and more concerned about what their peers think. So what is so different for Black kids?" Of course, she is right that all adolescents look at themselves in new ways, but not all adolescents think about themselves in racial terms. . . .

Why do Black youths, in particular, think about themselves in terms of race? Because that is how the rest of the world thinks of them. Our self-perceptions are shaped by the messages that we receive from those around us, and when young Black men and women enter adolescence, the racial content of those messages intensifies. A case in point: If you were to ask my ten-year-old son, David, to describe himself, he would tell you many things: that he is smart, that he likes to play computer games, that he has an older brother. Near the top of his list, he would likely mention that he is tall for his age. He would probably not mention that he is Black, though he certainly knows that he is. Why would he mention his height and not his racial group membership? When David meets new adults, one of the first questions they ask is "How old are you?" When David states his age, the inevitable reply is "Gee, you're tall for your age!" It happens so frequently that I once overheard David say to someone, "Don't say it, I know. I'm tall for my age." Height is salient for David because it is salient for others.

When David meets new adults, they don't say, "Gee, you're Black for your age!" If you are saying to yourself, of course they don't, think again. Imagine David at fifteen, six-foot-two, wearing the adolescent attire of the day, passing adults he doesn't know on the sidewalk. Do the women hold their purses a little tighter, maybe even cross the street to avoid him? Does he hear the sound of automatic door locks on cars as he passes by? Is he being followed around by the security guards at the local mall? As he stops in town with his new bicycle, does a police officer hassle him, asking where he got it, implying that it might be stolen? Do strangers assume he plays basketball? Each of these experiences conveys a racial message. At ten, race is not yet salient for David, because it is not yet salient for society. But it will be. . . .

What do these encounters have to do with the cafeteria? Do experiences with racism inevitably result in so-called self-segregation? While certainly a desire to protect oneself from further offense is understandable, it is not the only factor at work. Imagine the young eighth-grade girl who experienced the teacher's use of "you people" and the dancing stereotype as a racial affront. Upset and struggling with adolescent embarrassment, she bumps into a White friend who can see that something is wrong. She explains. Her White friend responds, in an effort to make her feel better perhaps, and says, "Oh, Mr. Smith is such a nice guy, I'm sure he didn't mean it like that. Don't be so sensitive." Perhaps the White friend is right, and Mr. Smith didn't mean it, but imagine your own response when you are upset, perhaps with a spouse or partner. He or she asks what's wrong and you explain why you are offended. Your partner brushes off your complaint, attributing it to your being oversensitive. What happens to your emotional thermostat? It escalates. When feelings, rational or irrational, are invalidated, most people disengage. They not only choose to discontinue the conversation but are more likely to turn to someone who will understand their perspective.

In much the same way, the eighth-grade girl's White friend doesn't get it. She doesn't see the significance of this racial message, but the girls at the "Black table" do. When she tells her story there, one of them is likely to say, "You know what, Mr. Smith said the same thing to me yesterday!" Not only are Black adolescents encountering racism and reflecting on their identity, but their White peers, even when they are not perpetrators (and sometimes they are), are unprepared to respond in supportive ways. The Black students turn to each other for the much needed support they are not likely to find anywhere else.

In adolescence, as race becomes personally salient for Black youth, finding the answer to questions such as, "What does it mean to be a young Black person? How should I act? What should I do?" is particularly important. And although Black fathers, mothers, aunts, and uncles may hold the answers by offering themselves as role models, they hold little appeal for most adolescents. The last thing many fourteen-year-olds want to do is grow up to be like their parents. It is the peer group, the kids in the cafeteria, who hold the answers to these questions. They know how to be Black. They have absorbed the stereotypical images of Black youth in the popular culture and are reflecting those images in their self-presentation. . . .

QUESTIONS

1. What is your earliest race-related memory? Was it about your own race or that of another person, child, or adult? Was it positive or negative?

2. Have you ever wondered, as Tatum asks, why African American high school students sometimes self-segregate? Do you find her answers persuasive?

3. Why do you think no one has written a book that addresses the question, "Why are all the White kids sitting together?" In what ways is the self-segregation of Whites the same as, or different from, the self-segregation of African American or Latino youth?

11

POLITICS
WHAT IS ITS PLACE IN

Although many efforts have been made to "keep politics out of our schools," such a phrase is virtually meaningless. It is within the political process that decisions are made in a democratic society. To most educators, it certainly seems desirable to keep certain kinds of political influence out of the schools. Teachers have fought hard so that they cannot be fired if their political party loses the next school board election, and, in general, teachers are not hired because of their **political affiliations**, either. It is rare (though not as rare as some would hope) for a government official to intervene directly in a hiring decision for a teacher

> **political affiliation** Active association with a political group or entity; registration to vote in a specific political party.

or in a promotion decision regarding a student, but most people also agree that this sort of political influence should be eliminated if professional educators are to do their jobs. Nevertheless, education is an intensely political activity, and it always will be.

The federal government—the federal courts, presidents, and members of Congress—have long had a significant impact on education in the United States. State and local governments have an even larger role, given that education is primarily a state and local responsibility in this country. Elected leaders in state and local governments are the final authorities on a range of educational issues, including developing the curriculum and standards, hiring top school officials such as district superintendents and state commissioners (who do most of the hiring of the rest of the educational staff), making decisions about mandated testing, and determining the funds available for schools. Elected or politically appointed school boards set the salaries and working conditions negotiated for teachers, and they determine the resources available for building schools and for buying everything from computers to books and pencils. In this chapter, we seek to understand better the inevitable place of politics in the American system of public education.

This chapter has two **Readings**. In the first, well-known educator Pedro Noguera reflects on what it will take to improve American education and the place of politics (locally and nationally) to help bring about those improvements. Drawing on his experience as a member of a local school board, Noguera understands the limits of what can be done at

EDUCATION?

- What is the role of federal officials?
- What are the politics behind the No Child Left Behind debate?
- What is the role of state and local politics in education?
- How do teachers make political decisions in the classroom?

that level, yet he is relentless in his call on people at all levels of the political process to do better. In the second **Reading**, Scott Franklin Abernathy looks at the No Child Left Behind (NCLB) legislation 5 years after it was passed. His goal is not so much to critique or support the legislation but rather to ask "what comes next?"

>> What Is the Role of Federal Officials?

When educators from Asia, Europe, or Latin America visit the United States, they are struck by the limited role of the national government in U.S. schools. Most other industrialized countries have a national curriculum and national policies about teacher qualifications and expected outcomes for students. Yet, even with the extraordinary expansion of the federal government's role in school issues in recent years, most educational decisions are made almost exclusively at the state level, such as specific standards in different fields, decisions about what constitutes a passing grade on state examinations (though the federal government mandates that the exams be offered), and the qualifications necessary to become a fully licensed teacher. Nevertheless, the federal government retains a significant role in school politics.

THE SUPREME COURT AND THE SCHOOLS

In 2007, the U.S. Supreme Court, led by a newly appointed chief justice, declared that voluntary efforts to racially desegregate public schools in Seattle, Washington, and Jefferson County (Louisville), Kentucky, were unconstitutional. Announcing the 5–4 decision, Chief Justice John G. Roberts, Jr., said that "the way to achieve a system of determining admission to the public schools on a nonracial basis is to stop assigning students on a racial basis." Fifty-three years earlier, another newly appointed chief justice,

Earl Warren, had announced the Supreme Court's decision that state-mandated segregation in the public schools of the United States was unconstitutional.

In the recent case, Seattle and Louisville had to move quickly to change their plans to foster racial integration, and leaders in many other school districts around the country realized that they too would have to either give up on the goal of racially inclusive schools or find new ways to accomplish the goal. The 1954 *Brown v. Board of Education of Topeka, Kansas* decision declared illegal the ways students were assigned to schools in every state in the South. Over the next decades, federal courts found that many northern districts had also illegally segregated their schools. After massive resistance in places as diverse as Little Rock, Arkansas, and Boston, Massachusetts, change came about slowly, and for a period of time, more students than ever attended school with others of different races.

The decisions in *Brown v. Board of Education* (1954), *Parents Involved in Community Schools v. Seattle School District* (2007), and *Meredith v. Jefferson County Board of Education* (2007) reflect the ongoing dominance of race as an issue in U.S. education policy, but they also illustrate the extraordinarily large role of the federal government, along with state governments and local authorities, in schools in the United States. In a democratic society, local, state, and federal policy makers are elected or are appointed by elected officials; thus, it is inevitable that school policy will be highly political.

Throughout the 20th century, the federal courts have decided many issues affecting schools. The best-known and probably most far-reaching court decisions have involved issues of race and racial segregation. In the 1930s, the National Association for the Advancement of Colored People (NAACP) Legal Defense Fund began a concerted effort to challenge school segregation. They decided that the federal courts were the place to make their case. The NAACP legal team won test cases in the federal courts against university-level segregation and against lower pay scales for African American teachers. In the 1950s, these civil rights lawyers, led by future Supreme Court Justice Thurgood Marshall, brought a case against a number of school districts that challenged segregation of elementary and high school students on the basis of their race. In 1954, the U.S. Supreme Court in *Brown v. Board of Education of Topeka, Kansas* ruled on these challenges, concluding that "'separate but equal' has no place" in public education. Many observers within the civil rights community had hoped that a unanimous decision by the justices of the nation's highest court would settle the issue, but many political leaders, initially in the South but in time around the nation, decided that the key to their own political futures was to promise "massive resistance" to the Court's order.

In September 1957, on the night before Central High School in Little Rock was to be integrated, Arkansas Governor Orval Faubus told the citizens of his state that "blood will run in the streets" if anyone attempted to integrate the school and called out the state units of the national guard to block African American students, even though they had a federal court order demanding their admission. When Elizabeth Eckford, one of the new students, tried to walk to school on opening day, the soldiers blocked her way and the White crowd jeered and taunted her. Due to the courage of children like Elizabeth and at the insistence of the federal courts, President Dwight Eisenhower sent regular U.S. Army troops to Little Rock. After some extraordinarily pain-filled months and years, Central High School and the schools of Arkansas were legally integrated. Some Whites created their own private academies, and some school districts found new ways to unofficially segregate the schools, but official policies of separate (and quite unequal) schools for European American and African American students were gone from the nation.

After the Seattle and Jefferson County decisions, the future of school integration seemed uncertain. Although Justice Clarence Thomas wrote in support of the majority decision that "It is far from apparent that coerced racial mixing has any educational benefits, much less that integration is necessary to Black achievement," another justice, Stephen G. Breyer, wrote in dissent, "The last half-century has witnessed great strides toward racial equality, but we have not yet realized the promise of Brown. . .to invalidate the plans under review is to threaten the promise of Brown. This is a decision that the court and the nation will come to regret."[1]

Many other Supreme Court decisions have had direct impacts on schools and teachers. In 1943, the Court in *West Virginia State Board of Education v. Barnette* ruled that public school students could not be compelled to recite the Pledge of Allegiance to the flag. In 1969, in *Tinker et al v. Des Moines Independent Community School District*, the

In Chapter 3, we looked at the individual cases that led to the *Brown* ruling.

Connections

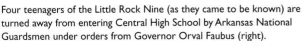

Four teenagers of the Little Rock Nine (as they came to be known) are turned away from entering Central High School by Arkansas National Guardsmen under orders from Governor Orval Faubus (right).

Court ruled that students at high schools in Des Moines, Iowa, and by implication the rest of the nation, could not be expelled for wearing black arm bands to school to protest the raging war in Vietnam. In that 7–2 decision, the Court ruled that "First Amendment rights, applied in light of the special characteristics of the school environment, are available to teachers and students." **Free speech**, the Court said, did not end at the schoolhouse door.

In another set of rulings, almost as controversial as those related to race, the Court ruled in *Engel v. Vitale* (1962) and *Abington v. Schempp* (1963) that schools could not offer officially sanctioned prayers or devotional readings from the Bible. In 1968, in *Epperson v. Arkansas*, the Court ruled that a state law disallowing the teaching of evolution was an unconstitutional infringement of the First Amendment separation of church and state. For some religious people, all three of these rulings meant that "God had been kicked out of the public schools," although many deeply religious people also believed that the Court, following the First Amendment prohibition of "any laws respecting an establishment of religion," protected religious beliefs by keeping specific religious practices out of the public arena.

Supreme Court decisions affect many different elements of schooling in the United States. Battles about free speech, the place of religion in public schools, the costs of schooling, and a dozen other issues are far from over, especially as the membership of the Supreme Court changes, reflecting the differing politics of presidents who appoint federal judges.[2]

free speech Ability to talk or exchange ideas without fear of censorship or limitation; guaranteed by the First Amendment.

Connections

Recall the Chapter 10 discussion of the *Rodriguez* case, in which the Supreme Court put the issue of inequality in school financing beyond the purview of federal courts, to the disappointment of those who wanted federal intervention.

PRESIDENTS AND THE U.S. CONGRESS

Early in November 2008, within days of the election of Barack Obama as president of the United States, *Education Week* ran a special story on the president-elect's views of the federal government's role in education. During his long presidential campaign, Obama had made several specific promises about the schools. Saying "the goals of this law were the right ones," he pledged to provide meaningful funding for a revised and improved NCLB Act. He had made a promise of federal funding "to recruit, prepare, retain, and reward" teachers. He had also proposed $18

Join the **Dialogue**

Is the court system the best vehicle for resolving educational debates? What happens to the wider public discussion of issues if the Court makes a ruling? If not the Court, who should resolve difficult questions, and under what circumstances should they do so?

billion for new elementary and secondary programs plus $10 billion more for the development of new preschool programs. The first months of the new administration saw significant federal spending for educational programs (such as the Teacher Quality Partnerships and Race to the Top) that will encourage school districts, universities, and states to take very seriously the quality of programs they offer. The federal government will be involved in the effort to develop new multistate standards for academic achievement and to help states find much more sophisticated ways to track data related to student achievement, and it will insist that they do so. The fact that many educators are watching the new president very closely speaks volumes about the increased role the federal government has assumed in education during the past 40 years.[3]

Although the Supreme Court may have had the greater impact on schools and the politics of schooling, recent U.S. presidents and Congress have been at the forefront of education politics. In 1917, Congress passed and President Woodrow Wilson signed the Smith-Hughes Act, starting a century-long policy of federal funding for vocational education.[4] As part of his campaign for a Great Society, President Lyndon Johnson proposed much more broad-based federal funding for schools. The Elementary and Secondary Education Act (ESEA) of 1965 passed Congress by large margins in record time. Not one given to understatement, Johnson was clear about how much he valued the act:

> As a son of a tenant farmer, I know that education is the only valid passport from poverty.
>
> As a former teacher—and I hope, a future one—I have great expectations of what this law will mean for our young people.

Did you know?

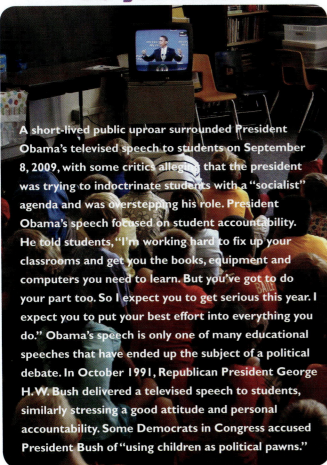

A short-lived public uproar surrounded President Obama's televised speech to students on September 8, 2009, with some critics alleging that the president was trying to indoctrinate students with a "socialist" agenda and was overstepping his role. President Obama's speech focused on student accountability. He told students, "I'm working hard to fix up your classrooms and get you the books, equipment and computers you need to learn. But you've got to do your part too. So I expect you to get serious this year. I expect you to put your best effort into everything you do." Obama's speech is only one of many educational speeches that have ended up the subject of a political debate. In October 1991, Republican President George H. W. Bush delivered a televised speech to students, similarly stressing a good attitude and personal accountability. Some Democrats in Congress accused President Bush of "using children as political pawns."

legislation at the federal and state levels has undermined many of the changes.

In the 1980s, the focus of federal policy shifted from a primary emphasis on equality of educational opportunity to the maintenance of high standards for students. In 1983, the National Commission on Excellence in Education, appointed by President Ronald Reagan, startled many observers with its report that "[o]ur Nation is at risk. . . . [T]he educational foundations of our society are presently being eroded by a rising tide of mediocrity. . . ." That report, *A Nation at Risk*, surprised many, as it had come from an administration that had promised to reduce if not eliminate the federal role in education. *A Nation at Risk* did not generate much in the way of federal legislation or, certainly, federal funding. It did, however, help to shift the terms of debates about education, from the 1960s' and 1970s' focus on equity to a new discussion of the meaning of educational excellence and the systems of standards and accountability that might produce a new level of educational attainment in the nation.[6]

The emphasis on educational standards gained momentum when the National Council of Teachers of Mathematics developed clear and specific standards for what every student in the United States should know about mathematics at different grade levels. Other professional organizations followed suit. These standards were first developed outside of government. Then, the administrations of George H. W. Bush and Bill Clinton yielded new federal legislation creating voluntary standards, known first as America 2000 and then Goals 2000, for what young people should know in different academic fields.[7]

To understand today's school curriculum, it is essential to understand the standards movement, but it is also important to realize that the standards movement is a prime example of the impact of federal politics on education. Without the strong support of Presidents George H. W. Bush and Clinton, the standards movement would not have had nearly the impact that it had. The movement laid the foundation for an even larger federal role in education, passage of NCLB early in George W. Bush's administration.

> **Connections**
> Chapter 4 detailed the succession of laws and court decisions that expanded educational rights to include all citizens.

> **YouDecide**
> Are education and politics always interconnected? How or when could they be separated?

> **Connections**
> Recall Chapter 2's discussion of President Johnson's war on poverty, how it used the ESEA to fund education, and subsequent debates about the ability of such funding to improve student achievement.

In the more than 40 years since ESEA passed, federal funding has continued to be important to local school districts and teachers in a number of ways.[5]

A flurry of federal legislation during the administrations of Johnson and, later, Richard M. Nixon transformed education. Teachers' jobs changed dramatically as a result of legislation from the 1960s and 1970s, as well as from other court decisions that built on the *Brown* decision and ruled that students could not be excluded from schools because of disabilities or an inability to speak English. These changes expanded teachers' responsibilities in requiring them to attend to this much more diverse group of students. None of these laws were passed without controversy, and, especially in the case of bilingual education, subsequent

Teachable Moment

Racing to the Top

President Barack Obama's administration released tentative rules concerning its competitive Race to the Top initiative, which promises $4.3 billion in grants to states that are aggressively working to improve student achievement, foster innovation, open more charter schools, and turn around failing schools.

Only a dozen or so states will benefit from the award, and some states have already been told that they are not eligible to apply. The ineligibility is most often linked to a specific restriction of the award in which states must have no "barriers to linking data on student achievement or student growth to teachers and principals for the purpose of teacher and principal evaluation." Following the often-made complaint during the Bush administration that NCLB relied too heavily on standardized testing, many teachers are protesting this rule as unfair, saying that it continues the excessive focus on such tests.

Many educators who were active supporters of Obama during the election were unhappy when they heard the rules concerning the Race to the Top, worrying that future rules may worsen the "test frenzy" that some observers associate with NCLB and could lead to a simplistic system for rewarding some teachers and punishing others. The two national teacher unions (the American Federation of Teachers and the National Education Association) have had no formal comment on the proposed rules, although unions have previously opposed the use of test scores in teacher evaluations.

Some states, such as New York, appealed the Education Department's plan, claiming their compliance

with a number of the rules. California is in the midst of debates about whether to continue to prohibit the use of student scores in teacher evaluations so that the state will be eligible, as a number of other states such as Indiana have already done. After states were notified that they needed to actively promote charter schools, Illinois, Louisiana, and several other states reworked their state policies to allow for more charter schools and for increases in the number of students allowed to attend them. A lot of money is at stake in these arguments, and cash-starved states want to be sure they are eligible for the funds.

QUESTIONS

- As a future teacher, how do you feel about legislation that uses student test scores on your career evaluation? Do you think this approach has merit, or is it unfair to teachers?
- How do we hold schools accountable? Do you think student test scores are an appropriate way to track school achievement and progress? Why or why not? What would be appropriate measures of accountability for schools and individual teachers?

>> What Are the Politics Behind the No Child Left Behind Debate?

The largest—and probably the most controversial—level of federal involvement in public education came much later and in a very different political context than the voluntary efforts for national standards and higher levels of school choice that

characterized the 1980s and 1990s. During the 2000 presidential campaign, both Democrat Al Gore and Republican George W. Bush campaigned for tougher accountability and higher standards in education. After the contested race was over, President Bush moved quickly to develop legislation that would fulfill his version of these campaign promises. Although initial planning was done within a relatively small circle, the new administration ultimately reached out to a wide range of liberal Democrats, especially Senator Edward

Teachable Moment

Charter Schools

One of the major developments in education since the mid-1980s was led by a group of educators who were skeptical of what the federal government could do to improve schools. These critics sought to create "charter" schools and educational vouchers that would allow parents to take the funds a public school might receive for their child's education to any private school they selected. Whereas the federal government sought standards for every school, charter school advocates sought to remove as many mandates as possible from individual schools so that they could prosper in their own way.

Charter schools are publicly funded and maintain autonomy from selected state rules and regulations, in return for meeting accountability standards. During the 2006–2007 school year, 410 new charter schools opened their doors, in addition to the 4,132 charter schools already operating. Of the 1.2 million students enrolled in charter schools, a higher percentage are of racial or ethnic minorities, compared to students in traditional public schools.

A split sometimes occurs between advocates of charter schools (which are public schools that usually operate outside the purview of traditional school districts) and advocates of vouchers (which have individualized educational choice more drastically). Although the initial impetus for charter schools and vouchers came from conservative theorists, many liberal, community-based critics of schools have joined in support of the proposals.

Pedro Noguera's essay in the **Readings** for this chapter reflects the split that has occurred among some liberal educators regarding **privatization** efforts. Noguera, a liberal voice in American education, sees a split between educational progressives who focus on system-wide change, and who therefore oppose any efforts that undermine the strength of school systems (such as privatizing efforts including charter schools and school

privatization Transition from government ownership to private-sector ownership. In education, refers to the use of vouchers and sometimes charter schools to encourage nonpublic ownership and control of schools.

vouchers), and those who have given up on school systems and have already opened their own independent schools. He notes that "independent school activists have been more likely to embrace vouchers as a means to provide educational alternatives to poor families." Terry M. Moe, one of the original advocates for privatization, says that, although the movement has not gone as far as he hoped, "Parents have many more choices today than they did ten years ago, and both choice and competition are expanding (especially through the increasing numbers of charter schools)."[8]

QUESTIONS

- Do you think it is more important to set clear national standards for all schools or to free educators from as many constraints as possible?
- What is the strongest argument in favor of charter schools? What is the strongest argument against them?

President George Bush and Margaret Spellings, Secretary of Education, during the Bush administration.

M. Kennedy, a long-time leader in the field of education in the U.S. Senate.

The bill that emerged from the inevitable compromises contained a number of significant provisions:

- Each state was given the responsibility for setting its own specific subject matter standards and for developing a clear and specific definition of adequate yearly progress (AYP), which each school was expected to achieve. For the first time, each state was expected, by federal law, to have clear standards and to administer the federal National Assessment of Educational Progress exam.

- If schools fail to make AYP (as defined by their state) for 2 years in a row, parents must be notified of their right to send their children to a nonfailing public school in the same district. (This has turned out to be difficult to enforce, since failing schools are often clustered near each other. The administration originally wanted to provide parents with vouchers they could use for private schools, but this provision was dropped.) Further failure means additional sanctions for schools and districts.

- Federal sanctions apply to schools and districts. States are not required to establish accountability standards that have sanctions for individual students or involve high school graduation requirements, although many states have also implemented high-stakes tests that require students to pass a specific exam or set of exams in order to be promoted or to graduate from high school.

- Each state had to develop a specific definition of a "highly qualified teacher," and only such teachers could

be employed in the future. The goal was to end the common practice of filling vacancies with teachers who are less than fully licensed, although the results have varied as districts found creative ways to define "highly qualified."

The federal government had never before asserted such a large role in public education in the United States.[9]

NCLB has generated extraordinary controversy since before the bill passed Congress and was signed by the president in January 2002. Some conservatives believe the bill does too little, that the accountability standards are too low, and that there are too many loopholes. Many liberals find several aspects of the bill to be objec-

Connections

Recall from Chapter 6 that high-stakes tests are one of the most controversial results of the NCLB legislation, although they are not formally part of it. Reauthorization of the act will likely be debated in 2010, with this issue addressed one way or another.

© 2007 Signe Wilkinson. Used with permission.

tionable. One judicious observer, Dana Grayson, supports some aspects of the legislation but worries about "the underlying logic of NCLB which seems to imply that the reason that schools are not achieving high test scores is because they are simply not exerting the effort or are 'lazy' or just not feeling pressured to do so." This logic, she writes, ignores the many larger social issues that shape what happens in many schools. Some critics of the legislation argue (1) that the accountability standards will lead to many young people being pushed out of school, (2) that teaching is being changed from a creative effort to help young people to understand and make meaning of their worlds into a massive test-prep program, and (3) that, unlike the ESEA, the NCLB federal regulations have never been matched by federal funding to give schools and teachers the resources needed to meet the standards. Some observers fear the result will be "many children left behind." How can you mandate certain results, they ask, and then not support the policy necessary to achieve the results?[10]

Debates about NCLB are not simple, and they are not likely to be resolved any time soon. Supporters and opponents of the legislation cannot easily be divided into two camps. Some critics of the law believe the legislation does not go far enough, whereas some see it as a veiled effort to destroy all of public education. Many others like some aspects of the legislation but take strong exception to other elements. President Obama has said that he supports the goals of NCLB—high standards and careful attention to the achievement of different groups of students—but he is critical of the lack of funding that has accompanied the law and is concerned that the tests used to measure progress have lacked attention to higher-order thinking skills.

Among authors traditionally viewed as educational conservatives, Frederick M. Hess and Chester E. Finn, Jr., are the most upbeat in their description of NCLB. However, they view the law as only a first small step in implementing a much larger accountability movement in education. Terry M.

Moe, more conservative than Hess and Finn, has grave doubts about NCLB. Moe, who has championed charter schools and educational vouchers, doubts that any government intervention can by itself undercut the deeply established traditions in contemporary school structures. For him, only a much higher level of **decentralization** linked to more powerful parental choice will bring about effective changes.

Educational liberals also disagree with each other about many aspects of NCLB, even if many (though certainly not all) share other aspects of a common critique. Linda Darling-Hammond describes NCLB as basically a set of good intentions gone awry, whereas Alfie Kohn sees the same law as, from the start, a calculated attack on all aspects of public education as we have known it in the United States. Whereas both authors are highly critical of the ways in which the testing aspects of NCLB can narrow the curriculum and, in their views, force teachers to "teach to the test," Darling-Hammond believes there is still a significant opportunity to reform the law and, if such reforms are linked to adequate funding, make a positive contribution to American education. Kohn, on the other hand, sees little hope in rescuing any aspect of NCLB and urges educators to do everything possible to ensure the repeal of the act.

No Child Left Behind was supposed to be reviewed by Congress in 2008, but no meaningful progress was made in this regard because of the presidential and congressional elections that year, followed by heated debates about the economic crisis and health care in 2009. Obama's administration and the Democratic majority in Congress will no doubt be defining their approach to this significant legislation in 2010.

In the meantime, many different voices are advocating what they believe should come next in place of NCLB,

> **decentralization** Transference of responsibility and authority from a concentrated power source to a number of smaller entities; for example, moving from district-wide school policies to allowing each school in a district to set its own policies.

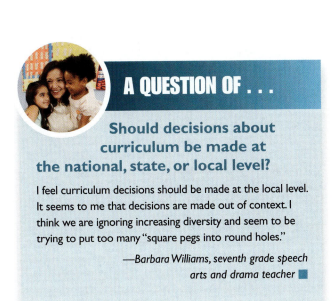

A QUESTION OF . . .

Should decisions about curriculum be made at the national, state, or local level?

I feel curriculum decisions should be made at the local level. It seems to me that decisions are made out of context. I think we are ignoring increasing diversity and seem to be trying to put too many "square pegs into round holes."

—Barbara Williams, seventh grade speech arts and drama teacher ∎

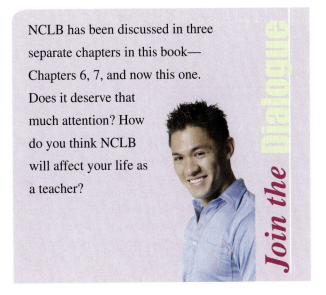

NCLB has been discussed in three separate chapters in this book—Chapters 6, 7, and now this one. Does it deserve that much attention? How do you think NCLB will affect your life as a teacher?

Join the Dialogue

There Are Many Opinions of NCLB

Four different voices, representative but hardly comprehensive, describe four different perspectives on the legislation, demonstrating the complexity of the legislation and the responses to it.

Alfie Kohn says:

If a single, powerful objection is reason enough to oppose a law, then we have multiple justifications for saying no to the legislation some have rechristened No Child Left Untested:

- NCLB usurps the power of local communities to choose their own policies and programs. It represents a power grab on the part of the federal government that is unprecedented in the history of U.S. education.
- It compromises the quality of teaching by forcing teachers to worry more about raising test scores than about promoting meaningful learning.
- It punishes those who most need help and sets back efforts to close the gap between rich and poor, and between black and white....

But to fully assess the impact of this law, we need to understand it in context. Some of NCLB's most energetic supporters are people and organizations opposed to the whole idea of public schooling—and, indeed, to public institutions in general. Their idea of "reform" turns out to entail some sort of privatization, such that education is gradually transferred to the marketplace. There, the bottom line is not what benefits children but what produces profit....

Jamie McKenzie, a former superintendent, put it this way on his website, Nochildleft.com: "Misrepresented as a reform effort, NCLB is actually a cynical effort to shift public school funding to a host of private schools, religious schools, and free-market diploma mills or corporate experiments in education."...Senator Jim Jeffords, who chaired the Senate committee that oversees education from 1997 to 2001, has described the law as a back-door maneuver "that will let the private sector take over public education, something the Republicans have wanted for years.[11]

Linda Darling-Hammond says:

Many civil rights advocates initially hailed the Bush administration's major education bill, optimistically entitled No Child Left Behind, as a step forward in the long battle to improve education for those children traditionally left behind in American schools—in particular, students of color and students living in poverty, new English learners, and students with disabilities. The broad goal of NCLB is to raise the achievement levels of all students, especially underperforming groups, and to close the achievement gap that parallels race and class distinctions....

This noble agenda seems unobjectionable on its face, but the complex 600-page law has affected states, districts, schools, and students in ways never envisioned by its authors.... As the evidence of NCLB's unintended consequences emerges, it seems increasingly clear that, despite its good intentions and admirable goals, NCLB as currently implemented is more likely to harm than to help most of the students who are the targets of its aspirations, and it is more likely to undermine—some would even say destroy—the nation's public education system than to improve it. These outcomes are likely because the underfunded bill layers onto a grossly unequal—and in many communities, inadequately funded—school system a set of unmeetable test score targets that disproportionately penalize schools serving the neediest students, while creating strong incentives for schools to keep out or push out those students who are low achieving in order to raise school average test scores.[12]

including Scott Franklin Abernathy, whose recommendations are in the second **Reading** for this chapter. At the same time, the U.S. Department of Education has launched significant new programs that should provide educators with much more data and will make much higher demands on school districts and states than in the past. The future of NCLB, or as it was originally named, the reauthorization of the Elementary and Secondary Education Act, will probably take many more months to play out.

>> What Is the Role of State and Local Politics in Education?

The former Speaker of the U.S. House of Representatives, Tip O'Neil, was famous for saying, "all politics is local." In no arena is that statement truer than in school politics. Decisions regarding education have generally been left to

Frederick M. Hess and Chester E. Finn, Jr., say:

NCLB represented a significant departure from past practice. For the first time, the federal government required that academic performance lead to concrete consequences for schools—and that children in inadequate schools have the opportunity to seek assistance or move elsewhere....

At NCLB's heart is the requirement that states annually test all public school students in grades 3–8 in reading and math and that every state measure whether its public schools (and school systems) are making "adequate yearly progress" (AYP) toward universal pupil proficiency in core subjects....

Crucially, schools must show gains not only for their overall student body but also for pupil subgroups delineated by grade level, ethnicity, gender, socio-economic status, English proficiency, and special needs. If schools do not make the progress mandated by the state, various sanctions and interventions are supposed to follow.

These twin provisions are intended both to provide better education options to students stuck in faltering schools and to create incentives for those schools to improve. Under NCLB, if a school fails to make AYP for two consecutive years, and it's a school that receives Title I dollars, its students must be offered "public school choice." Under that provision, the district is obliged to provide each child with options of alternative public (and charter) schools that are making satisfactory progress. If a child's (Title I) school fails to make AYP for a third consecutive year, the district is to provide him/her with the opportunity to enroll in supplemental educational services—essentially about 30 hours of free after-school tutoring. Such tutoring can be provided by a variety of suppliers, including private vendors of education services or the school system itself, and is to be paid for with a portion of the school's federal Title I dollars (money meant to promote learning for disadvantaged kids).[13]

Terry M. Moe says:

In state after state, governments have imposed new curriculum standards, new tests aligned to the standards, new requirements for promotion and graduation, new rules for ranking schools and publicizing test scores, and new systems of rewards and sanctions.... And President George W. Bush, a Republican not otherwise given to federal intervention, followed up by making his No Child Left Behind legislation a centerpiece of his domestic program—imposing, for the first time, a national accountability system of annual testing and performance-based rewards and sanctions....The movement for school accountability is essentially a movement for more effective top-down control of schools....The fact is the authorities are faced with a school system that...has never really been held accountable for student achievement. This long-standing lack of accountability is heavily reflected in the modern structure.With few exceptions, for instance, there is no connection between how much students learn and how much anyone gets paid....

So...the authorities are up against a control problem of formidable proportions. They do not know how to produce student achievement, nor do they necessarily know student achievement when they see it. But they must try to design a control structure that gets a resistant group of employees to apply their expertise in all the right ways to generate the desired outcomes. Over the last decade, the authorities have sought to do this through regimes of standards, tests, and rewards, and sanctions. They are fighting an uphill battle, though, and their prospects for success are not bright.[14]

QUESTIONS

- Which of these four different positions is closest to your own? If you were asked to add a fifth box with your own opinions about NCLB, what would you say?
- When so many thoughtful educators disagree so deeply about an issue such as NCLB, how is it possible to make wise decisions about education in a democratic way? How do you respond to people who disagree with you about educational issues?

---

the states, and many of the important decisions were left to the local communities. Elected or, occasionally, appointed local school boards set the curriculum, hire superintendents (who in turn hire the teachers), and generally decide what is taught by whom and on what schedule.

Even when it comes to responding to the vastly expanded federal role in schools since NCLB became law, many decisions about implementation happen at the local level. Some schools and school districts, and even state govern-ments, have resisted NCLB, but many localities have not only embraced the movement to tougher accountability but also have sought to stay ahead of the curve.

GOVERNORS, STATE LEGISLATURES, AND DEPARTMENTS OF EDUCATION

Governors, legislatures, and leaders in state departments of education have all responded to the change in national

Goals for ESEA

The Alliance for Excellent Education, a national policy and advocacy organization dedicated to making every child a high school graduate and preparing them for college and work, and to be contributing members of society, says that ESEA reauthorization should

- establish college and career readiness as the common goal for all students;
- ensure meaningful accountability for high school outcomes designed around common indicators of college and career readiness and high school graduation;
- replace the current flawed, one-size-fits-all school improvement process with requirements for state- and district-led systems that are differentiated and data driven, and prioritize addressing the lowest-performing high schools;

- support strategies that are necessary to implement high school improvement at a much larger scale, including districtwide efforts, maximizing the role of entities outside of the school system with expertise to contribute;
- build the capacity of the system to implement innovative solutions—bold approaches to teaching and learning, school organization, and system structure that result in higher expectations and achievement for all students; and
- provide new funding for the implementation of innovative solutions to address low-performing high schools.[15]

What About Me?

Your Views on No Child Left Behind

There are a variety of opinions about the No Child Left Behind Act. It is impossible to assess the act as simply good or bad, given the many factors and opinions on each side. Based on what you have gathered from the **Readings** and the text, your class discussions, and elsewhere, put a checkmark in the box that best describes how you feel about each given viewpoint.

	Strongly Disagree	Disagree	Neutral	Agree	Strongly Agree
The new standards, rankings, and requirements produce accountability and, therefore, progress in "a school system that...has never really been held accountable for student achievement."					
"[NCLB] compromises the quality of teaching by forcing teachers to worry more about raising test scores than about promoting meaningful learning."					
Despite its good intentions, NCLB cannot operate as intended at its current funding level.					
With the new requirements, students are given a "set of unmeetable test score targets that disproportionately penalize schools serving the neediest students."					
NCLB provides goals and a number of performance measurements for schools to help them work toward positive improvements.					
"NCLB represents a power grab on the part of the federal government that is unprecedented in the history of U.S. education."					
It is a positive that, under NCLB, "children in inadequate schools have the opportunity to seek assistance or move to another school."					

Teachable Moment

Evolving Standards

Since the governments of the 50 states have the final say on most matters that affect schools, a large array of strategies and solutions are often used to address the same issue. For example, different states have found various ways to approach the controversy surrounding how to teach evolution in a biology class.

In most states, biology, including evolutionary biology, is taught according to the tenets of the scientific community. Well-organized groups have fought against teaching evolution by seeking to undermine its scientific legitimacy. In Alabama, for example, as recently as 2005, the state board of education voted to continue requiring a disclaimer in biology textbooks describing evolution as a "controversial theory." In addition, anti-evolution bills were introduced in 2006, 2008, and 2009, all of which were intended to allow teachers to teach biblical explanations for the diversity of life. In 2005, stickers that stated evolution alone is "not adequate to explain the origins of life" were removed from Arkansas textbooks. In Cobb County, Georgia, the use of a similar sticker, claiming evolution to be "a theory, not a fact," was declared unconstitutional by a federal judge in 2005. Also in 2005, a coalition of Christian schools, along with a California Christian school and six of its students, sued the University of California system over its policy of not accepting certain biology classes as fulfilling high school science requirements for entry into the university system.

Other states have allowed the teaching of evolution as long as a complementary counter-theory is taught, whether it is **intelligent design** or **creationism**. Although Texas has gone back and forth on the teaching of evolution, changes were made to the state's science standards in 2009 that will significantly affect the teaching of evolution in that state. The Texas Board of Education called for changes to language about evolutionary theory and for questioning of the validity of evolution—and other scientific theories— in Texas classrooms.

creationism Religious belief that a supernatural being created humanity and all life on Earth.

intelligent design Belief that biological life on Earth was designed and created by an omnipotent entity; most often associated with the Christian God. Supporters of intelligent design claim it is a scientific theory that can stand against the study of evolution.

The Louisiana Science Education Act (2008) allows supplementary classroom materials to be used in teaching science. A provision that "materials that teach creationism or intelligent design or that advance the religious belief that a supernatural being created humankind shall be prohibited for use in science class" was deleted from a 2009 policy that sought to clarify the types of materials that could be used. Previously, in Ohio and New Mexico, students were encouraged to actively debate and investigate the merits of evolution, along with discussions concerning individual religious beliefs—though standards have been changed in both states as recently as 2009. Long court battles have ensued in states such as Pennsylvania, where a 2004 federal ruling rejected the teaching of intelligent design in high school classes because it represented an effort to include a religious issue, rather than a scientific one, in the school curriculum and thus violated the separation between church and state. In some instances, individual school districts in a state are given freedom to decide whether and how evolution will be taught in their schools.

Despite all the controversy, in the vast majority of states and in nearly all the largest districts, biology is taught in ways that include scientific evolution. Nevertheless, every teacher, whether planning to teach in one of the nation's largest urban districts, a small suburb, or an isolated rural area, needs to know that topics like evolution can lead quickly to fierce debates, not only at the policy level but also among parents and administrators in one's own school.

QUESTIONS

- How would you respond if you did not agree with an education policy that told you what to teach, or not teach? What resources do teachers have at their disposal to argue against these types of policies?
- What do you think is the correct way to handle an issue such as evolution in a classroom? Do you see merit in Alabama's textbook disclaimers, the ways that states like New Mexico or Ohio call for discussion of different perspectives, or the policy in most states that evolution should be taught as science and the controversy handled elsewhere in the curriculum?

Teachable Moment
Reconstituted Schools

In 1998, three years before NCLB was first proposed, the state of Oregon adopted its own tough accountability policies that called for "reconstituting" a school if it failed to meet specific state benchmarks. Linda Christensen, an editor of *Rethinking Schools*, describes what happened at her school, Jefferson High School in Portland, Oregon, when new state policies were implemented:

> *Jefferson High School teachers, cafeteria workers, custodians, secretaries, and administrators lined up to receive our official pink slips, notifying us to vacate our positions. Jefferson was being "reconstituted" because of low test scores and falling enrollment.... As part of the reconstitution process, staff could reapply for their positions. In meetings packed with emotion, Jefferson staff members struggled between staying for our students who did nothing to bring this about and leaving because it was an "insult to reapply for a job we did well." I always thought that I would retire from Jefferson. But instead, I packed my boxes because I refused to offer legitimacy to a shallow, mean-spirited education policy.*

According to Christensen, once Oregon had adopted the new "get-tough" policy, Jefferson was an obvious target. "Located in the heart of Portland's predominantly working-class African-American community, Jefferson is considered the only 'Black' high school in Oregon. One has to wonder how much this designation contributed to the student flight that has marked the school's enrollment patterns." Like many schools serving poor and working-class students and students of color, Jefferson had trouble maintaining its test scores. Promising efforts at smaller learning academies were moving Jefferson in the right direction, but not every teacher wanted to participate and neither the district nor the state wanted to allow more time

for the collaborative discourse that many educators believed was the only key to meaningful long-term change. "To embrace change," Christensen said, "teachers need support, time, and resources. They also need models of success, credible reform processes and leadership, and a sense of accountability to a mobilized student and community constituency."

In the aftermath of being reconstituted, the new principal and mostly new faculty tried to maintain the academies with some important successes. They also sought various short-term efforts to help students who were close to passing the state tests get "over the line." The result, however, was that large numbers of students who were further behind and now segregated into "Certificate of Initial Mastery reading classes" (known to their participants as the "retard class") became less engaged with school. Jefferson's enrollment continued to fall as students transferred to other schools and teachers and administrators left in large numbers. (The school had six principals in the 5 years following reconstitution.) All this happened before NCLB became law.

Source: "Reconstituting Jefferson: Lessons on School Reform," by Linda Christensen, in *Rethinking School Reform: Views From the Classroom*, edited by Linda Christensen and Stan Karp, 2003, *Rethinking Schools*, pp. 266–274.

QUESTIONS

- If you found yourself in the situation Christensen faced, do you think you would reapply for the job, or would you pack your boxes? Why?
- In what circumstances might it make sense for a school district or a state to "give up" on a specific school and virtually start over with new teachers and leaders? What would lead to such circumstances?

mood perhaps even more than the specific changes mandated in NCLB. Florida, for example, was far ahead of NCLB in developing tough state-level accountability systems. Thirty years before NCLB, and even before much of the national pressure, Florida passed its 1971 Educational Accountability Act that required statewide testing, the attainment of certain benchmarks to graduate from high school, and consequences for schools that did not perform well. By contrast, many states are like Colorado, where policy begins with the saying "Colorado is a strong local-control state" and, although the state government may enact policies as tough as or tougher than the federal regulations, local districts can ignore many of them and go their own way. A few states have debated rejecting the federal money to avoid having to meet the NCLB requirements, but the federal dollars are a strong incentive to find ways to function within the law's framework.[16]

State policy emanates from different power centers. Governors and legislatures control state spending on education and can also set basic legislative mandates for testing and standards. Most of the work of supervising education is left to state departments of education and to the chief state school officer (sometimes called the superintendent of public instruction or the commissioner of education). In some states, the commissioner or superintendent is an elected official. In other states, he or she is appointed by a state school board, whose members are often appointed by the governor. Since governors and members of state legislatures are elected by the voters, state education policy is always political. However, being "political" is not always a bad thing. It means that elected officials need to be attuned to public sentiment and teachers, parents, and others can influence state policy when they are well organized.

Although the way that state governments have chosen to implement NCLB has been the subject of great attention in recent years, state education officials are involved in all aspects of education. State education departments set academic standards in different subject areas. Each state determines the standards for becoming a teacher, and the state government licenses or certifies individuals to teach. The state approves certain university programs or alternative providers to prepare teachers. Special education regulations, policies for programs that teach English to non-English-speaking students, and a range of other regulations are set by state governments. State governments have the final authority to intervene in and even take over a local school district if they believe that the district is failing to serve the students as it should. In the end, states have the ultimate responsibility for public education in the United States.

Chapter 10 explained how a significant portion of a school's budget comes from state and local sources.

Connections

LOCAL SCHOOL DISTRICTS AND SCHOOL BOARDS

Schools are nearly always governed by an elected (or occasionally appointed) school board that sets overall policy for a school district and hires a superintendent to be the full-time senior administrator of the district, responsible for all day-to-day decisions about the schools in that area. There are 15,000 school boards governing districts as large as some of the nation's biggest cities and as small as districts that have only one elementary school. These boards have significant authority over the schools in their districts. As John Portz, a political scientist who studies school politics, writes:

The term "governance" refers to the authority structure by which major decisions are made and resources are allocated within a school system. As defined in a report by the Education Commission of the States, "governance arrangements establish the rules of the game, that is. . .who is responsible and accountable for what within the system." A long-time observer of school politics noted that "governance is about control—who drives the education bus." Put differently, a recent study of school boards describes governing as "steering" the school district. Governing involves the establishment of educational goals and policies that follow a vision and set of core beliefs about how academic achievement can be realized.

The diverse authorities that Portz cites seem to be saying the same thing: school boards govern schools in the United States. Portz also notes that

To be certain, school boards do not act alone or unfettered. They operate within numerous rules and regulations established by state governments and to a lesser extent, federal authorities. The superintendent also typically plays a role in school district governance and professional associations, particularly the teachers' union, might also have major governance responsibilities.

School boards have been criticized for being too actively involved in the details of school management, especially personnel decisions, that might better be left to professional educators, especially the superintendent that the board hires and should trust. They have been seen as too highly politicized and too anxious to cater to the immediate preoccupations of a portion of the electorate, such as activist teacher unions, anti-tax groups, activists concerned with one policy change or another, and so on. Some observers believe that school boards are merely an anachronistic leftover of a bygone era.[17]

Others question how much power school boards really have. As Pedro Noguera reflects from his own experience,

Teachable Moment

Halting a Collapse

In February 2009, Robert C. Bobb was appointed the emergency financial manager of Detroit's public school system by the Michigan governor's state financial-review team, thereby taking financial authority away from the city's school board. Bobb arrived in Detroit with unprecedented authority and with a grave task in front of him—turning around a district that had lost half of its students over the past 10 years and that carried with it a growing deficit that stood at $259 million. The district's student enrollment had been dropping partly because of the city's rapid loss of population but also because more and more families who stayed in the city were opting for other educational alternatives for their children. Making the job even more difficult, Bobb was given an initial appointment of only one year to carry out the changes.

While working through the problem, Bobb uncovered many instances of corruption, including a paper trail of "ghost" workers and employee theft. At the same time, teachers and students worked in dirty, unequipped classrooms. With little time and a school district on the verge of bankruptcy, Bobb began restructuring the district by cutting inefficiencies where he could and laying off staff that were no longer needed for the downsized student population. He scheduled 29 schools to close in the fall of 2009, and began restructuring an additional 40 underperforming schools. A former FBI agent was hired to recommend potential fraud cases for prosecution, while half of the top executive positions were eliminated and an additional 1,700 employees were laid off.

Even while the district was being downsized, plans were being made for future improvements. A total of 33,000 students participated in a free summer-school program, making it the largest such program ever offered. Bobb hired a former superintendent of the Cleveland school district to craft a long-term academic plan. Bobb's mission is to reform a damaged school district by closely scrutinizing areas of

Source: "Decline and Fall," by Dakarai I. Aarons, August 12, 2009, *Education Week*, http://www.edweek.org/ew/articles/2009/07/31/37detroit.h28.html?tkn=XQPFvNqE6FDOCMJaRjdRax/KljdENeAWRn4M.

The Enrollment Cliff

The number of students attending the Detroit public schools has declined sharply over the past decade. In 2010, the district is projected to have just more than half the number of students it had in 2001.

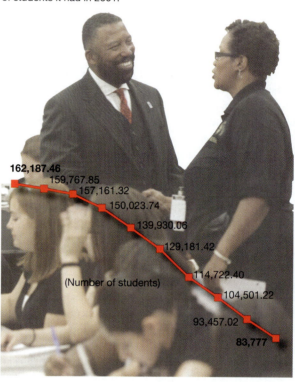

162,187.46
159,767.85
157,161.32
150,023.74
139,930.06
129,181.42
114,722.40
104,501.22
93,457.02
83,777

(Number of students)

2001 2002 2003 2004 2005 2006 2007 2008 2009 2010
(projected)

Source: www.edweek.org/media/2009/08/07/37detroit-c1.jpg

inefficiency and planning for a future that includes not possible bankruptcy and low enrollment but rather academic excellence and personal opportunity for the students who live in Detroit.

QUESTIONS

- What do you think of a state takeover of a school district such as happened in Detroit? Is it in some circumstances the best way to serve students? Is it a democratic way to make decisions?
- If Bobb asked your advice, what would you tell him was the single most important thing to spend money on, even if he had to cut other parts of the budget? What would your argument be for your favored expenditure?

I learned about the limitations of local government firsthand while working as assistant to the Mayor of Berkeley [California] during the 1980s and while serving as an elected member of the school board in the 1990s. Through direct experience, I learned that even with a relatively progressive local government in an affluent city, it was nearly impossible to solve problems such as chronic unemployment, drug trafficking, or homelessness.[18]

Defenders of local control and local school boards see the democratic control of school through local school boards as an essential political instrument in a democratic society. For an educator like Deborah Meier, the only solution to the problems of democracy and democratic control of schools is more democracy. Meier is deeply offended by the increasing centralization and professionalization of schools—the tendency to create larger and thus more impersonal school districts that can make school decision-making more removed from individual citizens. In 1930, there were 200,000 school boards, compared with 15,000 today. The result is that each school board governs many more teachers and students, and thus it is much harder for the voice of a parent or other concerned citizens to be heard. This problem is exacerbated by the fact that there are also three times as many students in school today, state educational bureaucracies are much more powerful, and the federal government is much more involved in educational decision-making. Meier insists,

> *We need to return schools to our fellow citizens—yes, ordinary citizens, with all their warts. The solution to the messiness of democracy is more of it—and more time set aside to make it work. . . . That's what local school boards are intended to be all about. If we can't trust ordinary citizens with matters of local K–12 schooling, whatever can we trust them with?*[19]

Others have a different opinion about the value of local school boards. Some of the nation's largest cities, including New York City, Chicago, Washington, D.C., Cleveland, Philadelphia, Baltimore, Los Angeles, and Boston, have abolished or drastically reduced the roles of elected boards, giving primary authority (and with it accountability) in school matters to the elected mayor. Mayoral control means that the city's political leader, who in most cities also controls the city budget, is responsible for the success of the schools. Having one point-person certainly avoids the finger pointing that can result when power is divided between an elected board (some of whose members may be interested in higher office) and a separate mayor.

In Chapter 12, we discuss the role of schools in a democratic society.

Connections

Portz explains the appeal of these changes:

> *Mayoral involvement in governance is intended to align political and financial resources in the city in support of public education. In almost every instance, these are mayors in strong-mayor systems who exercise considerable authority over the allocations of resources within the city. Involvement in school policy brings the mayor into a system of "integrated governance" in which political and financial control is centralized to create a more rational and systematic allocation of educational resources.*

The experiment of mayoral control versus the arguments in favor of control of schools at a much more community level seems destined to continue for the foreseeable future.[20]

For an aspiring or a new teacher, the politics of the school board, whether it is elected or abolished in favor of mayoral control, and what its powers are in relation to a professional superintendent or to state and federal officials, may all seem far beyond your immediate concerns. Nevertheless, all of us operate in political climates in which different people make decisions that affect our lives and the lives of our students. To ignore the politics of educational decision-making and to avoid the controversies about local control versus state versus national influence on educational decisions is to deal ourselves out of an important level of decision making that affects many aspects of our work.

Hiring Decisions Teachers are hired at the local level. Neither the state nor the federal government hires teachers. School boards hire superintendents. In larger districts, superintendents hire human resource directors and principals, and they hire the teachers. After a person has met all the qualifications for a teaching position, one of these people in authority still needs to decide whether the individual is the right person for the job before he or she can gain a signed contract and step in front of a classroom. Even when there is a teacher shortage, as there often is in certain fields such as mathematics, the sciences, or special education, or in "hard-to-staff" districts (which usually means districts serving poor students in urban or rural areas), you must connect with the right person in authority to get a teaching job.

Licensure Whereas hiring decisions are local, holding a license to teach—the formal certification that one is qualified to enter a classroom—means that one has also met qualifications set by other levels of educational authority. In general, teacher licensure is based on meeting specific qualifications for a license in one state. It used to be fairly easy for a person to become a teacher, but the requirements have risen steadily. Today, no state grants a teaching license to a person who does not hold a college degree and who has not completed some sort of program in education—usually a

highly qualified teacher As defined by No Child Left Behind standards, a highly qualified teacher is one who holds a bachelor's degree, full state certification or licensure, and verifiable knowledge of the subject taught.

college or university-based undergraduate or graduate program that includes education courses and student teaching, or occasionally an "alternative route" offered by a school district or an organization such as Teach for America. Until quite recently, many districts could arrange waivers so that they could hire teachers, especially in high-needs shortage areas, who did not have the required state license. However, one requirement of NCLB is that every child be taught by a **highly qualified teacher**, which has generally come to mean a teacher who is fully licensed in the state in which he or she plans to teach.

>> How Do Teachers Make Political Decisions in the Classroom?

It is easy to think of politics as something distant and even sometimes unsavory, but all aspects of teaching, large and small, are political. Fifth-grade teacher Bob Peterson writes:

All teaching is political whether we're conscious of it or not. We all make political decisions every day in the classroom. If we decide to put up a Halloween bulletin board instead of a bulletin board that indicts Christopher Columbus for being a war criminal, that's a political decision. If we decide to make Valentine's Day hearts with kids instead of celebrating Black History month, that's a political decision. And it's OK to do some of those things— I'm not against Halloween or hearts, although I oppose a holiday-driven curriculum— but we should do things self-consciously and recognize the political nature of our work.

You might think of Halloween as "unpolitical" while an indictment of Columbus would certainly involve taking a "political" stance, but every decision a teacher makes about raising or not raising an issue or taking or not taking a stand is also a political decision.[21]

Valentine's Day hearts and Black History month may be a long way from federal legislation and school board elections, but as Pedro Noguera reminds us in the **Readings**, "limit situations" can be important political opportunities for teachers to assert their limited but still very real power. When, as Noguera describes it, Paul Kurose decided to reach out to his student Jamila, first to prod her about unfinished work rather than let it slide, and then, when he realized the depth of what Jamila was facing at home, to intervene and help her get into the achievement program that helped her to gain college admissions, he made a political decision. There were, of course, risks involved. Jamila's mother might have objected or others might have thought he was exceeding his role. On the other hand, another teacher would have responded to Jamila's statement, "Do you think that you would be able to do your work if every night your mother was bringing a different man into your house to have sex and smoke crack?" by reporting the family to other authorities. All the options that Kurose might have pursued, and the one he did pursue, involved political calculations— what was required by law, what his conscience required, and what was possible within the limits of his own position and his time and energy. Clearly, in this story, Kurose's use of his power made an important difference.

Another example of working within perhaps even more limited situations is offered by teacher and author Gregory Michie. In "Resisting the Pull of School-as-Usual," he says, "It may be that you have to start with something small and seemingly insignificant—like bulletin boards." Michie says that though people rarely notice bulletin boards in schools, they can provide an opportunity, "the most visible one of all in many schools—to make a statement, to pose questions, to speak out on an issue, to bring kids' lives into classrooms or hallways." Michie describes seeing a bulletin board that said "They Were Here First," featuring American Indian tribes, another with information on the AIDS epidemic's impact in Africa, and another that invited students to share quotes they found challenging and inspiring. Of these very small-scale "limit situations," Michie writes:

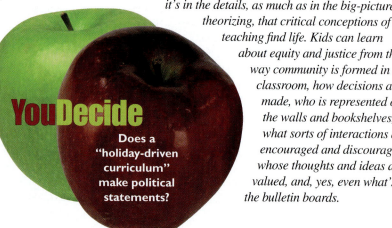

You Decide

Does a "holiday-driven curriculum" make political statements?

Those may not sound like such radical acts when placed alongside the more elaborate proposals of education's critical theorists. But once you're in a classroom of your own, you begin to realize that it's in the details, as much as in the big-picture theorizing, that critical conceptions of teaching find life. Kids can learn about equity and justice from the way community is formed in a classroom, how decisions are made, who is represented on the walls and bookshelves, and what sorts of interactions are encouraged and discouraged, whose thoughts and ideas are valued, and, yes, even what's on the bulletin boards.

How Can I Make a Difference?

Get Involved With Your School Board

School boards play a central role in setting the curricular standards and personnel policies for their districts. The board defines the vision of the community's schools, approves curriculum materials, maintains an annual budget, and chooses school superintendents. The policies they set have a significant impact on the lives of students and teachers in any given school system. In most communities, the local school board is an elected body. All residents over the age of 18 have the right to vote in school board elections,

and anyone can attend meetings and join a campaign to elect—or defeat—school board members. There is an old saying that "if you don't vote, you can't complain." Too many educators, including students studying to be teachers, may complain regularly but do not follow local elections and certainly do not participate. But you can.

Getting involved with a campaign to elect someone you admire to a local school board, or simply registering and voting and attending occasional school board meetings can have big payoffs. Your time and expertise can directly benefit students and teachers. Studies have found that school districts with underperforming school boards—especially those with members who do not work well together or who are underqualified—negatively affect students. Students in districts with troubled school boards often have lower test scores and higher dropout rates than those in districts with well-run boards. People of color are sorely underrepresented on school boards, as are members from low-income households.

To get a sense of how school boards interact and the issues they deal with, begin attending school board meetings in your community. You will learn a lot, even if you also witness a lot of tedious business being conducted. It could be an ideal way to become involved with a local campaign for a candidate you trust and respect. You will be a more informed teacher for the effort, and you might help make the schools better, too.

Sources: "School Boards' Worth in Doubt," by Jane Elizabeth, November 30, 2003, *Pittsburgh-Post Gazette*, http://www.post-gazette.com/localnews/20031130boardsmainlocal2p2.asp; "School Boards and Student Achievement," Iowa School Board Compass, Fall 2000, http://www.ia-sb.org/WorkArea/showcontent.aspx?id=570.

QUESTIONS

- What do you know about your local school board? Have you talked with any of its members, or asked them questions? Do you get involved during elections?
- Which issues or problems do you think are most pressing in your home community's schools? Why? What ideas or solutions would you suggest to deal with the specific problems?

PORTRAIT OF AN EDUCATOR

Ramon C. Cortines

Although Ramon Cortines is superintendent of the Los Angeles Unified School District, the second largest school district in the United States, when he is asked what he does, his answer is always, "I'm a teacher." He began his career as a sixth-grade teacher in a small school district near Monterey on the California coast just south of San Francisco. In a recent interview, he recalled,

> I was a damned good teacher but there were times when I needed help. I remember my first class—I certainly needed help then. I had 44 kids in my first class, all 6th graders. I didn't know that was too many. I was too green. I thought that was what I was dealt so I needed to deal with it, but I had people. I had a principal and a county supervisor that visited me once a month. They didn't visit to "get" me, but to find out how they could help and what I needed.

Cortines has tried to take that same attitude of "finding out how to help" into the senior administrative positions he has held. After Monterey, he moved to a position teaching English at a high school in Covina, California, one of the more distant suburbs of Los Angeles. Since his days as a teacher, Cortines has held

Source: "I've Always Been a Teacher: An Interview With Ray Cortines," by Travis Miller and Antero Garcia, April 14, 2008, http://manualarts.wordpress.com/2008/04/14/ive-always-been-a-teacher-an-interview-with-ray-cortines.

a very wide range of administrative and policy making positions in education. In the course of his career, he moved from being an assistant principal to superintendent of schools in Pasadena, San Francisco, and San Jose, California. He then served a term as New York City's chancellor of education (the city's title for the superintendent in the nation's largest district).

He has also held a number of other more political appointments in education including assistant secretary for intergovernmental and interagency affairs and human resources and, later, assistant secretary for educational research and improvement, both presidential appointments in the U.S. Department of Education. While he was in Washington, Cortines grew frustrated with the federal bureaucracy's distance from the everyday world of students and teachers, and he told his staff, "You people need to learn how to pick up the paper off of the playground." He has advised every U.S. president since Jimmy Carter on education matters. He also served a term as deputy mayor of Los Angeles for education, youth, and families. He is on the board of directors of the J. Paul Getty Trust, Scholastic, Inc. (a textbook publisher), and the Teachers Support Network. He has consulted with the Eli and Edythe Broad Education Foundation, served as a trustee of Brown University and Pacific Oakes College, and taught at Harvard and Brown Universities. Cortines is a teacher who understands all levels of political power in American education.

In a recent interview, Cortines outlined his approach to the politics of education. The key to being a strong leader, he says, is being a good listener:

> I think the educational staff needs to be listened to. My first year in New York, I held 30 community meetings with interpreters. People said that New Yorkers weren't interested in education; there were never less than 300 people in any one of those meetings. What I did was I didn't start talking. For the first 40 minutes, I just listened. And then we got back to them and I told them my focus. If I were taking over a school, I would create forums or focus groups where I listened to you. It's very difficult to be dumped on for an hour and a half, day after day, but it needs to happen.

For all the senior positions that Cortines has held in government, universities, and school districts, he believes that the most important work happens at the local level. He is critical of the large bureaucracy that he inherited in Los Angeles. "What we have now is you have an assistant to the assistant to the assistant. That's just b.s. [sic]." For him, education happens at a much more specific level: "It's between a teacher and a student. We need to create the conditions that are optimal for you to improve academic achievement."

As students learn from all these observations, they—and their teachers—are entering into a political process that is a key element in American public education.[22]

Education in the United States is highly political—from decisions made by the U.S. Supreme Court, Congress, or the president; to local school boards and superintendents and their human resource and budget offices; to teachers

who help a student in trouble or who change a bulletin board; to taxpayer and legislative decisions on adequate school funding. The teacher who recognizes the political nature of education will have the best chance not only to survive what can at times be a difficult political minefield but also to make a positive political contribution toward improving education and the lives of children.

Promising Practices

Mississippi Brings Civil Rights Into the Curriculum

Even a change to a school bulletin board can be a political act because it introduces a new way for students to think about an issue or historical period and to make their own voices heard. Educators in Mississippi, however, are taking a step past the bulletin board by implementing a curriculum program that promises to teach students about the "untold story" of the civil rights struggle.

Launched in 2009, the new curriculum requires civil rights instruction in high school and will extend to all students (K–12) by the 2010–2011 school year. Civil rights instruction is already in place in school districts in some states, such as Alabama, Georgia, and Arkansas, but Mississippi's program is more comprehensive than all existing programs.

Mississippi's program emphasizes the grassroots nature of the civil rights movement and explores the institutional nature of racism. Many students have traditionally been told the bare-minimum when it comes to civil rights—primarily learning about Martin Luther King, Jr., and Rosa Parks—without understanding that many important leaders, organizers, and activists laid the groundwork before the flowering of the movement in 1954 and 1955.

Students in Mississippi will now learn a more complex story through a variety of methods. Role-playing activities have students act out significant events, such as the Montgomery bus boycott. Local activists, relatives, and community members are invited into the classroom to provide their personal insight into the civil rights movement and the fight for integration. Younger children will discuss diversity and the equality of all people as an introduction into the subject.

By bringing the subject of civil rights and subsequent movements into the classroom, Mississippi is refusing to shy away from the more brutal periods of history, including its own history. Such efforts are intended to produce a better-informed and more well-rounded student body.

Source : "Miss. Making Civil Rights Part of K–12 Instruction," by Sheila Byrd, August 21, 2009, *Education Week,* http://www.edweek.org/ew/articles/2009/08/20/294299mscivilrightscurriculum_ap.html.

When we think of the Civil Rights Movement, images of leaders such as Martin Luther King, Jr. and Malcolm X quickly come to mind. However, the movement involved a long fight by many courageous citizens, such as these African American school children who in 1957 were turned away from attending a junior high school in Virginia because of their color.

REVIEW >>

- **What is the role of federal officials?**

  For better or worse, politics at the federal and local levels play a major role in education. At the federal level, the Supreme Court has handed down numerous rulings on issues that have affected how education is delivered and funded. Probably the most far-reaching court decisions have involved issues of race and racial segregation. The most notable of these cases, *Brown v. Board of Education of Topeka, Kansas*, legally ended segregation of the schools in 1954. Besides appointing Supreme Court justices, U.S. presidents, along with Congress, have had a significant impact on federal policies and funding for education, including the Elementary and Secondary Education Act of 1965, which was passed during the Johnson administration. The ESEA became the No Child Left Behind Act of 2002 and is up for reauthorization today.

- **What are the politics behind the No Child Left Behind debate?**

  The debate over accountability and standards, which began in the 1980s, led to the 2002 No Child Left Behind Act that outlined provisions for academic achievement for all public schools. Each state is responsible for setting standards for subject matter, adequate yearly progress (AYP), and the definition of a "highly qualified teacher," and states are expected to administer the federal National Assessment of Educational Progress exam.

  Sanctions apply to underperforming schools and districts. Both supporters and critics have debated a variety of issues surrounding the legislation, including whether standards should be set by the state or federal government (if at all), the impact of high-stakes testing on the quality of education, teacher accountability, and a host of other concerns.

- **What is the role of state and local politics in education?**

  Governors, state legislatures, and state departments of education play a significant role in deciding what is taught in a given state, how funds are used, how legislation such as NCLB is administered, and how teachers are licensed to work in their state. Local school boards select district superintendents, can govern local school districts that include anywhere from thousands of students to just a single school, and can have a tremendous impact on the education students receive, including hiring the classroom teachers.

- **How do teachers make political decisions in the classroom?**

  Whether or not they are aware of it, teachers make political decisions every day in the classroom, including what messages are conveyed on bulletin boards, what topics they teach or ignore in class, what holidays they choose to recognize or celebrate, and how they respond to the needs and concerns of their students.

What Is the Role of State and Local Politics?

From "WHAT IT WILL TAKE TO IMPROVE AMERICA'S URBAN PUBLIC SCHOOLS?"

BY PEDRO NOGUERA

Pedro Noguera is a professor at the Steinhardt School of Culture, Education, and Human Development at New York University. He has also taught at Harvard University, the University of California at Berkeley, and in K–12 schools in the San Francisco area. While a professor at the University of California, he also continued to teach a high school class. He was an elected member of the Berkeley, California, school board from 1990 to 1994. He has studied education and the politics of education from multiple perspectives: as a policy maker, teacher, and researcher. The following selection from the conclusion to his book *City Schools and the American Dream: Reclaiming the Promise of Public Education* reflects both his frustration and his underlying optimism with the schools he knows so well.

Throughout this book I have tried to make it clear that it will not be possible to improve urban public schools until our society is willing to address the issues and problems confronting the children and families in the communities where schools are located. Even though there are a small number of schools that manage to serve children well despite the harshness of conditions in inner-city neighborhoods (Education Trust, 2002; Sizemore, 1988), these will continue to be the rare exceptions. Unless concerted action is taken to alleviate the hardships and suffering related to poverty and to spur development that can lead to economic and social stability for communities and families, little change in the character and quality of urban schools in the United States will occur. Given the long history of failure in urban public schools, this point should be obvious. Yet, despite the track record of failure, we continue to hear slogans from the federal government like "Leave No Child Behind" without the political will needed to realize this goal.

Stating the obvious fact does not really help in furthering the development of solutions. The actions required—generating capital to bring economic development and social stability to urban areas—is relatively clear and straightforward, but the challenge of doing so is more complicated than it might seem. Local problems are frequently manifestations of larger societal problems. . .concentrated poverty severely limits the ability of communities to control and improve the quality of their schools. Larger issues such as the availability of housing and jobs, the location of industry, or the state of the regional or national economy have an impact on local conditions. Often, the effects of these larger forces cannot be mitigated at the local level. For example, because of the closure of several General Motors manufacturing plants in the 1970s and 1980s, the city of Flint, Michigan, is now bankrupt and its local government has been taken over by the state of Michigan (Casey, 2002). All observers acknowl-

edge that there is little that local government or the state's intervention can do to reverse downward trends in the city unless action is taken to address the economic roots of the problem. Unemployment rates in Flint are three times higher than the state average, and not surprisingly, Flint's schools are ranked among the worst in the state. Undoubtedly, it will be nearly impossible to improve the quality of public schools in Flint unless help is provided in restoring the viability of the local economy and bringing stability to the community.

I learned about the limitations of local government firsthand while working as assistant to the Mayor of Berkeley during the 1980s and while serving as an elected member of the school board in the early 1990s. Through direct experience I learned that even with a relatively progressive local government in an affluent city, it was nearly impossible to solve problems such

Source: "What It Will Take to Improve America's Urban Public Schools," by Pedro Noguera, in *City Schools and the American Dream: Reclaiming the Promise of Public Education*, 2003, Teachers College Press, pp. 142–157.

as chronic unemployment, drug trafficking, or homelessness. Although these were Berkeley's problems, their origin did not lie in the city but elsewhere—in a porous national border, in failed state and national policies for the mentally ill, in the lack of affordable housing, and in the flight of blue-collar jobs from the region. The situation was just as difficult in the school district, where declining revenue from the state required the school board to make deep and painful cuts in academic programs in order to balance the budget. At times we were able to rally the community around efforts to generate local funding for schools: through a bond measure and parcel tax, an initiative to save music programs, or an innovative approach to address juvenile crime. However, even when we could muster the will and the resources to address an issue, it was difficult to develop these into long-term solutions because of a variety of factors that could not be controlled at the local level.

The most disturbing fact about the persistence of failure is that the wealth and resources needed to support the work of schools are there. In an affluent region like the Bay Area, prospects for generating resources to address social and economic problems should be greater, even in high-poverty cities like Oakland and Richmond, than in less prosperous areas of the United States. An international center for biotechnology, communications, semiconductors, and finance, and with two of the largest research universities (UC Berkeley and Stanford) in the United States located there, it should be possible for schools to receive the technical and financial support they need. Schools in such an affluent region should never lack qualified teachers or suffer from a shortage of paper, textbooks, or computers. The fact that these shortages exist in Bay Area schools is a clear indication that the ties between schools and public and private institutions are not well developed. In the Bay Area and throughout the United States, we must stop pretending that public schools can solve the problems they face on their own. . . .

The problems I've analyzed in this book—racial inequality, poverty, and violence—certainly are not unique to the four cities of the Bay Area. Nor are they problems that typically are thought of as educational issues. These are societal issues for which a national strategy is needed if conditions in schools and communities in urban areas are to significantly improve. There is a vast body of research in education that has shown the importance of addressing environmental issues to solve educational problems, but rarely have we seen a concerted effort made to do so. Instead, policy makers and occasionally educators have tended to treat these environmental issues as though they were beyond the realm of education and have acted as if it were possible to improve schools without taking them on. Given the dismal record of failure in efforts to improve urban schools across the United States, it makes sense to try something new.

A new approach must be based on a framework that links educational issues to environmental issues, one that responds to the problems confronting schools in concert with those facing the local community. A small number of schools across the United States are doing this already by offering a broad range of services to students and their families on site (Dryfos, 2001). There are also a small but growing number of Beacon schools that remain open 10–12 hours a day and provide a safe haven for children (McLaughlin, 2000). Such approaches are showing signs of promise but they need to be significantly expanded so that larger numbers of children can be served. Anything less is unlikely to bring about the changes that are so desperately needed. We must stop pretending that we can avoid confronting and addressing urban conditions as we try to devise strategies for improving urban schools.

The call for a more comprehensive approach to addressing the issues confronting urban public schools is based on more than just wishful thinking. There is a vast body of research that shows that addressing basic human needs is essential to furthering other forms of development (National Research Council, 2002). Psychologist Abraham Maslow (1962) has shown through his research that unless basic human needs are met (e.g., security, housing, nutrition), it is difficult for children to develop and grow up to be healthy, well-adjusted adults. Similar arguments have been made for developing societies, such as those in the Sub-Saharan Africa that are besieged by civil war, food shortages, and debilitating diseases. Without assistance in bringing relief from these pressing concerns, it is unlikely that such societies will succeed in improving their economies, developing democratic institutions, and meeting the needs of their citizens (Sachs, 1989). The same arguments have been made for children and schools in economically depressed areas of the United States (Schorr, 1997).

Although they are located within the wealthiest nation on earth, many inner-city communities have not been able to attract the capital needed to bring about economic growth and social stability. In fact, on a number of indicators—infant mortality, homicide, and the rate of HIV infection—conditions in economically depressed urban areas of the United States often rival conditions in the Third World. For example, the infant mortality rate in Oakland surpasses that of Kingston, Jamaica, and the rate of HIV infection in New York City and Los Angeles is higher than that of Sao Paolo and Mexico City (Andrews & Fonseca, 1995). Proximity to wealth does not ensure access to wealth, resources, technology, or services. Even when impoverished communities are surrounded by wealth, as is the case in small cities like Poughkeepsie, New York, North Chicago, or East Palo Alto and Marin City, California, it has still not been possible to attract capital that might lead to development.

The economic empowerment zones created by the federal government in the 1980s, which remains the primary strategy for addressing urban poverty today, have largely not succeeded in luring private industry and jobs to the inner city. Although there are a few isolated examples of successful projects, the policy has had a very poor track record in revitalizing and bringing sustained improvements to the poorest communities (Gittel & Thompson, 2001). Even in Los Angeles where promises to rebuild the city were made following the devastation caused by the riots of 1991, there is little evidence of improvement in the neighborhoods with the highest levels of poverty (Valle & Torres, 2000). The track record of public and private efforts to improve the quality of life in impoverished urban areas is poor, and increasingly this is not even an issue that politicians raise during campaigns for public office. Urban poverty, like congested highways, homelessness, drug abuse, and the depletion of the ozone layer, increasingly are accepted as major problems that simply cannot be solved.

This was not always the case. In the 1960s and early 1970s both Republicans and Democrats campaigned on promises to eliminate poverty and joblessness (Phillips, 1983). Although the most ambitious and far-reaching social programs were created during the Johnson administration as part of his Great Society initiative, even the more conservative Nixon administration promised to create full employment through enlightened private-sector initiatives (Heyman, 2000; Phillips, 1983). Speaking in an address to the nation in the wake of several race riots that were raging in cities throughout the country in 1967, President Lyndon B. Johnson made the following call for reform:

> The only genuine, long-range solution for what has happened lies in an attack—mounted at every level—upon the conditions that breed despair and violence. All of us know what those conditions are: ignorance, discrimination, slums, poverty, disease, not enough jobs. We should attack these conditions—not just because we are frightened by conflict, but because we are fired by conscience. We should attack them simply because there is no other way to achieve a decent and orderly society in America. (Harris & Wicker, 1988, p. 484)

There were promises and the connections were made during an earlier era. It was an era characterized by a sense of optimism that a great nation could solve even the most pressing problems. Since the early 1980s, there has been no similar vision or commitment to fighting poverty or reviving America's urban centers. Surprisingly, although for the past 10 to 15 years there has been a sustained interest in improving the quality of education, this interest has not prompted policy makers to rethink the approach taken to address the issues and problems confronting economically depressed inner-city communities. It is widely known that these are the areas where educational problems are most acute and the conditions in schools most severe. Yet, policy makers continue to pretend that it is possible to improve the quality of education provided in these communities without simultaneously responding to the social and economic issues within the local environment, or that a policy gimmick like vouchers or charter schools will solve this problem. For children who are poorly nourished, sick, neglected, and abused, neither vouchers, charters nor increased academic standards and accountability will provide the educational opportunities and support that they need and deserve.

To a large degree, the retreat from more comprehensive approaches to addressing urban problems is ideological and reflects the low priority assigned to addressing the needs of the poor in the United States. The movement away from the interventionist policies of the 1960s began during the Carter administration at a time when cutbacks in social programs were rationalized as necessary because the economy was in recession and the federal government was faced with large budget deficits (Katz, 1989; Pinkney, 1984). Although it acted reluctantly, the Carter administration began cutting social programs like the Comprehensive Employment Training Act and enacted the first reductions in food stamps and housing assistance. Such programs could be treated as expendable and easily trimmed partially because they served constituencies that wielded little influence over government, and because increasingly social programs were regarded as "hand-outs" to the undeserving poor (Block, Cloward, Ehrenreich, & Piven, 1987).

With the election of Ronald Reagan in 1980, retrenchment in social services supported by the federal government accelerated. Eliminating social programs that served the "undeserving poor" and wiping out all other vestiges of liberalism became a central feature of the administration (Katz, 1989). During the 1980s, the Reagan and Bush administrations drew on the support of conservative scholars (Loury, 1995; Murray, 1984) who argued that social programs contributed to dependency among the poor and actually served to maintain poverty. Castigating welfare queens and poverty pimps who were accused of cheating the system, and liberals, who made excuses for the pathological behavior of the poor, conservatives demanded an end to the policies of indulgence, and called on the poor to help themselves.

The legacy of the Reagan Revolution has endured even during periods such as the 1990s when the prosperity of the national economy produced a budgetary surplus and the United States was led by President Clinton, who claimed to be genuinely interested in fighting poverty. Instead of a new set of Great Society programs, the Clinton administration enacted welfare reform—"ending welfare as we know it"—a political feat that even the Reagan and Bush administrations were unable to accomplish. Under Clinton, the idea that poverty could be eliminated by reducing federal subsidies to the poor and extolling the virtues of hard work and self-help became the essence of federal social welfare policy once again.

For all of these reasons, our society is less willing to tackle the broad array of problems related to poverty in urban areas today. Even as indicators of policy failure in urban areas have become more apparent—with crime, unemployment, poverty, and incarceration rates still extremely high or rising in many urban areas (Heyman, 2000)—a change of course in federal policy appears unlikely. Thus far President George W. Bush's proclaimed commitment to "compassionate conservatism" has not produced any new, comprehensive national initiatives to address urban poverty. Although he has pledged to "Leave No Child Behind," the needs of many children continue to be neglected and child poverty rates in the Unites States continue to be the highest among Western industrialized nations (Terry, 1995). Only one out of seven children in the United States has access to quality preschool programs, and over 30% lack medical insurance coverage (Schorr, 1997). Even Head Start, which has been acclaimed as one of the most successful federal programs (Andrews & Fonseca, 1995), has not been significantly expanded. We know from research that cognitive and neurological development that occurs during infancy plays a crucial role in long-term developmental outcomes for children (Diamond, 1999). Yet, we continue to treat child care workers as babysitters and provide minimal training and abysmally low wages to those who do this vital work. . . .

Working Within the Limits and Possibilities of Change

In Chapter 1, I suggested that those who have not given up hope in the possibility of improving urban schools could benefit by adopting Paulo Freire's (1972) approach to viewing the problems confronting these institutions as "limit situations." Such an approach requires that our hopes in the possibility for change be tempered by a strong dose of pragmatism, given how formidable the problems that need to be addressed are. It starts with the recognition that while sweeping solutions to the problems confronting urban schools and communities are needed, they are not likely to be enacted at this time. Instead, partial solutions that alleviate the most severe hardships must be devised based on an understanding of the limits and possibilities of the historic period we are living in. This is not the same as working for piecemeal reforms or introducing palliative treatments to make poverty less painful. Rather, even as we attempt to figure out how to take action in particular urban schools and communities, we must never lose sight of the need to work toward more ambitious goals—justice, equality, and genuine empowerment of the most downtrodden and marginalized citizens. For this to occur, each act of gradualism must be based on a willingness to engage in a process of change that aims at transforming relationships between those who have power and those who do not. Unless this transformation occurs, it is unlikely that even ambitious reforms will lead to lasting change.

Let me offer a few examples to explain how this might work by citing cases that demonstrate how it is working already on small (interpersonal) and even not so small (community) levels. My friend and colleague, Paul Kurose, an exceptional math teacher and a committed educator, described a situation he encountered with a student while working at Castlemont High School in east Oakland. One of his tenth-grade students, a quiet girl named Jamila, showed considerable academic promise based on her performance in his class. However, she rarely turned in her homework and frequently missed several days of school. As a caring teacher, Paul pressed her, insisting that she turn in her work and attend class regularly. He did so out of concern for her education and welfare, and he did so persistently, thinking that his constant pressure would produce the change in behavior that he hoped for. Finally, exasperated by Paul's urgings, Jamila explained why she failed to turn in so many assignments: "Do you think that you would be able to do your work if every night your mother was bringing a different man into your house to have sex and smoke crack?"

Jamila's clarification of her situation shocked him. He had no idea that this student was coping with such a difficult situation at home and his initial response was to back off. Repulsed by what he heard and having difficulty imagining how he would have put up with such a circumstance, he gained new respect and appreciation for the fact that she made it to school at all. However, rather than pulling back altogether out of fear that deeper involvement would entangle him in this student's difficult life, Paul thought about how he could serve as a source of support to this needy student. To address the fact that Jamila was unable to work at home, he offered to provide her tutoring after school in his classroom so that she would have a place to complete assignments. Then he helped her to enroll in the Mathematics, Engineering, and Science Achievement program (MESA), a program sponsored by the University of California that provides minority students with extra counseling and academic enrichment to help them gain admission to 4-year colleges. MESA offered Saturday classes and a residential summer program that would give Jamila a chance to get away from her home. Finally, Paul told Jamila that if she ever needed help, she should call him and he would do what he could to assist her. His efforts on behalf of this student paid off. Despite the tremendous obstacles she faced, Jamila graduated from high school and was admitted to a local public university.

The actions taken by my friend Paul Kurose are illustrative of what it means to work within the limits and possibilities of the current situation in urban schools and communities. Although he could not save Jamila from the depressing situation she was in, Paul took steps to help her to eventually find a way to get out of it herself. Instead of retreating when he heard about the terrible situation she faced in her home, Paul extended himself and offered to be a source of support. He could not offer an immediate solution to the situation she faced at home, but he thought long and hard about partial solutions that could bring hope and long-term relief to the student. . . .

What Is to be Done?

Education, Civil Rights, and Community Empowerment

In Chapter 1, I cited the example of my old friend, Amateka Morgan, the teacher at the Islamic school in Brooklyn who had left the public schools because he was tired of seeing educators accept the failure and loss of large numbers of students. His efforts to create a genuine educational alternative

for students outside of public education is representative of an important trend in American education. Historically, efforts to provide poor children of color with access to quality education have been the preoccupation of activists and educators who connected their work in education to broader efforts to improve and uplift the condition of downtrodden and disadvantaged people. Recognizing the consistent failure of federal and state governments to ensure access to quality public schools, such individuals have played a crucial role in making educational opportunities available to the disenfranchised.

At the end of the Civil War many of the educators who traveled to the South to establish schools for the former slaves were driven by a missionary zeal to help those recently freed from bondage (Anderson, 1988). While their efforts led to some of the first schools and universities created for the purpose of educating African Americans, several critics now question the goals and intentions of these educators. Rather than conceiving education as a means to empower those who had been enslaved, some of the early architects of African American education appear to have settled for an education designed to create a docile but useful servant caste (Watkins, 2001). Similar arguments have been made about the boarding schools that were set up for Native American children as part of their effort to "civilize" them and free them from their "savage cultures" (Prucha, 1973). As the German philosopher and playwright Berthold Brecht (1965) has written, "Education is a double-edged sword: It can be used to oppress or to liberate". Similar arguments were made by Carter G. Woodson (1933), an African American historian and educator, who argued that the "mis-education" of Black people was instrumental in their oppression.

There is also a long legacy of educators who have dedicated themselves to serving subordinate populations in the United States and have envisioned their work as part of the effort to liberate and empower the oppressed. For some, this has taken on an overtly political dimension because they have attributed the cause of inadequate educational opportunities to an indifferent and unresponsive political system. Such a view has led many to take up the struggle for educational opportunity in the courts, an arena where, at certain times, overt forms of discrimination and institutional indifference have been challenged (Wolters, 1984). Others, like my friend Amateka, have focused their energies on establishing independent schools where they have sought to address the needs of children by providing them with the attention, love, and support they cry out for and deserve. Despite differences in approach, both strategies have conceptualized the educational dilemma in political terms, and both strategies have been linked to broader social movements aimed at improving the lives of the poor and disenfranchised in American society.

Since the U.S. Supreme Court's *Brown* decision in 1954, public education has been at the center of struggles for expanding and redefining civil rights in American society (Carnoy, 1994; Orfield & Eaton, 1996). The Court's landmark ruling to end apartheid in public education opened the door to protracted conflict and debate over the meaning of equality and equal opportunity in education and how these were to be achieved (Kirp, 1980). Although *Brown* failed to provide clarity to communities and school districts with regard to how the Court's mandate should be fulfilled, the Court's decision did bring about significant changes at the federal, state, and local level with respect to policies governing access to public education. With federal assistance and court enforcement, many public schools have been desegregated, and legally sanctioned racial segregation has been largely eliminated.

Yet, despite this significant accomplishment, the limitations of *Brown* are glaring and obvious: Nearly 50 years after the Court's decree, large numbers of schools throughout the United States remain segregated, not only on the basis of race, but also on the basis of class (Orfield & Eaton, 1996). Segregation remains because in many parts of the United States *Brown* was never fully implemented. In cities like San Francisco, Berkeley, Richmond, and Oakland, the majority of White middle-class residents simply opted out of the system altogether, even though they continue to reside in the city. Now, with the courts increasingly less willing to support desegregation plans that were adopted in the past, the limitations of *Brown* are even more obvious. [This was written before the Seattle and Louisville decisions that are discussed at the beginning of this chapter.]

This is not to say that the changes brought about as a result of the *Brown* decision have not been significant. The precedent set by *Brown* and related court rulings has created a legal basis for promoting educational equity that extends well beyond racial justice. Since the *Brown* ruling, public education has become the most democratic and accessible institution in the United States. Gradually but steadily, groups and individuals that historically have been subject to discrimination and exclusion have been able to use the courts to press for the elimination of unjust barriers (Cuban & Tyack, 199; Katznelson & Weir, 1985; Spring, 1994). Discrimination on the basis of language, disability, and gender has been eliminated, and even the rights of undocumented children have been upheld. Genuine progress has been made in expanding the rights of children, and even those who decry the continued neglect and mistreatment of millions of children across the United States should acknowledge the gains.

Despite these advances, it would be a mistake to grow complacent, because conservative groups continue to challenge these victories through lawsuits and ballot initiatives. Relying on justice from the courts clearly has its limitations. I was reminded of this by a recent conversation with the principal of Central High School in Kansas City, Missouri. In the 1980s and 1990s the district received nearly $500 million from that state as a result of a federal court order to upgrade facilities. In a novel approach to desegregation, Judge Clark ruled that in order to integrate the city's long-neglected schools, improvements would have to be made in facilities so that Whites would be attracted back into the system. The controversial court order resulted in significant physical improvements to the schools in the district, including Central High School, a place described by *60 Minutes* as the "Taj Majal" of schools. I visited the school in 1995 and was extremely impressed by its features: an Olympic-sized pool, a computerized robotics lab, and a fully equipped Greek-styled amphitheater. Yet, when I spoke recently with the new principal, I was shocked to learn that the robotics lab no longer existed because the equipment had been stolen (he believed by adults who worked at the school). He also informed me that the school had no swim team or drama club to make use of the other facilities. "If I could have had some say in how to spend all that money back then I would have told them to invest in some competent teachers who knew how to teach our students. That's what we really need" (interview, July 30, 2002).

The limitations of legal remedies have become obvious elsewhere as well. For example, there are several cities, such as Boston, where schools continue to be segregated even after a bloody and protracted struggle to integrate them in the 1970s. This is why the approach epitomized by the work of my friend Amateka or the struggle for community-controlled schools in Brooklyn, New York, in 1968, is appealing to so many people. For those frustrated by the slow pace of change in public schools or whose experience with these flawed institutions has led them to believe change is not possible, working outside of the system by creating independent alternatives has been attractive. While some pressed the courts to desegregate schools in the 1970s, other activists and educators formed the Council of Independent Black Institutions, representing a network of independent Black schools throughout the United States. The success of schools like Shelton's Primary in Oakland and Marcus Garvey in Los Angeles reminds us that providing quality education to poor children in the inner city is possible. The tireless efforts of the educators who keep these schools going also show that those who are unhappy about the state of urban schools can do more than wring their hands in despair as we wait for the courts or the government to do the right thing.

Yet, over 20 years later, many of these independent institutions no longer exist due to lack of funds or because the activists who created them have burned out, passed away, or

moved on. For this reason, even as we applaud their efforts, we must remember that the small number of successful independent schools do not constitute a genuine alternative to public schools. There simply aren't enough of them to address the needs of millions of poor children. . . .

Those who seek to hold the government accountable for aiding urban schools, and those who direct their efforts toward grassroots community-building initiatives, share a common goal: to make quality education available to all poor children. Differences in outlook often have separated and divided these camps, but both strategies are important. While civil rights activists continue to pursue the goal of integration and access to all of the rights and privileges children deserve, independent educators and activists can continue to focus their efforts on community empowerment. Often, the differences between the two camps seem to mirror the divisions that separated W. E. B. Du Bois and Booker T. Washington as the two leaders debated the best way forward for African Americans after the end of Reconstruction (Twombly, 1971). Today, there is no need for the rivalry or acrimony that characterized the previous debate because there is simply too much to do.

Presently, some of the differences between the two camps have become manifest in conflicting stances toward the issue of vouchers and privatization. Whereas civil rights activists generally have opposed vouchers on the grounds that they would further undermine public support for education, independent school activists have been more likely to embrace vouchers as a means to provide educational alternatives to poor families. Vouchers also have been embraced by some as representing a means to obtain more stable support for financially strapped independent schools.

Although I am firmly opposed to vouchers, it is not because I oppose the idea of educating poor children in private schools. If vouchers would guarantee all children who need them access to high-quality schools of any kind, my conscience would require that I support the policy. However, this is far from the case. Rather than framing solutions to the educational problems facing poor children of color in dichotomous terms, I believe that concerned individuals should adopt a pragmatic approach as we consider various possibilities for change. Polarization on these issues often has had the effect of blurring the important commonalities shared by the two camps and undermining possibilities for concerted action.

As an educator and activist, I have worked without a sense of conflict, within both camps. My personal commitment has been to put the needs of children first, and I have worked in a variety of ways to provide quality education to poor children of color. For this reason I have experienced no sense of contradiction in supporting independent private and charter schools, even while working to support public schools. I am opposed to vouchers, not for ideological reasons but for practical ones: I know that few private schools have the space or the desire to serve poor children. When we put the needs of children first, defending an ideological position on how schooling should be provided becomes less important than doing whatever it takes to make quality education available to poor children.

Education is a political issue, and the question confronting all of those who are disturbed over the state of education for poor children in America is: "Which side are you on?" Education plays a special role in American society because it operates on more democratic principles than any other social institution (Carnoy & Levin, 1985). As the only public institution required to serve the needs of all children, it is all that remains of the social safety net for poor children in the United States. Without a doubt it would be a major blow to child welfare and civil rights generally if the flawed and feeble institution of public education were to be dismantled.

We can make significant improvements in the quality of public education available to poor children in urban areas. We have the resources, the know-how, and the models to do this. What is lacking is the will and conviction to make it happen. Those who understand the importance of education must work with creativity and a sense of urgency to find ways to generate the will, to make those who are presently indifferent or unconcerned understand what is at stake. What is at stake are children's lives and the kind of society we will become. For those who do not want to see entire cities written off as dangerous "no man's lands," who do not want to see incarceration rates continue to rise and executions of the most vulnerable continue to escalate, who are afraid of becoming a society that fears its own children, working to improve urban education is an imperative. The future of American society will be determined in large measure by the quality of its urban schools. We have the responsibility and the obligation to try to make that future far better than the present we now know.

QUESTIONS

1. When Noguera says, "building civic capacity in support of public education is essential," what does he mean? What specifically needs to be built? What do you think a teacher's role is in such an effort, if any?

2. If, as Noguera says, the 1960s and early 1970s were "characterized by a sense of optimism that a great nation could solve even the most pressing problems" including problems of poverty and violence that undermine the work of schools, what would it take to recreate that sense of optimism? Do educators have a role in such a large-scale change?

3. Can you imagine making change in the kinds of "limit situations" that Noguera describes, like the teacher in Oakland, California? What would it take to do something similar now, as a student preparing to teach, or as a new teacher?

4. Noguera says, "Education is a political issue, and the question confronting all of those who are disturbed over the state of education for poor children in America is: 'Which side are you on?'" Do you agree? Should a teacher take sides?

What Are the Politics Behind the No Child Left Behind Debate?

From *NO CHILD LEFT BEHIND AND THE PUBLIC SCHOOLS*

BY SCOTT FRANKLIN ABERNATHY

Although much of the material written about No Child Left Behind appeared within the first few years of the act's passage, Scott Franklin Abernathy, who had developed his own understanding of the complexity of educational change, attempted a more dispassionate analysis 5 years after the legislation was signed. Looking primarily at the law's impact in the state of Minnesota, Abernathy attempted an even-handed analysis of the law, praising its overall goals and yet providing a tough critique of many of the details contained in the law itself and in its implementation by federal, state, and local school authorities. Not everyone will agree with Abernathy. Nevertheless, Abernathy's discussion of how it is working provides a useful status report on the impact of the law and represents one educator's plea for what should come next. The next step in the story will depend on the current administration, members of Congress, and thousands of school leaders, teachers, parents, and students in the course of another decade.

How's It Working?

Among the disagreements and controversies that surround the No Child Left Behind Act of 2001, researchers and policymakers agree on two things. First, the act's goals are laudable, even necessary. Ensuring that our public schools demonstrate improved performance for all students and for those students who have traditionally underperformed—including students of minority ethnicity, those from low-income households, and those with disabilities or limited English proficiency—is absolutely essential on the grounds of fairness, national economic interests, and fulfillment of the American dream. Second, the law's effects are likely to be far-reaching. The sanctions to be imposed on schools that fail to make AYP clearly are significant, since they include restructuring

Source: No Child Left Behind and the Public Schools, by Scott Franklin Abernathy, 2007, University of Michigan Press, pp. 10–20.

and reconstituting failing public schools, perhaps under private management.

Beyond these points of agreement, however, very little is known about how the law will play out, not only because we remain in the early stages of implementing NCLB but also because the problem is both undertheorized and lacking in enough solid, nonpartisan, empirical research. Though recent work has examined the politics surrounding the law's passage and how and why it came to be, much less work, at least by political scientists, has focused on the political and policy consequences of the law's implementation.

The little empirical evidence that exists on the achievement effects of No Child Left Behind is mixed. A March 2005 national survey of state and district education officials found that 72 percent of school districts reported that academic achievement was improving on the state-designed tests. School district personnel uniformly reported that they were "aligning curriculum and instruction with standards and assessment (99%), and providing extra or more intensive instruction to low-achieving students (99%)." The authors of an analysis of 320,000 student test scores from twenty-three states also found some evidence of improvement of mathematics and reading scores between the 2001–2 and 2003–4 school years. However, they observed that recent year-by-year growth in student test scores had declined since NCLB was put into place. More alarmingly, the authors found that although growth in achievement levels has been declining for all ethnic groups, Hispanic students appeared to be falling behind white non-Hispanic students.

In contrast to the relative lack of findings on the achievement effects of No Child Left Behind, an already large and still growing literature documents what is wrong with the law and what incremental fixes might be applied to it. Attacks on and critiques of No Child Left Behind are proliferating and are coming from many different sources focusing on many different consequences, intended and unintended. These worries center on a variety of issues that can be grouped into seven categories: the use of standardized tests; the use of cross-sectional test score data; the requirement for 100 percent proficiency; implementation, incentives, and uneven playing fields; unfunded mandates; lack of flexibility in implementation; and secondary provisions.

The Use of Standardized Tests

One group of critics focuses on the challenge of measuring anything as complex as student achievement with any set of standardized tests—no matter how thoroughly or thoughtfully implemented—and the consequences of these tests on the curricula and learning environments of schools. The danger is that in their single-minded desire to improve test scores, schools and teachers will damage the breadth and quality of the curriculum. This issue had been a topic of discussion ever since these tests were first implemented . . . . Decisions about what to include on these tests are themselves highly political and often result in a watered-down consensus curriculum that fails to make any real cognitive or evaluative demands on students.

Deborah Meier, a former teacher and principal in Boston and New York and one of the strongest critics of No Child Left Behind, calls the curriculum push for high-stakes standardized testing "fundamentally misguided," primarily because of the damage it will cause education as students experience it. Rather than encourage the same kinds of qualities of leadership and governance that we would like to see in our students—the support and encouragement of local decision-making and citizen involvement—NCLB takes all power away from those closest to the creation of education and places it in the hands of distant "experts." As Meier observes, the use of standardized tests to improve education is based on a list of assumptions, none of which has been established beyond doubt:

There is a definition of what we mean by a good education.

Experts can know what this definition is.

Experts can measure it.

We can trust the experts more than we can trust the teachers and principals.

The system will produce equity in education, without major resource shifts.

The system will work.

[See Deborah Meier, "Educating a Democracy," in *Will Standards Save Public Education*? Edited by Joshua Cohen and Joel Rogers (Boston: Beacon, 2000).]

To which I would add:

We will know whether all this is working.

The Use of Cross-Sectional Test Score Data

Even if one believes that standardized tests can accurately and benignly measure student achievement, extracting what the school is doing for that student's achievement is much trickier than simply asserting how well one group of students is doing. No Child Left Behind currently relies on what is often called a "status model" of educational achievement that bases its assessments on a one-time snapshot of all of the students in a grade and in the grade-level subgroups.

Using status models to measure the quality of education within a school has three main drawbacks. The first is the likelihood that schools will be designated as failing even though they are making gains: schools starting from extremely low levels of average proficiency cannot possibly expect to hit the targets before identification and sanctions kick in. Theoretically, the "safe harbor" provision should protect such schools, but they must still reduce the number of students failing by 10 percent every year. If only one sub-group realizes smaller gains than other groups or schools as a whole, a school can still fail.

A further complication is the issue of where to set the cutoff for triggering the inclusion of scores from specific subgroups in assessing whether a school is making AYP. Setting the trigger low (for example, ten students minimum per grade in any of the eight subgroups) increases the number of schools that qualify and, therefore, fail. Setting the trigger higher (fifty students in any given subgroup) runs the risk of ignoring the needs of minority students, since their results may not be directly looked at in schools with too few minority or high-need students to trigger the AYP evaluation for that subgroup. If the needs of specific subgroups of students are ignored, the basic premise of No Child Left Behind is lost.

The most important risk, however, is that basing sanctions on a status model also runs the considerable risk of identifying and sanctioning schools based mostly on the characteristics of the students rather than on the school's contribution to students' academic achievement, since many things outside of a school's control show up in the cross-sectional aggregation of student test scores. . . . . it is useful to note that determining a school's success or failure based on these kinds of cross-sectional tests appears to result in incorrectly singling out schools with high-need populations.

One Hundred Percent Proficiency

Closely related are potential problems resulting from the law's insistence on full proficiency as of 2013-14, when 100 percent of each school's and each district's students must be proficient in reading and mathematics. Critics have argued that this goal is at best overly ambitious and at worst is completely unattainable, leading to the prospect of failure for nearly all of the nation's public schools. "In 2003, no state or large district had anything close to 100% of their students performing at the *basic* level, much less the *proficient* level." To attain 100 percent proficiency by 2013–14 would require a rate of improvement many times that which has been observed in recent years in even the most promising schools.

The prospect of inevitable and widespread failure has led some observers and researchers to assert that the real goal of No Child Left Behind is the destruction of public schools. The challenge of 100 percent proficiency is especially problematic when one considers the prospect of full proficiency for special education students. Researchers have also pointed out that many special education students

are so labeled because their disabilities prevent them from attaining grade-level proficiency, producing an inherent contradiction between definitions and goals.

Implementation, Incentives, and Uneven Playing Fields

All policies have the potential for unforeseen and unwanted consequences, and No Child Left Behind is no different. Critics have focused mostly on the skewed incentive structure that state, district, and school officials will face—that is, states face powerful incentives to set the proficiency bar as low as possible, given the costs involved in instituting the sanctions regime. Teachers have incentives to cheat, while their leaders have incentives to look the other way if they feel that they will not be caught. Districts have few incentives to accept poor and minority students from other districts (unless they are forced to do so), and schools might be encouraged to move their lowest-performing students out of regular education and into alternative learning centers or high school equivalency programs. Given the malleability of and tremendous variance in how states define academic proficiency, many potential problems arise with the utility and reliability of data. A report by the U.S. General Accounting Office cautioned that "more than half of the state and school district officials. . .interviewed reported being hampered by poor and unreliable student data."

Although the federal Department of Education must approve states' plans, the standards and assessments that states use are typically based on preexisting accountability systems, which may or may not have overlapped with NCLB's goals and methods, creating a very messy patchwork of tests. This tremendous state variation in baseline levels of proficiency means that a successful school in one state could easily be classified as failing in another state that set its initial proficiency targets at a higher level. The General Accounting Office also found a great deal of variance in how and how well states were measuring academic proficiency in these early stages of implementation, leading, for example, California to require that only 14 percent of its elementary students be proficient and Colorado to require 78 percent proficiency in the same year. According to Minnesota's Office of Legislative Auditor, "Due to inter-state differences in proficiency standards, testing practices, and 'adequate yearly progress' calculations, there is no meaningful way to use AYP data to make multi-state comparisons of educational performance."

Other implementation worries focus not on the failure of the law, its goals, or its methods but on the school, district, and state officials who are supposed to be carrying out NCLB's reforms. Of particular concern are levels of compliance and the pace of implementation of parental exit options in failing schools (which apply to schools that have failed to make AYP for two consecutive years). Very small percentages of parents who are eligible to send their children to successful schools appear to be doing so, and only a slightly larger percentage of parents whose children are eligible for supplemental services take advantage of that option. Lack of capacity in successful schools, lack of information on the part of parents, and active district resistance may have combined to prevent large numbers of parents from exercising their exit options.

Unfunded Mandates

Claims that No Child Left Behind does not adequately fund the ambitious goals and requirements that it places on states and districts have come from all levels of the public educational system. At the district level, such costs include the requirement to comply with the fully trained teacher requirement, the provision of supplementary services, and the task of administering and grading the ever-increasing volume of tests. At the state level, these costs include implementing all of the corrective action and restructuring provisions as well as overseeing the testing regimen. Ted Kennedy, who helped steer the bill through the Senate, later lamented, "The tragedy is that these long overdue reforms are finally in place, but the funds are not."

In April 2005, school districts in several states joined the National Education Association in suing Secretary of Education Margaret Spellings on the basis of insufficient funding for NCLB. Though the law states, "Nothing in this Act shall be construed to. . .mandate a State or any subdivision thereof to spend any funds or incur any costs not paid for under this Act," the plaintiffs argued that the compliance requirements placed an unfunded and undue financial burden on local schools and districts. The U.S. General Accounting Office concluded that No Child Left Behind was not an unfunded mandate because participation in NCLB is technically voluntary and the conditions laid out in the law "were a condition of federal financial assistance," thus disqualifying NCLB as an unfunded mandate as defined by law. A February 2005 report by the National Council of State Legislatures argued that No Child Left Behind's ambiguous and coercive provisions fail to pass constitutional muster. In addition, observers have expressed concern that rigidities in the provisions for schools that fail to make AYP will make academic improvements less rather than more likely as insufficient monies are spread too thinly and are used only in crisis mode.

Lack of Flexibility in Implementation

Reports from the field also indicate a great deal of frustration on the part of school, district, and state officials regarding their lack of flexibility in complying with the law's underlying goals. Of particular concern are rigid and unrealistic targets of academic success, particularly for students receiving special education services and those with limited English proficiency. In its 2005 task force report, the National Conference of State Legislatures concluded that "states should be allowed to develop any system they choose as long as it meets the spirit of NCLB." The report also argued that a preexisting statutory basis for this much-needed flexibility lies in provisions allowing the U.S. Department of Education to offer statutory waivers to states, districts, and schools.

Secondary Provisions

Small but significant provisions continue to come to light such as the withholding of all federal funds for school districts that fail to notify their state's educational administration that "no policy of the local educational agency prevents, or otherwise denies participation in, constitutionally protected prayer in public elementary schools and secondary schools." Funds are also to be withheld from districts that "deny equal access [to] any group affiliated with the Boy Scouts of America" or any other group listed as a "patriotic society" as well as from districts that fail to "provide, on a request made by military recruiters or an institution of higher education access to secondary school students' names, addresses, and telephone listings."

In response to these concerns, researchers and policymakers have proposed a series of modifications to No Child Left Behind.

1. **Fully funding the law**

   No Child Left Behind's passage was accompanied by promises of significant increases in funding. Officials in several states are now complaining that the additional monies allocated by the federal government do not even cover the costs of compliance, much less those necessary to achieve meaningful progress in closing the achievement gap. The combined concerns of unfunded mandates and the increased federal intrusion into state policy-making have sparked legal and political opposition among a very diverse group of stakeholders that runs the gamut from teachers' unions to Republican governors and legislators.

   On April 20, 2005, the Utah legislature voted to instruct state school leaders to focus on Utah's goals and priorities and to ignore provisions of NCLB that conflicted with the state's plan; Utah's governor signed the measure the following month. The bill did not directly withdraw Utah from NCLB but increased the likelihood of a showdown over the state's autonomy and put $76 million in federal education funding at risk. Republican U.S. Representative Steve Mascaro was quite blunt: "I'd just as soon they take the stinking money and go back to Washington with it. Let us resolve our education problems by ourselves. I will not be threatened by Washington over $76 million." The following August, Connecticut sued the federal government to reclaim $50 million in state money spent on compliance. Though the amount was small, observers cited the symbolic importance of the suit, arguing that the "real battle is over who will make key education decisions—local officials or policymakers in Washington." These political rifts are likely only to deepen as NCLB's sanctions sweep up more and more schools, thereby forcing states to cope with the attendant costs.

2. **Moving away from status models of measurement**
   Many reform proposals focus on the way in which achievement is measured. One proposed change is to look at the year-by-year changes in percentages of students who achieve academic proficiency rather than the percentages of students who are or are not meeting the targets. This approach is usually referred to as a "growth model." A second approach is to use what is called a "value-added" model of achievement, which attempts to extract the value a school adds to a given student's achievement by tracking the changes in test scores over time for individual students. . . . Neither is perfect, and each raises its own challenges, but either might be preferable to the status model currently embodied in the law.

3. **Providing more flexibility and realism**
   Some observers have argued that the requirement for 100 percent proficiency should be amended or scaled back to account for the almost impossible nature of its attainment: "there should be evidence that the goal does not exceed that [which] has previously been achieved by the highest performing schools." Others have argued for a more realistic and flexible approach to the testing of and achievement standards for students with limited English proficiency and those with disabilities. Critics have also declared that the 10 percent growth requirement necessary to achieve safe harbor cannot be attained by all but a very small number of schools not making AYP.

4. **Increasing coherence and consistency between states, particularly in the definition of academic proficiency**
   More standardization of accountability systems would not only be fairer but also provide researchers with much more reliable data on which to base any evaluations of NCLB's effects on achievement.

What Is Still Missing From the Debate?

Of all the problems with No Child left Behind, the ultimate success or failure of its ambitious agenda will likely come down to how the law interacts with two unavoidable realities in American education.

The first reality is that the United States has a very unequal and class-stratified society. Most children go to school with children from families with similar incomes. However ambitious, No Child Left Behind does nothing to address these long-standing resource inequalities in the United States and its educational system. To the extent that these resource inequalities—rather than failures by administrators, principals, and/or teachers—are responsible for

unequal academic achievement, No Child Left Behind is destined to fail to live up to its liberal promises.

The second reality is that education involves a great deal of uncertainty on the part of those who would evaluate it and a great deal of discretion on the part of those who perform its tasks. In other words, it is very hard to know what is actually happening at the moment of "education." In all of the debate about No Child Left Behind, policymakers have failed to ask the most basic and most important question: Can we ever really know if a child's education is good?

So many factors contribute to and confound what ultimately happens at the interface between a student's mind and the school's products that policymakers should think very carefully about how to measure "educational quality." Doing so will require a deeper and more thorough investigation of the underlying problems of producing and measuring quality in education. It may seem like an obscure task, but, as I hope will become apparent, it represents the first step on an interesting and necessary journey to achieve a vision of equality of educational outcomes for all students, especially for those students whose dreams have been continually deferred.

This book argues primarily that policy makers must begin with the goal of producing quality in education and move from there rather than assume that any test can accurately measure "good" education. This approach is radical in the literal sense of getting to the roots of the challenge at hand. We cannot succeed without doing so. If—and this is a big if—we accept the limitations of our evaluative capabilities, and if we get beyond the magical thinking of NCLB's punishment-driven philosophy, then we can make the law live up to its liberal promises.

QUESTIONS

1. How would you compare Abernathy's ideas to those of Kohn, Darling-Hammond, Hess and Finn, and Moe presented in this chapter? Does Abernathy find a middle way? A new way? Or does he side with one author?

2. If you were asked to be an education advisor to President Obama, would you make the same recommendations as Abernathy does or propose something different when Congress turns to the next reauthorization of the NCLB bill?

3. How does what Abernathy says fit with what you have previously heard or read about NCLB?

4. As you think about beginning your own teaching career, are there things you would like Abernathy to add or subtract from his recommendations that might make life better for you and your students?

12

PUBLIC EDUCATION

WHAT IS ITS PURPOSE IN A DEMOCRATIC SOCIETY?

LIBERTY!
FREEDOM!
DEMOCRACY!
True anyhow no matter how many
Liars use those words.

—Langston Hughes[1]

More than 50 years ago, poet Langston Hughes spoke to a worldwide movement of people he called "the folks with no titles in front of their names" who were rising up for rights in the United States and in Asia, Africa, and South America. His words also could have been applied to two centuries of debates about the purposes of public schooling in the United States.

Helping young people become active and engaged citizens and giving them the tools needed to participate actively in democratic institutions—from voting to speaking and acting on what they believe to be right—is a core purpose of schooling if democratic institutions are to survive and thrive in future generations. More than preparing students for jobs or teaching basic skills, fostering democracy has been at the heart of public education in the United States for as long as Americans have cared about their school systems. However, in many ways this nation is deeply undemocratic, and schools have often been structured to perpetuate inequity and undemocratic social arrangements. Great strides have been made to make schools more inclusive, but many observers would say that our schools are organized to perpetuate the advantage of the few and the **marginalization** of too many young people.

> **marginalization** To demote populations of people based on economic or racial differences and push them to the lower edges of society or the sidelines in a policy debate.

In this chapter, we look at both the historic role that schools have been assigned in fostering a more democratic society and the ways that schooling, as an institution, has failed to live up to that assignment. In the midst of this discussion, we keep asking, "What is a teacher's role. . .in making schools and the larger society more democratic?"

FOCUS >>

- What does a democratic society expect of its schools?
- What is the relationship between a universal education and democratic citizenship?
- How can we make our schools more democratic?

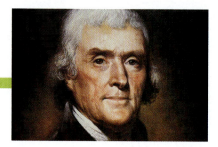

Four **Readings** look at what schools ought to do in a democratic society. Over a century ago, the philosopher John Dewey wrote "My Pedagogic Creed," outlining his basic beliefs about the importance of schools to a **democracy**. Following that piece is a short essay written by the civil rights leader W. E. B. DuBois entitled, "The Meaning of Education," and then a chapter from David T. Hansen's recent book *Exploring the Moral Heart of Teaching*. The **Readings** conclude with "An Agenda for Change," an essay by the editors of the journal *Rethinking Schools*, which leads us back to a focus on what needs to be done by teachers to help make schools more democratic in the future.

> **democracy** Political system in which decisions and laws are put into place by the vote of the whole community and in which everyone's voice matters.

>> What Does a Democratic Society Expect of Its Schools?

DEFINING DEMOCRACY

At one level, a democracy refers to a system of government "of the people, for the people, and by the people," as Abraham Lincoln said. Defined that way, democracy seems to mean, at minimum, a government based on the consent of the governed, as opposed to a **dictatorship** or an **oligarchy** based on birth, wealth, or power. Throughout the history of the United States, many observers have argued that to give (or withhold) informed consent, all citizens need a basic education that will enable them to be familiar with the issues and debates of the day.

However, to many others, democracy means much more than merely giving informed consent. It means the active involvement of all citizens in constantly re-creating the

> **dictatorship** Government rule by an individual who holds absolute power without hereditary lineage.
>
> **oligarchy** Political system in which power rests with a small group of elite, often wealthy, individuals.

Did you know?

A recent partnership between YouTube.com and the U.S. State Department provided the spark for an international discussion about the meaning of democracy. The Democracy Video Challenge asked applicants to complete the phrase "Democracy is …" in a short video. In the first year, the contest received more than 900 applications from over 95 countries. Six winners were chosen by online voters. This contest reflects a recent change in the State Department's overall mission and conduct. The Bureau for International Information Programs revised its "tagline" from "Telling America's Story" to "Engaging the World." The Democracy Video Challenge is one way the State Department is seeking to create a worldwide conversation about key issues. A second Democracy Video competition was posted in September 2009. For more information and contest rules, visit www.videochallenge.america.gov.

meaning of a good society for all—government *of* and *by* the people as well as *for* the people. Such an expanded definition of democracy goes far beyond voting, important as that is, and involves active engagement in our communities. It involves a certain way of living in the world, insisting on equality for ourselves and for all other citizens.[2]

THE SCHOOL'S ROLE IN A DEMOCRATIC SOCIETY

Maintaining and expanding the notion of democracy is one of the oldest and most important roles that society has assigned to its schools throughout the more than 200-year history of the United States. From the time the political leaders of the 13 British colonies on the mainland of North America declared their independence from King George, the language of democracy has been essential in shaping the nation's public schools. A democratic society needs to renew democracy continually through the education of its next generation of citizens. Since the time of the American Revolution, many of the nation's leaders have recognized that making democracy a reality requires educated citizens and voters, not only at election time but also in the daily lives of the people.

In our own time, when noted education professors James A. Beane and Michael W. Apple make the case for democratic schools, they naturally include issues like the democratic structure of social institutions, the open flow of ideas "regardless of their popularity," and concern for the welfare of others. They also argue that democratic schools should foster "faith in the individual and collective capacity of people to create possibilities for resolving problems." This is a much larger understanding of the meaning of democracy and of the relationship between democracy and education. It is not sufficient to provide freedom to individuals and services to all, important as these are. A real democracy is more than this. A truly democratic society is structured around the belief that the solutions to contemporary social concerns reside with the people and that all of the people, if fully empowered—and well educated— will be wiser than any small minority or vanguard. Such a democracy cannot be taught through lectures and textbooks. Schools must create classrooms where the young will experience such a democracy, if they are to grow into adult citizens who can also practice it.[3] Thus, teachers have a key role in building democracy, but only if they are informed, reflective, thoughtful, and ultimately engaged themselves.

It is ironic that the question of what most Americans expect their schools to accomplish in terms of fostering a larger democracy is seldom at the center of public debates about education. Everyone seems to assume that the answer to that question is obvious and then they move on to other questions, such as how to raise standards and test scores,

As you consider a career in teaching, you also need to develop your own answers to the questions regarding the purpose of schools. What should schools accomplish? What is the relationship of schooling to the needs of a larger democratic society? What is included—and excluded—in the responsibilities that society properly gives to its schools and to teachers? What would constitute success for all students in the kind of schools we hope for? How are your answers to these questions reflected in your own philosophy of education, or when you think about the way you would like to conduct your first class?

Join the Dialogue

Creating Responsible Citizens

What should be a school's role in creating responsible citizens? Some of the following issues are controversial among various parts of society for different reasons, for example, because of limited funding or understaffing. Particular problems arise, however, when certain groups believe that what a school is teaching oversteps the boundaries of what many people assume to be the domain of family or religious community. Put a checkmark next to the items that you believe students should learn or that should be offered during a public school education:

Sexual and puberty education	
Out-of-school field trips or recreational activities, such as dances	
Social studies courses that address controversial issues	
Advanced courses in math and engineering	
Advanced Placement classes and computer courses	
Physical education and nutrition	
After-school tutoring and summer courses	
Classes on child-rearing skills for pregnant students	
Technical courses such as auto shop or welding	
World languages	
Arts: band, visual arts, creative writing, ceramics, theater, photography, dance, etc.	
College and ACT/SAT prep courses	
Sports programs	
Independent study in research areas chosen by students	
Before- and after-school child care	
Drivers' education	
Encouraged voter registration among eligible students	
Online classes	
All-day kindergarten and preschool	
Tuition-free college courses for high school students	
Required community service hours	
GED preparation	

improve teacher preparation, and reduce dropout rates. Or they ask the schools to address myriad other social problems—for example, by offering sex education and drivers' education, by tackling the current epidemic of obesity through the regulation of what food is available at schools and through education about good nutrition, or more generally by discouraging a range of adolescent behaviors that trouble adults.

YouDecide

Is "teaching democracy" an appropriate expectation for our schools, along with all the core material that has to be covered?

Schools appropriately have many roles, including ensuring basic literacy, developing students' higher-order knowledge and thinking skills, helping young people lead safe and productive lives, *and* inducting young people into full democratic citizenship. Nevertheless, the purpose of schooling in a democratic society needs to be central in our discussion of schooling and teaching.

Teachable Moment

What Does It Mean for Schools to Teach Democracy?

In a recent article, "Reconnecting Education to Democracy," Joel Westheimer of the University of Ottawa in Canada and Joseph Kahne of Mills College in Oakland, California wrote,

For more than two centuries, democracy in the United States has been predicated on citizens' informed engagement in civic and political life. For much of that time, public schools have been seen as essential to support the development of such citizens. "I know of no safe depository of the ultimate powers of society but the people themselves," Thomas Jefferson wrote in his famous 1820 letter to William Jarvis, "and if we think [the people] not enlightened enough to exercise their control with a wholesome discretion, the remedy is not to take it from them, but to inform their discretion by education." Belief in the fundamental importance of civic education for democracy has been long-standing. But if educators can agree that schools have a role to play in educating democratic citizens, they can't seem to agree on what that means.

Students are no more in agreement on what good citizenship means than are teachers, policy makers, and politicians. When asked what it means to be a good citizen, one student from a focus group we conducted in an urban California school replied, "Someone who's active and stands up for what they believe in. If they know that something's going on that is wrong, they go out and change it." But a student from a different urban California school told us that to be a good citizen, you need to "follow the rules, I guess, as hard as you can, even though you want to break them sometimes. Like cattle." This lack of consensus around the civic goals of schooling underscores the challenge and complexity of deciding what we want schools to accomplish and how to make this happen.

*Increasingly, politicians, policy makers, and educators are forging connections between civic education for democracy and symbolic school practices that seek to instill a love of country and an ethic of service. These programs and policies equate **patriotism** with democratic commitment and community service with democratic citizenship.*

> **patriotism** Love, devotion, and willingness to sacrifice for one's country.

To say that many have promoted patriotism and service as educational goals tied to democratic ideals is not to say that this view has been universally accepted. The vision of patriotism and service put forward in recent pronouncements has been criticized for its disconnection from democratic values and institutions. Patriots in a democracy, for example, should be encouraged to challenge as well as support the government. Democracy requires more than community service; it requires citizen participation in the affairs of state. "Charity is a matter of personal attributes," wrote the Rev. William Sloan Coffin, "justice a matter of public policy." Moreover, many people see service as an alternative to politics and government programming, thus limiting further the links between a service-related curriculum and preparation for democratic citizenship. Like these social critics, the authors … argue that democratic societies are strengthened, not weakened, by providing space for debate between critics and supporters of various policies. Indeed, it is the basic conflicts of values in society that make democracy essential, and it is the ability to discuss these differences in an informed and productive manner that must be a priority for civic educators. Therefore, forms of patriotism that squelch debate and "patriotic" curricula that obscure the need for debate are, in important ways, antidemocratic.

QUESTIONS

- What do you think it means for schools to teach democracy? Do you agree with the authors' concerns about community service? Do you see yourself preparing to teach democracy?
- If educators and policy makers disagree as deeply as these authors say, how is a teacher supposed to carry out the mandate to teach democracy? How do you plan to handle the situation?

Sources: "Reconnecting Education to Democracy: Democratic Dialogues," by Joel Westheimer and Joseph Kahne, September 2003, *Phi Delta Kappan,* pp. 9–14.

PORTRAIT OF AN EDUCATOR

Sheldon Berman

Sheldon Berman is superintendent of the Jefferson County Public Schools in Louisville, Kentucky. The Louisville system has 98,000 students and 6,000 teachers. Just after Berman arrived in 2007, the U.S. Supreme Court ruled that the way the district assigned students to schools to ensure racial integration was unconstitutional, and Berman had only a few months to design a new system while ensuring that Louisville did not return to a racially segregated system.

Prior to his move to Louisville, Berman was superintendent of schools in the small Massachusetts town of Hudson, an old mill town in the middle of the state. Before taking on leadership positions for public school systems, Berman was one of the founders and the president of an organization called Educators for Social Responsibility, which not only advocated for more just and democratic approaches to schools but also encouraged teachers to be leaders in such advocacy. In the course of his career, Berman has emerged as one of the leading advocates of a more democratic approach to education and to the organization of schools and their curricula.

Jefferson County's goals are to "strengthen school culture, advance character development, and promote the social and emotional growth of students by creating inclusive, caring school communities that nurture respectful, supportive relationships among students, educators, support staff and parents." This sounds like standard school-talk until one looks at Berman's track record during his years in Hudson, where he made school an experience in democracy—for students, teachers, and parents. In 2003, he wrote,

Sources: "Jefferson County (Kentucky) Public Schools 2009–2010 District Goals and Strategies," retrieved from www.jefferson.K12.ky.us/AboutUs/Mission/html; "Sheldon Berman Helps Implement Change in First Year at JCPS," by Ben Adkins, September 4, 2008, *Business First of Louisville*, http://louisville.bizjournals.com/louisville/stories/2008/09/01/story17.html; "Respect and Responsibility: Building a Caring High School Community," by Sheldon H. Berman, January 2003, *Perspectives: The Journal of the Massachusetts Association for Supervision and Curriculum Development*.

In an environment of standards, testing, and accountability, we often forget that public education serves a larger purpose. That larger mission is to help young people develop the convictions and skills to shape a safe and sustainable and just world. Preserving and promoting a democratic society was the founding precept of our public education system and, if we are to continue to preserve our democracy, this mission must remain central to our efforts.

Serving as a longtime superintendent in Massachusetts, one of the states with the strongest accountability systems, Berman was in no position to ignore "standards, testing, and accountability." But he was also determined to do more and to ensure that his concern with "promoting a democratic society" not be mere rhetoric.

As he reflected on his experience in Hudson, Berman remembered that soon after he arrived, a number of elementary teachers asked him to tighten the discipline procedures because of the disruptive behavior of young children. Rather than adopt the often-popular "get tough" approach, Berman formed a committee to develop a more inclusive approach. Elementary schools in Hudson began to focus some of their instruction on teaching young children conflict-resolution skills and anger management. But they also moved beyond that to be sure that the classrooms were small learning communities that modeled what was being taught. The structure of elementary classrooms was changed fundamentally so that children could solve problems through collaborative class meetings, engage in service learning, and "develop an ethic of care and service through direct experiences of helping others and the community."

As successful as the elementary experience was, Berman knew that adolescents needed something different. "We have been developing a high school program to create a sense of community that embodies the concepts of respect and responsibility. It began with the integration of service-learning into many of our high school courses as a way to help young people develop an ethic of care and service." Many studies have shown that high school students respond well when asked to serve, and Berman put service at the core of the culture he was developing for his high school. He then turned to the academic curriculum, developing four-person teaching teams that would work with a group of ninth-grade students so that all students entering the high school were part of a small learning community with teachers who knew their names and cared for them. Finally, the high school teachers, with Berman's leadership, developed a curriculum that included "an ethics-based English and Social Studies course for all students focused on civic judgment and civic engagements." At the core of this course was the question "What is a just society and an individual's responsibility for creating such a just society?" In addition, the high school created a participatory governance structure in which each student and faculty member had one vote. The new governance addressed issues as diverse as the menu in the school cafeteria to the way the school responded to new international students who arrived in Hudson. At the same time, the system of school governance taught students a great deal about the workings of democracy, the need for compromise and consensus, and deep **civic engagement**.

civic engagement The active involvement of people who come together to address common issues and improve their community.

>> Historically Speaking: What Is the Relationship Between a Universal Education and Democratic Citizenship?

THE EDUCATIONAL PHILOSOPHY OF THOMAS JEFFERSON

Whereas it appeareth that however certain forms of government are better calculated than others to protect individuals in the free exercise of their natural rights, and are at the same time themselves better guarded against degeneracy, yet experience hath shewn, that even under the best forms, those entrusted with power have, in time, and by slow operations, perverted it into tyranny; and it is believed that the most effectual means of preventing this would be, to illuminate, as far as practicable, the minds of the people at large, and more especially to give them knowledge of those facts, which history exhibiteth, that, possessed thereby of the experience of other ages and countries, they may be enabled to know ambition under all its shapes, and prompt to exert their natural powers to defeat its purposes.

—Thomas Jefferson[4]

At the time of the American Revolution, Thomas Jefferson proposed a new system of education for his home state of Virginia. He reminded his fellow legislators that even the best governments (including the new one they were in the middle of creating through their revolution) had a dangerous tendency to be "perverted into tyranny." The best protection against such a development would be "to illuminate, as far as practicable, the minds of the people at large." In addition, Jefferson proposed an educational system that he believed would promote public happiness by ensuring that "those persons, whom nature hath endowed with genius and virtue, should be rendered by liberal education worthy to receive, and able to guard the sacred deposit of the rights and liberties of their fellow citizens, and that they should be called to that charge without regard to wealth, birth or other accidental condition or circumstance."[5] The bill did not become law, but Jefferson's words nevertheless became famous as a call to his fellow American rebels about the importance of education for the kind of democracy they were attempting to create.

Jefferson believed education and democracy were inextricably linked. Unless all the people had a basic education so that they could participate in the democratic process and would know and recognize tyranny when it appeared, and unless leaders were developed from among all the people, not just those who could afford to pay for a college education, the experiment in democracy launched by the American Revolution would surely fail. Jefferson never wavered in his belief that education was the key to preserving democracy. Over 40 years later, long after he had retired from his two terms as the nation's third president, Jefferson wrote, "I know no safe depository of the ultimate powers of the society but the people themselves; and if we think them not enlightened enough to exercise their control with a wholesome discretion, the remedy is not to take it from them, but to inform their discretion by education."[6] Thus, from the beginning of the United States, education was given a central role in expanding and preserving the nation in the words if not in the actions of the founders.

In spite of Jefferson's noble words, the Constitution of the United States does not guarantee education for all, as the Supreme Court reminded the nation in 1973 in the *Rodriguez* decision. In fact, the words *education* and *school* do not appear anywhere in the nation's founding documents. Jefferson himself had a very narrow definition of "the people" who were supposed to benefit from the kind of education he proposed. He really meant free White males. Women were not included in the educational system that Jefferson proposed. Slaves, of whom Jefferson himself had many, the few African Americans who were free, and Native Americans had no meaningful role

Thomas Jefferson, author of the Declaration of Independence, believed the country's new promise of democracy would fail if its citizens weren't active, educated participants.

in the society that Jefferson envisioned. In addition, neither Jefferson nor any of the founding fathers were successful in establishing schools that would deliver on their goals. Jefferson established the University of Virginia, but the lower-level schools he wanted did not materialize in his lifetime. For the most part, neither Jefferson nor the other founders expanded their vision of whom the schools should serve. Nevertheless, the generation that founded the United States as a nation described a vision of the role of education in a democratic society that would, in future hands, be expanded far beyond their wildest dreams.

STRUCTURING A DEMOCRATIC SCHOOL SYSTEM

The successive generations of men, taken collectively, constitute one great Commonwealth. . . . [E]mbezzlement and pillage from children and descendants are as criminal as the same offences when perpetrated against contemporaries.

Without undervaluing any other human agency, it may be safely affirmed that the Common School, improved and energized as it can easily be, may become the most effective and benignant of all the forces of civilization.

—*Horace Mann*[7]

In the early 1800s, there were quite a few schools in many parts of the country, but they were often private and limited either to those who could pay or, in some instances, to the White male citizens of towns that taxed themselves for their support. Almost from the beginning, others argued for a wider definition of "schooling for all" and for the inclusion of women, African Americans, Native Americans, more recent immigrants, poor children, children living in isolated rural communities, and the like. Throughout the 19th century, women fought long and difficult battles for inclusion in schools as students and then as teachers. At the end of the Civil War, recently freed African Americans began a major drive to expand the educational opportunities available to them.

When Horace Mann became the first secretary to the newly created Massachusetts state Board of Education in 1837, he began almost immediately to institutionalize the Jeffersonian vision, while also expanding it. Mann consciously echoed Jefferson, writing in one of his annual reports that "the necessity of general intelligence, under a republican form of government, like most other very important truths, has become a very trite one." Yet trite or not, Mann believed that it was essential, indeed "that a republican form of government, without intelligence in the people, must be on a vast scale, what a mad house, without superintendent or keepers, would be on a small one."

Mann also expanded the Jeffersonian argument about the link of schooling and democracy in two important

THE PERRY PICTURES.   138.   COPYRIGHT, 1908, BY E. A. PERRY.

HORACE MANN.

Horace Mann believed that education should be funded for all citizens and should be inclusive regardless of class (although not race).

ways. First, whereas Jefferson unsuccessfully called on his state legislature in Virginia to support schools, Mann argued with much greater success for public funding of education. He did not mince words. If the schools were essential to the future of the republic, and if every child had a right to an education (Mann included girls as well as boys, though he did not include the African American or American Indian residents of Massachusetts), then failure to adequately support the schools was a crime. Paying taxes for the schools was a fundamental part of citizenship, and failure to do so was theft from the next generation. More than a century and half after Mann, school funding remains an issue and writers like Stan Karp might see the current financial arrangements as "embezzlement from children" even today.

Mann also rejected the Jeffersonian plan for a modest basic education for all followed by an elite education for the future leaders. "The very terms, *Public School*, and *Common School*, bear upon their face, that they are schools which the children of the entire community may attend," he argued. The

Connections

Recall Stan Karp's *Reading* in Chapter 10 and his examples of how school funding is unequal.

only way to make a democracy function, Mann believed, was for citizens to know each other, to mix with each other, and to be educated in common. Mann, a middle-class Whig politician and abolitionist, disliked **elitism** in any form. He was convinced that, in a democratic nation, leaders could not rise above the electorate. "By a natural law, like that which regulates the equilibrium of fluids, elector and elected, appointer and appointee, tend to the same level," he said. If that is true, he believed, then leaders and followers, legislators and voters needed the same education in the same institutions so that they could together create a unified democratic society.

elitism Attitude that people of a higher intellect or ability are considered more worthy than others or should be given power and responsibility.

Mann has come to be known as the father of public education in the United States. That is certainly an overstatement, for schools existed long before his term of office in Massachusetts. He was, however, a powerful advocate for a state-supported system of common schools, available to all citizens, that was far broader than that advocated by any of his predecessors.[8]

EDUCATION, SLAVERY, AND FREEDOM

Few people who were not right in the midst of the scenes can form any exact idea of the intense desire which the people of my race showed for education. It was a whole race trying to go to school. Few were too young, and none too old, to make the attempt to learn.

—*Booker T. Washington*[9]

One reads in vain the words of Jefferson or Mann, or many of their contemporary education reformers, for any meaningful discussion of the education of African Americans. Although they and so many other Americans of their generation were deeply committed to expanding educational opportunity and to ensuring that the American democracy was founded on a literate and well-read **electorate**, and while Mann was also deeply committed to the abolition of slavery, both he and Jefferson and nearly all of their contemporaries were amazingly silent on the education of the 10–20% of the nation's people who were not free. This is true despite the fact that both wrote a great deal about African Americans in other contexts: Jefferson, as the sometimes-ambivalent slaveholder, and Mann, as the courageous advocate for the abolition of slavery. It was as if to them, and the vast majority of their fellow European American citizens, African Americans existed in a completely different universe.

electorate Population of voters in a country or geographic region.

However, the African American population did not passively accept the dominant culture's lack of interest in their education. Two decades before slavery ended in the United States, a group of free Blacks in Boston, Massachusetts, petitioned for an end to racially segregated schools in their city. The petitioners wrote "that the establishment of exclusive schools for our children is a great injury to us, and deprives us of those equal privileges and advantages in the public school to which we are entitled as citizens." In 1846, these African American citizens understood that

since all experience teaches that where a small and despised class are shut out from the common benefit

Booker T. Washington, Frederick Douglass, and W. E. B. DuBois, shown here as young men, were early civil rights activists and leaders who championed education for African Americans.

African Americans stand outside a Freedman's Village school in Arlington, Virginia, in the 1860s. Note that each person, young and old, is reading from a book.

of any public institution of learning and confined to separate schools. . .the teachers and the scholars are soon considered, and of course, become, an inferior class.

It took another decade, but in 1855, the public schools of Boston were desegregated by state law, though the city would spend the next 150 years dealing with less formal but very real forms of school segregation.[10]

During and after the Civil War, northern Whites in the union army and agents of the federal government's Freedmen's Bureau, created to respond to the needs of newly freed slaves, were continually amazed by newly freed Blacks' passion for education.[11] One northern teacher, who had gone to Florida to teach, told of a 60-year-old woman who, "just beginning to spell, seems as if she could not think of any thing but her books, says she spells her lesson all the evening, then she dreams about it, and wakes up thinking about it." A teacher in North Carolina said of a student, "[H]e thought a school-house would be the first proof of their *independence*."[12]

That so many recently freed slaves saw the schoolhouse as "proof of their *independence*" surprised many White observers. However, this isn't surprising considering the nature of southern slavery during the previous half-century. According to James Anderson, the foremost historian of 19th-century African American education,

During the three decades before the Civil War slaves lived in a society in which for them literacy was forbidden by law and symbolized as a skill that contradicted the status of slaves. As former slave William Henry Heard recalled: "We did not learn

to read nor write, as it was against the law for any person to teach any slave to read; and any slave caught writing suffered the penalty of having his forefinger cut from his right hand; yet there were some who could read and write."[13]

Even before the end of the Civil War, and with it the end of slavery, one of the most famous runaway slaves had explained the lessons he had learned early in life about the power of literacy. As he later told the story, a kindly woman had begun to teach the young Frederick Douglass how to read, but his White master quickly stopped the lessons. Douglass overheard him telling her that such lessons "would forever unfit him to be a slave. . . ."[14] Douglass remembered that "the argument which he so warmly urged, against my learning to read, only served to inspire me with a desire and determination to learn."[15] Learn he did, so that in the years after he escaped from slavery, Douglass became one of the great writers and orators of his time.

John W. Alvord, the federal government's chief administrator for setting up schools for the newly freed slaves during and after the Civil War, arrived in the South thinking he would have to start the very first schools. He found, however, that "throughout the entire South, an effort is being made by the colored people to educate themselves."[16] Soon the work of these schools was supplemented by the northern teachers like Charlotte Forten Grimké and so many others who were part of a vast crusade in the 1860s and 1870s to bring literacy to the newly freed slaves and to institutionalize a system of schools for them.[17] Sent by churches and the government, the best of these teachers became allies of the teachers who were already in the field.

PRIMARY SCHOOL FOR FREEDMEN, IN CHARGE OF Mrs. GREEN, AT VICKSBURG, MISSISSIPPI.—[See Page 504.]

This illustration depicts a White teacher instructing a class of freed slaves in Vicksburg, Mississippi, around 1865.

Connections

Recall Charlotte Forten Grimké's teaching experiences, as relayed in her diary entries in Chapter 1.

Sometimes there were tensions between the White northern educators and their southern Black counterparts. One White teacher, William Channing Gannett, reported, "There is jealousy of the superintendence of the white man in this matter. What they desire is assistance without control."[18] People who had recently been enslaved were not about to cede to anyone control over something as important as their education.

In time, the initial informal efforts were transformed into schools, school districts, and the development of teacher preparation colleges. After the Civil War, every southern state added to its constitution a provision for free public education. However, the creative energy of the first years did not last. Beginning not long after the end of the Civil War, there was an assault on the fundamental meaning of democracy as state after state effectively took away African American citizens' rights to vote, to participate in the larger society, or to receive a quality education. It is impossible to overstate the difficulties African American educators experienced in the years between the 1870s and the 1960s. As W. E. B. Du Bois wrote in 1934, "Public education for all at public expense was, in the South, a Negro idea."[19] It was not surprising that the civil rights movement of the 20th century would embrace equal educational opportunity with such commitment. For people who had known the absence of both schools and democracy, the link was indeed essential.[20]

MAKING DEMOCRACY "COME ALIVE" IN SCHOOL

We are apt to look at the school from an individualistic standpoint, as something between teacher and pupil, or between teacher and parent. That which interests us most is naturally the progress made by the individual child of our acquaintance, his normal physical development, his advance in ability to read, write, and figure, his growth in the knowledge of geography and history, improvement in manners, habits of promptness, order, and industry— it is from such standards as these that we judge the work of the school. And rightly so. Yet the range of the outlook needs to be enlarged. What the best and wisest parent wants for his own child, that must the community want for all its children. Any other ideal for our schools is narrow and unlovely; acted upon, it destroys our democracy. . . . To do this means to make each one of our schools an embryonic community life, active with types of occupations that reflect the life of the larger society and are permeated throughout with the spirit of art, history, and science. When the school introduces and trains each child of society into membership within such a little community, saturating him with the spirit of service, and providing him with the instruments of effective self-direction, we shall have the deepest and best guaranty of a larger society which is worthy, lovely, and harmonious.

—John Dewey[21]

At the beginning of the 20th century, some progressive educators, such as John Dewey, were arguing that the link between education and democracy was more sophisticated and more complicated than earlier writers had suggested. Schools needed to be the model of the inclusive and **egalitarian** society that they were supposed to teach students to honor. Dewey noted that only about 5% of the population finished high school and the majority dropped out by the end of fifth grade. Universal schooling had a long way to go. Progressive education, in the hands of Dewey and others, was a means of engaging more students in their schooling so that they would stay and participate for a longer period of time. It was even more fundamentally a philosophy that demanded a complete rethinking of the purposes and goals of schooling in a democratic nation. Preparing informed citizens was important, Dewey and his allies argued, but the goal was preparing citizens who would continually remake society in ways that were more democratic for all citizens.

egalitarian The belief that all people are equal and should have the same political, economic, social, and civil liberties.

Connections Progressive education is discussed in a number of contexts throughout this book, including Chapter 1 (history of the teaching profession), Chapter 5 (John Dewey and the philosophy of progressive education), and Chapter 7 (motivation as a key factor to student success).

If democracy is more than a system of government and a way of living in a community, then the implications for education are significant. As Dewey wrote in 1899 in *The School and Society*,

When the school introduces and trains each child of society into membership within such a little community, saturating him with the spirit of service, and providing him with the instruments of effective self-direction, we shall have the deepest and best guarantee of a larger society which is worthy, lovely, and harmonious.[22]

Dewey was also clear as he said in "My Pedagogic Creed" that "I believe that education, therefore, is a process of living and not a preparation for future living." Democratic citizenship began when the child entered school, not when he or she graduated. He also said, "I believe, finally, that the teacher is engaged, not simply in the training of individuals, but in the formation of the proper social life." The progressive education movement, as defined by Dewey, was a means of preparing self-confident, active citizens who were ready to engage in the continuing process of social evolution and community building, and progressive teachers who understood this were the key players.

Join the **Dialogue**

Write your own "pedagogic creed"—a statement of your basic philosophical beliefs about education, using the statements by Dewey and other educators as models. Think carefully about your deepest beliefs about schooling and the links of schooling to democracy and fairness for all.

Active learning, self-directed study, and participation in school governance were not merely new and more effective means of instruction; they were ways of creating in the school the small-scale model of the larger democratic society—a society that is not only well governed but also "worthy, lovely, and harmonious." In a sense, Dewey was the first American philosopher of education to take seriously Alexis de Tocqueville's observation in his 1835 *Democracy in America* that the American democracy always threatened to degenerate into anarchic individualism unless the forces of community were as central to democracy as those of individual liberty.[23]

EDUCATION IS A CIVIL RIGHT

Our goal is First-Class Citizenship, and we will settle for nothing less.

—*Ruth Batson*[24]

Ruth Batson was the chairman of the education committee of the Boston branch of the NAACP when she testified before the Boston School Committee in 1963. Her demand for full equality in the treatment of African American students in the Boston public schools is a reminder that the civil rights movement had an impact on schools in every part of the United States. We've discussed the Supreme Court's *Brown* decision that ended legalized racial segregation in U.S. schools in 1954. However, the battle for *Brown*—the decades of litigation that preceded it and the ensuing decades of efforts to implement it—was part of a much larger national civil rights movement that included a deep commitment to a more democratic system of education.

For many civil rights leaders, ending racial segregation in the schools was but a first step—whether it was the "separate but equal" segregation of African Americans in the South, the effective segregation of Latino students (especially in the Southwest), the segregation of Asian students in California that lasted into the 1920s, or the informal racial segregation that was practiced in schools in every part of the United States. The larger goal was the creation of a society that allowed all its citizens full participation in democracy at all levels, in the "beloved community" as Martin Luther King, Jr., said. Education was considered the key to such participation.

Whether it was the creation of Freedom Schools across the South by educators such as Septima Clark, the quiet dignity with which young African Americans made *Brown* real by entering often hostile and dangerous White schools, or the creation of the kinds of independent Black schools described by Pedro Noguera in the **Readings** for Chapter 11, civil rights organizers were also educational organizers.

Ruth Batson was a civil rights and education activist, a NAACP leader, and the first Black female member of the Democratic National Committee.

RECENT VISIONS OF DEMOCRATIC SCHOOLING

The classroom, with all its limitations, remains a location of possibility. In that field of possibility we have the opportunity to labor for freedom, to demand of ourselves and our comrades, an openness of mind and heart that allows us to face reality even as we collectively imagine ways to move beyond the boundaries, to transgress. This is education as the practice of freedom.

—*bell hooks*[25]

Writing in response to the 1983 federal report that declared the nation to be at risk because of "a rising tide of mediocrity" in our schools, Ann Bastian and her colleagues challenged the assumptions behind the report as reinforcing "competitive structures of achievement modeled on and serving the economic marketplace." To these writers, such a focus "misconstrues the crisis in education." Bastian and her colleagues then named what they saw as the real crisis in education at the end of the 20th century:

There is a catastrophic failure to provide decent schools and adequate skills to low-income students; there is also a chronic failure to provide reasoning and citizenship skills among all students. . . . In establishing a framework for progressive alternatives, it is necessary to project a concept of education in which quality and equality are mutually inclusive standards.[26]

Did you know?

President Barack Obama voiced sentiments similar to those voiced in the past by leaders in the Reconstruction era, education reformers, and leaders of the civil rights movement when he claimed that education was "the most important issue for the black community" because educational equality works against economic inequality. By providing a comprehensive plan that provides educational opportunities and support for all children from early childhood through college, the Obama administration hopes to bridge the current achievement gap between African American and Latino students and White students. Implementing and funding programs such as Head Start, Promise Neighborhoods, and Pell Grants is a major component of his current education plan.

Teachable Moment

Organizing a Movement

In *Teaching U.S. History: Dialogues Among Social Studies Teachers and Historians,* Diana Turk and her colleagues interviewed Adam Green, one of the foremost historians of the civil rights movement. Green says,

> I think the single best way to look at the accelerated phase of black freedom—the era from the 1940s until at least the 1960s and possibly the 1970s—is to say that before you pay attention to leaders you have to pay attention to organizers. Of course, certainly it's important to think about the rank and file and the ways in which these were very much mass movements. But I think seeing the alternative to a leader-centric notion of history as being a mass-centric notion of history seems to me to be replacing one essentialism with another essentialism. So, for example, for many many years people thought about the Civil Rights Movement as a pantheon of great male leaders, like Martin Luther King and Malcolm X—and then there was Rosa Parks, who is often represented as a woman who stood up momentarily, and basically through her humble, quiet dignity created a certain kind of turn or spark or paradigm shift that gave rise to the kind of mass component of the movement.

....

For more than a year, the African American citizens of Montgomery, Alabama, boycotted the public transit system, choosing to walk rather than ride at the "back of the bus." The Montgomery Bus Boycott ended in December 1956 and led to the United States Supreme Court declaring that segregated buses were unconstitutional.

In their book, *Choosing Equality: The Case for Democratic Schools,* Bastian and her colleagues developed an argument that was grounded in the ideals of the civil rights movement and of Jefferson, Mann, Dewey, and many other philosophers of a democratic system of education. Like their predecessors, they demanded a system of education in which "quality and equality are mutually inclusive standards" because anything less was undemocratic and unfair to the young citizens who received less than a top-quality education. It was also undemocratic because it failed to prepare citizens who could take an active place in shaping the larger society into which they were moving.

The journal *Rethinking Schools* has emerged as a strong voice for social justice in education. As the editors say in "Rethinking Our Classrooms" in the **Readings** for this chapter, their work begins with "the premise that schools and classrooms should be laboratories for a more just society than the one we now live in." Their goal is not only to help teachers serve the students and families who are in their classes but also to understand their obligations to

But you know, one of the things that had to be understood in relation to making sense of Rosa Park's role was that she had been an organizer. She had been someone who had worked within the NAACP as a very important member. And she had a deep understanding of the full operation that had been waiting for a case, basically, to kind of move the bus boycott campaign in Montgomery forward.

Reflecting on this interview, "Suzie," who teaches Advanced Placement U.S. History at a large urban high school, decided on a different approach than the standard lecture and discussion. After ensuring that her students had read about the Montgomery bus boycott and knew the stories of the major players, she proceeded with a new approach, described in the book:

"Imagine 99% of people in New York City decided to boycott public transportation," Suzie posed to her class. "In order to do so, what would we need to put in place to ensure our success?" Writing "bus boycott" in a center circle, she drew lines radiating out from the center, each line marking a different aspect that would need to be planned. "A team to lead," one student offered. "A charismatic leader," another followed. "People to join the group," a third proposed. "Funds for alternative transportation for publicity" another put forth. Each of these, along with "clearly outlined goals," "widespread publicity," and "communications network" Suzie wrote next to a single spoke emerging from the center circle. "Is this the job of one person?" she asked. A chorus of "no!" filled the room. "We need a lot of people!" "We need a leader!" "We need a hierarchy!" "We need

Source: Teaching U.S. History: Dialogues Among Social Studies Teachers and Historians, by Diana Turk, Rachel Mattson, Terrie Epstein, Robert Cohen, 2009, Routledge.

technology!" "OK, now let's apply this to the whole Civil Rights Movement," Suzie proposed. "Were the masses as important as the leaders?" What about the organizers? What does it take to have a successful movement?" Discussion fairly flew from there.

Students began to think seriously about what it took to organize the Montgomery bus boycott and what democratic activism might look like and the range of people that would need to be involved for meaningful social change to take place. They moved from what Green calls a "leader-centric" view of history, which tends to breed passivity in students who learn that the only thing they can do is wait for the next great leader, to a far deeper understanding of the role of everyday people who have the courage to take on extraordinary roles, organizing, planning, and working together to make democracy a reality.

Because they were so deeply engaged, the students learned the material about this important moment in U.S. history far better than if Suzie had merely lectured or given a quiz based on the textbook (and subsequent test results showed that this was the case).

QUESTIONS

- Did you learn about the civil rights movement in your high school U.S. history class? Was it taught in a way that was similar to Suzie's or different? What would have happened if your teacher had used Suzie's methodology?
- Think about a lesson you want to teach someday at the elementary, middle, or high school level. In what ways could you teach it so that students would not only learn the material but also connect it to democratic activism in the way Suzie's lesson did?

"society as a whole" and their role in helping to create "a multiracial democracy capable of addressing the serious social and ecological problems that cloud our future."

Many educators have found ways to both embrace and expand the links between what happens in schools—or the potential for what could happen in schools—and the fostering of a larger democratic society. For example, Deborah Meier has worked tirelessly to create smaller schools that can be democratic learning communities within the large and bureaucratized school systems of New York City

and Boston. For Meier, the key to building democracy is through face-to-face communities of students, parents, teachers, and others who can build trust among themselves, not just respond to outside pressures. Only in this way is it possible to build "a community-wide consensus about the essential purposes of schools and education—about what comes first." It is not important to do this just for purposes of governance, Meier insists, but because schools, which are supposed to teach democracy, can teach it effectively only if they model that same democracy. Thus,

Schools need to be governed in ways that honor the same intellectual and social skills we expect our children to master and—ideally—in ways the young can see, hear, and respect. At every point along the way we must connect the dots between our practice and democracy. It's nice when ends and means can come together in this way, and it's the most powerful form of education when they do. Will it be neat and orderly? Probably not. But democracy is and ever was messy, problematic, and it is always a work in progress.

Meier would insist it is also the point of public education.[27]

Lisa Delpit created a significant controversy when in 1986 she asked,

Why do the refrains of progressive educational movements seem lacking in the diverse harmonies, the variegated rhythms, and the shades of tone expected in a truly heterogeneous chorus? Why do we hear so little representation from the multicultural voices which comprise the present-day American educational scene?

Delpit was not turning her back on progressive pedagogy, although she certainly found some elements of that pedagogy highly questionable. However, in her continuing discussion of the education of *Other People's Children*, she insisted that a democratic education could not be governed by theories and research cut off from the voices and the lived experiences of the children and their parents in specific communities shaped as they were by their own culture and tradition.

Delpit's work has led her to be critical of Dewey's call for an education for all that reflects what "the wisest and best parent" wants. She cautions, "To provide schooling for everyone's children that reflects liberal, middle-class values and aspirations is to ensure the maintenance of the status quo, to ensure that power, the culture of power, remains in the hands of those who already have it." The status quo, she reminds us, is profoundly undemocratic.[28]

More recently, Delpit has focused on the need for schools to respect the home language of their students, whether it is a "recognized" language or the speech patterns of the African American community, or another so-called dialect. Delpit has called for a much more respectful embrace of all students that not only demands high standards but also begins with respect and love. She says,

We must treat all with love, care, and respect. We must make them feel welcomed and invited by allowing their interests, culture, and history into the classroom. We must reconnect them to their own brilliance and gain their trust so that they will learn from us. We must respect them, so that they feel connected to us. Then, and only then, might they be willing to adopt our language form as one to be added to their own.[29]

"Reconnecting students to their own brilliance" is also part of what it means for schools to be places where a democratic society is built.

The list could go on. There are as many disagreements as there are agreements among educators who seek to build more democracy in classrooms, schools, and society. Some seek only full integration into one culture, while others seek at least temporary separation in order to create the space to build a vibrant, if small-scale, culturally relevant democracy. However, viewing the schools as a foundation for an ever-expanding democratic culture has been one of the core purposes of public education in the United States for over 200 years. There have been terrible failures, and the goal remains elusive, but it is one that every teacher needs to take seriously.

>> How Can We Make Our Schools More Democratic?

SCHOOLS ARE NOT ALL EQUAL

Most citizens believe in the principle that every child has the right to the best possible education, and this belief has fueled reform movements in every generation. Important progress has been made. For example, a century ago, only 5% of adolescents received a high school diploma, and half a century ago, only 50% of this age group did so. Today, over 95% of young people receive either a high school diploma or a GED by the time they are in their mid-20s. Of course, a high school diploma alone is not the key to success that it was in 1900 or 1950. For most people, some higher education, if not a college degree, is a requirement for financial success in adult life. Not all high school diplomas offer equal access to higher education or a quality job.

Unfortunately, the democratic ideal of a quality education for every child is far from being realized. Many students do not receive the kind of quality education that most people believe is their birthright because the community in which they live does not have sufficient resources to hire the best teachers or invest in buildings, technology, or laboratories. Students are still excluded from school or made to feel terribly uncomfortable because of their race, gender, or sexual orientation; because of a disability; or because their first language is not what is known as "standard English." Policies are invented that make schools less equal, and individuals in authority tolerate discrimination, often because they simply do not notice it or because it would take a larger supply of courage than they have at the moment. The external things that make for a good education—safe streets, supportive families, a larger community of concerned adults—are not distributed evenly in this country, and schools are far from being able to make up for the inequities that exist in other parts of society, even if they were fully equal in the resources they provided for every child who attended them.

In 2004, on the 50th anniversary of the U.S. Supreme Court's *Brown* decision, considered at the time to be a landmark in democratizing schools by ending government-sanctioned racial segregation, Pedro A. Noguera and Robert Cohen wrote,

> *Throughout the country, the more common experience for students is to attend schools that are separate and unequal—schools that are well-equipped and cater to the children of the affluent, and schools that barely function and serve the poor, white and nonwhite. Throughout America, a majority of poor children attend schools where learning has been reduced to preparation for a standardized test, where failure and dropping out are accepted as the norm, and where overcrowding and disorder are common.*[30]

Noguera and Cohen have named a reality in American public education that is too often more accurate than the hopes of those who see schools as the nation's great equalizer.

According to the historian James Anderson, "Both schooling for democratic citizenship and schooling for second-class citizenship have been basic traditions in American education."[31] As a future teacher, you need to think about what is fair and unfair or democratic and undemocratic in the way that schools operate and ask how schools would be organized if they truly reflected our democratic commitments. What does the connection among school, democracy, and fairness mean in terms of what should be taught and how students should be treated? What policies should individual teachers and teacher-dominated organizations, such as unions and professional associations, advocate? Who is included in a democratic system of education? Perhaps most important, what can teachers—individually and collectively—do to help make our schools more democratic?

Few observers of public schools have probed as deeply as Jonathan Kozol. Kozol began his career as an elementary school teacher in Boston and has spent most of his life writing about children and the way adult society fails those young people. In *Savage Inequalities: Children in America's Schools*, published in 1991, he reported on the frightening state of education and the desperate unfairness that he saw in many schools that served the poorest of the nation's children.

To begin with, the majority of schools that serve poor children, despite some wonderful exceptions, are not happy places. Kozol summarized his own research, saying,

> *My deepest impression, however, was less theoretical and more immediate. It was simply the impression that these urban schools were, by and large, extraordinarily unhappy places. With few*

These two schools could be only a few miles apart, yet the buildings themselves tell a tale of inequality that is still all too evident in American education.

Take a look at the some of the educators profiled in this text, and consider the following:

- Deborah Meier (Chapter 9): To what extent do Meier's ideas represent a Jeffersonian approach to education? To what extent might she differ from Jefferson?
- Marian Wright Edelman (Chapter 10): How would Edelman's ideas represent a version of Horace Mann's approach to education? How does she differ from Mann?
- Septima Clark (Chapter 3): To what extent do Clark's ideas represent a continuation of the concerns of the Reconstruction era? To what extent might she differ from them?
- The philosophers and psychologists described in Chapter 5: Who (no matter when he or she lived) do you think would be counted as part of the progressive movement? Who would not?
- Edith Greene (Chapter 4): How have Greene's hopes and ideas been met in the years since she worked for the Title IX legislation? How might she still be disappointed if she visited schools today?

exceptions they reminded me of "garrisons" or "outposts" in a foreign nation. . . . [T]heir doors were guarded. Police sometimes patrolled the halls. The windows of the schools were often covered with steel grates . . . . I often wondered why we would agree to let our children go to school in places where no politician, school board president, or business CEO would dream of working.

And the children, Kozol discovered, knew how unhappy these places were.

Kozol recently returned to some of the same schools and found that things are even worse in many places. In his 2005 book, *The Shame of the Nation*, Kozol describes two terrible failures of the democratic ideal that he sees in today's schools. First, he says,

One of the most disheartening experiences for those who grew up in the years when Martin Luther King and Thurgood Marshall were alive is to visit public schools today that bear their names. . .and to find how many of these schools are bastions of contemporary segregation.

Kozol relays stories that are nothing short of "apartheid schooling"—one set of schools for the well-off, mostly White children and another set of very different schools for the overwhelmingly poor students of color.

The second thing Kozol noticed in his recent visits to these segregated schools was how very different the education being offered to these students really was. It was not just a second-rate education—it was a profoundly distinct education. In observing one class, Kozol noticed, "No one laughed. No child made a funny face to somebody beside her." Every moment seemed tightly scripted. It is as if, Kozol says, "the differentness of children of minorities is seen as so extreme as to require an entire inventory of 'appropriate' approaches built around the proclamation of their absolute uniqueness from the other children of this nation."

Part of the power of Kozol's writing is his ability to listen carefully to the children who attend these schools and live in poor neighborhoods and to record their wisdom. The students tell Kozol that they understand what is going on:

"It's like we're being hidden," said a 15-year-old girl named Isabel I met some years ago in Harlem, in attempting to explain to me the ways in which she and her classmates understood the racial segregation of their neighborhoods and schools. "It's as if you have been put in a garage where, if they don't have room for something but aren't sure if they should throw it out, they put it there where they don't need to think of it again."

How much farther could a society stray from building school communities that are microcosms of a larger society that is "worthy, lovely, and harmonious?"

THE TEACHER'S ROLE IN A DEMOCRATIC SOCIETY

Teachers have been at the forefront of making schools more democratic for the past two centuries; however, much remains to be done. Whether one teaches in a school

Promising Practices

In the Zone

As Geoffrey Canada, the creator of Harlem's Children's Zone, knows, a smattering of after-school programs and tutors cannot provide the necessary support for students in low-income areas. To start the Harlem Children's Zone project, Canada had to reform his own thinking about programs for at-risk students. Instead of creating a number of programs and trying to make them work together in a cohesive manner, Canada decided to reverse the process by establishing the outcomes he wanted to achieve and reworking separate programs until they matched the results.

Geoffrey Canada of the Harlem's Children's Zone.

What Canada accomplished was, and still is, inspiring. Harlem Children's Zone now offers over 20 individual programs to more than 8,000 children in 100 blocks of Harlem. The programs focus on every area of a child's life: The Baby College instructs parents of children aged 0–3 on prenatal issues and childhood development; Harlem Gems is a preschool program with a low 4:1 child-to-adult ratio that prepares children for school and teaches them English, Spanish, and French; the Promise Academy is the charter school centerpiece of the program; Employment and College Success services round out the transition from childhood to college and employment. Additional programs offer sports as well as health-care, asthma, obesity, and counseling services.

Students are required to work harder and longer than students at other schools. To subvert the current paradigm of underachieving students in disadvantaged areas, educators continually reinforce their students'

ability to achieve anything and instill discipline in students to help them attain these goals. The results of this comprehensive approach to education are impressive. Sixth-grade students entering the Promise Academy previously scored in the 39th percentile among New York City students in math. Their scores moved up to the 74th percentile by the eighth grade. English Language Arts scores jumped from the 39th percentile to the 53rd percentile. The Promise Academy all but eliminated the achievement gap in math between Black students and the city average for White students.

To reach his final goal, Canada hopes that the effects of students leaving the Children's Zone program and attending college transform the entire Harlem community by ending intergenerational poverty in these neighborhoods. President Obama's 20 proposed Promise Neighborhoods, replications of Canada's model, can be used to compare the effects of these programs in different communities.

Sources: *Whatever It Takes: Geoffrey Canada's Quest to Change Harlem and America*, by Paul Tough, 2008, Houghton Mifflin Harcourt Publishing Company; "Harlem Program Singled Out as Model," by Robin Shulman, August 2, 2009, *Washington Post*, http://www.washingtonpost.com/wp-dyn/content/article/2009/08/01/AR2009080102297_3.html?sid=ST2009080102632, "The Baby College," The Harlem Children's Zone Project Web site, http://www.hcz.org/programs/the-hcz-project#baby_college

that serves poor youth or the more fortunate children of the middle class, every teacher has a responsibility to make schools fairer for all.

Beyond the economic issues, a democratic society now, as 200 years ago, requires well-educated citizens who can understand public issues, make informed choices, and respond to the call to leadership in their communities. The challenge continues to be bringing practice closer to that belief while resisting more recent policies in many schools that seem to imply such diverse access is not, after all, such an appropriate goal. In a variety of ways, issues of access, inclusion, equality, and excellence are going to dominate the lives of the next generation of teachers just as they have most previous generations. Those entering the teaching profession need to be clear about their own beliefs and their expectations and the role they can play in a democratic system of education.

Half a century ago, the U.S. Supreme Court ordered that racial segregation in schools be dismantled "with all deliberate speed." However, schools remain segregated not only by race but also by huge divides between the schools for rich children, middle-class children, and poor children. In addition, within the same school, even the same classroom sometimes, students experience a vastly different education depending on their gender, sexual orientation, religion, perceived academic abilities, language of origin, or disabilities. Many students, teachers, parents, and advocates grow impatient for the coming of greater equity.

This chapter began with one poem by Langston Hughes. In another poem, "Democracy," Hughes spoke of this healthy impatience:

> Democracy will not come
> Today, this year
>   Nor ever
> Through compromise and fear.
> I have as much right
> As the other fellow has
>   To stand
> On my two feet
> And own the land
> I tire of hearing people say,
> Let things take their course.
> Tomorrow is another day.
> I do not need my freedom when I'm dead.[32]

This democratic urgency is part of every teacher's professional responsibility.

How Can I

Creating Citizens in the Classroom

According to the 2003 report *The Civic Mission of Schools*, schools should continue to be the primary vehicle for encouraging civic duties because schools have the capacity to reach almost every young person in the country and because the country needs citizens who understand their civic responsibilities. Through class discussions and critical thinking exercises, teachers have the opportunity to lay the groundwork for future informed debate about key civic issues, one of the hallmarks of a democracy.

All teachers—not only social studies teachers—have a responsibility for providing their students with civic knowledge. What techniques or lessons can you use to bring this knowledge into your classroom? *The Civic Mission of Schools* study suggests the following:

- *Incorporate current news events and issues into everyday discussion*
- *Implement mock trials and debates in the classroom*
- *Design a service-learning program and encourage meaningful work*
- *Offer extracurricular activities that take lessons beyond the classroom walls*
- *Encourage participation in school government*

In addition, you can find teacher resources at the Web site "Facing History and Ourselves" (http://www.facinghistory.org/resources). Resources include lesson plans, videos, and online modules that help students embrace the larger national and international communities and understand their own responsibility to be active participants in history, not passive witnesses.

Source: Campaign for the Civic Missions of Schools, The Center for Information and Research on Civic Learning and Engagement and Carnegie Corporation of New York, 2003, http://www.civicmissionofschools.org/site/campaign/cms_report.html.

QUESTIONS

- Do you remember a school lesson that dealt directly with what it meant to be a citizen? What was the lesson? Was it effective in getting you to be more engaged in your community? Why or why not?
- What other community organizations or institutions also foster civic engagement and knowledge? Are they effective in producing knowledgeable citizens?

REVIEW >>

- **What does a democratic society expect of its schools?**

  The full definition of democracy includes more than just educated voters. It involves an active citizenry that strives to create a government that is not only *for* the people but *of* and *by* the people as well. Schools have been considered an integral player in creating educated, responsible citizens to fulfill this ideal.

- **What is the relationship between a universal education and democratic citizenship?**

  Since the founding of the United States, the concept of democracy has imposed great expectations on schools and teachers. Thomas Jefferson believed the country's new promise of democracy would fail if its citizens weren't active, educated participants. Horace Mann similarly believed that education was the key and should be funded for all citizens and inclusive regardless of class. However, African Americans typically were not covered under that "inclusive" expectation and were often denied the right to an education, whether formal or informal. Thus, upon the abolition of slav-

ery, former slaves embraced education as the means to becoming active participants in shaping a democratic government and their future. John Dewey and progressive educators saw the role of schools as not only teaching the tenets of democracy but also engaging and motivating students for lifelong involvement in the democratic process. The civil rights movement challenged a system that supported equality for all but did not in fact provide it, especially in education. Today's vision for democracy seems to point to schools being models of ideal democratic societies—although this ideal has yet to be realized in many places.

- **How can we make our schools more democratic?**

  National leaders from the American Revolution to the present day have argued that schooling for all of the nation's youth is essential to the success of a democratic society, but in every generation, young people have been excluded from schools or placed in second-class school situations where they do not have the opportunities of their more fortunate counterparts. The next generation of teachers will be challenged to play their part in ensuring that the schools of the United States truly leave no child behind.

How Can We Make Our Schools More Democratic?

The following statements are examples of the kind of personal creed—a philosophical and ethical statement of belief—that every teacher should be able to write. John Dewey, arguably the nation's foremost philosopher of education, wrote "My Pedagogic Creed" in 1897. W. E. B. Du Bois, one of the founders of the NAACP and a foremost advocate for African American rights during the first half of the 20th century, spoke to a group of educators at the end of World War II. David T. Hansen is a contemporary educator who has written extensively about the moral and ethical aspects of teaching. Finally, the editors of *Rethinking Schools* publish some of the leading materials on social justice education today.

From "MY PEDAGOGIC CREED"

BY JOHN DEWEY

I believe that education, therefore, is a process of living and not a preparation for future living.

I believe that the school must represent present life—life as real and vital to the child as that which he carries on in the home, in the neighborhood, or on the playground.

I believe that much present education fails because it neglects this fundamental principle of the school as a form of community life. It conceives the school as a place where certain information is to be given, where certain lessons are to be learned, or where certain habits are to be formed. The value of these is conceived as lying largely in the remote future; the child must do these things for the sake of something else he is to do; they are mere preparation. As a result they do not become a part of the life experience of the child and so are not truly educative.

I believe that the discipline of the school should proceed from the life of the school as a whole and not directly from the teacher.

I believe that education is the fundamental method of social progress and reform.

I believe that all reforms which rest simply upon the enactment of law, or the threatening of certain penalties, or upon changes in mechanical or outward arrangements are transitory and futile.

I believe that the community's duty to education is, therefore, its paramount moral duty. By law and punishment, by social agitation and discussion, society can regulate and form itself in a more or less haphazard and chance way. But through education society can formulate its own purposes, can organize its own means and resources, and thus shape itself with definiteness and economy in the direction in which it wishes to move.

I believe, finally, that the teacher is engaged, not simply in the training of individuals, but in the formation of the proper social life.

I believe that every teacher should realize the dignity of his calling; that he is a social servant set apart for the maintenance of proper social order and the securing of the right social growth.

I believe that in this way the teacher always is the prophet of the true God and the usherer in of the true kingdom of God.

From "ON EDUCATION"

BY W. E. B. DU BOIS

You are of course aware that a new branch of learning has recently become popular which is called Semantics. Semantics has to do with the meaning of words and takes up the fact that very often we use the same word unconsciously with different meanings so that what is true of the word in one meaning is quite untrue in another meaning. I want to call your attention this morning to some differences of meaning in the word education. . . .

In order to make clearer what I mean I want to go over first the meaning of education in my life. From the age of five through my twenty-sixth birth-day, over twenty years, were spent almost entirely in receiving an education according to the preconceptions of the late nineteenth century. . . . Now at the end of these twenty years of study and travel . . . I was not prepared to do any specific piece of work; I could not make a table or cook a meal or sew on a button. I could not carve nor paint; and the art of writing and revealing my thought had not been developed. On the other hand, I did have a rather firm grasp, and idea of what this world was, and how it had developed in the last thousand years. I knew something of the kind of human beings that were on earth, what they

Source: "My Pedagogic Creed," by John Dewey, January 1897, *School Journal* 54, pp. 77–80.

Source: "On Education," by W. E. B. Du Bois, in Herbert Aptheker, ed., *Against Racism: Unpublished Essays, Papers, Addresses, 1887–1961 by W. E. B. Du Bois,* University of Massachusetts Press, 1985, pp. 249–252.[33]

were thinking and what they were doing. I was able to reason rather accurately, and whatever there was that I had not been trained to do, the specific training that was necessary came rather easily because I had this general grasp.

Nevertheless, as I came into the twentieth century, I was aware of the widespread criticism of the sort of education which I had had, and the questioning in the minds of men as to how far that sort of education was really valuable and how far it could be applied to the youth of today. More especially during the present war [this speech was given late in World War II], this criticism has been sharpened and emphasized in the United States. We have seen young people who had training in mechanics easily get jobs that paid wages almost fabulous.

This has made the people say and doubtless you have had it emphasized here, that what education ought to do, is to prepare young people for doing work of this sort; and that it is a great waste of time to study what we used to call the humanities and art and literature, over periods which counted up into decades, rather than in a few years of intensive work made a man a capable workman in some trade or art where he could get an immediate and comfortable salary.

Now despite this, we look upon a curiously contradictory world. The technical advance of western European civilization in the last century has been the most marvelous thing which the world has seen. It can without exaggeration be called miraculous. Personally I never can get over the unreality of travel by airplane. When I was a boy we typified the impossible by comparing it to flying. Now we fly easily and with astonishing safety around the world. But not only that; we talk over immeasurable distances. We transport goods and ideas. We have a world whose technical perfection makes all things possible. And yet, on the other hand, this world is in chaos. It has been organized twice in the last quarter of a century for murder and destruction on a tremendous scale, not to mention continual minor wars. There is not only this physical disaster, there is the mental and moral tragedy which makes us at times despair of human culture.

Now when we compare the technical mastery which man has over the world, with the utter failure of that power to organize happiness, and peace in the world, then we know that something is wrong. Part of this wrong lies in our conception of education. There are two different things that we have in mind in education: One is training for mastery of technique; the other is training the man who is going to exercise the technique and for whom the technique exists. If, regardless of the man himself, we train his hands and his nervous system for accomplishing a certain technical job, after that work is done we still have the question as to why it is done, and for whom, and to what end. What is the work of the world for? Manifestly it is for the people who

inhabit the world. But what kind of people are they? What they are depends upon the way in which they have been educated, that is, the way in which their possibilities have been developed and drawn out.

It is a misuse of the word education to think of it as technical training. Technical training is of immense importance. It characterizes civilization. But it is of secondary importance as compared with the people who are being civilized and who are enjoying civilization or who ought to enjoy it. Manifestly the civilized people of the world have got to be characterized by certain things; they must know this world, its history and the laws of its development. They must be able to reason carefully and accurately. Attention must be paid to human feelings and emotions which determine and guide this knowledge, and reason and action must follow a certain pattern of taste. These things: knowledge, reason, feeling and taste make up something which we designate as Character and this Character it is which makes the human being for which the world of technique is to be arranged and by whom it is to be guided.

Technique without character is chaos and war. Character without technique is labor and want. But when you have human beings who know the world and can grasp it; who have their feelings guided by ideals; then using technique at their hands they can get rid of the four great evils of human life. These four evils are ignorance, poverty, disease and crime. They flourish today in the midst of miraculous technique and in spite of our manifest ability to rid the world of them. They flourish because with all our technical training we do not have in sufficient quantity and for a long enough time the education of the human soul; the training of men to know and think and guide their feelings by science and art.

From *EXPLORING THE MORAL HEART OF TEACHING*

BY DAVID T. HANSEN

Conceptions of teaching have consequences. They influence how teachers think about and conduct their work. They shape what researchers investigate. They guide how teacher educators prepare new candidates. They play a role in what students come to expect from their teachers. And they underlie how administrators, policy makers, politicians, businesspersons, and parents perceive and judge teachers. In short, conceptions of what teaching is, and of what it is for, make a difference in educational thought and practice.

My aim in this book is to contribute to a conception of teaching that does justice to its time-honored importance in human life. I investigate why teaching is a moral and intellectual practice with a rich tradition. Those terms help capture why teaching has been such a long-standing priceless human activity. I mean "priceless" in the sense of having no substitute. No other practice, be it medicine, parenting, law, or social work, accomplishes what teaching does, even though there may be occasional overlap between them. This viewpoint turns attention to the importance of the person—the distinctive, irreproducible human being—who inhabits the role of teacher. It spotlights, in turn, why teaching entails paying attention to the persons who fill the role of student. These persons, whether they be children or adults, are themselves unique and noninterchangeable. They need teachers, at timely moments, to help them fulfill their promise.

In this introductory chapter, I outline this perspective on the practice by, first, examining the current conceptions of teaching. I raise the questions about them that center on the issue of whether teaching is an "empty cell" whose terms and meaning derive from outside the practice, in various political, economic, social, or other interests. I argue that teaching is an enduring practice whose moral and intellectual terms can be derived, to a vital degree, from *within*. Teaching has its own integrity, just as do the individual men and women who occupy the role in a serious-minded, thoughtful way. I discuss why the integrity of both the practice of teaching and of individual teachers threatens to fall out of sight whenever people cast teaching as merely a means to an end, with that end shaped from outside the practice. Public concerns and interests do merit a permanent place in talk about teaching. But such talk should be balanced by a grasp of why teaching is a moral and intellectual endeavor. . . .

Do ideals and idealism have a role to play in teaching? Two quick answers come to mind. The first is that they have no place, or at most a very limited place. According to this line of thinking, teaching is a well-defined occupation with well-defined goals. Our romantic impulses may tell us otherwise. They may lead us to envision teachers as artists and as transformers of the human spirit. However, a critic might argue, teaching is not an artistic endeavor because teachers are not artists, save from the point of view of method and even then only in a metaphorical sense. Unlike painters at their easels, teachers cannot create whatever they wish in the classroom. They are public servants beholden to the public to get a particular job done. Idealism is warranted as a source of motivation, but teachers' vision had better not take them away from the job itself. According to this point of view, the only ideal teachers should hold is, ideally, that of fulfilling their publicly defined obligations in a responsible and effective manner.

The second answer advances the opposite position. Teachers must have ideals, and their ideals must reach beyond mere social expectations. According to this argument, teachers are not bureaucratic hired hands whose only charge is to pass on to the young whatever knowledge and skills the powers that be have sanctioned. Teachers do play an important role in socializing students into expected custom and practice. However, as teachers, rather than as mere socializers, they also help equip students to think for themselves, to conceive their own ideals and hopes, and to prepare themselves for the task of making tomorrow's world into something other than a tired copy of today's.

Both answers contain truth. Teaching is not an empty cell to be filled in any fashion one wishes. The individual who occupies the role does not own teaching as if it were a possession that can be manipulated to suit personal taste. It is one thing to paint one's own canvases. It is another thing to paint, metaphorically speaking, with the hearts and minds of other people's children. Teachers have publicly defined tasks, ranging from teaching knowledge to

Source: *Exploring the Moral Heart of Teaching: Toward a Teacher's Creed*, by David T. Hansen, 2001, Teachers College Press, pp. 1–2, 157–158, 173, 175.

treating students with respect. They must uphold these if they are to deserve the right to remain in the classroom.

However, teaching is also more complicated and more important than occupational language alone can capture. Teaching comprises more than a series of discrete tasks whose content and presentation can be prefabricated. Teaching is a moral and intellectual practice whose outcomes cannot just be punched in, at least if we associate teaching with education rather than with a narrow version of training. Moreover, to the extent that teachers exercise autonomy and initiative, their individuality comes to the fore. Issues addressed in previous chapters—person, conduct, and moral sensibility, crafting an environment for teaching and learning, developing a sense of tradition—all point to the ideals and attitudes teachers can bring to their work.

Neither of our initial answers to the question about ideals in teaching is sufficient. Moreover, both answers polarize functional and moral aspects of teaching that, in the final analysis, need to be brought into a working accord. . . .

Teachers will differ in the big ideals that guide their work, whether they be to help create a better society or to produce smart and caring people. Such ideals are warranted—for example, as sources of motivation—albeit within limits

tailored by the terms of the practice. What teachers can agree on, it seems to me, is an ideal that will enable them to become the kind of person who can indeed have a beneficial rather than harmful or random, impact on students. Such an ideal will describe at one and the same time a disposition. Tenacious humility is a mane for this ideal. . . .

Tenacious humility does not tell teachers what materials or instructional methods to employ, all of which are discrete, specific decisions. Rather, in taking tenacious humility seriously as an ideal of personhood, teachers can build into their working lives continuity, or what some scholars call narrative unity. In reaching toward the ideal, teachers will be more likely to make specific educational choices that add up to a meaningful pattern rather than to a haphazard or random series. If they are tenacious about teaching well, and humble in their pretensions, they will be more rather than less likely to become a force for good in students' lives. Striving for this ideal will not prevent teachers from making mistakes and misjudgments. But it will enable them to learn and to keep working to improve. Tenacious humility constitutes a practical, humanizing ideal that can guide both big ideals and everyday practice, keeping them in the service of teaching and learning.

From "RETHINKING OUR CLASSROOMS: TEACHING FOR EQUITY AND JUSTICE"

BY THE EDITORS OF RETHINKING SCHOOLS

In rethinking our classrooms we begin from the premise that schools and classrooms should be laboratories for a more just society than the one we live in now. After more than a decade of high-profile national debate on school reform, we think this proposition is more central than ever to the success, perhaps even the survival, of public education.

Schools have crucial obligations not only to individual students and families, but to our society as a whole. Their success or failure is tied not just to personal well-being, but to the prospects of creating a multiracial democracy capable of addressing the serious social and ecological problems that cloud our future. We live in a world plagued by economic inequality, endemic violence, and racial injustice. A me-first, dollar-driven culture undermines democratic values, and seems to invent daily new forms of alienation and self-destruction. Over the long term, the production and consumption patterns of industrial over-developed and underplanned economies like ours threaten global ecological disaster.

Given such unpleasant but inescapable realities, education reform must be driven by a far broader vision than it has been in recent years. What happens every day in our classrooms both shapes and is shaped by the larger social currents that define who we are as a society and where we are headed. Accordingly, to be truly successful, school reform must be guided by democratic social goals and

values that provide a deeper context for more traditional academic objectives.

Unfortunately, too many schools foster narrowly self-centered notions of success and "making it." Too many, especially in poor areas, provide a dismal experience based on tests, tracking, and a sanitized curriculum that lacks the credibility or sense of purpose needed to engage students or to connect with their communities. Too many schools fail to confront the racial, class, gender, language, and homophobic biases woven into our social fabric.

Years of classroom experience have convinced us that these shortcomings are intimately connected to low student achievement. The problems many schools have in teaching children to read, write, and think are, to a large extent, symptoms of the inequality that permeates our educational system. In fact, we would argue that unless our schools and classrooms are animated by broad visions of equity, democracy, and social justice, they will never be able to realize the widely proclaimed goal of raising educational achievement for all children.

Historically, efforts to expand the reach of public education or to democratize curriculum have been accompanied by extensions of the sorting and labeling mechanisms schools use to preserve pockets of privilege. . . .

Today the standardized testing crusade threatens to play a similar role. It professes to raise the bar for all children,

Source: "Rethinking Our Classrooms: Teaching For Equity and Justice," by the editors of *Rethinking Schools*, in Linda Christensen and Stan Karp, eds., 2003, *Rethinking School Reform: Views From the Classroom*, Rethinking Schools, pp. 3–9.

yet without dramatic increases in resources and radical improvements in teaching and learning inside classrooms, the testing crusade is more likely to create a new credentialing maze that continues to channel some students to lives of privilege and others to educational oblivion.

Teachers are often simultaneously perpetrators and victims in this process. They typically have little individual control over many of the factors that shape the conditions of schooling. But in their classrooms they often have a measure of autonomy to create a space that can profoundly affect the lives of young people. Teachers can create classrooms that are places of hope, where students and teachers gain glimpses of the kind of society we could live in, and where students learn the academic and critical skills needed to make it a reality.

This effort to rethink our classrooms must be both visionary and practical: visionary, because we need to go far beyond the prepackaged formulas and narrow agendas now being imposed on our schools and classrooms; and practical, because the work of reshaping educational practice and countering the agendas imposed from above requires daily, school-based efforts at learning, teaching, organizing, and educational activism by those with the most at stake— teachers, students, parents, and local communities. . . .

For all its flaws, public education exists because generations of people have fought to improve the future for themselves and their children. Whether public education continues to exist, and whether it rises to the challenges before it, remains an open question. How we as teachers respond will help determine the answer.

A classroom veteran once told younger colleagues that teachers had two choices: "We can teach for the society we live in, or we can teach for the one we want to see." *Rethinking Schools* is for those with the vision to reach for their dreams.

13

DEVELOPING A PLAN AND A PERSONAL PHILOSOPHY

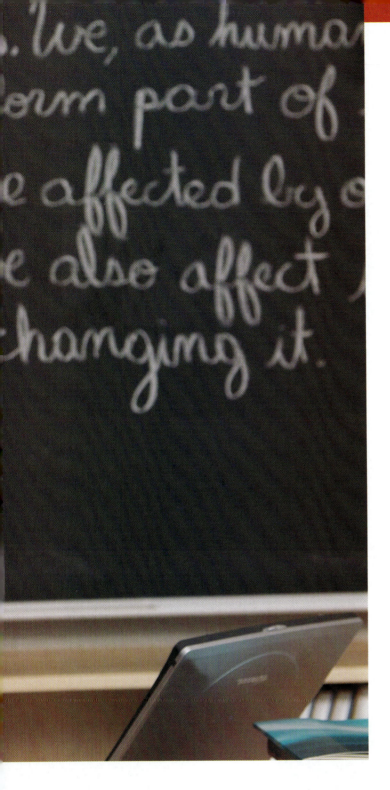

At the beginning of this book, we posed the simple question, "Why do I want to do this?" That question most likely did not have a simple answer. Or maybe you hadn't even considered your reasons for pursuing a career in teaching. By now, however, you may have formulated a complex response, taking into account all the benefits, opportunities, challenges, issues, and obstacles related to teaching.

As you continue to explore the rewarding field of teaching, you need to find the best path to get the skills, experiences, and licenses that will help you land your first job. It is also critical for you to determine the kind of teacher you want to be and your own personal philosophy about education. You should consider how you will manage the challenges of the initial years on the job. Your goal will be to establish a successful routine that evolves continually and allows you to grow in both skills and personal satisfaction.

The **Readings** for this chapter are written by people who have spent many years teaching and finding ways to answer these same questions for themselves. In her book *What Keeps Teachers Going?*, Sonia Nieto reflects on how her own experiences and those of other teachers can help to answer the question, "How will I survive as a new teacher?" The other two **Readings** focus on the question "What kind of teacher do I want to be?" In the first piece, Robert Fried talks about the characteristics of the "passionate teacher." Though Fried finds that passion comes in many forms, he concludes that every successful teacher is marked by passion—for his or her subject and students—and calls on all new teachers to become passionate teachers. Finally, Jacqueline Jordan Irvine discusses the characteristics of caring and competent teachers. Like Fried, Irvine finds that care and competence come in many different forms. What may look caring in one instance may not seem so caring in another. Nevertheless, Irvine concludes that while each teacher needs to define care and competence in his or her own way, no one should enter teaching who does not want to be identified by these significant characteristics.

WHERE DO I GO FROM HERE?

FOCUS »

- How do I get my first teaching job?
- How will I survive as a new teacher?
- What kind of teacher do I want to be?

» How Do I Get My First Teaching Job?

I spoke recently with a newly appointed director of human resources in a large urban school district. Upon starting her new job, she discovered that the district's personnel office was not very friendly to new applicants. She heard the phone answered with "What do you want?" . . . hardly a way to encourage applicants. When she witnessed a young, enthusiastic applicant being turned away because "no one has time to conduct job interviews today," she intervened quickly. She took the applicant into her own office and conducted a job interview on the spot. The city gained a new and enthusiastic teacher that it otherwise might have lost. The policy for answering the telephone was also changed quickly; the new greeting: "How may I help you?"

In some years and in some school districts, there are lots of jobs for new teachers; in others, opportunities may be limited. It is hoped that when you begin the search for your first teaching job, you will be greeted with "How may I help you?" rather than "What do you want?" and that someone will want to interview you. Whatever initial greeting you receive, however, remember that it takes patience and perseverance to land the job you want.

Two different sets of authorities govern entrance into the teaching profession. The fifty states plus the District of Columbia grant licenses (or certification as it is called in some states) to be a teacher. The decision to grant a license is based on your having completed the required course of study, usually at a university-based teacher preparation program. Teachers are hired by the 15,000 different school districts or often by the principals of individual schools. Except in unusual circumstances, a school or district cannot hire anyone to teach who does not have the appropriate state license or certificate. However, the license does not guarantee a job; only the individual district or school can offer a paid position as a classroom teacher.

You never know what kind of reception to expect when you apply for your first job.

Connections

In Chapter 11, we discussed how the issues of licensure and hiring are handled at the state and local levels, respectively, even though the federal government has become more involved in accountability issues and in defining a "highly qualified teacher."

STATE LICENSURE AND EXAMINATIONS

The vast majority of teachers gain their **state licensure** by completing a college- or university-based state-approved teacher preparation program. If you are reading this text for a college course, the odds are good that you are enrolled in such a program. In most states, the state department of education creates a set of standards for teacher licensure. The state then enters into agreements with colleges and universities offering teacher preparation programs in which the institution of higher education ensures that its curriculum for aspiring teachers meets the state requirements and the state reviews the school's curriculum (usually every 5 years). Many teacher preparation programs also have accreditation through the National Council for the Accreditation of Teacher Education (NCATE) or the Teacher Education Accreditation Council (TEAC). If the college offers a state-approved program, then its graduates are essentially promised that the state will honor the institution's recommendation and they will be licensed as teachers if they complete all the requirements.

If you are a college student studying to be a teacher, you should ask an advisor about the rules and regulations in your state and for your college. In addition to asking if you are enrolled in a state-approved program, you should also be clear about the specific license your curriculum will lead you to. Many states offer a variety of teaching licenses, not just for elementary or high school teachers, but for early elementary grades versus later elementary grades or middle school, and specific licenses for high school teachers according to the subjects taught, such as chemistry, mathematics, history or social studies, English, biology, and the like. Other licenses are issued for special education teachers; for teachers of bilingual education or English as a second language; and for teachers of theater, art, dance, and so on. Knowing the kinds of licenses offered in your state and the specific license for which your curriculum is preparing you will help you to avoid serious disappointment in the future.

You may also find it useful to secure more than one license before beginning to look for a job. An elementary teacher who is also licensed in special education, a secondary chemistry teacher who can also teach physics, or a social studies teacher who has state approval to teach at both the middle and high school levels has a much better chance of finding a position than someone who can do only one thing. Many teachers add a second or third license after they have already begun teaching, but others use their undergraduate or graduate preparation programs to secure more than one license from the beginning.

> **state licensure (called state certification in some states)** A formal document issued by the state that indicates the holder has met the teaching standards in a particular state—most often graduating from a state-approved teacher preparation program in a college or university—and has met any other requirements such as passing a state-approved exam.

Although most teachers gain their initial license through a state-approved college or university program, there are many "alternative routes" to teaching. Some alternative routes are through free-standing organizations such as Teach for America. Many school districts have their own in-district programs that recruit college graduates and offer an apprentice-style program that leads to teacher licensure. Finally, some states award licenses to individuals who can demonstrate experience in or advanced knowledge of a subject in which the demand for teachers is high (often mathematics, one of the sciences, or a foreign language). A major debate is ongoing between advocates of such alternative routes and those who believe that all prospective teachers should be required to complete a university-based program. Nevertheless, the vast majority of the nation's teachers (over 90%) qualify for their jobs by completing a college- or university-based program, either as part of their baccalaureate program or as a one- or two-year graduate program. The key for anyone aspiring to a career in teaching is

> **specialization** Focused area of study and skill used in a specific teaching field; elementary teacher, high school chemistry teacher, special education teacher, or teacher of English as a second language are all recognized specializations.

Join the **Dialogue**

Map out your plan. What other courses, field placements, or experiences do you need to become a fully qualified teacher? Which level (elementary, middle school, or high school) are you interested in teaching? Is there a content area you are interested in teaching (such as math or history)? Is there an additional **specialization** you could obtain that would broaden your opportunities and interests? Have you discussed different options with your advisor? If you haven't already done so, draft an academic plan and determine everything you want and need to accomplish (and when you need to do it) in order to be fully licensed as a teacher in your state.

to be sure that the specific path you are following will enable you to realize your goals.

During the past decade, most states have also added one more step in the process for earning a state license or certification: a state examination. State teacher examinations were popular in the United States during much of the first half of the 20th century. After World War II, most states phased out these exams, replacing them with the program approval agreements with colleges and universities that ensured much higher standards for new teachers than simply passing one examination. During the 1990s, however, as a new national debate emerged about the quality of the nation's teaching force, many states began to create new examinations designed to ensure that the graduates of all programs met a single state standard for literacy, knowledge of subject matter, pedagogy, and often also an understanding of human development and other aspects of schooling.

The majority of states that instituted examinations used an already well-respected examination offered by the Educational Testing Service (home of the SAT tests) called PRAXIS. PRAXIS exams test an applicant's general knowledge, specific subject matter knowledge in the area in which one wants to teach, and understanding of pedagogy—what works and what does not work in helping young people learn. (For more information on the PRAXIS examination visit www.ets.org/praxis5.) Some states have created new examinations. The federal government currently provides a national "report card" listing the passing rate on the teacher examinations for each state and for each teacher preparation program, but because the fifty states use many different examinations, and states using the same examination use different scores to determine a passing grade, meaningful judgments across the states cannot be made. Many instructors within the teacher preparation programs are critical of these exams.

You need to know the rules in the state where you want to teach. Do you have to take an examination? Does the program in which you are enrolled offer workshops or other means of preparing for the exam? When do you need to take the exam to avoid any delays in securing your initial teaching license? Others may engage in an extended debate about teacher examinations, but if you want to teach and your state requires such an examination, you still need to take *and pass* it.

GETTING HIRED

After completing a state-approved program and passing the required exams, you should be the proud holder of a state license to teach. However, a critical step remains before you can enter your first classroom as a paid teacher: You need to get hired. Making a good impression is essential and involves assembling the right **credentials**. No prin-

You Decide

Is it fair to test job candidates who have already completed a state-approved teacher education program?

cipal or district human resources office wants to hire someone who barely passed his or her courses or state exams. Given the organizational skills demanded for successful management of a classroom, no one wants to hire a teacher who does not demonstrate careful organizational skills in submitting an application for a job. In some high-needs areas (such as mathematics, special education, and foreign languages), many school districts will hire almost all applicants. In other areas (such as elementary education or history or social studies), although the jobs are just as important, those who are doing the hiring can be more selective. Some school districts can afford to be selective, whereas others have a hard time finding enough qualified teachers. No matter what, you need to be the strongest possible candidate for the job you want.

> **credentials** Certificates or awards that attest to the qualifications, skills, and knowledge learned through a course of study or some other measure.

A QUESTION OF . . .

What job hunting tip would you pass along to a recent graduate?

Have several people look over your résumé before you present it to a potential employer. If you know principals or English teachers who would be willing to review it, then by all means make sure that they do. I was recently on a committee of teachers selected to screen potential candidates for our new principal, and it was painfully obvious which ones had carefully edited their résumés and which ones had not. As a screening committee, our belief was that the unorganized résumés with glaring errors were written by people who did not pay much attention to detail nor cared to use professionalism within the one document that was supposed to make them stand out from all of the other candidates. A poorly constructed résumé does not leave a good impression and is more likely to end up in the "reject" pile. Remember that your résumé is a reflection of who you are and may reveal more about you than you realize.

—*Renee Notaro, sixth-grade English and visual/performing arts teacher* ■

Teachable Moment
Developing a Teaching Portfolio

A teaching portfolio is a collection of materials and information that serves as a record of what you have taught, the impact of your teaching, and your development as a teacher. William Cerbin writes, "At its best a portfolio documents an instructor's approach to teaching, combining specific evidence of instructional strategies and effectiveness in a way that captures teaching's intellectual substance and complexity."

The Center for Instructional Development and Research at the University of Washington describes two types of teaching portfolios: a developmental teaching portfolio, which "is your own reflective record of your teaching [that] provides a place for you to document and reflect on various aspects of your teaching," and an evaluative teaching portfolio, which "you present to someone else to provide them with evidence for a decision about your teaching."

Whereas a résumé captures where you have worked and what you have done there, a teaching portfolio provides greater details about your teaching experience. A teaching portfolio should also be a living document that "does more than simply list what you have done as a teacher. It is both a product and a process. The product is a set of papers that documents and reflects on your teaching effectiveness, your students' learning, and your teaching development over time. It is also a continuous process of editing, taking material out and adding new material, and, generally, reflecting on your progress as you grow as a teacher."

Thus, a teaching portfolio can be valuable not only when you are pursuing a teaching position but also when you are being evaluated in your current position and as a developmental tool that can support your progress as a teacher.

What should a teaching portfolio include? The contents of your teaching portfolio may be dictated by whether you are building a developmental, an evaluative, or an all-purpose portfolio, but in general, a teaching portfolio will include the following:

- **A reflective statement.** Outline your teaching philosophy, give examples of how you put this philosophy into practice, and explain your growth and evolution as a teacher.
- **Sample curriculum materials.** Include class syllabi, lesson plans, or assignments.
- **Examples of teaching outcomes.** Include samples of graded essays with your comments explaining the grading, or other student work that illustrates the impact of your teaching.
- **Evaluations of your teaching.** Include formal evaluations from students or supervisors, or letters of evaluation from fellow teachers or administrators.
- **Additional supporting material.** Include a video of you teaching, an explanation of ways you are involved in the school outside of the classroom, or illustrations of how you have used technology as a teaching tool.

Be sure to update your portfolio continually. According to the Second Language Teaching and Curriculum Center at the University of Hawaii at Manoa, "Increasingly, employers are asking for various portfolio elements before, during, and after the hiring process. By putting together an organized, cohesive, reflective, and ever-growing portfolio, you better prepare yourself to show who you are as a teacher and what you offer to a potential employer."

Sources: Center for Instructional Development and Research, University of Washington, "Developing a Teaching Portfolio," http://depts.washington.edu/cidrweb/Bulletin/TeachingPortfolio.html; "Developmental Teaching Portfolios," http://depts.washington.edu/cidrweb/portfolio/developmental.html; "Evaluative Teaching Portfolios," http://depts.washington.edu/cidrweb/portfolio/evaluative.html; Graduate Student Instructor Teaching & Resource Center, University of California–Berkeley, "What Is a Teaching Portfolio?" and "What Should Be Included in a Teaching Portfolio?," http://gsi.berkeley.edu/resources/portfolio/index.html; Teacher Portfolio & Preparation Series, Second Language Teaching & Curriculum Center, University of Hawaii at Manoa, "TiPPS for Teacher Portfolios," http://www.lll.hawaii.edu/sltcc/tipps/portfolio.html

QUESTIONS

- What materials do you already have that you could put in your teaching portfolio? What materials would you need to prepare or develop to put in your portfolio?
- What would you hope to communicate through your teaching portfolio?

Teachable Moment

The Interview

Edward Eggleston wrote *The Hoosier Schoolmaster* as a fictional account of the life and adventures of a schoolteacher in rural Indiana in the early 19th century. The book opens with the story's hero and soon-to-be-teacher, Ralph Hartsook, enduring his job interview with "old Jack Means," who seemed to be the only authority who mattered in the schools of Flat Creek, Indiana:

> Want to be a school-master, do you? You? Well, what would you do in Flat Crick deestrick, I'd like to know? Why the boys have driv off the last two, and licked the one afore them like blazes. You might teach a summer school, when nothin' but children come. But I 'low it takes a right smart man to be a school-master in Flat Crick in the winter. They'd pitch you out of doors, sonny, neck and heels, afore Christmas.

It was clear what the priorities were in Flat Creek, just as it was clear who made the decisions. Means soon resolved the issue, saying that he had no objection if Hartsook thought he could "trust [his] hide in Flat Crick school-house." Means added that, although there were other school trustees, since he paid the most taxes in the district, the others let him make the decisions. So Hartsook got the job.

In describing Hartsook's job interview, Eggleston captured what was far too often the reality of the life of a rural 19th-century school teacher in the United States—the requirements for the job, the expectations, the daily experiences, and the power relationships with the rest of the community. Luckily, the rules for getting hired have changed. School board members don't hire individual teachers. Those who do the hiring usually want to know much more than whether the prospective teacher can handle a class and can avoid getting "pitched" out the door before Christmas—though classroom management remains a key skill asked about in many interviews. Perseverance, sometimes in the face of someone as difficult

as "old Jack Means" or others who might make the hiring process less than pleasant, remains the key to landing a good teaching job.

QUESTIONS

- Have you ever been interviewed for a job (e.g., a summer job, part-time work)? Was the experience pleasant or unpleasant? What did the person interviewing you really want to know about you? If you got the job, did you think the questions you were asked related to the work you had to do?

- As you think ahead to a possible interview for your first teaching job, what is the most important thing you would want a prospective school leader to know about you? How would you make sure he or she found out that information, whether or not you were asked about it directly?

In Chapter 12, you were asked to write your own philosophy of education. Take another look at what you wrote. Are you clear on the kind of teacher you want to be (not just the grade or subject matter you want to teach, but the style—the particular kind of care, compassion, and passion—that you want to bring to your work with young people)? Update your philosophy if need be so that it makes clear what you believe and what you want for yourself and your students. Make this paper the first draft of the one you might submit as part of a portfolio for a job interview. There is a good chance you may be asked for it.

Join the Dialogue

how a school and a district *want* to be perceived. Almost every school and school district has its own Web site, and these contain a great deal of information about where the schools are located, how well the students are performing, and what the school and the school district value the most. You will make a strong impression if you come to an interview having looked carefully at the available Web sites and any other information you can find. It will help you decide if this is a good place for you to work. When you get to your interview, ask a lot of questions. Principals and other administrators respect someone who comes to the interview well informed and curious. Few people mind answering questions about the place where they work.

Those who do the most hiring of teachers note that successful candidates have had some meaningful experience in teaching and can speak about that experience with a sense of personal authority and confidence. Nearly everyone applying for a teaching job has done some amount of **student teaching**. The person who has done more, or who has worked with young people in other circumstances, is going to be the most appealing candidate. It also helps if you can describe moments of success

> **student teaching** Program in which a student in a teacher preparation program spends time teaching in a real classroom under the supervision, and occasional direction, of an experienced teacher; usually done in the last semesters of a program.

Finding a Supportive School

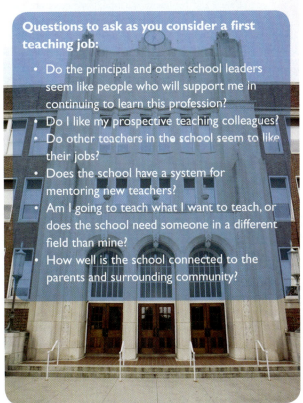

Questions to ask as you consider a first teaching job:

- Do the principal and other school leaders seem like people who will support me in continuing to learn this profession?
- Do I like my prospective teaching colleagues?
- Do other teachers in the school seem to like their jobs?
- Does the school have a system for mentoring new teachers?
- Am I going to teach what I want to teach, or does the school need someone in a different field than mine?
- How well is the school connected to the parents and surrounding community?

When asked what they look for in selecting a new teacher, principals and human resources officers usually say similar things. They want to know that the person will be a good "fit" for the position. Not all teachers and all schools are interchangeable parts. Different schools have different philosophies of education. Different districts, schools, and departments want teachers with different ways of teaching. Many school districts will ask you to submit a paper on your own philosophy of education as part of a portfolio of materials about you. Whether you submit it in writing or are asked the question in an interview, you need to be able to present yourself as a candidate who has a clear, well-thought-out, and specific philosophy of education when seeking a first job and establishing a successful career. Being vague or presenting yourself as someone who has not thought about these issues is not a strong starting point.

The question of "fit" is important, not just to those doing the hiring but also to the person seeking a position. Nothing could be worse than teaching in a place where you feel you simply do not belong because of differences in philosophy or approach to the education of young people. Research the district and school before you show up for an interview. Using the Internet, you can determine

Ten Tips for Interviewing for Your First Teaching Job

1. In order to get the interview, your cover letter is the chance to sell yourself to the screening/**hiring committee** and set yourself apart from the many other applicants they may be considering. Address it directly to the school principal *by name*, make sure it is absolutely error free, and give the readers a sense of who you are and what you have to offer. A bland formulaic letter won't make the cut if the market is competitive. On the other hand, don't make it too long—no more than two pages in a font size that respects the readers' varying acuity.

2. Another thing to spend time on before interviewing is question and answer rehearsal. You may have a chance to do some mock interviews as part of your program or with a friend. If not, do it on your own by getting a good interviewing book or by finding a Web site that provides typical questions. Write responses out or use a voice-recording tool or a friend as a sounding board. The more you can anticipate and prepare, the more relaxed and confident you'll be. Have concrete examples or illustrations in mind to accompany your responses.

3. Create a "leave behind" portfolio—whether or not you've also created a larger one-of-a-kind professional portfolio. Not all committees are interested in, or have time for, a thorough review of all applicants' portfolios. Bring along your full portfolio to pass around if asked to do so, or for you to make reference to a particular item in response to a question. Get attractive, professional copies made of just the essential items—cover letter, résumé, letters of recommendation, one or two other items—and put them together in a nice folder that you can leave behind. Creating a CD version will demonstrate your technology skills, but you can't count on people taking the time to look at it until you reach the finalist stage.

4. Make sure you know where you're going! If possible, make a trial run before your interview. If you get lost or delayed on the day of your interview, you'll be late and stressed out—not a good way to start. Much better to arrive with time to sip the water you've remembered to bring and use a restroom.

5. Think professionally when you choose your clothing and your language. You may have heard or observed that a particular school is casual. There is plenty of time to further assess the school culture, rules, and administrative standards and adjust your style *after* you've been hired.

6. When you arrive, remember that you are creating a first impression for everyone you see: the security guard, parents in the hallway or office, the secretaries, students, a visiting school board member, PTA president, and other potential employers or co-workers—before you even meet with the hiring committee. All encounters should give people evidence of your professionalism, friendliness, confidence, and poise. Meanwhile, you are getting a sense of what is called the "school climate" by seeing how various interactions occur in the school and if you feel it is a place for you.

7. Do your best to relax and "be yourself." If you know that your hands shake when you're nervous, fold them in front of yourself and don't attempt to pick up the coffee or water you've been offered. Give people a sense of your personality as you warm up. The committee wants to get a sense of what you will be like as a colleague and you want them to know who you are—and choose you over others. You won't be happy for long in a place where you can't be yourself.

8. Just as the committee members are "sizing you up" as a potential colleague and teacher of their students, you should be alert to the social dynamics in the room. Do you feel comfortable or intimidated? Are people treating you and each other with respect? Does the principal or other leader seem to have positive relationships with the committee members? One effective way to convey your "people skills" while you assess body language and other indicators is to be generous with your eye contact. When responding to a question, share your eye contact with all in the room, rather than responding only to the individual who posed the question.

9. Provide evidence that you are positive, respectful, and nonjudgmental. You may have had difficult, even terrible, situations with cooperating teachers, students, parents, and professors along the way. In response to a question that asks about a challenge, convey your understanding of multiple perspectives and the complexities of dealing with conflict. That's a person they will want to work with—not someone who seems quick to judge or blame others. Save the venting for your journal or friends.

10. Finally, be prepared to figure out what to say when you don't know what to say. You're a beginner and can't possibly know everything about curriculum, special programs, or how to handle a particular situation. If you're really thrown a curve ball, it's generally better to talk about your eagerness to learn more from your mentor, colleagues, or professional development than it is to pretend you know more than you do and be "found out" later, or to give an opinion that you regret after the interview.

Source: Courtesy of Elizabeth McDonald, New York University (former elementary school principal)

hiring committee Designated group of people who hold authority in the school and decide which potential teacher applicant to place in an open position or to make appropriate recommendations to a principal or other administrator who makes the final decision.

with students as well as moments of failure, especially if you can also say what you would do to be sure that the failures are not repeated. Teachers have an extraordinary level of freedom from supervision once they are hired and in their own classroom. Those doing the hiring want to be sure that the person they are selecting will use that freedom correctly.

>> How Will I Survive as a New Teacher?

THE CRITICAL FIRST YEAR

Kelley Dawson Salas teaches fourth grade in Milwaukee, Wisconsin. She recalls when she began teaching:

My alarm had not yet gone off, but I was wide awake. My stomach was in knots and I knew I

Promising Practices

Get a Foot in the Door

Through my own experiences, if your goal is to obtain a teaching position completely on your own merit (that is, you do not have any inside pull to get you through the door), there is one tried and true method that is sure to impress the hiring principal. What I have done (successfully in two different states) is to give the principal a call in the early spring and express my desire to visit his or her school. It is best to point out your specific interest in the school at this time. For example, after teaching at the elementary level for five years, I was ready for a change and decided that I wanted to teach middle school students. Thus, I explained to the principal that I would love an opportunity to observe the teachers in his middle school while they interacted with their own students. In doing so, I was making sure that this would be the right move for me.

Once invited, equip yourself with a professional-looking folder or portfolio containing a list of questions that you would like to ask the teachers and the principal. Most importantly, include a copy of your résumé, but do not present it to the principal until you have completed your tour and have had most of your questions answered. If you are a gracious guest and remember to thank your host for taking time away from a very busy schedule to accommodate you, chances are pretty good that your "visit" will end in an interview, or you may

be invited back for one at a later date. Whatever the outcome, do not leave without offering your résumé to the principal. Furthermore, don't forget to point out what aspects of the school most impressed you and how you would be honored to become a part of this particular educational team.

With this approach, not only do you "get your foot in the door" and have an excellent opportunity to make a positive impression with your potential employer, but you are also making sure that the school is the right fit for you. You, in your own way, are "interviewing" the people with whom you may be working. Consider this to be the "hands-on" approach in job hunting.

Source: Renee Notaro, sixth-grade teacher

would not be able to eat breakfast. I longed to turn over, go back to sleep, wait for the alarm, hit snooze.

But there was no way. It was September, a school day, a few weeks into my first year of teaching. . . .

I dragged myself out of bed and called a friend. My worries poured forth: I'm no good at this. It's too hard for me to learn the things I need to learn. There are so many jobs that would be easier and pay better. Finally, I called the question: Should I just walk away from this whole thing?[1]

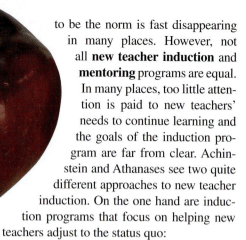

You Decide

How long should you stay in a job or profession before you know if it's the right fit for you?

Few teachers cannot identify with these words—the wide-awake moments, the nausea, the self-doubt, the question "Should I just walk away?" They all seem to go with the territory of entering one of the most rewarding, and most challenging, professions.

The first year in any new field of endeavor is usually difficult. All the colleagues and routines are new. Other people seem to have knowledge and expectations that are not shared immediately. Fair or not, the new person is always being watched to see if he or she measures up. These issues can be exacerbated in the teaching profession. As educational researchers Betty Achinstein and Steven Z. Athanases note in their book *Mentors in the Making: Developing New Leaders for New Teachers*, "Most teachers still experience the 'sink-or-swim' career introduction, isolated in their classrooms, unsupported by colleagues, with little power over decision making and few opportunities for learning." Recall the discussion in Chapter 1 in which researchers noted that approximately 30% of new teachers leave within the first 3 years and the proportion rises to 50% in five years. The numbers can be even higher in high-poverty, urban, and rural districts where the need for first-rate teachers is the greatest.

More school districts are taking seriously the problems facing new teachers. The "sink-or-swim" model that used

to be the norm is fast disappearing in many places. However, not all **new teacher induction** and **mentoring** programs are equal. In many places, too little attention is paid to new teachers' needs to continue learning and the goals of the induction program are far from clear. Achinstein and Athanases see two quite different approaches to new teacher induction. On the one hand are induction programs that focus on helping new teachers adjust to the status quo:

If one believes that the new teacher is a survivor in a challenging context, trying to impart basic knowledge to well-managed kids, then mentoring entails helping novices adjust to new environments, learn routines, keep management plans in place, and learn some tips and techniques of teaching. . . . These conceptions identify the purposes of induction as enculturating new teachers into the current system to help novices fit into their new environments, rather than critiquing or challenging existing schooling practices.

For most novices, there are certainly days on which this approach seems like it might be enough. Learning some tips and fitting in can seem appealing. In teaching, however, "survival" is never sufficient. Achinstein and Athanases ask for much more:

Recent reforms necessitate different norms than those identified in the survival models. These call for teachers to be change agents, reflective practitioners, collaborative colleagues, and lifelong learners—educators who are student-centered, equity-focused, and constructivist. These calls challenge the status quo of teaching and schooling and, therefore, of mentoring.

Idealistic as they may sometimes sound, only these kinds of norms for new teachers (or for any teachers) can move them from being cogs in a wheel to professional educators who take charge of their work and hold themselves accountable for the success of all their students. These norms are also absolutely essential if one is to resist some of the pressures to merely conform to the kind of deadening, highly scripted curriculum that is found in some schools today.[2]

One of the most effective means of addressing this problem has been the development of a robust system of teacher mentoring. In many school districts, every new teacher

A QUESTION OF . . .

What do you wish someone had told you before you began teaching?

I wish someone had told me it's not about how smart you are in your graduate school courses—it's how you execute in your own classroom when you teach."

—*Nekia Wise, first grade teacher* ■

new teacher induction System of support and guidance offered to novice teachers in the beginning of their careers.

mentoring Act of serving as an advisor and trusted guide to a less experienced person; often part of a new teacher induction program.

New Teacher Survival Guide

Antonio Ramírez, a middle and high school teacher in Milwaukee, Wisconsin, developed a number of tips for how to survive as a new teacher—many things he learned the hard way or just needed to persevere through until he "found his groove." Although he wrote this piece for teachers of color, his advice can apply to all new teachers who are similarly learning to "find their groove":

1. **Communicate with students in nontraditional ways.** Your relationships with students are the best part about being a teacher. Every day, talk with students about things that have nothing to do with the classroom. Know what they like. Ask about and get to know their families. Attend a birthday party, quinceañera, or poetry reading after school.

2. **Don't fear discipline.** Don't think you can be a classroom teacher without learning how to discipline. Some new teachers command an interesting mix of respect and fear from the minute they step in a classroom. Some, including myself, don't. If you are like me, be aware of it and be aware that you can change it. Ask those teachers that discipline out of love and respect if you can sit in and watch them. The best way to learn how to teach well is sitting and watching an excellent teacher.

3. **Educate yourself.** Although it's difficult during the first hectic years as a teacher, don't leave all the theories you studied in teacher education courses back at school. Theories are tools that help reflect on the past and prepare for future experiences. Hours of sleep I lost by reading Paulo Freire, Gloria Ladson-Billings, Herbert Kohl, and bell hooks were more than made up for by a rejuvenated sense of purpose and energy.

4. **Have realistic expectations for yourself.** Throughout my first year, I'd feel like a master teacher one day and the next I'd be seriously considering what other career I should pursue after quitting. But a piece of advice that kept me sane through the first year of teaching came from a fellow teacher who said, "Your first year's goal is to survive. Nothing more." While this may seem a bit scary, it definitely helped to remember that simple goal on late Sunday nights when I had a mountain of papers and piles of unfinished lesson plans on my desk.

5. **Get to know your allies.** Meet other young teachers and like-minded teachers and staff as soon as possible. In my first year of teaching, I didn't have a support network of other teachers. Preoccupied with crafting the perfect lesson plan and keeping up with grading, I had lost contact with most of my university classmates. I didn't go out of my way to establish strong friendships with other teachers in my new school. As a result, I struggled in silence my first year.

6. **Don't be afraid to ask.** Some schools have a natural culture of "being in it together," where lesson plans, resources, and sympathy are spread around liberally.

Source: Antonio Ramírez, "A Survival Guide for New Teachers of Color," *The Nation,* August 31, 2009.

Most don't. Many new teachers in the latter situation fall into the trap of thinking they'll look incapable if they have to ask a question or for advice. In my experience, the reverse is true. The most successful teachers share, borrow, and steal colleagues' ideas and inspiration.

7. **Know your union.** Teachers' unions have also made consistent calls for increased support for new teachers and better recruitment of teachers of color. Teachers active in our union were committed, serious educators who fought for students and took time to mentor younger teachers.

8. **Take time to reflect.** Teaching has emotional, physical, and psychological aspects that are overwhelming, especially in your first years. Be sure to take time to truly reflect on successes and failures in the classroom and to congratulate yourself on your achievements. Think about your most difficult students and develop strategies on how to get through to them.

9. **Take time to not reflect.** The first years of teaching can easily take over your life. In my first year, I worked seven days a week, usually until nine or ten every night, and was miserable. Remember to continue to make time for parts of life that have nothing to do with school and that you truly enjoy. Stay connected with family and friends. Doing things to relax and take your mind off teaching will allow you to return to the classroom refreshed.

10. **Teach for at least two years.** I remember going to school just as the sun was coming up and being jealous of construction workers, bus drivers, and cashiers who didn't have to face classrooms full of students and desks full of papers every morning. I seriously considered quitting several times the first year. But by the end of my second year, I started to imagine myself as a truly good teacher. I was engaging more students in serious conversations about the meanings of race, history, and culture. I felt like I was really becoming a teacher.

Did you know?

Acknowledging how much support first-year teachers need, Texas A&M University–Corpus Christi developed a program called SOS: Strategies of Success, designed to support beginning teachers. The program has been working: The school conducted a study in 2005 to determine how likely program participants were to stay in teaching.[4] For the three cohort groups studied, SOS program participants had a 98 percent retention rate, compared to 88 percent for graduates of the teacher education program who did not participate in SOS, and 70 percent for new teachers across the state of Texas.

is assigned a senior colleague to act as a mentor. In some districts, the school or the school district selects the mentor. In other cases, the teacher union plays a major role. Some colleges and universities that prepare teachers have developed new programs to stay in touch with their graduates and to get them actively involved in the mentoring process. Recent research sponsored by the Carnegie Corporation of New York has demonstrated that multiple modes of mentoring—from the school in which the novice teacher is employed and from the university from which she or he graduated—may be the most effective. Some issues are so school specific that only someone intimately involved with the school can be an effec-

Connections

Recall the discussion in Chapter 1 about the effectiveness of the mentoring system used in Toledo, Ohio.

Teachable Moment
Required Reading

A valuable resource for any new teacher is Jonathan Kozol's *Letters to a Young Teacher.* Addressing Francesca, who represents several novice teachers whose rooms Kozol has visited and with whom he has talked, this long-time veteran critic of the public schools offers wise, warm, and thoughtful advice on everything from coping with young students who have "decided in advance that we are someone they won't like and who probably should not be trusted" to wondering "whether anyone I know who's setting education policy these days ever speaks about the sense of fun the children have, or ought to have, in public school or the excitement that they take when they examine interesting creatures such as beetle-bugs and ladybugs and other oddities of nature that they come upon—or even merely whether they are happy children and enjoy the hours that they spend with us in school." In the end Kozol concludes his advice by saying:

Source: Letters to a Young Teacher, by Jonathan Kozol, 2007, Three Rivers Press.

Resist the deadwood of predictability. Embrace the unexpected. Revel in the run-on sentences. Celebrate silliness. Dig deep into the world of whim. Sprinkle your children's lives, no matter how difficult many of those lives may be, with hundreds of brightly colored seeds of jubilation. Enjoy the wild flowers!

These are words of wisdom and encouragement that every first-year teacher, as well as every 20- or 40-year veteran, needs to hear.

QUESTIONS

- Why does a teacher need to be prepared for students who have "decided in advance that we are someone they won't like and who probably should not be trusted"? What is a teacher's responsibility in this situation?
- Kozol tells us to "celebrate silliness." Do you agree with this advice?

What About Me?

Preparing for the Challenges Ahead

If you read enough of the statistics about teacher **attrition rates**, you might think somebody is trying to scare you from entering the field entirely. Yet educators are open and honest about these data not only to raise awareness of the challenges of retaining teachers but also to find solutions. A report from the National Center for Education Statistics projects that an additional half-million teachers will be needed in elementary and secondary schools by the year 2017. How much easier would it be to meet that increased demand if retention rates were increasing instead?

> **attrition rate** Amount of shrinking or loss in number of participants in a venture; can refer to the loss of students through dropping out of high school or the loss of practicing teachers over a period of time.

Of course, as a potential teacher, you are about to become part of that statistic. Will you be one of the teachers who stays in the field for a long career, or will you be a teacher who leaves after just a few years? It's easy today, with your whole career in front of you, to imagine the best. But sometimes, it's best to prepare for the worst, so that you can think about how you might handle the trials and struggles that most teachers face. Take a few minutes now to think about how you deal with challenges, and how the lessons you have learned from your experiences might help you once you get to the classroom:

- What is the biggest challenge you have faced in your life so far? Why was it such a challenge for you?
- How did you respond to this challenge? Are you happy with the way you responded? What lessons can you learn from the experience of facing this challenge that might help you when you face a challenge as a teacher?
- Who is in your support network? Who do you turn to when you need advice, support, feedback, or encouragement? Have you talked with those people about how they might support you as a teacher, or how you might lean on them? If yes, how did the conversations go? If no, what might be the benefits of those conversations?
- Who might you add to your support network that could make it even stronger? What fellow teachers can you include whose experience and wisdom would prove valuable to you? How else might you expand your support network?
- What stress management or other coping strategies have been successful for you in the past? Do you exercise? Write in a journal? Visit a friend? How might you use these strategies to help you through a challenging situation at school?

Source: "Number of teachers in elementary and secondary schools, and instructional staff in postsecondary degree-granting institutions, by control of institution: Selected years, fall 1970 through fall 2017," table 4 in *Digest of Education Statistics: 2008*, U.S. Department of Education, Institute of Education Sciences, National Center for Education Statistics, http://nces.ed.gov/programs/digest/d08/index.asp.

tive mentor; for other issues, especially in those moments of failure and frustration that every teacher experiences, a mentor who is a little more distant and not an employee of the school or district can be more helpful.[3]

STAYING, SURVIVING, THRIVING, CONTRIBUTING

Kelley Dawson Salas's friend gave her some important advice for the first year of teaching: "Don't add to your difficulties by beating up on yourself. Let up a little so you have the time and the space to become a good teacher." She fought the tendency to become isolated by taking advantage of professional development activities, collaborating with colleagues at her school, and joining with other education activists to engage in issues that were important to

her. She also received plenty of less helpful advice of the "you need to be a drill sergeant" variety. Through it all, she created space and support for herself that allowed her to do much more than survive. She knows her own doubts and shortcomings, but she is much better at coping. According to Salas,

> *Whenever I feel overwhelmed by the lack of support, I fight the urge to leave teaching. Instead, I try to speak up about what teachers need to succeed.*
>
> *As I struggle toward my vision of good teaching, I remind myself of what I have accomplished so far. I am less isolated and have close ties with other progressive teachers. I am more confident about developing curriculum and a teaching style that reflects my politics. I still need time and guidance,*

How Can I Make a Difference?

A Personal Learning Network

Many organizations and institutions are trying to address the challenges teachers face, but a Personal Learning Network (PLN) puts the power in your hands—both for you to help yourself and for you to help fellow teachers.

A PLN is "a collection of resources assembled by an individual to enhance and enrich" his or her own personal learning, according to education blogger Jason Epstein. Those resources can be information based, such as blogs you read (or write), or people based, such as other educators whose insight and perspective you seek out regularly.

The Internet, and social networking in particular, has made it possible to expand your PLN well beyond people you've met face to face. Kelly Tenkely, a technology teacher and blogger, recommends using Twitter to build your PLN online. "Twitter is an excellent place for new teachers to connect, collaborate, share ideas and struggles with educators around the world," she says. "When joining Twitter, make sure to fill out your profile with information related to education."

As the name implies, a PLN is personalized, something you can customize to your evolving needs. What's more, as you build a PLN to support your own development, you can also become a part of someone else's PLN, making a difference in the professional development of other teachers, and contributing to the larger education conversation.

Sources: "The Personal Learning Network (PLN)," by Jason Epstein, August 16, 2009, The Educators' Royal Treatment, http://www.educatorsroyaltreatment.com/2009/08/the-personal-learning-network-pln.html; "Top 10 Technology Tips for New Teachers," by Kelly Tenkely, The Apple, http://www.theapple.com/benefits/articles/8506-top-10-technology-tips-for-new-teachers.

QUESTIONS

- How could a PLN be most helpful to you? What information or topics would you like to learn more about?
- Do you already have a PLN? What Web sites, blogs, newspapers, or magazines do you read regularly to stay on top of current issues in education? Who do you talk with about teaching strategies and ideas? How could you expand your PLN, or start one if you don't have one already?

---

but some of the conditions are in place for me to someday become the teacher I want to be.

I have a long way to go. But I'm on my way.[5]

This attitude, and not an attempt to be a "hero," is the key to success for nearly all teachers.

In the first **Reading** for this chapter, Sonia Nieto offers her own thoughts and those of other teachers she has interviewed in *What Keeps Teachers Going?* Nieto says that, although teaching is hard work, it is also possible to get good at it quite soon. As you face difficulties in teaching, especially in the beginning, it is important to remember Junia Yearwood's sense that the "light in [her students'] eyes" keeps her going after 20 years of city teaching and Mary Cowhey's report that a combination of parents, principals, students, colleagues, and the opportunity to continue her own life as a student help to keep her going. In reading these stories and many others, two conclusions quickly become clear. First, there is no magic bullet that sustains teachers year after year in the sometimes very difficult work of teaching. Second, a number of recurring themes—most of all, taking delight in your students, finding other teachers who can be a support network, and finding a school that is supportive of your approach to the profession—are absolutely essential if you are to survive and thrive in teaching over the long term.

As a former principal and current teacher educator, Elizabeth McDonald also has some suggestions for surviving during that difficult first year and beyond. Among other things, she recommends:

- Maintain a life and interests outside of school. As important as it is to work hard and maintain a thoughtful commitment to your work, it is also important to your physical and mental well-being that you set boundaries, take breaks, and exercise.

- Maintain a sense of humor and perspective.

- Keep a journal as an outlet for your frustration and as grist for reflection.

- Network and find other teachers and all the resources available for teachers through the Internet.

Generations of teachers have found ways to survive and flourish in their careers while also maintaining a full life outside school. In the end, it is all a matter of balance and finding ways to maintain enthusiasm—for teaching and for life.

>> What Kind of Teacher Do I Want to Be?

During that challenging first year of teaching, merely surviving as a teacher and overcoming fears may seem like quite enough. In the end, however, every aspiring teacher wants to do more—to be not just an adequate teacher but an excellent one. As Robert Fried says in the first **Reading**, "good enough" is never really good enough. Any teacher truly worthy of his or her profession wants to be remembered as more than "a 'pretty good teacher' who made chemistry or algebra or tenth-grade English 'sort of interesting.'" We all want to be like the teachers Fried describes who "opened up the world of the mind to some students who had no one else to make them feel that they were capable of doing great things with test tubes, trumpets, trigonometry, or T. S. Eliot."

In the final **Reading**, Jacqueline Jordan Irvine describes one of the key elements in teacher greatness. As Irvine reports, more and more policy makers are calling for the preparation of what are now called "caring and competent teachers." The trick, as she notes, is to be clear about what the words *caring* and *competent* mean and then prepare yourself to meet that standard.

In her article, "Caring, Competent Teachers in Complex Classrooms," Irvine describes two very different teachers, both of whom in her judgment meet the high standard she would set for being a caring and competent teacher. There is Ms. Little, the White teacher who has a strong social consciousness that leads her to define being a caring teacher as well as a competent teacher as making sure that "her students pass the English Advanced Placement (AP) exam so that they can succeed in college and leave behind the desolation of the urban community in which they live." Little is clear that her caring and her competence drive her to focus on her students' academic success. As she says at one point, "I'm not their damn mama, I'm their English teacher."

The other teacher that Irvine describes, Ms. Moultrie, has a very different definition of both care and competence. As a caring, African American teacher working with mostly African American students, Ms. Moultrie, who is known as Mama Moultrie, sees her role very much as a surrogate parent. She uses her classroom as "a pulpit from which she uses literature to teach values, racial pride and uplift, and hard work." The focus of all her work is on preparing her students for college *and* for life.

Irvine regards both Moultie and Little as models of caring, competent teachers; she believes there is no one definition of a caring, competent, or excellent teacher. She asks, "Is it possible to determine if one is more caring or more competent than the other?" The answer, it seems, is no. Both women are caring, effective teachers in spite of their different approaches to their work.

Part of being successfully caring *and* competent may be the third element that Robert Fried introduces into the equation: passion. Observing Maria Ortiz, a middle school teacher in Hartford, Connecticut, and then other elementary, middle, and high school teachers, Fried notices that it is hard to name the unique essence of the best of them:

PORTRAIT OF AN EDUCATOR

Top Teachers

What makes a top teacher? Is it dedication to students? Creativity in the classroom? Perseverance in engaging the community? It's all this and more, as shown by the following examples of three Teachers of the Year. Since 1952, the National Teacher of the Year Program has honored exemplary teachers for their work. A committee of leaders in the field of education choose the National Teacher of the Year from the winners of State Teacher of the Year awards.

Alex Kajitani was recognized as 2009's California Teacher of the Year and one of the top four finalists for the National Teacher of the Year award. Known as the Rappin' Mathematician, Kajitani's major focus is bridging the achievement gap that occurs in low-income schools. Realizing that his middle-school students could remember the words to their favorite rap songs, but not rules for improper fractions, Kajitani decided to craft raps for math fundamentals. The idea caught on and he began creating more raps, eventually putting together a "Routine Rap" that reminded students of the daily classroom routine and why it was important. Students are required to create their own math raps, as well, and often create and film their own music videos for the raps. As an excellent communicator and creative thinker, Kajitani reached out to students who otherwise might have given up on school. As a result, the math scores in his classrooms have shot up and are now above average for the district.

Alex Kajitani

Washington state music educator Andrea Peterson received the 2007 National Teacher of the Year award, which was unusual because winners are not often specialists in one discipline. Peterson's teaching skills, however, far outweighed any doubts about her receiving the award. When Peterson began teaching in the Granite Falls School District in 1997, the music program had little funding and few resources—the secondary band owned only six percussion instruments, two of which were broken. To provide for her students, she lobbied the school board and administration for extra

Andrea Peterson

funds. After canvassing parents and the community, Peterson was able to revitalize the elementary and high school programs with more than $55,000 in new music equipment. Students now perform in state and national music competitions and can choose from a number of school programs, such as elementary choir, marching or jazz band, and high school chorus. Peterson believes in the ability of music to aid with other subject areas and, as such, has implemented cross-curriculum classes. In one of these classes, students are asked to create and perform an interpretive musical based on a book they have read in another class. Peterson knows that music can unlock a student's potential, whether by providing self-confidence and creativity, reinforcing mathematical concepts, or giving them discipline.

The third profiled top teacher, Kimberly Oliver, received the National Teacher of the Year award in 2006. In her Maryland kindergarten classroom, Oliver holds the philosophy that every student learns in different ways and her teaching style must adapt to each. In a school where 9 out of 10 students qualify for free or reduced-cost meals and three-fourths speak a language other than English at home, Oliver has had to adapt her teaching style to a variety of learning styles and challenges. She believes that for students to achieve they must have the support and compassion of an entire community. When she became a teacher, Oliver was faced with a school in danger of being restructured due to declining academic performance. She built up a professional learning community for staff that emphasized collaboration and began reaching out to parents

Kimberly Oliver

with reading events, such as "Books and Supper Night," and regular phone calls. Through her creation of several programs focused on consistency in curriculum, the school improved substantially and in 2001 had the greatest percentage increase in test scores in the school system. No Child Left Behind requirements were met, or exceeded, at the school from 2003 to 2005. Because of Oliver's persistence and determination, an entire community became involved with their children's education.

So, what do all of these educators have in common? What makes them top teachers? They all noticed problems and found unique solutions to them. They all used creative and persistent means to get their communities and administrations involved. In the end, however, despite differences in location, grade levels, and socioeconomic factors, these three educators stayed focused entirely on one thing—the academic achievement of their students.

Sources: National Teacher of the Year Program. Council of Chief State School Officers, http://www.ccsso.org/projects/National_Teacher_of_the_Year; "A California Teacher of the Year, 'The Rappin' Mathematician' Is One of Four Finalists for Top National Teaching Honor," California Department of Education, January 14, 2009, http://www.cde.ca.gov/nr/ne/yr09/yr09rel8.asp; "Andrea Peterson, 2007 National Teacher of the Year," Council of Chief State School Officers, http://www.ccsso.org/projects/national_teacher_of_the_year/national_teachers/9842.cfm; Grace Rubenstein, "Kimberly Oliver: National Teacher of the Year," Edutopia, September 2006; http://www.edutopia.org/kimberly-oliver; "Kimberly Oliver: 2006 National Teacher of the Year," Council of Chief State School Officers, http://www.ccsso.org/projects/national_teacher_of_the_year/national_teachers/8144.cfm.

Our inability to translate great stories into a useful pedagogy is due to our encountering something that people find hard to identify, talk about, or hold onto intellectually. I believe that what we are dealing with is passion.

Fried gives many examples of the kind of passionate teaching he is talking about. Irvine's Little and Moultrie certainly each have passion. Perhaps it is the combination of all three attributes—caring, competence, and passion—that makes for great teaching.

If both Irvine and Fried agree on anything, it is that the best teachers can be very different from each other. Neither essay puts forth one model of great teaching. Moultrie and Little are very different teachers. Ortiz and Ervine, Griffin, Clarke, Fuentes, Bisaccio, Lukas, and Sullivan—some of the other passionate teachers Fried describes—are very different from each other. But all these teachers bring something special to their work. They know their subject, they know how to teach it, and they care deeply that their students will learn, succeed, and prosper—in school and beyond. Perhaps the right word for this is, indeed, passion.

Arriving in your first classroom, milestone though it is, is only the first of many steps. Much more will remain to be done to achieve the kind of professional mastery that makes a teacher feel comfortable in front of a class, confident in the management of the room, and sure that the students are learning what they need to be learning. Much more beyond that is needed to be the kind of teacher every teacher yearns to be—the caring, competent, and passionate teacher who is remembered for making a difference in the lives of many, many young people. Continuing to grow in that direction is part of the challenge, and the joy, of teaching.

We began this book by asking you, the aspiring teacher, to join in a conversation involving a series of questions that many people considering a career in teaching ask their instructors, their classmates, their families and peers, and themselves. As we've explored potential answers to these questions, we have read and reviewed a range of material from many different authors. Some of the authors agree with each other; others disagree sharply. In many instances, they agree with certain nuances but find other aspects that set their beliefs apart. Researchers and educators can look at the same data and often come up with different interpretations or solutions.

You were also asked to reflect carefully on your own education—all those years you spent in K–12 classrooms observing teachers and experiencing schools as institutions with their own unique customs and values. You also may have had the opportunity to observe classrooms more recently, examining what you remember, have read, or thought about what goes on in schools and what *should* go on in schools, and how schools are different from each other. It is hoped that you now have a more informed understanding of teaching and schooling and the role of professional educators. This experience of reading, observing, and pondering should leave you with a much clearer sense of your own educational philosophy and your own views about teaching. You should also be in a much stronger position to answer what are probably the most critical questions for you at the conclusion of this book:

- Do I still want to be a teacher?
- What kind of teacher do I want to be?
- How can I best prepare myself to be that kind of teacher?

The answers to these questions are yours and yours alone and will continue to evolve in the years to come. It is hoped that you feel more prepared and empowered to embrace that process as you seek to find and develop your own answers and personal philosophies about teaching and your role and responsibilities as an educator.

Join the Dialogue

Although every textbook provides core material that you need to learn and master in order to pass a course, it's important for you to stop and think about what you *really* learned from the whole experience:

- Based on what you read, what surprised you the most about teaching?
- What events or statistics were the most eye-opening?
- What topics or issues had you not heard of prior to taking this course?
- Did your opinions change after reading different viewpoints? For which issues and why?

- Which authors or researchers inspired you the most? Whose philosophies resonated with you and seemed to mimic your own beliefs about teaching and education? Which ones did you disagree with the most?
- Most important, what questions do you have that weren't addressed in the text?

Keep the dialogue going and look for those answers in your next courses and your career.

REVIEW >>

- How do I get my first teaching job?

  Each state grants teaching licenses (or certification) based on the completion of a required course of study, usually in a university-based teacher preparation program. Most states also require applicants to pass a state examination, the most widely used of which is the PRAXIS exam. After receiving a teaching license, you will apply directly to a school district for a teaching position and may be interviewed by someone at the district as well as school level.

- How will I survive as a new teacher?

  As for anyone entering a new career, the initial year can be extremely challenging, and teaching can be more challenging than many fields. Because of the high attrition rate, schools are providing more resources, such as mentoring, to support new teachers and help them transition into the profession. Although there is no one set of guidelines for how to survive and thrive as a teacher, every successful teacher has found his or her own way to balance the challenges of the profession with the goal of providing the most supportive environment and the most effective education possible for all students.

- What kind of teacher do I want to be?

  A number of adjectives could be used to describe a great teacher or great teaching. Just about everyone entering the profession aspires to become that kind of teacher or to deliver that kind of teaching. As described by Robert Fried and Jacqueline Jordan Irvine, it is most likely a combination of caring, competence, and passion that makes for great teaching.

How Will I Survive as a New Teacher?

From *WHAT KEEPS TEACHERS GOING?*

BY SONIA NIETO

Sonia Nieto has spent her life in education, teaching, writing, talking with other teachers. She is among the leaders in the field of multicultural education, but she also cares deeply about the lives of teachers and values their voices much more than the opinions of those who want to tell teachers what they should be doing. In her book *What Keeps Teachers Going?*, she asks, "How do you stick with it, given that teaching is such hard work?" Her own answers and those of the many teachers with whom she spoke and corresponded provide encouraging answers to this basic question.

From that day in 1965 when I first stepped into the fourth-grade classroom where I would start my student teaching, I have experienced the exhilaration, anguish, satisfaction, uncertainty, frustration, and sheer joy that typify teaching. Years later, when I began teaching teachers, I fell in love with the profession all over again. Working with teachers who would in turn prepare young people for the future seemed to me a life worth living. I am as certain today as I was then that this is true.

Yet I also am perplexed about why teachers remain in teaching, why they dedicate their lives to a profession ostensibly honored but generally disrespected by the public in a climate increasingly hostile to public education and fixated on rigid conceptions of "standards" and accountability. There is nothing wrong with standards; on the contrary, it is high time that this concept was used in reference to urban public schools. But unfortunately, the call for standards too often results in a climate that does little besides vilify teachers and their students. This is a punitive climate that may have ominous repercussions not only for many students but also for talented teachers, those who care most deeply about students.

Experience alone, as John Dewey reminds us, is hollow without reflection. My own evolution as a teacher might not have resulted in any particular insights were it not for the ongoing opportunities I've had to think about my experiences as part of the larger context in which education takes place. In what follows, I share my thinking as a teacher and teacher educator and the lessons I've learned along the way. . . .

Lessons Learned Along the Way

I became a teacher in 1966. But I am not now the same teacher I was in 1966, or in 1975, or 1990. As we all do, I have changed a great deal over the years, and so have my practices and ideas about teaching. These changes did not occur without warning; they have been responses to experiences that I have had as a teacher, teacher educator, mentor, mother, grandmother, scholar, and researcher. I have lately become more introspective about where I began, where I am now, and why and how I have changed along the way.

Teaching Is Hard Work. I studied elementary education in college knowing that I wanted to teach young children. But my first assignment was to Junior High School 278, a troubled school in Ocean Hill/Brownsville in Brooklyn. . . . I was one of 35 new teachers in a teaching staff totaling about 75. . . . I was young and naïve. As the only Puerto Rican staff member in the school, I thought I'd have a fairly easy time of it. I hadn't expected discipline to be so arduous; after all, I had been a student at similar schools. Yet the kids I faced every day seemed angrier and more oppositional than what I remembered. Most of all, I was not prepared for the hopelessness that permeated the school on the part of the students and staff. I often went home and cried.

Source: What Keeps Teachers Going? by Sonia Nieto, 2003, Teachers College Press, pp. 9–15, 26–28, 101–105, 128–129.

Becoming a Good Teacher Takes Time. But I didn't give up. I vowed to improve my teaching and to create an affirming climate in my classroom. I worked hard to develop strong and positive relationships with my students and their families.... I also sought out teachers who believed in the young people, and I talked with them about my hopes and fears.... I knew I had a long way to go, but by that first winter, I began to notice a change: My students were listening and paying more attention, and they appeared to be more engaged in their learning.

Social Justice Is Part of Teaching. Two years after I began teaching in that junior high school in Brooklyn, I found out about an elementary school in the Bronx that was beginning an experimental program in bilingual education, only the second such school in the nation.... I was enthusiastic but wary ... For example, I had many questions about the feasibility of bilingual education (after all, I had never been in a bilingual program and I had done well, hadn't I?) and about the school's almost militant support for parental and family involvement. Within a short time, however, I saw with my own eyes the value of both, and I became one of the staunchest advocates for these innovations. I realized that although I had "made it," most others had not; I was one of the lucky ones.... After having come face to face with the effects of inequality at JHS 278, I began to think more seriously about what social justice meant for public education.

There Is No Level Playing Field. Given my own experiences growing up in a struggling, working-class Puerto Rican family in New York City in the 1940s and 1950s, I thought I knew firsthand about inequality. But my work as a teacher with my students whose lives were far more difficult than mine had ever been opened my eyes to the impact of daily, unrelenting injustice and hopelessness. I saw that successful student learning was not simply a matter of positive interactions between individual teachers and their students. I began to understand that conditions outside the control of most classroom teachers, including inequality in schools and outside them, prevented many students from learning.

Education Is Politics. "Education is always political" is a statement that the late Paulo Freire made famous in his landmark book, *Pedagogy of the Oppressed*. A few years after he wrote those words, he pointed out even more directly the relationship between education and politics. "This is a great discovery," he wrote, "education is politics!" And he added, "The teacher has to ask, What kind of politics am I doing in the classroom? That is, in favor of whom am I being a teacher?" These words became riveting to me as my own political awareness developed.... to work with future teachers, and to help them understand teaching as political and ethical work was exhilarating.

Teacher Autobiographies

A number of years ago, I began to experiment with what I called teacher autobiographies. In my work with teachers I asked them to write about how their backgrounds or experiences have influenced their decision to pursue a career in teaching. [Two of the responses to Nieto's request for autobiographies follow.]

My Journey   Junia Yearwood

I was born on the Caribbean Island of Trinidad and was raised and nurtured by my paternal grandmother and aunts on the island of Barbados. My environment instilled in me a strong identity as a woman and as a person of African descent. The value of education and the importance of being able to read and write became clear and urgent when I became fully aware of the history of my ancestors. The story of the enslavement of Africans and the horrors they were forced to endure repulsed and angered me, but the aspect of slavery that most intrigued me was the systematic denial of literacy to my ancestors....

This revelation made my destiny clear. I had to be a Teacher.

My resolve to someday become a teacher was strengthened by my experiences with teachers who had significant and lasting positive effects on my personal and academic growth. I gradually came to realize that the teachers whose classes I was eager to get to and in whose classes I excelled were the ones who treated and nurtured me as an individual, a special person. They pushed, challenged, and cajoled me to study and perform to my full ability. They believed in me; they identified not only my weaknesses but also my strengths and talents. They encouraged me to think, question, and enter into the "conversation" on an equal intellectual footing. They respected my thoughts and opinions and they showed me that they cared. In addition, and just as important, they looked like me. They shared my ancestry, my culture, and my history. They were my role models....

The "light in their eyes," that moment when students are fully engaged and excited about learning, that Sonia Nieto has written about energizes, revitalizes, and keeps me focused. I share my students' successes, their challenges, their hopes, and their dreams. My commitment and passion for learning and teaching wax and wane, sparkle and flicker, but stubbornly keep burning like an eternal flame, a flame that I hope burns bright and helps guide my students on their academic and personal journey through life. In the words of Robert Frost, "I am not a teacher. I am an awakener."

A Way to Live in the World   Mary Cowhey

Teaching is a way to live in the world. I just can't see myself living in this world if I am not doing something positive. Size and effectiveness do not matter too much to me, if I nurture one plant or a large garden, if I help one person well, if I reach 20 children and their families in a year or thousands, what is important is that I do it and do it well, that I do it with heart. The process of teaching, of organizing, of caring, of nurturing—I believe it makes me a better person. . . .

I am thinking of your title/idea, what keeps teachers going in spite of everything. One thing that strikes me as I write this is the importance of the relationships with parents, with families. (By parents I mean all of their loving adults and caregivers). Children are such a mystery. . . . From the start of each school year, even before the school doors open, I work to build that relationship with families. Whether it is done by home visits or arranging some unhurried conversations with families early in the year, that foundation is vital. . . . I care about these families.

What else keeps me going in spite of everything? My principal. I have the most wonderful principal in the world. . . . She creates a climate in our school that allows me to teach and grow the way I do. . . .

Intellectual work—of course there is that. . . . New ideas, new questions to find answers to, new people to ask and find out, new problems to solve, new angles to see things from, motivation to do something that I might not have been passionate about before. . . .

Children. I teach my students like I want my children taught. I want them challenged and loved. . . . They need good teaching, the best. That drives me on.

Good teachers. I often think of teachers who really loved their subject or who really loved me or listened to me or encouraged me or took me seriously or pushed me to do my best work. . . .

[After many such conversations, Nieto concludes her book.]

It is by now a truism that the profession of teaching, although enormously significant in the lives of so many people, is terribly undervalued, undercompensated, and underrespected. We see signs for this everywhere: Teachers take second jobs as cashiers in convenience stores and clean houses during their summer vacations; they spend hundreds and sometimes thousands of dollars of their own money each year on classroom materials; and they spend even more on their continuing education, usually with no compensation from their school districts. Yet the current policy climate at both state and national levels is permeated by a profound disrespect for teachers, especially teachers in urban schools, and for the children they teach. Most politicians, for instance, although they speak often about education, rarely step foot in schools. They tend to stress only accountability, and the tone they use to speak about teachers is sometimes disparaging and unforgiving. But no first-year signing bonus, no teacher test, and no high-stakes test can take the place of a true, enduring respect for teachers. In fact, these things often get in the way of retaining good teachers because they question the intelligence, ability, and commitment of teachers.

One thing we learned from the inquiry group project that we are certain about is this: *No amount of decontextualized "best practices" will keep teachers engaged or committed.* The current discourse in education reform focuses on developing "best practices" as the antidote to both teacher burnout and student underachievement. Our work departs in an essential way from this stance. We have come to the conclusion that it is only when teachers are treated as professionals and intellectuals who care deeply about their students and their craft that they will be enticed to remain in the profession and that new teachers will be attracted to join. We hope that our work illustrates that, rather than a focus on dehumanized "best practices," we need to focus on students and those who best teach them. . . .

Teachers such as Junia need to be supported by teacher educators, administrators, school committees, politicians, and citizens who care about and support with words, deeds, and money the work of schools in our society. If we are really serious about expanding the opportunities for students in our urban public schools, rather than concentrating on high-stakes tests, we should be focusing our efforts on high standards, high expectations, and high finance.

This is the challenge that lies ahead. If we are as concerned about education as we say we are, then we need to do more to change the conditions faced by teachers, especially those who work in underfinanced and largely abandoned urban schools. We need to support those teachers who love their students, who find creative ways to teach them, and who do so under difficult circumstances. We need to celebrate teachers who are as excited about their own learning as they are about the learning of their students. And we need to champion those teachers who value their students' families and find respectful ways to work with them. Above all, we need to expect all teachers to do these things. The children in our public schools deserve no less.

QUESTIONS

1. Nieto says, "We need to celebrate teachers who are excited about their own learning." Think back to your own teachers—in school and in more informal settings—and think of one who was especially excited about learning. What difference did he or she make in your life?

2. Imagine that you have been teaching for 3 years. What kind of letter would you want to be able to write in answer to the question "What keeps teachers going?"

What Kind of Teacher Do I Want to Be?

From "PASSIONATE TEACHING"

BY ROBERT L. FRIED

Robert Fried is a former school teacher and principal who now teaches at Northeastern University. He has spent many hours sitting in elementary and high school classrooms in rural, suburban, and urban high schools asking the question "What is the ingredient of teaching and learning at their best?" The answers have resulted in two books, *The Passionate Teacher*, from which this selection is taken, and the subsequent *The Passionate Learner*, which describes students who are most deeply engaged in their own learning.

I believe I make a difference not only by helping kids connect math and science to their lives, but also in understanding how to reach their goals in life—how to be somebody.

> —Maria Ortiz, science teacher

The destiny of Maria Ortiz, now in her twenty-second year of teaching science at Lewis B. Fox Middle school in an inner-city neighborhood of Hartford, Connecticut, was probably decided on the very day she entered first grade, back in the village of Canovanas, Puerto Rico, and encountered the woman she still refers to as "Mrs. Betancourt."

She was not only a teacher, but a kind of mother to us—so loving to each kid that I can remember almost every single moment of first and second grade (I had her for two years) even though it was more than forty years ago. Every morning, she was waiting for us outside in the school yard. She hugged each kid like we were her long-lost children. Then she would gather us around her, like a mother hen with her chicks, and lead us inside.

And waiting for us would be hot cocoa and soda crackers—she didn't believe we should have to wait for mid-morning snack time; we got our snack first thing. Then she would get us singing, all of us. And her songs were full of tricks to make us learn things even while we were singing and having fun: songs about the alphabet, about animals and numbers. We would get so involved in her projects— drawing, building things, making a doll out of an old sock with buttons for its eyes—that we didn't realize how much we were learning. We knew we had to do schoolwork, but because of her warmth it didn't seem like work, it seemed like fun.

You see, I never planned to be a teacher. Since I liked science and was good at it, my parents wanted me to be a doctor. Instead, I studied pharmacology for four years in college and then started an apprenticeship in a drugstore. But as soon as I started practicing, I knew it wasn't for me. I didn't want to spend my life putting labels on bottles and selling them to customers for high prices.

So I went back to my dean and told him I was in the wrong profession and was quitting. He asked why, and I said, "A highly regarded doctor sent in a prescription for a woman, and although it was only for aspirin, he gave it a scientific name, and the druggist told me to cover over the 'Bayer Aspirin' label and charge her $20. I told him I wouldn't do it. If that's the kind of business it is, pharmacy is not for me. I have to have an opportunity to live!"

Then I thought I would change my major and become a science researcher. But my sister-in-law said, "Why don't you become a teacher?" Immediately Mrs. Betancourt flashed into my mind. And I said to myself: "Maybe that's what I really want to be—I want to be like her!"

So I began teaching right away. There was such a shortage of math and science teachers that they were willing to hire me even though I had never taken an education course and didn't know any methodology. I had to create everything myself, without relying on theories.

I started teaching science to students in grades 7 and 9, in a middle school in Hato Rey, near San Juan. As the newest teacher, naturally they gave me what they thought were the worst classes. (They didn't tell me that nine other teachers had already quit because they could not handle the kids.) I can still remember one of the students, Ismari Rivera. Our class was held in the art room, and when I came in, he was sitting atop the pottery wheel, slowly spinning around before an admiring audience of classmates. He gave me a look that said: "I dare you to get me off, or make me stop,"

I decided to ignore him and busied myself at my desk. After a while, Ismari looked up and said: "Are you the new teacher?" I said, "Yes." He paused, and then asked, "Are you going to leave us, too?" I said, no, I wasn't going to leave. And he continued to spin on the wheel and I continued to ignore him and began talking to the kids.

For the first week or two, I said nothing at all about science. I was operating totally on instinct, and my instinct told me that I needed first of all to

Source: "Passionate Teaching," in *The Passionate Teacher: A Practical Guide*, by Robert L. Fried, 1995, Beacon Press, pp. 11–23.

get to know who these kids really were. The principal had said that they were mentally retarded, but I soon found out that they were not that at all, just angry. We talked about the kind of sports and music they liked, and they told me all about who was in their families, and of course they asked about mine, and I told them.

At the end of the first week, I knew so much about their lives, and somehow, that *changed their behavior*. They probably saw me as the kind of older teenager that they might want to be, and they were grateful that I was so interested in them. They saw themselves as rebels in the school because there was so much anger around them, in their lives, in school, in their homes.

After a while, I could tell them that I was a science teacher and that my job was to teach the science curriculum. But I promised that we would take one day each week and pull our chairs into a circle and talk about whatever was on their minds. We set some rules: everybody had to promise to listen to each other and to take turns if they wanted to talk. When somebody mentioned a problem they were having, one by one the other kids could give suggestions or make helpful comments.

Ismari didn't like this. He had gotten down from the pottery wheel when the other kids stopped paying attention to him. But now he just sat in the corner and sulked. And I still decided it was best to ignore him. So eventually, he moved closer and closer, until he was in the circle.

I remember one girl, named Waleska, who told us she hated her father because he had killed her little sister. She said that he had backed up his car and it had run over her sister. She couldn't understand how he could have done that. And so we talked about it, and we all decided that it had been an accident, and that her father didn't mean it. Slowly, with our help, Waleska was able to understand this too. The circle gave them a chance to let their emotions out and deal with them. There was some crying, at times, by all of us. But there was also a lot of laughter.

And so I became a teacher, just like that. After a few years I was offered a chance to come to America and teach for a year. I came to this school, in Hartford, in 1972. And I'm still here. I believe I make a difference not only by helping kids connect math and science to their lives, but also in understanding how to reach their goals in life—how to be *somebody*. It's strange: in Puerto Rico the kids seem so proud of themselves. But when they come here, they suffer a great blow to their esteem. We have to work very hard to help them convince themselves that their goals still mater, that nothing

is impossible, that they can do it, that to be bilingual is to have power.

I don't feel fifty years old. I can still think like a teenager. There are three teachers in Hartford schools who were my students, here at Fox Middle, and another who's at the university, studying to be a teacher. And we owe it all to Mrs. Betancourt.

When I hear stories like this—and almost every school has its stories of inspired and devoted adults who reach out in ways that change people's lives—it occurs to me that we educators and social scientists have not yet found a way to capture what we hear and see. When we try to synthesize what has inspired us, to generalize from these individual stories and draw them into a theory or a technique, the images don't survive, like certain wildflowers that won't bloom if you try to transplant them.

We boil the stories down into their essences but their power slips away. We try to draw from them a methodology that seems so personal as to be nearly impossible to transmit to others, leaving us with fleeting impressions that can only be admired from a distance. We hear about the legendary Mrs. Betancourt in Puerto Rico, or about the work of Maria Ortiz amid the urban blight of Hartford, and we somehow end up putting a frame around their unique gifts and placing it up on a shelf, so it won't get trampled when the next bunch of kids comes storming or slouching into the classroom.

Our inability to translate great stories into a useful pedagogy is due to our encountering something that people find hard to identify, talk about, or hold onto intellectually. I believe that what we are dealing with is *passion*. And it all feels too special, too intense, too outside the boundaries of professional consideration.

But I am convinced that passion—our own as well as other people's—can be analyzed and put to work. The examples, strategies, and techniques I describe in these pages are instances of passion-in-action, ways of transforming those images into use in our daily work with children and young adults. I hope to celebrate passionate teaching and make it accessible to us in whatever roles we are called upon to play. My challenge is to enable readers to translate potentially exciting ideas and models in to their own practical idioms, so that these will survive the inevitable clash with our workaday constraints.

Why passion, when we have so many other ways of thinking about teaching and learning? Passion seems a rather odd way to characterize what teachers ought to bring to their work. Bumping into one another on a Monday morning, not many of us are likely to ask: "So, are you feeling passionate enough for your classes today?" Isn't there enough irrationality and fool-headedness in education and most everywhere else these days without adding passion to the soup?

Yet as I look into hundreds of classrooms, watch teachers working with all kinds of students, when I ask myself what makes the greatest difference in the quality of student learning—it is a teacher's passion that leaps out. More than knowledge of subject matter. More than variety of teaching techniques. More than being well-organized, or friendly, or funny, or fair. *Passion*.

With teachers, as with anyone else who has a goal in life to do great things—to create works of art or defend the environment or right social wrongs or create new technologies—passionate people are the ones who make a difference in our lives. By the intensity of their beliefs and actions, they connect us with a sense of value that is with—and beyond—ourselves.

Sometimes that passion burns with a quiet, refined intensity; sometimes it bellows forth with thunder and eloquence. But in whatever form or style a teacher's passion emerges, students know they are in the presence of someone whose devotion to learning is exceptional. Even when that devotion has an intensity that may make students uncomfortable, they still know it is something important. It's what makes a teacher unforgettable.

Of some of our teachers, we remember their foibles and mannerisms; of others, their kindness and encouragement, or their fierce devotion to standards of work that we probably did not share at the time. And of those who inspired us most, we remember what they cared about, and that they cared about us and the person we might become. It is this quality of caring about ideas and values, this fascination with the potential for growth within people, this depth and fervor about doing things well and striving for excellence, that comes closest to what I mean in describing a "passionate teacher."

Here I can imagine an experienced teacher, someone with a pretty good reputation among colleagues and students, slamming this book shut and tossing it onto the teacher's room table: "What's this guy want from us now—blood? For eighteen years I've done my job, and done it pretty damn well. I not only teach them the stuff, I take the time to try to get to know the kids in my classes. Isn't it enough to be a caring teacher who's got the students' interests at heart, who helps them learn each in their own way, who gives everybody a chance to succeed? What business does anybody have asking me to be 'passionate' on top of everything else?"

Obviously, no business at all. We should be more than grateful for each of the skilled, dedicated, caring teachers in our schools who do good enough work under conditions that are often demanding and stressful. I am tempted to say: "Oh, but this is not a book for *you*—it's for those other teachers, the ones who are just putting in their time and doing the minimum they need to get by."

But maybe it is part of my job in this book to make good teachers feel dissatisfied with being "good enough." Passion may just be the difference between being remembered as a "pretty good teacher" who made chemistry or algebra or tenth-grade English "sort of interesting"—or as the teacher who opened up a world of the mind to some students who had no one else to make them feel that they were capable of doing great things with test tubes, trumpets, trigonometry, or T. S. Eliot.

How, then, is a teacher "passionate"?

You can be passionate about your field of knowledge: in love with the poetry of Emily Dickinson or the prose of Marcus Garvey; dazzled by the spiral of DNA or the swirl of van Gogh's cypresses; intrigued by the origins of the Milky Way or the demise of the Soviet empire; delighted by the sound of Mozart of the sonority of French vowels; a manic for health and fitness or wild about algebraic word problems. . .

You can be passionate about issues facing our world: active in the struggle for social justice or for the survival of the global environment; dedicated to the celebration of cultural diversity or to the search for a cure for AIDS. . .

You can be passionate about children: about the rate of violence experienced by young black males; about including children with disabilities in all regular school activities; about raising the low rate of high school completion by Latino children; about the insidious effects of sexism, racism, and social class prejudice on the spirits of all children; about the neglect of "average" kids in schools where those at the "top" and "bottom" seem to get all the attention; about the decline of literacy in an age of instant electronic gratification; about the wealth of hidden talent that goes unnoticed in so many children.

To be avowedly passionate about at least some of these things sets one apart from those who approach each day in a fog of fatigue, ritual, routine, or resignation, or who come to work wrapped in self-protective cocoon. The passion that accompanies our attention to subjects, issues, and children is not just something we offer our students. It is also a gift we grant ourselves: a way of honoring our life's work, our profession. It says: "I know why I am devoting this life I've got to these children."

I want to distinguish passionate teaching from mere idiosyncrasies or foibles. Lots of teachers have "pet peeves" or fixations: points of grammar, disciplinary practices, eccentricities of dress or diction. These may, indeed, make them memorable to their students (for better or worse). But the passions I am speaking about convey much more. It is teachers' passions that help them and their students escape the slow death of "business as usual," the rituals of going through the motions, which in schools usually means checking that the homework was done, covering the curriculum, testing, grading, and quickly putting it all behind us. The example we set as passionate adults allows us to connect to young people's minds and spirits in a way that can have a lasting positive impact on their lives.

For me, passionate teachers include all those who ever entered the classroom because they loved kids, because they loved learning, because they wanted in some small way to change the world. Sadly, many who entered with high hopes have not been able to hold onto their passion for very long, because of the conditions under which they work. Others nurse their passions quietly, almost embarrassed to care so much or to hold to such high standards in a climate of school and society that looks for compromises and shortcuts. Still others have become embittered by the whole scene: students who won't do any work, administrators who manipulate, colleagues who complain all the time, officials who won't provide adequate funds, parents who can't seem to be bothered, and a society that would rather blame its schools than fund them.

Many disillusioned teachers began their careers as passionate people, only to have their spirits dampened, depleted, ground to dust. The passion I talk about belongs as much to them as to the brightest-eyed newcomers or the cheeriest veterans. It is their struggle, too. Our nation of children, faced with the ever changing demands of being citizens, family members, and bread winners in a twenty-first-century world, cannot afford for any of their teachers' passions to be eroded or squelched.

Who Are the Passionate Teachers?

What does passion look like when we see it at work in the classroom? Let's look briefly at some of the people whose stories appear in these pages.

We've just met Maria Ortiz. As I see it, her passion is to make sure that the students in her middle school, especially the girls, almost all of whom are African American or Latina, come to view science as a part of their lives and a part of their future. At a moment when so many forces around them are pushing these girls to abandon their education and their intellectual potential, Maria is determined to be that other voice—friendly and warm, but fiercely protective of the right of these young people to pursue a life of the mind.

For Tim Sullivan, the passion lies in a resolve that his fourth graders are going to be players on the field where classroom learning meets the real world: whether it's in lobbying for a seat-belt law, organizing and running a school store, or spray-painting "Stop, Look, Walk" on the sidewalk of every street corner near every elementary school in town.

David Ervin is a middle school music teacher in a middle-class college town who inspires the entire seventh grade to imagine, create, write, compose, organize, and stage an original musical play each year, with each of them playing a part.

Yvonne Griffin is passionately committed to her students' making choices in their relationships with other people. She is determined that they become young people who *make* things happen, rather than becoming people that things happen *to*.

Ed Clarke will not let any student he works with in his English classes write anything that is less than the best they can do. He flunks students in honors classes who try to slide by, while publishing the best poems and stories of even his least-skilled writers. Many of those who flunk come back the following year to work with him to get it right.

Alfredo Fuentes teaches math and wages a passionate struggle to convince everybody in the school that algebra is for *every* student, even those who have trouble with long division or don't yet know their multiplication tables.

When Dan Bisaccio was teaching science in a rural, working-class town in New Hampshire, his job was to show his students how to think and act like scientists, rather than simply to learn about science. The passion I witnessed in his teaching of evolution showed in his skill at coaching students to actively discover and debate Darwin's theories for themselves, not merely to read about and memorize them.

Susan Lukas teaches literature at an independent school with a diverse student body. She also writes poetry and fiction and edits manuscripts for other writers. Her passion as a teacher lies in assigning to her students works of literature that have very great meaning for her, and finding a way to encourage honest discussion about them with all her students, even those who are hostile to the authors and their message.

Christine Sullivan teachers writing to students in all four academic levels of a traditional rural/suburban high school. Her passion about student portfolio writing has led her students to discover their own learning styles, to minimize concern for letter grades while adopting a performance-based approach to learning, and to advocate for their own individual approaches to assignments given by other teachers.

Some of the most passionate teachers are quiet, intense, thoughtful people. They patiently insist on high standards of quality in a language lab or drafting class. They talk with students in conference about their work and where their talents and persistence might lead them. They stop to respond to a comment thrown out by a student that has more than a germ of truth in it. They bring in something from their current reading or their personal history that demonstrates the power of ideas.

On the other hand, a certain amount of abandon can also deliver the message. One teacher from Georgia announced at a workshop: "Ah intend this year to be jest a little bit *craaazy* about what ah'm teaching!" What he wanted his fellow teachers to hear was that he was eager to break out of the competent but comfortable mold he had built around himself, and to break up the unimaginative complacency of his students.

What impresses me about such teachers is that no particular set of teaching tricks or topics, much less a common personality type, epitomizes them. As individual as they are, what unites them are some ways they approach the mission of teaching; they organize their curricula and their daily work with students in practical ways that play to those different strengths. These practical observations—the tools of the passionate craft teaching—will emerge as the book progresses, but let's look at two of them here:

1. Passionate teachers *organize and focus* their passionate interests *by getting to the heart of their subject* and sharing with their students some of what lies there—the beauty and power that drew them to this field in the first place and that has deepened over time as they have learned and experienced more. They are not after a narrow or elitist perspective, but rather a depth of engagement that serves as a base for branching out to other interests and disciplines.

2. Passionate teachers *convey their passion* to novice learners—their students—by acting as partners in learning, rather than as "experts in the field." As partners, they invite less experienced learners to search for knowledge and insightful experiences, and they build confidence and competence among students who might otherwise choose to sit back and watch their teachers do and say interesting things.

From "CARING, COMPETENT TEACHERS IN COMPLEX CLASSROOMS"

BY JACQUELINE JORDAN IRVINE

Jacqueline Jordan Irvine is the Charles Howard Candler Professor of Urban Education Emerita at Emory University in Atlanta. Through her leadership of the CULTURES program at Emory, and in more than a dozen books and innumerable speeches and articles, she has become a national voice for insisting that excellence in teaching involves "seeing with a cultural eye" and respecting and engaging all students by understanding the full diversity of today's students.

Policymakers and teacher educators frequently refer to the National Commission on Teaching and America's Future (NCTAF) recommendation that every child deserves a competent teacher (Darling-Hammond, 1997). Recently, the descriptor *caring* was added to the call for competent teachers, meaning that our students need, not just competent teachers, but *caring*, competent teachers. I believe, however, that the appeal for caring and competent teachers does not unearth the complexities of teaching, particularly in urban, culturally diverse classrooms. Educating educators is a daunting, persistent challenge. Unless we understand the complexity of the task and articulate a convincing mission in carefully crafted language, words such as care and competence easily will be reduced to being used in laudable yet shallow clichés and homilies.

No one would disagree that teacher education programs should produce caring, competent teachers, and we are challenged to train significant numbers of these teachers in a rela-

Source: "Caring, Competent Teachers in Complex Classrooms," in *Educating Teachers for Diversity: Seeing With a Cultural Eye*, by Jacqueline Jordan Irvine, 2003, Teachers College Press.

tively short period of time. If we solely focus on the absolute number of teachers needed, we may note that demographers have informed us that school systems will have a demand for 2 million caring, competent teachers during the coming decade. Certainly, colleges of education will be unable to prepare enough teachers to fill these projected vacancies. There are only 1,300 teacher education programs in the nation, and one half of all graduates will not be teaching 4 years after they graduate (Olsen, 2000). Even if districts are successful in recruiting 2 million new teachers (which is questionable), more than 30% of beginning teachers will leave within their first 5 years. According to the National Center for Education Statistics (NCES) (1997), the situation is even more complex than these remarkable figures reveal:

- Forty-four percent of all schools do not have any teachers of color on their faculty.
- Teacher shortages do not exist in all subject matter fields. There are acute needs in science, mathematics, English for speakers of other languages (ESOL), and special education.
- Wealthy schools have more applicants than they need.

- Urban, culturally diverse, low-income schools, even those that offer so-called combat pay; magnet schools; and other innovative structural configurations have many vacancies and cannot attract and retain certified and experienced teachers.

Therefore, what seems to be a rather benign and commendable goal—preparing caring, competent teachers—is laden with issues of definition, interpretation, and assessment. As we know, the devil is in the details. First, I will address the complexity of the issue of care.

And Still We Rise: The Trials and Triumphs of Twelve Gifted Inner-City High School Students, written by a journalist (Corwin, 2000), illustrates the complexity of defining caring, competent teachers. There are two veteran caring, competent English teachers in the inner-city African American school of which Corwin writes. One is a White teacher, Ms. Little, who has a strong social consciousness and believes that her students' race and family income are irrelevant. The other equally caring, competent teacher is an African American woman, Ms. Moultrie, who is affectionately called Mama Moultrie by her students. Moultrie assumes the role of a surrogate parent and her classroom resembles a pulpit from which she uses literature to teach values, racial pride and uplift, and hard work. Little believes that her mission is to help her student pass the English Advanced Placement (AP) exam so that they can succeed in college and leave behind the desolation of the urban community in which they live. Little believes that Moultrie talks too much about race and social inequities and too little about essay structure and thesis development. She does not see herself in a parental role. "I'm not their damn mama," Little says, "I'm their English teacher". Moultrie responds to Little's criticism that she spends too little time teaching content and too much on preaching by proclaiming that she is preparing Black students not merely for college, but for life.

These two caring and competent teaches have different philosophies about their personal and professional roles as teachers, their mission, efficacy, practice, beliefs, students, and the communities in which they work. Is it possible to determine if one is more caring or more competent than the other? How will we decide? By what criteria will we measure degrees of competence and care? To answer these questions, an examination of the concepts of care and competence is required.

Complexity of the Issue of Care

I believe that teaching is synonymous with caring. Care as an essential quality of effective teachers was affirmed in a Gallup poll that developed an extensive personality profile of successful urban teachers (Van Horn, 1999). Responses in the poll revealed that of the 11 qualities presented, commitment and dedication were especially important. But what does it mean to say that a teacher cares? How do you identify a caring teacher? Who should define it? Can you teach it? Should we use care as an entrance or exit criteria in teacher education programs? And more important, how do you measure care?

Caring comes in many forms and manifests itself in different ways. In describing her favorite teacher, an African American student in my research (Irvine, 2002) used the typical adjectives, *caring, sympathetic, dedicated, friendly,* and *funny.* But the student quickly added, "My teacher has all these wonderful qualities, but don't be fooled. She was in control."

The student proceeded to describe a particular incident in which everyone in the class failed a test. The student recalled:

> The word passed quickly that Mrs. Washington was "P-Oed." When we walked into her class Mrs. Washington said, "Well, I guess that you heard that you have ticked me off." One student tried to explain and she told him to be quiet. Mrs. Washington ordered one student to open the windows because it was "getting ready to get hot in here." Then on the spot Mrs. Washington made up a rap about self-esteem, confidence, and hard work. We were clapping and laughing (and still scared) but Mrs. Washington had made her point.

Another African American student in my research (Irvine, 2002) wrote the following excerpt about teachers:

> I wish school had been more challenging for me. Some students don't like strict teachers. But I do. When I say strict I mean in the academics. They stress that you must complete all assignments. And when you do not complete the assignments, they aren't just nice to you and let you just slide by.

These students did not equate caring with being nice or friendly. None of them felt that they had been silenced or demonstrated any resentment toward their teachers. Caring for these students means firm, fair discipline, high standards and expectations, and an unwillingness on the part of teachers to let students "slide by." These "warm demanders" (Kleinfeld, 1975) are caring, competent educators whose public "take no prisoner" demeanor may lead some to conclude incorrectly that such teachers do not care about their students. It has been my experience that naïve classroom observers and evaluators often misinterpret the caring in what appears on the surface to be rather harsh disciplinary tactics.

My colleague and I provided the following example of warm-demander caring in an article that we wrote about why so few African American teachers are certified by the National Board for Professional Teaching Standards (NBPTS):

> "That's enough of your nonsense, Darius. Your story does not make sense. I told you time and time again that you must stick to the theme I gave you. Now sit down." Darius, a first grader trying desperately to tell his story, proceeds slowly to his seat with his head hung low. The other children snicker as he looks embarrassed and hurt. What kind of teacher could say such words to a child? Most would agree that the teacher would not meet any local or national performance standards.

Ironically, Irene Washington, an African American teacher with 23 years of experience, is a recognized model teacher in her predominantly African American school and community. Similar to thousands of African American educators across the country, Washington teaches her African American students with a sense of passion and mission that is rooted in cultural traditions and a common history that she shares with her students. African American warm demanders, as well as other teachers of color, provide a tough-minded, nononsense, structured, disciplined classroom environment for young people whom society has psychologically and physically abandoned. Strongly identifying with their students and determined to give them a future, these teachers believe that culturally diverse children not only *can* learn but *must* learn. These previous descriptions are reminiscent of the acclaimed teaching style of Marva Collins, the African American teacher who started her own school in Chicago, and Jaime Escalante, the Hispanic teacher in Los Angeles who produced amazing results with his high school math students.

When asked about the teaching episode involving Darius, Irene Washington provided insight into the culturally responsive style that she uses:

> "Oh that little Darius is something else. Now he knows that there are times I will allow them to shoot from the hip. But he knows that this time we're working on themes. You see, you've got to know these students and where they're coming from—you know, talk the talk. He knows what's expected during these activities, but he's trying to play the comedian. I know he knows how to develop a theme and I won't let him get away with ignoring my instructions."

She explained that her comments to Darius were motivated by a particular set of negative environmental circumstances and a sense of urgency not only to teach her children well but also to save and protect them from the perils of urban street life. She continued:

> "Darius is street smart, street wise. You see he has older brothers who are out there on the streets, selling and using [drugs]. I know if I don't reach him, or if I retain him, I may lose him to the streets this early. That's what I'm here for—to give them opportunities—to get an education and the confidence. I certainly don't want them to meet closed doors."

She ended her interview on a pensive and reflective note, declaring that, "I know what it means to grow up Black" (Irvine & Fraser, 1998), p. 56.

Research on Latino educators (Henz & Hauser 1999) documents another type of caring called *carino*. Examples of *carino* included instances in which teachers refer to their Latino students with kinship terms such as *mijo/mija* (son/daughter) or *mi amor* (my love). The Latino teachers thought that it was important to establish and foster a sense of *confianza*, which includes sharing cultural experiences with their students, listening to them, and relating to them as culturally connected relatives.

I am sure that many teachers who are demanding and who chastise and even punish students care about their pupils as much as do teachers who dialogue, co-construct, facilitate, negotiate, and celebrate voices. The task of teacher educators is to make sure that teacher education students and the people who evaluate and assess them understand the complexity of a term that seems so simple—*care*. We should continue to speak and write about our profession so that policy makers understand how teacher characteristics and traits, such as being caring, are influenced by the multiple layers and enigmatic nature of classroom practice.

Complexity of the Issue of Competence

The second term in our lexicon that needs further refinement and lucid thought is *competence*. Let's set the record straight. I believe that teachers should be competent and that their competence should be assessed with valid and

multiple measures. Furthermore, I support high standards. Again, the issue is not whether teachers should be competent. Of course, they must be. No teacher should be allowed to enter a classroom without documented evidence of competence in literacy, numeracy, technology, and his or her subject matter field. However, similar to what occurs in the case of the term *care*, issues of measurement, validity, and reliability complicate the discussion of competence.

Unfortunately, such murky measurement issues have not discouraged or prevented the media's insatiable appetite for stories about teacher incompetence, particularly teachers' performance on state and national assessments. Although conventional wisdom insists that teacher education students are "idiots," as Massachusetts's Speaker of the House said (Laitsch, 1998, p. 1), recent data from the educational Testing Service (ETS) (Gittomer, Latham & Ziomek, 1999) confirm that teacher education students are not less talented than their peers in other majors. Although teacher educators maintain varying positions on the merits of mandated competency, almost all agree with Berliner's (2000) contention that "raw intelligence is insufficient for accomplished teaching" (p. 358).

Complexities of Teaching

The complexities of teaching are revealed in the observation that teaching involves four essential elements:

1. some person
2. teaching something,
3. to some student,

4. somewhere.* (*Many thanks to Judith Lanier, former president and chair of the Holmes Group, for our conversation on this subject.)

First, let's talk about "some person." It does matter who the teacher is. Indeed, we teach who we are. Teachers bring to their work values, opinions, and beliefs; their prior socialization and present experiences; and their race, gender, ethnicity, and social class. These attributes and characteristics influence teachers' perceptions of themselves as professionals. I am not purporting that there is a simplistic interpretation of this finding. People—including teachers—are not mere representatives of their ethnic group or passive recipients of their cultural experiences. However, we should understand that teachers are influenced by their past and present cultural encounters.

In addition to these cultural variables, teachers have preferences for the type of student whom they want to teach. They do not treat all students the same or have similar expectations for their success and achievement. In my research (Irvine, 1990a), I have found that when teachers were asked to describe their favorite students, they used descriptors such as *above average, friendly, cooperative, curious, affectionate*, and *outgoing*.

One of the teachers said, "I like working with Matt the best. He is well behaved and doesn't act up. He does what he is told and gives me no problems. He is very soft-spoken and tries hard to please me." Another admitted, "I found that I prefer to teach a more physically attractive kid who follows directions well. Most importantly, I like the ones that respond to me."

Second, it does matter what the "something" is that is being taught. Effective teachers love and care about the students whom they teach, and they also love and are excited about the subject that they teach. A thorough, deep understanding of the content contributes to teachers' ability to represent and deliver that content in various ways. Competent teachers know how to employ multiple representations of knowledge that use students' everyday lived experiences to motivate and assist them in connecting new knowledge to home, community, and global settings. Multiple representations of subject matter knowledge involve finding pertinent examples, comparing and contrasting, bridging the gap between the known (students' personal cultural knowledge) and the unknown (materials and concepts to be mastered).

My colleague and I edited a book in which we present culturally responsive, transformative lesson units in four subject areas that are aligned with content area standards (Irvine & Armento, 2001). Examples include the following:

- Teaching language arts by helping culturally diverse students to comprehend, interpret, evaluate, and appreciate text by drawing on the resources of their family and community

- Teaching mathematics by identifying geometric shapes and patterns in African textiles and Navajo pottery
- Teaching weather and other scientific concepts by first helping students to understand the connections between their culture and weather as portrayed in myths, folklore, and family sayings
- Teaching social studies by arranging mock presidential elections in selected historical periods for which students assume various roles, such as women, slaves, Whites, and property owners; in addition, helping them to transform their own community by analyzing and reporting voting patterns in their neighborhood and executing a voter education project.

Effective teachers do not falsely dichotomize students as learners in school and nonlearners out of school (Moll, Amanti, Neff, & Gonzalez, 1992). Teachers' ability to demonstrate the connection between school and community knowledge is an essential element of subject matter competence. Students learn best when teachers' content knowledge is so deep and extensive that they help students to interpret knowledge, store and retrieve it, and make sense of the world in which they live. I believe that students fail in schools not because their teachers do not know their content, but because their teachers cannot make connections between subject-area content and their students' existing mental schemes, prior knowledge, and cultural perspectives.

Third, it does matter who is being taught—the student. The student's age, developmental level, race and ethnicity, physical and emotional states, prior experiences, interests, family and home life, learning preferences, attitudes about school, and a myriad of other variables influence the teaching and learning process. How many times do teacher educators remind students to "meet the needs of the learners in their classroom"? It's mind-boggling and humbling to contemplate the complexities of this much heralded precept of effective teaching (Schulman, 1987).

Teachers are accountable for instructing students who are unmotivated, angry, violent, hungry, homeless, shy, and abused. Policymakers, and some school administrators, seem oblivious to the fact that students are not passive recipients of teaching. Students have preferences regarding the subject matter that they are taught and the people who teach them.

Fourth, it does matter where one is teaching. Urban, suburban, and rural schools differ from one another. Larger and small schools have different climates and teacher-student relationships. Private versus parochial, low-income versus privileged, elementary versus middle, charter versus non-charter, are not mere labels for schools. These distinctions matter. An all–African American school, for example, differs from a culturally diverse or all-White school. School policies, organizational structures, and personnel are relevant pieces of the context of teaching.

Ponder the powerlessness and ineffectiveness of caring, competent teachers (even those certified by the National Board for Professional Teaching Standards) working in overcrowded, underfunded schools with low-tracked curricula and insensitive, incompetent administrators. We have produced hundreds of caring, competent teachers in our programs who do not choose to stay in the profession for these very reasons. In a North Carolina study (Southeast Center for Teaching Quality, 2002), 14,000 teachers were surveyed to determine the type of incentives that would convince them to work in low-performing schools. Seventy percent of the teachers stated that they would not work in such schools, even with incentives such as increased compensation. What the teachers wanted were responsive, effective administrators, extra planning periods, and instructional support.

Hence, teaching is clearly a complex act involving some person teaching something to some student somewhere. Context is the operative word here. Caring, competent educators understand context and the complexity of teaching and do not use a set of rigid pedagogical principles in their classrooms. Instead, they modify what they have learned in teacher education, recognizing that mastery of pedagogical principles and subject matter content are necessary but not sufficient conditions for effective teaching. Caring, competent teachers recognize that they do not instruct culturally homogenized, standardized students in a nonspecified school setting. Teachers armed with such generic teaching skills often find themselves ineffective and ill prepared when faced with a classroom of diverse learners.

For a complete listing of the references for this Reading, go to **www.mhhe.com/teach1e2010**.

QUESTIONS

1. Which teacher, Ms. Little or Ms. Moultrie, best meets your own definition of a caring, competent teacher? Do you agree with Irvine that two such different teachers can both be caring and competent? What do you think Fried would say?

2. Do you think, as Irvine implies, that a teacher can be caring, sympathetic, friendly, and yet tough and "in charge"? Is this asking too much?

3. In the example Irvine gives, do you think Darius's teacher was fair to him?

4. Do you agree with Irvine that "context is the operative word" and that teachers need to teach quite differently in different cultural contexts, or do you ultimately think "good teaching is good teaching"?

Chapter 1

1. National Education Association. Status of the American Public School Teacher, pp. 67–68.

2. Ayla Gavins, "Being on a Moving Train," in Sonia Nieto, ed., *Why We Teach* (New York: Teachers College Press, 2005), pp. 101, 103–104.

3. William Ayers, *To Teach: The Journey of a Teacher* (New York: Teachers College Press, 2001), p. 8.

4. Parker J. Palmer, *The Courage to Teach: Exploring the Inner Landscape of a Teacher's Life* (San Francisco: Jossey-Bass, 1998), p. 1.

5. Ayers, p. 8.

6. Jennifer Welborn, "The Accidental Teacher," in Sonia Nieto, ed., *Why We Teach* (New York: Teachers College Press, 2005), p. 17.

7. Jean Anyon, "Putting Education at the Center," in William Ayers, Gloria Ladson-Billings, Gregory Michie, and Pedro A. Noguera, eds., *City Kids City Schools* (New York: New Press, 2008), pp. 310–311.

8. Welborn, p. 20.

9. Robert L. Fried, *The Passionate Teacher: A Practical Guide* (Boston: Beacon Press, 1995), pp. 11–23.

10. Welborn, p. 22.

11. Richard M. Ingersoll and Thomas M. Smith, "The Wrong Solution to the Teacher Shortage," *Educational Leadership,* May, 2003, Vol. 60, Issue 8, pp. 30–33. For a more detailed discussion of these issues see Richard M. Ingersoll, *Who Controls Teachers' Work? Power and Accountability in America's Schools* (Cambridge: Harvard University Press, 2003).

12. Ellen Moir, "The Santa Cruz New Teacher Center Teacher Induction Model," presentation at New York University, March 1, 2006. For more information on the important work of the New Teacher Center, see http://www.newteachercenter.org.

13. Linda Molner Kelley, "Why Induction Matters," *Journal of Teacher Education,* 2004, Vol. 55, Issue 5, pp. 438–448.

14. Barbara McEwan in Ronald E. Butchart and Barbara McEwan, eds., *Classroom Discipline in American Schools: Problems and Possibilities* (Albany: State University of New York Press, 1998).

15. Rury, p. 14.

16. John Adams, entry for Monday, March 15, 1756, in L. H. Butterfield, ed., *Diary and Autobiography of John Adams, 1755–1770.* Vol. 1 (Cambridge: Belknap Press of Harvard University Press, 1961), pp. 13–14.

17. Rury, in Warren, pp. 17, 23.

18. Catharine E. Beecher, "An Essay on the Education of Female Teachers for the United States" (1835), reprinted in James W. Fraser, *The School in the United States: A Documentary History* (New York: McGraw-Hill, 2001), p. 61.

19. Michael B. Katz, *The Irony of Early School Reform: Educational Innovation in Mid-Nineteenth Century Massachusetts* (reissued with a new Introduction, New York: Teachers College Press, 2001), p. 91.

20. Nancy Hoffman, *Woman's "True" Profession: Voices from the History of Teaching* (Old Westbury, NY: Feminist Press, 1981), offers some wonderful first-person accounts of what it meant to be a woman teacher at different periods of this nation's life.

21. Second Annual Report of the General Agent of the Board of National Popular Education (Cleveland, OH: Steam Press of M. C. Younglove & Co., 1849), pp. 29–32.

22. Linda M. Perkins, "The History of Blacks in Teaching: Growth and Decline Within the Profession," in Warren, pp. 344–369; for citations, see pp. 347, 356.

23. Stanley K. Schultz, *The Culture Factory: Boston Public Schools, 1789–1860* (New York: Oxford University Press, 1973), pp. 256, 260.

24. Rury, in Warren, p. 23.

25. Marian Dogherty, *'Scusa Me Teacher* (Francestown, NH: Marshall Jones, 1943), cited in Hoffman, pp. 257–258.

26. See Chapter 7, "The Progressive Era," in Fraser, pp. 181–221; Dewey quote is on p. 207, Young quote on p. 193.

27. David F. Labaree, "Career Ladders and the Early Public High-School Teacher: A Study of Inequality and Opportunity," Chapter 6 in Warren, pp. 157–189; Persons story is on p. 178.

28. For more on the historical development of high schools, see William J. Reese, *The Origins of the American High School* (New Haven, CT: Yale University Press, 1995).

29. For a thorough study of the Peace Corps and its early 20th century predecessors, see Jonathan Zimmerman, *Innocents Abroad: American Teachers in the American Century* (Cambridge, MA: Harvard University Press, 2006).

30. For a detailed study of the changing expectations for entering teaching, see Fraser, *Preparing America's Teachers: A History* (New York: Teachers College Press, 2007), especially chapter 10, pp. 173–194.

31. Elaine P. Witty, "The Norfolk Conference on Diversity," in Susan Cimburek, ed., *Leading a Profession: Defining Moments in the AACTE Agenda, 1980–2005* (Washington, DC: American Association of Colleges for Teacher Education, 2005), pp. 18–20.

32. Herbert Kohl, *The Discipline of Hope: Learning from a Lifetime of Teaching* (New York: Simon & Schuster, 1998), pp. 331–333.

Chapter 2

1. Sonia Nieto, *What Keeps Teachers Going?* (New York: Teachers College Press, 2003), p. 21.

2. Horace Mann, *Fourth Annual Report* (1840), in Lawrence A. Cremin, *The Republic and the School: Horace Mann on the Education of Free Men* (New York: Teachers College Press, 1957), pp. 45–52.

3. Margaret Haley, "Why Teachers Should Organize," *Addresses and Proceedings* (St. Louis, MO: NEA, 1904), pp. 145–152.

4. See interviews with Glenn Seaborg and Alan Friedman, "Sputnik's Legacy," http://whyfiles.org/047sputnik/main3.html; see also "Janet Whitla on the Evolution of EDC's Thinking," http://main.edc.org/about/evolution.asp.

5. Lyndon B. Johnson, "Remarks in Johnson City, Texas, Upon Signing the Elementary and Secondary Education Bill, April 11, 1965," Public Papers of the Presidents, Lyndon B. Johnson, 1965, Book I, (Washington, DC: 1966), pp. 413–414.

6. Ellen Condliffe Lagemann, *The Politics of Knowledge: The Carnegie Corporation, Philanthropy, and Public Policy* (Chicago: University of Chicago Press, 1989), pp. 244–248.

7. Kati Haycock, "Good Teaching Matters: How Well-Qualified Teachers Can Close the Gap," *Thinking K–16,* Summer 1998, Vol. 3, Issue 2, p. 11–12.

8. Ibid.

9. Steve Farkas, Jean Johnson, and Tony Foleno, "A Sense of Calling: Who Teaches and Why" (New York: Public Agenda, 2000), p. 33.

10. Nieto, p. 19.

11. Ella Flagg Young, Isolation in the School (Chicago: University of Chicago Press, 1901); John T. McManis, *Ella Flagg Young and a Half Century of the Chicago Public Schools* (Chicago: A.C. McClurg, 1916), retrieved from Google Books, June 9, 2009; Jackie M. Blount, "Ella Flagg Young, 1845–1918," *The Columbia Encyclopedia*, Sixth Ed., 2007, retrieved online, June 9, 2009.

12. Ronald F. Ferguson, "Evidence That Schools Can Narrow the Black-White Test Score Gap," 1997, p. 32; Ronald F. Ferguson and Helen F. Ladd, "How and Why Money Matters: An Analysis of Alabama Schools," in *Holding Schools Accountable: Performance Based Reform in Education*, Washington, DC: The Brookings Institute Press, 1996; Dan D. Goldhaber and Dominic J. Brewer, "Evaluating the Effect of Teacher Degree Level on Educational Performance," in *Developments in School Finance,* 1996, p. 199; Eva L. Baker, "Report on the Content Area Performance Assessments (CAPA): A Collaboration Among Hawaii Department of Education, the Center for Research on Evaluation Standards and Student Testing, and the Teachers and Children of Hawaii," 1996, p. 109; Jeff Archer, "Students' Fortune Rests With Assigned Teacher," *Education Week,* February 18, 1998.

13. Linda Darling-Hammond, "What Matters Most: A Competent Teacher for Every Child," in *The Right to Learn: A Blueprint for Creating Schools That Work* (San Francisco: Jossey-Bass, 1997), chap. 3.

14. John D. Bransford, Ann L. Brown, and Rodney R. Cocking, eds., *How People Learn: Brain, Mind, Experience, and School* (Washington, DC: National Academy Press, 2000), pp. 5–6.

15. See Lee Shulman, *The Wisdom of Practice: Essays on Teaching, Learning, and Learning to Teach* (San Francisco: Jossey-Bass, 2004).

16. Robert L. Fried, *The Passionate Teacher* (Boston: Beacon Press, 1995), p. 16.

17. Richard Light, *Getting the Most Out of College* (Cambridge, MA: Harvard University Press, 2002).

18. Jacqueline Jordan Irvine, *In Search of Wholeness: African American Teachers and Their Culturally Specific Classroom Practices* (New York: Palgrave-Macmillan, 2002), p. 142.

19. James P. Comer, "The Rewards of Parent Participation," *Educational Leadership,* (March 2005), Vol. 62, Issue 6, p. 38.

20. J. B. Diamond, L. Wang, and K. Gomez, "African-American and Chinese American Parent Involvement: The Importance of Race, Class and Culture," *FINE Network at Harvard Family Research Project,* (2004), http://www.gse.harvard.edu/hfrp/projects/fine/resources/digest/race.html; G. Valdez, "The World Outside and Inside Schools: Language and Immigrant Children," *Educational Researcher,* (1998), Vol. 27, Issue 6, pp. 4–18; Fabienne Doucet, "Divergent Realities: The Home and School Lives of Haitian Immigrant Youth," *Journal of Youth Ministry,* (2005), Vol. 3, Issue 2, pp. 37–65. I am very grateful to my colleague Fabienne Doucet for pointing me to these articles and for opportunities to discuss these issues.

21. James P. Comer, "Parent Participation: Fad or Function?" *Schools,* p. 136.

22. Comer, "The Rewards of Parent Participation," p. 41.

23. Robert D. Putnam, *Bowling Alone: The Collapse and Revival of American Community* (New York: Simon & Schuster, 2000), p. 367.

24. Putnam, pp. 403–404.

Chapter 3

1. National Commission on Teaching and America's Future, "Learning Teams: Creating What's Next" (NCTAF Report, April 2008), p. 12.

2. Ronald Takaki, *A Different Mirror: A History of Multicultural America* (Boston: Little Brown, 1993), p. 1.

3. Clara C. Park, A. Lin Goodwin, and Stacey J. Lee, *Asian American Identities, Families, and Schooling* (New York: Information Age Publishing, 2003), pp. vii, 16–21.

4. Shirley Brice Heath and Milbrey W. McLaughlin, eds., *Identity and Inner-City Youth: Beyond Ethnicity and Gender* (New York: Teachers College Press, 1993), pp. 18, 21.

5. Heath and McLaughlin, p. 6.

6. All of the data in this section, including charts, are from National Center for Educational Statistics, *The Condition of Education, 2008* (Washington, DC: U.S. Government, 2008), http://nces.ed.gov/programs/coe/2008

7. Gary Orfield, *Reviving the Goal of an Integrated Society: A 21st Century Challenge* (Los Angeles: Civil Rights Project/Proyecto Derechos Civiles, UCLA, 2009).

8. Heath and McLaughlin, p. 25.

9. Harris Interactive and GLSEN, *From Teasing to Torment: School Climate in America: A Survey of Students and Teachers* (New York: GLSEN, 2005).

10. For a much more detailed discussion of the issue of religion—and religious and nonreligious students—in today's schools, see James W. Fraser, *Between Church and State: Religion and Public Education in a Multicultural America* (New York: St. Martins, 1999); Nel Noddings citation from p. 231.

11. Public Agenda, "New Teachers: 'I wasn't prepared for the challenges of teaching in a diverse classroom," http://www.publicagenda.org/LessonsLearned3

12. Tessie Liu, "Teaching the Differences Among Women from a Historical Perspective: Rethinking Race and Gender as Social Categories," in Vicki L. Ruiz and Ellen Carol DuBois, eds., *Unequal Sisters; A Multicultural Reader in U.S. Women's History* (New York: Routledge, 2000), p. 628.

13. Lisa Delpit, *Other People's Children: Culture Conflict in the Classroom* (New York: New Press, 1995), pp. 21–26.

14. Peggy McIntosh, *White Privilege and Male Privilege: A Personal Account of Coming to See Correspondences Through Work in Women's Studies* (Wellesley, MA: Wellesley College Center for Research on Women, 1988).

15. Jacqueline Jordan Irvine, *Educating Teachers for Diversity; Seeing With a Cultural Eye* (New York: Teachers College Press, 2003), pp. xv–xvii.

16. Delpit, pp. 28–29.

Chapter 4

1. Martha Ziegler, testimony to the National Coalition of Advocates for Students Board of Inquiry, cited in *Barriers to Excellence: Our Children at Risk* (Boston: National Coalition of Advocates for Students, 1985), p. 26.

2. Cited in Herbert M. Kliebard, *The Struggle for the American Curriculum, 1893–1958* (Boston: Routledge and Kegan Paul, 1986), p. 141.

3. William H. Chafe, "The Road to Equality, 1962–Today" in Nancy F. Cott, ed., *No Small Courage: A History of Women in the United States* (New York: Oxford University Press, 2000), pp. 547–549; Marlyn E. Calabrese, "What Is Title IX?" in Anne O'Brien Carelli, ed., *Sex Equity in Education: Readings and Strategies* (Springfield, IL: Charles C. Thomas, 1988), pp. 83–93; Barbara Bitters, "Sex Equity in Vocational Education," in Carelli, *Sex Equity in Education*, pp. 231–232; T.J. Wirtenberg, "Expanding Girls' Occupational Potential: A Case Study of the Implementation of Title IX's Anti-Sex-Segregation Provision in Seventh Grade Practical Arts," unpublished doctoral dissertation, University of California, Los Angeles, 1979, cited and discussed in Helen S. Farmer and Joan Seliger Sidney, with Barbara A. Bitters and Martine G. Brizius, "Sex Equity in Career and Vocational Education," in Susan S. Klein, ed., *Handbook for Achieving Sex Equity through Education* (Baltimore: Johns Hopkins University Press, 1985), pp. 348–349; Karen Blumenthal, *Let Me Play: The Story of Title IX* (New York: Atheneum Books, 2005), pp. 3, 23–40.

4. An excellent discussion of these issues can be found in D. B. Tyack and E. Hansot, *Learning Together: A History of Coeducation in American Public Schools* (New York: Russell Sage Foundation, 1992), pp. 242–292; Sexton is cited on p. 290.

5. Myra and David Sadker, *Failing at Fairness: How America's Schools Cheat Girls* (New York: Scribner's, 1994), p. 1.

6. Diego Castellanos, *The Best of Two Worlds: Bilingual-Bicultural Education in the U.S.* (Trenton: New Jersey State Department of Education, 1983).

7. James Crawford, *Bilingual Education: History, Politics, Theory, and Practice* (Trenton, NJ: Crane Publishing, 1989), pp. 18–36; Crawford is citing Castellanos, *The Best of Two Worlds*.

8. Crawford, pp. 35–38.

9. Crawford, pp. 38–43.

10. See National Coalition of Advocates for Students, *Barriers to Excellence: Our Children At Risk* (Boston: NCAS, 1985), pp. 20–21.

11. Don Soifer, "Bilingual Education: Where Do We Go from Here?" Issue Brief, The Lexington Institute, June 19, 1998, http://lexingtoninstitute.org.

12. John Espinoza, "Speak the Truth About 227," October 17, 1998, http://www.humnet.ucla.edu/humnet/linguistics/people/grads/macswan/espinoza2.htm.

13. Tom Parrish et al., "Effects of the Implementation of Proposition 227 on the Education of English Learners, K–12 Findings from a Five-Year Evaluation," final report for AB 56 and AB 1116, submitted to the California Department of Education (Palo Alto, CA: American Institutes for Research, 2006).

14. Jill Kerper Mora, "From the Ballot Box to the Classroom," *Educational Leadership*, 66 (April 2009), pp. 14–19.

15. U.S. Department of Commerce, Minority Business Development Agency, "The Emerging Minority Marketplace" (Washington, DC: U.S. Department of Commerce, September 1999), p. 4; American Institutes for Research and WestEd, "How Are English Learners Faring Under Proposition 227" (Palo Alto, CA: American Institutes for Research, 2006).

16. For an excellent study of how the ideal of an inclusive classroom came to be the norm in U.S. schools, see Robert L. Osgood, *The History of Inclusion in the United States* (Washington, DC: Gallaudet University Press, 2005).

17. Edward Moscovitch, *Special Education: Good Intentions Gone Awry* (Boston: Pioneer Institute, 1993), pp. 1–6.

18. Osgood, p. 166; Robert A. Henderson, "What Is This 'Least Restrictive Environment' in the United States?" in Roger Slee, ed., *Is There a Desk with My Name on It? The Politics of Integration* (London: The Falmer Press, 1993).

19. Moscovitch, p. 19.

20. Ellen C. Guiney, Mary Ann Cohen, and Erika Moldow, "Escaping from Old Ideas: Educating Students with Disabilities in the Boston Public Schools," in S. Paul Reville with Celine Coggins, eds., *A Decade of Urban School Reform: Persistence and Progress in the Boston Public Schools* (Cambridge, MA: Harvard Education Press, 2007).

21. Osgood, p. 197.

22. Marilyn Friend, "The Coteaching Partnership," *Educational Leadership* 64 (February 2007), pp. 48–51.

23. From Katherine Hanson, Vivian Guilfoy, and Sarita Pillai, *More Than Title IX: How Equity in Education Has Shaped the Nation* (Lanham, MD: Rowman & Littlefield, 2009), pp. 232–233.

Chapter 5

1. Morris L. Bigge and S. Samuel Shermis, *Learning Theories for Teachers*, 6th ed. (New York: Longman, 1999), p. 5.

2. My discussion of the philosophy of education has been helped greatly by reading Tony W. Johnson and Ronald F. Reed, *Philosophical Documents in Education* (Boston: Allyn and Bacon, 2008). I recommend the book as an excellent place to start to learn more about the subject.

3. Plato, *Apology* cited in Tony W. Johnson and Ronald F. Reed, *Philosophical Documents in Education* (Boston: Allyn and Bacon, 2008), p. 25.

4. Plato, *The Republic*, Book VI, cited in Johnson and Reed, pp. 29–31; I am grateful to Jane Roland Martin (see note below) for the reminder that Plato attended to the education of women as well as men.

5. Aristotle, *Nicomachean Ethics*, cited in Johnson and Reed, pp. 35–43.

6. Jean-Jacques Rousseau, *Emile*, cited in Johnson and Reed, pp. 76–81.

7. John Dewey, *The School and Society* (Chicago: University of Chicago Press, 1899); *Democracy and Education* (New York: Macmillan 1916); *Experience and Education* (New York: Macmillan, 1938).

8. Mortimer J. Adler, *The Paideia Proposal: An Educational Manifesto* (New York: Macmillan, 1982).

9. Maxine Greene, *Releasing the Imagination: Essays on Education, the Arts, and Social Change* (San Francisco: Jossey-Bass, 1995); William Pinar, *The Passionate Mind of Maxine Greene* (London: Falmer Press, 1998); "Maxine Greene: the Importance of Personal Reflection," http://www.edutopia.org/maxine-greene, accessed May 15, 2009.

10. Jane Roland Martin, *Reclaiming a Conversation: The Ideal of the Educated Woman* (New Haven: Yale University Press, 1985).

11. bell hooks, *Teaching Community: A Pedagogy of Hope* (New York: Routledge, 2003), p. 91; see also *Teaching to Transgress: Education as the Practice of Freedom* (New York: Routledge, 1994); and her forthcoming *Plantation Culture* (New York: Routledge, 2010).

12. Kwame Anthony Appiah, *The Ethics of Identity* (Princeton: Princeton University Press, 2005), see especially pp. 212 and 268–269.

13. Jean Piaget, *The Moral Judgment of the Child* (New York: Free Press, 1997), pp. 31, 36–37, 42, 47–50.

14. Ruth M. Beard, An Outline of Piaget's Developmental Psychology for Students and Teachers (New York: Basic Books, 1969), p. 139.

15. B. F. Skinner, *Science and Human Behavior* (New York: Macmillan, 1953), p. 91, cited in Bigge and Shermis, p. 102. Bigge and Shermis provide a useful text for further study of all the people and theories presented in this chapter.

16. B. F. Skinner, *Recent Issues in the Analysis of Behavior* (Columbus, OH: Merrill Publishing, 1989), pp. 99–103.

17. L. Vygotsky, *Mind in Society: The Development of Higher Psychological Processes*, M. Cole, V. John-Steiner, S. Scribner, and E. Souberman, editors and translators (Cambridge: Harvard University Press, 1978), p. 86.

18. Jerome S. Bruner, *Toward a Theory of Instruction* (Cambridge: Harvard University Press, 1966), pp. 5 and 27. See also Bruner's *Acts of Meaning* (Cambridge: Harvard University Press, 1990), and the discussion of Bruner in Bigge and Shermis, pp. 133–153.

19. Bruner, *Toward a Theory of Instruction*, p. 126; *The Relevance of Education* (New York: Norton, 1973), p. 131; *Toward a Theory of Instruction*, p. 53.

20. John D. Bransford, Ann L. Brown, and Rodney R. Cocking, editors, *How People Learn: Brain, Mind, Experience, and School* (Washington, DC: National Academy Presses, 2000), pp. vii and 358–359.

21. Eugene E. Garcia, *Hispanic Education in the United States: Raices y Alas* (Lanham, MD: Rowman & Littlefield, 2001), p. 146.

22. Victoria Purcell-Gates, "'. . . As Soon as She Opened Her Mouth!': Issues of Language, Literacy, and Power," in Lisa Delpit and Joanne Kilgour Dowdy, eds., *The Skin That We Speak: Thoughts on Language and Culture in the Classroom*, revised ed. (New York: New Press, 2008), pp. 121–141.

23. Diana B. Erchick, "Women's Voices and the Experiences of Mathematics," *Focus on Learning Problems in Mathematics* 18 (Winter–Summer): 105–122; Joanne R. Becker, "Women's Way of Knowing in Mathematics Education," *Equity in Mathematics Education: Influences of Feminism and Culture*, ed. Pat Rogers and Gabriele Kaiser (London: Falmer, 1995), both cited and discussed in Karen N. Bell and Elaine Kolitch, "Voices of Mathematical Distress and Resilience," *Women's Studies Quarterly* 28 (Fall/Winter 2000), pp. 233–248.

24. Peter Senge et al., *Schools That Learn* (New York: Doubleday, 2000), pp. 35–42.

25. Howard Gardner, "Multiple Lenses on the Mind," paper presented at the ExpoGestion Conference, Bogotá, Colombia, May 25, 2005.

26. Sharon K. Ferrett, *Peak Performance: Success in College and Beyond* (Boston: McGraw-Hill, 2010), pp. 13–17. *Peak Performance* is a useful source for learning more about the differences in learning styles.

Chapter 6

1. See William F. Pinar, "'A Lingering Note' Comments on the Collected Works of Ted T. Aoki," *Educational Insights* 8:2. See also William F. Pinar, *Understanding Curriculum* (New York: Peter Lang, 1995).

2. Meredith Houle, "Investigating the Role of Educative Curriculum Materials in Supporting Teacher Enactment of a Field-Based Urban Ecology Investigation," unpublished Ph.D. dissertation, Boston College, May 2008, pp. 8–14, citing p. 238 of J. T. Remillard, "Examining Key Concepts in Research on Teachers Use of Mathematics Curricula," *Review of Educational Research*, 75:2 (2005), pp. 211–246.

3. Ralph W. Tyler, *Basic Principles of Curriculum and Instruction* (Chicago: University of Chicago Press, 1950), pp. 1–2, cited in

Herbert M. Kliebard, *Forging the American Curriculum: Essays in Curriculum History and Theory* (New York: Routledge, 1992), p. 154.

4. Tyler, p. 3, cited in Kliebard, *Forging the American Curriculum*, p. 154.

5. Tyler, p. 69, cited in Kliebard, pp. 162–163.

6. Elliot W. Eisner, "Educational Objectives—Help or Hindrance?" reprinted in David J. Flinders and Stephen J. Thornton, eds., *The Curriculum Studies Reader* (New York: Routledge Falmer, 2004), pp. 85–91.

7. Herbert M. Kliebard, *The Struggle for the American Curriculum*, 3rd ed. (New York: Routledge Falmer, 2004), see especially pp. 1–25, though this is, in fact, a summary of the book.

8. Kliebard, *Struggle for the American Curriculum*, p. 25, see also pp. 229–230.

9. Larry Cuban, *How Teachers Taught: Constancy and Change in American Classrooms*, 1890–1990, 2nd ed. (New York: Teachers College Press, 1993), xix.

10. For a particularly thoughtful analysis of the hidden curriculum, see Michael W. Apple, "The Hidden Curriculum and the Nature of Conflict," in Michael W. Apple, *Ideology and Curriculum*, 3rd ed. (New York: Routledge Falmer, 2004), pp. 77–97.

11. James A. Banks, "Multicultural Education: Characteristics and Goals," in James A. Banks and Cherry A. McGee Banks, eds., *Multicultural Education: Issues and Perspectives*, 6th ed. (Hoboken, NJ: Wiley, 2007), pp. 6–7.

12. Sonia Nieto, *Affirming Diversity: The Sociopolitical Context of Multicultural Education* (Boston: Pearson, 2004), p. 346.

13. Banks.

14. Albert Shanker, "The Pitfalls of Multicultural Education," *Education Digest* (December 1991).

15. For a thoughtful and even-handed discussion of these concerns, see David Tack, *Seeking Common Ground: Public Schools in a Diverse Society* (Cambridge: Harvard University Press, 2003).

16. Banks, pp. 7, 20–25.

17. My views of the standards movement are elaborated in more detail in my book, *Reading, Writing, and Justice: School Reform as If Democracy Matters* (Albany: State University of New York Press, 1997). See especially pp. 21–29, from which some of this material is adapted.

18. National Commission on Excellence in Education, *A Nation at Risk: The Imperative for Educational Reform* (Washington, DC: U.S. Government Printing Office, 1983), p. 5.

19. One of the best critiques of *A Nation at Risk*, by a group of authors who saw it as undermining a national commitment to educational equity is Ann Bastian, Norm Fruchter, Marilyn Gittell, Colin Greer, and Kenneth Haskins, *Choosing Equality: The Case for Democratic Schools* (New York: The New World Foundation, 1985).

20. Cynthia McCallister, "Toward 'An Education on Equal Terms': Standards, Assessments and the Challenge of Educational Equity," unpublished paper, New York University, January 2007, p. 4; Edmund W. Gordon, *Education & Justice: A View From the Back of the Bus* (New York: Teachers College Press, 1999); Edmund W. Gordon and Associates, *Human Diversity and Pedagogy* (New Haven: Yale University Center in Research on Education, Culture and Ethnicity, Institution for Social Policy Studies, 1988).

21. See National Council of Teachers of Mathematics, "Standards 2000 Project," retrieved September 12, 2009, from http://standards.nctm.org/document/prepost/project.htm

22. Jonathan Zimmerman, *Whose America? Culture Wars in the Public Schools* (Cambridge: Harvard University Press, 2002), p. 73.

23. Contract With America, p. 79.

24. Marge Scherer, "Perspectives/Making Standards Work," *Educational Leadership* 59:1 (2001), p. 5.

25. James Banks's brief "Foreword" to Christine Sleeter, *Un-Standardizing Curriculum: Multicultural Teaching in the Standards-Based Classroom* (New York: Teachers College Press, 2005), pp. vii–xi, offers an excellent look at these debates.

26. Linda Darling-Hammond and Joan Baratz-Snowden, "A Good Teacher in Every Classroom: Preparing the Highly Qualified Teachers Our Children Deserve," *Educational Horizons* 85:2 (Winter 2007), pp. 111–132.

27. Michael W. Apple, "Do the Standards Go Far Enough? Power, Policy, and Practice in Mathematics Education," *Journal for Research in Mathematics Education* 23:5 (1992), p. 412.

28. Sleeter, p. 3.

29. Deborah E. Burns and Jeanne H. Purcell, "Tools for Teachers," *Educational Leadership* 59 (September 2001), pp. 50–52.

30. Vito Perrone, *A Letter to Teachers: Reflections on Schooling and the Art of Teaching* (San Francisco: Jossey-Bass, 1991), pp. 12–13.

31. C. Dudley-Marling and P. Paugh, "The Rich Get Richer: The Poor Get Direct Instruction," in B. Altwerger, ed., *Reading for Profit: How the Bottom Line Leaves Kids Behind* (Portsmouth, NH: Heinemann, 2005), pp. 156–171.

Chapter 7

1. National Governors Association, "Redesigning the American High School: Rate Your Future," Winter/Spring 2005, Horatio Alger Association of Distinguished Americans, Inc., "State of Our Nation's Youth 2005," August 2005.

2. John Dewey, *Experience and Education* (New York: Touchstone, 1997, originally published 1938).

3. There are many excellent studies of Leonard Covello's educational work. The best place to start is Leonard Covello with Guido D'Agostino, *The Heart Is the Teacher* (New York: McGraw-Hill, 1958). Also useful are Vito Perrone, *Teacher With a Heart: Reflections on Leonard Covello and Community* (New York: Teachers College Press, 1998), Paula S. Fass, *Outside In: Minorities and the Transformation of American Education* (New York: Oxford University Press, 1989), and especially Michael C. Johanek and John L. Puckett, *Leonard Covello and the Making of Benjamin Franklin High School* (Philadelphia, Temple University Press, 2007).

4. See Vito Perrone, *Lessons For New Teachers* (Boston: McGraw-Hill, 2000), pp. 104–119.

5. Paulo Freire, *Teachers as Cultural Workers: Letters to Those Who Dare Teach* (Boulder, CO: Westview Press, 1998), p. 56.

6. Lee Canter & Associates, *Back to School With Assertive Discipline* (Santa Monica, CA: Lee Canter & Associates, 1990), pp. 9 and 29.

7. Landon E. Beyer, "'Uncontrolled Students Eventually Become Unmanageable': The Politics of Classroom Discipline," in Ronald E. Butchart and Barbara McEwan, editors, *Classroom Discipline in American Schools: Problems and Possibilities for Democratic Education* (Albany: State University of New York Press, 1998), pp. 51–81.

8. Barbara McEwen, "Contradiction, Paradox, and Irony: The World of Classroom Management," in Butchart and McEwan, pp. 135–155.

9. Vito Perrone, *Lessons for New Teachers* (Boston: McGraw-Hill, 2000), pp. 120–128.

10. Gloria J. Ladson-Billings, "I ain't writin' nuttin': Permissions to Fail and Demands to Succeed in Urban Classrooms," in Lisa Delpit and Joanne Kilgour Dowdy, eds., *The Skin That We Speak* (New York: The New Press, 2002), pp. 109–110.

11. Pedro Noguera and Jean Yonemura Wing, eds., *Unfinished Business: Closing the Racial Achievement Gap in our Schools* (San Francisco: Jossey-Bass, 2006), pp. 121–122.

12. Terry Meier, "Standardized Tests: A Clear and Present Danger," in David Levine, Robert Lowe, Bob Peterson, and Rita Tenorio, eds., *Rethinking Schools: An Agenda for Change* (New York: The New Press, 1995), p. 175.

13. Martin R. West and Paul E. Peterson, "The Politics and Practice of Accountability," in Paul E. Peterson and Martin R. West, eds., *No Child Left Behind? The Politics and Practice of School Accountability* (Washington, DC: The Brookings Institution Press, 2003), p. 3.

14. Monty Neill, "Leaving No Child Behind," in Deborah Meier and George Wood, eds., *Many Children Left Behind: How the No Child Left Behind Act Is Damaging Our Children and Our Schools* (Boston: Beacon Press, 2004), p. 103.

15. Arthur Costigan, *Teaching Language Arts in a Test Driven Era* (New York: Routledge, 2008).

16. Judith McVarish, *Infusing Mathematics Reasoning Into Elementary School Classrooms* (New York: Routledge, 2008).

17. Greene's book offers a practical, thoughtful, and understanding approach to one of the most difficult issues every teacher faces—how to manage a classroom and how to deal with the occasionally disruptive kids that make such management such a challenge.

Chapter 8

1. Rosemary E. Sutton, "Equity and Computers in Schools: A Decade of Research," *Review of Educational Research* 61:4 (1991), pp. 475–503; Dennis Evans, "Can Web-based Learning Transform the Classroom?" in Evans, ed., *Taking Sides: Clashing Views on Controversial Issues in Teaching and Educational Practice* (Dubuque, IA: McGraw-Hill/Dushkin, 2005), p. 94.

2. Larry Cuban, *Oversold and Underused: Computers in the Classroom* (Cambridge: Harvard University Press, 2001); and Diana G. Oblinger, "The Next Generation of Educational Engagement," *Journal of Interactive Media in Education* 8, Special Issue on the Educational Semantic Web, http://www-jime.open.ac.uk/2004/8/oblinger-2004-8pdf, cited in Katherine Hanson and Bethany Carlson, *Effective Access: Teachers' Use of Digital Resources in STEM Teaching* (Newton, MA: Education Development Center, 2005), pp. 5–7.

3. See New Tech web site (http://www.newtechfoundation.org), as well as the article included in the **Readings** for this chapter. I also visited the New Tech High School in Rochester, Indiana, in spring 2008.

4. Marie Leech, "All Alabama High Schools This Year Have State Distance Learning Program," *Birmingham News*, August 13, 2009, http://www.al.com/news/birminghamnews/metro.ssf?/base/news/125015138188440.xml&coll=2

5. Seymour Papert, *The Children's Machine: Rethinking School in the Age of the Computer* (New York: Basic Books, 1993), pp. ix and 4.

6. Ibid., p. 43.

7. Ibid., pp. 2–3.

8. Larry M. Dooley, Teri Metcalf, and Ann Martinez, "A Study of the Adoption of Computer Technology by Teachers," *Educational Technology and Society* 2(4): 107–115, cited in Hanson and Carlson, p. 5.

9. Larry Cuban, *Teachers and Machines: The Classroom Use of Technology Since 1920* (New York: Teachers College Press, 1986), pp. 4–11.

10. *BizVoice*/Indiana Chamber of Commerce, November/December 2007, pp. 72–76.

11. Andrew Trotter, "Technology Educators Decry New Digital Divide," *Education Week* 26, published online June 26, 2007.

12. National Center for Educational Statistics, "Libraries and Educational Technology," in *Digest of Educational Statistics*, 2003, http://nces.ed.gov//programs/digest/d03/tables/dt429.asp.

13. H. Wenglinsky, *Does It Compute: The Relationship Between Educational Technology and Student Achievement in Mathematics* (Princeton, NJ: Educational Testing Service, Policy Information Center, 1998), cited in Committee on Increasing High School Students' Engagement and Motivation to Learn, *Engaging Schools: Fostering High School Students' Motivation to Learn* (Washington, DC: National Academies Press, 2004), pp. 84–85. See Michael W. Apple, *Teachers and Texts: A Political Economy of Class and Gender Relations in Education* (New York: Routledge, 1986), p. 169.

14. American Association of University Women Educational Foundation, "Tech Savvy: Educating Girls in the New Computer Age," 2000, http://www.aauw.org/research/upload/TechSavvy.pdf.

15. Children NOW, "Fair Play? Violence, Gender and Race in Video Games," 2001, http://publications.childrennow.org/publications/media/fairplay_2001b.cfm.

16. Tony Scott, Michael Cole, and Martin Engel, "Computers and Education: A Cultural Constructivist Perspective," *Review of Research in Education* 18 (1992), pp. 229–230.

17. NPD Group, "Video Gaming Attracts Larger Female Audience in 2009," press release, June 29, 2009, http://www.npd.com/press/releases/press_090629b.html.

18. Entertainment Software Association, "Essential Facts About the Computer and Video Game Industry: 2009 Sales, Demographic and Usage Data," http://www.theesa.com/facts/pdfs/ESA_EF_2009.pdf.

19. Gwen Solomon and Lynne Schrum, "Much to Gain, and Many Barriers," *Education Week*, May 29, 2002, pp. 48, 34–35.

20. Common Sense Media, "Is Technology Changing Childhood? A National Poll on Teens and Social Networking," August 10, 2009, http://www.commonsensemedia.org/teen-social-media.

21. Peter H. Kahn, Jr., and Batya Friedman, "Control and Power in Educational Computing," in Hank Bromley and Michael W. Apple, eds., *Education/Technology/Power: Educational Computing as Social Practice* (Albany: State University of New York Press, 1998), pp. 157–173.

22. Kelly Tenkely, "Using Technology to Differentiate Instruction," http://www.theapple.com/benefits/articles/8484-using-technology-to-differentiate-instruction.

Chapter 9

1. Dan C. Lortie, *Schoolteacher* (Chicago: University of Chicago Press, 2002; originally published, 1965), p. 65.

2. Margaret A. Haley, "Why Teachers Should Organize," National Educational Association, *Addresses and Proceedings*, St. Louis, 1904, pp. 145–152.

3. Amelia Allison, "Confessions of Public School Teachers," *Atlantic Monthly* (July 1896), pp. 107–108, cited in Nancy Hoffman, *Women's "True" Profession: Voices From the History of Teaching* (Old Westbury, NY: The Feminist Press, 1981), p. 271.

4. "Salary Survey for All K-12 Teachers," http://www.payscale.com/research/US/All_K-12_Teachers/Salary/by_Degree and http://www.payscale.com/research/US/All_K-12_Teachers/Salary/by_Certification.

5. Juan Williams, *Thurgood Marshall: American Revolutionary* (New York: Three Rivers Press, 2000), pp. 89–91, 198.

6. As used here, real salaries are adjusted by the Consumer Price Index to reflect 2007 values.

7. See the Web sites of the nation's two teacher unions, http://www.nea.org and http://www.aft.org. For more background on the history and growth of teacher unions in the United States, see Marjorie Murphy, *Blackboard Unions: The AFT and the NEA, 1900–1980* (Ithaca, NY: Cornell University Press, 1992).

8. Lortie, p. viii.

9. Susan Moore Johnson, *Teachers at Work: Achieving Success in Our Schools* (New York: Basic Books, 1990), pp. 151–164.

10. Linda Christensen, "Voices From the Classroom," in Salas et al., p. 39.

11. Frank McCourt, *Teacher Man* (New York: Scribner, 2005), pp. 11–18.

12. See, for example, Ronald Edmonds, "Effective Schools for the Urban Poor," *Educational Leadership* 37 (October 1979), pp. 15–24.

13. Sara Lawrence Lightfoot, *The Good High School: Portraits of Character and Culture* (New York: Basic Books, 1983), pp. 325–333.

14. Sonia Nieto, *What Keeps Teachers Going?* (New York: Teachers College Press, 2003), p. 102.

15. "I Want Schools Small Enough to Fail as They Learn on the Job: An Interview With Deborah Meier," by John Merrow, July 14, 2009, http://learningmatters.tv/blog/op-ed/i-want-schools-small-enough-to-fail-as-they-learn-on-the-job-an-interview-with-deborah-meier/2243/

16. Bill Bigelow, cited in Salas et al., p. 214.

17. Lola Glover, "We Must Act as If All the Children Are Ours," in Salas et al., pp. 218–219.

18. Lightfoot, p. 322.

19. Chela Delgado, "White Teacher to the Rescue: A Review of Freedom Writers," *Rethinking Schools* 21:3 (Spring 2007).

20. Jennifer Medina, "Class Size in New York City Schools Rises, but the Impact Is Debated," *New York Times,* February 21, 2009, http://www.nytimes.com/2009/02/22/education/22class.html; Health & Education Research Operative Services, "Project STAR: The Student/Teacher Achievement Ratio Study," n.d., http://www.heros-inc.org/new-fact.pdf; Michelle Krupa, "Class Size Is Not So Important, Study Says," *Times-Picayune,* February 10, 2003, http://www.freerepublic.com/focus/news/840353/posts.

21. Judy Logan, *Teaching Stories* (New York: Kodansha International, 1997), p. xxi.

Chapter 10

1. Sean P. Corcoran and William N. Evans, "Equity, Adequacy, and the Evolving State Role in Education Finance," in Helen F. Ladd and Edward B. Fiske, eds., *Handbook of Research in Educational Finance and Policy* (New York: Routledge, 2007).

2. *Serrano v. Priest,* 5 Cal, 3d 584, 96 Cal Rptr. 601, 487 p. 2d 1241 (1971) cited in David Fellman, ed., *The Supreme Court and Education* (New York: Teachers College Press, 1976), p. 283.

3. *San Antonio School District v. Rodriguez,* 411 U.S. 1 (1973), Mr. Justice Powell delivered the opinion of the Court, Mr. Justice Marshall dissenting, cited in Fellman, pp. 284–296.

4. Stan Karp, "Money, Schools, and Justice," *Rethinking Schools* 21:4 (Summer 2007), pp. 27–30.

5. James Traub, "It's Elementary," *The New Yorker,* July 17, 1995, p. 77.

6. Paul Wellstone, "If We Are Not for Our Children, Who Are We For?" epilogue in Carl Glickman, ed., *Letters to the Next President: What We Can Do About the Real Crisis in Public Education* (New York: Teachers College Press, 2004), pp. 257–259.

7. The Census of Governments: School Districts, 2005–2006.

8. Karp.

9. National Working Group on Funding Student Learning, *Funding Student Learning: How to Align Education Resources With Student Learning Goals* (Center on Reinventing Public Education: University of Washington, Bothell, 2008).

10. My own views on many of these issues of educational fairness are discussed in my book, *Reading, Writing, and Justice: School Reform as if Democracy Matters* (Albany: State University of New York Press, 1997). See, especially, Chapter 4, "Toward a New Kind of Child-Centered Curriculum: The Individual Child and a Democratic Society."

11. Two important voices in the research that has shown the negative impact of tracking have been John I. Goodlad and Jeannie Oakes. See, especially, John I. Goodlad, *A Place Called School: Prospects for the Future* (New York: McGraw-Hill, 1984), and Jeannie Oakes, *Keeping Track: How Schools Structure Inequality* (New Haven: Yale University Press, 1985). For a useful look at parental resistance to ending tracking, see Amy Stuart Wells and Irene Serna, "The Politics of Culture: Understanding Local Political Resistance to Detracking in Racially Mixed Schools," *Harvard Educational Review* 66 (Spring 1996), pp. 93–118.

12. Wheelock, p. 71.

13. Wheelock, pp. 283–284.

14. Jeannie Oakes, "Foreword," in Wheelock, p. xiii.

15. Leonard Covello, *The Heart Is the Teacher* (New York: McGraw-Hill, 1958), pp. 52–53.

16. D. B. Tyack and E. Hansot, *Learning Together: A History of Coeducation in American Public Schools* (New York: Russell Sage Foundation, 1992), pp. 248–249.

17. National Center for Education Statistics, *Dropout Rates in the United States: 2000* (Washington, DC: National Center for Education Statistics, 2001), retrieved from http://nces.ed.gov/pubs2002/droppub_2001/.

18. Michelle Fine, *Framing Dropouts: Notes on the Politics of an Urban Public High School* (Albany: State University of New York Press, 1991), pp. 1–2, 21–25.

19. Office of Multiple Pathways to Graduation, "Developing and Strengthening Schools and Programs That Lead to High School Graduation and Post-Secondary Opportunities for Overage, Under-credited Youth," New York City Department of Education, June 22, 2006; Division of Assessment & Accountability, "An Examination of the Relationship Between Higher Standards and Students Dropping Out," New York City Department of Education, March 1, 2001.

20. Jacqueline Jordan Irvine, "Still Standing in the Schoolhouse Door," and Pedro Noguera and Robert Cohen, "The Legacy of 'All Deliberate Speed'," as well as Richard Rothstein, "Social Class Leaves Its Imprint," in *Education Week* 23 (May 19, 2004), pp. 38–40.

21. Beverly Daniel Tatum, "Why Are All the Black Kids Sitting Together in the Cafeteria?" And Other Conversations About Race (New York: Basic Books, 2003), p. 52.

22. Tatum, p. 54.

23. Asa G. Hiliard III, "If We Had the Will to See It Happen," in Glickman, p. 29.

24. Shirley Brice Heath and Milbrey W. McLaughlin, eds., *Identity & Inner-City Youth: Beyond Ethnicity and Gender* (New York: Teachers College Press, 1993), pp. 6, 25–30, and 222.

25. Heath and McLaughlin, p. 59.

26. Robert Infantino and Rebecca Wilke, *Tough Choices for Teachers: Ethical Challenges in Today's Schools and Classrooms* (Lanham, MD: Rowman & Littlefield, 2009).

27. Infantino and Wilke, pp. 22–23, 46–49, 59–60, 76–79, 104–105.

28. Kelley Dawson Salas, cited in *The New Teacher Book* (Milwaukee: A Rethinking Schools Publication, 2004), p. 81.

Chapter 11

1. Daisy Bates, *The Long Shadow at Little Rock* (Fayetteville: University of Arkansas Press, 1962); U.S. Supreme Court, *Parents Involved in Community Schools v. Seattle School District,* No. 5, Supreme Court of the United States 908 (2007); and *Meredith v. Jefferson County Board of Education,* No. 5, Supreme Court of the United States 915 (2007).

2. U.S. Supreme Court, *Tinker et al. v. Des Moines Independent Community School District et al.,* No. 21, Supreme Court of the United States 393 U.S. 503 (1969); *Engel et al. v. Vitale et al.,* No. 468, Supreme Court of the United States 370 U.S. 421: 82 S. Ct. 1261 (1962); *Abington School District v. Schempp,* Supreme Court of the United States 374 U.S. 203 (1963); *Epperson v. Arkansas,* Supreme Court of the United States 393 U.S. 97 (1968). For more discussion of these issues, see David Fellman, ed., *The Supreme Court and Education,* 3rd ed. (New York: Teachers College Press, 1976). For a detailed discussion of the religion-related decision, see Jim Fraser, *Between Church and State: Religion and Public Education in a Multicultural America* (New York: Palgrave-Macmillan, 1999).

3. David J. Hoff, "Obama Gets to Work on Transition," *Education Week,* November 7, 2008, http://www.edweek.org.

4. Herbert M. Kliebard, *The Struggle for the American Curriculum, 1893–1958,* 2nd ed. (New York: Routledge, 1995), pp. 144–149.

5. Lyndon B. Johnson, "Remarks in Johnson City, Texas, Upon Signing the Elementary and Secondary Education Bill, April 11, 1965," Public Papers of the Presidents, Lyndon B. Johnson, 1965, Book I, Washington, DC, pp. 413–414.

6. National Commission on Excellence in Education, *A Nation at Risk: The Imperative for Educational Reform* (Washington, DC: U.S. Government Printing Office, 1983), p. 5; for a thoughtful discussion of the impact of this report and the changing national dialogue about education, from a critical perspective, see Ann Bastian, Norm Fruchter, Marilyn Gittell, Colin Greer, and Kenneth Haskins, *Choosing Equality: The Case for Democratic Schools* (New York: New World Foundation, 1985).

7. Edmund W. Gordon, *Education & Justice: A View From the Back of the Bus* (New York: Teachers College Press, 1999); Andrew Rudalevige, "No Child Left Behind: Forging a Congressional Compromise," in Paul E. Peterson and Martin R. West, eds., *No Child Left Behind? The Politics and Practice of School Accountability* (Washington, DC: The Brookings Institution Press, 2003), pp. 23–54.

8. Pedro Noguera, *City Schools and the American Dream: Reclaiming the Promise of Public Education* (New York: Teachers College Press, 2003), p. 156; Terry M. Moe, "Politics, Control, and the Future of School Accountability," in Paul E. Peterson and Martin R. West, eds., *No Child Left Behind? The Politics and Practice of School Accountability* (Washington, DC: The Brookings Institution Press, 2003), p. 101.

9. For a good summary of NCLB legislation, as well as the politics leading up to its passage, see Paul E. Peterson and Martin R. West, eds., *No Child Left Behind? The Politics and Practice of School Accountability* (Washington, DC: The Brookings Institution Press, 2003).

10. I am grateful to former NYU graduate student Dana Grayson for insightful commentary on this material. Helpful background can be found in John Chubb's *Within Our Reach*, and Deborah Meier's *Many Children Left Behind*.

11. Alfie Kohn, "NCLB and the Effort to Privatize Public Education," in Deborah Meier and George Wood, eds., *Many Children Left Behind: How the No Child Left Behind Act Is Damaging Our Children and Our Schools* (Boston: Beacon Press, 2004), pp. 79–80.

12. Linda Darling-Hammond, "From 'Separate but Equal' to 'No Child Left behind': The Collision of New Standards and Old Inequities," in Meier and Wood, eds., *Many Children Left Behind*, pp. 3–4.

13. Frederick M. Hess and Chester E. Finn, Jr., "Introduction," in *Leaving No Child Behind? Options for Kids in Failing Schools* (New York: Palgrave Macmillan, 2004), pp. 2–4.

14. Terry M. Moe, "Politics, Control, and the Future of School Accountability," in Paul E. Peterson and Martin R. West, eds., *No Child Left Behind? The Politics and Practice of School Accountability* (Washington, DC: The Brookings Institution Press, 2003), pp. 80–86.

15. Alliance for Excellent Education, "Reinventing the Federal Role in Education," policy brief, July 2009, http://www.all4ed.org.

16. Jane Hannaway and Kendra Bischoff, "Florida: Confusions, Constraints, and Cascading Scenarios," and Alex Medler, "Colorado: Layered Reforms and Challenges for Scale," both in Frederick M. Hess and Chester E. Finn, Jr., *Leaving No Child Behind? Options for Kids in Failing Schools* (New York: Palgrave Macmillan, 2004), pp. 89-111, 113-136.

17. Portz, pp. 63–65.

18. John, Portz, "Governing and the Boston Public Schools," in S. Paul Reville with Celine Coggins, eds., *A Decade of Urban School Reform* (Cambridge: Harvard Education Press, 2007), pp. 63–64, citing Education Commission of the States "Governing America's Schools: Changing the Rules," (Denver: Education Commission of the States, 1999), Joseph Murphy, "Governing America's Schools: the Shifting Playing Field (paper presented at the annual meeting of the American Educational Research Association, Montreal, Canada, April, 1999), Donald R. McAdams, *What School Boards Can Do: Reform Governance for Urban Schools* (New York: Teachers College Press, 2006).

19. Deborah Meier, "NCLB and Democracy," in Meier and Wood, eds., *Many Children Left Behind*, pp. 66–73.

20. Portz, pp. 64–65.

21. Bob Peterson, cited in Rethinking Schools, *The New Teacher Book* (Milwaukee, WI: Rethinking Schools, 2004), p. 206.

22. Gregory Michie, "Teaching in the Undertow: Resisting the Pull of School-as-Usual," in *The New Teacher Book*, p. 194.

Chapter 12

1. Langston Hughes, "Freedom's Plow," in *Selected Poems of Langston Hughes* (originally published 1959; republished New York: Vintage Classics, 1990), p. 291

2. For an expanded discussion on the issue of the relationship between democracy and education, from which these paragraphs are partly drawn, see James W. Fraser, *Reading, Writing, and Justice: School Reform as if Democracy Matters* (Albany: State University of New York Press, 1997).

3. Michael Apple and James A. Beane, *Democratic Schools* (Alexandria, VA: Association for Supervision and Curriculum Development, 1995).

4. Thomas Jefferson, "A Bill for the More General Diffusion of Knowledge" (1779), in Gordon C. Lee, *Crusade Against Ignorance: Thomas Jefferson on Education* (New York: Teachers College Press, 1961), pp. 83–84.

5. Ibid.

6. Jefferson to William C. Jarvis, September 28, 1820, in Lee, p. 17.

7. Horace Mann, Tenth and Twelfth Annual Reports (1846 and 1848) in James W. Fraser, *The School in the United States: A Documentary History* (New York: Routledge, 2009), p. 50.

8. Citations from Horace Mann's Tenth (1846) and Twelfth (1848) Annual Reports in Fraser, pp. 49–57.

9. James D. Anderson, *The Education of Blacks in the South, 1860–1935* (Chapel Hill: University of North Carolina Press, 1988), p. 5.

10. "Report to the Primary School Committee on the Petition of Sundry Colored Persons for the Abolition of schools for Colored Children," Boston, June 15, 1846, p. 2.

11. The best analysis of the 19th-century Black community's commitment to literacy and schooling is found in Anderson. See also Chapter 5 of James W. Fraser, *A History of Hope* (New York: Palgrave, 2002), for more on this issue. These paragraphs owe much to that work.

12. Eric Foner, *Reconstruction: America's Unfinished Revolution, 1863–1877* (New York: Harper Collins Perennial, 2002), pp. 96–97.

13. Anderson, pp. 15–16.

14. Frederick Douglass, *Narrative of the Life of Frederick Douglass: An American Slave* (1845; Cambridge: Harvard University Press, 1967), p. 58.

15. Douglass, p. 59.

16. John W. Alvord, *Inspector's Report of Schools and Finances. U.S. Bureau of Refugees, Freedmen and Abandoned Lands.* (Washington, DC: U.S. Government Printing Office, 1866), pp. 9–10, cited in Anderson, p. 7.

17. W. E. B. DuBois, *The Souls of Black Folk* (1903, reprinted New York: Crest, 1961), p. 31.

18. Anderson, p. 5.

19. W. E. B. DuBois, *Black Reconstruction in America, 1860–1880* (originally published 1935; republished New York: Free Press, 1992), pp. 641–649.

20. Anderson, p. 278.

21. John Dewey, *The School and Society*, 2nd ed. (Chicago: University of Chicago Press, 1915), p. 7.

22. Ibid, p. 29.

23. Alexis de Tocqueville, *Democracy in America*, edited and abridged by Richard D. Heffner (New York: New American Library, 1956).

24. Ruth Batson, "NAACP Boston Branch, Statement to Boston School Committee, June 11, 1963," in Fraser, *The School in the United States*, p. 305.

25. bell hooks, *Teaching to Transgress: Education as the Practice of Freedom* (New York: Routledge, 1994), p. 18.

26. Ann Bastian, Norm Fruchter, Marilyn Gittell, Colin Greer, and Kenneth Haskins, *Choosing Equality: The Case for Democratic Schools* (Philadelphia: Temple University Press, 1985).

27. Deborah Meier, "NCLB and Democracy," in Deborah Meier and George Wood, eds., *Many Children Left Behind: How the No Child left Behind Act Is Damaging Our Children and Our Schools* (Boston: Beacon Press, 2004), pp. 76–78.

28. Lisa Delpit, *Other People's Children: Cultural Conflict in the Classroom* (New York: The New Press, 1995), pp. 11, 28.

29. Lisa Delpit, "No Kinda Sense," in Lisa Delpit and Joanne Kilgour Dowdy, eds., *The Skin That We Speak* (New York: The New Press, 2002), p. 48.

30. Pedro A. Noguera and Robert Cohen, "The Legacy of 'All Deliberate Speed,'" *Education Week* 22 (May 19, 2004), p. 39.

31. Anderson, p. 1.

32. Langston Hughes, "Democracy," in *Selected Poems of Langston Hughes* (originally published 1959; republished New York: Vintage Classics, 1990), p. 285.

33. Aptheker notes that this speech was found among Du Bois's papers with no indication of where or exactly when it was delivered, although it seems to have been a lecture to future teachers given late in World War II, that is, in 1944 or 1945.

Chapter 13

1. Kelley Dawson Salas, "Time to Learn," in *The New Teacher Book*, edited by Kelley Dawson Salas, Rita Tenorio, Stephanie Walters, and Dale Weiss (Milwaukee, WI: Rethinking Schools, 2004), pp. 11–12.

2. Betty Achinstein and Steven Z. Athanases, *Mentors in the Making: Developing New Leaders for New Teachers* (New York: Teachers College Press, 2006), pp. 1–8.

3. Daniel Fallon and James W. Fraser, "Rethinking Teacher Education in the 21st Century: Putting Teaching Front and Center," in Thomas L. Good, ed., *21st Century Education: A Reference Handbook*, vol. 2 (Thousand Oaks, CA: Sage, 2008), pp. 58–67.

4. "Statistics and Rationale, SOS: Strategies of Success," Texas A&M University–Corpus Christi, College of Education, http://sos.tamucc.edu/statistics.html.

5. Salas, p. 19.

Chapter 13

Text Credits

Key term page numbers are in bold.

INTASC Model Standards for Beginning Teacher Licensing, Assessment, and Development

Developed by the Council of Chief State School Officers, the INTASC Standards reflect a broad consensus about what preservice teachers need to learn when preparing to become teachers. This material is covered throughout the text, including the specific topics cited below:

INTASC PRINCIPLE	TEACH TOPIC/CHAPTER/PAGE
Principle #1 The teacher understands the central concepts, tools of inquiry, and structures of the discipline(s) he or she teaches and creates learning experiences that make these aspects of subject matter meaningful for students.	Defining Curriculum, Ch. 6, p. 180 The Goals of Curriculum, Ch. 6, p. 181 Different Approaches to Curriculum, Ch. 6, p. 183 The Standards Movement, Ch. 6, p. 191 Project-Based Learning, Ch. 6, p. 182 It All Adds Up, Ch. 6, p. 194 On A Need-to-Know (and Be-Able-To-Do) Basis, Ch. 6, p. 196 Motivating Students, Ch. 7, p. 216 Keeping it Fresh, Ch. 7, p. 217 Merging Test Prep with the Curriculum, Ch. 7, p. 234
Principle #2 The teacher understands how children learn and develop, and can provide learning opportunities that support their intellectual, social, and personal development.	How Children Learn, Ch. 5, p. 142 Philosophies about Human Learning, Ch. 5, p. 144 Psychological Theories about Human Learning, Ch. 5, p. 149 Constructivism, Ch. 5, p. 156 Brain Research and School Practice, Ch. 5, p. 157 Serving a Range of Learning Styles, Ch. 5, p. 158 The Psychology of It, Ch. 5, p. 159 Race, Ethnicity, Class, Culture, and Gender, Ch. 5, p. 160 "Normal" Learning, Ch. 5, p. 161 Multiple Intelligences, Ch. 5, p. 162 See, Listen, Move, Ch. 5, p. 164 Motivating Students, Ch. 7, p. 216 Keeping it Fresh, Ch. 7, p. 217
Principle #3 The teacher understands how students differ in their approaches to learning and creates instructional opportunities that are adapted to diverse learners.	Student Diversity, Ch. 3, p. 67 Race and Ethnicity, Ch. 3, p. 69 Fueling the Pipeline, Ch. 3, p. 75 Gender and Sexuality, Ch. 3, p. 81 Sexual Orientation, Ch. 3, p. 82 Religious Diversities, Ch. 3, p. 71 Seeing Diversities, Ch. 3, p. 85 Including Everyone, Ch. 4, p. 98 Multicultural Education, Ch. 6, p. 184 Gender Fairness, Ch. 4, p. 102 Bilingual Education, Ch. 4, p. 108 Three Tiers for English Learners, Ch. 4, p. 114 Special Needs Education, Ch. 4, p. 115 Gifted Students, Ch. 4, p. 121 Serving a Range of Learning Styles, Ch. 5, p. 158 Race, Ethnicity, Class, Culture, and Gender, Ch. 5, p. 160 "Normal" Learning, Ch. 5, p. 161 Multiple Intelligences, Ch. 5, p. 162 See, Listen, Move, Ch. 5, p. 164 Sorting and Tracking, Ch. 10, p. 322 To Track or Not to Track? Ch. 10, p. 324 Achievement Gap, Ch. 10, p. 330
Principle #4 The teacher understands and uses a variety of instructional strategies to encourage students' development of critical thinking, problem solving, and performance skills.	Teachers Need to Understand How to Teach, Ch. 2, p. 42 Constructivism, Ch. 5, p. 156 Rethinking Our Schools, Ch. 6, p. 186 Project-Based Learning, Ch. 6, p. 182 Motivating Students, Ch. 7, p. 216 Keeping it Fresh, Ch. 7, p. 217 The Jigsaw, Ch. 7, p. 222 Bloom's Taxonomy, Ch. 7, p. 229 Merging Test Prep with the Curriculum, Ch. 7, p. 234 Technology and Schools, Ch. 8, p. 250 Using Technology to Improve Teaching, Ch. 8, p. 265 Using Podcasting in the Classroom, Ch. 8, p. 267 The Cell Phone as a Teaching Tool, Ch. 8, p. 268 Achievement Gap, Ch. 10, p. 330
Principle #5 The teacher uses an understanding of individual and group motivation and behavior to create a learning environment that encourages positive social interaction, active engagement in learning, and self-motivation.	Motivating Students, Ch. 7, p. 216 Keeping it Fresh, Ch. 7, p. 217 Motivated Inside and Out, Ch. 7, p. 221 Classroom Management, Ch. 7, p. 221 The Jigsaw, Ch. 7, p. 222 Zero-tolerance, Ch. 7, p. 223 Establishing Expectations, Ch. 7, p. 224 Teacher Behaviors in the Classroom, Ch. 7, p. 225 Equal Expectations, Ch. 7, p. 226 Creating a Democratic Classroom, Ch. 12, p. 400